Lecture Notes in Computer Science 9970

Commenced Publication in 1973
Founding and Former Series Editors:
Gerhard Goos, Juris Hartmanis, and Jan van Leeuwen

More information about this series at http://www.springer.com/series/7409

Ralf Dörner · Stefan Göbel
Michael Kickmeier-Rust · Maic Masuch
Katharina Zweig (Eds.)

Entertainment Computing and Serious Games

International GI-Dagstuhl Seminar 15283
Dagstuhl Castle, Germany, July 5–10, 2015
Revised Selected Papers

 Springer

Editors
Ralf Dörner
RheinMain University of Applied Sciences
Wiesbaden
Germany

Stefan Göbel
Technische Universität Darmstadt
Darmstadt
Germany

Michael Kickmeier-Rust
TU Graz
Graz
Austria

Maic Masuch
University of Duisburg-Essen
Duisburg
Germany

Katharina Zweig
TU Kaiserslautern
Kaiserslautern
Germany

ISSN 0302-9743   ISSN 1611-3349   (electronic)
Lecture Notes in Computer Science
ISBN 978-3-319-46151-9   ISBN 978-3-319-46152-6   (eBook)
DOI 10.1007/978-3-319-46152-6

Library of Congress Control Number: 2016950885

LNCS Sublibrary: SL3 – Information Systems and Applications, incl. Internet/Web, and HCI

This Springer imprint is published by Springer Nature
The registered company is Springer International Publishing AG
The registered company address is: Gewerbestrasse 11, 6330 Cham, Switzerland

Preface

According to the CEO of Activision Blizzard Inc., their computer game "Destiny," which was published in 2014, had a budget of U.S. $500 million. In comparison, even blockbuster movies from the same year such as "The Hobbit" are estimated to have had only half of this budget. Analysts assume that the global game market was worth more than U.S. $90 billion in 2015 with a growth rate exceeding 9 % compared with 2014. Digital games are at the core of a booming market that attracts more than a billion players. However, digital games are rich not only in financial opportunities but also in research questions. The relevance of these research questions increases as computer games affect the lives of more and more people and as their societal and economic significance grows rapidly.

The range of research questions can be broadened when not only computer games that aim to entertain players are the subject of scientific research but computer games that pursue additional goals, for example, educating the players about economic effects. Here, even more scientific disciplines are concerned. In the case of an educational game, for example, research questions may lie in the disciplines of pedagogics and didactics as well as the discipline that deals with the game's subject (e.g., business sciences). For this type of game, the term "serious game" has been coined. While all educational games are serious games, the goals that can be pursued with serious games are more than education. For instance, health games can aim at increasing the fitness of the player. Serious games can be used for advertising, for behavior change, or for medical treatment. Additional disciplines such as sport sciences, marketing, psychology, or medicine become involved in research questions that relate to serious games.

Not surprisingly, many research questions cannot be addressed in isolation but an interdisciplinary approach or at least some basic understanding of the interdisciplinary context of serious games and entertainment computing is essential. Moreover, the whole field is quite unstructured and there are many different scientific communities that conduct research from their own perspective. In general, this is an obstacle for scientific advancements. In particular, this makes it difficult for young researchers who want to start a PhD with a research question related to serious games and entertainment computing. Even their supervisors may be faced with difficulties as this area of research is quite new.

The aim of this book is to collect and to cluster research areas in the field of serious games and entertainment computing – and to provide an introduction as well as a state-of-the-art analysis. This is meant to serve as a starting point for people who want to start research in this area. At the same time, it can be seen as a contribution toward establishing and structuring research in this exciting field. As this is a comparatively young field, the underlying idea of this book was to select authors who are young researchers in the area, still working on their PhD thesis or having just finished it. They were provided with the task of conceiving and writing a book that will introduce and guide the next generation of researchers. The book should provide their successors with a better basis for research, easing their way to tackle new research questions. As a starting point, the perspective of computer science on serious games and entertainment computing was chosen.

With the support of the German Society for Computer Science (GI) and the Leibniz Center for Computer Science, Dagstuhl Castle, a renowned international meeting place for computer science research, was made available for a seminar where all prospective authors could meet and discuss the book for a whole week. A call for participation was internationally distributed in 2014 for this seminar and the associated book project. The resonance was overwhelming. As the number of seminar spaces was limited, it was necessary to conduct a highly competitive selection process. As a result, 25 young researchers from universities and research institutes from 12 countries worldwide were invited. During July 5–10, 2015, these 25 young researchers, and the three organizers of the GI-Dagstuhl seminar supported by two senior researchers, worked (and played) together at Dagstuhl Castle in Germany. The GI-Dagstuhl seminar "Entertainment Computing and Serious Games" proved to be very lively and all participants were enthusiastic to present and discuss research questions, to select suitable content for the envisioned book, and to conceive its structure. After the seminar, the participants worked in virtual teams to flesh out and finalize each chapter of this book according to the structure and the work plan that was drawn up at the end of the seminar.

This book is the result of this process. The authors of the book are mainly the young researchers who participated in the GI-Dagstuhl seminar. The organizers (Ralf Dörner, Stefan Göbel, and Katharina Zweig) and the senior researchers (Michael Kickmeier-Rust and Maic Masuch) served as editors. The book is more than the proceedings of this GI-Dagstuhl seminar. It represents the fruits of the labor of all the participants who invested in the extensive preparation of the seminar, the intensive week at Dagstuhl Castle, and particularly the months of hard work after the seminar. The young researchers who participated are Mohamed Abbadi, Nataliya Bogacheva, Eelco Braad, Paolo Burelli, Rahul Dey, Katharina Emmerich, Benjamin Guthier, Susanne Haake, Antonia Kampa, Johannes Konert, Hector Martinez, Bernhard Maurer, Betty Mohler, Leif Oppermann, Alyea Sandovar, Michaela Slussareff, Jan Smeddinck, Heinrich Söbke, Björn Straat, Alexander Streicher, Henrik Warpefelt, Viktor Wendel, Philip Wilkinson, Diana Xu, and Gregor Zavcer.

We as editors would like to thank the GI, the Leibniz Center for Computer Science, the staff at Dagstuhl Castle, as well as our universities for the support of this book project. Moreover, we would like to thank Springer for their support in publishing this book. And, of course, special thanks go to the 25 passionate young participants – without them this book would not exist.

August 2016

Ralf Dörner
Stefan Göbel
Michael Kickmeier-Rust
Maic Masuch
Katharina Zweig

Contents

VIII   Contents

Introduction to the GI-Dagstuhl Book on Entertainment Computing and Serious Games

Ralf Dörner[1]([⊠]), Stefan Göbel[2], and Michael Kickmeier-Rust[3]

[1] Department Design – Computer Science – Media,
RheinMain University of Applied Sciences, Wiesbaden, Germany
ralf.doerner@hs-rm.de
[2] Multimedia Communications Lab – KOM, Technische Universität Darmstadt,
Darmstadt, Germany
stefan.goebel@kom.tu-darmstadt.de
[3] Knowledge Technologies Institute,
Graz University of Technology, Graz, Austria
michael.kickmeier-rust@tugraz.at

Abstract. This chapter contains an introduction to this book which aims at providing guidance to people who are interested in conducting or dealing with research in the area of entertainment computing and serious games. The chapter starts with defining key terminology. It then illustrates benefits and challenges in this area of research by discussing the development of educational games, one of the most recognized subsets of serious games. Describing and characterizing the current state of the research communities involved in entertainment computing and serious games, an overview of the research landscape is presented. Finally, an overview of the structure of this book is given and the individual chapters of this book are briefly summarized.

Keywords: Entertainment computing · Serious games · Games with a purpose · Gamification · Educational games · Terminology · Benefits · Research challenges

1 Scope and Terminology

As already stated in the preface, this book is the result of a GI-Dagstuhl seminar, i.e. a seminar with 30 participants that was held at Dagstuhl castle in Germany, supported by the Leibniz Center for Computer Science and the German Society for Computer Science (GI). The topic of the seminar was "entertainment computing and serious games". The seminar's goal was to publish this book that offers guidance to everybody who is interested in researching the field of entertainment computing and serious games. This is accomplished by providing introductory texts in the chapters of this book that survey the current state-of-the-art, structure the research field, identify current research challenges, and list good starting points in literature. The intended audience for the book is researchers, e.g. persons who aim to start their PhD thesis in the area of entertainment computing or want to develop their research in this area, and everybody who is

R. Dörner et al. (Eds.): Entertainment Computing and Serious Games, LNCS 9970, pp. 1–16, 2016.
DOI: 10.1007/978-3-319-46152-6_1

interested in the research aspects of entertainment computing and serious games. For undergraduate students and people who want to familiarize themselves with the topic first, we recommend the textbook "Serious Games - Foundations, Concepts and Practice" [1].

The participants of the GI-Dagstuhl seminar discussed the topic "entertainment computing and serious games" in various forms. During the seminar, several important subtopics in the field of entertainment computing and serious games were identified and the remaining chapters are devoted to these subtopics. This chapter serves as an introduction to these remaining chapters. First, we will describe the scope of this book and define some fundamental terminology. In Sect. 2, we will illustrate fundamental benefits and challenges that are often associated with the research field "entertainment computing and serious games". We do this by examining one of the most researched and well-known applications in this research field: educational games. Section 3 gives an introduction to the research communities that are involved in the topics of this book. An overview of dedicated conferences and journals that contain original literature is also given. Finally, Sect. 4 describes the structure of the remaining chapters and characterizes them briefly.

1.1   Entertainment Computing

"Der Mensch ist nur da ganz Mensch, wo er spielt." (Human beings are only fully human when they play) – this classic quote from the German poet Friedrich Schiller (1759 – 1805) captures nicely the sentiment that games play a vital role in everyone's life. Humans play games for fun, entertainment and other intrinsic reasons. Playing games is a constituent part of human culture. Thus, it is not surprising that the computer as a technical artefact has not only been used to perform sophisticated calculations or to query large amounts of data but also for entertainment and playing.

In fact, using computer systems for entertainment purposes is a major application field for methodologies and algorithms developed in computer science. The dynamic growth of this application field is fueled by the advent of mobile devices such as smartphones and tablets as well as special purpose hardware (game consoles) making attractive online games and collaborative games feasible in particular. Computer games have matured from addressing only teenage male audiences with a limited number of genres and serving entertainment purposes only. Computer game software has wide user demographics that ranges from toddlers to users well advanced in years, encompassing all societal groups. In the industry, this large consumer market is a driving force for technical innovations, for example graphical processing units (GPUs) or depth cameras. The low cost hardware becoming available due the economies of scale in the game market has a tremendous impact on a broader applicability of research results from computer science. For example, inexpensive GPUs facilitate a more extensive use of parallel computing as they can not only be used for computer games but for general-purpose computing. As a result, entertainment and computing are affecting each other.

"Entertainment Computing" is a term that aims to capture this interdependency between entertainment and computing. It is a term that is somewhat loosely defined.

Usually, it is used quite broadly encompassing topics such as the usage of new media in entertainment and their creation, technical artefacts used for entertainment (not only computers but also robots, for example), the architecture and authoring of systems for entertainment, or the impact of entertainment based on computing machinery. Consequently, not only researchers in computer science are shaping the field of entertainment computing, but also social scientists, engineers, artists, storytellers and representatives of various applications areas for entertainment computing among others. Entertainment computing is inherently interdisciplinary.

One key term in entertainment computing is "digital game". We define a digital game as a game that uses some kind of computing machinery (e.g. a personal computer, a smartphone or a piece of electronics usable for playing games such as a video game console or a robot). Today, digital games complement traditional games such as cardboard games. An important subset of digital games is serious games. The term "serious games" describes software that offers additional benefits for their users beside entertainment. For instance, edutainment software is able to support users in learning and training; exergames encourage people to become physically active and sustain a healthy lifestyle; advergames are used for marketing purposes or recruiting and may raise awareness of certain topics.

Similar to entertainment computing, serious games open up a whole range of new research questions, for example "How do we enable authors such as teachers or marketing experts to create content for computer games?" or "What are the factors that determine whether a serious game is able to achieve its anticipated benefits while still being entertaining?" In the following, we will focus on serious games since the set of research questions associated with them is a superset of the research questions concerned with computer systems solely for entertainment. From a research perspective, serious games are the most interesting subset of digital games as they aim for entertainment as all other digital games do, they cover all game genres, and the "serious" aspects add a level of complexity.

1.2 Serious Games

Some years ago, a new kind of digital games entered the stage combining entertainment and fun on the one hand and training, education, science etc. on the other hand: serious games. Serious games describe games which help to achieve desired goals while they are played. So each serious game pursues at least two different goals. One of these goals is always entertainment. The other goals characterize which type of serious game we have – for instance, if this goal is education, we have an educational game; if it is physical fitness, we have an exergame. We use the following definition of a serious game by Dörner et al. [1]: "A serious game is a digital game that was created with the intention to entertain and to achieve at least one additional goal (e.g., learning or health). These additional goals are named characterizing goals."

There are several definitions of serious games used in literature. One difference between these definitions is the entity who decides whether a game is "serious". While our definition sees the intention of the game's authors as decisive, other definitions use the fact whether a game actually achieves a characterizing goal or not as main criterion to determine whether a game is a serious game or not. For instance, if an ego shooter was created with the only intention to entertain and it is used by some players as a training device to improve their reaction time, this ego shooter would not be a serious game according to the definition above, but would meet other definitions of serious games. Another example would be an educational game to teach children basic mathematics. If it is that bad that it fails to teach children anything, it would be still a serious game according to the definition given above, but not according to other definitions. A second major difference between definitions of the term "serious game" is the importance attributed to the goal to entertain. In our definition, all serious games need to pursue the goal to entertain, while other definitions do not specify this. Our definition does not rank the goals of a serious game, while other definitions demand that the characterizing goals are primary and the goal to entertain is secondary.

Figure 1 visualizes the approach of serious games: serious games combine game technology and game concepts (inner circle) with further technologies and interdisciplinary concepts from different disciplines (second level) and apply it to a broad spectrum of application areas and market sectors for serious games (outer circle).

This means serious games can be seen as instruments to achieve their characterizing goals (e.g. learning, training, health benefits, or fitness) in a pleasant and enjoyable manner. The development of serious games demands the knowledge of game technologies and game theory as well as further application specific technologies and

Fig. 1. Understanding of Serious Games: Game technology/concepts plus further concepts/technologies applied to application domains. Source: derived from S. Göbel, Serious Games Conference (2010).

concepts. Among those are information and communication technologies (ICT), digital media, psychology and pedagogy, or sociology and economics.

The application fields of serious games include, but are not limited to game-based training and simulation, digital educational games ranging from kindergarten to university, vocational or workplace training, marketing and advertisement games, games for (mental and physical) health and sports or persuasive and social impact/awareness games covering any societal relevant topic such as politics, security, energy or climate – cf. the serious games taxonomy provided by Sawyer and Smith [2].

Serious games are also called "applied games" with the same meaning. "Educational games" or "games for health" represent subgroups of serious games, tackling the educational sector (from kindergarten and schools to higher education, vocational training and collaborative workplace training) respectively the health(care) sector with its facets of prevention and rehabilitation, mental and physical health. "Games with a purpose" sometimes is also used as synonym for serious games, but usually games with a purpose are focused on a game-based approach for solving computational and scientific problems that employs crowd sourcing. A prominent example of a game with a purpose is Foldit [3] where tasks in the area of protein structure prediction are transformed in a game and players contribute en passant to solving scientific problems. Another concept sometimes confused with serious games is "gamification". It describes game-based concepts and/or elements to 'gamify' existing applications and processes – whereby that kind of gamified applications typically are less than a full (serious) game. The idea behind gamification consists of using playful concepts from game design in non-playing contexts, e.g. to spice up monotone tasks at work [4]. Although the term gamification has been introduced by Nick Pelling in 2002 already [5], it gained its popularity in 2010 in several scientific publications. While different from serious games, games with a purpose and gamification are still important topics within the scope of entertainment computing.

2 Example "Educational Games": Benefits and Challenges

Entertainment computing if often found to be an inspiring and attractive area of research because of its large application potential – who does not want to be entertained after all? Moreover, many potential benefits are associated with entertainment computing ranging from better user acceptance to higher levels of motivation. In addition, there are still grand challenges in this research field including socio-economic aspects such as efficient production of entertainment content, quality, security and privacy issues, e.g. concerning user-generated content, methods and concepts for game creation such as collaborative authoring processes, control and personalization (interaction, adaptation, artificial intelligence, player and learner models) as well as the evaluation (usability, user experience, game experience, effects and affects) of entertainment computing applications in general and serious games in particular. Thus, there is a considerable motivation for researchers to work in this field.

In this section we want to illustrate potential benefits on the one hand and interesting research challenges by looking at the example of one of the most prominent subset of entertainment computing and serious games: educational games. In fact, in education we can see an increasing fascination and believe in serious games. Educators often have high hopes about the capacities of using "cool" computer games for educational goals. There is no doubt that learning by playing is one of the most natural and reasonable forms of learning. Likewise, there is little doubt that computer games are an outstanding and incredibly successful part of the present entertainment landscape.

Educational games aim at bringing both worlds together; education is seen from the two different perspectives - the learning and the gaming perspective. However, it is still matter of debate whether "serious games" is a genre that is a positive "more" than the sum of its parts or whether it is an ineffectual chimaera. To find an answer, we need to reduce exaggerated expectations, on the one hand. Serious games are just another learning medium that has certain strength here and certain weaknesses there. On the other hand, research must increasingly address a solid evaluation about the effects specific games have for specific persons, focusing on specific topics, and posed in specific context conditions. Just as an example, from research we know very well that there are clear gender differences what concerning the acceptance of learning games and the learning performance within those games. We must also not underestimate the complexity of using computer games for serious purposes. To apply the right games in the right situation, a vast array of characteristics and features must be addressed: Target audience, subject matter, game genre, game mechanics, learning mechanics, personalization, the learning curve, motivational aspects, storytelling aspects, etc. Of course, the same goes for a solid evaluation of games and, ultimately, a justification of the high costs of development. In previous work, certain frameworks for the classification and evaluation of serious games have been proposed (e.g., by Kickmeier-Rust [6]). Also large initiatives such as the European Network of Excellence GALA (Games and Learning Alliance; www.galanoe.eu) contributed to such concerns.

A substantial concern in the context of serious games is the high design and development costs as opposed to the costs of conventional educational media. Equally, the ratio between "serious" activities (such as learning) and gaming have been discussed in-depth in the past, leading to a complex and fragile balance of game and education. As a consequence, the high development costs and an uncertain market for educational innovations make investments in developing learning games similar to commercial video games too risky for the video game and educational materials industries (see also Moreno-Ger et al. [7]). Education organizations are cautious to give up textbooks or purchase educational technologies that have not proven their efficacy, especially in terms of today's education standards.

The current problem is that educators as well as game industry demands simple, even overly simple answers about efficacy. Usually the question "Does it work?" is posed. But, as said, in assessing and gauging serious games, there is more than meets the eye.

The usual approach to serious game evaluation is designing a single game to achieve serious, measurable, sustained changes in performance and behavior [8]. However, to date there is no comprehensible consensus regarding an evaluation framework and metrics for estimating the benefit of a serious game. In fact there is a lack of standardized evaluation methods and performance indicators. When it comes to evaluating the effectiveness of a serious game, the focus of previous research concentrates predominantly on the measurement of learning achievement or motivation.

However, by focusing mainly on the academic benefits of educational games, other important aspects happen to be disregarded, for example the effect of game-play on attitude and self-concept.

Another important critical aspect regarding game research comprises in the generalization of results. The results of a certain study are often related to individual differences like gender and psychosocial factors [9]. A more accurate classification scheme would be able to address this problem. Thus, in implementing a new technology, the absence of a standardized evaluation methodology can lead to a serious dilemma: In the case of serious games policy makers and procurers are on the one hand responsible for the money spent on education programs and so they question costs. On the other hand, teachers are concerned about programs which actually have an impact on the pupils' learning performance, so they question effectiveness. According to these arguments, assessment tools and techniques for estimating the benefit of serious games are urgently required. All in all, justifying the application of serious games is a highly complex problem that cannot be addressed on the surface only. A strong indicator that too vague approaches are impairing the take up of serious games comes from Smith, Blackmore, and Nesbitt [10], who argue that more standardized and better-validated techniques are required for a better comparison of serious games outcomes between different studies and, lately, for a strong justification of benefits. Key challenges, so they argue, include "how to collect data without influencing its generation, and more fundamentally, how to collect and validate data from humans where a primary emphasis is on what people are thinking and doing" [10]. Their work [10] presents a meta-analysis of data collection activities in serious games research.

A comprehensive framework for the measurement and justification of serious games was proposed by Kickmeier-Rust et al. [11], just as one example. This approach acknowledges the complexity of the field, the diversity of metrics and it differentiates three types of outcomes which must influence a final statement as a whole, that is, primary (the direct learning goal), secondary (potential side effects such as attitude towards the subject) and tertiary (learning unintended, perhaps wanted and unwanted competencies) outcomes of applying serious games. These authors also argue that many evaluation studies fail to provide objective interpretation of results. As an example, some studies found that gaming improves multitasking abilities. This can be sold as a positive aspect; however, it could be interpreted as the inability to focus on a single task, which definitely is a negative result. Stizmann [12] is backing this argument, saying "[there is] strong evidence of publication bias in simulation games research [towards positive learning effects]".

Now, do serious games constitute a promising, maybe successful educational genre per se? A meta-review by Wouters et al. [13] indicates that serious games are an effective genre for promoting learning and facilitating retention. Other meta-analyses (e.g., Connolly et al. [14]) found that serious games are not superior to equivalent no-gaming instruction. What we can conclude in general is that serious games are just an educational medium, there are good ones and bad ones, and we also can conclude that gaming per se is not success factor for learning. What literature says is basically that gaming support learning best, when the gaming experience (storytelling, game-play, game and learning mechanics) are tailored to the individual preferences, expectations, and abilities (in terms of gaming and in terms of learning) and when games are embedded in a global didactic concept [15, 16]. This view is also reflected in recent initiatives such as the European RAGE project (www.rageproject.eu) which aims at providing game industry with an ecosystem of educationally relevant assets for producing serious games.

To sum up, this example of educational games illustrates that the research field of entertainment computing needs very differentiated research approaches and methods and that various research disciplines need to cooperate. It also shows that not only the game software itself or the phase when it is used should be subject of research but also the conception and production of entertainment computing applications. Then entertainment computing has great potential to not only bring joy and fun to people but it is able to offer novel and sustainable solutions to a whole set of real-world problems - a subject worth of conducting research in.

3   Researching Entertainment Computing and Serious Games

Often resulting in highly complex IT systems, entertainment computing software is based on research results from a wide range of scientific disciplines such as computer science. Even within each discipline such as computer science, several fields are involved such as graphics, artificial intelligence, software engineering, programming techniques, simulation and modeling, database management, computer communication networks or computer security. However, computer games themselves are not often subject of research and merely seen as an application field. As a result, only single aspects of entertainment computing are often researched (e.g. real-time aspects in computer graphics research) and no holistic view is adopted. Also, it is often neglected that research that is directly concerned with entertainment computing can provide valuable contributions to established research disciplines as there are not only dependencies but interdependencies. For example, in computer game development extensive playtesting is conducted as this is of key importance for a game's commercial success. The results of these tests could provide highly valuable input for research efforts in the field of human computer interaction or multimedia. But dedicated scientific methods for playtesting are lacking as they have not been addressed by research that focuses on the interconnection between entertainment (serious) games and computing.

Because it is inherently multidisciplinary – bringing together disciplines such as psychology, art & design, computer science, pedagogics or social studies – research in this area always has the potential to cross-fertilize research and identify novel directions in research. For example, since almost all subfields of computer science are valuable contributors to research in entertainment computing and serious gaming, this field has the potential to open new research questions in other subfields of computer science and identify connections between them.

One strength of the field of entertainment computing and serious gaming is that it is able to generate interest and support from industry because of its economic relevance. Conversely, research results in this field have a high potential for directly benefitting industry in particular as well as culture and society in general. Internationally, work in the field of serious gaming can be characterized as being currently very active, with creative new technologies and interesting new game ideas being born continuously.

Recently, numerous game-specific conferences have been established – among others the Game Developers Conference (GDC), International Conference on Entertainment Computing (ICEC), Foundations of Digital Games (FDG), Games for Health or the GameDays. The ACE – Advances in Computer Entertainment Technology conference serious that started in 2004 is one of the few conferences dedicated fully to entertainment computing. Further, particular game aspects are discussed at well-known, highly ranked academic conferences such as the ACM conferences on Computer Graphics (SIGGRAPH) or on Human Factors in Computing Systems (CHI), the Artificial Intelligence for Interactive Digital Entertainment Conference (AIIDE) or the International Conference on Computer-supported Cooperative Learning (CSCL).

Figure 2 depicts the conference landscape of research that is associated with serious games. It is not surprising that according to the diversity of serious games and underlying variety of interdisciplinary concepts and technologies, serious games aspects are tackled in a broad spectrum of conferences and journals. Only a few conferences – namely the Joint Conference of Serious Games that is based on the Int'l Conference on Serious Games initiated and hosted by TU Darmstadt since 2010 in the context of the GameDays science meets business event series and the Int'l Conference on Serious Games, Development and Applications – address the characteristics of serious games in its core. Other conferences address serious games as application area from well-established technology fields, e.g., learning technologies, artificial intelligence, human computer interaction, mobile computing and sensor technologies or multimedia technologies and computer graphics. Game research conferences such as DIGRA, ICEC or FDG are not focused on serious games, but on game analysis (DIGRA), entertainment computing and (foundations of) digital games in general. Further application oriented conferences such as the European Conference on Games-based Learning or Games for Health (Europe) address serious games in specific application areas. Other research communities such as the multimedia research community do not consider computer games and game technology much.

To sum up, the research landscape is fragmented. Moreover, there are no highly ranked national or international conferences or journals in the area of entertainment computing yet, let alone serious games. This is an indicator that there is no established research community in the field, but it is instead dispersed in various subgroups. This fragmentation of the research community is a serious shortcoming of the field. As a consequence, no clear visions and directions of research can be located in the field, synergies are not properly exploited. Not only the research community is cluttered, research funding in the field stems from various sources (e.g. contract research from industry, public promotion of trade and industry, and to a lesser extent public funding from research agencies). Those initiatives are not coordinated, resulting in a suboptimal use of resources. It only starts that first prestigious policy makers like the Canadian NSERC recognized entertainment computing and games as a strategic ICT field in its own right.

Another shortcoming of entertainment computing is that it is sometimes just perceived as an application area of computer science and not as a discipline on its own. There are other research fields that are comparable, for example bioinformatics.

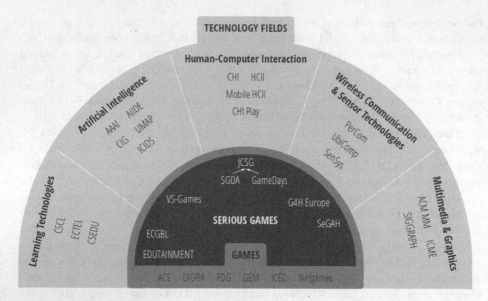

Fig. 2. Conference landscape in the field of serious games – technology-driven perspective. Source: Serious Games group at TU Darmstadt, 2016.

Is bioinformatics "just" an application of computer science to biology or is a simple application not enough and biology and computer science need to become more deeply coupled in a field on their own in order to define new questions and approaches? To achieve results in entertainment computing successfully, it becomes evident that computer science needs to be deeply coupled to other disciplines from the arts and the humanities. Even more, synergies between established sub-disciplines within each discipline need to be deeply coupled together with game related expertise in order to find solutions in entertainment computing. One example are sophisticated non-player characters where a common effort in research in artificial intelligence, computer graphics, virtual reality, image processing, human-computer interaction together with perception and psychology, storytelling and design is indispensable. Multidisciplinary cooperation like this will make significant contributions to shape the research field of entertainment computing and serious games.

4   Topics and Organization of the Book

A major undertaking of this book project is the survey of the state-of-the art as well as the identification, discussion and elaboration of core challenges in the field of entertainment, serious games and computing. The discussion of these challenges addresses promising approaches to solve them. Research efforts and resources needed that would lead to significant breakthroughs in the field are also a topic. Finally, visions for the field were collected and prerequisites for their achievement were formulated.

Being a non-established and fragmented research field and being characterized by the involvement of a wide range of disciplines, it is no wonder that the topics being associated with entertainment computing are very diverse. Thus, a first important step in the project that led to the publication of this book was to structure the research field. In the GI-Dagstuhl seminar where all prospective authors of this book met face-to-face for a week, the discussion started with five focal points that were identified in preparation for the workshop by the participants:

- Applications of Serious Games (e.g. Learning/Didactics, Health, ...)
- Game Design (e.g. Balancing, Social Aspects, Collaboration, Motivation, Affective Computing)
- Player-Game Interaction (e.g. User Interface, Design of User Experience, AR-Games, Mobile Games, ...)
- Game Development (e.g. Authoring, System Architectures, Content Generation...)
- Evaluation & Impact (e.g. Assessment, Analytics, Impact Modelling, Cognitive Theories...)

In a second step, working groups were formed and significant topics were mapped to chapters in this book. In Fig. 3 the typical iterative approach is depicted that is often adopted when entertainment software is developed. Each iteration has four major steps. In the design phase, game design (but also media design, interaction design etc.) is conceived and the whole authoring process for the development is planned. In the second phase, the design is implemented. For example, content including assets such as 3D models, textures, or sounds are created, software is written and tested. The resulting entertainment computing system is then used in the third phase. One special case is that the resulting system is a serious game that can be categorized according to its characterizing goal (e.g. an educational game or a health game). In the fourth and final phase, the usage of the system is evaluated. One of the most important questions here is to figure out whether the system is really found to be entertaining by the intended target group. In the case of serious games, it is also important to evaluate in how far the characterizing goals are met. Usually, the evaluation results are not satisfactory after the first iteration. Therefore, a next cycle is started where design, development, usage or even the evaluation methods are modified or adapted in order to obtain a better evaluation result. These iterations are repeated until the evaluation shows the system to be satisfactory. In order to speed up the process, the first iterations are often conducted with prototypes instead of fully developed and tested systems. Even paper prototypes may be used in the first iterations. The adaptation process depicted in the middle of the cycle in Fig. 3 does not only refer to the adaptation of all phases due to the evaluation results. Often software employing entertainment computing methodologies is also adaptive, e.g. for personalizing a gaming experience or for adapting game play based on evaluations conducted during the use of the software (e.g. an adapting the difficulty level of a health game to the player's heart rate). This type of adaptation effects all phases because (1) it needs to be designed carefully, (2) it needs to be implemented using appropriate adaptation mechanisms, (3) it needs to be executed during the usage of the game, and (4) it needs evaluation results (or even conduct evaluations during usage) that serve as basis for the adaptation.

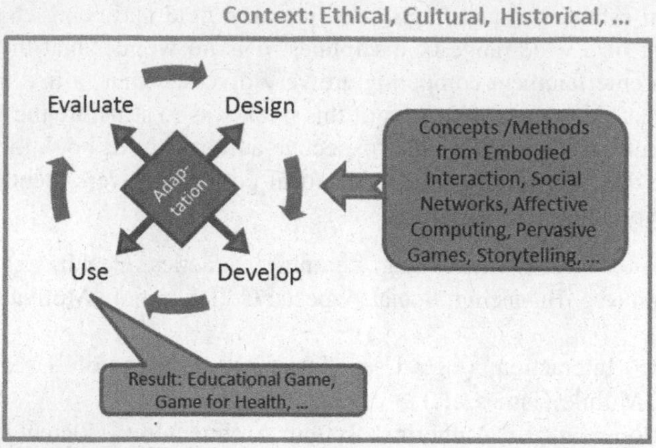

Context: Ethical, Cultural, Historical, ...

Fig. 3. A graphic map for explaining the organization of this book

Figure 3 also shows that the whole iterative process is informed by concepts and methods from various fields such as human computer interaction (e.g. methodologies for embodied interaction), social networks (e.g. for bringing in a social component in the entertainment), affective computing (e.g. to react on the player's emotional state), pervasive computing (e.g. to take the location of the player into consideration), or storytelling (e.g. to conceive non-linear stories that entertain the players and engaging them in the entertainment software). As shown in Fig. 3, this cycle and its sources of influence are framed in a context, e.g. an ethical context, a cultural context, or a historical context.

This book begins with discussing the context in its next three chapters. In Chap. 2 "A Brief History of Games" by Phil Wilkinson (responsible editor: Ralf Dörner) the history of serious gaming since Clark Abt introduced this term in 1970 is briefly reviewed. In this historical review, connections are made to research and practice in the contemporary field of serious games. After focusing on the historical context in Chap. 2, in Chap. 3 the ethical context is the major subject. Alyea Sandovar, Eelco Brad, Alexander Streicher, and Heinrich Söbke describe in this chapter that is entitled "Ethical Stewardship: Designing Serious Games Seriously" an ethical framework for serious game design. Moreover, they put forward four guidelines that support ethical stewardship and highlight the different areas where ethics play a role in serious game design. Responsible editor for Chap. 3 is Katharina Zweig. Chapter 4 also addresses the ethical context as well as the interdisciplinary context of serious games. Chapter 4 is entitled "The Serious Games Ecosystem: Interdisciplinary and Intercontextual Praxis" and written by Phil Wilkinson and Thomas Joseph Matthews (responsible editors: Stefan Göbel and Ralf Dörner). The chapter also looks at the relation between academia one the one hand and commercial production and contextual adoption on the other hand. With this, Chap. 4 strives to make researchers aware of the context of their work and help them to recognize that academic research of serious games does not occur in a vacuum.

After dealing with the context, the next chapters are about topics related to the cycle depicted in Fig. 3. The next two chapters address the design phase. "Processes and Models for Serious Game Design and Development" is the title of Chap. 5 written by Eelco Brad, Gregor Žavcer, and Alyea Sandovar (responsible editor: Katharina Zweig). In Chap. 5, various approaches are reviewed how the design and development process can be organized. Different models are presented that support specific design decisions concerning setting, mechanics, or gameplay. Moreover, the usage of design patterns for serious games is discussed. The approach to game development is then discussed on a more technical level in Chap. 6. Here, Mohamed Abbadi provides a "Taxonomy of Game Development Approaches" (responsible editor: Stefan Göbel). Chapter 6 discusses several languages that can shape the development process for entertainment software such as specific domain specific languages.

Chapters 7 und 8 address the second phase in the cycle shown in Fig. 3: the development phase. Chapter 7 is named "Serious Games Architectures and Engines". It is written by Heinrich Söbke and Alexander Streicher (responsible editor: Stefan Göbel). Chapter 7 covers the basic software engineering principles that are used in the development of software for entertainment. It presents typical software architectures. Chapter 7 also explains and illustrates the concept of a game engine and its characteristic components. But game development is not only about software development. Content that contains assets such as object models, textures, or sound also needs to be produced. Rahul Dey and Johannes Konert address this aspect in Chap. 8 "Content Generation for Serious Games" (responsible editor: Michael Kickmeier-Rust). In Chap. 8, they show how authors of entertainment software can create large amount of content quickly and efficiently. In particular, automatic content generation is discussed. Chapter 8 focuses on types of content that is specific to serious games.

The next two chapters delve deeper in the "usage phase" of the cycle shown in Fig. 3. They are concerned with a prominent type of serious games each. "Games for Learning" is the title of Chap. 9. It is written by Michaela Slussareff, Eelco Brad, Philip Wilkinson, Björn Stråått (responsible editor: Michael Kickmeier-Rust). It draws on recent meta-reviews to provide a comprehensive inventory of known learning and affective outcomes in serious games. Chapter 9 discusses different theoretical frameworks for learning, classifications for learning outcomes, and principles for designing serious games for learning. "Games for Health" are another noticeable example of serious games. "Games for Health" is the title of Chap. 10 by Jan D. Smeddinck (responsible editor: Stefan Göbel). This chapter gives an overview how entertainment computing has been applied to foster and improve personal and public health. It summarizes the basic promises and challenges in this application area. In addition, Chap. 10 examines example projects in the area of games for health.

The final phase of the cycle shown in Fig. 3, the evaluation phase, is the topic of the next three chapters. Chapter 11 has the title "Serious Games Evaluation: Process, Models and Concepts". It is written by Katharina Emmerich, Mareike Bockholt (responsible editor: Katharina Zweig). It deals with a major question always associated with serious games: In how far does the serious game achieve its characterizing goals? Chapter 11 familiarizes the reader with typical evaluation challenges and acquaints them with a framework of evaluation-driven design that offers guidance in the evaluation process. This is complemented with other models. Moreover, Chap. 11 examines three examples of best practice in serious game evaluation and illustrates how the abstract evaluation models can be used in a concrete evaluation. The next chapter focuses on a certain research method: experiments. For researchers in this area, the knowledge how to conduct and interpret scientific experiments in entertainment computing is valuable. Nataliya V. Bogacheva gives an introduction in Chap. 12 that is named "The Experimental Method as an Evaluation Tool in Serious Games Research and Development" (responsible editor: Maic Masuch). It explains the difference between true experiments, quasi-experiments and correlational studies. Moreover, Chap. 12 shows how experiments can be used to testify causal hypotheses employing an approved scientific paradigm. The next chapter, Chap. 13, is devoted to measuring and quantifying abstract concepts. For this, methods for data gathering are discussed and main psychological concepts and evaluation constructs are introduced. The chapter contains a compilation of concrete techniques (e.g. questionnaires) that address concepts relevant for the evaluation of serious games such as motivation, player experience, learning outcomes, health, well-being, or attitudes. Chapter 13 is named "Operationalization and Measurement of Evaluation Constructs" and it is written by Katharina Emmerich, Nataliya Bogacheva, Mareike Bockholt, and Viktor Wendel (responsible editor: Katharina Zweig).

Figure 3 illustrates that adaptation is a central concept in the area of entertainment computing and serious games. Alexander Streicher and Jan D. Smeddinck discuss this topic in Chap. 14 that is named "Personalized and Adaptive Serious Games" (responsible editor: Stefan Göbel). They present basic techniques for adaptability and adaptivity in serious games and highlight the challenges associated with employing them. Chapter 14 also contains examples that illustrate how these approaches for personalization and adaptation work in practice.

Lastly, the last 5 chapters deal with topics that inform and influence the development process in the context of entertainment computing (see the right-hand side in Fig. 3). Bernhard Maurer starts in Chap. 15 with looking at "Embodied Interaction in Play: Body-Based and Natural Interaction in Games" (responsible editor: Ralf Dörner). Beside examining example games that use body-based interactions, he presents fundamental bridging concepts between gameplay and various interaction paradigms that employ the human body, e.g., natural and tangible interaction. Chapter 15 also introduces the concept of sensorimotor couplings and illustrates design strategies that strive for using the human body as a resource for game interaction design. The human body cannot only be used to interact with entertainment software but also to convey emotions that can be used as a specific input. Chapter 16 deals with human emotions and their relevance in entertainment computing. This chapter is named "Affective Computing in Games" and is written by Benjamin Guthier, Ralf Dörner, and Hector P. Martinez (responsible editor: Ralf Dörner). The chapter provides an overview of different psychological models of affect, e.g. models of emotions or models of personality. Chapter 16 also discusses approaches how to obtain information about the affective states of users based for example on sensing physiological data that stem from the heart, the brain, the skin, the respiration, or the peripheral nervous system. Other sources of information about emotions of the users are body posture and movements, facial expressions, eye tracking, voice analysis, and text analysis. Chapter 16 examines examples how these pieces of information obtained by sensors can be exploited in serious games. While Chaps. 15 and 16 are concerned with an individual human player, Chap. 17 looks at social aspects of gaming. Social networks are an area that is highly relevant for entertainment computing. Accordingly, Chap. 17 is named "Social Network Games". It is written by Johannes Konert, Heinrich Söbke, and Viktor Wendel (responsible editor: Katharina Zweig). The authors introduce underlying theoretical models and concepts for utilizing social networks such as Facebook in entertainment software. Best practice examples illustrate potential usages. In addition, Chap. 17 discusses specific design and development aspects of social network games, e.g. the establishment of deep learning or toxic behavior of players. Similar to the ubiquity of social networks, the broad availability of mobile devices and advances in positioning technology such as GPS lead to a specific type of games. This type of games fosters technology mediated experiences in the players' local context. Games of this type are called "Pervasive Games" and it is the title of Chap. 18. The authors are Leif Oppermann and Michaela Slussareff (responsible editor: Ralf Dörner). They present and analyze examples of pervasive games, e.g. alternate reality games. Moreover, Chap. 18 provides an introduction to enabling technologies as well as to development aspects of serious games, specific authoring concepts, and considerations for the design process. Finally, Antonia Kampa, Susanne Haake, and Paolo Burelli look at "Storytelling in Serious Games" in Chap. 19 (responsible editor: Stefan Göbel). Chapter 19 briefly describes storytelling basics. Moreover, it presents the current state of the art in interactive storytelling addressing aspects such as example experiences, authoring tools and challenges in the field.

All chapters have in common that they have a section where further readings are recommended for delving deeper into the topics addressed in the book. Moreover, most chapters explicitly identify research challenges. This book is for persons interested in research aspects of entertainment computing and serious games. In particular, it is for persons who want to conduct research in this area themselves. Thus, the chapters not only provide their readers with valuable basic information and guidance but with a cornucopia of ideas where future research would be valuable. It shows that entertainment computing and serious games are a rich, exciting, and rewarding field for research that is even sometimes, but not always, fun.

References

1. Dörner, R., Göbel, S., Effelsberg, W., Wiemeyer, J.: Serious Games – Foundations, Concepts and Practice. Springer, Cham (2016)
2. Sawyer, B., Smith, P.: Serious Games Taxonomy. Game Developers Conference (2008). http://www.dmill.com/presentations/serious-games-taxonomy-2008.pdf
3. Cooper, S., Khatib, F., Treuille, A., Barbero, J., Lee, J., Beenen, M., Leaver-Fay, A., Baker, D., Popović, Z.: Predicting protein structures with a multiplayer online game. Nature **466** (7307), 756–760 (2010)
4. Deterding, S., Khaled, R., Nacke, L.E., Dixon, D.: Gamification: toward a definition. In: Proceedings of ACM CHI (2011)
5. Marczewski, A.: Gamification: A Simple Introduction & a Bit More, self-published as eBook on Amazon Digital Services (2013)

6. Kickmeier-Rust, M.D. (ed.): Proceedings of the 1st International Open Workshop on Intelligent Personalization and Adaptation in Digital Educational Games, 14 October 2009, Graz, Austria (2009)
7. Moreno-Ger, P., Burgos, D., Torrente, J.: Digital games in eLearning environments: current use and emerging trends. Simul. Gaming 40(5), 669–687 (2009)
8. Boyle, E.A., Connolly, T.M., Hainey, T.: The role of psychology in understanding the impact of computer games. Entertainment Comput. 2(2), 69–74 (2011)
9. Stege, L., Van Lankveld, G., Spronck, P.: Teaching high school physics with a serious game. Int. J. Comput. Sci. Sports 11(1), 123–134 (2012)
10. Smith, S.P., Blackmore, K., Nesbitt, K.: A meta-analysis of data collection in serious games research. In: Loh, C., Sheng, Y., Ifenthaler, D. (eds.) Serious Games Analytics: Methodologies for Performance Measurement, Assessment, and Improvement, pp. 31–55. Springer, Berlin (2015)
11. Kickmeier-Rust, M.D., Mattheiss, E., Braunecker, J., Albert, D.: Cool and popular? Yes! But are educational computer games useful? In: Proceedings of the International Conference on Education, Research and Innovation, ICERI 2011, Madrid, Spain (2011)
12. Stizmann, T.: A meta-analytic examination of the instructional effectiveness of computer-based simulation games. Pers. Pyschol. 64, 489–528 (2011)
13. Wouters, P., van Nimwegen, C., van Oostendorp, H., van der Spek, E.D.: A meta-analysis of the cognitive and motivational effects of serious games. J. Educ. Psychol. 10(2), 249–265 (2013)
14. Connolly, T.M., Boyle, E.A., MacArthur, E., Hainey, T., Boyle, J.M.: A systematic literature review of empirical evidence on computer games and serious games. Comput. Educ. 59, 661–686 (2013)
15. Kickmeier-Rust, M.D., Albert, D. (eds.): An Alien's Guide to Multi-adaptive Educational Games. Informing Science Press, Santa Rosa (2012)
16. Kickmeier-Rust, M.D., Albert, D.: Educationally adaptive: balancing serious games. Int. J. Comput. Sci. Sport 11(1), 15–28 (2012)

A Brief History of Serious Games

Phil Wilkinson[✉]

The Centre for Excellence in Media Practice, Bournemouth University, Bournemouth, UK
pwilkinson@bournemouth.ac.uk

Abstract. Serious Games are now an established field of study. In this field most would attribute the rise of Serious Games to Clark C Abt's creation of the term in 1970, or indeed Ben Sawyer's popularization of it in 2002. However, considering the rich history of purposing non-digital games, itself preceded by discussions of purposing play that are traceable to the work of Plato, it can be said that Serious Games is a contemporary manifestation of centuries old theories and practices. In this chapter, we explore the pre-history of Serious Games, beginning with the suggested purpose, and purposing of play. Throughout this historical review we identify key in research and practice that are apparent in the contemporary Serious Games field.

Keywords: Serious games · Play · Simulation-based learning · Game-based learning · Games for social change · Games for health · Playful learning

1 Introduction

"As important new research begins in such matters as the cognitive implications of play, the sociology of sport, simulations in education, and interaction behavior, it is vital that researchers and students have easy access to some of the major historical and current information on the study of games, and of play." [1]

Serious Games as a field of study did spring into existence. There is a rich, interdisciplinary history that has converged into the current Serious Games ecosystem. Tracing back this convergence reveals historical trends emerging from fundamental discussions exploring the very notion of play itself. Furthermore, concepts prevalent in contemporary Serious Games discussion are often concepts from historical fields that have been reapplied. Therefore, to take the study of serious game seriously it is necessary to consider these historical origins. These trends and concepts are apparent when exploring the application of games, their conceptualisation, and their evaluation.

For instance, exploring the application of games for purposes other than entertainment has a historical precedence in the application of play – especially in educational contexts. Plato, for example, philosophised that reinforcing certain behaviours exhibited in play would reinforce those behaviours as an adult. Indeed, it can be argued that from the 19th century onwards it has been assumed that children's play and games are a developmental imperative. Seminal development psychologist Jean Piaget even goes so

R. Dörner et al. (Eds.): Entertainment Computing and Serious Games, LNCS 9970, pp. 17–41, 2016.
DOI: 10.1007/978-3-319-46152-6_2

far as to suggest "play is the work of children" [2] - a philosophy apparent in contemporary Serious Games development. Other contexts that have become key adopters and developers of Serious Games have a similar history.

Chaturgana – argued by historians to be the precursor to chess – developed in 7th Century India, was the first game, on record, to explicitly apply a militaristic metaphor to a board game [3]. Taking this as a starting point, we can then trace this militaristic application of games to more recognisable *digital* Serious Games such as America's Army. Paralleling this historical application of games in educational and military contexts, there are examples of pre-digital games designed to enact social change and the governmental application of games for serious purposes. For instance, the Landlord's Game, created in 1902 and precursor to Monopoly, was designed to illustrate the dangers of capitalist approaches to land taxes and property renting [3].

Interweaving this historical contextual adoption of Serious Games, both analogue and digital, is the development of conceptualisations relating to their application. For instance, the often repeated notion of the 'magic circle' developed by play theorist Johan Huizinga was conceived to describe imaginary play spaces [4]. Additional key terms such as engagement, interaction, or flow emerged from the fields of education, computer scie nce, and positive psychology. These cross-over terms applied in Serious Games can be viewed as the attempted ludic framing of theories, models, and frameworks from other fields.

This development and dismissal of theories and approaches can be applied to Serious Games development and evaluation. The field of Serious Games sometimes suffers for its interdisciplinarity due to inconsistent definitions, evaluation methods, and multiple conceptualisations. However, there is potential for Serious Games research to benefit from the historical precedents set out by its converging disciplines. As a recent meta-analysis suggests [5], the majority of educational Serious Games do not explicitly adopt a key learning theory. Additionally, the same methodological problems of ecological invalidity and prescriptive, lab-based play evaluations in the 1970s [2] are apparent in some contemporary Serious Games evaluative studies [6, 7].

2   Chapter Overview

"Yet individuals can once again become involved, and thought and action can again be integrated, in games created to simulate these social processes. The zest for life felt at those exhilarating moments of history when men participated in effecting great changes on the models of great ideas can be recaptured by simulations of roles in the form of Serious Games" [8]

Given the intercontextuality and interdisciplinarity of Serious Games, it would be impossible for any researcher to be familiar with the rich, dynamic history of every informing discipline. The goal of this chapter is to retroactively apply contemporary discussions, approaches, and applications of Serious Games onto historical precedents. In this we will map a developmental trajectory for Serious Games research, beginning with early philosophical discussions.

Plato's early discussions regarding the purpose of play – and to an extent, the purposing of play – mark a starting point in a millennia old debate. This debate surrounding play's purpose has direct implications for the study of Serious Games, especially in relation to educational applications. Of course part of this play-debate is the conceptual difficulty in defining play resonated with contemporary difficulties in defining Serious Games. In addition, lessons can be taken forward from attempts to research and measure play during the height of the behaviourist psychological paradigm.

Paralleling and interweaving with this debate are, of course, discussions about the applications of games. The distinction between play and games is as contentious as their singular definitions. Application of games - specifically for serious purposes - throughout history will be highlighted. From this we will see a pattern of purposing and contextual adoption that emerges. Moreover, when we cast current, generally accepted definitions of a serious game back, we can reveal a rich history of purposing games that reflect current, formalised approaches.

The term Serious Games can be traced to the seminal work of Clark Abt [8]. Through this work, coupled with the rising popularity of video games in popular culture, contemporary uses of the term Serious Games imply a digital form. As will be demonstrated there historically, multiple non-digital examples. For the sake of posterity this chapter will view the Serious Games development trajectory in relation to the development of digital Serious games – that is, pre- and post-digital. Pre-digital will include the aforementioned debates surrounding play, key examples, and related fields of simulation-based learning. Post-digital will highlight the continuation of historical trends as they converge on contemporary research into Serious Games.

In addition, the development of Serious Games will be discussed in relation to the increased legitimization of entertainment games. As media theorist Henry Jenkins suggests:

> *"Games represent a new lively art, one as appropriate for the digital age as those earlier media were for the machine age. They open up new aesthetic experiences and transform the computer screen into a realm of experimentation and innovation that is broadly accessible"* [9]

Henry Jenkin's framing of the development of the digital games field as creating increased capacity for experimentation and innovation directly speaks to contemporary understandings of Serious Games. It illustrates the link between the development of entertainment game technologies and their application in Serious Games.

Finally, writing on the emerging field of pre-digital games-based learning, particularly in reference to his own city administration game *Metropolis* Richard Duke suggested that *"gaming is a future's language, a new form of communication emerging suddenly and with great impact across many lands and in many problem situations."* [10] Converging this with Jenkin's assertion that games are *"the thing that pushes forward innovation and experimentation."* [9], we are well positioned to take the developmental trajectories discussed in this chapter and make reasonable speculations about future trends.

3   Purpose of Play

> *"[I]f a boy is to be a good farmer or a good builder, he should play at building toy houses or at farming and be provided by his tutor with miniature tools modelled on real ones. . . . One should see games as a means of directing children's tastes and inclinations to the role they will fulfil as adults."* – [11]

Plato's proposal that play can be used to guide a child's development and, by extension, suggests that play can be educationally purposed [11]. However, despite this proposal of purposing, up until the end of the 18th century play was viewed as something to be curtailed in children. It was only with the works of Enlightenment philosophers Friedrich Schiller and Jean-Jacques Rousseau that we began to consider play a right of childhood [2]. Through their work we began to recognise a contemporary framing of play as an intrinsically purposeful activity.

In play theorist David Cohen's extensive review of play he suggests that the early 19th century saw the development of *"enlightened laws [giving] children a kind of freedom which they had never had before. If they used some of that freedom to play, then play had to have some purpose."* [2] He argues that there is an implicit assumption – not often examined – that play must serve some purpose, even after removing the suggested guided structuring of play put forward by early play-based educationalist Frobels and Montessori.

Through this ongoing discussion regarding the purposing of play, it appears there is an increase in perceived complexity regarding play. Moving from play is a necessity for expelling excess energy, towards an evolutionary perspective of play as the development of skills needed for survival or the cathartic practice of primitive behaviours [2, 12]. As playful behaviour is exhibited across the animal kingdom – with greater frequency in youth – Groos' evolutionary theory is still present even in neuroscientific enquiries into play [13].

Taking an, admittedly, much broader and encompassing understanding of the purpose of play, Johan Huzinga argued that play itself is a foundational necessity of cultural development. In his seminal work Homo Ludens – or playing man – he begins from a similar starting point to Hall and Groos, that is, examining what meaning we can take from existence of play in the animal kingdom. For Huzinga this demonstrated that play predates cultured society and play itself is culturally generative, that is *"culture arises in the form of play, that it is played from the very beginning"* [4].

In addition to Huzinga's exploration of the play element of culture – that is how culture itself exhibits playful qualities – he is perhaps best known for his conception of the magic circle. This conception was an attempt to capture the physical or metaphysical boundaries of play spaces - *"All play moves and has its being within a play-ground marked off beforehand either materially or ideally, deliberately or as a matter of course"* [4]. In contemporary digital game studies, this notion of a distinct space in which play happens is readily applied to the virtual spaces of digital games [14–16].

Although the magic circle has become a key concept in game studies - popularised by game studies researchers Katie Salen and Eric Zimmerman [14] it has seen limited application to Serious Games [17]. One example creates a salient discussion of the necessity of understanding the magic circle, or how this play space can be broken, in games-based learning [18]. Although the magic-circle can be blurry, increasingly so with the rise of pervasive games [19], it has interesting implications for Serious Games. For instance, the notion that boundaries between playing and not playing are *"fuzzy and permable"* [14] directly speaks to the inherent tension of balancing fun and purpose in Serious Games design [20].

While the magic circle is especially relevant today, current discourse has also been informed by other early theories of play – especially those that discuss play's purpose. Social learning theorist Lev Vyogtosky conceptualised play as wish fulfilment in which children use their imaginations to free themselves from immediate situational constraints [21]. In addition, Vygotsky believed that *"[i]n play a child always behaves beyond his average age, above his daily behavior; in play it is as though he were a head taller than himself"* [21].

Vygotsky's contemporary, Jean Piaget, argued that play affords the consolidation of existing skills through repetition – as well as developing a sense of mastery. Counter to the other theorists mentioned here, Piaget paid little direct attention to the role of play. However, his focus on cognitive stages of development informs the work of psychologists who seek to categorise play stages [2]. As such children's play - or capacity for specific types of play – is used as a means of assessing their developmental stage (Broadhead, 2006). Following the work of early educational-play theorists is a pervasive notion of play's role in children's cognitive, emotional, and social developmental (Bergen, 2002; Pellegrini, 2009).

Furthermore, pretend play in which a child roleplay societal characters – a doctor or fireman for example – can be seen as the child exploring cultural norms [2, 22, 23]. This underlying assumption of play's purpose is apparent in modern digital play activities – as evidenced by contemporary discussions exploring the role of digital games in expressing and reinforcing socio-civic norms [24, 25]. As play has been repeatedly framed as having an intrinsic developmental purpose, this same notion of purpose has been applied to modern digital video games [26–28].

Given the pervasiveness of this assumed purpose of play, it is perhaps inevitable the same assumption has extended to digital games. As seminal sociologist Erving Goffman suggests – *"[t]he function of play has been commented on for many centuries, to little avail"* [29]. Reflecting this functionalist approach to understanding play – assuming that it must serve some purpose – is the functionalised approach. Following the logic that play must indeed be a purposeful activity, and therefore serves a purpose, it can be assumed that play can indeed *be purposed*. Here we have an emergence of the key tension of between play, fun, and entertainment and the underlying purposes of Serious Games.

Reflecting the inherent tension of balancing fun and purpose in Serious Games is the work of French Sociologist Roger Caillois. In Man, Play and Games [30] Caillois comprehensively develops the work of Johan Huzinga through categorizing play. For Calliois, play existed on a spectrum from *ludus* (etymological origin for the term ludology, frequently applied to the field games studies) or game to *padia* or free play. He also argued here there is a human tendency to move from *paida* to *ludus* play. This has interesting implications for the Serious Games field, perhaps an extreme example of moving from free-play to purposeful rule-based games. In addition, it also speaks to the historical approach of functionalising play.

4 Purposing Play for Learning

"The playing adult steps sideward into another reality; the playing child advances into new stages of mastery. I propose the theory that the child's play is the infantile form of the human

ability to deal with experience by creating model situations and to master reality by experiment and planning." [31]

Given Plato's assertion that the play of the child shapes their development into adulthood, in conjunction with humanistic psychologist Erik Erikson suggestion of the developmental potential of play, it is understandable that play has so frequently been purposed for learning. As previously touched upon, this notion of purposing play has existed alongside the idea that play has an intrinsic – if ineffable – purpose. Revisiting Rousseau we see that his advocacy for the rights of citizens, and for the right for children to *"eat, run, and play as much as they please"* [2] touches upon a blurred notion of children's play as work. This notion of the child's right to play is now legally mandated in under the United Nations Convention on the Rights of the Child [32].

For Rousseau *"to a child of 10 or 12, work or play are all one"* [2]. The influence of Rousseau's work is apparent in the *playful* approach to early years' education pioneered by Frobel and Montessori. It is worth noting however, that both educationalists believed in the need for purposing, or controlling, play. Frobel's kindergartens predominantly used teacher-directed imaginative play. For Montessori, her often misinterpreted quote *"play was the work of the child"* [2] referred to her encouraged practice of object-based real-world interaction, not to free, unguided play.

This notion of harnessing the captivating nature of play and by extension the stratification of different types of play in terms of their development value has persisted. For instance, Montessori's focus on object-based real-world play stood in opposition to the teacher-guided imagination-based play of Frobel [2] In the western cultures this attitude pervades as an expectation of parents to play with their children, an expectation that frequently places the developmental nourishment of real-world play in opposition to digital-play.

Indeed, digital technology is often framed as destroying childhood [33, 34]. Of course, this has direct implications for the perception of digital games as developmentally important in play [27, 28, 35]. When discussing the role of digital Serious Games in children's education it is worth considering this cultural context. It should, however, be noted that this attitude is not universal. As described by Gaskins, Haight, and Lancy [36], we can categorise cultural expectations of play's developmental significance into three areas.

Western society broadly fits into a cultural category of cultivating play, in that play is actively encouraged in children. This is in opposition to 'culturally curtailed play', where children are dissuaded from play; and 'culturally accepted play', in which play is expected but not encouraged. Viewing the Western development of play expectations then, it is perhaps little surprise that the expectations placed on parents to encourage play with their children are mirrored in parents' expectation of schools. A 2009 report funded by the UK Government Department for education found out of 952 parents surveyed *"over 90 % [were in] agreement that young children should have fun and learn through play at primary school"* [37]. Moreover, it is worth considering that advances in Serious Games have typically emerged from this western cultural context, particularly the US [8, 38].

Given this expectation of younger children to learn through play perhaps explains the prevalence of Serious Games – particularly learning games – for younger learners

[39]. Of course this expectation of play-based learning has created a tension in marrying curricular expectations and playful pedagogies [40]. It is worth recognising that just as the popularity of purposing play for learning reflects the popularity of educational Serious Games, there are other historical purposes of play that are reflected in contemporary Serious Games. Education therefore is not the only purposing of play that directly speaks to current applications of Serious Games.

5   Purposing Play for Therapy

"Play is the highest development in childhood, for it alone is the free expression of what is in the child's soul. ... Children's play is not mere sport. It is full of meaning and import". [41]

This position of play, interpreted by early educational-play theorist Frobel, is the core of the historical development of play as therapy. For Froebel, play can be seen as an expression of internal experiences – especially through symbolic or imaginative play [2]. However, the notion of play's internal reflectivity can be traced, again, back to the 18th century work of Jean-Jacques Rousseau. In his seminal text Emile, or On Education, Rosseau highlights the importance of understanding children through observing them in play [2, 42].

Tracing the historical development of play as a therapeutic medium we reveal two justifications for play's application here. First, as Rosseau and Froebel suggested, play can be viewed as a window into the child's inner experiences – a justification that is used for current therapeutic Serious Games [43]. Secondly, it is also suggested play is the natural behaviour of the child, so engaging in therapeutic activity through play allows for a naturalistic approach that puts the child at ease [42]. It is interesting that this second justification has familiar echoes in the justification for the use of games in therapeutic settings, and indeed education [44] due to children's familiarity and comfort with the medium.

Given the assumption that play provides a window into the internal representations of the child, it is of little surprise that this approach was adopted in early psychoanalytical approaches. In fact, the first case of applying play in a therapeutic setting can be traced to Sigmund Freud. In his treatment of a young boy suffering from a phobia he suggestion to the parent to observe the boy's play at home to provide insight into his mental state [2, 42]. As well as this play-analysis approach developed by Freud – and further expanded by Madeleine Klein - was Anna Freud's use of play as a means of developing child-therapist relationships [2, 42, 45].

It is perhaps the work of humanist psychologist Carl Rogers in play therapy that has the greatest significance for play therapy today – and by extension the therapeutic use of Serious Games. Rogers pioneered the client-centred approach to therapy, highlighting notions of self-determination and an internal desire for self-actualisation on the part of the client [46]. This was developed by the work of Viginia Axline who – in effect - operationalised the humanist paradigm set-forth by Rogers in the form of child-centred play therapy [47].

For Axline *"A play experience is therapeutic because it provides a secure relationship between the child and the adult, so that the child has the freedom and room to state himself in his own terms."* [47]. Currently, this child-centred play therapy is the most popular approach, with the largest body of research, in therapeutic practice [42, 48]. Taking this historical perspective of play therapy into account, in addition to an awareness of current practices, we can see multiple implications for the application of Serious Games for therapeutic purposes.

The assumption of children's natural desire to be playful in the current context of digital games' prevalence is often used a justification which is frequently made explicit [43, 49]. Similarly, the justification of play-based therapies as allowing for the child to freely express themselves resonates with current discourse arguing that Serious Games application affords degrees of freedom not otherwise available. Furthermore, it has direct implications for therapeutic Serious Games developers as they consider player agency [50], or the creation of virtual safe-spaces [51].

Blurring the line between the – admittedly already blurry – boundary of Serious Games and serious application of entertainment games, we can see the application of play based therapies in other therapeutic contexts such as cognitive behavioural therapies [49, 52]. There is indeed increasing interest in the use of entertainment game as a means of building rapport, or fostering therapist-child relationships [49, 53]. However, counter to historical applications of play as a means of developing positive researcher-client relationships, it has been suggested that current uses of digital-play based interventions may undermine this relationship [54].

We must acknowledge that, like playful learning and the broader Serious Games eco-system, we have predominantly focussed on the child. However, in the current social construction of childhood as an opportunity for play - even if it is directed - it is perhaps now little surprise that the number of Serious Games reflect this. Returning to our original quotation of Plato – *"one should see games as a means of directing children's tastes and inclinations to the role they will fulfil as adults."* [11] – we see traces of our final historical play-precedent for Serious Games.

6 Purposing Play for Social Control

"No society has ever really noticed how important play is for social stability. My proposal is that one should regulate children's play. Let them always play the same games, with the same rules and under the same conditions, and have fun playing with the same toys. That way you'll find that adult behavior and society itself will be stable." [11]

Although this is third time we return to Plato, it is because his self-proclaimed ground-breaking work has such implications for the purposing of play. In this instance though, we refer to his specific suggestion of the need to, or the potential of, regulating play. Play theorist David Cohen's review of play is, at times, critical of the attitudes informing early play conceptions [2] He argued that the work of Froebel and Montessori were largely informed by puritan attitudes of the time, in that it was expected that leisure time was to be spent bettering oneself. This notion frames the motivation play-based learning less as less rooted in pedagogic rationale, and more in reflecting the societal expectations of the time.

Prescribing playful activities, as Plato directly suggests and Cohen implies in the approach of early play theorists, can be viewed as a means of directing and controlling children's behaviour such that you control their developmental trajectory. This readily reflected in the discourse surrounding cognitive, physical, and socio-emotional development of children through play-based learning. It can also be argued that through prescriptive play you are able to control the development of their socio-cultural attitudes.

For play theorist David Cohen, the early work of play educationalists and practitioners was an attempt at control – a perspective reflected in Brian Sutton-Smith's extensive historical and rhetorical unpacking of play [55]. Between 1890 and 1920, the American government spent $100million creating playgrounds across America. Suttonsmith argues that this investment was predominantly a means of implicitly training youngsters to become integrated into, and productive members of, society.

This notion of play-spaces as a means of cultivating desired cultural and societal values can be traced to the work of Henry Curtis. In Curtis' *Education Through Play*, we see the purpose of play for social cultivation emerge – Curtis suggests that *"the idleness of the street... is morally dangerous"* [2]. Developing Sutton-Smith's argument, Cohen surmises that *"Western societies have used play to make children conform"* [2]. Following this, there is indeed a rise in the use of Serious Games for changing or cultivating social attitudes [27, 56, 57].

In addition, when applying this notion of *control* to Serious Games more broadly, we can begin to unpack implicit societal messages. For instance, the frequently referenced America's Army – a training and recruitment game – we can see a societal message promoting militarism [58]. The notion of using play to encourage children to conform can be seen as echoing, on a societal level, the application of play in mediating learning or therapy. It can be argued that this same philosophy of purposing play as a means of cultivating desired behaviours can be applied to Serious Games. Frequent justifications for the use of Serious Games are their perceived *'holding power'* [59], and ability to engage and motivate players [60, 61].

From this we can see how this historical approach to purposing play has direct implications for the application areas of Serious Games. Play is well established, from the perspective of academic inquiry and socio-cultural expectations, as a means of engaging children in educational, developmental, and therapeutic activities. Perhaps most significant, however, is the broader approach of *purposing* play and games. Therefore, the rich history of inquiry and discussion surrounding the purpose and purposing of play directly resonates with contemporary applications of Serious Games.

Having established that there is indeed antecedence in historical research - and broader socio-cultural expectations of play - that informs current approaches to Serious Games, it is necessary to narrow our focus to games specifically. The following sections will outline approaches to purposing non-digital games, before moving on to the purposing of digital games – or what we would recognise as Serious Games research. First however, it is worth considering historical research into games more broadly as there are parallels to be drawn with the contemporary legitimization of Serious Games research.

7   Emerging Study of Games

"The comparative study of games is one that deserves a high place among our inquiries into the history and development of culture. Their origin belongs to the time preceding that of written records; and many games were not only the product of primitive conditions, but represent the means by which man endeavored to bring himself into communion with and to penetrate the secrets of the natural powers that surrounded him." [62]

The historical study of non-digital games has seen an oscillation of regard. Stewart Culin's seminal work in the late 19th and early 20th elevates games as something worthy of study. Despite the historical antecedents and contemporary elevation of the significance of play at the time of Culin's work, games were still seen as having limited significance for research. This is remarked upon by W. H. Holmes, the Director of the Bureau of American Ethnography, when reporting on Culin's exploration of the Games of North American Indians in 1903:

"The popular notion that games ... are trivial in nature and of no particular significance as a subject of research soon gave way, under the well-conducted studies of Mr Culin, to an adequate appreciation of their importance as an integral part of human culture" [63]

Culin's work preceded Johan Huizgina's book *Homo Ludens* [4], Roger Caillois work *Man, Play and Games* [30], and seminal games studies such as *The Kissing Games of Adolescents in Ohio* [64] or *Children's Games in the Street and Playground* [65]. With regards to Huizinga and Caillois especially, their work directly builds upon Culin's position that games are significant for cultural inquiry as their origin *"preced[es] that of written records"* [62]. For Huizinga and Caillois play and games both formed and are informed by culture, as evidenced by their existence prior to human civilization.

In theory then, it could be said that Culin's work provide a turning point in promoting serious academic inquiry into games. However, as discussed in the preceding section, there is still non-trivial philosophical discussion of games. Even if this philosophical inquiry doesn't hold the same rigour as the ethnographic study of Culin's and those that followed, it still demonstrates that games were seen as worth 'serious' consideration.

It can be argued that Culin's pioneering studies of games - counter to notions of games triviality at the time - are reflected in the contemporary pioneering of Serious Games and advocates of their legitimacy [66, 67]. Additionally, this movement towards taking games - and Serious Games - 'seriously' is not a linear process but one of ebbs and flows. As suggested by Jasper Juul [68], supported by the work of Elliot Avedon and Brian Sutton Smith [1], there is a historical oscillation of regard for the significance of games. When mapping this historical antecedent onto contemporary work in Serious Games it is perhaps not surprising then that Clark Abt's foundational work [8] was comparatively ignored until the beginning of the 21st century.[1]

Within this broader academic shifting of priorities is a field specific changing of priorities in what is considered 'serious' inquiry. Current academic focuses on Serious Games can be considered interdisciplinary but there are dominant disciplines within this eco-system. What is evident when exploring historical academic consideration of non-digital games is there is dominance of anthropological and ethnographic approaches [1].

---

[1] Based on number of Citations from 1970 to 1990 compared with 1991 to 2016.

This stands in contrast to the current study of Serious Games research dominated by social sciences, psychology, and, naturally, fields from computing.

What does this mean for the study of Serious Games? Firstly, like historical studies of games, Serious Games has not followed a consistent linear path of legitimisation, but instead moves in stops and starts. For instance, the Clark Abt introduced the term 'Serious Games' in 1970, however, according to Tarja Susi [69] and Damien Djaouti [38] it wasn't until 2002 that 'Serious Games' came into wide usage. This dynamism is reflected in the shifting consensus on what constitutes 'serious' Serious Games research – that is, which research should be prioritised in the field. Additionally, there is again historical precedent for the purposing of games – which will be explored here - amongst the broader shifting academic landscape.

8   Origins of the Purpose and Purposing of Games

"[Here] the general position taken is that a game performs something of a bridge function in development. It allows for the expression of given impulses but at the same time safeguards the players by putting limits on the way in which those impulses can be expressed." [64]

The above quote is taken from *The Kissing Games of Adolescents in Ohio* by Brian Sutton-Smith [64], in this he concludes that games do indeed serve a role in children's development. For Sutton-Smith, games offer an opportunity for children to express themselves in a safe-space that provides rule-based boundaries to help shape their expressions. This notion of games as providing a space for children's safe exploration of necessary skills or social practices builds directly on notions of play's purpose in their development. There is however, a distinction to be made here that follows Roger Caillois's conception of a *ludus – paida* spectrum [30].

The distinction between play and games can be centred on the introduction of rules – systematic boundaries, taking different forms, that shape playful activities. It is in this distinction that we move away from the perceived *intrinsic purpose* of free-play, and the *intentional purposing* of games through the intentional construction of game-rules. This purposeful construction of games as rule-based systems formed a key starting position in the rise of 'simulation gaming' throughout the mid-20th century.

According to Wolf and Crookall, *"the modern era of simulation/gaming began in the late 1950s"* [70]. They argue that it emerged through a combination of 'war-gaming' practices, and new educational theories that prioritised active participation – such as experiential learning [71]. Indeed, these same theories of experiential learning are apparent in contemporary Serious Games approaches [60, 69, 72]. Wolf and Crookall also acknowledge a historical precedence in this as they suggest war-games were formerly introduced in the 17th and 18th century – discounting war-themed *"parlour games"* chess and Chaturanga [70].

Given this historical integration of game-based training in military contexts across multiple centuries, it is perhaps unsurprising that this would have a role in the development of simulation-gaming. Even less surprising then is its consideration as the forefront of modern Serious Games practices, as exemplified by leading Serious Game *America's*

Army. The rise of simulation-based learning - and the rise of Serious Games - perhaps owes much to historical military training practices. From the 1950s onwards commercial organisations began to adopt simulation-based learning practices.

Simulation-based learning, with its military origins and supported by the emergence of participatory theories of learning, was seen as a necessity given the rising complexity of real-world practices. However, simulation-game rules could be constructed to accurately reflect complex social, economic, and political systems. Writing on the subject, simulation-based learning pioneer Richard Duke suggests that:

> *"Gaming/Simulation is one device that is useful for presenting a dynamic model which is an abstraction of complex reality .... Games can be viewed as abstract symbolic maps of various multidimensional phenomena."* [10]

In Duke's writing we can again see a justification for the use of non-digital games-based learning practices, which also hold true for modern Serious Games practices. However, it can be suggested that Serious Games extends and builds upon this justification, as digital technologies offer greater representational affordances.

As touched upon earlier in this chapter, Duke became an advocate for simulation-based learning practices, as evidenced by his seminal book *Gaming: The Future Language*. Here again we can draw parallels with the same - at times - evangelical rhetoric surrounding the *'power'* of Serious Games, and an anticipatory excitement for their potential across multiple domains [6, 57, 69, 73–76]. Writing on the subject of Simulation gaming in 1995, taking a historical perspective of the preceding 35 years, Wolfe and Crookall identified several impediments to the field - directly related to this sense of interdisciplinary excitement:

> *"The field [Simulation-Based Learning] often celebrates its interdisciplinary nature and recognizes it's diverse origins. This very nature, however, encourages a lack of independent structure, a lack of recognition by the established disciplines and sciences, and a free-form orientation that often attracts the temporary interest of dilettantes who soon move onto other fancies without leaving much of an important."* [70]

Interestingly, this passage can be readily applied to the current Serious Games ecosystem. An excitement across multiple disciplines has created a fractured field of study [72]. Moreover, this fractured excitement has a role in creating somewhat superficial - or as Wolf and Crook describe, 'dilettante' - research and developmental practices. This is evidenced by limited empirical Serious Games evaluations [60, 77] and a lack of integration of theories of learning into educational Serious Games [5].

A justification for the purposing of simulation based learning, alongside following theories of experiential learning, is the affordance of holistic representation. Learners participating in a simulation of policy and resource management with Richard Duke's *Metropolis* [10] for example, would be presented with a representation of all of the processes inherent in this. Therefore, this would lead to a gestalt understanding of the overall system. Again, this follows comparable justifications for Serious Games – especially those that attempt to develop appreciation for social systems, or an empathy for the social issues that arise in these systems [57, 73].

With analogous simulation-based learning then, there are parallels to be drawn with contemporary Serious Games. There is a comparable diversity of application domains and interest across academic disciplines – in itself leading to tensions as the field develops. Moreover, contemporary Serious Games follow similar justifications of experiential, problem-based, and situated learning theories. Serious Games indeed follows the same trajectory of simulation-based learning. Moreover, the frequency with which the two fields are discussed together, or conflated, speaks to an intertwined ongoing development [72].

Serious Games as understood today, however, is built on the rise of digital technologies. With this rise of digital learning practices, Serious Games' focus extends beyond representation of social systems and includes individualistic approaches to knowledge acquisition and skills development, following behaviourist and cognitivist theories of learning. At this point we can follow the trends identified in the foundational - yet analogous - pre-history of Serious Games towards their digital manifestation. Before doing so however, it is necessary to consider the seminal work of Clark C Abt.

In his book *Serious Games* Clark Abt [8] identifies justifications, contextual applications, and conceptual definitions of contemporary Serious Games that are predictive, if not directly foundational. Moreover, this work provides an historically situated anchor point that illustrates both the movement from simulation-based learning to games-based learning as separate practices and the seemingly natural transition from analogous to digital Serious Games.

9   Emergence of Serious Games as a Field

"Games may be played seriously or casually. We are concerned with 'Serious Games' in the sense that these games have an explicit and carefully thought-out educational purpose and are not intended to be played primarily for amusement. This does not mean that serious game are not, or should not be, entertaining." [8]

Abt is often credited with coining the term 'Serious Games' [38, 69]. From the above quote we can see that he provided the foundation for modern definitions of Serious Games that frame them as games designed for a purpose beyond entertaining – though these games are indeed still entertaining. What is striking however, when reading Abt's seminal work *Serious Games,* is his identification of the key justifications for using contemporary Serious Games.

For Abt, Serious Games provide an opportunity to address the *"motivational inadequacies"* of the American educational system. They also provide representational affordances, and therefore different opportunities for engagement, of complex organizational or socio-political systems. Finally, bridging the historical purposing of play as 'safe exploration' and modern justifications of Serious Games, he suggests that *"Simulations or games offer an inexpensive and relatively unthreatening means of experimentation"* [8].

Moving on from the specific form of Serious Games, Abt also discussed their contextual adoption. For instance, with educational Serious Games, Abt discusses the teacher's practices of their adoption arguing that: *"the timing of a classroom game should be made to maximize the game's dramatic impact on the students"* and the importance of debriefing or *"postgame analysis"* [8]. Moreover, he paints the use of these educational Serious Games as decidedly social affairs with learners collaborating or competing within the game. The contextual consideration and social approach of the Serious Games Abt describes stands in near-contrast to contemporary practices, which prioritise personalised and individualistic Serious Games design.

More broadly, Abt also identifies that one of the key considerations for Serious Games adoption is not just their effectiveness, but their cost-effectiveness.

"[A]ssessing the value of games and whether they are, in fact, 'worth the trouble' means that we must assess their cost-effectiveness, their efficiency in comparison to other instructional and research methods." [8]

Indeed, Abt's broader considerations of an emerging Serious Game eco-system also extend to the necessity of answering *"skeptics"* [8] – a process of legitimization that is still apparent in contemporary work [66, 67]. Furthermore, in Abt's initial unpacking of the notion *Serious*, he refers to the games themselves, but also the pursuit of Serious Games research. This, of course, has implications for the broader field of Serious Games studies:

"The term 'serious' is also used in the sense of study, relating to matters of great interest and importance." [8]

It is worth noting that although Abt has a clear history in the field, his seminal work which has become foundational in contemporary Serious Games pursuits is written largely anecdotally. Moreover, his work still predominantly focussed on analogous simulation games, speaking to his experience and the broader popularity of the approach [78]. However, he does include digital Serious Games in his discussion and does so rather straightforwardly. He states that *"It is possible, of course, to make a computer simulation of a game"* [8]. Throughout his book *Serious Games* references to computer based simulations as a logical, and expected extension of pre-existing simulation-based learning practices.

America's military had been experimenting with computer simulation-based learning since the end of World War 2. In 1948, AIR DEFENSE SIMULATION was completed and actively used for military training [79]. Of course this was a rather rudimentary visual representation, overlapping sophisticated mathematical models, of enemy aircraft and anti-air weapons. This was followed by the development of CARMONETTE (Combined Arms Computer Model) in 1953 and deployed in 1956 which expanded upon AIR DEFENSE SIMULATION to include a richer virtual representation, including infantry, radio-communications, and tanks [79].

Considering the historical military application of simulation gaming and early military experiments with computer-modelling, it is not surprising that they began developing what we may consider Proto-Serious Games as early as 1948. Moreover, at the time of Abt's writing updated *Serious Games* in 1985, it is less surprising that there were *"400 major computer war games"* [8] already developed. For Abt then, digital Serious Games were merely an extension of the previous simulation-based learning approach.

Writing in 1985 he was, however, disappointed when reflecting upon the previous 15 years of computer simulation-based learning development. In updating *Serious Games,* Abt reflected on the 15 years since his original publication and lamented a lack of progress in the *"analytical, educational, evaluative and predictive quality"* [8] of computer simulation games. Furthermore, although he acknowledged that digital

Serious Games were indeed being used in the classroom, they were overshadowed by the development of computer games primarily for entertainment.

At this point in the chapter, with Abt's *Serious Games* as our historical nexus, we will move from discussing the non-digital incarnation of Serious Games and narrow our focus onto the contemporary field. From the 1970s onwards, the development of Serious Games became an increasingly reified field, distinct from both analogous play or game-based practices; and other computer based instructional methods. During this time there was the rise of the video game industry and human-computer interaction fields of study occurring in parallel with the rise of the contemporary Serious Games research field.

10   From Analogue to Digital Serious Games

"[C]omputer games have become a larger mix of entertainment rather than instruction, and the market for entertainment games with minimal instructional content has completely outdistanced the market for instructional games, however entertainingly computerized". [8]

At the time of writing *Serious Games* there was a tentative adoption of educational Serious Games in the classroom. Lemonade Stand, a text based business simulation game, was developed and used in the classroom in 1973; followed by, the now famous, Oregan's Trail in 1974 [38]. It is interesting that Abt expresses a disappointment in the rise of games that prioritise entertainment, seemingly at the cost of instructional content. This creates an interesting point of departure for the work of Abt for two reasons.

First, Abt was perhaps unable to predict the use of commercially available entertainment games in an educational context [80]. Secondly, most importantly, there is a lack of consideration here for the potential of the rising entertainment games industry in driving forward the Serious Games eco-system. There was indeed a rise of arcade games and personal home consoles towards the latter end of the 20th century [81]. For some this presented an opportunity for developing Serious Games that build upon pre-exiting games and can be more widely disseminated through at-home consoles.

Following the trend of military experimentation, *The Bradley Trainer* was a game developed in cooperation with the US Military and Atari. In 1980 Atari had just published their arcade cabinet game *Battlezone*, in which players would use a periscope attachment to target and shoot enemy vehicles. For the US Army's *The Bradley Trainer,* this same game mechanic was seen as a training simulator for, then new, Infantry Fighting Vehicles (IFV). However, custom assets were added to the game including replacing the fantasy shells of *Battlezone*, with ammunition types carried by actual IFVs and enemy tank models were changed to reflect the silhouettes of real-world tank types [82].

During this same time period, commercial organisations also began to repurpose exiting game technologies for advertising. For instance, *Pepsi Invaders* was developed in 1983 for sales employees of Coca-Cola as a means of fostering company moral in relation to their Coca-Cola's rival. As the title suggests, *Pepsi Invaders* was a near identical copy of the classic video game *Space Invaders* - with alien spaceships replaced with the letters P-E-P-S-I [38]. However, *Pepsi Invaders* was intended for internal usage whereas its contemporaries *Kool-Aid Man*, or *Chex Quest* were designed specifically for brand promotion through home video game consoles [38].

With the examples of *Kool-Aid Man* and *Chex Quest* we see the emergence of Serious Games designed for advertising commercial products specifically to children – a trend that is apparent in modern advergaming research [83]. With these games, *The Bradley Trainer* included, we can see the burgeoning influence of the commercial video games market on Serious Games. In these cases, we can again see the historical trend of using the engagement or motivational potential of games.

In the healthcare context, the early examples of using video games for rehabilitative practices were framed around their engagement potential [84, 85]. For rehabilitation, video games were seen as a way of overcoming initial resistance to therapy, distracting the patients focus away from pain, and avoiding repetitive or boring rehabilitative exercises [84, 85]. Furthermore, video game usage in psychotherapeutic settings were initially justified following the same logic of using play-based therapy. That is, video games were seen as a means of building rapport, managing behaviour, or observing children's internalised thought processes through their game-play behaviour [53, 86].

Given the rising popularity of video games and the perceived engagement of the player, there was an outcry discussing their potential addictive nature [87, 88]. As media theorist, and socio-technological commentator Sherry Turkle describes it:

"There has been controversy about video games from the days of Space Invaders and Asteroids, from the time that the games' holding power provoked people who saw it as a sign of addiction to become alarmed. The controversy intensified as it became clear that more than a "games craze" was involved. This was not the Hula-Hoop of the 1980s" [88]

It is this notion of the video games *"holding power"* as described by Turkle that has particular relevance here. For all of the discussion of video games engagement potential, this was indicative of early scholarly works specifically discussing this engagement potential. Indeed, Turkle's work *The Second Self* is perhaps the first instance in which Mihaly Csikszentmihalyi's theory of *'flow'*, now ubiquitous in Serious Games research [89, 90], was specifically applied to video games.

Preceding Turkle, Thomas W. Malone in 1980 had already begun researching the underlying intrinsic motivational potential of video-games form a cognitive psychologist perspective [91]. With this work Malone created a taxonomy of motivational principles from games that could be used to inform instructional design. This psychological perspective of motivation was paralleled in *Minds at Play,* a book written by Geoffrey and Elizabeth Loftus. In this they argue that part of the *'holding power'* of video games is due to their *'partial reinforcement'* [87] of play behavior.

Loftus and Loftus argue that the rewarding but unpredictable nature of video games feedback leads to a continued desire from the player. Interestingly, this is reflected in modern neuroscience studies tracking the release of dopamine – understood as the 'desire' chemical – during game play [92]. Furthermore, this approach of random reward intervals has been adopted by Serious Games to promote engagement [93, 94]. Therefore, as exemplified in Malone's discussion of applications of instructional video games, there was a rise of Serious Games that adopted this 'games-as-motivation' approach.

As identified by the work of Damien Djaouti and others, there was a rise in the number of Serious Games for education from 1980 to 2002 [38]. However, there was an expression of dissatisfaction by some educational technology theorists, and researchers, at the rather simplistic form of these games. For Seymour Papert – founder of constructionism and pioneer of games design as a pedagogic approach – educational Serious Games of the time were Shavian reversals [95]. That is, they adopted the worst practices of their parent disciplines thus forming games that were primarily drill and practice quizzes in which the player is motivated through behaviourist notions of reinforcement [96].

It is worth noting that this, unfortunate, trend towards ludic incentivised quizzes – or rote skills practices – is apparent today [75]. Indeed, the popular framing of Serious Games as *'chocolate-covered brocoli'*, initially conceived by Amy Bruckman and presented at the 1999 Games Developers Conference [97], is readily apparent in contemporary Serious Games discourse [98]. Indeed, this approach is now often, derisively, referred to as *edutainment* – the field of designing typically traditional media for educational purposes. However, during this time period there were other independently constructivist notions of educational Serious Games.

Seriously Considering Play [99], the seminal work of Lloyd Rieber was published in 1996. In this work Rieber maps the constructivist notion of a microworld – a self-contained, complete, and internal representation of a domain of interest – with the fantastical representations of games. Rieber, and others [100] argued that his fantasy element leads to engagement with the learning content. Here then, in the work of Rieber we have a logical extension of the approach of Malone – that is the segmenting of 'games' into a set of heuristics that can be used to form Serious Games design.

This work to unpack, stratify demarcate, or otherwise categorize games into a set of heuristics or design principles to be applied to educational games was a significant focus for researchers at the time [101]. Moreover, when reviewing the modern trends in Serious Games research, it is apparent that this trend has continued – though the models are now more formalised [38, 102–104]. From the mid-1980s to late 1990s the continued research into stratifying game elements to be purposed for their learning was paralleled with a marked decline in the number of studies looking at non-digital educational Serious Games [96] – emphasizing a shift towards the digital.

In 2001 Espen Aarseth published the article *Computer Game Studies, Year One* in the first *"first academic, peer-reviewed journal dedicated to computer game studies"* [105]. In this, as the title suggests, he positions 2001 as *Year 1* of computer games studies. That is, computer games had become a credible, international, academic field as evidenced by the founding of the first peer-reviewed journal and international scholarly conference dedicated to the field [105].This illustrates a step in academia to legitimize the field of Game Studies – with obvious implications for the field of Serious Games. Following the work of Aarseth, and borrowing his moniker, the following year can be framed as *Year One* of Serious Games.

11 Serious Games Studies, Year One

In 2002, Rosemary Garris, Robert Ahlers, and James Driskell produced a comprehensive review of pre-existing research into educational Serious Games [101]. This review is illustrative for three reasons. Firstly, Garris and Ahlers published the work whilst working for the US Naval Air Warfare Center for Training Systems Division – demonstrating the military's continued role in driving forward Serious Games research. Secondly, they review the work of existing researchers with a view to develop a model for educational Serious Games, in itself illustrative, but also it represents a shift towards more formalised models. Finally, in the article though they describe their work as developing *instructional games* they highlight the oxymoronic tensions of their terminology:

> *"Huizinga argued that the "fun element" underlies the intensity, absorption, and power of games and that play is the direct opposite of seriousness. As we adapt games for serious purposes, we must be aware of this tension between the world of play and the world of work. Thus, in one sense, the term instructional game is an oxymoron."* [101]

In the article though they refer to their field as *instructional games*, their repeated reference to the notion of 'serious' is very timely. In the same year Ben Sawyer would release the foundational white paper *Serious Games: Improving Public Policy through Game-based Learning and Simulation* [38, 69]. This paper and the soon to follow launch of the Serious Games Initiative would cement the term Serious Games in popular academic discourse when discussing the purposing of games. Here then, we enter what is framed by most as the contemporary era of Serious Games [38, 69].

In 2002 the commercial video game market had grown significantly [106]. Therefore, in Ben Sawyers discussion of the potential of Serious Games, he identified a need to link the commercial video game industry with contextual applications [38, 69]. This approach of comparing the approaches of the video game industry with educational practitioners, highlighting how the former can inform the latter, became a key pillar at the foundation of Serious Games.

Mark Prensky popularised this comparative discourse in his first book *Digital Game-Based Learning* [44]. In this he explicitly compares the entertainment game and educational trainer industries – highlighting the energy and excitement on display at the Electronic Entertainment Expo (E3):

> *"Today's trainers and trainees are from totally separate worlds. The biggest underlying dynamic in training and learning today is the rapid and unexpected confrontation of a corps of trainers and teachers raised in a pre-digital generation and educated in the styles of the past, with a body of learners raised in the digital world of Sesame Street, MTV, fast movies and "twitch speed" videogames."* [44]

For Prensky then it was not so much an opportunity for educational practitioners to borrow from the games design principles and practices of the commercial video games industry, it was a necessity. Of course, Prensky is now well-known in educational Serious Games circles for furthering this rhetoric. Though perhaps slightly dogmatic, in 2001 he captured a desire – that had been growing since the work of Malone and Turkle in the early 1980s – to apply commercial digital game design in educational contexts. Currently, this same inter-contextual sharing of practices is readily apparent and formalised through the establishment of academia, industry, and application domain networks.

At this point in this chapter it is necessary to acknowledge that since starting the discussing of the Serious Games history, post invention of the computer, we have focused primarily on educational Serious Games. As is now apparent however, this is fitting with the historical development of purposeful analogous or digital games and simulations. That is, the historical analogous games, and indeed the computer-based proto-Serious Games were primarily designed for learning.

In Damien Djaouti and others [38] historical review of Serious Games, starting with early computer games, from 1980 to 2002 they identified 953 Serious Games. Moreover, of these 953 Serious Games 'ancestors' 65.8 % could be categorised as educational [38]. From Serious Games' *Year One*, 2002, through to 2010 there was a marked increase in the total number of Serious Games however, the proportion of educational games dropped to 25.7 %. This reduction of the proportion of educational Serious Games was of course the result of an increased diversity of purpose in the emergent field of Serious Games.

Here then, we have a dramatic shift in the field of Serious Games as the diversity of their application grew. For instance, as identified in their work Djaouti [38] identifies that between 2002 and 2010, 30.7 % of the Serious Games developed were designed for advertising. Indeed, following 2002 the newly founded Serious Games Initiative had a role in developing the application of Serious Games in social activism, and healthcare. In 2004 the first Games for Change conference was held and thus a formalised network of non-profits and experts emerged to explore the potential of Serious Games for tackling social issues [57]. In this same year the Games for Health conference was also first held to explore the potential of Serious Games in healthcare [107].

Given the increasing application of Serious Games across multiple contexts scholars in the emerging field began to wrestle with Serious Games definition. Currently, the issue of defining Serious Games is still prevalent. However, definitions that are presented are frequently a derivative or slight re-interpretation of *'games that have a purpose beyond entertainment'* [38, 69]. Indeed, these definitions are often traced to works of David Michael and Sande Chen [108] or Michael Zyda [109]:

"Games that do not have entertainment, enjoyment, or fun as their primary purpose." [108]

"Serious game: a mental contest, played with a computer in accordance with specific rules, that uses entertainment to further government or corporate training, education, health, public policy, and strategic communication objectives." [109]

As with the other critical periods of history identified here, this wrestling over defining the term Serious Game is a trend with historical origin that continues to this day. The difficulty of defining 'play' or 'games' – or even the impossibility of the task [110] - only adds to the difficulty of defining both 'serious' and 'games' in conjunction. As Crookall suggests however, despite this difficulty in definition the field as a whole will continued to move forward:

"I am sure that some dust will continue to fly for the next few years, maybe decades, and that researchers and developers will continue to do their thing, despite the arguments one way or the other with regard to the term 'serious'." [72]

12 Conclusion

"Serious gaming seems to have captured the imagination of, and drawn strong support from, many well beyond the actual gaming world. Even governments are providing support for serious games, with recent examples including a major thrust by the French Government, funding by

the U.S. Institutes for Health and a European Union grant for the GaLA network. Surely that is a good thing." [72]

In Crookall's review of the current state of Simulations and Gaming at the 40th Anniversary Symposium of S&G, he directly acknowledges the rise of Serious Games. In his article, as illustrated in his quote here, he optimistically addresses the popularity of Serious Games and their inter-contextual appreciation. At the time of Crookall's writing this review, Serious Games had already become an established academic field of study evidenced by the founding of The Serious Games Institute at Coventry University in 2007.

Currently, as signposted by Crookall, Serious Games are an increasingly interwoven practice across multiple domains. Indeed, Serious Games had transitions from exploratory, or fringe, experiments, to an increasingly legitimized medium for education, healthcare, and social change. In the coming together of these domains, the field of study has become increasingly interdisciplinary. Starting with rather simple origins in the convergence of computational modelling and non-digital game-based learning, now the field of Serious Games is a nexus for multiple other disciplines – as evidenced by the breadth of topics covered in this book.

If we were to revisit the slightly romanticised rhetoric of Richard Duke and Henry Jenkin's,their positioning of games as a *'language of the future'* [10] and *'the new lively art'* [9] has become manifest in the contemporary field of Serious Games. Serious Games research and practices are beginning to shape the practices of the contexts they are used in. However, as we have identified in this chapter, like Duke and Jenkins, perhaps we could have seen this coming. There are historical antecedents to Serious Games in the form of purposing of play and games. Additionally, beginning with these antecedents, we can see trends emerge, and the same challenges facing previous researchers are still apparent.

There is still a pre-eminence of educational applications for Serious Games and the research field itself is still driven forward by external partnerships – particularly the military. Moreover, the difficult of pin-pointing the first Serious Game as we understand it today, speaks to current debates in their definition. Again, a debate that has existed since the researchers began to study 'play'. Another key characteristic that is apparent through the history and pre-history of Serious Games is an optimistic sense of expectancy of the potential of games. This sense of expectancy was perhaps best captured by the work of Duke and Jenkins – written 33 years apart. So it can be said then that games and by extension Serious Games are a language and a medium of the future but with a rich and storied past.

References

1. Avedon, M.E., Sutton-Smith, B.: The Study of Games. Ishi Press International, California (2015)
2. Cohen, D.: The Development of Play, 3rd edn. Routledge, London (2007)
3. Parlett, D.S.: Oxford History of Board Games. Oxford University Press, Oxford (1999)

4. Huizinga, J.: Homo Ludens: A Study of the Play-Element in Culture. Beacon Press, Boston (1971)
5. Wu, W.H., Hsiao, H.C., Wu, P.L., Lin, C.H., Huang, S.H.: Investigating the learning-theory foundations of game-based learning: a meta-analysis. J. Comput. Assist. Learn. **28**, 265–279 (2012)
6. DeSmet, A., Van Ryckeghem, D., Compernolle, S., Baranowski, T., Thompson, D., Crombez, G., Poels, K., Van Lippevelde, W., Bastiaensens, S., Van Cleemput, K., Vandebosch, H., De Bourdeaudhuij, I., Hospital, G., Street, T., Gard, T., Hoge, E.A., Kerr, C.: A meta-analysis of serious digital games for healthy lifestyle promotion. Prev. Med. (Baltim) **69**, 95–107 (2014)
7. Mayer, I., Bekebrede, G., Harteveld, C., Warmelink, H., Zhou, Q., Van Ruijven, T., Lo, J., Kortmann, R., Wenzler, I.: The research and evaluation of serious games: toward a comprehensive methodology. Br. J. Educ. Technol. **45**, 502–527 (2014)
8. Abt, C.C.: Serious Games. University Press of America (1987)
9. Jenkins, H.: The Wow Climax: Tracing the Emotional Impact of Popular Culture. New York University Press, New York (2007)
10. Duke, R.D.: Gaming, the Future's Language. Wiley, New York (1974)
11. D'Angour, A.: Plato and play: taking education seriously in ancient Greece. Am. J. Play **5**, 293–307 (2013)
12. Wood, W.: Children's Play and Its Place in Education. Routledge, New York (2012)
13. Wang, S., Aamodt, S.: Play, stress, and the learning brain. Cerebrum **2012**, 12 (2012)
14. Salen, K., Zimmerman, E.: Rules of Play: Game Design Fundamentals. The MIT Press, Cambridge (2003)
15. Juul, J.: The magic circle and the puzzle piece. In: Conference Proceedings of the Philosophy of Computer Games 2008, pp. 56–67 (2008)
16. Rodriguez, H.: The playful and the serious: an approximation to Huizinga's Homo Ludens. Game Studies **6** (2006)
17. Klopfer, E., Osterweil, S., Salen, K.: Moving learning games forward. Flora. **3**, 58 (2009)
18. Remmele, B., Whitton, N.: Disrupting the magic circle: the impact of negative social gaming behaviours. In: Psychology, Pedagogy, and Assessment in Serious Games, pp. 111–126. IGI Global (2014)
19. Montola, M.: Exploring the edge of the magic circle: defining pervasive games. In: Proceedings of DAC, p. 103 (2005)
20. Franzwa, C., Tang, Y., Johnson, A.: Serious game design: motivating students through a balance of fun and learning. In: 2013 5th International Conference on Games and Virtual Worlds for Serious Applications (VS-GAMES), pp. 1–7. IEEE (2013)
21. Vygotsky, L.: Interaction between learning and development. In: Gauvain, M., Cole, M. (eds.) Readings on the Development of Children, vol. 23, pp. 34–41. Scientific American Books, New York (1978)
22. Schwartzman, H.: Transformations: The Anthropology of Children's Play. Springer Science & Business Media, New York (2012)
23. Lillard, A.S., Lerner, M.D., Hopkins, E.J., Dore, R.A., Smith, E.D., Palmquist, C.M.: The impact of pretend play on children's development: a review of the evidence. Psychol. Bull. **139**, 1 (2013)
24. Flanagan, M., Nissenbaum, H.: Values at Play in Digital Games. MIT Press, Cambridge (2014)
25. Saomya, S.: Kurt Squire on civic engagement through digital games. https://edtechreview.in/e-learning/558-civic-engagement-through-digital-games

26. Verenikina, I., Harris, P., Lysaght, P.: Child's play: computer games, theories of play and children's development. In: Proceedings of the International Federation for Information Processing Working Group 3.5 Open Conference on Young Children and Learning Technologies, vol. 34, pp. 99–106 (2003)

27. Prensky, M.: Don't Bother Me Mom, I'm Learning! How Computer and Video Games are Preparing Your Kids for Twenty-First Century Success and How You Can Help!. Paragon House, St. Paul (2006)

28. Gee, J.P.: What video games have to teach us about learning and literacy (2003)

29. Goffman, E.: Replies and responses. Lang. Soc. **5**, 257–313 (1976)

30. Caillois, R., Barash, M.: Man, Play, and Games. University of Illinois Press, Champaign (1961)

31. Erikson, E.H.: Childhood and Society, 2nd edn. W. W. Norton, New York (1963)

32. Detrick, S.: A Commentary on the United Nations Convention on the Rights of the Child. Martinus Nijhoff Publishers, The Hague (1999)

33. Buckingham, D.: After the Death of Childhood. Blackwell, Oxford (2008)

34. Buckingham, D., Chronaki, D.: Saving the children? (2014)

35. Gee, J.P.: Learning and games. In: The Ecology of Games: Connecting Youth, Games, and Learning, pp. 21–40 (2008)

36. Gaskins, S., Haight, W., Lancy, D.F.: The cultural construction of play. In: Göncü, A., Gaskins, S. (eds.) Play and Development: Evolutionary, Sociocultural, and Functional Perspectives, pp. 179–202 (2007)

37. Department for Education: Working Together, Achieving More. London (2009)

38. Djaouti, D., Alvarez, J., Jessel, J., Rampnoux, O.: Origins of serious games. In: Ma, M., Okionomou, A., Jain, L.C. (eds.) Serious Games Edutainment Application, pp. 25–43. Springer, New York (2011)

39. Ritterfeld, U., Cody, M., Vorderer, P.: Serious Games: Mechanisms and Effects. Routledge, New York (2009)

40. Fisher, K.R., Hirsh-Pasek, K., Golinkoff, R.M., Gryfe, S.G.: Conceptual split? Parents' and experts' perceptions of play in the 21st century. J. Appl. Dev. Psychol. **29**, 305–316 (2008)

41. Froebel, F.: The Education of Man. A. Lovell & Company, New York (1885)

42. Landreth, G.L.: Play Therapy: The Art of the Relationship. Routledge, New York (2012)

43. Martins, T., Carvalho, V., Soares, F., Moreira, M.F.: Serious game as a tool to intellectual disabilities therapy: total challenge. In: 2011 IEEE 1st International Conference on Serious Games and Applications for Health (SeGAH), pp. 1–7. IEEE (2011)

44. Prensky, M.: Digital Game-Based Learning. McGraw-Hill, New York (2001)

45. Roos, J., Roos, M.: Play is the key. In: Thinking from Within, pp. 25–40. Springer (2006)

46. Rogers, C.R., Dorfman, E.: Client-Centered: Its Current Practice, Implications, and Theory. ICON Group International (1951)

47. Axline, V.M.: Play therapy experiences as described by child participants. J. Consultation Psychol. **14**, 53 (1950)

48. Crenshaw, D.A., Kenney-Noziska, S.: Therapeutic presence in play therapy. Int. J. Play Ther. **23**, 31 (2014)

49. Horne-Moyer, H.L., Moyer, B.H., Messer, D.C., Messer, E.S.: The use of electronic games in therapy: a review with clinical implications. Curr. Psychiatry Rep. **16**, 1–9 (2014)

50. Sherlock, L.: Toward a rhetoric of serious game genres. In: Interdisciplinary Models and Tools for Serious Games: Emerging Concepts and Future Directions, vol. 50 (2010)

51. Brahnam, S., Brooks, A.L.: Two innovative healthcare technologies at the intersection of serious games, alternative realities, and play therapy. Stud. Health Technol. Inf. **207**, 153–162 (2014)

52. Wilkinson, N., Ang, R.P., Goh, D.H.: Online video game therapy for mental health concerns: a review. Int. J. Soc. Psychiatry **54**, 370–382 (2008)
53. Gardner, J.E.: Can the Mario Bros. help? Nintendo games as an adjunct in psychotherapy with children. Psychother. Theory Res. Pract. Train. **28**, 667 (1991)
54. Barrett, M.S., Gershkovich, M.: Computers and psychotherapy: are we out of a job? Psychotherapy **51**(2), 220–223 (2014)
55. Sutton-Smith, B.: The Ambiguity of Play. Harvard University, Cambridge (1997)
56. Misuraca, G.: Digital Games for Empowerment and Inclusion (DGEI) D3 Final Vision and Roadmap A Roadmap for Action on Digital Games for Empowerment and Inclusion in Europe A Report of the Study, pp. 1–20 (2012)
57. Klimmt, C.: Serious games and social change why they (should) work. In: Ritterford, M. (ed.) Serious Games: Mechanisms and Effects, pp. 249–270. Routledge, New York (2009)
58. Martin, G., Steuter, E.: Pop Culture Goes to War: Enlisting and Resisting Militarism in the War on Terror. Lexington Books, Lanham (2010)
59. Turkle, S.: The Second Self. MIT Press, Cambridge (2005)
60. Connolly, T.M., Boyle, E.A., Macarthur, E., Hainey, T., Boyle, J.M.: Computers & education a systematic literature review of empirical evidence on computer games and serious games. Comput. Educ. **59**, 661–686 (2012)
61. McGlarty, K.L., Orr, A., Frey, P.M., Dolan, R.P., Vassileva, V., McVay, A.: A literature review of gaming. In: Gaming Education, pp. 1–36 (2012)
62. Culin, S.: Retrospect of the Folk-Lore of the Columbian exposition. J. Am. Folklore **7**, 51–59 (1894)
63. Holmes, W.H.: Twentieth Annual Report of the Bureau of American Ethnology, 1898–1899 (1903)
64. Sutton-Smith, B.: The kissing games of adolescents in Ohio. Midwest Folklore **9**, 189–211 (1959)
65. Opie, I.A., Opie, P.: Children's Games in Street and Playground: Chasing, Catching, Seeking, Hunting, Racing, Duelling, Exerting, Daring, Guessing, Acting, Pretending. Clarendon Press, Oxford (1969)
66. Sinclair, B.: Serious games stigmatized in and out of the industry, says Schell
67. DiCebro, K.: Taking Serious Games Seriously in Education
68. Juul, J.: Games telling stories. Game Stud. **1**, 45 (2001)
69. Susi, T., Johannesson, M., Backlund, P.: Serious games: An overview (2007)
70. Wolfe, J., Crookall, D.: Developing a scientific knowledge of simulation/gaming. Simul. Gaming **29**, 7–19 (1998)
71. Kolb, D.A.: Experiential Learning: Experience as the Source of Learning and Development. FT Press, Englewood Cliffs (2014)
72. Crookall, D.: Serious games, debriefing, and simulation/gaming as a discipline. Simul. Gaming. **41**, 898–920 (2010)
73. Bogost, I.: How to do things with videogames. Univertiy of Minnesota Press (2011)
74. Squire, K., Jenkins, H.: Harnessing the power of games in education. Insight **3**, 5–33 (2003)
75. Van Eck, R.: Digital game-based learning: it's not just the digital natives who are restless. Educ. Rev. **41**, 16–30 (2006)
76. Kahne, J., Middaugh, E., Evans, C.: The Civic Potential of Video Games. MIT Press, Cambridge (2008)
77. Young, M.F., Slota, S., Cutter, A.B., Jalette, G., Mullin, G., Lai, B., Simeoni, Z., Tran, M., Yukhymenko, M.: Our princess is in another castle: a review of trends in serious gaming for education. Rev. Educ. Res. **82**, 61–89 (2012)

78. Boocock, S.S., Schild, E.: Simulation Games in Learning. Sage Publications, California (1968)
79. Smith, R.: The long history of gaming in military training. Simul. Gaming **41**, 6–19 (2009)
80. Groff, J., Howells, C., Cranmer, S.: The Impact of Console Games in the Classroom: Evidence from Schools in Scotland. Futurelab, Bristol (2010). Learning 98
81. Kent, S.: The Ultimate History of Video Games: from Pong to Pokemon and Beyond: The Story Behind the Craze that Touched Our Lives and Changed the World. Three Rivers Press, New York (2010)
82. Stone, R.J.: Serious gaming—virtual reality's saviour. In: Proceedings of Virtual Systems and MultiMedia Annual Conference, VSMM, pp. 773–786 (2005)
83. Harris, J.L., Speers, S.E., Schwartz, M.B., Brownell, K.D.: US food company branded advergames on the internet: children's exposure and effects on snack consumption. J. Child. Media **6**, 51–68 (2012)
84. Griffiths, M.: The therapeutic use of videogames in childhood and adolescence. Clin. Child Psychol. Psychiatry **8**, 547–554 (2003)
85. Griffiths, M.: Video games and clinical practice: issues, uses and treatments. Br. J. Clin. Psychol. **36**, 639–642 (1997)
86. Spence, J.: The use of computer arcade games in behaviour management. Mal. Ther. Educ. **6**, 64–68 (1988)
87. Loftus, G.R., Loftus, E.F.: Mind at Play: The Psychology of Video Games. Basic Books, Inc., New York (1983)
88. Turkle, S.: Video games and computer holding power. In: The Second Self: Computers and the Human Spirit, pp. 64–92 (1984)
89. Chen, J.: Flow in games and everything else. Commun. ACM **50**, 31–34 (2007)
90. Bowman, N.D., Weber, R., Tamborini, R., Sherry, J.: Facilitating game play: how others affect performance at and enjoyment of video games. Media Psychol. **16**, 39–64 (2013)
91. Malone, T.: What Makes Things Fun to Learn? A Study of Intrinsically Motivating Video Games. Palo Alto (1980)
92. Howard-Jones, P.: Neuroscience and Education: Issues and Opportunities. Seminar Series 28 (2007)
93. Richter, G., Raban, D.R., Rafaeli, S.: Studying gamification: the effect of rewards and incentives on motivation. In: Reiners, T., Wood, L.C. (eds.) Gamification in Education and Business, pp. 21–46. Springer, Switzerland (2015)
94. Nagle, A., Wolf, P., Riener, R., Novak, D.: The use of player-centered positive reinforcement to schedule in-game rewards increases enjoyment and performance in a serious game. Int. J. Ser. Games **1**, 35–47 (2014)
95. Papert, S.: Does easy do it? Children, games, and learning. Game Dev. Mag. (1988)
96. Egenfeldt-Nielsen, S.: Third generation educational use of computer games. J. Educ. Multimedia Hypermedia **16**, 263 (2007)
97. Bruckman, A.: Can Educational Be Fun? (1999)
98. Chen, S.: Facing edutainment's dark legacy. http://www.gamesandlearning.org/2016/01/25/facing-edutainments-dark-legacy/
99. Reiber, L.: Seriously Considering play. Educ. Technol. Res. Dev. **44**, 43–58 (1996)
100. Cordova, D.I., Lepper, M.R.: Intrinsic motivation and the process of learning: beneficial effects of contextualization, personalization, and choice. J. Educ. Psychol. **88**, 715 (1996)
101. Garris, R., Ahlers, R., Driskell, J.E.: Games, motivation, and learning: a research and practice model. Simul. Gaming **33**, 441–467 (2002)

102. Arnab, S., Lim, T., Carvalho, M.B., Bellotti, F., De Freitas, S., Louchart, S., Suttie, N., Berta, R., De Gloria, A.: Mapping learning and game mechanics for serious games analysis. Br. J. Educ. Technol. **46**, 391–411 (2015)
103. Gunter, G.A., Kenny, R.F., Vick, E.H.: Taking educational games seriously: using the RETAIN model to design endogenous fantasy into standalone educational games. Educ. Technol. Res. Dev. **56**, 511–537 (2008)
104. Bedwell, W.L., Pavlas, D., Heyne, K., Lazzara, E.H., Salas, E.: Toward a taxonomy linking game attributes to learning: an empirical study. Simul. Gaming **43**, 729–760 (2012)
105. Aarseth, E.: Computer game studies, year one. Game Stud. **1**, 1–15 (2001)
106. Clements, M.T., Ohashi, H.: Indirect network effects and the product cycle: video games in the US, 1994–2002. J. Ind. Econ. **53**, 515–542 (2005)
107. Howell, K.: Games for health conference 2004: issues, trends, and needs unique to games for health. CyberPsychology Behav. **8**, 103–109 (2005)
108. Michael, D.R., Chen, S.L.: Serious Games: Games that Educate, Train, and Inform. Muska & Lipman/Premier-Trade, Roseville (2005)
109. Zyda, M.: From visual simulation to virtual reality to games. Computer **38**, 25–32 (2005). (Long. Beach. Calif)
110. Wittgenstein, L., Anscombe, G.E.M., Hacker, P.M.S., Schulte, J.: Philosophische Untersuchungen: Philosophical Investigations. Wiley-Blackwell, New York (2009)

Ethical Stewardship: Designing Serious Games Seriously

Alyea Sandovar[1(✉)], Eelco Braad[2], Alexander Streicher[3],
and Heinrich Söbke[4]

[1] School of Leadership Development, Fielding Graduate University,
Santa Barbara, CA, USA
asandovar@email.fielding.edu
[2] School of Communication, Media and IT,
Hanze University of Applied Sciences, Groningen, The Netherlands
e.p.braad@pl.hanze.nl
[3] Fraunhofer IOSB, Karlsruhe, Germany
alexander.streicher@iosb.fraunhofer.de
[4] Bauhaus-Institute for Infrastructure Solutions,
Bauhaus-Universität Weimar, Weimar, Germany
heinrich.soebke@uni-weimar.de

Abstract. In this chapter, we propose an ethical framework for serious game design, which we term the *Ecosystem for Designing Games Ethically* (EDGE). EDGE expands on Zagal's categorization of ethical areas in game design by incorporating the different contexts of design and their use. In addition, we leverage these contexts to suggest four guidelines that support *Ethical Stewardship* in serious game design. We conclude by discussing a number of specific areas in which ethics plays a role in serious game design. These include games in (a) a military context, (b) the consideration of privacy issues, and (c) the evaluation of game design choices.

Keywords: Serious game design · Information ethics · Ethical stewardship · Military games · Educational games · Ethical intelligence · Design politics · Values in design · Data privacy · Video game design · Values at play · Game design values

1 Introduction

Games themselves are complex cultural artifacts and designed systems—they are designed objects [1]. So, too, is the study of digital games ethics—it is as complex and nuanced as are games. Often ethics and digital games are associated with the violence in games and subsequent aggressive behavior in players [2–4]. This association solely focuses on how the players are implicated by the artifact, that is, by the game—not on the ethics of the development process, the industry, nor on the developers.

As an information system, the game experience is in part defined by the design and in part by the player's interaction with the design of the game [1]. A comprehensive

R. Dörner et al. (Eds.): Entertainment Computing and Serious Games, LNCS 9970, pp. 42–62, 2016.
DOI: 10.1007/978-3-319-46152-6_3

Table 1. Zagal's ethical variables

The cultural artifact	Business ethics	Ethical play	Frameworks
The cultural artifact itself – is the game good or bad?	What does it mean to create the game ethically?	What does it mean to play fair/ethically?	What actions do games define for the player?

description is illustrated by Zagal [5] who makes a strong case for the consideration of certain variables (Table 1).

Each of these variables reflect aspects of digital games, including serious games. For example, in a learning history game by the Danish Studio Serious Games Interactive, *Playing History 2 - Slave Trade* (H2ST), players are slaves tasked to enslave others by their owner. Each of Zagal's variables can be considered in the following manner in H2ST: As a cultural artefact—an object created by humans which informs about the object's culture and use—is H2ST a good or bad game? After all, it is a game designed to question moral choices in the player, such as collecting slaves and loading them into a ship. The player is a slave herself and is being forced to place others in a similar position. In addition, the game uses appealing visuals such as a cartoon-like mouse and a friendly dragon to draw the player into performing these acts. Is a game which elicits such conduct good or bad? Next, the business ethics can also be evaluated. What were the business motivations to create such a game? What are the moral implications of selling a game that portrays a sensitive aspect of human history? Is this perception influenced by the location of the company? The game company, Serious Game Interactive, garnered media attention with a questionable play mechanic in which the slaves needed to be stored in the ship in a Tetris-like manner (see Fig. 1). While it is historically accurate that slaves were treated as cargo, is it ethical for a company to address the topic in such a manner?

Fig. 1. Playing History 2 - Tetris Gameplay (2013).

Ethical play can showcase players' relationships to one another and the moral boundaries they are willing to cross or not. A player might choose to play the role of the slave with an intention to do as little as demanded of them to escape later and free others, for example. Frameworks are defined by the design of the game itself. The player might decide to play ethically (be an ethical player), but if the game parameters are such that unethical behavior is rewarded and ethical behavior is not, then the player is limited in her ethical play.

Entertainment games are designed for engagement and achievement, sometimes with the goal of increasing profit margins. By contrast, serious games aim to provoke thinking, elicit self-awareness, simulate experiences, support healing, or engage players in learning. The vision of serious game designers is intentional and goal oriented. Often with the to elicit behaviour change in the player. Such a focus requires a higher degree of moral intelligence in design. Thus this chapter proposes a process that enhances ethical intelligence in serious games. We term the framework for the ethical design of serious games *Ecosystem for Designing Games Ethically* (EDGE) and its corresponding guidelines, *Ethical Stewardship*.

2   An Ethical Framework

This chapter expands upon Zagal's variables [5] to include the designer and the context of use into the development process (Fig. 2). The integration of the designer [10, 11] and the context of use into Zagal's [5] variables, creates a more complete picture of the ethical ecosystem navigated in games. We use the MDA model (a formal approach to game design that includes mechanics, dynamics, and aesthetics) as a way to organize these variables into what we term an *Ecosystem for Designing Games Ethically* (EDGE) (see Fig. 2). This ecosystem serves as an organizing framework for this chapter, which is divided into five sections as follows: the two contexts of design and use, and the negotiations that occur between the designer, the serious game and the player.

Why then include the game designer herself as a variable in the framework? Discussing the ethics of digital games can include the concept that morality in games may be informed by a game designer's ethical perspective. In addition, except for business ethics, Zagal's [5] variables address aspects of post-production (after the game is created). Information systems literature offers serious games a bridge that supports the inclusion of the designer as an ethical variable. The information system field places the emphasis of ethics on pre-production (design) and extends a consideration of morality to values and beliefs in design [6, 7]. If digital games reflect ethical perspectives of those who design them, then digital game ethics would do well to expand on current definitions, by including game designer's ethical perspectives that inform: (a) ethical play, (b) actions of the player, and (c) the game itself. For example, it might be challenging to fully address how race informs the degree of ethical play for the player in H2ST, if the ethical evaluation of the game does not also include an exploration of the designers and their values. For this reason, scholars in digital games ethics now address how a game designer's values inform design [8, 9].

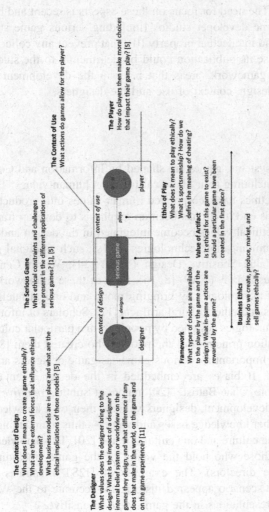

The Context of Use
What actions do games allow for the player?

The Player
How do players then make moral choices that impact their game play? [5]

Ethic of Play
What does it mean to play ethically? What is sportsmanship? How do we define the meaning of cheating?

Value of Artifact
Is it ethical for this game to exist? Should a particular game have been created in the first place?

The Serious Game
What ethical constraints and challenges are present in the different applications of serious games? [1], [5]

context of use

plays

serious game

designs

context of design

player

designer

Framework
What types of choices are available to the player by the game and the design? What in-game actions are rewarded by the game?

Business Ethics
How do we create, produce, market, and sell games ethically?

The Context of Design
What does it mean to create a game ethically? What are the external forces that influence ethical development? What business models are in place and what are the ethical implications of those models? [5]

The Designer
What values does the designer bring to the design? What is the impact of a designer's internal belief system or worldview on the games they design, and what difference if any does that make in the world, on the game and on the game experience? [11]

Fig. 2. Ecosystem for designing games ethically (EDGE).

In addition to the designer and the player, two important contexts should also be considered. Within the context of design, the designer makes the design choices that define the game. Within the context of use, the player interacts with the game. Much literature is already devoted to the ethics in the games themselves, in game play, and to the ethical considerations by players [1, 5, 8]. However, very little attention is given to the design contexts and the designers themselves. Within the scholarly literature of game design, there is a paucity of attention focused on the game creation process [12] and on serious games. The need for focus on these aspects is recent and has to do with the accessibility to game developer studios (including serious game studios); many have secrecy clauses and intellectual property (IP) that prevent any collected data to be used in a study, because its publication could be detrimental to the studio [13]. This section will focus on gamework, areas that refer to the development of the game including: context of design, context of use and the designers.

3 The Designer

As designed software systems, games are shaped by Information and Communication Technologies (ICTs), including their historical focus on human values. The domain of computer information ethics has incorporated human values into product design since its inception [6]. To this end, there has been an emphasis to develop frameworks that ensure that moral and ethical values become integrated in the design and development of information and communication technologies (ICTs), such as digital games. These frameworks include Value Sensitive Design (VSD) [14], Worth Centered Design (WCD) [15], and Values at Play (VAP) [8, 16]. Each of these frameworks attempts to influence the design of technologies by bringing moral and ethical intelligence to the creation of technologies and other cultural artifacts [17]. Scholars of information ethics (IE) also claim that technologies designed by people from a particular culture reflect the values and communication principles of the people who created them [8, 18, 19].

This is particularly important for serious games as game designers are tasked with an agenda and a goal. If biases are embedded in the design, then unknowingly, designers could promote what Battiste [20] names a subtle *cognitive imperialism*. Through digital game development, designers validate their own knowledge base, and cognitively disclaim other knowledge bases and values—thus maintaining the primacy of the one language, one culture and one cultural frame [20]. This knowledge base may also be validated by those who hold the vision of the game (including designers, producers and creative directors). The example of H2ST illustrates this type of imperialism. While the scenario appeared historically accurate to the Western developers, some of the representations in the game were insensitive.

Designers therefore have a choice in the selection and presentation of the game content, and the interactions and choices that the game offers or does not offer to its users. These design choices need to be in line with the overarching purpose of the game; designers ought to consider what is conveyed with the gameplay, narrative, and the visual elements of the game. For example, in *America's Army*, a multiplayer first-person shooter, it is not possible to play as the enemy—a specific and deliberate design choice that allows particular content, while limiting access to other views.

How then can serious game designers balance project and design demands, with ethical stewardship? The next section facilitates an understanding of ethics in design.

3.1 Ethical Considerations in Design

It has become clear that ethical considerations are an important aspect of designing serious games. While similar design choices need to be addressed in the production of other media, such as film and writing, the interactive aspect of games complicates the considerations that must be made. In addition to which content to present, and in what way to present it, a designer must also attend to the choices a player can make within the game, and how these choices are rewarded within the game. For example, design dilemmas exist in which roles a player is allowed to play, and which actions are available to the player within a role. An example can be found in *Assassin's Creed*, a series of action-adventure games in a fictional historical setting. The series does not contain playable female characters—even when history provides ample examples of strong female roles [21, 22]. These examples demonstrate that in the presentation of the environment to play in, and what options are available to a player, ethics are at play.

As all designers do, game designers can anticipate the effects brought forward by the artefacts they create and can become accountable for their designs. However, there are a number of barriers that stand in the way of adopting this stance as regular practice. First, there is tension between ethical considerations for the design and the project constraints such as time and budget. Anticipating possible effects beyond the intended goals of the serious game is often low priority in an already complex process. Second, within game studios it is not common practice to include the ethical perspective in design. In addition, the game development literature does not include ethical thinking into the game design process nor does the literature point to the available frameworks that support ethical thinking in design [1, 5, 8]. For a nascent serious game developer, there is little material to guide their decision-making process from an ethical perspective. For example, of the current leading game design books none addresses ethics in any chapter. We propose that ethics could easily be discussed in parallel with introductions to the different stages of the game development cycle (concepting, prototyping, building and evaluating). Third, and last, the game industry at large, whether focused on serious games or entertainment games, is a relatively young field and considering the intended and unintended effects of the games produced is only starting to become regular practice. That said, there are some ways in which the designer can attempt to bring moral and ethical intelligence through design. We refer to these self-reflective and practice guidelines as *Ethical Stewardship* (ES) in design. These guidelines are modeled after Deardorff's intercultural competence model [23] and design models from information ethics [10].

3.2 Ethical Stewardship in Design

Ethical Stewardship in design requires a shift in the game designer's internal state to a reflective stance. This is achieved through: (a) developing requisite attitudes (such as respect, openness, and curiosity) which serve as the basic unit of *Ethical Stewardship*,

(b) critical reflection on values, (c) developing ethical knowledge and skills through bricolage, and (d) developing an informed frame of reference through understanding stakeholders. The last level produces a desired external outcome which leads to more reflection in design.

1. *Ethical stewardship requires developing requisite attitudes as design practice.* In intercultural communication, requisite attitudes of respect, openness and curiosity comprise basic units of a reflective stance [23]. Each of these attitudes are defined in the following manner: (a) Respect refers to valuing other perspectives; (b) openness refers to the ability to withhold judgment; and (c) curiosity refers the ability to tolerate ambiguity. We propose to adopt these same attitudes as a starting point for ES. One way to increase designers' openness and curiosity is to actively seek out and include existing ethical tools [24]. One such tool is Taylor and Dempsey's RPG game, *Ethical Quest* [25]. Through the role-playing mechanics in *Ethical Quest* members of a design team learn to define their own ethical stance. The goal of *Ethical Quest* is to collaboratively define a code of ethics with other players. The challenge however, is that players must negotiate a code of ethics while role playing a character that is part of a design team (designer, programmer, manager, player, etc.). In ethical stewardship, a designer can include these types of tools to support their development of requisite attitudes.

2. *Ethical stewardship requires critical reflection on values.* A model that supports game designer reflection on their personal ethical frameworks and values during design is Values at Play (VAP) designed by Mary Flanagan and colleagues [10]. Values at Play is an iterative process that designers utilize to discover, translate and verify their values within their game design. One tool developed by the VAP team is the *Grow A Game* cards which provide a method for designers to critical analyze and think about how to incorporate certain values into a game. Through this exercise designers gain a deeper understanding of how including values in a game from the beginning alters the game design. Another method for designers to develop critical reflection about values is to build towards understanding the influence of their own historical context on their design. To gain critical reflection, a game designer would employ a variety of interaction design tools usually used with users for self-understanding, including cultural analysis, collages and cognitive mapping [26]. By doing so she would understand better her own history and background informs her values and her worldview.

3. *Ethical stewardship requires bricolage.* Ethical knowledge and understanding requires intellectual bricolage [27]—what Claude Levi-Strauss calls "making do with what is at hand" [28]. A bricoleur may gather materials, knowledge and tools for future use without knowing when these will be used. In cultural anthropology the concept of bricolage occurs when new ideologies emerge from current myths and social realities. Bricolage thinking involves being resourceful and adaptable within a given context. Ethical bricoleurs: (a) are flexible and responsive—they employ a variety of research methods to gain a deeper understanding of users; (b) remain intellectually informed and stay abreast of interpretive paradigms; and (c) are multi-skilled and technically competent by enlisting different tools for gathering user information (interviews, focus groups, etc.) Additionally, a bricoleur

should understand and be informed about the variety of methods available to gather diverse user data.

To gain deeper ethical knowledge in design, a game designer employing bricolage would gather materials and resources that would support a deeper understanding of differing perspectives in design. There is a Dutch saying, "vreemde ogen dwingen," which roughly translates to "strange eyes have stronger voices than eyes that look through familiar glasses." Such a saying illustrates the importance of keeping an open mind to include perspectives outside of our own. For example, ethical designers can include non-Western tools as a means for including broader perspectives. While the dichotomy of Western and non-Western is a Western construct itself [29], non-Western refers to systems of thoughts outside of European traditions including, for example, African, African American, Asian, Latin American, and indigenous populations [30]. Other design fields, like architecture, have been successful at introducing diversity in design by including examples of non-Western designers in their work and learning from the contributions of "invisible designers" [30, 31]. Western game design process could benefit not only from the inclusion of collaborative methods during design. For example, if game designers were to develop a game based on a historical event, all those involved in the project would learn about the geography, people and history of the event from multiple perspectives [32]. When creating a game based on the U.S. Gold Rush, for example, designers would incorporate learning about the history from the perspective of indigenous nations, and not solely as accounted historically in Western texts [33].

4. *Ethical stewardship requires including stakeholders as co-creators of games from the beginning.* Developing an informed frame of reference requires an understanding of the people for whom the game is intended for. While it is common practice to include players in the development cycle to test a game, we propose including all appropriate stakeholders from the beginning. This approach fits well with the user-centered design process. As the design process should inherently assess and address the user, several methods supporting user advocacy have been developed and widely adopted. These approaches range from evaluating game prototypes with focus groups representing the target audience (passive participation), to actively including end users in the design team (participatory design or co-creation). Game designers can partner with stakeholders to co-create the designs, rather than perceive stakeholders in subject position, participating solely as "inputters," not partners. Furthermore, the type of stakeholder that contributes to the design of game can be selected for their skill and their creative capacity [34]. For example, in the development of an educational game to be used in schools, it is important to include teachers and parents as part of the design team.

Additionally, inclusion of co-creating with stakeholders requires much more than an implementation of design strategies, and instead asks the designer to become a facilitator of the relational process [35]. Intellectual facilitation is based upon the notion that well-understood design practices might not be appropriate for a given audience, and instead requires a mutual learning process between designer and user [35, 36]. Through this sort of facilitation, game designers understand the conditions needed for a successful ethical design and allow space for each design to arise out of specific situations. This includes extending the same understanding to users in the context being designed for. For example, a game designer might create a collage of the history of transportation in the city. The player might be asked to do the same. In doing so, not only does the game designer place herself in the global context, but allows for self-reflection and understanding of the differences and commonalities between her values and those of the player.

4   The Contexts

In the previous section we discussed the ethical considerations for the design and development of serious games from the perspective of the designer: which questions to ask and what steps to take. We suggested that the design choices that a designer makes during the design process define the serious game. Some of these design choices and ethical dilemmas are similar regardless of the application context. We defined context as the environment and circumstances in which the game is designed (context of design) and intended to be used (context of use). However, some particular application contexts present their own ethical discussions, stemming from the nature of that context. From our perspective, the contexts of design and use do not operate in isolation (as Fig. 2 shows), rather, they are closely linked to other variables in the ethical ecosystem. In this section, two relationships between contexts and variables are explored. The first is the relationship between context of design and context of use through discussions on education and military games. The second relationship discussed in this section, is the connection between context of use and business ethics in privacy aspects of serious games.

4.1   Serious Games and Education

In education, serious games support learning through a variety of methods, such as providing practice-with-feedback scenarios in a motivating environment, integrating learning environments with instruction, adaptation to the learner's individual needs, and integrated assessments. A number of ethical issues in serious games for learning are becoming apparent but are left largely unaddressed.

The goal of learning games is primarily to help a learner achieve a set of learning goals, through interactive experience and real time feedback. Often associated with such educational games is the opportunity to provide individualised or personalised learning, by adapting content to the needs of the learner. The introduction of so-called virtual coaches, with realistic affective behaviour towards the learner, begs the question of whether the goal is becoming to replace traditional teachers with technology. While there is much to say in favor of taking advantage of technology in education, there is an inherent ethical discussion on the appropriate extent of this use.

This closely relates to the variation in educational materials used within a curriculum: how much of a curriculum should be gamified? It is unclear whether game-based learning suits some learners better than others. Thus, as an extension of ethical stewardship in game design for specific courses or learning goals, there is a broader need for stewardship in the design of an educational program as a whole.

Learning with digital tools such as serious games allows the mass collection of data about the learner and the learning process. Such game analytics and learning analytics may be used to monitor progress, provide feedback, and support a learner with personalised feedback. However, the ownership of the collected data is often unclear and outside of the learner's control. Moreover, it can be debated whether personalised learning is always in the best interest of the learner: perhaps a different choice in the automatically selected level of difficulty, learning materials, and exercises may be more effective. There is a possibility that a learner is denied access to educational resources that are made available to other students.

The goals of a learning game may not always be clear. *America's Army* is positioned as an entertainment game as well as a training tool; yet if we regard the game from a business ethics perspective, it is not transparent that the intended use of the game is to recruit the best players to work for the U.S. army [37, 38]. The average player is likely unaware of that and hence not in a position to consider the implications of this hidden purpose. Laying open agendas of an algorithm and making choices on an algorithm transparent is the goal of an area recently termed *IT Algorithm Accountability* [39, 40].

One of the areas in which serious games for learning are particularly popular is in medical training. Serious games and simulations offer effective environments to practice without real-world consequences, as particularly in this context of use, the cost and impact of a mistake is high. However, the fidelity of the simulation to the real world situation is crucial in providing effective training. If it turns out that using the serious game as a training tool produces unwanted effects, who is responsible for the resulting consequences? For example, a serious game about medical triage procedures is used to train staff in performing the correct steps [41]. If a mistake would be made in actual triage procedures because of a misrepresentation in the serious game, it is unclear where liability falls.

Another area of training in which serious games are being used is in the training of intercultural awareness and communication. For example, in the graphic adventure game *It's a Deal!*, Spanish men and women in international trade are trained in general awareness of cultural differences, as well as specific rules that apply to British culture [42]. The question is whether the design is accurate: are the scenarios representing the cultures involved correctly, or are there underlying assumptions that may be detrimental in real life situations? Using the Hofstede model of synthetic cultures [43] as the basis for the game play, the game design implicitly assumes that cultures are bounded or binary (e.g. collectivist vs. individualist), whereas the real life situation is more varied and complex. This may cause players to over-generalize based on their training. A similar example can be found in the Adaptive Thinking and Leadership (ATL) training game, a multiplayer simulation game used as part of the training for U.S. Army Special Forces Officers [44]. The accuracy of the scenarios, actions, and feedback within the game have a significant impact on how well the training outcomes transfer to real life situations.

These examples showcase the delicate relationship between context of use and context of design. Designers require an understanding of underlying assumptions that they may have about the context for which they are designing (context of design). Equally critical is reflecting on how these assumptions are transferred to the design of the serious game, and how these then influence the player (context of use).

4.2 Serious Games and the Military

"A military convoy is traveling on a rough desert road in Iraq. Suddenly there is a deafening noise: a Humvee explodes ahead, black smoke rises. Rebels attack the vehicles from all sides - shots are heard, screams fill the night. The smell of burning rubber impregnates the air." [45]

This story illustrates the typical manner in which military serious games present their narratives. In contrast to games for entertainment, these narratives reflect real events. Military games simulate actions which have ramifications in real life; therefore serious games for the military raise ethical issues. This section reviews the ethical issues for digital serious games with military applications. Specifically we present a historical summary of military serious games followed by a look at the application context and the linked cultural aspects; we examine the difference between simulations and games; and we discuss how these computer programs are aligned in the military decision-making process.

In the field of ethics and moral, military serious games reflect multiple variables from our ethical framework (cf. Sect. 2). In particular we focus on three variables: (a) cultural aspects, (b) business ethics and (c) ethical play. The term *military ethics* encompasses these variables. Military ethics is typically understood as applied professional ethics and concerns questions regarding the application of force by military armed forces [46].

There is a long connected history between serious games and the military [47], as the first serious games were developed for military training. These games were designed, developed and used by the military, like the U.S. Army, during the Cold War [48]. One of the most famous examples is the arcade game *Army Battlezone* and its specialized version *The Bradley Trainer* by Atari in 1980, used by the U.S. Army as a targeting training simulator for a specific tank type. In the game the user views a plane with hostile enemy tanks and mountainous horizon from a first-person perspective. The goal is to target and destroy moving enemy tanks and collect reward points. The game displays the objects with wireframe vector graphics on a black and white screen. The game *Battlezone* represents one of the early provocations of cultural and moral differences between the military and game developers: several of Atari's employees were opposed to the "game" content and refused to make further games for the military [48]. The original designer of *Battlezone,* Ed Rotberg, stated: "We didn't want anything to do with the military. I was doing games. I didn't want to train people to kill." [48]. Serious games for the military have since become a huge industry. *America's Army, Virtual Battlespace, Steel Beasts* or *Combat Flight Simulator* are recent games with large budgets made for the U.S. military [49].

The narratives and scenarios of games for the military are clear: war or war-like conflicts and their serious ramifications. Hence, those games are not just for entertainment with fictional narratives, but rather have serious application contexts and events. Serious games for military train people to ultimately support martial actions. The usage of realistic and violent first-person shooters (FPS) which train people how to kill raises ethical issues. There is empirical data providing evidence that people's personality structures are significantly altered when playing these shooter games [2]. That is, in the short-term, violent games affect aggression by priming aggressive thoughts, and in the long-run the repeated exposure to computer game violence can lead to increases in aggressive affect, which can negatively influence everyday social interactions [2]. Obviously this is of high relevance when such games are directly linked with real war-like application scenarios, like the training of combat situations which include killing actions. Of course, in the military such training is inherently part of the profession itself. However, the ultimate intended outcome of such training is not only for defensive actions but could also lead—directly or indirectly—to offensive attack actions. Again, in the formal military context and with military personnel this is part of the profession. But for a general audience it is questionable whether games which can change the personality structure and could affect aggression are tolerable for society. At this point questions arise whether it is ethical to design and develop games for the military (which are open to the general public) since they can negatively influence multiple people's lives.

An example for a military first-person shooter game is the often-cited recruiting game *America's Army*, developed and published by the United States Army. It is a subject of ongoing criticism and controversy [37, 50]. *America's Army* is the name of a technology platform used to create free realistic army games permitting (young) Americans to virtually explore typical combat situations with other players in multi-player scenarios. As a strategic communication device, the game is designed to collect usage data used by the U.S. Army for recruitment purposes. In the same manner, China's People's Liberation Army (PLA) has released the similar first-person shooter game *Glorious Mission* with the dual purpose of recruiting soldiers and training personnel in combat skills and technological awareness. In some societies such games are generally more or less accepted, whereas in others the topic is highly controversial. In Germany, contentious discussions arose over 3D shooter games which have human-like characters being harmed or killed; the games are often discredited as "Killerspiele" ("killer games") [51]. Of course, there are also military serious games designed for more positive purposes, i.e., which not only concern the application of force but train social skills like inter-cultural communication [52, 53] or games for psychiatric rehabilitation targeting post-traumatic stress disorder (PTSD) [45].

In the military, the term *simulation* is more often used than *serious game*. The political acceptance level is much higher for serious simulations (even with game-like concepts like narratives etc.) than for computer games which are explicitly declared as such. Typically, no one wants to talk about gaming when it comes to ethically questionable activities. From a technical perspective, there exist distinct differences between military computer simulations and entertainment games. In military computer simulations, the focus is not on the explicit display of violence or of harmed bodies, neither the killing action nor the display of use of force from a first person perspective. Military simulations focus primarily on high realism of equipment or processes, and not on the most realistic use of force. Whereas entertainment games have their realism focus on the realistic display of violence (blood detail, weapon details etc.), military simulations focus mostly on correct (realistic) physics or validity of processes. These simulations capture the physics and aerodynamics present in the use of equipment such as weapons, vehicles, tanks or aircraft. Understanding and learning how these work is essential for the training of soldiers to safely operate real, complex equipment.

Often mentioned in discussions of this topic is the analogy to the application of weapons: a gun itself is not dangerous, but the human using it could be. Hence, it is the responsibility of people to make proper use of tools. This is often applied to software as well: the military computer simulation for training itself is at first not directly linked to any killing. But, of course, it could be used to facilitate the process of harming others. For example, in the computer simulation, soldiers could have been trained to steer weaponized military drones, be they manually steered or semi-autonomous [54, 55]. Those type of weapons enable soldiers to participate in wars and conflicts, but from a very remote location and not in direct, life-threatening contact. It is important that soldiers are also trained to never forget their responsibility for their remotely executed actions. They are always part of the military kill-chain [56]. Localizing a military computer program in the military decision-making process, like the military kill-chain model, is difficult; it depends on the nature of the software, i.e., whether it is an educational serious game or a tactical simulator. An educational serious game (or a computer simulation for just training) could be seen at the very beginning of a military decision process. The educational serious game is right at the front disconnected from any killing action and only used in a formal education context, e.g., training at the military academy. Typically, it is not part of a combat situation, i.e. it is not part of any killing action. In contrast, the link in the kill-chain is much stronger for an operational military tactical simulator which is used right before the soldier continues with the real weaponized drone. In this case, this computer simulator is actually part of the military kill-chain and the ethical issues apply.

The application of military games are multiple and broad, and can include infantry, flight simulators, tanks, submarines, tactics, strategy, trauma management and others [47–49]. Such applications of military games therefore merit an exploration of the ethical issues of their use. As long as there are conflicts, the military and its industrial partners will continue to produce military serious games for recruitment, training, and education. Those games will always be subject to the aforementioned ethical issues. As researchers and designers of serious games it is important to critically question their proper and ethical use since serious games for military use appear to be permanently embedded in society, for now.

4.3 Serious Games and Data Privacy

With the number of users and strategies for sharing and storing data about them increasing, data privacy becomes an important issue in serious games design. However, there is no common definition of the term *data privacy*. In general, it refers to the efforts to control any access of user-related data by any third party. Video games can be considered rich origins of data: they are interactive software systems by design. Games receive input data via various channels such as interactive interfaces and controllers, which potentially can be collected and stored digitally by the game software.

The following example demonstrates how much data is produced by games. Eggert et al. [57] exploit replay files of a real time strategy game to classify player types, using behavioral low-level data during game play. Even if replay files may not be stored by default, it demonstrates the ability of the game software to log each small game interaction, which is sufficient to reproduce a complex game play. Another kind of data available for use are *player stats* - data that defines the current status of the player in the game. The massively multiplayer online game (MMOG) *EVE Online* [57] serves as an example. *EVE Online* contains a comprehensive data model - a great amount of game related (player status) data has to be managed. For example in the market a player has submitted offers and bids. Player skills have to be developed in order to gain certificates, therefore optimized schedules of (time-based) skill training have to be developed. There is even a data interface, which has led to the emergence of a number of third party tools with the purpose of user-friendly administration of game-related data [58]. Thus, video games collect, aggregate and store large amounts of player data.

Whenever data is collected and stored, there is the potential for misuse. In general, data protection laws have been enacted in order to protect data privacy. However, those laws do not provide regulations specific to video games. In the context of video games, misuse could be defined as using game data for other purposes than entertainment by this game. Serious games are by definition videogames with further purposes besides pure entertainment, thus such a definition seems to be insufficient in the context of serious games. Those further purposes might require collection and processing of even more user-related data. For example, in adaptive learning games, the current user status has to be stored. In the learning game *Doctor's Cure* [59], students assume the role of a reporter investigating the details of a moral dilemma narrative hint by hint. Collected data from measuring learning progress is provided to the teacher through the *Teacher Dashboard*, and the teacher takes on the role of editor in communicating with the students. So, in order to support the goals of the game, there is an inherent requirement to generate and store additional data, i.e., the information needed in the Dashboard and the communication log between student and teacher.

For a serious game this definition has to be extended: data should be used only for this game's purposes—including and besides entertainment. However, the definition continues to seem incomplete, as the following examples should illustrate. Fliplife [60] is a social network game (SNG), used also as a storytelling platform for companies, making it a so-called advergames, a kind of a serious game. In Fliplife aspects of daily life are simulated: work, education and spare-time. The player chooses a career she wants to pursue and works on it in projects, which are timer-based activities, together with other players, the co-workers. Careers are provided by companies in order to implement a narrative corporate presentation in the game. Furthermore, a German trust has been said to consider the game as as a source for potential employees [61]: based on game-collectible data, a list of candidates for job interviews can be generated. From a methodological point of view such an attempt to identify candidates for a job can be considered as completely feasible [62]. From an ethical point of view, there remain at least doubts: players are not explicitly aware of the collection of data which does not support game mechanics, but enables third parties to trace their personality traits like reliability, engagement or leadership qualities of players. Using the proposed ethical ecosystem, this kind of data exploitation falls under the category of Business Ethics and can be a part of a business model for the game supplier. Observing players in this way appears unproductive if they are aware of this surveillance and act accordingly. Consequently, this collection and use of data should not be revealed to players. Then it becomes hidden surveillance, which is ethically problematic. Another example in this context of the ethical ecosystem in the category Business Ethics is the smartphone-based augmented reality game INGRESS [63]. This game requires gamers to walk around in the neighbourhood and visit locations with virtual portals in order to interact with those portals virtually. During the game play, a great deal of data could be collected, which would be useful in other contexts [64]. So for example, preferred routes and activity times could be tracked. Much of that data is already available at mobile providers, but now it would be exploitable for the game provider at a much more detailed level. Among the positive imaginable results of player's actions are pictures with attached position data, which could augment online map services and WLAN identifiers. These artifacts may be highly useful for tracking services. Actually, such a use is denied by the game developer [65], although it is not explicitly excluded by the Terms of Service and Privacy Rules [66]. Therefore, there is a high likelihood that a sudden change of data usage would go unnoticed by users.

Although the importance of data privacy is valued differently across countries and cultures, the disclosures of Edward Snowden [67] have raised it to wide public attention. The increasing use of online games and mobile apps further establishes the relevance of data privacy in the context of games. A recent German study about data privacy in online games "found several breaches of data protection rules. Most of the privacy policy statements did not meet the required strict German standard of comprehension and completeness" [68]. Further, the study claims data privacy is handled heterogeneously, mostly depending on the country where the servers are based. On the other hand, the results indicate that "many users are interested in data protection and privacy issues."

As there are no widely accepted standards, and as it seems that such a standard will not be established in the near future, serious game developers must proactively address data privacy responsibly, i.e., carefully taking ethical considerations into account. As already indicated, in the context of serious games, data privacy is a matter of *Business Ethics* based on the above defined variables of the ethical ecosystem. As serious games are intended to pursue further purposes than pure entertainment, the needs for these purposes guide the development and application of those games. At the same time, these purposes limit the degrees of freedom regarding design and implementation of a serious game. "Enjoyment" is the goal which must be achieved by pure entertainment games; for serious games, entertainment and enjoyment are employed, but not for the primary purpose of the games. Therefore, within the categories of our proposed Ethical Ecosystem (see Fig. 2), *Business Ethics* might be the dominant variable, as the examples of *Fliplife* and *INGRESS* illustrate. There might be an inherent drive to the exploitation of generated data, which has to be reviewed in its ethical dimensions carefully and leads to data privacy being an ethical matter. However, the three central elements of the Ethical Ecosystem can be used to categorise the concerns of data privacy. Mainly, *The Serious Game* provides a frame for adherence to ethical implementation of data privacy concerns. Furthermore, *The Designer* is in charge of negotiating a reasonable balance of data privacy requirements and serious games goals, and *The Player* should be made aware of the privacy policies implemented in the game.

Responsible data privacy at least comprises implementing national data protection laws of those countries where the game is rolled out, and revealing clearly and precisely the actual procedures of collection, storage and use of data in a meaningful data policy. The user should be informed about the current ways to utilize the game's data. Even if the issue of data privacy is raised by quite a few games (e.g., *Data Dealer* [69] or *Privacy Pirates* [70]) there is no commonly accepted guideline. This missing regulation may endanger the acceptance of (serious) online games in the long term: if players hesitate to play a game due to privacy concerns, this would be an unnecessary obstacle of the game developers' own doing. All the more, game developers are required to adhere to a clear and responsible data privacy guideline.

5 Conclusions and Outlook

The purpose of this chapter is to highlight the importance of moral intelligence in game development with a special focus on serious games. To support moral intelligence in game development, we proposed an *Ecosystem for Designing Games Ethically (EDGE)*. The ethical ecosystem integrates the work of previous scholars such as Zagal and Flanagan into one system that includes the designer and the contexts of use as necessary to ethical reflection. We defined these contexts of design and use. The context of design is one in which the designer makes the design choices that define the game and the context of use is one within which the player interacts with the game. Context considerations for specific design contexts were reviewed including contexts of educational games, and games with military game play. Data privacy considerations were also included.

In addition to EDGE, we provided a process for serious game designers to implement moral intelligence in design which we termed, *Ethical Stewardship* (ES). A primary aim of ES is to strengthen relationships between designers, players and stakeholders throughout the entire process of moral competence in designers. Ethical stewardship does not negate the business of digital games—the need for institutions, or game studios to be profitable, nor the practices required to expand serious games to new markets. Ethical stewardship also does not blindly affirm that every ES guideline must be met for moral intelligence. We acknowledge that constraints exist in the development process and that it is not always possible to include all components of ES. Rather, we offer ES as a way to embrace ethical ethnorelativism and moral design in serious games. In practice, ethical stewardship can be addressed through education and training. The myriad of university curricula addressing the design and development of serious game bear the responsibility to actively address ethical design considerations in their projects.

In closing, we wish to contribute some remarks on the importance of moral intelligence in digital game design. As socially constructed artifacts, digital games influence social, psychological, political and economic contexts [8, 71]. Several design perspectives assume that embracing ethical competence is vital for good design [32, 35]. Some argue that game designers, as creators of art, media and cultural artifacts, have a moral and social obligation to understand the impact their design choices have on society—that there are consequences to what is designed and therefore consumed by others [19, 40, 72–74]. Others argue that self-reflection in design is essential for personal and professional growth. Deardorff [23, 24] and others [75] claim that embracing moral intelligence is an important part of human development and of "good" citizenship. Alternatively, it could be said that neglecting "ethics" contributes to the lack of moral intelligence in game creation, and that in itself undermines the success of serious design efforts and contributes to questionable design decisions such as those in H2ST [32].

Instead, this chapter's authors assert that ethical stewardship ought to be embarked upon because richness of artifact creation—the creation of new forms of serious games—lies in the constraints an ethical stance affords. Ethical stewardship is not simply a methodology for moral competence as good action or self-growth. Nor a method to pursue what others identify as good design. Rather, ethical stewardship makes a commitment to reflecting upon moral intelligence as critical to creativity and innovative action. Greater moral competence in design ultimately results in a more integrated player experience for its respective market, improved game content quality and stronger partnerships with stakeholders. At a larger scale, ethical considerations need to become standard practice in game design and development frameworks and a topic of discussion in the respective academic journals and conferences, as well as in the field of practice.

6   Reflective Questions

- What challenges present themselves to the designer who wishes to include an ethical perspective?
- What ethical considerations would be most difficult to integrate and why?
- In what manner can the suggested tools be integrated in your design process to develop alternative perspectives and critical reflection?
- Should all games require an ethical certification or course? Which usages of player-related data can be considered as ethically appropriate?
- What impact has a clear data privacy term on the usage of a serious game in comparison to the absence of such terms?
- What recent developments in technology require new approaches in data privacy (e.g., health data [63, 64], location based data, and route tracking)?
- How to systematically assess the influence of serious games designed for specific contentious purposes (e.g. military)? How to define an ethical assessment framework?

Acknowledgement. In addition to Prof. Katharina-Anna Zweig (zweig@cs.uni-kl.de), our chapter editor, we would like to thank Dr. Cheri Gurse, founder of Scholar Builder, for her time and dedication in editing this chapter. Dr. Gurse works as a professional editor in the Social Sciences and can be reached at cgurse@fielding.edu.

Further Reading

To develop a deeper understanding of the perspectives mentioned in this chapter, the following list is suggested for further reading:

Values in Game Design: Flanagan, M., & Nissenbaum, H. (2014). *Values at play in digital games*. Boston, MA: MIT Press.
Information Ethics: Floridi, L. (Ed.). (2010). *The Cambridge handbook of information and computer ethics*. Boston, MA: Cambridge University Press.
Digital Game Ethics and Models: Schrier, K. (Ed.). (2010). *Designing games for ethics: Models, techniques and frameworks*. Hershey, PA: IGI Global.
Player Ethics: Sicart, M. (2011). *The ethics of computer games*. Boston, MA: MIT Press.
Digital Game Ethics: Zagal, J. P. (2011). *The videogame ethics reader*. San Diego, CA: Cognella Academic Publishing.

References

1. Sicart, M.: The banality of simulated evil: designing ethical gameplay. Ethics Inf. Technol. **11**(3), 191–202 (2009)
2. Anderson, C.A., Dill, K.E.: Video games and aggressive thoughts, feelings, and behaviour in the laboratory and in life. J. Pers. Soc. Psychol. **78**(4), 772 (2000)
3. Sherry, J.L., Lucas, K., Greenberg, B.S., Lachlan, K.: Video game uses and gratifications as predictors of use and game preference. In: Playing Video Games Motives Responses Consequences, pp. 213–224 (2006)
4. Vessey, J.A., Lee, J.E.: Violent video games affecting our children. Pediatr. Nurs. **26**(6), 607–609 (2000)
5. Zagal, J.P.: Ethically notable videogames: moral dilemmas and gameplay. In: Proceedings of DiGRA 2009: Breaking New Ground: Innovation in Games, Play and Practice and Theory, p. 9 (2009)
6. Bynum, T.W.: Computer ethics: basic concepts and historical overview. In: The Stanford Encyclopedia of Philosophy (2001)
7. Bynum, T.W.: Flourishing ethics. Ethics Inf. Technol. **8**(4), 157–173 (2006)
8. Flanagan, M., Nissenbaum, H., Howe, D.C., Nissenbaum, H.: Embodying Values in Technology: Theory and Practice. Cambridge University Press, Cambridge (2008)
9. Shaw, A.: What is video game culture? Cultural studies and game studies. Games Cult. **5**(4), 403–424 (2010)
10. Flanagan, M., Nissenbaum, H.: Values at Play in Digital Games. MIT Press, Cambridge (2014)
11. Sandovar, A., Street, D.L.V.: Cultural narratives in game design, pp. 4–6 (2015)
12. Whitson, J.R.: Game Design by Numbers: Instrumental Play and the Quantitative Shift in the Digital Game Industry. Carleton University, Ottawa (2012)
13. O'Donnell, C.: Developer's Dilemma: The Secret World of Videogame Creators. MIT Press, Cambridge (2014)
14. Friedman, B., Kahn, P., Borning, A.: Value sensitive design: theory and methods (2002)

15. Cockton, G.: Designing worth—connecting preferred means to desired ends. Interact. ACM **15**(4), 54–57 (2008)
16. Flanagan, M., Howe, D.C., Nissenbaum, H.: Values at play: design tradeoffs in socially-oriented. In: Chi 2005, pp. 751–760 (2005)
17. Manders-Huits, N., Zimmer, M.: Values and pragmatic action: the challenges of introducing ethical intelligence in technical design communities. Int. Rev. Inf. Ethics **10**, 37–44 (2009)
18. Ess, C.: Digital Media Ethics. Polity Press, Cambridge (2009)
19. Nissenbaum, H.: Values in the design of computer systems. Comput. Soc. **28**(1), 38–39 (1998)
20. Battiste, M.: Indigenous knowledge: foundations for first nations (2005)
21. Rath, R.: The historical case for playable women in Assasin's creed: unity. The Escapist (2014)
22. Leboeuf, S.: Editorial: omitting women from games because 'It's Too Hard' is unacceptable. The Escapist (2014)
23. Deardorff, D.K.: Assessing intercultural competence. New Dir Inst. Res. **149**, 65–79 (2011)
24. Deardorff, D.K.: Identification and assessment of intercultural competence as a student outcome of internationalization. J. Stud. Int. Edu. **10**(3), 241–266 (2006)
25. Taylor, C., Dempsey, S.: Ethics quest: harnessing the power of an RPG to help interdisciplinary teams. Presented at the Games for Change Conference (2016)
26. Hannington, B.: Methods in the making: a perspective on the state of human research in design. Des. Issues **19**(4), 9–18 (2003)
27. Kamppuri, M., Tedre, M., Tukiainen, M.: Towards the sixth level in interface design: understanding culture. In: Proceedings of the CHI-SA, pp. 1–6 (2006)
28. Lévi-Strauss, C.: The Savage Mind. University of Chicago Press, Chicago (1967)
29. Merriam, S.B., Kim, Y.S.: Non-western perspectives on learning and knowing. New Dir. Adult Continuing Edu. **119**, 71–81 (2008)
30. Asojo, A.O.: A model for integrating culture-based issues in creative thinking and problem solving in design studios. J. Inter. Des. **27**(2), 46–58 (2001)
31. Grant, B.: Cultural invisibility: the African American experiences in architectural education. In: Dutton, T.A. (ed.) Voices in Tribal Education: Cultural Politics and Pedagogy, pp. 149–164. Bergin & Garvey, New York (1991)
32. Edwards, K.: Culturalization: the geopolitical and cultural dimension of game content. Trans **15**, 19–28 (2011)
33. Acharya, A., Buzan, B. (eds.): Non-Western international relations theory: perspectives on and beyond Asia. Routledge, London (2009)
34. Czarnota, J.: Designing player-studio interactions for co-creation: reviewing academic theory with industrial practice. In: Multi.Player 2 Conference Abstract (2014)
35. Winschiers-Theophilus, H.: The art of cross-cultural design for usability. In: Stephanidis, C. (ed.) Universal Access in HCI, Part I, HCII 2009. LNCS, vol. 5614, pp. 665–671. Springer, Heidelberg (2009)
36. Lee, J., Sayed, S.: Culturally sensitive design. In: Levanto, Y., Sivenius, P., Vihma, S. (eds.) Design Connections: Knowledge, Value and Involvement Through Design, pp. 54–63 (2008)
37. Turse, N.: Zap, Zap, You're Dead… TomDispatch.com (2003). http://www.tomdispatch.com/post/1012/
38. Morris, C.: Your Tax Dollars at Play. CNN Money (2002)
39. Diakopoulos, N.: Algorithmic accountability: journalistic investigation of computational power structures. Digit. J. **3**, 398–415 (2015)
40. Diakopoulos, N.: Accountability in algorithmic decision making. Commun. ACM **59**, 56–62 (2016)

41. van der Spek, E.D.: Experiments in serious game design: a cognitive approach, vol. 36 (2011)
42. Guillén-Nieto, V., Aleson-Carbonell, M.: Serious games and learning effectiveness: the case of it's a deal! Comput. Edu. **58**(1), 435–448 (2012)
43. Hofstede, G.J., Pedersen, P.B., Hofstede, G.: Exploring Culture: Exercises, Stories and Synthetic Cultures. Intercultural Press, Yarmouth (2002)
44. Raybourn, E.M., Deagle, E., Mendini, K., Heneghan, J.: Adaptive thinking and leadership simulation game training for special forces officers. In: Interservice/Industry Training, Simulation and Education Conference (I/ITSEC) (2005)
45. Rizzo, A.: Bravemind: virtual reality exposure therapy. University of Southern California Institute for Creative Technologies (2005)
46. Cook, M.L., Syse, H.: What should we mean by 'Military Ethics'? J. Mil. Ethics **9**(2), 119–122 (2010)
47. Prensky, M.: True believers: digital game-based learning in the military. In: Digital Game-Based Learning, pp. 1–18 (2001)
48. Kent, S.: The Ultimate History of Video Games: From Pong to Pokemon and Beyond… The Story Behind the Craze that Touched our Lives and Changed the World. Three Rivers Press, New York (2010)
49. Roman, P.A., Brown, D.: Games - just how serious are they. In: The Intersevice/Industry Training, Simulation and Education Conference (I/ITSEC) (2008)
50. Schulzke, M.: Rethinking military gaming: America's army and its critics. Games Cult. **8**(2), 59–76 (2013)
51. Nauroth, P., Bender, J., Rothmund, T., Gollwitzer, M.: Die 'Killerspiele'-Diskussion: Wie Die Forschung Zur Wirkung Gewalthaltiger Bildschirmspiele in Der Öffentlichkeit Wahrgenommen Wird. In: Porsch, T., Pieschl, S. (eds.) Neue Medien Und Deren Schatten. Mediennutzung, Medienwirkung Und Medienkompetenz, pp. 81–100. Hogrefe, Göttingen (2014)
52. Buch, T., Egenfleldt-Nielsen, S.: The learning effects of global conflicts: palestine. In: Medi@ Terra Conference (2006)
53. Johnson, W.L., Wang, N., Wu, S.: Experience with serious games for learning foreign languages and cultures. In: Proceedings of the SimTeT Conference (2007)
54. Lin, P., Bekey, G., Abney, K.: Autonomous military robotics: risk, ethics, and design (2008)
55. Borenstein, J.: The ethics of autonomous military robots. Stud. Ethics Law Technol. **2**(1) (2008)
56. Azuma, R., Daily, M., Furmanski, C.: A review of time critical decision making models and human cognitive processes. In: IEEE Aerospace Conference (2006)
57. Eggert, C., Herrlich, M., Smeddinck, J., Malaka, R.: Classification of player roles in the team-based multi-player game Dota 2. In: Chorianopoulos, K., et al. (eds.) ICEC 2015. LNCS, vol. 9353, pp. 112–125. Springer, Heidelberg (2015). doi:10.1007/978-3-319-24589-8_9
58. CCP, "3rd Party Tools," EVElopedia (2015). https://wiki.eveonline.com/en/wiki/3rd_party_tools
59. Arici, A., Barab, S.: Transformational play; Using 3D game-based narratives to immerse students in literacy learning. In: European Conference on Games Based Learning, p. 35 (2013)
60. Fliplife (2012). Game discontinued 30 Sept 2014. http://fliplife.com/
61. Meyer, M.: Per Spiel zum Traumjob? FORUM - Das Wochenmagazin (2011). https://web.archive.org/web/20111130094810/http://www.magazin-forum.de/per-spiel-zum-traumjob
62. Söbke, H., Hadlich, C., Müller, N., Hesse, T., Henning, C., Schneider, S., Kornadt, O.: Social game fliplife: digging for talent – an analysis. In: Proceedings of the 6th European Conference on Games Based Learning, pp. 487–494 (2012)

63. Niantic Labs, "Ingress." Google (2013). http://www.ingress.com/
64. Lobo, S.: S.P.O.N. - Die Mensch-Maschine: Google macht die Welt zum Spielfeld. Spiegel Online (2013). http://www.spiegel.de/netzwelt/web/google-ingress-die-ganze-welt-als-spiel-a-902267.html
65. Janssen, J.-K.: Ingress-Erfinder: 'Visionär zu sein ist uns wichtiger als Datensammeln' c't Mag. für Comput. **15**, 41 (2014)
66. Ingress Terms of Service. Niantic, Inc. (2015). https://www.ingress.com/terms
67. Greenwald, G.: No Place to Hide: Edward Snowden, the NSA, and the U.S. Surveillance State. Picador, USA (2015)
68. Unabhängiges Landeszentrum für Datenschutz Schleswig-Holstein (ULD) (2010). https://www.datenschutzzentrum.de/projekte/dos/results/
69. Cracked Labs, "Data Dealer. Legal? Illegal? Whatever" (2013). http://datadealer.com/
70. Privacy Pirates: An Interactive Unit on Online Privacy. MediaSmarts (2015). http://mediasmarts.ca/sites/mediasmarts/files/games/privacy_pirates/flash/-PrivacyPirates_English/main.html
71. Kerr, A.: The culture of gamework. In: Deuze, M. (ed.) Managing Media Work. Sage, London (2011)
72. Akrich, M.: Beyond Social Construction of Technology: The Shaping of People and Things in the Innovation Process. Campus/Westview (1992)
73. Flanagan, M., Belman, J., Nissenbaum, H., Diamond, J.: A method for discovering values in digital games. Paper presented at Situated PLay DiGRA 2007, Tokyo, Japan (2007)
74. Van den Hoven, J.: Information technology and moral philosophy (2008)
75. Spitzberg, B.H., Changnon, G.: Conceptualizing intercultural competence. In: Deardorff, D. K. (ed.) The Sage Handbook of Intercultural Competence, pp. 2–52. Sage, Thousand Oaks (2009)

The Serious Games Ecosystem: Interdisciplinary and Intercontextual Praxis

Phil Wilkinson[1](✉) and Thomas Joseph Matthews[2]

[1] The Centre for Excellence in Media Practice, Bournemouth University, Bournemouth, UK
pwilkinson@bournemouth.ac.uk
[2] The Centre for Digital Entertainment, Bournemouth University, Bournemouth, UK
tmatthews@bournemouth.ac.uk

Abstract. This chapter will situate academia in relation to serious games commercial production and contextual adoption, and vice-versa. As a researcher it is critical to recognize that academic research of serious games does not occur in a vaccum. Direct partnerships between universities and commercial organizations are increasingly common, as well as between research institutes and the contexts that their serious games are deployed in. Commercial production of serious games and their increased adoption in non-commercial contexts will influence academic research through emerging impact pathways and funding opportunities. Adding further complexity is the emergence of commercial organizations that undertake their own research, and research institutes that have in-house commercial arms. To conclude, we explore how these issues affect the individual researcher, and offer considerations for future academic and industry serious games projects.

Keywords: Serious games · Applied games · Educational games · Games for health · Academia · Commercial games · Games for change · Application domains · Academic partnerships · Research evaluation

1 Introduction

The intention of this chapter is for you – as a researcher – to reflect on your role in the serious games eco-system. Although traditional models of abstract knowledge creation and dissemination apply in this instance, there is the opportunity to adopt different perspectives on research practice. It can be seen as enhancing knowledge creation capacity; the critical capture of knowledge; and the facilitation of praxis – the process by which research informs practice.

From the authors' experience, we – as researchers – often presume that we are the creators and distributors of knowledge. However, we often fail to take into account the importance of situated knowledge and practices surrounding the design, production, development, and indeed, application of serious games.

© Springer International Publishing AG 2016
R. Dörner et al. (Eds.): Entertainment Computing and Serious Games, LNCS 9970, pp. 63–91, 2016.
DOI: 10.1007/978-3-319-46152-6_4

2   Chapter Overview

This chapter will provide an overview and a snapshot of the current eco-system. We will first attempt to establish the different positions – ontologies – that one as researcher might adopt. Building upon this we will negotiate our epistemological position; as before, with discussing the different contextual and inter-contextual practices of knowledge construction, it is necessary to consider the different conceptualisations of 'knowledge'. Additionally, we will re-articulate the definition of serious games that we will be using.

Narrative linearity will be imposed on the interconnected complexity of the serious games eco-system through first discussing academic research practice. The commercial serious games sector will then be outlined, before moving onto the contextual adopters of serious games. There are of course numerous contexts [1], so for the purposes of detailing intercontextuality and interdisciplinarity this chapter will focus on both industrial – advertising, military, and corporate training – and non-commercial – social change, education, and healthcare – contexts. Explicit links will then be drawn with serious games commercialisation and exemplar studies research practice in these contexts.

Following the contextual overview, this chapter will discuss – with reference to specific instances of industry-academic partnerships - typical models and working practices used, suggested benefits, and emerging tensions. Equipped with this understanding, this chapter will finish with a reflective discussion of the serious games eco-system and the implications for the individual, doctoral or early career researcher.

3   Positioning in the Serious Games Academic Context

A useful allegory for the evolution of serious games research is the general scientific method:

It began with a general hypothesis – games can be used for serious purposes: inherently evidenced in the introduction (or at least popularization) of the term 'serious games' itself [2]. This is followed by testing – how can this be proved: the first established focussed institute – Serious Games Institute Coventry in 2007 [3] – and first dedicated journal – EAI Endorsed Transactions on Serious Games in 2013 [4] - demonstrate the beginning of a structured pursuit of answers to this query. Finally, establishing theory for further testing – serious games are effective given a clear definition of 'effectiveness' and under certain conditions: a current research trend that will be explored further in this chapter.

Serious games research is now intersected with multiple fields of study. For the sake of creating an introductory text, these fields can be abstracted into academic interests chiefly concerned with one of four interlinked areas: conceptualisation, production, evaluation, and contextualisation. These areas can be further broken down.

3.1   Conceptualisation

Conceptualisation – including definition modelling and sub-categorization is predominantly concerned with the framing of serious games.

Exploring conceptualisation closely illustrates the different epistemological positions that one can adopt as a researcher. For instance, game designers and researchers Mary Flanagan [5], James Paul Gee [6], and Ian Bogost [1], adopt a discursive, constructivist, approach to serious games conceptualisation. They highlight the complexity of games as a socially-situated medium, and rely on large bodies of writing in their framing of serious games. Conversely, the work of researchers Jan-Paul van Staalduinen [7], Damien Djaouti [8], and Pauline Rooney [9] adopt an instrumentalist approach - seeking to distil the rhetoric and broader conceptualisations of serious games into replicable frameworks.

Like the work of Staalduinen [7], serious game frameworks often centre on the mapping of purpose driven concepts with game mechanics – such as rehabilitative criteria with games used in healthcare [10], therapeutic benefits of digital applications [11], theories of learning in games-based learning [12]. It is worth noting that in works specifically framing games-based learning, the term 'serious games' is often used rather narrowly: interchangeably with 'games-based learning' instead of an inclusive meta label [7, 8, 12]. The instrumentalist approach of developing readily deployable serious games is apparent in academic serious games production and evaluative research that focusses on replicability.

3.2   Production

Much like the conceptualization, serious games production is typically focussed on linking purpose-relevant theories with games development practice [10, 12]. This is perhaps best illustrated through the development of the Ludens Modi Varetas model [13] through, again, the mapping of game elements with the Behaviour Change Support System (BCSS) to provide a theoretical basis for developing games for social change.

Whilst most serious games fields typically do this - affective computing will link emotionally representative game mechanics with the importance of emotionality in learning [14], and games for health will link the affordance of different interactive modalities in human computer interaction with frameworks for health goals [10, 15], for example – this is not always the case. With games-based learning, a systematic review undertaken by Wu et al. [16] found a lack of design backed by established learning-theories.

This usage of domain or purpose specific theory linked to design practice, perhaps through necessity, is also apparent in the evaluation of serious games.

3.3   Evaluation

Serious games evaluation is currently a key focus in academia. A rise in serious game usage has led to multiple serious game categories, use-cases, and adopted domains [17]. Demonstrating the efficacy of games-based learning in particular is a deeply explored but contentious field in academia with multiple meta-analysis papers demonstrating effectiveness [18–20]. However, these studies are often plagued by difficulties in replicability [21], a lack of contextual ecological validity [22], and prescriptive measures of effectiveness [23, 24].

Games-based learning measurability is problematic due to a diversity of different measures used [23]. In this instance, the notion of measurability positions the researcher as a positivist, seeking to objectively prove a tangible outcome from a game's usage. Given this positivist epistemology, outcomes are frequently measured in terms of knowledge acquisition and increases in motivation [25]. Perhaps ironically, though there is an implicit agreement to prove effectiveness through measuring outcomes, there is little agreement regarding what these measures should be or what methods should be used [22, 23]. In the field of games for social change, this fragmentation is also apparent in the narrow, sometimes ideologically driven, definitions of impact [24].

Of course this heterogeneity of effective measures and methods in broader serious games research is further confounded by multiple application domains and therefore domain-specific measures [10, 12, 24]. There are however developments of domain agnostic serious game evaluation methods - either systematically analysing game design [12], or through the application of 'user-centred validation techniques from other disciplines [26, 27]. Again, these methods demonstrate an instrumentalist approach that seeks to provide consistent academic evaluative practices. Additionally, they attempt to move beyond positivistic definitions effectiveness towards a more interpretivist approach.

For instance, heuristic evaluation techniques are regularly applied to serious games evaluation, frequently drawing on pre-existing heuristics for evaluating games or technology systems such as playability and usability [28, 29]. This approach of adapting heuristic evaluation techniques from related disciplines was also adopted in the development of a holistic approach to serious games evaluation as part of the Realising an Applied Gaming Ecosystem (RAGE) project [30].

Not only does the holistic approach put forward by Steiner et al. [30] situate learning outcomes with the pedagogic values of the institution, it also accounts for institutional experiences with serious game co-development and deployment. This holistic contextualisation of serious games evaluation is illustrative of academic efforts to contextualise all aspects of serious games research.

3.4   Contextualisation

A key justification for the contextualisation of academic research – and indeed for the existence of this very chapter - is the necessity of understanding inter-contextual knowledge production. As already established, it is necessary to understand domain-specific intended outcomes of a serious game before said game's effectiveness can be evaluated [10, 19, 24]. Additionally, it is necessary to explore the adoption and deployment practices surrounding serious games [31–34] less we subscribe to notions of technological determinism, meaning the technology itself is the driving factor, not the practices surrounding it [35].

3.5   Conclusion

Returning to the concept of epistemology introduced at the beginning of this section, with the nature of knowledge, in the instance of academic research into serious games we see a mixture of positivistic and interpretivistic positions on knowledge creation that is then, frequently, instrumentalised. In contrast to this, and as the RAGE project appears to support, a question arises regarding where this knowledge originates. Given the industry interest in the development of serious games, and their different contextual usages, it is suggested that it is necessary for academia to position itself as a facilitator of knowledge creation, instead of just a creator of knowledge. As Eraut suggests:

"[Academia must] extend to its role from that of creator and transmitter of generalizable knowledge to that of 'enhancing knowledge creation capacities' of individuals and professional communities. This would involve recognising that much knowledge creation takes place outside the higher education system, but is nevertheless limited by the absence of support structures and the prevailing action-orientation of practical contexts" [36].

At this stage then it is worth considering the systems outside of higher education. To begin, we will explore more deeply the industrial, production-orientated, practices surrounding the development of serious games. These practices will be interlinked with the research areas already discussed. However, before looking deeply into the minutia of the serious games industry it is necessary to unpack what we mean by 'industry', understand its size and scale, and have an awareness of the types of organisation that can be said to constitute this industry.

4   Academic Industrial Serious Games Partnerships

Since the late 19th century, the university as educational institute has undergone three revolutions of purpose. This first revolution was an expansion of their remit from the capture and dissemination of knowledge, to active production of new knowledge through research [37].

According to Etzkowitz [38], a second revolution of academia has resulted in increased academic-industrial partnerships as governmental science policy agendas attempt to translate research findings into economic development [39]. This, of course, has direct corollaries for the serious games eco-systems as we witness an increase in the number and sophistication of academic-industrial partnerships. This increase in partnerships is perhaps best exemplified by the rise of academic-industrial networks such as the Games and Learning Alliance [40], the Serious Games Institute Community [41], or the Serious Games Society [42].

Perhaps best representing the third academic revolution [39] is the Realising an Applied Games Eco-System [30]. Among other goals, RAGE aims to develop a "social space that connects research, gaming industries, intermediaries, education providers, policy makers and end-users" and a central depository for the 'assets' used in the production of serious games – in this instance referred to as applied games. Therefore, RAGE embodies an academic purpose to create economic development through engagement with industrial partners. In addition to this direct partnership with industry to create economic value, there is an entrepreneurial spirit underlying the third revolution of academic purpose [43].

4.1 Entrepreneurialism

As universities engage with industrial partners in a policy driven culture of prioritizing economic development they develop their capacity for generating economic value - through translating research findings into intellectual property or products that are monetized. It follows then, that universities are able to have direct economic agency through a spirit of entrepreneurialism, rather than indirectly through partnerships with industry [43]. This notion is apparent in the RAGE project, with the development and dissemination of "a business model and launch plan for exploiting RAGE results beyond project's duration" as one of the projects deliverables [44].

As university funding is squeezed through increased student populations and the present shadow of global economic downturn, universities themselves have increasing interest in offering commercial service. Sara de Freitas, through her work as founder of the Serious Games Institute [3] - a research centre that offers applied research consultancy and bespoke serious games design – developed the Innovation Diffusion Model (IDM) [45].

It is the intention that this model for academic-industrial partnerships will afford universities direct financial reward for their research – through commercial income, and knowledge exchange targeted funding – whilst industry benefits from new intellectual property and access to a highly-skilled workforce [45]. This commercialised approach to research, has also been expanded in the form of Serious Games International [46] – an international, commercial spin-out.

This notion of entrepreneurialism in academic research centres - resulting from industrial partnerships; research centres offering commercial services; and the emergence of spin-out commercial organisations - exemplifies a challenge when discussing the serious games industry. That is, this industry is a heterogeneous collection of research, commercial, not-for-profit, individual practitioners and governmental organisations – often with blurred lines of demarcation. Therefore, before we begin to make generalised sweeping statements about serious games industry's experience with serious games conceptualisation, production, evaluation, and contextualisation – it is worth considering this heterogeneity.

4.2 Heterogeneity

Typically, a serious game production company will either develop serious games on a consultancy basis for specific project (Business to Business), or as products for release in the serious games marketplace (Business to Consumer). PlayGen [47] for instance is a UK-based studio that creates serious games bespoke for client needs, such as raising awareness of flood risks [48], or promoting prosocial behaviours and criticality of violent extremism [49]. In addition, international consultancy firms not typically associated with games development, such as IBM [50] or Deloitte [51], offer comparable services.

For games-based learning in particular, the Business to Consumer business model is common. In 2014 games-based learning industry was reportedly worth $1.8 billion - with $1.4 billion of this coming from consumer purchases as opposed to institutional, governmental, or commercial purchasing [52]. It is difficult to ascertain the total worth of entire serious games market - again, due to difficulties in categorization [53]: for example, Interpret valued the entire serious games market at $10 billion in 2012 [53], whereas Ambient Insight valued the entire market at $4 billion for the same year [54], moving up to $6 billion in 2014 [52]; finally, Marketsandmarkets estimated that the serious games market will only be valued at $5 billion by 2020 [55]. Typically, these figures are linked to corporate, health, military training, institutional, and/or consumer education products, but the estimations fluctuated depending on the definition of serious games used, reflecting the existing epistemological issues discussed earlier in this chapter.

Not all of the serious games industry is framed around commercial gain, however. Games of Change is a non-for-profit organisation that "facilitates the creation and distribution of social impact games that serve as critical tools in humanitarian and educational efforts" [56]. It has created a network of organisations invested in the development or adoption of social impact games – also known as 'impact games' [24] or 'games for social change' [57]. In addition, they host competitions for game ideas designed around specific topics such as 'safe sex' [58] or 'nuclear weapons' [59]. This activist approach to developing serious games is also typical of other charitable, international, and inter-governmental organisations [60–62].

Paralleling this organisational development of games for social change, coinciding with the rise in popularity of projects not funded by traditional publishing sources - or 'indie games' - in entertainment games production, is the independent creation of 'social awareness' games such as *Depression Quest* [63] or *That Dragon, Cancer* [64]. It is worth noting that these 'indie games' do not typically analyse the social impact of their content and messages in the same fashion that consultancies or organisations do, and instead often originate from personal artistic messages.

From the individual socially motivated developer, to the studio developing corporate training games, and finally the multinational governmental organisation furthering a political agenda, all can be said to be a part of the serious games industry and broader eco-system.

4.3   Conceptual Blurriness

The muddiness of conceptualisations and definition apparent in academic discussions of serious games is reflected by similar problems in the industry. As previously mentioned, 'games for social change' are also categorized as 'impact games', 'games for change', 'purposeful games', or 'transformational games' depending on your perspective and field. With this instance of serious games specifically, there is further blurriness as with the notion that 'transformational games' can be applied to general entertainment games as well [65].

This conceptual blurriness has created obstacles for serious game developers seeking funding calls, as the descriptions of such calls impress a sense of consensus on topics that require further debate. As one game developer put it "D'you know what my biggest obstacle is? Just knowing what a 'game for change' is and knowing if the thing I'm making fits the criteria" [24]. Of course there are knock-on effects of this fragmentation for production and evaluation practices. In an interview, Jessie Schell – founder of serious games company Schell Games – on the subject of serious games described a problem of perception:

"[T]here's often a kind of inauthenticity that surrounds these kinds of games. They make promises about taking this boring thing and making it fun, but if they fail, you just go, 'This really is bad.... Teaching is really hard. Making an entertaining game is really hard. And now we're proposing that we're going to do both of them simultaneously'" [65].

Schell raises two relevant points here. Firstly, the difficulty of melding complex interdisciplinary theories and practices, and, secondly, a notion of inauthenticity, or a lack of rigour, in the industrial production of serious games. This lack of rigour is supported by a research report commissioned by Games for Change [24]. According to this report, game developers do not have the development time available for rigorous pre-production research integrated design, due to limited resources and a necessity to prioritise income-producing activities. Perhaps due to this time constraint, a report produced through the RAGE project suggests surveyed games developers expressed a desire for pedagogic strategies [66].

Interestingly, the same RAGE report that highlights a desire for pedagogic strategy resources from developers also seems to suggest a superficial understanding of pedagogic strategies on the part of these developers [66]. This lack of deep integration of theories of learning with games production is not isolated to industry however. According to Wu et al.'s [16] meta-analysis, a majority of games-based learning projects do not explicitly align with the one of the four key learning theory paradigms.

4.4 Learning Theories

MeTycoon [67] provides an example of the use of learning theories in the production of digital learning games. The game uses the concept of variable interval reinforcement as outlined in the behaviourist theory of learning established by B.F. Skinner [68]. However, although this notion of reward schedules is critical in behaviourist learning theory, it is deployed primarily as a means of maintaining player engagement, rather than fostering learning [69]. Additionally, this example demonstrates the challenge of intercontextual praxis, marrying academic theory and professional practice – with interdisciplinarity adding further difficulty. This is shown with the choice of *MeTycoon*'s learning theory being behaviourism, despite the fact that behaviourism has mostly fallen out of favour - due its reductionist conception of learning - in contemporary pedagogic practices, replaced instead by cognitivism and a rising interest in constructivism (see chapter on games-based learning).

It is of course facetious to make sweeping statements regarding approaches to the development key for serious games. Even the industry-led reports referenced in this section only provide a limited snapshot. For instance, the romantic image of a games development studio as a perennially playful environment with free-flowing creative process not constrained by traditional industry project management or business practices is readily challenged in a study undertaken by the British Educational Communications and Technology Agency [70]. Instead, games developers will often utilize a systematic, iterative rapid prototyping, agile development approach.

4.5   Conclusion

Therefore, it is not the intention of this section to critically appraise the serious games industry, but instead to equip the reader with a criticality that can be used when engaging with the broader serious games eco-system. For instance, there are suggestions that serious games developers over-represent the benefits of their games and lack robust evaluation practices [24, 71]. As suggested by an Impact report in 2015:

"If the lack of evaluated games is any indication, a common scenario is to focus on creating the game and worry about evaluation once it is done (if at all)" [24].

It is easy to reach the conclusion that games developers do not wish to invest in evaluating their game as it may prove its ineffectiveness [71]. However, going back to Eraut's notion of industrial action-orientation [36], for commercial organisations it may not be a lack of willingness but a lack of capacity. A robust evaluation of a serious game's effectiveness requires a non-trivial investment of resources. In addition to this challenge of limited resources in organisations that are profit-driven; there is also the challenge in finding commercially appropriate evaluation methods.

Reflecting the challenges in academic approaches to evaluation, there is a suggestion that commercial organisations experience a similar debate regarding how to prove serious games' effectiveness. For instance, a report, commissioned by Games for Change, suggests that there is a narrow definition of 'impact' – a conception of effectiveness – relying instead on the superficial use of evaluation methods [24]. It is perhaps for these reasons – both the narrow definition of 'impact' and lack of capacity for evaluation – that games developers express a desire for easily implemented evaluation approaches [66].

Of course evaluation approaches used in commercial settings – just as in academia – will be reflective of the outcomes desired by the context the serious games are deployed in. In addition, production practices such as user-centred design, or agile development, prioritise the consistent involvement of the end-user and stakeholders. Furthermore, the conceptualisations of games will also be contextually focused. For instance, games-based learning games used in corporate training sectors may elevate their return on investment [72], whereas in educational settings they may discuss their alignment with standardised national curriculums [73]. It is therefore necessary to consider the context adopting serious games in more detail.

5   Contextual Application Domains for Serious Games

A consistent theme of the academic and industry practice discussed in this chapter is the need for situating such practice in context. Additionally, from the perspective of academic practice specifically, increasingly the onus is on demonstrating the 'impact' of research in terms of influencing discourse, behaviours, or practice outside of academia [74]. Additionally, serious games are often classified in relation to their adopted contexts or market areas [75]. This section will therefore discuss the adoption of serious games in different contexts - specifically advertising, social change, military, corporate training, education, and healthcare.

We will discuss these contexts as they are the largest contemporary adopters of serious games [52]. Additionally, these contexts will demonstrate the pre-eminent motivations behind the use of serious games. However, a problem of classification occurs – as with the term 'serious games' itself – as the classifications used are broad and refer to intertwined contexts. For instance, the educational contexts for the use of serious games – in this instance – refer to both formal and informal education.

As we will see, motivations for the use of serious games in these contexts predominantly rely on the 'holding power' of games [76] - also referred to as 'flow' [77] or 'engagement' [78] – to achieve their aims. The topic of 'engagement' is relevant here as it, again, highlights the difficulty of modelling serious games terms as well as tensions inherent in inter-contextual practices. Defining 'engagement' in serious games research has become a key focus for academics, as it forms a core argument for the utilization of games over other interactive mediums, and therefore will inform design [79] and the metrics used to determine effectiveness [79–81]. However, the term 'engagement' has set meaning in educational contexts, so the meaning of this term does blur within the games-based learning field. This kind of engagement is not just applied to educational serious games however.

5.1 Advertising

Advergames – advertising games - seek to exploit the engaging nature of games to for the purposes of advertising [82]. This includes both the use in-game advertising in entertainment games - such as virtual billboards or branded in-game items [83] - and the bespoke development of games designed to engage players with a commercial brand [82]. For instance, *The Scarecrow* [84] is a game designed by US fast-food company Chipotle to promote the values of the company [85]. Of course, this has raised ethical considerations as these predominantly web-based games are accessible by, and frequently designed for, children. Therefore, in the case of fast-food advertisements there are concerns regarding this form of brand engagement [86].

5.2 Social Change

The 'advergames' approach to brand engagement through digital games is reflected by the production of games for social change. These games, often produced by commercial, industry studios on behalf of charitable organisations, seek to engage the users with social issues for the purposes of raising awareness, challenging beliefs, or changing behaviours [75].

An example of a more direct approach, *Freerice* [87], is an ad-supported, free-to-play 'game' supported by the World Health Organisation that donates 10 grains of rice for every correct answer from the player in a simple vocabulary quiz. *Freerice*'s approach to generating donations through crowdsourced player engagement is reflected by a broader movement to crowdsource donations through in-game purchases. Furthermore, *Freerice* is evidence of blurring between social change and educational with its language learning focus [88].

Though not strictly related to serious games, just as advertisers are able to purchase advertising space in entertainment games, charitable contributions can be made through purchasing virtual products in-game [89, 90]. Similarly, there are some serious game projects which crowdsource beneficial data analysis through playful mechanics: *Citizen Science* [91], for the analysis of cancer cells data, and *Foldit* [92], for the analysis of protein folding, are two such examples.

Games for social change and advergames both seek to exploit the engagement potential of games. Such games that are designed to raise awareness, challenge beliefs, change behaviours [75], or create direct, crowdsourced, contributions to a cause [91, 92], along with advergames that seek to promote a brand or commercial values, rely on player engagement.

5.3 Military

Another application promoting values through player engagement - not commercial or charitable values but military values - is evidenced with *America's Army*, a serious games published by the United States Armed Forces which aims to use "computer game technology to provide the public a virtual Soldier experience that was engaging, informative and entertaining" [93].

The popularity of *America's Army*, now a platform of media tools used for recruitment and virtual training [94], has given rise to much critical discussion regarding its ethical deployment. It is of course a controversial topic with those arguing the game is a rather disingenuous piece of propaganda [94], that provided an insincere sense of realism [95], with additional criticisms over its use in schools [96]. However, the game itself has additionally received much praise for its changing of perceptions in 16 to 24 year olds, with studies suggesting that 29 % of this group saw the US Army more positively as a result [97].

From these examples of advergames and games for social change we can see the notion of engagement framed both as a creation of new engagement opportunity, and of providing longer term engagement. In addition, this usage of engagement, frequently framed as 'motivational capacity' [99] or 'holding power' [100], is a key argument for their usage for corporate training and – as in the case of *America's Army* – recruitment.

5.4 Corporate Training

In corporate training there are two adjacent methods – simulation-based learning, and gamification. Simulation-based learning refers to the provision of a virtual learning environment that is able to be explored. Again, this definition is also not sacrosanct.

With this definition in mind, we can then differentiate games-based learning from simulation-based learning through the presence of game mechanics. Furthermore, gamification refers to the application of game mechanics and tropes – such as leaderboards, goals, or points – to, in the context of corporate training, business processes.

To further complicate matters there is also a rising use of game mechanics within simulation-based learning. It is therefore difficult to paint a clear picture of how serious games are being used, and to what degree they have been adopted [34]. In addition, it is difficult to gather empirical evidence regarding their effectiveness in commercial contexts [101]. Continuing the pattern of applying contextually relevant assessments of effectiveness, there are, however, examples of applying corporate training evaluation frameworks. For instance, Johnson and Wu [102], O'Neil et al. [103], and Martínez-Durá et al. [104] have all applied the Kirkpatrick [105] levels of learning effectiveness to assessing serious games.

Given the complexity of defining serious games in a corporate training context, stratifying these serious games in terms of learning needs can help our understanding [106]. For instance, the training needs of a commercial organisation may range from the development of generalizable prosocial skills, often referred to as soft skills - such as communication, team-work, or empathy – to sector specific knowledge of compliance regulations, physical layouts of working environments, or role-orientated continued professional development. As a conceptual mapping of these needs, we can adopt Bloom's taxonomy.

Bloom's taxonomy [107] demarcates learning into three domains – cognitive, psychomotor, and affective. Therefore, in the instance of serious games in corporate training, cognitive will refer to acquisition of knowledge and development of mental skills – such as compliance training, and the development of marketing professionals. It is of course worth noting that this application of Bloom's taxonomy to serious games modelling is not unique to corporate contexts [12, 108] and is frequently applied to games used in education.

5.5 Education

As with other applications of serious games, as discussed in this chapter, the difficulty in evaluating the effectiveness of serious games re-emerges for the training and learning applications (for a more detailed discussion of the theoretical underpinning behind games in education see the chapter on games-based learning in this volume). To evaluate the effectiveness of games designed for training or learning, often context-specific measures or frameworks will be used. For instance, in the case of serious games for corporate training, the game may be evaluated in terms of a return on investment, as well as in relation to key performance indicators [72]. For games used in state-education settings, they may be aligned with curriculum standards [73].

Games-based learning's classroom adoption is often justified through perceived motivational ability - of 1600 UK primary and secondary school teachers surveyed, 60 % would use games in their lessons for this reason [109]. Furthermore, as 99 % of 8- to 15-year-olds have played some form of video game in the last six months [110] – combined with a prolific notion of the 'digital generation' [111] – there is the argument that the education of this age group must be digitally supported; including the use of digital games [112]. Although the efficacy of games-based learning techniques has been empirically proven – when compared with traditional instruction methods, under given conditions, for certain subjects [25, 113] - there are still challenges to their adoption.

From the perspective of professional praxis, the biggest challenge is perhaps educators changing role – moving from leader to facilitator [114]. Questions are also raised regarding game-related expertise. In 2006, a 72 % majority of teachers (at both primary and secondary level) surveyed by Futurelab state they never play video games in their spare time, with only 36 % of primary teachers and 27 % of secondary teachers having used games in the classroom in the past [115].

Combined with this is the expectation from teachers that their pupils are gaming experts [116]. In some cases, this has created a sense of shared expertise, as pupils show teachers how to play games and teachers show pupils how to analyse their content in media subjects [117]. Furthermore, lack of supporting materials, availability of resources, and the inflexibility of the curriculum are cited as barriers to adoption [118].

Teachers citing of a lack of supporting materials is indicative of the current approach in, at least, the industry's development of serious games. They are often developed to be engaged with as independent activities, relying on behaviouristic notions of learning, without taking into account the role or the learner's peers or teachers. However, in the case of educational game platforms like *MyMaths* [119] and *Lexia* [120], there is additional functionality for teachers, like measuring and tracking the engagement and performance of their learners.

Acquiring those metrics relevant to the educational context, and meaningfully presenting them to educators, is an emerging topic of research [121] – somewhat reflecting broader movements in education towards data-driven, or 'big-data' practices. In addition to this is development of educational games that are not only designed to educate but also to assess learner's progress. Moreover, there are recent efforts in educational game development to account of the changing emotional states of the learners and how this relates to their engagement with learning activities [14]. This accounting for the role of data-capture, continuous assessment (or performance observation), and emotional acuity indicates an awareness of the educational context that serious games are adopted in. There is however, scope for this to be expanded.

Research is emerging from the Joan Ganz Cooney centre that explores the notion of joint media engagement: the design of apps for co-viewing by children and parents [122, 123]. In this case, reflecting the Sesame Workshop's broader purpose of at-home education through media [124], the research refers to using co-engagement as a strategy for learning at home. However, given the rise of digital media resulting in a shift from teachers as leaders to facilitators of learning, drawing on social theories of learning such as Vygotksy's More Knowledgeable Other [125], there are still ways in which serious games design can be aligned with pedagogic practice to be designed as such that teachers or peers can play an actual, often supporting, role.

As previously discussed, the marrying of theories of learning with serious games design principles is often dependent on the subject matter of the game. For instance, the practice of mental mathematical skills is often supported through a behaviourist game design – sometimes referred to as drill-and-practice learning [126]. Whereas constructivism suggest learners actively construct knowledge as they make sense of their experiences [127]: more fitting to general problem solving skills.

This notion of constructivism in serious games has been both theoretically, and pedagogically, developed by the work of constructionist Seymour Papert. In his work on the pedagogic potential of project-based production he closely explored the role of digital games:

"I have found that when they get the support and have access to suitable software systems, children's enthusiasm for playing games easily gives rise to an enthusiasm for making them, and this in turn leads to more sophisticated thinking." [128]

Furthermore, Kafai – proponent of games making as a learning approach and former student of Papert - suggested that "videogames, because of their prevalence in youth culture, present a particularly promising application for creative production." [129]. In the book *Connected Code* [130], early learner-led serious games development pioneer Yasmin Kafai discusses her experience of using the education-driven programming language LOGO – created by Papert [131] - in a games development environment. Over the course of a year, based in a school, students used the LOGO language to create mathematical educational games for other students to use. This use of game authoring tools for developing serious games for traditional curriculum subjects – especially mathematics – is apparent today [132–135].

In addition, there are frequently commercially backed ventures that attempt to use digital games development as a means of developing digital literacy skills. Kodu [136] – Microsoft's visual game programming environment – is designed to "teach creativity, problem solving, storytelling, as well as programming" [136] through game development software that is, in itself, 'game-like'. Additionally, Microsoft also runs the software development competition 'Imagine Cup' [137], in which a recurring category involves students aged 6-18 developing games around a common theme and/or accessible development tool. Additionally, the Joan Ganz Cooney centre runs 'The Video Game Challenge' [138] yearly in which high-school aged students are invited to create and submit games designed to teach a Science, Technology, Engineering, or Maths (STEM) subject.

Just as there is confusion regarding the role of serious games in corporate training settings, due to the prevalence of gamification, simulation-based learning and e-learning solutions, there is also the same conceptual confusion in education. To discuss the role of games in education invites interdisciplinary perspectives on: the purposing of commercially available off-the-shelf games; the design, production, and development of games - both serious and non-serious - as a constructionist pedagogy; and the adoption and utilization of educational serious games. However, at the centre of this complexity is the purposing of digital games for learning.

5.6 Healthcare

As will become apparent there is a difficulty in consistently framing the discussion of serious games in healthcare. Attempting to provide a broader review of the modelling, design, development, and evaluation of serious games in healthcare is challenging due to the multitude of purposes for these games.

According to Tom Baranowski et al. [139] – editor of the newly-emerging Journal for Health Games – there are currently 4 classifiable types of health games. Games for health to increase knowledge for health and wellbeing, games for health to explicitly alter behaviours, games for health to subversively promote behaviour change through game play, and games for health that influence negative health precursors. Again these suggested types are related to the purpose of the game itself, and we can see a degree of overlap with serious game definitions from other context.

As with other domains, the primary use of serious games in healthcare revolves around training and learning – or games that increase knowledge. However, there are different motivations for their adoption. Serious games have been developed for multiple aspects of healthcare. For surgery [140] there are serious games for training in laparoscopic techniques [141], knee-replacements [142, 143], and blood management [144]. In addition, there are examples of serious games used for the training of nurses to manage pain [145].

Virtual Pain Manager [145], was designed as an opportunity for nursing staff to gain practical understanding of managing a patient's pain overtime. This game is intended to be used as a training tool following instruction in pain management theory. Similar to this, *Florence* [146] is a serious game designed to train nurses in the necessary practice surrounding three challenging areas – blood transfusion, fire safety, and hazardous materials handling. These serious games demonstrate a key motivation for the adoption of serious games in healthcare: they allow for practice and training given in simulations of real-world conditions in otherwise dangerous areas.

A recent review of the current state of games in healthcare suggested that they are more common place in some areas than others – one of these areas was basic first aid training [147]. In the domain of first aid-training there are again examples, like *Virtual Pain Manager* and *Florence*, that are designed to give training for situations difficult to replicate in the real-world. For instance, *Code-Orange* [148] is a serious game designed for medical staff and first-responders to gain experience in the management of crisis following the use of a weapon of mass destruction. Following this training for healthcare professionals, there of course multiple examples of serious games designed for the patient education.

Given the requirement for consistent adherence to insulin injections there has been great interest in using video games for diabetes self-management, especially in the case of Type-1 diabetes [149]. With diabetes there are multiple approaches adopted with serious games. For instance, *The Diabetic Dog* [150] is a game in which the player must care for a pet dog with diabetes, which includes the management of insulin levels. This use of serious games to educate the player in diabetes self-management can even be traced back to 1997 [151, 152].

Didget [153] is a physical blood glucose reader that interfaces directly with a Nintendo DS handheld console and game associated with it. Through checking and maintaining acceptable glucose levels regularly, they are rewarded with in-game items. Interestingly, this is perhaps an example of both a serious game and of gamification, as it has layered a reward schedule over a real-world process, but such rewards are virtual in-game items.

In any case, this game serves as an illustration of the broader purpose behind these health training games designed for patients. That is, they are designed to change behaviours. As suggested by seminal social learning theorist Albert Bandura [154], and subsequently summarised by Debbie Thompson: "Knowledge and skill provide the foundation for behavior change" [155].

This approach is not specific to the development of health games for diabetes. *Remission* [156] is a serious game ostensibly designed to inform adolescents about their ongoing cancer treatments. From the use of this game they found patients were more knowledgeable about their treatment, more likely to adhere to their treatment regime, and exhibit a more positive outlook than pre-intervention [156].

It has been suggested that empowerment through playing games, prior to surgery, can reduce physiological reactions associated with fear and anxiety, and enhance resilience - therefore reducing post-recovery time [157]. Taking this a step further, there are examples of serious games designed as clinical tools in treating underlying psychological conditions. *SPARX* [158] is a 3D adventure game that has Cognitive Behavioural Therapy embedded in its gameplay. It has been demonstrated that this approach is as effective – in the short term – as compared to face-to-face counselling [158], although long term data has yet to be collected. Relating to this, there is scepticism towards the usage of such games as/in interventions [159].

At this point we again witness the diffusion of serious games definitions and categories. Games for health that are designed to increase knowledge can also have the aim of changing behaviours through this increase in knowledge. This overlap of purpose can also be applied to the typical approach of games for social change. That is, behaviour change is achieved through educating the player – in the case of health games – of good health self-management habits. Following the focussed application of serious games for behaviour change in specific groups, this has also been applied more broadly to target the general public.

Riccardi et al. [147] suggests that, as with the justification for their commercial adoption, serious games can be more cost effective – than traditional approaches - for preventative healthcare. Typically, these games focus on the promotion of healthy lifestyles and have been proven – again, in the short term - to be effective in encouraging healthy behaviours in players [151]. So rather than providing training or education for those already living with medial issues, these serious games adopt a preventative stance to curb medical issues before they arise. As with the application of serious games generally, there is a particular focus on designing health games for children [139].

Yummy Tricks [160] and *Squire's Quest* [161] are both designed to promote healthy diets in young children through centring mechanical metanarratives around ideal culinary behaviours. Whilst *Yummy Tricks* and *Squire's Quest* have a comparable purpose, with a similar target group, they adopt different challenges. *Yummy Tricks* was offered as a classroom-based activity whereas *Squire's Quest* was made available online for individual play. This illustrates a dilemma on the part of the serious game developer: capturing children's attention when their activities are already controlled, for instance at school, is easier than capturing their attention at home when they have more freedom and indeed choice in which media they consume [162, 163].

Perhaps most clearly demonstrating the overlapping contextual domains of serious games – and perhaps the futility of this chapter's attempt to demarcate them – is the development of serious games for change focussing on health. Not necessarily developed for use by healthcare professionals, or for use in healthcare contexts, these games attempt to address a societal problem relating to healthcare. For instance, both *Depression Quest* [63] and *Elude* [164] are games focussed on representing the experience of living with depression. *Elude*, specifically, was designed for family and friends of a person living with depression to gain more understanding, knowledge, and empathy [164].

Reflecting educational practices in games adoption, healthcare professionals are exploring the capacity of non-serious games to support mental health, rehabilitation, and pre-empt cognitive degradation. In one such example, there was a randomised control trial conducted in which casual video games had been demonstrated to have a positive impact on depression and anxiety [165, 166]. Again, citing the motivational potential of video games, there is evidence demonstrating game-based interventions can be used as a means of maintaining patient engagement with effective rehabilitative practices [167]. Additionally, this 'clinical' application of casual or typical games allow patients to replicate these practices at home [168, 169], and demonstrate the capacity of existing non-serious games for health to include the preferential behaviours as part of the gameplay, fulfilling the same purpose as serious games for health.

Paralleling the interest in developing game-based health interventions and games designed to change behaviours in children, there is increasing interest in the application of digital games for the elderly [170]. A systematic review found several positive health benefits emerging from this area of commercial, off-the-shelf games, including mental, physical, and social health benefits [171]. Focussing on the application of digital games for persons living with dementia, a review revealed that the majority of games used are, again, commercial games [172]. Despite this, serious games – as opposed to off-the-shelf games – have been identified as a potential clinical tool for dementia [173].

When reviewing the adoption of serious games vs non-serious games in healthcare contexts, we can see a general trend of the latter outnumbering the former. Where the purpose is to enhance knowledge or promote a specific behaviour, games are predominantly 'serious' – perhaps as their content is required or recommended to be specific and precise, not muddied by entertainment or narrative goals. Conversely, where the purpose is to engage the player in the desired behaviour during gameplay, or where the game is designed to address influence health precursors, 'non-serious' games are more popular. Specifically looking at physical rehabilitation, the proliferation of exergames and associated, low-cost, feedback technologies makes their application appropriate [15, 174, 175].

Regardless of the purpose behind the adoption of serious or indeed non-serious games, there is a stringent necessity in healthcare for robust evaluation processes. This is perhaps a key difference between the adoption of serious games in other contexts and in healthcare. For instance, there are several randomised control trials attempting to prove the efficacy of serious games in interventions for depression [165, 169], anxiety [176], and positive physical health outcomes in rehabilitation [175, 177]. Additionally, a series of meta-analyses across these areas focus on the ability to draw conclusions regarding game efficacy [178, 179].

A propensity for adopting randomised controlled trials does not mean that healthcare is not subject to the same evaluation methodological draw-backs demonstrated in other contexts. For instance, these studies often have small sample-sizes, do not take into account cultural or other demographical differences, and are undertaken over a short period [180–182]. Furthermore, several meta-analyses demonstrated a range of mostly positive results in regards to efficacy in the fields of exercise [183], promoting healthy lifestyles [184], and diabetes self-management [185]. Therefore, we can see the same challenges in healthcare that are apparent in educational and other contexts within this chapter – satisfactorily proving the efficacy of an amorphous medium across multiple use-cases.

6   Conclusion

This chapter has highlighted not only contextual commonalities, but also the diffusion and fluidity of the serious games ecosystem. It is now worth considering: what does this mean for the researcher? As a researcher you are likely to come across comparable justifications for serious games adoption, specifically through notions of 'engagement', 'motivation', or 'cost-effectiveness'. However, the actual effectiveness of these serious game interventions is currently a contentious issue due to the contextual specificity of measurements, and frequently inadequate research protocols. In addition to this difficulty of evaluation, due to the multifaceted purposing of serious games, is the problem of inconsistent conceptualisation.

Games, in themselves, are a broad media capturing multiple instantiations of aesthetic, ludic, and narrative elements. Furthermore, serious games have a significant overlap with other fields such as simulation-based learning or gamification such that these terms are often conflated. Adding to this taxonomical confusion is the inconsistent use of the term 'serious games' itself. As repeatedly touched upon in this chapter there are several examples directly conflating 'serious games' – an umbrella term – with 'games-based learning', without making a distinction. Furthermore, there are multiple emerging, adjacent, umbrella terms used in place of 'serious games' such as 'applied games', 'purposed games', or 'procedural rhetoric'.

The sub-categories that exist within these umbrella terms of 'serious games' are themselves, again, a contentious field. 'Digital games-based learning' is used alongside 'educational games', or 'playful learning' and – occasionally – terminology such as an 'edutainment' that is used more prominently in other, non-games, fields, extending the intercontextual blur to an intermedia one. Reflecting this 'serious games' identity crisis is the changing role of serious games research as a contextually sensitive interdisciplinary field, meaning it is unlikely to be undertaken in a purely academic vacuum.

Increasingly, inter-contextual serious games practice blurs the line between serious games academic research, commercial development, and contextual adoption. It is necessary to be contextually sensitive, as context will often dictate motivations and practices surrounding adoption, the theories and frameworks underlying the serious game's design, as well as the ways in which its efficacy is measured. These contexts are in a constant conversation with each other – fluidly overlapping but with a strong commercial driving force - as industry developmental trends shift. Additionally, these individual fields are in a constant state of flux themselves.

Some resources exist to smooth these transitions and connect these entities, like the RAGE project, which aims to "develop, transform and enrich advanced technologies from the leisure games industry into self-contained gaming assets (i.e. solutions showing economic value potential) that support game studios at developing applied games, and make these assets available along with a large volume of high quality knowledge resources through a self-sustainable Ecosystem, which is a social space that connects research, gaming industries, intermediaries, education providers, policy makers and end-users." [186]

The contextual application of serious games is influenced by social, cultural, and political factors – from the perception of video games, to systematic frameworks governing effectiveness, to the access to, and familiarity with, technologies. In addition to the context specific fluctuations there also exist socio-cultural and technological factors that impact all contexts. For instance, governmental polices mandating national education frameworks will, to a degree, impact research directions, commercial development, and adoption of educational games. In addition, perhaps most obviously, but not yet acknowledged, is the development and access to technology itself.

In the last 10 years we have seen a trend of mobile devices gaining popularity as the preferred gaming platform of individuals [187], particularly amongst under-18 s [188], and all roads point towards this trend continuing. Despite this, games for learning academic research projects are predominantly built for the PC platform, and other serious games areas seem to follow suit [73]. This illuminates a key-part of one of the main tensions of conducting research in this area – the different expectations of time-frames. It can be argued that academia is cursed to be playing perpetual catch-up with the adoption and development of serious games. The technological, commercial, and contextual specific factors create an action-orientated approach that isn't easily mapped on to the fastidious, reflective, and rigorous approach of academia.

The researcher can therefore consider themselves a facilitator of praxis, as researchers are frequently positioned at the intersection of theory and practice. For instance, there is renewed interest in participatory research methods – that value and empower research participants and context practitioners to become a part of the research and development process [189]. In addition, the research studies mentioned throughout this chapter, even if not explicitly linked, have reflected the research practices of action-oriented, practice-based, and practice-led research. Revisiting Eraut's pivotal quote from the beginning of this chapter highlights an ontological shift on the part of the researcher:

"[Academia must] extend to its role from that of creator and transmitter of generalizable knowledge to that of 'enhancing knowledge creation capacities' of individuals and professional communities." [36]

This notion of praxis, when applied to serious games, attempts to capture the processes by which the relevant theories of academic, industry, and adoptive contexts come together to inform the contexts relative practices. These processes are multifaceted, depending on the adoptive contexts and academic disciplines involved, however their goal is the same – to generate impactful research. Given a shifting socio-political landscape, higher education research is frequently evaluated in terms of its impact [190].

For instance, at €80billion, Horizon 2020 the largest EU research and innovation programme ever [191]. Horizon 2020 has two streams directly relevant to research into serious games - ICT 20: Technologies for better human learning and teaching and ICT 21: Advanced digital gaming/gamification technologies - and as a programme has made "marks a shift towards the use of indicators that aim to capture results and impacts" [192].

Therefore, to undertake impactful research that has "an effect on, change or benefit to the economy, society, culture, public policy or services, health, the environment or quality of life, beyond academia'' [193] requires an appreciation and sensitivity to both the interdisciplinary and intercontextual nature of the serious games ecosystem.

References

1. Bogost, I.: Persuasive Games: The Expressive Power of Videogames. MIT Press, Cambridge (2007)
2. Abt, C.: Serious Games. Abt Associates Inc., New York City (1970)
3. Coventry University: About Serious Games Institute. http://www.coventry.ac.uk/events/games-for-health-uk-conference-2016/about-serious-games-institute/
4. European Union Digital Library: EAI Endorsed Transactions on Serious Games. http://www.eudl.eu/issue/sg/1/1
5. Flanagan, M.: Critical Play: Radical Game Design. MIT Press, Massachusetts (2009)
6. Gee, J.: What Video Games Have to Teach Us About Learning and Literacy, 2nd edn. Palgrave Macmillan, London (2007)
7. van Staalduinen, J.-P., de Freitas, S.: A game-based learning framework: linking game design and learning outcomes. In: Learning to Play: Exploring the Future of Education with Video Games, pp. 29–55. Peter Lang, Bern (2011)
8. Djaouti, D., Alvarez, J., Jessel, J.-P.: Classifying serious games: the G/P/S model. In: Handbook of Research on Improving Learning and Motivation through Educational Games: Multidisciplinary Approaches, pp. 118–136. IGI Global, Hershey (2011)
9. Rooney, P.: A theoretical framework for serious game design: exploring pedagology, play and fidelity and their implications for the design process. Int. J. Game-Based Learn. 2(4), 41–60 (2012)
10. Rego, P., Moreira, P., Reis, L.: A serious games framework for health rehabilitation. Int. J. Health. Inf. Syst. Inform. 9(3), 1–21 (2014)
11. Horne-Moyer, H., Moyer, B., Messer, D., Messer, E.: The use of electronic games in therapy: a review with clinical implications. Cur. Psychiatry Rep. 16(12), 1–9 (2014)
12. Arnab, L.T., Carvalho, M., De Gloria, A.: Mapping learning and game mechanics for serious games analysis. Br. J. Educ. Technol. 46(2), 391–411 (2015)
13. Wartena, B., Kuipers, D., van Dijk, H.: Ludo Modi varietas: a game-architecture inspired design approach for BCSS. In: Öörni, A., Kelders, S., van Gemert-Pijnen, L., Oinas-Kukkonen, H., (eds.) Proceedings of the Second International Workshop on Behavior Change Support Systems (BCSS 2014), Padua, Italy, pp. 77–84. CEUR (2014)
14. Wilkinson, P.: Affective educational games: utilizing emotions in game-based learning. In: 2013 5th International Conference on Games and Virtual Worlds for Serious Applications (VS-GAMES 2013), Bournemouth, pp. 1–8. IEEE (2013)

15. O'Neill, O., Gatzidis, C., Swain, I.: A State of the Art Survey in the Use of Video Games for Upper Limb Stroke Rehabilitation. In: Ma, M., Jain, L.C., Anderson, P. (eds.) Virtual, Augmented Reality and Serious Games for Healthcare 1, pp. 345–370. Springer, Heidelberg (2014)
16. Wu, W.-H., Hsaio, H.-C., Wu, P.-L., Lin, C.-H., Huang, S.-H.: Investigating the learning-theory foundations of game-based learning: a meta-analysis. J. Comput. Assist. Learn. **28**(3), 265–279 (2012)
17. Ratan, R., Ritterfeld, U.: Classifying serious games. In: Serious Games: Mechanisms and Effects, pp. 10–24. Routledge, London (2009)
18. Sitzmann, T.: A meta-analytic examination of the instructional effectiveness of computer-based simulation games. Pers. Psychol. **64**(2), 489–528 (2011)
19. Wouters, P., van Nimwegen, C., van Oostendorp, H., van der Spek, E.: A meta-analysis of the cognitive and motivational effects of serious games. J. Educ. Psychol. **105**(2), 249–265 (2013)
20. Ke, F.: A qualitative meta-analysis of computer games as learning tools. In: Handbook of Research on Effective Electronic Gaming in Education 1, pp. 1–32. IGI Global, Hershey (2008)
21. All, A., Castellar, E., van Looy, J.: Measuring effectiveness in digital game-based learning: a methodological review. Int. J. Serious Games **2**(1), 3–20 (2014)
22. All, A., Castellar, E., van Looy, J.: Assessing the effectiveness of digital game-based learning: best practices. Comput. Educ. **92**(C), 90–103 (2014)
23. All, A., Castellar, E., van Looy, J.: Defining effectiveness of digital game-based learning: a socio-cognitive approach. In: Busch, C., (ed.) Proceedings of the 8th European Conference On Games Based Learning (ECGBL 2014), Berlin, Germany, pp. 669–675. Academic Conferences and Publishing (2014)
24. Stokes, B., O'Shea, G., Walden, N., Nasso, F., Mariutto, G., Hill, A., Burak, A.: Impact with Games: A Fragmented Field. Report, Games for Change (2016)
25. Connolly, T., Boyle, E., MacArthur, E., Hainey, T., Boyle, J.: A systematic review of empirical evidence on computer games and serious games. Comput. Educ. **59**(2), 661–686 (2012)
26. Yusoff, A., Crowder, R., Gilbert, L.: Validation of serious games attributes using the technology acceptance model. In: Debattista, K., Dickey, M., Proença, A., Santos, L., (eds.) 2010 Second International Conference on Games and Virtual Worlds for Serious Applications (VS-GAMES), Braga, pp. 45–51. IEEE (2010)
27. Rao, V.: A framework for evaluating behavior change interventions through gaming. In: Reidsma, D., Katayose, H., Nijholt, A. (eds.) ACE 2013. LNCS, vol. 8253, pp. 368–379. Springer, Heidelberg (2013)
28. Desurvire, H., Wiberg, C.: Game usability heuristics (PLAY) for evaluating and designing better games: the next iteration. In: Ozok, A., Zaphiris, P. (eds.) OCSC 2009. LNCS, vol. 5621, pp. 557–566. Springer, Heidelberg (2009)
29. Jerzak, N., Rebelo, F.: Serious games and heuristic evaluation – the cross-comparison of existing heuristic evaluation methods for games. In: Marcus, A. (ed.) DUXU 2014, Part I. LNCS, vol. 8517, pp. 453–464. Springer, Heidelberg (2014)
30. Steiner, C., Nussbaumer, A., Kluijhout, E., Nadolski, R., Bazzanella, B., Mscarenhas, S., Ger, P., Dascalu, M., Trausan-Matu, S., Becker, J., Yuan, L., Hollins, P.: RAGE Evaluation Framework and Guidelines. Project Deliverable, Graz University of Technology (2016)
31. Arnab, S., Riccardo, B., Earp, J., de Freitas, S., Popescu, M., Romero, M., Stanescu, I., Usart, M.: Framing the adoption of serious games in formal education. E-J. E-Learn. **10**(2), 159–171 (2012)

32. Arnab, S., de Freitas, S., Bellotti, F., Lim, T., Louchart, S., Suttie, N., Berta, R., de Gloria, A.: Pedagogy-driven design of Serious Games: An overall view on learning and game mechanics mapping, and cognition-based models. Research Report, Serious Games Institute (2012)

33. Ulicsak, M., Williamson, B.: Computer Games and Learning. Futurelab, London (2011)

34. Azadegan, A., Riedel, J.C., Baalsrud Hauge, J.: Serious games adoption in corporate training. In: Ma, M., Oliveira, M.F., Hauge, J.B., Duin, H., Thoben, K.-D. (eds.) SGDA 2012. LNCS, vol. 7528, pp. 74–85. Springer, Heidelberg (2012)

35. Watt, J.: Improving methodology in serious games research with elaborated theory. In: Serious Games: Mechanisms and Effects, pp. 374–388. Routledge, London (2009)

36. Eraut, M.: Developing Professional Knowledge and Comptenence. Routledge, London (1994)

37. Jencks, C., Riesman, D.: The Academic Revolution. Doubleday, New York (1968)

38. Etzkowitz, H.: The norms of entrepreneurial science: cognitive effects of the new university-industry linkages. Res. Policy 27(8), 823–833 (1998)

39. Etzkowitz, H., Webster, A., Gebhardt, C., Terra, B.: The future of the university and the university of the future: evolution of ivory tower to entrepreneurial paradigm. Res. Policy 29(2), 313–330 (2000)

40. Bellotti, F., Berta, R., De Gloria, A.: Games and learning alliance (GaLA) supporting education and training through Hi-Tech gaming. In: 12th International Conference on Advanced Learning Technologies, Rome, pp. 740–741. IEEE (2012)

41. Serious Games Institute: SGI Community. http://www.seriousgamesinstitute.co.uk/community/

42. Serious Game Society: About. http://www.seriousgamessociety.org/index.php/joomla-pages/about-us

43. Etzkowitz, H.: Research groups as 'quasi-firms': the invention of the entrepreneurial university. Res. Policy 32(1), 109–121 (2003)

44. Riestra, R., Westera, W.: The Rage Project Aims at Boosting Games Development for Education and Training in Europe. Press Release, Hull College (2015)

45. de Freitas, S., Mayer, I., Arban, S., Marshall, I.: Industrial and academic collaboration: hybrid models for research and innovation diffusion. J. High. Educ. Policy Manage. 36(1), 2–14 (2014)

46. Serious Games International: About us. http://www.seriousgamesinternational.com/about-us/

47. PlayGen: About PlayGen. http://playgen.com/company_index/

48. PlayGen: FloodSim. http://playgen.com/play/floodsim/

49. PlayGen: Choices & Voices. http://playgen.com/play/choices-and-voices/

50. IBM Corporation: Serious Solutions with Serious Games. Whitepaper, IBM Global Services (2011)

51. Deloitte: Serious Games. http://deloitte-learning.com/?page_id=438

52. Adkins, S.: The 2014–2019 Global Edugame Market. Whitepaper, Ambient Insight (2015)

53. Cai, M.: Serious Games, Serious Play. Presentation, Interpret (2012)

54. Adkins, S.: The 2012–2017 Worldwide Game-based Learning and Simulation-based Markets. Presentation, Ambient Insight (2012)

55. Marketsandmarkets: Serious Game Market by Vertical (Education, Corporate, Healthcare, Retail, Media and Advertising), Application (Training, Sales, Human Resource, Marketing), Platform, End-User (Enterprise, Consumer), and Region - Forecast to 2020, Market Research, Marketsandmarkets (2015)

56. Games for Change: About. http://www.gamesforchange.org/about/

57. Swain, C.: Designing games to affect social change. In: Baba, A., (ed.) Proceedings of the 2007 DiGRA International Conference (DiGRA 2007). JAPAX, Tokyo (2007)
58. Games for Change: G4C13 Sex Etc. Game Design Competition. http://www.gamesfor change.org/learn/g4c13-sex-etc-game-design-competition-results/
59. Games for Change: N Square Challenge $10,000 Game Design Competition Around Nuclear Weapons. http://www.gamesforchange.org/2015/10/n-square-game-design-challenge/
60. Reckian, D., Eisenack, K.: Climate change: gaming on board and screen. Simul. Gaming **44**(2–3), 253–271 (2013)
61. Arora, P., Itu, S.: Arm chair activism: Serious games usage by INGOs for educational change. Int. J. Game-Based Learn. **2**(4), 1–17 (2012)
62. Pereira, G., Brisson, A., Prada, R., Paiva, A., Bellotti, F., Kravcik, M., Klamma, R.: Serious games for personal and social learning & ethics: status and trends. In: de Gloria, A., de Freitas, S., (eds.) 4th International Conference on Games and Virtual Worlds for Serious Applications (VS-GAMES 2012), Genoa, pp. 53–65. Elsevier Procedia (2012)
63. Quinn, Z.: Depression Quest An Interaction (non)Fiction About Living With Depression. http://www.depressionquest.com/
64. Numinous Games: That Dragon Cancer. http://www.thatdragoncancer.com/
65. Sinclair, B.: Serious games stigmatized in and out of the industry, says Schell. http://www.gamesindustry.biz/articles/2013–05-30-serious-games-stigmatized-in-and-out-of-the-industry-says-schell
66. Saveski, G.L., Westera, W., Yuan, L., Hollins, P., Manjón, B.F., Ger, P.M., Stefanov, K.: What serious game studios want from ICT research: identifying developers' needs. In: de Gloria, A., Veltkamp, R., de Gloria, A. (eds.) GALA 2015. LNCS, vol. 9599, pp. 32–41. Springer, Heidelberg (2016). doi:10.1007/978-3-319-40216-1_4
67. PlayGen: MeTycoon. http://playgen.com/play/me-tycoon/
68. Skinner, B.: The Technology of Teaching. Meridith Corporation, New York (1968)
69. Dunwell, I., Lameras, P., de Freitas, S., Petridis, P., Star, K., Hendrix, M., Arnab, S.: MeTycoon: a game-based approach to career guidance. In: 5th International Conference on Games and Virtual Worlds for Serious Applications (VS-GAMES 2013), Bournemouth, pp. 1–6. IEEE (2013)
70. BECTA: Engagement and motivation in games development processes. Research Report, BECTA (2006)
71. Culyba, S.: Report response Sabrina of Schell Games. http://gameimpact.net/response-culyba-schell/
72. Bachvarova, Y., Bocconi, S., van der Pols, B., Popescu, M., Roceanu, I.: Measuring the effectiveness of learning with serious games in corporate training. In: de Gloria, A., de Freitas, S., (eds.) 4th International Conference on Games and Virtual Worlds for Serious Applications (VS-GAMES 2012), Genoa, pp. 221–232. Elsevier (2012)
73. Cheng, M.-T., Chen, J.-H., Chu, S.-J., Chen, S.-Y.: The use of serious games in science education: a review of selected empirical research from 2002 to 2013. J. Comput. Educ. **2**(3), 353–375 (2015)
74. REF: About the REF. http://www.ref.ac.uk/about/
75. Klimmt, C.: Serious games for social change: why they (should) work. In: Serious Games: Mechanisms and Effects, pp. 248–270. Routledge, London (2009)
76. Turkle, S.: The Second Self. Simon & Schuster, New York (1984)
77. Csikszentmihalyi, M.: Flow: The Psychology of Optimal Experience. Harper & Row, New York (1990)
78. Iacovides, I., Aczel, J., Scanlon, E., Taylor, J., Woods, W.: Motivation, engagement and learning through digital games. Int. J. Virtual Pers. Learn. Environ. **2**(2), 1–16 (2011)

79. Kiili, K., de Freitas, S., Arnad, S., Lainema, T.: The design principles for flow experience in educational games. In: de Gloria, A., de Freitas, S., (eds.) 4th International Conference on Games and Virtual Worlds for Serious Applications (VS-GAMES 2012), Genoa, pp. 78–91. Elsevier (2012)
80. Kiili, K., Perttula, A., Arnab, S., Suominen, M.: Flow experience as a quality measure in evaluating physically activating serious games. In: Gloria, A. (ed.) GALA 2013. LNCS, vol. 8605, pp. 200–212. Springer, Heidelberg (2014)
81. Bellotti, F., Kapralos, B., Lee, K., Moreno-Ger, P., Berta, R.: Assessment in and of serious games: an overview. Adv. HCI **2013**, 1–11 (2013)
82. Terlutter, R., Capella, M.: The gamification of advertising: analysis and research directions of in-game advertising, advergames, and advertising in social network games. J. Advert. **42**(2–3), 95–112 (2013)
83. Nelson, M.: Exploring consumer response to "advergaming". In: Online Consumer Psychology: Understanding and Influencing Consumer Behavior in the Virtual World, pp. 156–182. Lawrence Erlbaum Associates, New Jersey (2005)
84. Chipotle: The Scarecrow. http://www.scarecrowgame.com/game.html
85. Weed, A.: Engaging consumers with advergames: case study of Chipotle's "The Scarecrow". In: Conference Presentation, MBAA (2015)
86. Harris, J., Speers, S., Schwartz, M., Brownell, K.: US food company branded advergames on the internet: children's exposure and effects on snack consumption. J. Child. Med. **6**(1), 51–68 (2012)
87. World Food Programme: About. http://freerice.com/about
88. Mariana, C.: Freerice.com - free education based on appealing level-based english tests. In: Roceanu, I., (ed.) Proceedings of the 8th International Scientific Conference "eLearning and Software for Education", Bucharest, p. 6. Editura Universitara (2012)
89. Zynga: Give the gift of play this holiday season. https://blog.zynga.com/2012/11/28/toys-for-tots/
90. Birkwood, S.: Video game industry 'could be a goldmine for charity fundraisers'. http://www.thirdsector.co.uk/video-game-industry-could-goldmine-charity-fundraisers/fundraising/article/1347151
91. Cancer Research UK: Citizen Science. http://www.cancerresearchuk.org/support-us/citizen-science
92. Center for Game Science at University of Washington: The Science Behind Foldit. http://fold.it/portal/info/about
93. America's Army: America's Army Backgrounder. Press Release, United State's Army (2013)
94. Nieborg, D.: America's Army: more than a game? In: Eberle, T., Kriz, W., (eds.) 35th Annual Conference of the International Simulation and Gaming Association (ISAGA 2004), Munich, p. 2. SAGSAGA (2004)
95. Galloway, A.: Social realism in gaming. Int. J. Comput. Games. Res. **4**(1) (2004)
96. American Civil Liberties Union: Soldiers of Misfortunate: Abusive U.S. Military Recruitment and Failure to Protect Child Soldiers. Report, American Civil Liberties Union (2008)
97. Wardynski, E.: Informing popular culture: the America's Army game concept. In: America's Army PC Game Vision and Realization, pp. 6–8. The Wecker Group, Monterey (2004)
98. Smith, R.: The long history of gaming in military training. Simul. Gaming **41**(1), 6–19 (2010)
99. Haworth, R., Sedig, K.: The importance of design for educational games. In: Education in a Technological World: Communicating Current and Emerging Research and Technological Efforts, pp. 518–522. Formatex, Badajoz (2011)

100. Squire, K., Jenkins, H.: Harnessing the power of games in education. Insight **3**(1), 5–33 (2003)
101. Riedel, J.C., Feng, Y., Azadegan, A., Romero, M., Usart, M., Baalsrud Hauge, J.: Measuring the commercial outcomes of serious games in companies – a review. In: Ma, M., Oliveira, M.F., Baalsrud Hauge, J. (eds.) SGDA 2014. LNCS, vol. 8778, pp. 176–191. Springer, Heidelberg (2014)
102. Johnson, W., Wu, S.: Assessing aptitude for learning with a serious game for foreign language and culture. In: Woolf, B.P., Aïmeur, E., Nkambou, R., Lajoie, S. (eds.) ITS 2008. LNCS, vol. 5091, pp. 520–529. Springer, Heidelberg (2008)
103. O'Neil, H., Wainess, R., Baker, E.: Classification of learning outcomes: evidence from the computer games literature. Curric. J. **16**(4), 455–474 (2005)
104. Martínez-Durá, R., Arevalillo-Herráez, M., García-Fernández, I., Gamón-Giménez, M., Rodríguez-Cerro, A.: Serious games for health and safety training. In: Serious Games and Edutainment Applications, pp. 107–124. Springer, London (2011)
105. Kirkpatrick, D.: Techniques for evaluating training programs. Train. Dev. J. **33**(1), 78–92 (1979)
106. Donovan, L.: The Use of Serious Games in the Corporate Sector. Report, Learnovate Centre (2012)
107. Bloom, B.: Learning for Mastery. Eval. Comment **1**(2), 1–12 (1968)
108. Hays, M., Ogan, A., Lane, H.: The evolution of assessment: learning about culture from a serious game. In: Lynch, C., Ashley, K., Mitrovic, T., Dimitrova, V., Pinkwart, N., Aleven, V., (eds.) ITS 2010. LNCS, vol. 6094, pp. 37–44. Springer, Heidelberg (2010)
109. Williamson, B.: Computer Games, Schools, and Young People: A Report for Educators on Using Games for Learning. Futurelab, Bristol (2009). Research Report
110. Internet Advertising Bureau UK: Gaming Revolution. Research Report, Internet Advertising Bureau UK (2014)
111. Buckingham, D.: Is there a digital generation? In: Digital Generations: Children, Young People, and the New Media, pp. 1–18. Lawrence Erlbaum Associates, New Jersey (2006)
112. Prensky, M.: Digital Game-Based Learning. McGraw-Hill Education, New York (2001)
113. de Freitas, S., Rebolledo-Mendez, G., Liarokapis, F., Magoulas, G., Poulovassilis, A.: Learning as immersive experiences: Using the four-dimensional framework for designing and evaluating immersive learning experiences in a virtual world. Br. J. Educ. Technol. **41**(1), 69–85 (2010)
114. Sandford, R., Facer, K., Williamson, B.: Constructions of games, teachers and young people in formal learning. In: Digital Games and Learning, pp. 175–199. Continuum, New York (2011)
115. Sandford, R., Ulicsak, M., Facer, K., Rudd, T.: Teaching with Games: Using commercial off-the-shelf computer games in formal education. Futurelab, Bristol (2006). Research Report
116. Sandford, R., Williamson, B.: Games and Learning: A Handbook. Futurelab, Bristol (2005)
117. Berger, R., McDougall, J.: Reading videogames as (authorless) literature. Literacy **47**(3), 142–149 (2013)
118. Baek, Y.: What hinders teachers in using computer and video games in the classroom? exploring factors inhibiting the uptake of computer and video games. CyberPsych. Behav. **11**(6), 665–671 (2008)
119. Oxford University Press: MyMaths - Bringing maths alive. https://www.mymaths.co.uk/index.html
120. Lexia Learn: Why Lexia. http://www.lexialearning.com/why-lexia

121. Loh, C., Sheng, Y., Ifenthaler, D.: Serious Games Analytics: Methodologies for Performance Measurement, Assessment, and Improvement. Springer International, Switzerland (2015)
122. Takeuchi, L., Stevens, R.: The New Coviewing: Designing for Learning Through Joint Media Engagement. The Joan Ganz Cooney, New York (2011). Center Research Report
123. Rideout, V.: Learning at Home: Families' Educational Media Use in America. The Joan Ganz Cooney Center, New York (2014). Research Report
124. Sesame Workshop: workshop at a glance. http://www.sesameworkshop.org/about-us/work shop-at-a-glance/
125. Vygotsky, L.: Mind in Society: Development of Higher Psychological Processes. Harvard University Press, Cambridge (1978)
126. Egenfeldt-Nielson, S.: Third generation educational use of computer games. J. Educ. Med. Hypermed. **16**(3), 263–281 (2007)
127. Driscoll, M.: Psychology of Learning for Instruction. Allyn and Bacon, Boston (1994)
128. Papert, S.: Does easy do it? children, games, and learning. Game Developer Mag. (1998). Article
129. Peppler, K., Kafai, Y.: From SuperGoo to Scratch: exploring creative digital media production in informal learning. Learn. Med. Technol. **32**(2), 149–166 (2007)
130. Kafai, Y., Burke, Q.: Connected Code: Why Children Need to Learn Programming. MIT Press, Cambridge (2014)
131. Papert, S.: Mindstorms: Children, Computers, and Powerful Ideas. Basic Books, New York (1980)
132. Kafai, Y.: The classroom as living laboratory: design-based research for understanding, comparing, and evaluating learning science through design. Educ. Technol. **45**(1), 28–34 (2005)
133. Marchiori, E., Torrente, J., del Blanco, Á., Moreno-Ger, P., Sancho, P., Fernández-Manjón, B.: A narrative metaphor to facilitate educational game authoring. Comput. Educ. **58**(1), 590–599 (2012)
134. Robertson, J., Howells, C.: Computer game design: Opportunities for successful learning. Comput. Educ. **50**(2), 559–578 (2008)
135. Li, Q., Vandermeiden, E., Lemieux, C., Nathoo, S.: Secondary students learning mathematics through digital game building: a study of the effects and students' perceptions. Int. J. Technol. Math. Educ. **23**(1), 25–34 (2016)
136. Microsoft: What is Kodu? http://www.kodugamelab.com/about/
137. Microsoft: About Imagine Cup. https://www.imaginecup.com/custom/About
138. The Joan Ganz Cooney Center: National STEM Video Game Challenge. http://www.joanganzcooneycenter.org/initiative/stemchallenge/
139. Baranowski, T., Blumberg, F., Buday, R., DeSmet, A., Fiellin, L., Green, C., Kato, P., Lu, A., Maloney, A., Mellecker, R., Morrill, B., Peng, W., Shegog, R., Simons, M., Staiano, A., Thompson, D., Young, K.: Games for Health for Children—Current Status and Needed Research. Games Health J. **5**(1), 1–12 (2016)
140. Graafland, M., Schraagen, J., Schijven, M.: Systematic review of serious games for medical education and surgical skills training. Br. J. Surg. **99**(10), 1322–1330 (2012)
141. Tommaso De Paolis, L., Ricciardi, F., Giuliani, F.: Development of a serious game for laparoscopic suture training. In: Paolis, L.T., Mongelli, A. (eds.) AVR 2014. LNCS, vol. 8853, pp. 90–102. Springer, Heidelberg (2014)
142. Sabri, H., Cowan, B., Kapralos, B., Porte, M., Backstein, D., Dubrowskie, A.: Serious games for knee replacement surgery procedure education and training. Soc. Behav. Sci. **2**(2), 3483–3488 (2010)

143. Park, S., Yoon, Y., Kim, L., Lee, S.: Virtual knee joint replacement surgery system. In: Geometric Modeling and Imaging (GMAI 2007), Zurich, pp. 79–84. IEEE (2007)
144. Qin, J., Chui, Y.-P., Pang, W.-M., Choi, K.-S., Heng, P.-A.: Learning Blood Management in Orthopedic Surgery through Gameplay. Comput. Graph. Appl. **30**(2), 45–57 (2009)
145. Parsons, G., Richards, B.: Virtual Pain Manager. http://vpm.glam.ac.uk/
146. Sante Training: Florence: Blood Transfusion. http://www.sante-training.com/catalogue/19-serious-games/8-serious-game-transfusion-sanguine
147. Ricciardi, F., De Paolis, L.: A Comprehensive Review of Serious Games in Health Professions. Int. J. Comput. Games Technol. **11**(9), 1–11 (2014)
148. BreakAway Games: Code Orange. http://www.breakawaygames.com/games/code-orange/
149. Lieberman, D.: Video games for diabetes self-management: examples and design strategies. J. Diab. Sci. Technol. **6**(4), 802–806 (2012)
150. Nobel Media AB: Diabetes and Insulin. https://www.nobelprize.org/educational/medicine/insulin/index.html
151. Lieberman, D.: Digital games for health behavior change: research, design, and future directions. In: eHealth Applications: Promising Strategies for Behavior Change, pp. 110–127. Routledge, London (2012)
152. DeShazo, J., Harris, L., Pratt, W.: Effective intervention or child's play? a review of video games for diabetes education. Diab. Technol. Ther. **12**(10), 815–822 (2010)
153. Klingensmith, G., Aisenberg, J., Kaufman, F., Halvorson, M., Cruz, E., Riordan, M., Varma, C., Pardo, S., Viggiani, M., Wallace, J., Schandner, H., Bailey, T.: Evaluation of a combined blood glucose monitoring and gaming system (Didget®) for motivation in children, adolescents, and young adults with type 1 diabetes. Pediatr. Diab. **14**(5), 350–357 (2013)
154. Bandura, A.: Social Foundations of Thought and Action: A Social Cognitive Theory. Pearson, London (1986)
155. Thompson, D.: Designing Serious Video Games for Health Behavior Change: Current Status and Future Directions. J. Diab. Sci. Technol. **6**(4), 807–811 (2012)
156. Tate, R., Haritatos, J., Cole, S.: HopeLab's approach to re-mission. Int. J. Learn. Med. **1**(1), 29–35 (2009)
157. Govender, M., Bowen, R., German, M., Bulaj, G., Bruggers, C.: Clinical and neurobiological perspectives of empowering pediatric cancer patients using videogames. Games Health J. **4**(5), 362–374 (2015)
158. Merry, S., Stasiak, K., Shepard, M., Frampton, C., Fleming, T., Lucassen, M.: The effectiveness of SPARX, a computerised self help intervention for adolescents seeking help for depression: randomised controlled non-inferiority trial. Br. Med. J. **344**(7857), 16 (2012)
159. Bruce, V., Kutcher, S.: Electronic interventions for depression in adolescents: hot idea or hot air? S. Afr. J. Psychol. **1**(1), 1–13 (2016)
160. Inglés-Camats, G., Presno-Rivas, M., Antonijoan, M., Garcia-Panella, O., Forrest, T.: Yummy tricks: a serious game for learning healthy eating habits. Stud. Health Technol. Inform. **172**(1), 185–190 (2012)
161. Thompson, D., Bhatt, R., Lazarus, M., Cullen, K., Baranowski, J., Baranowski, T.: A serious video game to increase fruit and vegetable consumption among elementary aged youth (Squire's Quest! II): rationale, design, and methods. JMIR Res. Protoc. **1**(2), e19 (2012)
162. Baranowski, T., Buday, R., Thompson, D., Lyons, E., Lu, A., Baranowski, J.: Developing games for health behavior change: getting started. Games Health J. **2**(4), 183–190 (2013)
163. Peng, W.: Design and evaluation of a computer game to promote a healthy diet for young adults computer game as a medium for health promotion. Health Commun. **24**(2), 115–127 (2009)

164. Rusch, D.: "Elude": designing depression. In: El-Nasr, M.S., Consalvo, M., Feiner, S., (eds.) Proceedings of the International Conference on the Foundations of Digital Games (FDG 2012), Raliegh, pp. 254–257. ACM (2012)

165. Russoniello, C., Fish, M., O'Brien, K.: The efficacy of casual videogame play in reducing clinical depression: a randomized controlled study. Games Health J. 2(6), 341–346 (2013)

166. Fish, M., Russoniello, C., O'Brien, K.: The efficacy of prescribed casual videogame play in reducing symptoms of anxiety: a randomized controlled study. Games. Health J. 3(5), 291–295 (2014)

167. Swanson, L., Whittinghill, D.: Intrinsic or extrinsic? using videogames to motivate stroke survivors: a systematic review. Games Health J. 4(3), 253–258 (2015)

168. Szturm, T., Reimer, K., Hochman, J.: Home-based computer gaming in vestibular rehabilitation of gaze and balance impairment. Games Health J. 4(3), 211–220 (2015)

169. Roepke, A., Jaffee, S., Riffle, O., McGonigal, J., Broome, R., Maxwell, B.: Randomized controlled trial of superbetter, a smartphone-based/internet-based self-help tool to reduce depressive symptoms. Games Health J. 4(3), 235–246 (2015)

170. Larsen, L., Schou, L., Lund, H., Langberg, H.: The physical effect of exergames in healthy elderly—a systematic review. Games Health J. 2(4), 205–212 (2013)

171. Hall, A., Chavarria, E., Maneeratana, V., Chaney, B., Bernhardt, J.: Health benefits of digital videogames for older adults: a systematic review of the literature. Games Health J. 1(6), 402–410 (2012)

172. McCallum, S., Boletsis, C.: Dementia games: a literature review of dementia-related serious games. In: Ma, M., Oliveira, M.F., Petersen, S., Hauge, J.B. (eds.) SGDA 2013. LNCS, vol. 8101, pp. 15–27. Springer, Heidelberg (2013)

173. Robert, P., König, A., Amieva, H., Andrieu, S., Bremond, F., Bullock, R., Ceccaldi, M., Dubois, B., Gauthier, S., Kenigsberg, A., Nave, S., Orgogozo, J., Piano, J., Benoit, M., Touchon, J., Vellas, B., Yesavage, J., Manera, V.: Recommendations for the use of serious games in people with Alzheimer's Disease, related disorders and frailty. Front. Aging Neurosci. 6, 54 (2014)

174. Burns, M., Andeway, K., Eppenstein, P., Ruroede, K.: Use of the Wii gaming system for balance rehabilitation: establishing parameters for healthy individuals. Games Health J. 3(3), 179–183 (2014)

175. Sato, K., Kuroki, K., Saiki, S., Nagatomi, R.: Improving walking, muscle strength, and balance in the elderly with an exergame using Kinect: a randomized controlled trial. Games. Health J. 4(3), 161–167 (2015)

176. Pham, Q., Khatib, Y., Stansfeld, S., Fox, S., Green, T.: Feasibility and efficacy of an mHealth game for managing anxiety: "Flowy" randomized controlled pilot trial and design evaluation. Games Health J. 5(1), 50–67 (2016)

177. Bower, K., Clark, R., McGinley, J., Martin, C., Miller, K.: Feasibility and efficacy of the Nintendo Wii gaming system to improve balance performance post-stroke: protocol of a phase II randomized controlled trial in an inpatient rehabilitation setting. Games Health J. 2(2), 103–108 (2013)

178. Jinhui, L., Theng, Y.-L., Foo, S.: Game-based digital interventions for depression therapy: a systematic review and meta-analysis. Cyberpsychology Behav. Soc. Network. 17(8), 519–527 (2014)

179. Theng, Y.-L., Lee, J., Patinadan, P., Foo, S.: The use of videogames, gamification, and virtual environments in the self-management of diabetes: a systematic review of evidence. Games Health J. 4(5), 352–361 (2015)

180. Rahmani, E., Boren, S.: Videogames and health improvement: a literature review of randomized controlled trials. Games Health J. 1(5), 331–341 (2012)

181. Kato, P.: Evaluating efficacy and validating games for health. Games Health J. **1**(1), 74–76 (2012)
182. Kharrazi, H., Lu, A., Gharghabi, F., Coleman, W.: A scoping review of health game research: past, present, and future. Games Health J. **1**(2), 153–164 (2012)
183. Gao, Z., Chen, S., Pasco, D., Pope, Z.: A meta-analysis of active video games on health outcomes among children and adolescents. Obes. Rev. **16**(9), 783–794 (2015)
184. DeSmet, A., Ryckeghem, D., Compernolle, S., Baranowski, T., Thompson, D., Crombez, G., Poels, K., Van Lippevelde, W., Bastiaensens, S., Van Cleemput, K., Vandebosch, H., De Bourdeaudhuij, I.: A meta-analysis of serious digital games for healthy lifestyle promotion. Prev. Med. **69**(1), 95–107 (2014)
185. Coyle, M., Francis, K., Chapman, Y.: Self-management activities in diabetes care: a systematic review. Aust. Health Rev. **37**(4), 512–522 (2013)
186. Riestra, R., Urbina, M., Guaylupo, S., Westera, W., Star, K.: RAGE Dissemination Plan. Project Deliverable, INMARK (2015)
187. Entertainment Software Association: Essential Facts about the Computer and Video Game Industry. Market Research, Entertainment Software Association (2016)
188. NPD Group: Kids and Gaming 2015. Market Research, NPD Group (2015)
189. Khaled, R., Vasalou, A.: Bridging serious games and participatory design. Int. J. Child-Comput. Interact. **2**(2), 93–100 (2014)
190. Penfield, T., Baker, M., Scoble, R., Wykes, M.: Assessment, evaluations, and definitions of research impact: A review. Res. Eval. **23**(1), 21–32 (2014)
191. European Commision: What is Horizon 2020? https://ec.europa.eu/programmes/horizon2020/en/what-horizon-2020
192. European Commission: Horizon 2020 indicators: Assessing the results and impact of Horizon 2020. Project Documentation, European Commission (2015)
193. Research Excellence Framework: Assessment framework and guidance on submissions. Documentation, Research Excellence Framework (2011)
194. Crookall, D.: Serious games, debriefing, and simulation/gaming as a discipline. Simul. Gaming **41**(6), 898–920 (2010)

Processes and Models for Serious Game Design and Development

Eelco Braad[1]([⊠]), Gregor Žavcer[2], and Alyea Sandovar[3]

[1] School of Communication, Media and IT, Hanze University of Applied Sciences, Groningen, The Netherlands
e.p.braad@pl.hanze.nl
[2] Mei:CogSci–University of Ljubljana, Ljubljana, Slovenia
gregor@plur.si
[3] Department of Human and Organizational Development, Fielding Graduate University, Santa Barbara, CA, USA
asandovar@email.fielding.edu

Abstract. A serious game needs to combine a number of different aspects to help the end user in reaching the desired effects. This requires incorporating a broad range of different aspects in the design, stemming from a broad range of different fields of expertise. For designers, developers, researchers, and other stakeholders it is not straightforward how to organize the design and development process, to make sure that these aspects are properly addressed. In this chapter we will discuss a number of ways of organizing the design and development process and various models that support specific design decisions during this process, concluding with a discussion of design patterns for serious games.

Keywords: Serious game design · Game development process · Design science research

1 Introduction

A serious game incorporates play as well as a myriad of other aspects: motivation, learning content, feedback. For designers, developers, but also researchers and other stakeholders, it is not straightforward what steps to take from a problem statement towards a game that can be played by the intended users. This chapter provides an overview of various approaches, models, and frameworks that can be used to support the design and development of serious games.

This chapter is organized into four main sections. In the first section, we will discuss a number of important aspects pertaining to the context in which a serious game is designed and the context in which the game is intended to be used. Subsequently, we will take on a high level perspective and discuss a number of processes that are being used to design and develop serious games. In the third section, we will present a number of design models that assist in making design choices to achieve particular effects with the resulting game. This approach is becoming more and more formalized using a design patterns approach, which are discussed in the final section.

© Springer International Publishing AG 2016
R. Dörner et al. (Eds.): Entertainment Computing and Serious Games, LNCS 9970, pp. 92–118, 2016.
DOI: 10.1007/978-3-319-46152-6_5

At the end of the chapter, a number of future research questions and suggested reading material are included.

2 Context

A serious game only becomes an effective tool to foster learning, promote healthy behavior, or change behavior, when it is played by players. Necessarily, playing takes place in a specific context and it is often hard for a game designer to foresee the time, place, culture, and other contextual aspects that affect the player experience. Considering this context for which a serious game is designed is therefore an important step of the design process: from this context stems an important set of specific design requirements for the serious game.

Before we can discuss particular development process frameworks or more detailed design models to support design decisions, we will first explore the context. We will do so by pointing out a number of different, and often opposing, perspectives. From a user perspective, we will start with the different views that designers and users have of the game. From a game perspective, we emphasize that they differ a large amount in the audience and purposes that they address. From a market perspective, we briefly discuss some differences between the field of entertainment and serious games.

2.1 Differences in Designers and Users

The MDA-framework addresses the dichotomy between designers and players by defining how the mechanics, dynamics, and aesthetics of a game work together to create the player experience [1]. The game designer is in direct control of establishing the mechanics, while the aesthetics that players perceive are separated from them in time, space, and context. Reversely, the player directly perceives the aesthetics while the mechanics can only be experienced through the dynamics of gameplay. This conceptualization of game design as a second-order design problem emphasizes the complexity of predicting how design choices affect the player experience.

Considering the possible contexts in which the game will be played during the design process, requires the designer to investigate and form a model of the intended user. As the design process itself takes place in its own context as well, designers additionally need to be aware that values of their own design context may become part of the game design. Therefore, a critical view towards the design choices and underlying design assumptions needs to be taken.

A model for providing insight into and making the transfer of values explicit for game designers is Values at Play [2, 3]. Supporting current design practices and iterative processes, it helps designers identify, reflect upon, and embed their values in their designs in a conscious, rather than an unconscious, manner. The integration of ethical considerations and cultural values into the design process is further discussed in [4] and in the chapter on ethical stewardship elsewhere in this book.

Combining the views we have discussed, we can discern the context of design and context of use around the implementation of a serious game and (see Fig. 1).

This visualization extends one of the diagrams from [1], however, in order to emphasize the interactive nature of play, the relationship between the player and the serious game has been visualized as a bi-directional arrow.

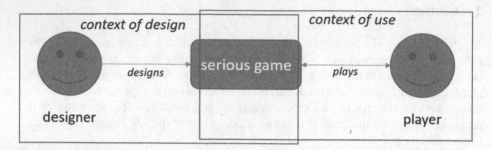

Fig. 1. The context of design and the context of use in serious games.

In the design of artefacts such as serious games, it is important to consider the situation in which the artefact is meant to be used: in many cases, the design also necessarily encompasses aspects of the context of use [5]. For example, when playing a game in the classroom is embedded between an introductory briefing and a concluding debriefing, the design of the game itself, as well as the design of the surrounding activities, are of interest. Klabbers [6] refers to this as design-in-the-small (DIS) and design-in-the-large (DIL). Here, design-in-the-small refers to the game or simulation being designed as a digital artefact in itself, whereas design-in-the-large refers to changing the existing situation and embedding the artefact in its context of use. In serious games, the term game-based learning addresses this inclusion of the larger context of use as part of the design [7].

The use of computer games in a classroom is one example of embedding serious games in a particular context, and while it may be easy to bring a game into the class and play it, it is no silver bullet for education if the context is not adapted to accommodate the game [8, 9]. The experiences of both teachers and researchers in embedding serious games into a curriculum have provided useful insights for how the class context can be adapted [10], arguing for a focus on the underlying concepts and ideas behind the learning activities, of which playing games may be one example. Specific examples of tuning the context to improve the effectiveness of a serious game can be found when addressing higher-order cognitive learning and attitudinal or affective goals. The reflection step in learning can be accommodated by organizing a debriefing to make sense of the experience of play [11] and metacognition may be improved by discussing play in groups [12]. Thus, the design of serious games may extend beyond the design of the game itself: often other interventions in the context of use are required as well.

2.2 Differences in Audience and Purpose

Serious games are being proposed, designed, built, and evaluated across an increasingly wide range of application domains. An early serious games taxonomy distinguishes between seven domains, ranging from government, education and health care through to marketing, defense and industry applications [13]. The same taxonomy loosely introduces a number of serious games categories, such as games for health, games for training and games for work. More recently, a classification scheme that distinguishes between gameplay, purpose, and scope of serious games has been proposed [14] to classify serious games. Of this latter G/P/S-model, the dimension of scope addresses two of the most salient areas from which design requirements stem: the intended audience and intended purpose of the game.

The audience targeted by a serious game is an important source of design requirements: gameplay, look-and-feel and suitable technology need to be in tune with the future players. Traditionally, games are often associated with kids and henceforth many serious games target children before, in, or after primary school. However, more recently much attention has been given to so-called silver gaming: using serious games to improve the quality of life of the elderly [15]. While the games targeting the younger audience often have an education-related goal, games targeting the elderly often have health-related goals such as promoting regular exercise or improving cognitive function. Although other target audiences, such as adolescents in specific work situations or students in higher education, have seen less attention, the notion that the average age of gamers is rising has led to increasing attention for different ages in recent years. Some serious games focus on very specific audiences with specific design requirements, such as children with autism-spectrum disorders [16] or visually impaired persons [17, 18].

The purpose targeted by a serious game is another important source of design requirements: gameplay and other content and interactions within the game need to support the overarching purpose of the game. One of the most outstanding uses is for education and training, leading to the term educational games. In this case, the purpose of the game is to help a learner achieve a given set of learning goals by playing the game. However, the content and activities afforded by the games may differ widely: some provide training and instruction as well as performance assessment, others are limited to repeated practice with automated feedback (skill drill). Another well-known purpose of serious games is to stimulate exercise, leading to the derived term exergame. In this case, the game is designed to let the player perform certain behaviors by providing them with engaging game mechanics [19]. While some exergames have the behavior itself as the main goal, other games strive to increase a user's self-efficacy to maintain this behavior over longer periods [20] or try to generate enough content to keep a user motivated over a longer period of time [21]. Where exergames normally address behavior change in individuals, one final well-known application of serious games is to elicit social change and attitude change, leading to the terms games for change [22] and persuasive games [23]. Outside this scope falls a category of games used to support research itself by gathering data or exploring a solution space. A typical example is FoldIt, which crowdsources possible protein folding solutions through gameplay [24].

The wide range of purposes of serious games, target audiences addressed by serious games, and ways of embedding serious content into a serious game, makes it complicated to discuss the design of serious games in general: in almost all cases the specific area of application or the specific goals of the game need to be taken into account. The classification of learning outcomes distinguishes between cognitive, skill-based and affective learning outcomes [25], and provides a suitable framework to address the different goals we find in serious games. For cognitive outcomes, a further subdivision into verbal knowledge, knowledge organization, and cognitive strategies is made, which can be related to many educational games. For skill-based outcomes, the focus is on maintaining the skills through compilation and automaticity, which can be related to many exergames. For affective outcomes, attitudinal goals may be set, relating closely to persuasive games. Additionally, the affective outcomes include motivation, and links this with motivational disposition, goal-setting, and self-efficacy, providing a basis for the motivational aspect in many serious games (see Table 1). With these notions, in the following serious games are discussed from this broader perspective of addressing particular types of learning outcomes.

Table 1. Subdivision of learning goals into cognitive, skill-based and affective outcomes [25].

Learning outcomes		
Cognitive	Skill-Based	Affective
– Verbal knowledge – Knowledge organization – Cognitive strategies	– Compilation o proceduralization o composition – Automaticy	– Attitudinal – Motivational o motivational disposition o self-efficacy o goal setting

2.3 Differences Between Entertainment Games and Serious Games

Whereas games for entertainment are probably best known by the general audience of consumers, serious games are more known for being used in specific contexts and for specific audiences. This trait has two side effects. First, as the target audience is more specific and hence less in numbers, in general budgets or return-on-investment may be lower. Second, this has the consequence that the business-to-consumer (B2C) model, prevalent in entertainment game market, is nearly absent in serious games. Rather, a business-to-business (B2B) model, often combined with subsidized consortia of business and academic partners, is seen more often.

However, certain serious game projects seem to succeed in combining a solid business case with an academic underpinning. Quest Atlantis has had the benefit of having a long development time, a good budget and consecutive revisions [26]. Moreover, it was received well and discussed in various published articles [27–29]. Other games appear to completely cross over the entertainment/serious games boundary: America's Army is used in army training courses, but also played for entertainment. For a further discussion of differences between entertainment and serious games, and alternative classifications, see [14].

2.4 Conclusions

In this section we have identified a number of contextual aspects that influence the design and development of serious games. In particular, the distinction between the context of design and the context of use provides insight into the considerations for the designer.

Identifying and taking into account the requirements that stem from these aspects improves the suitability of the design for the selected purpose and audience.

3   Processes

In the previous section we have seen a wide range of aspects to consider in the design and development of serious games. Therefore, it is not straightforward how to approach such a complex task: the effects of many design choices are uncertain under different conditions and even more so in conjunction with other design choices. To remedy this complexity, various frameworks that describe design and development processes have been proposed, and in this chapter we will discuss a number of them.

According to Khaled and Ingram [30], there are at least five active perspectives within serious game projects in general: project organization, technology, domain knowledge, user research, and game design. In this section we will focus on the processes used for organizing the design and development process, and how to integrate domain knowledge and user information through the use of research and user-centered design methods. Aspects pertaining to the specific game design choices will be discussed in the next section on models.

3.1   Including Phases and Iteration

The design and development of serious games includes various phases with different purposes: there is a difference between designing (producing a concept) and developing (producing a product). The ADDIE-model is an often-used high-level organization of

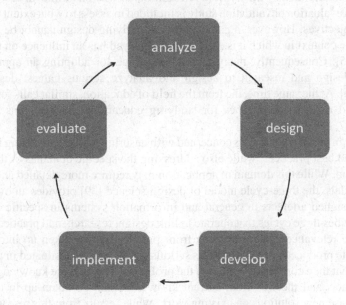

Fig. 2. A visualization of the cyclic ADDIE process.

the design and development process, distinguishing between phases of analysis, design, development, implementation (in the context of use), and evaluation [31]. Additionally, it supports an iterative approach where results from a previous evaluation feed into the analysis and design phases of the next iteration and hence incrementally improves the design and/or the product (see Fig. 2).

This cyclic and phasic approach underlies various other existing approach to serious game design. In an attempt to reduce design complexity, and hence development costs, the EMERGO-toolkit and associated approach are based on the ADDIE-cycle [32] and focus on how to address case requirements in the design. Similarly, but focusing on the evaluation phase instead, the ADDIE-cycle underlies an approach to improve usability, playability, and learnability in games [33].

In practice, this cyclic approach is often supported by a software development methodology known as Scrum (see for example [34]). This emphasizes incremental development and evaluation of prototypes during the development process and integrates well with the ADDIE-approach. The use of Scrum has seen significant rise in recent years, particularly in the field of game development.

3.2 Including Research

General consensus is that research has a definite and prerequisite role in the design and development of serious games. In particular domain-specific analysis as part of the design, and effectiveness studies as part of the evaluation or validation, are commonplace. However, how to combine research throughout the design and development process is less clear.

The goals of transfer of the learning content beyond playing the game call for a design that can be underpinned by theory from relevant fields, as well as known best practices, and often an evaluation or validation study is included to assess to what extent the design meets its objectives. However, a game and its underlying design cannot be studied in isolation; the context in which it is employed and played has an influence on the results obtained [35]. Consequently, many researchers argue for adopting an approach that integrates design and research to design and analyze serious games: design-based research [36]. At the same time, the from the field of education, similar calls for applying design-based research approaches for studying educational interventions are being proposed [37, 38].

The design of serious games is concerned with ensuring a solid embedding in existing literature and best practices, while also addressing the specific demands of the domain of application. While this domain of application may require more detailed and domain-specific models, the three-cycle model of design science [39] provides an overarching view for designed artefacts in general and information systems in specific [40]. This model describes three cycles that operate to link design, research, and practice together. Through the relevance cycle, problems from practice can be taken up into a design process while produced artefacts, such as serious games, can be evaluated in practice to make sure that they contribute to solving the problems. Through the knowledge or rigor cycle, artefacts and theories from current knowledge can be taken up in the design process to base new solutions on existing work, while results from this research can be added to the knowledge base (see Fig. 3). The design cycle, then, is at the heart of the design process and refers to an iterative approach to design and developing the artefacts.

Fig. 3. A three-cycle view of design science research [39].

Focusing prominently on the research and evaluation aspects, Mayer and colleagues [41] argue for a more coherent approach to research, and offer concrete advice on the development of a corresponding research framework. They specifically aim to address the broad application scope of serious games, while being useable in practice. They define further comparative analysis of serious games, improving evaluation constructs and scales, and digital tooling integrated into games as the next steps forward. While this seems like a promising direction, an overarching and game-specific research framework is still lacking.

3.3 Including Users

As discussed earlier, there is wide support in literature and practice for a user-centered design methodology in designing and developing serious games: in an attempt to bridge the designer-player dichotomy, it is paramount to involve members of the target audience in the design process. In recognition of the need for specific design frameworks, Rankin et al. [42] describe how they used a user-centered design approach for evaluating second language acquisition in existing games. In this model of user-centered game design, phases such as conceptualization, prototyping, and playtesting can be distinguished and are explicitly associated with user-focused research steps and outcomes. As they use existing entertainment games such as EverQuest II to embed learning scenarios, this is also an example of repurposing: using the game for a purpose it was not originally designed for.

The role of the user in the design process may differ: sometimes, like in the previous model, the user input is gathered through focus groups and evaluations. In other cases, the user takes on a more active role and actually actively contributes to the design [43]. In the latter case, we label this as participatory design, rather than just user-centered design.

Including users in the design process is particularly hard when there is not yet a playable version of the game. The observation that it is hard to address design problems in a concept before it is developed into a playable game is widely recognized [44]. In order to gather the feedback from playing with users as early as possible, an iterative approach that creates early prototypes of the game is preferable – such a player-centric approach is fully outlined in the book entitled Game Design Workshop by Fullerton [45]. As digital prototypes require more effort to construct and change, often paper prototyping is used in early iterations: using physical papers, cards, die, pawns, and such to simulate future gameplay early on.

Whereas physically prototyping digital games definitely has its place in the design process, there limitations in representing for example real-time action components [46]. To make the transition from written design document to playable prototype easier, several authors have noticed a lack of design vocabulary and argued for more formalized ways of defining game designs in terms of their mechanics [47–49]. The introduction of so-called game design patterns [50] can be viewed as another effort to capture the effects and interactions of different game design choices, and will be explored for serious games later in this chapter. This formalization approach has been further elaborated in the Machinations framework [51], which combines a model-based theoretical perspective with digital tools to allow designers to alter design choices and see their effects in practice.

Taking the previous perspectives into account, we will use the ADDIE phases of analysis and design, and then those of development and evaluation to discuss a number of existing frameworks.

3.4 Analysis and Design

The coming together of different disciplines, particularly game design and instructional design, is one of the main topics in designing educational games. In an effort to combine pedagogy and play, as well as retaining fidelity to the subject matter, Rooney proposes a triadic framework that integrates these aspects [52]. She addresses different learning methodologies, such as situated learning and experiential learning, as part of this framework and further argues for theoretical underpinnings of designing games within these contexts. A conceptual approach that identifies similar dimensions of Game vs. Learning, Game vs. User, and User vs. Learning addresses further details of designing and analyzing educational games [53]. Another approach aimed at integrating didactic and game design perspectives focuses specifically on the iterative nature, as addressed in the previous section. In this approach, the authors emphasize the didactic perspective throughout the various phases of the design process [54].

Such a theory-based design approach was used in the design and development of a serious game to reduce cognitive biases [55]. In this study, an explicit link between the domain knowledge of cognitive biases to the game mechanics and in-game narrative is made, and subsequently evaluated the game with users to test for effect and efficacy. When the domain knowledge is not present in the designers or the researchers involved, integrating domain knowledge into the game becomes more complicated and may require active consideration as to how to involve the experts [56]. The integration of serious content within the mechanics, balancing fun and education, is a widely debated topic and even practitioners have varying methods and processes for approaching this problem [57], which only further emphasizes a key problem in serious game design: a common framework for the effective design of serious games is lacking [58].

3.5   Development and Evaluation

The phases of development and evaluation have similar complexities that influence the effectiveness of the game. For example, in the development of a science education game, the authors/researchers worked together with a number of different roles: domain experts in biology, immunology, experts in pedagogy and learning science, and game designers [59]. They did face a number of design choices where the game designers had different ideas from the educational experts, for example when interspersing the gameplay with the option to ask questions. The team overestimated the features that could be implemented and underestimated available time, ending up having to cut a number of design aspects, such as a full 3D simulation or soft-body physics.

In order to assess the qualitative and/or quantitative results found through evaluation of a game, an interpretation of what the results mean must be made. This includes tracing back the effects found to specific elements in the design of the game. One method is to underpin design decisions from theory and trace them to the evaluation phase [60], allowing the subsequent iteration to be informed by previous choices. Another, more formalized and labor-intensive method, is to code specific game stimuli and responses and assess these during evaluation [61]. This latter approach was shown to work within the setting of an exergame, making it highly relevant to include physical responses in the evaluation.

There are many different approaches, methodologies, and techniques to gather data for the evaluation of games. They range from physiological measurements, such as facial muscle activity (via EMG) or heart beat intervals, to audio/visual technologies, such as video and online or retrospective talk-a-loud protocols, to in-game assessments, such as route logging and game analytics [62].

Some evaluation frameworks specifically address the aforementioned player context, player background and application to serious games [63]. When the evaluation is specifically focused on the player experience or gameplay experience, specific evaluation methods such as the Gameplay Experience Questionnaire (GEQ) [64] may be used. More often, a combination of methods is used, such as combining observations and self-reports. For example, in a study after game design for the elderly, the GEQ was combined with qualitative observations [65]. Adaptations to make the GEQ suitable for serious games are being researched, but have thus far concluded that the variation in context of playing had large impact on the results obtained, finding that the various design stages did improve usability but not gameplay experience [66].

A typical example of the evaluation of serious game is found in the comparison of an educational game to traditional instructional methods in teaching computer programming [67]. This evaluation addresses the effectiveness of both the game design and the learning. Tying into the design-based research approach discussed earlier, specific assessment frameworks for games and simulations have been developed [36]. Specifically for serious games, a step-based approach that integrates usability and playability into the process is described by Olsen et al. [33]. Other scholars focus on online or in-game evaluation, by developing learning analytics systems as an integrated part of educational game design [68, 69]. This approach stretches beyond the design process:

it also provides end-users such as learners and teachers with insights into the performance of both the learners and the game itself.

3.6 Integrated Process Frameworks

Considering all the aspects of context, process, involving users, and embedding research, creating an encompassing process that supports most serious games projects is complex. Moreover, a process framework must be academically sound as well as feasible for use in practice. Notwithstanding these challenges, a number of such integrated frameworks have been put forward and further elaborated upon.

An approach of combining design-based research, information system design, has been further adapted for serious games into the Simulation-game Instructional Systems Design (SG-ISD) Model [70], by paralleling game development phases from the traditional Waterfall-model of software engineering with information systems design methods based on the iterative ADDIE-model (see Fig. 4). In the analysis phase, they emphasize the integration of instructional theory into the game design, and in the design phase learning methodology and game features need to be integrated. This design framework provides further guidelines for testing (formative evaluation), prototyping and playtesting and evaluation in practice (summative evaluation). Later, they extensively discussed the use of the model in practice [71]. While this framework is intended specifically for the design and development of educational simulation games, it includes many of the features discussed earlier, and hence seems like a good step towards a more general-purpose process framework.

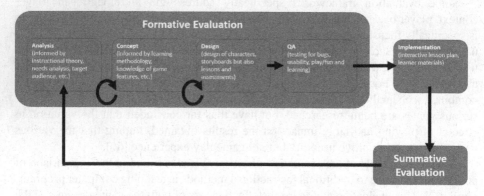

Fig. 4. The integration of design-based research with game development phases in the simulation-game instructional systems design model [70].

In the absence of process frameworks that address the design and development of serious games across the broad range of application areas, several authors have proposed specific, instantiated frameworks for particular areas of serious games. Focusing specifically on educational adventure games, an early effort to define a coherent design approach is found in the work of Moser [72]. In this approach the ADDIE model is iteratively expanded with specific adventure game design choices such as which characters, what puzzles, and what user interface to include.

In an effort to reduce the design complexity involved in addressing increasingly complex learning outcomes, a study that focuses on scenario-based games has provided a framework that links conceptual design aspects with an underlying technical architecture [32]. In this model, the game itself is embedded within a larger game-based learning framework that includes supportive views for both learners and teachers, as well as analytics and monitoring of learning integrated in the game world. Two alternate approaches and examples of applications of such models can be found in collaborative decision making games [26], and games for cultural heritage [73].

In an attempt to standardize development approaches for particular user group, and improving consistent game design, evaluation, and efficacy, the game-based learning development approach was proposed [74]. This approach distinguishes between three perspectives on the design and development process. At the process level, the project runs from a case through the ADDIE-phases, towards a designed learning activity. At the principles level, a number of guidelines for learning with games are emphasized, such as fostering positive attitudes and using game-based learning only when appropriate. At the tools & techniques level, these phases and principles are aligned with particular practices, such as questionnaires, prototype evaluation and trials.

While an iterative approach is hinted upon with the arrow extending from evaluation at the process level, the other levels do not support a similar iteration. Moreover, including stakeholders and users only in later phases is at odds with most user-centered design practices.

3.7 Conclusions

In this section we have identified a number of requirements for a process framework that supports the design and development of serious games. Such a framework must support different phases such as analysis, design, development, and evaluation, in an iterative fashion. Furthermore, such a framework must facilitate the integration of domain knowledge and support the evaluation of effects achieved through playing the game. User-centered design seems like an appropriate framework to draw upon, as it emphasizes including the user within the process – either passively (focus groups) or actively (participatory design). While integrated design and development frameworks are emerging, currently each framework is suitable only for a specific set of serious games and a general design and development framework is lacking.

4   Models

In the first part of this chapter we have presented a number of ways to approach the design and development of a serious game. The focus has been on the overarching process: which steps to take and how to evaluate whether these steps are working out towards a final product. However, this leaves unaddressed the question of how to make the right design choices in the design of the game itself. This section discusses a number of models that attempt to describe what choices in setting, mechanics, and gameplay have what kind of effects on the motivation and learning of the user.

When designing a serious game, the designers must consider both the learning goals that the user needs to achieve and the motivational factors that help the user to continue playing. Some models for serious game design emphasize either the learning or the motivational characteristics of games, whereas other models try to integrate both aspects more coherently. We will first discuss some of the main motivation-focused models and learning-focused models and then present some of the integrated models.

4.1 Motivation

One of the first studies to systematically explore what makes computer games fun, and how to use their features for learning identifies a number of motivational factors in games [75, 76]. A number of games were modified, compared, and evaluated to identify the motivational elements of challenge, fantasy, and curiosity. Challenge seems to relate to intrinsic motivation when it meets particular standards – for example a balance between player ability and game difficulty. Fantasy refers to the representational part of games, regardless of whether the depiction is realistic or non-realistic; fantasy here is used to set it apart from an abstract game. Curiosity refers to the uncovering of feedback and auditory and visual aspects.

Whereas the previous study analyzed games to identify design principles, others have taken the approach of using motivational theories to explain how players are engaged by games. In one such study, self-determination theory [77] was used to analyze motivation in games from a perspective of a player satisfying their needs. In single-player games, perceived competence and autonomy were shown to indeed explain game enjoyment and preference for future play, whereas in multiplayer games the aspect of relatedness served the same role [78]. Later on, this approach was extended to include explanations for short-term well-being, the appeal of in-game violence, and post-play aggressive behavior as well [79].

Acknowledging that research literature was lacking clear principles on how to engage users with particular game features, while achieving the desired instructional goals, Garris et al. have put forward a research-and-practice model [80]. This model identifies key game features and types of learning outcomes, and links these to a game cycle of user judgments, behavior, and feedback that supports learning. This input/output-model emphasizes the integration of instructional content and game characteristics to help achieve the learning outcomes in the player. Based on existing studies, this model also expands the aforementioned game features challenge, fantasy, and curiosity with rules, goals, and control, and tries to link them with learning outcomes in the skill-based, cognitive, and affective categories [25]. The authors, however, stress that while games offer the instructional opportunities to learn by doing, not everyone learns by doing and not everything can be learnt by doing.

4.2 Learning

With the increasing attention for serious games, the need for using sound educational principles to design them also increased: motivational and educational effectiveness needed to be integrated into the serious game design process [81]. By combining existing pedagogical models, such as the ARCS model of attention, relevance, confidence, and satisfaction [82], Gagné's nine events of instruction [83], with a number of common game elements, the RETAIN-model defines a three-level motivational model of games: relevance, embedding of the learning content, transfer, adaptation to the player, immersion, and naturalization of the learning goals [84]. This can be seen as a model that can be used both to analyze and design serious games using these principles. A similar approach compares four lenses (motivation, flow, learning environment, and gameplay) to a number of common game elements (interest, goals, challenge, and feedback) in a comparison [85]. This comparison shows that key features of games are in line with factors promoting motivation and learning (see Table 2).

Table 2. Similarities between game features and factors promoting motivation and learning [85].

	Motivation	Flow	Learning environments	Game design/Play
Focus/ Interest	Attention strategies for arousing and sustaining curiosity and interest	Attention is completely absorbed in the activity	Avoid distractions and disruptions that intervene and destroy the subjective experience	Sensory and cognitive curiosity within the learner
Goals	Relevance strategies that link to learner's needs, interests, and motives	The activity has clear goals	Have specific goals and established procedures	Goal reaching and feedback
Challenge	Confidence strategies that help students develop a positive expectation for successful achievement	Challenge is optimized	Provide a continual feeling of challenge that is neither so difficult as to create a sense of hopelessness and frustration, nor so easy as to produce boredom	The learner should continually feel challenged as difficulty increases in concordance to increased skills
Feedback	Satisfaction strategies that provide extrinsic and intrinsic reinforcement for effort	The activity provides clear and consistent feedback as to whether one is reaching the goals	Provide a high intensity of interaction and feedback	The learner should feel a sense of control through endogenous feedback provided by the game

The models discussed so far have taken motivation as the main emphasis, but necessarily identified learning as one of the other required serious game components. Other models have completely focused on how learning can take place through games and how existing and new pedagogical models can help to understand and improve the effectiveness of serious games. Taking learning-by-doing or experiential learning as a starting point, the experiential gaming model [86] links the four stages of experiential learning [87] to particular game activities and features. Specific emphasis is placed on storytelling, game balance, and optimizing cognitive load, in order to improve effectiveness of learning and as such this model emphasizes learning through the core mechanics and the design of the game.

Another route to approach the problem of designing effective serious games is by taking the intended learning outcomes as a start point. This directly raises the questions of which game activities are best suited to help a learner achieve those outcomes. The Game Object Model [88] tries to identify elements and objects within game design and creates a taxonomy of these elements as a design tool. The learning mechanic/game mechanic, or LM-GM model [89] then tries to match particular learning mechanics to particular game activities. Similar approaches of aligning gameplay with learning exist [90, 91]. These can be viewed steps towards finding a relation between the design aspects of a game and the effects and effectiveness of that game as a tool for learning.

4.3 Integration and Alignment

In the previous discussion we have seen that the models for designing serious games have incorporated aspects such as motivation and the learning objectives. This leaves the question of how to integrate these in an effective manner unanswered. In an experiment comparing intrinsic embedding of the learning content with the gameplay to an extrinsic embedding, Habgood et al. found an increased motivation for the activities [92]. The integration of learning with gameplay, and hence the alignment of gameplay activities with learning activities, is a topic of ongoing research.

Where the LM-GM model focus specifically on the design of the game, the motivation and goals of the user playing the game must also be considered as part of the design space. Drawing from activity theory, Carvalho et al. [93] have put forward a multi-layered model that extends the LM-GM-model by addressing different motives and contexts. This model distinguishes between actions and motives outside of and inside of the game, as well as aspects of the context of use, such as community, rules, and culture. For the design of serious games, this model is a recent and comprehensive basis to link design decisions to intended effects from an integrated perspective.

In the context of evaluating existing serious games, a four-dimensional framework that takes into account learner specifics, pedagogic considerations, mode of representation, and context of use is proposed [94]. This work is further expanded upon by distinguishing between the learning question, the instruction question, the assessment question, and the alignment question and then incorporating a number of the previous approaches into an integrated model [95].

In this game-based learning framework, the motivational aspects and the learning cycle of user engagement, user learning, user behavior and player feedback are made explicit, as well as the integration of learning objectives and content. However, a further specification of the game elements or mechanics to include, and to what effect, is omitted.

It seems that a further elaboration on serious game design and evaluation models is still required in order to support integrated design with an integrated framework.

These latter and more recent examples show a currently emerging approach in serious game design: that of aligning the gameplay with the goals of the game at different levels [96]. A more recent and further analysis of promises and challenges in aligning gameplay content with learning goals has led to a number of principles for achieving this match [91], such as making mental models of what the player needs to learn, and supporting strategic thinking and cognitive skills by teaching more than just the content itself.

4.4 Conclusions

In this section we have discussed a number of models that assist in making design choices as part of an overarching design and development processes. Whereas earlier models focused on motivational aspects, more recently the emphasis has come to lie on the alignment of gameplay activities and the goals of the game. This approach of integrating learning and playing, and linking specific design choices to specific effects, seems like a promising next step in serious game design research.

5   Serious Game Design Patterns

As mentioned, a major challenge for the designers of serious games is to create an engaging gameplay that is also effective in achieving desired purpose. If serious games are designed only by game designers, they may be entertaining but may lack the effect of primary purpose; if they are designed by teachers and trainers, they might be very efficient, but lack the motivational appeal [97], which is one of the key reasons to use serious games in the first place [98]. Therefore, in order to address this issue, stakeholders from the "serious" side and "game" side should cooperate in the design process. However, lack of a shared design vocabulary and tool box containing both broad application solutions and solutions specific to certain genres of games is a major issue and limitation [99], even though such shared and unified vocabulary can bring significant benefits to the area [100]; this was pointed out already in the past by several authors such as Costikyan and Church [47, 48]. Serious game design patterns seem to be a promising approach and solution to address this challenge and to facilitate collaboration, cooperation and mutual understanding between different stakeholders [101].

5.1 What Are Game Design Patterns?

A design pattern is a general reusable solution to a commonly occurring problem after it has been successfully applied in specific contexts in response to specific design problems, such as learning in the affective domain [102]. As a method patterns were first introduced in architecture by Alexander: "Each pattern describes a problem which occurs over and over again in our environment, and then describes the core of a solution to that problem, in such a way that you can use this solution a million times over, without ever doing it the same way twice" [103].

Later, Gamma et al. introduced the use of design patterns in software engineering [104], however, design patterns are today used in various fields such as, for example, human-computer interaction and interaction design [105]. In education they are applied in active learning, management systems and intelligent tutoring systems [97]. Nonetheless, none of these uses takes in account the game-playing dimension [97].

In game design, the use of patterns was introduced by Kreimeier [106] and put forward by Björk et al. [107]. Unlike in software engineering where patterns provide strict solutions, game design patterns should not be seen as such as game design is a creative process which often does not have one right solution [107]. Important to note is that game design patterns are used for an earlier stage than actual application development [108]. In this regard, the game design pattern description itself is just a summary of causes and effects, describing one way to reach a given objective [106].

There have been various approaches in researching and documenting game design patterns. Currently, the most significant attempt to set up a database of design concepts is Björk and Holopainen's collection of more than 200 design patterns [99] and it is also considered as most coherent and functional [97]. Their structure of the pattern can be seen as an evolution over the Formal Abstract Design Tools (FADT) suggested by Church and consists of (1) name, (2) concise description, often with notes in which game the pattern was identified, (3) consequences of applying the solution suggested by pattern, (4) how to use the pattern, and (5) relations to other patterns [107]. Moreover, it should be mentioned, that some researchers used the proposed pattern structure also as basis in formalising and expanding serious game design patterns, linking it with the "serious" part of the game [108–111]. Kelle, for example, introduced the concept of "game learning patterns" (GLP) as a methodology for the design of learning games by using game design patterns and matching these with corresponding learning functions [108] while Reuter et al. researched design patterns for collaborative player interactions [110].

5.2 Why Use Patterns for Serious Games Design?

Game design patterns create a shared design vocabulary and can be used for problem-solving during development, idea generation, as creative design tool, to communicate with peers and with other professions [105], for analysis and categorization of games, for exploration of new mediums and platforms [107], such as, for example, mixed reality games [112]. In this regard, game design patterns become even more useful not only for analysis but further extend themselves into areas like authoring, content, software development and testing as these games introduce new design aspects compared to traditional videogames (e.g. reliance on inaccurate sensor data, close coupling to the real world context they are played in) [112]. Furthermore, recently, Dahlskog et al. identified a set of patterns at different sizes and levels of abstractions (micro-, meso- and macro-) for procedural content generation which also further strengthens the link between game design patterns and software development [113].

The usability and advantages of design patterns have also been recognized in the serious games community [101]. Dormann et al. proposed using game patterns as a conceptual tool to initiate discussions about the role of affect in games and to support the design of games situated in the affective domain [102]. In their research, they used game patterns to "bridge the gap between theories and high-level affective principles to their representation or actualization through games" [102]. Thus, developing a collection of game patterns helped gaining insights into the design of affective learning in games and raised a number of issues to take into consideration [102]. Moreover, Mader et al. argue that patterns help to better understand features that make play engaging and motivating which helps maximize patients' intrinsic motivation and smooth out the medical aspect of therapeutic games, consequently making a serious game more effective for treatment or therapy [114]. Not engaging gameplay was also a common critique of games designed to address brain injury rehabilitation and patterns might be a solution [109]. Moreover, Cheng et al. argue that investigating patterns in games for rehabilitation is beneficial for researchers and designers for several reasons: (1) game design patterns have the capacity to capture the qualitative information about brain injury rehabilitation, (2) have the ability to distill abstract game design knowledge from a large amount of data about how well existing games worked in therapy into a set of coherent and tangible exemplars, and (3) patterns as a common language can serve as a valuable tool to facilitate effective communication and mutual understanding among game designers and therapists [109].

In this regard, as patterns are a formal means of documentation [106], we can argue that they are key enablers for structured research in the serious game domain. Game design patterns seem to be a promising choice as they provide a means of capturing existing successful design practices, expand knowledge about game design and provide a shared design vocabulary for communication between researchers, game designers, and developers [102]. In addition, lack of such procedures can slow down production of serious games and likely has a negative impact on the quality of the products as currently each project is more a new challenge than the re-use of established and well-grounded procedures [101]. Research findings also suggest that design patterns help various stakeholder to faster acquire new knowledge that is outside their expertise. This is supported by an interesting observation from Marne et al. fieldwork research which showed that teachers were more interested in game related patterns while game designers were more interested in pedagogical patterns [97]. Moreover, findings also supports Björk et al. claims that game design patterns are beneficial to multidisciplinary groups as they ease communication [107].

Lastly, structured research can be supported with expanded documentation of game design patterns which also covers more in-depth "scientific part" with additional information such as for example ethical concerns, serious purpose, data gathered, etc. Serious games Design Pattern Canvas (DPC) (see Fig. 5) is such proposal towards unifying serious games design patterns with strong grounding in research. DPC is a visual chart with elements describing a pattern's purpose, mechanics, audience, consequences, collected data, related research, and ethical considerations [111]. The chart can be looked at from the center, where the left side is aimed at design questions ("serious" part) and the right side is dedicated to interaction design ("game" part). An example of such relevant and reusable information would be a research done in 2009 which demonstrated that the popular game Tetris is a visuospatial task that can reduce PTSD flashbacks if played after a traumatic event [115].

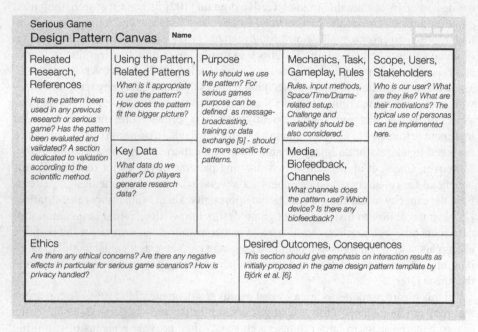

Fig. 5. Serious game design pattern canvas (alpha proposal) [111], inspired by the business model canvas [116].

5.3   Criticism of Patterns

Most criticism of design patterns, such as considering them a fad and either too formal or not formal enough, comes from other fields, but can be also applied to game design patterns [105]. Still, these objections do not really criticize the notion of patterns, but rather the quality of their current conceptualization, use, and unspecified level of analysis they address; also, game design patterns are only useful as long they can be used and applied with reasonable effort to support development of a game or solve particular design problems [105].

In this regard Almeida & Silva criticize game design patterns proposed by Björk et al. as not being enough documented, having contradictory documentation on patterns with disagreements between title, definition and usage examples while also lacking graphical models which together results in less intuitive use [99].

However, these objections do not really criticize the notion of patterns but rather the quality of their current conceptualization, use and unspecified level of analysis they address. Furthermore, it can be argued that with standardized design language and taxonomy the quality and usability of game design patterns could be improved. Nonetheless, as we can consider the game design patterns method still in its beginning, critiques like this should be addressed in future development of serious game design patterns. In addition, game design patterns need to be validated or it has to be at least specified in which development phase they are. As there is not much research on game design patterns validation, this can be considered as a major limitation and future research should also address this question.

5.4 Conclusion

To summarize, besides creating a shared vocabulary for various stakeholders, game design patterns have many benefits ranging from problem-solving during development, idea generation, as a creative design and communication tool for better collaboration with peers and other professions [105]. In addition, design patterns support analysis, categorization of games and exploration of new mediums and platforms are listed [107].

For the domain of serious games, we can argue that some of these advantages are even more beneficial. The documentation of design guidelines can assist in the knowledge transfer between generations of professionals [99] and different communities to a greater extent than before [105] which is a key factor for structured research built upon best and proven practices.

Lastly, design patterns provide means for structured evaluation and validation of serious games [114].

6 Future Challenges

Within the broader topics of this chapter, a number of future challenges or future research topics can be identified:

- How to integrate process frameworks with specific design models – thereby linking software development with creativity, pedagogical consideration, research and specific domain or field expert knowledge.
- How to integrate pedagogy and instructional design with game activities and specific game aspects – thereby focusing not so much on if serious games can work but how to make specific designs work.
- How to form an accurate model of the end user throughout the design process and how to cater to this user – thereby focusing on adaptiveness of the game to the motivational and learning needs of the user.
- How to reap benefits from formalized approaches such as game design patterns, while leaving room for creativity and innovation.

Further Reading

A number of books can be suggested as further reading on the topics addressed in this chapter.

- Fullerton, T. (2014). Game Design Workshop: A Playcentric Approach to Creating Innovative Games. CRC Press. This book presents a pragmatic approach to creating games, emphasizing early (paper) prototyping, evaluation with players, and using the feedback obtained to improve the game iteratively.

- Kapp, K. M. (2012). The Gamification of Learning and Instruction: Game-Based Methods and Strategies for Training and Education. John Wiley & Sons. This book brings together underlying theory and practical examples of using game design for learning.
- Schell, J. (2014). The Art of Game Design: A book of lenses. CRC Press. This book presents an extensive overview of game design theory through the use of a large number of different lenses to view to game through.
- Adams, E., & Rollings, A. (2007). Game design and development. Person Education, Inc., Upper Saddle River, New Jersey. This book presents both game design theory and development approaches, detailing specific considerations for a wide number of established genres.

References

1. Hunicke, R., LeBlanc, M., Zubek, R.: MDA: a formal approach to game design and game research work. In: Challenges Game AI, pp. 1–4 (2004)
2. Flanagan, M., Nissenbaum, H., Howe, D.C., Nissenbaum, H.: Embodying Values in Technology: Theory and Practice. Cambridge University Press, Cambridge (2008)
3. Flanagan, M., Nissenbaum, H.: Values at Play in Digital Games. MIT Press, Cambridge (2014)
4. Sandovar, A.: Ph.D. Dissertation
5. Marklund, B.B.: Out of context – understanding the practicalities of learning games. In: Proceedings of DiGRA 2014 Conference (2014)
6. Klabbers, J.H.G.: A framework for artifact assessment and theory testing. Simul. Gaming **37**, 155–173 (2006)
7. Pivec, M., Dziabenko, O., Schinnerl, I.: Aspects of game-based learning. In: 3rd International Conference on Knowledge Management, Graz, Australia, pp. 216–225 (2003)
8. Squire, K.D.: Changing the game: What happens when video games enter the classroom. Innov. J. Online Educ. **1**(6), 1829–1841 (2005)
9. Stieler-Hunt, C., Jones, C.M.: A model for exploring the usefulness of games for classrooms. In: Proceedings of the 2015 DiGRA International Conference (2015)
10. Popescu, M.-M., Roceanu, I., Earp, J., Ott, M., Moreno-Ger, P.: Aspects of serious games curriculum integration - a two-folded approach. In: 8th International Scientific Conference on eLearning and Software for Education, pp. 359–366 (2012)
11. Feinberg, J.R.: Debriefing in simulation games: An examination of reflection on cognitive and affective learning outcomes. University of Georgia (2003)
12. Kim, B., Park, H., Baek, Y.: Not just fun, but serious strategies: using meta-cognitive strategies in game-based learning. Comput. Educ. **52**(4), 800–810 (2009)
13. Sawyer, B., Smith, P.: Serious games taxonomy. In: Game Developers Conference (2008)
14. Djaouti, D., Alvarez, J., Jessel, J.-P.: Classifying serious games: the G/P/S model. In: Handbook of Research on Improving Learning and Motivation Through Educational Games: Multidisciplinary Approaches, no. 2005, pp. 118–136 (2011)
15. Imbeault, F., Bouchard, B., Bouzouane, A.: Serious games in cognitive training for alzheimer's patients. In: IEEE 1st International Conference on Serious Games and Applications for Health (SeGAH), pp. 1–8 (2011)

16. Zakari, H.M., Ma, M., Simmons, D.: A review of serious games for children with autism spectrum disorders (ASD). In: Ma, M., Oliveira, M.F., Baalsrud Hauge, J. (eds.) SGDA 2014. LNCS, vol. 8778, pp. 93–106. Springer, Heidelberg (2014)
17. Yuan, B., Folmer, E.: Blind hero: enabling guitar hero for the visually impaired. In: Proceedings of the 10th International ACM SIGACCESS Conference on Computers and Accessibility, pp. 169–176 (2008)
18. Morelli, T., Foley, J., Columna, L., Lieberman, L., Folmer, E.: VI-Tennis: a vibrotactile/ audio exergame for players who are visually impaired categories and subject descriptors. In: Foundations of Digital Games, pp. 147–154 (2010)
19. Whitehead, A., Johnston, H., Nixon, N., Welch, J.: Exergame effectiveness: what the numbers can tell us. In: Proceedings of the 5th ACM SIGGRAPH Symposium on Video Games, pp. 55–62 (2010)
20. Song, H., Peng, W., Lee, K.M.: Promoting exercise self-efficacy with an exergame. J. Health Commun. **16**, 148–162 (2011)
21. Degens, N., Braad, E.: Keep on moving: designing a physiotherapeutic exergame for different devices and exercises. In: DiGRA 2015: Diversity of Play (2015)
22. Swain, C.: Designing games to effect social change. In: Situated Play, Proceedings of DiGRA 2007 Conference, pp. 805–809 (2007)
23. Bogost, I.: Persuasive Games: The Expressive Power of Videogames. MIT Press, Cambridge (2007)
24. Khatib, F., Cooper, S., Tyka, M.D., Xu, K., Makedon, I., Popovic, Z., Baker, D.: Algorithm discovery by protein folding game players. Proc. Natl. Acad. Sci. **108**(47), 18949–18953 (2011)
25. Kraiger, K., Ford, K., Salas, E.: Application of cognitive, skill-based, and affective theories of learning outcomes to new methods of training evaluation. J. Appl. Psychol. **78**(2), 311– 328 (1993)
26. Azadegan, A., Sutherland, S., Harteveld, C.: Design approach for collaborative decision making games. In: Foundations of Digital Games (2015)
27. Barab, S., Thomas, M., Dodge, T., Carteaux, R., Tuzun, H.: Making learning fun: Quest Atlantis, a game without guns. Educ. Technol. Res. Dev. **53**(1), 86–107 (2005)
28. Barab, S., Dodge, T., Tuzun, H., Job-Sluder, K., Jackson, C., Arici, A., Job-Sluder, L., Carteaux, R., Gilbertson, J., Heiselt, C.: The quest atlantis project: a socially-responsive play space for learning. In: The Design and Use of Simulation Computer Games in Education, pp. 153–180 (2007)
29. Thomas, M.K., Barab, S., Tuzun, H.: Developing critical implementations of technology-rich innovations: a cross-case study of the implementation of Quest Atlantis. J. Educ. Comput. Res. **41**(2), 125–153 (2009)
30. Khaled, R., Ingram, G.: Tales from the front lines of a large-scale serious game project. In: Proceedings of the 2012 ACM Annual Conference on Human Factors in Computing Systems, CHI 2012, pp. 69–78 (2012)
31. Molenda, M.: In search of the elusive ADDIE model. Perform. Improv. **42**(5), 34–37 (2003)
32. Westera, W., Nadolski, R.J., Hummel, H.G.K., Wopereis, I.G.J.H.: Serious games for higher education: a framework for reducing design complexity. J. Comput. Assist. Learn. **24**(5), 420–432 (2008)
33. Olsen, T., Procci, K., Bowers, C.: Serious games usability testing: how to ensure proper usability, playability, and effectiveness. In: Marcus, A. (ed.) HCII 2011 and DUXU 2011, Part II. LNCS, vol. 6770, pp. 625–634. Springer, Heidelberg (2011)
34. Keith, C.: Agile Game Development with Scrum. Pearson Education, Boston (2010)

35. Barab, S., Squire, K.D.: Design-based research: putting a stake in the ground. J. Learn. Sci. **13**(1), 1–14 (2004)
36. Klabbers, J.H.G.: Gaming and simulation: principles of a science of design. Simul. Gaming **34**, 569–591 (2003)
37. Bannan-Ritland, B.: The role of design in research: the integrative learning design framework. Educ. Res. **32**(1), 21–24 (2003)
38. Faiola, A., Boyd Davis, S., Edwards, R.L.: Extending knowledge domains for new media education: integrating interaction design theory and methods. New Media Soc. **12**(5), 691–709 (2010)
39. Hevner, A.R.: A three cycle view of design science research a three cycle view of design science research. Scand. J. Inf. Syst. **19**(2), 87–92 (2007)
40. Hevner, A.R., March, S.T., Park, J.: Design science in information systems research. MIS Q. **28**(1), 75–105 (2004)
41. Mayer, I., Bekebrede, G., Harteveld, C., Warmelink, H., Zhou, Q., Van Ruijven, T., Lo, J., Kortmann, R., Wenzler, I.: The research and evaluation of serious games: toward a comprehensive methodology. Br. J. Educ. Technol. **45**(3), 502–527 (2014)
42. Rankin, Y.A., McNeal, M., Shute, M.W., Gooch, B.: User centered game design: evaluating massive multiplayer online role playing games for second language acquisition. In: Proceedings of the 2008 ACM SIGGRAPH Symposium on Video Games, pp. 43–49 (2008)
43. Khaled, R., Vasalou, A.: Bridging serious games and participatory design. Int. J. Child-Computer Interact. **2**(2), 93–100 (2014)
44. Mitgutsch, K., Alvarado, N.: Purposeful by design: a serious game design assessment framework. In: Proceedings of the International Conference on the Foundations of Digital Games, FDG 2012, pp. 121–128 (2012)
45. Fullerton, T.: Game Design Workshop - A Playcentric Approach to Creating Innovative Games, 3rd edn. CRC Press, Boca Raton (2014)
46. Sigman, T.: The siren song of the paper cutter: tips and tricks from the trenches of paper prototyping. Gamasutra (2005). http://www.gamasutra.com/view/feature/130814/the_siren_song_of_the_paper_.php
47. Church, D.: Formal abstract design tools. Gamasutra (1999). http://www.gamasutra.com/view/feature/131764/formal_abstract_design_tools.php
48. Costikyan, G.:I have no words but I must design: toward a critical vocabulary for games. In: Computer Games and Digital Cultures Conference, pp. 9–33 (2002)
49. Koster, R.: A grammar of gameplay. In: Game Developers Conference (2005). http://www.theoryoffun.com/grammar/gdc2005.htm
50. Björk, S., Holopainen, J.: Patterns in Game Design. Charles River Media, Boston (2005)
51. Dormans, J.: Engineering Emergence - Applied Theory for Game Design. University of Amsterdam (2012)
52. Rooney, P.: A theoretical framework for serious game design: exploring pedagogy, play and fidelity and their implications for design process. Int. J. Game Based Learn. **2**(4), 41–60 (2012)
53. Degens, N., Bril, I., Braad, E.: A three-dimensional model for educational game analysis and Design. In: Foundations of Digital Games (2015)
54. Wagner, M.G., Wernbacher, T.: Iterative didactic design of serious games. In: 1st International Workshop on Intelligent Digital Games for Empowerment and Inclusion (2013)
55. Barton, M., Symborski, C., Quinn, M., Morewedge, C.K., Kassam, K.S., Korris, J.H.: The use of theory in designing a serious game for the reduction of cognitive biases. In: DiGRA 2015: Diversity of Play (2015)

56. Marchiori, E.J., Serrano, Á., Del Blanco, Á., Martinez-Ortiz, I., Fernández-Manjón, B.: Integrating domain experts in educational game authoring: a case study. In: Proceedings 2012 4th IEEE International Conference on Digital Game and Intelligent Toy Enhanced Learning, DIGITEL 2012, pp. 72–76 (2012)

57. Ryan, W., Charsky, D.: Integrating serious content into serious games. In: Foundations of Digital Games (2013)

58. Nacke, L.E., Drachen, A., Kuikkaniemi, K., Niesenhaus, J., Korhonen, H., Van den Hoogen, W.M., Poels, K., IJsselsteijn, W.A., De Kort, Y.A.W.: Playability and player experience research. In: Proceedings of the IEEE BT - Breaking New Ground: Innovation in Game, pp. 1–11 (2009)

59. Kelly, H., Howell, K., Glinert, E., Holding, L., Swain, C., Burrowbridge, A., Roper, M.: How to build serious games. Commun. ACM **50**, 44 (2007)

60. Braad, E.P., Folkerts, J., Jonker, N.: Attributing design decisions in the evaluation of game-based health interventions. In: Proceedings of the 3rd European Conference on Gaming and Playful Interaction in Health Care, pp. 61–74 (2013)

61. Adams, M.A., Marshall, S.J., Dillon, L., Caparosa, S., Ramirez, E., Phillips, J., Norman, G.J.: A theory-based framework for evaluating exergames as persuasive technology. In: Proceedings of the 4th International Conference on Persuasive Technology - Persuasive 2009, p. 1 (2009)

62. Bellotti, F., Kapralos, B., Lee, K., Moreno-Ger, P., Berta, R.: Assessment in and of serious games: an overview. Adv. Hum. Comput. Interact. **2013**(1), 11 (2013)

63. Drachen, A., Göbel, S.: Methods for evaluating gameplay experience in a serious gaming context. Int. J. Comput. Sci. Sport **9**, 1–12 (2010)

64. IJsselsteijn, W., De Kort, Y., Poels, K., Jurgelionis, A., Bellotti, F.: Characterising and measuring user experiences in digital games. In: International Conference on Advances in Computer Entertainment Technology, vol. 620, pp. 1–4 (2007)

65. Gerling, K.M., Schulte, F.P., Masuch, M.: Designing and evaluating digital games for frail elderly persons. In: Proceedings of the 8th International Conference on Advances in Computer Entertainment Technology - ACE 2011, p. 1 (2011)

66. De Grove, F., Van Looy, J., Courtois, C.: Towards a serious game experience model: validation, extension and adaptation of the GEQ for use in an educational context. Play. Play. Exp. **10**, 47–61 (2010)

67. Eagle, M., Barnes, T.: Experimental evaluation of an educational game for improved learning in introductory computing. In: Proceedings of the 40th ACM Technical Symposium on Computer Science Education - SIGCSE 2009, p. 321 (2009)

68. Serrano, Á., Marchiori, E.J., Del Blanco, Á., Torrente, J., Fernández-Manjón, B.: A framework to improve evaluation in educational games. In: IEEE Global Engineering Education Conference, EDUCON (2012)

69. Serrano-Laguna, Á., Torrente, J., Moreno-Ger, P., Manjón, B.F.: Tracing a little for big improvements: application of learning analytics and videogames for student assessment. Procedia Comput. Sci. **15**, 203–209 (2012)

70. Kirkley, S.E., Tomblin, S., Kirkley, J.: Instructional design authoring support for the development of serious games and mixed reality training instructional design authoring support for the development of serious games and mixed reality training. In: Interservice/Industry Training, Simulation and Education Conference (I/ITSEC), pp. 1–11 (2005)

71. Kirkley, J., Kirkley, S.E., Heneghan, J.: Building bridges between serious game design and instructional design. In: Shelton, B.E., Wiley, D.A. (eds.) The Design and Use of Simulation Computer Games in Education, pp. 59–82. Sense Publishers, Rotterdam (2007)

72. Moser, R.B.: A Methodology for the Design of Educational Computer Adventure Games (2000)
73. Chen, S., Pan, Z., Zhang, M., Shen, H.: A case study of user immersion-based systematic design for serious heritage games. Multimed. Tools Appl. **62**(3), 633–658 (2013)
74. De Freitas, S., Jarvis, S.: Towards a development approach to serious games. In: Games-Based Learning Advancements for Multi-Sensory Human Computer Interfaces: Techniques and Effective Practices, pp. 215–231 (2009)
75. Malone, T.W.: What Makes Things Fun to Learn? A Study of Intrinsically Motivating Computer Games (1980)
76. Malone, T.W.: Toward a theory of intrinsically motivating instruction. Cogn. Sci. Multidiscip. J. **5**, 333–369 (1981)
77. Deci, E.L., Ryan, R.M.: The 'what' and 'why' of goal pursuits: Human needs and the self-termination of behavior. Psychol. Inq. **11**, 227–268 (2000)
78. Ryan, R.M., Rigby, C.S., Przybylski, A.: The motivational pull of video games: a self-determination theory approach. Motiv. Emot. **30**, 347–363 (2006)
79. Przybylski, A.K., Rigby, C.S., Ryan, R.M.: A motivational model of video game engagement. Rev. Gen. Psychol. **14**(2), 154–166 (2010)
80. Garris, R., Ahlers, R., Driskell, J.E.: Games, motivation, and learning: a research and practice model. Simul. Gaming **33**(4), 441–467 (2002)
81. Gunter, G., Kenny, R.F., Vick, E.H.: A case for a formal design paradigm for serious games. J. Int. Digit. Media Arts Assoc. **3**(2004), 1–19 (2006)
82. Keller, J.M., Kopp, T.W.: Application of the ARCS model to motivational design. In: Reigeluth, C.M. (ed.) Instructional Theories in Action: Lessons Illustrating Selected Theories, pp. 289–320. Larence Erlbaum, New York (1987)
83. Gagne, R.: Domains of Learning (1971)
84. Gunter, G., Kenny, R.F., Vick, E.H.: Taking educational games seriously: Using the RETAIN model to design endogenous fantasy into standalone educational games. Educ. Technol. Res. Dev. **56**, 511–537 (2008)
85. Paras, B. Bizzochi, J.: Game, motivation, and effective learning: an integrated model for educational game design (2005)
86. Kiili, K.: Digital game-based learning: towards an experiential gaming model. Internet High. Educ. **8**, 13–24 (2005)
87. Kolb, D.: Experiential Learning: Experience as the Source of Learning and Development. Prentice-Hall, New Jersey (1984)
88. Amory, A.: Game object model version II: a theoretical framework for educational game development. Educ. Technol. Res. Dev. **55**(1), 51–77 (2007)
89. Arnab, S., Lim, T., Carvalho, M.B., Bellotti, F., de Freitas, S., Louchart, S., Suttie, N., Berta, R., De Gloria, A.: Mapping learning and game mechanics for serious games analysis. Br. J. Educ. Technol **46**, 391–411 (2014)
90. Bedwell, W.L., Pavlas, D., Heyne, K., Lazzara, E.H., Salas, E.: Toward a taxonomy linking game attributes to learning: an empirical study. Simul. Gaming **43**(6), 729–760 (2012)
91. Boyan, A., Sherry, J.L.: The challenge in creating games for education: aligning mental models with game models. Child. Dev. Perspect. **5**(2), 82–87 (2011)
92. Habgood, M.P.J., Ainsworth, S.E.: Motivating children to learn effectively: exploring the value of intrinsic integration in educational games. J. Learn. Sci. **20**(2), 169–206 (2011)
93. Carvalho, M.B., Bellotti, F., Berta, R., De Gloria, A., Sedano, C.I., Hauge, J.B., Hu, J., Rauterberg, M.: An activity theory-based model for serious games analysis and conceptual design. Comput. Educ. **87**, 166–181 (2015)

94. de Freitas, S., Oliver, M.: How can exploratory learning with games and simulations within the curriculum be most effectively evaluated? Comput. Educ. **46**, 249–264 (2006)

95. De Freitas, S., Van Staalduinen, J.-P.: A game based learning framework linking game design and learning outcomes. In: Learning to Play: Exploring the Future of Education with Video Games, pp. 1–37 (2009)

96. Shelton, B.E., Wiley, D.A.: The Design and Use of Simulation Computer Games in Education, vol. 21(2) (2007)

97. Marne, B., Wisdom, J., Huynh-Kim-Bang, B., Labat, J.-M.: The six facets of serious game design: a methodology enhanced by our design pattern library. In: Ravenscroft, A., Lindstaedt, S., Kloos, C.D., Hernández-Leo, D. (eds.) EC-TEL 2012. LNCS, vol. 7563, pp. 208–221. Springer, Heidelberg (2012)

98. Wouters, P., van Nimwegen, C., van Oostendorp, H., van der Spek, E.D.: A meta-analysis of the cognitive and motivational effects of serious games. J. Educ. Psychol. **105**, 249–265 (2013)

99. Almeida, M.S.O., da Silva, F.S.C.: A systematic review of game design methods and tools. In: Anacleto, J.C., Clua, E.W., da Silva, F.S., Fels, S., Yang, H.S. (eds.) ICEC 2013. LNCS, vol. 8215, pp. 17–29. Springer, Heidelberg (2013)

100. Neil, K.: Game design tools: time to evaluate. In: Proceedings of 2012 DiGRA Nordic (2012)

101. Huynh-Kim-Bang, B., Wisdom, J., Labat, J.-M.: Design Patterns in Serious Games: A Blue Print for Combining Fun and Learning Introduction (2010)

102. Dormann, C., Whitson, J.R., Neuvians, M.: Once more with feeling: game design patterns for learning in the affective domain. Games Cult. **8**, 215–237 (2013)

103. Alexander, C., Ishikawa, S., Silverstein, M.: A Pattern Language: Towns, Buildings, Construction. Structure, vol. 2 (1977)

104. Gamma, E., Helm, R., Johnson, R., Vlissides, J.: Design patterns: abstraction and reuse of object-oriented design. Games Cult. **8**(4), 215–237 (2013)

105. Kreimeier, B., Holopainen, J., Björk, S.: Game design patterns. In: Lecture Notes from GDC 2003 (2003)

106. Kreimeier, B.: The case for game design patterns. Gamasutra (2003)

107. Björk, S., Lundgren, S., Holopainen, J.: Game design patterns. In: Proceedings of Level Up-1st International Digital Games Research Conference, pp. 180–193 (2003)

108. Kelle, S.: Game Design Patterns for Learning (2012)

109. Cheng, J., Putnam, C., Rusch, D.C.: Towards efficacy-centered game design patterns for brain injury rehabilitation: a data-driven approach. In: Proceedings of the 17th International ACM SIGACCESS Conference on Computers and Accessibility, pp. 291–299 (2015)

110. Reuter, C., Wendel, V., Göbel, S., Steinmetz, R.: Game design patterns for collaborative player interactions. In: DiGRA 2014 (2014)

111. Žavcer, G., Mayr, S., Petta, P.: Design pattern canvas: towards co-creation of unified serious game design patterns. In: VS-Games 2014: 6th International Conference on Games and Virtual Worlds for Serious Applications, pp. 134–136 (2014)

112. Wetzel, R.: A case for design patterns supporting the development for collaborative player interactions. In: Foundations of Digital Games (2013)

113. Dahlskog, S., Togelius, J., Björk, S.: Patterns, dungeons and generators. In: Proceedings of the 10th Conference on the Foundations of Digital Games (2015)

114. Mader, S., Natkin, S., Levieux, G.: How to analyse therapeutic games: the player/ game/ therapy model. In: Herrlich, M., Malaka, R., Masuch, M. (eds.) ICEC 2012. LNCS, vol. 7522, pp. 193–206. Springer, Heidelberg (2012)

115. Holmes, E.A., James, E.L., Coode-Bate, T., Deeprose, C.: Can playing the computer game 'Tetris' reduce the build-up of flashbacks for trauma? A proposal from cognitive science. PLoS ONE **4**(1), 41–53 (2009)
116. Osterwalder, A., Pigneur, Y.: Business Model Generation: A Handbook for Visionaries, Game Changers, and Challengers. Wiley, Hoboken (2010)

Taxonomy of Game Development Approaches

Mohamed Abbadi[✉]

Ca'Foscari University, Venice, Italy
mohamed.abbadi@unive.it

Abstract. While it might seem desirable to "program" games "close to a high-level specification", the pragmatic reality has not, until very recently, allowed this. In this chapter we discuss the fundamental aspects that define a game and show how these aspects are captured by means of the so-called game development tools. In particular, we show: (i) how the various historical tools have always been intrinsically inspired by the dominant programming languages/paradigms that were the most popular at the time when the tool was developed; and (ii) we discuss these tools by comparing their pro and cons (typically imposed by the chosen language/paradigm or the available hardware) in order to understand the most important requirements for their next generations.

Keywords: Serious games · Game engine · Game development · Languages

1 Introduction

In the following chapter we discuss what a game is (from a formalized perspective) and its fundamental aspects. We begin with a formal mathematical introduction to what a game is and how its state changes according to the flow of time, and provide an example of a game structure (Sect. 2). We then discuss the issues arising from implementing such formalizations as a computer program. We present incremental solutions to these issues by relating each of these solutions to a specific period of historical evolution in computer and programming languages (Sect. 3). Through the whole chapter we will use a simple running example, a moving particle, to show how aspects of a game would be programmed with the different game development tools that we study. The goal of such examples is to show the difficulties arising from expressing high-level concepts into game code, and the evolution of such game development tools. Only recently (Sect. 3.6) we are starting to have game code that is close to the high-level mathematical description discussed in Sect. 2.

2 What Is a Game?

A game is any voluntary activity where people interact in order to achieve some goals within some constraints (described as *game rules*). Players come with

© Springer International Publishing AG 2016
R. Dörner et al. (Eds.): Entertainment Computing and Serious Games, LNCS 9970, pp. 119–147, 2016.
DOI: 10.1007/978-3-319-46152-6_6

different expectations, which might be provided externally, for example by an instructor, or are self-motivated, like achieving entertainment [3]. The purpose of a game is now to provide tools for the players that allow them to capture their challenging expectations.

2.1 Video Game

Within the panorama of games we find *video games*. A video game is a specialized kind of game where the interaction is carried out by means of electronic devices. Precisely, a video game, from now on a *game*, is a *computer program* that indefinitely interacts with hardware components to carry out the game logic. The game automates the game rules mentioned above, therefore enforcing the structure of the experience [15]. Moreover, the program also handles rendering, user input, the flow of time (frame rate dependent or independent), etc. by providing a real-time experience that helps users to experience a "virtual reality" feeling [39].

2.2 Formal Definition of a Video Game

In order to implement a game, we need a precisely and formally detailed definition of its rules. Without such a definition we will not be able to "explain" to the machine what it is supposed to do. Therefore, in what follows we now give a "pure" mathematical definition of a game that is technology independent and helps us to focus on the game definition only.

A game is made up of objects (each represented by a series of numbers), which we call *state*. In this formalization we can see a state $w(t)$ as a vector of all numbers C_i^t that describe the game at some time t.

$$w(t) = C_1^t, C_2^t, \ldots, C_N^t \tag{1}$$

The dynamics of the game define how the state changes over time. We can represent the evolution of the state by an integrator that approximates each component of the state at all times of a game[1]:

$$w(T) = \int_{t=0}^{t=T} \frac{\mathrm{d}w(t)}{\mathrm{d}t} dt \tag{2}$$

The integrator above computes the value for all components of the state. In what follows we see a *trivial* application of the above integrator to find the position of a particle over time.

Example. Consider a state $w(t)$ made up of a particle with velocity $v(t)$ and position $p(t)$:

$$w(t) = (p(t), v(t)) \tag{3}$$

---

[1] Components of the state might behave as discrete functions, for example a number that changes according to a timer. To treat such dynamics we treat their functions as *piecewise functions*.

According to (2), for this example computing the value of $w(t)$ requires first to solve the differential equation:

$$\frac{dw_t}{dt} = \left(\frac{dp_t}{dt}, \frac{dv_t}{dt} \right) \tag{4}$$

In this example, the velocity is defined as the rate of change of position with respect to time, and acceleration is defined as the rate of change of velocity with respect to time according to Earth gravity:

$$\frac{dp_t}{dt} = v(t) \qquad \frac{dv_t}{dt} = (0, -9.81, 0) \tag{5}$$

According to (5) at any time t, in this example, integrating the velocity $v(t)$ gives the position at time t, whereas integrating the gravitational acceleration returns the velocity at time t.

It might seem, at a first glance, from this example that solving the integral for each component of the state in isolation is sufficient to determine the value of the state. Unfortunately, this is typically not true. Typically games come with more complex dynamics: in a game, the value of an object (the position for example) could be the result of combining different values of the state (imagine if we applied friction, or of the particle collides with other objects of the world). Therefore, in most of cases, since components of the state are tightly related to each other (with respect to time) the derivative of each component of the state depends on many elements of the state. For these cases, the function to integrate is too complex and requires numerical methods to determine its values over time. In the following we discuss this issue and discuss the solution used for games.

2.2.1 Numerical Vs. Analytic Solutions

The fact that we are able to model the evolution of the state by means of a function does not mean that finding an exact solution is possible or simple. This happens because the functions to integrate for the game will usually be too complex to allow analytical solutions: analytical solutions work only for simple models [35]. When the game becomes complex (imagine a city simulator, or a driving simulator with lots of physics) or the model is influenced by the user input, then it is (in general) not possible to identify a closed form solution [17].

We need to use numerical methods for solving game model equations such as the Euler method [5] (which is meant for solving systems of differential equations), where the initial values are the initial state and the update describes the changes of the state over a short amount of time.

We can use Euler to find the solution for the evolution of our particle. Consider again (5):

$$\frac{d\mathbf{p}(t)}{dt} = \lim_{dt \to 0} \frac{\mathbf{p}(t + dt) - \mathbf{p}(t)}{dt} = \mathbf{v}(t)$$

$$\frac{d\mathbf{v}(t)}{dt} = \lim_{dt \to 0} \frac{\mathbf{v}(t + dt) - \mathbf{v}(t)}{dt} = (0, -9.81, 0) \tag{6}$$

By applying the Euler's method to approximate the two limits in (6) we obtain the following:

$$\mathbf{p}(t + \Delta t) = \mathbf{p}(t) + \mathbf{v}(t) * \Delta t \qquad \mathbf{v}(t + \Delta t) = \mathbf{v}(t) + \mathbf{a}(t) * \Delta t \qquad (7)$$

At this point, by taking many steps with small Δt (and an initial given value for time $t = 0$) for every component of the *State*, we achieved an approximated solution for the original integral shown in (2).

Of course this is an approximation. If we need higher precision methods then we could use better approximation methods such as those in the Runge-Kutta family [10].

2.2.2 Implementable Formal Specification

We now provide an algorithm that can effectively compute the state at any time t, given an initial state s_0.

With Euler we managed to describe how the dynamics of a game determine the evolution of the state for a very small amount of time. Unfortunately, if we try to increase by a larger time interval, then Euler alone is not enough[2] [36]. Ideally, we wish to apply Euler, starting from an initial state, enough times until we reach a cumulative approximation of the state for the desired time.

For example, if we need the state for a time T, starting from an initial given state s, we apply once Euler to s for a small step dt and use the resulting approximation of the evolved state for all successive applications of Euler. We keep repeating this operation until the amount of steps is enough to "cover" the whole desired time T.

We observe from the above example that Euler is used **at most once** per step. This is important for us, since we can now define a function *loop* that, given a state s_0 and an amount of time t, returns:

- s_0 in case t is less or equals to zero;
- the application of a new state (obtained by evolving s_0 for a very small amount of time dt according to an Euler step) and an a decreased t (from which we remove exactly dt, the amount of time consumed by the Euler step) to a function ϕ. ϕ a high order function that unfolds a step of *loop*, by applying an Euler step once.

$$loop_\phi(s, t) = \begin{cases} s, & \text{if } t \leq 0 \\ \phi(euler\_step(s, dt), t - dt), & \text{otherwise} \end{cases} \qquad (8)$$

Of course, the above definition does not specify what happens after the single step of Euler: the ϕ function. To achieve the desired result, we need ϕ to continue with the very same process described by `loop` itself. This process, known as recursion, can be explicated by taking the *fixpoint* of the `loop` function [6]. The

---

[2] Euler is a numerical approximation, small steps made of small amounts of time are necessary so to avoid to end into a wrong state.

fixpoint operator will care to reapply `loop` to itself so that calling ϕ effectively calls `loop` again:

$$fix\ loop = loop_{(fix\ loop)} \tag{9}$$

In the following, we show how the above formalism has been captured since the beginning of the game development "era".

3   Game Development

In Sect. 2.1 we showed a symbolic representation of the dynamics of a moving particle and an equivalent numerical interpretation. Both descriptions are valid, although they differ in precision. The advantage of using the numerical approach is that we can implement it into a computer. Research in game development in the past decades was focused on finding suitable high-level interpretations for numerical solutions that work for all those "non-functional" pragmatic requirements such as real-time performance, networking, etc. [23]. All these non-functional requirements add yet an additional challenge to research.

3.1   Evolution

While, of course, it might seem desirable to "program" games "close to the high-level specification", the pragmatic reality has not, until very recently, allowed this.

3.1.1   Expression Tools

Expression tools used to build actual games can be seen, in the substance, as ways to encode abstractions. The various historical tools have always been intrinsically linked with the dominant programming languages and paradigms that were the most popular at the time of the expression tool in question. Each tool, with its language (and therefore paradigm [44]), imposed a set of limitations that ultimately were lifted by the next generation tools [30].

This progression has clearly marched towards finally being able to write code against the mathematical specification and further away from hardware considerations.

3.1.2   Programming Paradigms

Historically, as hardware has become more and more powerful, programing paradigms less focused on hardware details have become usable in the practice of game development [33]. Among the possible paradigms used for making games we find: functional, declarative, object-oriented (OO), and procedural [16,22,29,32]. By choosing a specific programming paradigm, game developers have to decide in advance how to design the architecture of the implementation for their games. These designs are shaped by the features offered by the chosen paradigm(s).

For example procedural programming is "performance-oriented", OO programming is by some considered to be cognitively closer to the way humans perceive the real-world, declarative programming is meant for querying sets of facts and rules, functional programming treats "all" computations as mathematical functions. Of course, every paradigm comes with disadvantages, which should be known in advance. For example procedural programming is not suitable for designing very complex architectures with clear separation of concerns, OO programming tends to add lots of overhead to the CPU, declarative programming is confined only on query operations, and functional programming programs are typically more complex to use, thus require a bit more of planning before writing the actual implementations.

3.1.3   Game Making Systems

Nowadays, we often see systems for making games that not only support programming paradigms for dealing with the game specification, but also providing sophisticated editors for building game content, kinematics, etc. [7,13,24,25]. A chronological evolution of these systems for making games (inspired by [19]) is roughly reported in Table 1.

The fact that an item in the table is listed in an older location does not mean that its philosophy is not used anymore. All the categories of tools and systems presented in Table 1 are still to some extent used nowadays, with a tendency to use elements from older layers embedded into frameworks made according to the newest layer considerations. It is also worthy of notice that for many systems

Table 1. Game development tools evolution

Period	Design philosophy	Languages	Paradigms
1950s	Hand made everything	Assembly, C	Procedural
1980s	Construction sets (no programming knowledge). User-derived, drag-and-drop visual interface engineered for the rapid prototyping of games	-	Visual
1980s	Graphic APIs. Developer oriented tools that provide a series of domain abstractions to deal with different hardware sharing similar functionalities	HLSL, GLSL, PSSL, etc	Declarative
mid -1990s	Low-level game engines. Developer oriented libraries that provide basic game functionalities in the shape of composable and reusable classes (such as physics, game loop, etc.) used inside developers game code	C/C++, Java, C#, etc	OO
late -1990s	High-level Game engines. Typically in the shape of tools that combine visual interface with actual coding. The visual interface is meant to deal with the common tasks of making games (assigning path finding properties to game entities, placing the game models on the map, defining the characters animations flow, etc.). Code is required to define special algorithms or game structures that are difficult to express with just the visual interface	SGL, LUA, GML, Python, Casanova, etc	Declarative, Functional, OO, Visual

(independent of the level of abstraction) to achieve high performance multiple forms of ad-hoc optimizations have to be done by hand.

In what follows we discuss the elements of Table 1. In particular, for each element we discuss the pros and cons of using it, and show how the particle would be implemented in each them (Sect. 2.1).

3.2 Assembly Language (Hand Made Everything)

Assembly language is the language closest to machine code [9, 11]. As for machine code, programs written in assembly can directly deal with CPU components such as registers. The goal of assembly is to provide developers an abstraction over the binary format of machine code without, at the same time, losing the ability to directly manipulate hardware components such as the CPU or memory. This abstraction is achieved since assembly uses mnemonic operands to implement machine code.

Between the 1950 s and the early 1990 s most of the games were written in assembly code. The reason was that most of games used to run on consoles, which used to come with limited hardware resources in terms of storage and computational power. Because of these limitations assembly language used to be the most suitable tool. Assembly instructions are limited in terms of CPU overhead and can produce high speed programs that work with limited storage space. Later, as hardware became more sophisticated and powerful, games started to feature higher level code such as C, confining assembly to the graphics and most performance sensitive code. For example, in Commander Keen the logic is written in C whereas code for drawing is written in assembly; in the following link you can find the code for Commander Keen: https://github.com/keendreams/keen.

Successful Examples. Among the games written in assembly we find all those written for the Atari 2600, Apple II, Commodore 64, Atari 800, SEGA Genesis, the SNES, etc. Many of the arcade systems from the 1970 s until the early 1990s (for example Definitive Combat) were also written in assembly. In Fig. 1 we can see some screenshots of games written in assembly.

Nowadays, assembly is almost never used anymore, since dealing with the low-level hardware components of the computer is achieved by means of standardized libraries. However, we occasionally find some traces of assembly code in libraries (although this is getting less and less common) from a few modern game engines.

Particle Example - Assembly. We now show how the "particle" example presented in Sect. 2.1 could be have been written in assembly[3]. Specifically, since the assembly code necessary to express the dynamics of our particle is not large, due to the intrinsic verbosity of the language, in the following we only present code for the position and velocity update.

---

[3] For this example we use the syntax of x86 assembly. The x86 assembly language differs from other assemblies, like MIPS assembly for example, and is meant for the class class of x86 processors.

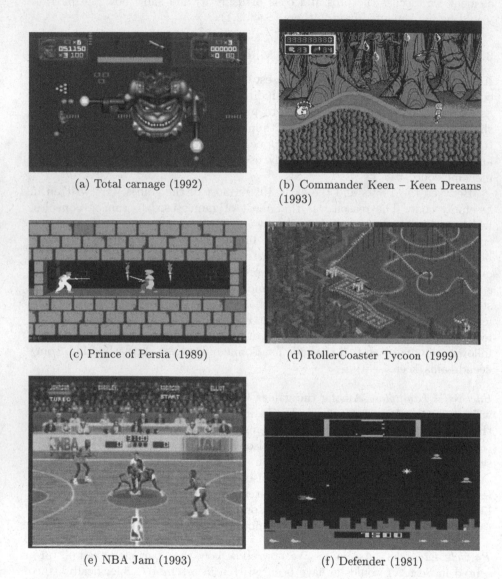

(a) Total carnage (1992)

(b) Commander Keen – Keen Dreams (1993)

(c) Prince of Persia (1989)

(d) RollerCoaster Tycoon (1999)

(e) NBA Jam (1993)

(f) Defender (1981)

Fig. 1. Some assembly games

Listing 1.1: Particle velocity and position update in the Assembly lanugage

```
; 24    :       p = p + v * dt;
lea       eax, DWORD PTR _dt$[ebp]
push      eax
lea       ecx, DWORD PTR $T5[ebp]
push      ecx
lea       ecx, DWORD PTR _v$[ebp]
call      Vector2_times               ; Vector2::operator*
push      eax
lea       edx, DWORD PTR $T4[ebp]
push      edx
lea       ecx, DWORD PTR _p$[ebp]
call      Vector2_plus                ; Vector2::operator+
mov       ecx, DWORD PTR [eax]
mov       edx, DWORD PTR [eax+4]
mov       DWORD PTR _p$[ebp], ecx
mov       DWORD PTR _p$[ebp+4], edx

; 25    :       v = v + Vector2(0, -9.81f) * dt;
lea       eax, DWORD PTR _dt$[ebp]
push      eax
lea       ecx, DWORD PTR $T2[ebp]
push      ecx
push      ecx
movss     xmm0, DWORD PTR __real@c11cf5c3
movss     DWORD PTR [esp], xmm0
push      ecx
movss     xmm0, DWORD PTR __real@00000000
movss     DWORD PTR [esp], xmm0
lea       ecx, DWORD PTR $T3[ebp]
call      Vector2                     ; Vector2::Vector2
mov       ecx, eax
call      Vector2_times              ; Vector2::operator*
push      eax
lea       edx, DWORD PTR $T1[ebp]
push      edx
lea       ecx, DWORD PTR _v$[ebp]
call      Vector2_plus               ; Vector2::operator+
mov       ecx, DWORD PTR [eax]
mov       edx, DWORD PTR [eax+4]
mov       DWORD PTR _v$[ebp], ecx
mov       DWORD PTR _v$[ebp+4], edx
```

Advantages. The main feature of assembly is the ability to provide machine instructions to exactly specify all that the hardware must do, in extreme detail. The *absolute control* over hardware allows developers to write very high performance code. This performance was crucial in games, especially, when consoles featured limited amounts of computational resources.

Disadvantages. As we can see from the code listed above is very verbose even to express a very simple operation such as updating the position of the particle. This is due to the fact that assembly does not provide effective abstractions for expressing high-level behaviors. By using assembly, developers are left the only choice of using low-level constructs that are tightly related to the underneath hardware.

This limited choice pushes developers towards developing code that requires a lot of effort to be coded, as developers have to specify every single behavior of the underneath hardware, including dealing with CPU registers or other hardware components. As a result of this, the chances of making mistakes are significant. Portability is also limited, since the choice of the assembly version is derived by the chosen hardware and different assembly versions come with different instruction sets.

Moreover, as CPU's become more powerful, bigger games and more complex low-level assembly instruction sets have slowly made it impossible to contain development costs without moving to more advanced tools.

3.3   Multimedia API

A multimedia API (Application Programming Interface), such as OpenGL [37] or DirectX [28], is a set of routines, protocols, and tools. These API's were introduced in the early'90s for handling multimedia tasks (such as GUI, input, etc.) standardized across a variety of hardware platforms. Through appropriate abstractions, developers could access the hardware of the computer, like the GPU, and make their code portable to different hardware.

3.3.1   Graphics API

A graphics API is the best known example of a multimedia API centered around rendering tasks. The evolution of graphics API's on personal computers followed a very fast evolution curve that started in the'80s. Until the early'80s most of the graphics of games were written by manipulating the VGA (video graphics array) pixel by pixel in assembly or in C. By providing developers an array that represents the pixels of a monitor, developers could plot the desired colors into specific pixels (writing into that memory area would also write to the screen). Further evolutions allowed developers not only to deal with single pixels on the screen but also to draw textures, introducing the concept of 2.5D games, which featured 3D worlds rendered with no (or very limited) graphical hardware support. Among these software rendered 2.5D games we find Wolfenstein 3D and Quake (see Fig. 2).

The CPU load of software-rendered games was a known issue. As the necessity of high performance games and advanced 3D graphics started to become widespread among developers, modern GPU's came in to help with graphics

(a) Quake (1996)   (b) Wolfenstein 3D (1992)

Fig. 2. Some software rendered games

acceleration. Thanks to graphics acceleration, developers could finally delegate rendering tasks to the GPU while offloading the CPU. This made it possible to achieve higher performance, since the GPU is designed to process graphics commands in parallel and has dedicated memory. Moreover, this would free the CPU to process game logic such as AI, physics, networking, and other tasks, therefore significantly improving the overall game experience.

Graphics API's for Accelerated Hardware. In the early'90s, because of the increasing complexity of GPU's, a new generation of graphics API's was introduced. The goal of such API's was to abstract the complex hardware of modern accelerated GPU's in favour of a high-level model of its behavior. Such a model would help developers with expressing graphics directives with little effort, and help developers stay focused on the design of graphics effects algorithms rather than having to think constantly about specific hardware details.

Among such API's we find IRISGLP, OpenGl (an improved version of IRIS-GLP), Glide, and DirectX. Nowadays DirectX and OpenGL are the most used graphics API for rendering games contents.

FFP (Fixed Function Pipeline). Abstracting the complex hardware of GPU's became possible due to the introduction of the so-called FFP (fixed function pipeline). Fixed functions are a series of functions that map directly to dedicated drawing logic that can only be used on GPU's designed to support them. By editing a set of hardware switches, developers could customize those functions. However, this customization comes with some expressiveness limitations, since editing the hardware switches allows developers to customize single or small groups of instructions but not the fundamental shape of the underlying algorithms. Moreover, since the hardware switches are shared among several functions, making predictions on the algorithmic behavior of the algorithms became complex and hard: changing just one switch might affect the behavior of the FFP dramatically.

These limitations pushed the community towards the development of better abstraction mechanism that would lift the artificial limitations of the FFP.

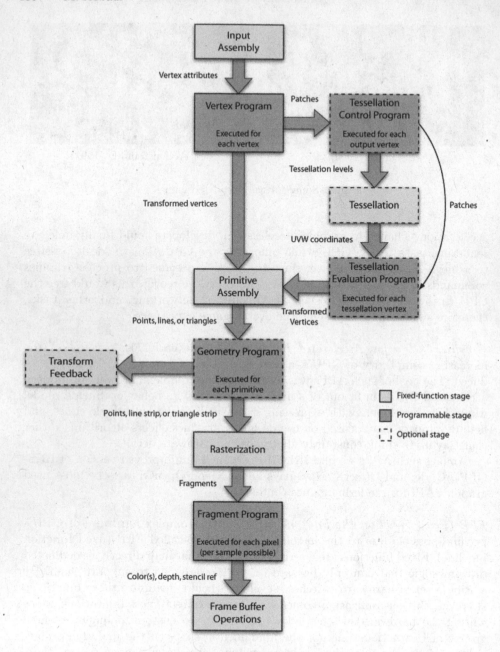

Fig. 3. Graphics pipeline of a modern GPU

Shaders. To overcome the FFP limitations, customizable pipelines were made programmable through the system known as "shaders", or "programmable pipeline". By introducing shaders, which are small programs that are run on the GPU pipline, developers could design their own algorithms and have a clear control over the pipeline process (huge variation space, no "weird" interactions between variables). Figure 3 shows the programmable parts of a modern GPU.

With shaders, a developer could manipulate the pipeline in two different processing stages: vertex processing and pixel processing (Fig. 4). For vertex processing, the developer has the task of designing an algorithm for placing every game element from model space to world space. For pixel processing, the developer has the task of designing an algorithm to draw the game elements that are inside the frustum of the camera to the screen (pixel by pixel). New shader models have more stages that are programmable.

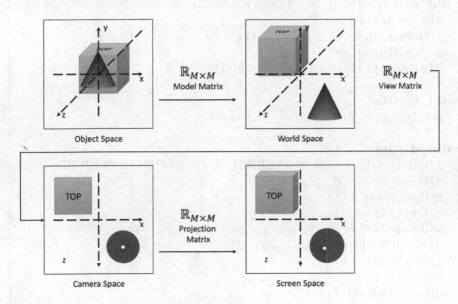

Fig. 4. Drawing stages of modern GPU's

Fixed functions vs Shaders. Fixed functions represent the first attempt to make customizable GPU pipelines by providing developers with a series of functions that can be customized to specific drawing scenarios. Shader systems are programmable instead and allow developers to deal with graphics data (or game geometries) by means of user-defined algorithms that define how those graphics data are transformed and rendered.

Particle Example - FFP/OpenGL/C++. We now show a complete solution to the "particle" example presented in Sect. 2.1 written in C++ and using OpenGL as graphics API with the FFP.

Particle Example - Shader/OpenGL/C++. To benefit from shaders, the previous code requires some adjustments. First we need to define our vertex and fragment shader. In this example we wish to change the color of our particle to green and to make it smaller.

Listing 1.2. Particle written with C++/OpenGL

```cpp
#include<GL/glut.h>
#include"math.h"

Vector2 position = Vector2(0, 0), velocity = Vector2(0,
    ↪ 0.0001);
void glutInitRendering() {
  glEnable(GL_DEPTH_TEST);
}
void reshaped(int w, int h) {
  glViewport(0, 0, w, h);
  glMatrixMode(GL_PROJECTION);
  glLoadIdentity();
  gluPerspective(45, 0, 1, 200);
}
void update() {
  position = position + velocity;
}
void display() {
  glClear(GL_COLOR_BUFFER_BIT | GL_DEPTH_BUFFER_BIT);
  glClearColor(0, 0, 1, 0);
  glPushMatrix();
  glColor3f(0, 1, 1);
  glTranslatef(position.x, position.y, 0);
  glutSolidSphere(0.1, 23, 23);
  glPopMatrix();
  update();
  glutSwapBuffers();
}
int main(int argc, char **argv) {
  glutInit(&argc, argv);
  glutInitDisplayMode(GLUT_DOUBLE | GLUT_RGB |
      ↪ GLUT_DEPTH);
  glutInitWindowSize(400, 500);
  glutCreateWindow("Bouncing_Ball");
  glutInitRendering();
  glutDisplayFunc(display);
  glutIdleFunc(display);
  glutReshapeFunc(reshaped);
  glutMainLoop();
}
```

– The following vertex shader scales all vertices in x and y direction.

Listing 1.3. A simple vertex shader

```
void main(void)
{
  vec4 a = gl_Vertex;
  a.x = a.x * 0.5;
  a.y = a.y * 0.5;
  gl_Position = gl_ModelViewProjectionMatrix * a;
}
```

– The following fragment shader sets to green the color of all pixels corresponding to the particle on the screen.

Listing 1.4. A simple fragment shader

```
void main (void)
{
  gl_FragColor = vec4(0.0, 1.0, 0.0, 1.0);
}
```

Once the shaders are defined, we need to load them into a shader object within the glutInitRendering function.

Listing 1.5. Loading the shaders

```
void glutInitRendering() {
  glEnable(GL_DEPTH_TEST);
  //SM is properly initialized variable of type
     ↪ glShaderManager
  shader = SM.loadfromFile("vertexshader.vs", "
     ↪ fragmentshader.ps");
}
```

To use the shader object, we need (inside the display function) to call in order the methods "begin" and "end" of the shader object and to put the actual drawing calls within these two calls.

Listing 1.6. Calling the shader

```
void display() {
  glClear(GL_COLOR_BUFFER_BIT | GL_DEPTH_BUFFER_BIT);
  glPushMatrix();
  glTranslatef(position.x, position.y, 0);

  shader->begin();
```

```
glutSolidSphere(1.0,32,32);
shader->end();

glPopMatrix();
update();
glutSwapBuffers();
}
```

Advantages. API's set a new stage in game development, by providing developers an easier abstraction experience compared to coding everything in assembly. By means of a shader, for example, customizing the behavior of the GPU becomes more accessible. Moreover, hardware considerations are, to some extent, hidden to developers. Indeed, developers are not required to master memory, CPU vector instructions, etc. to achieve high performance (every operation in a shader maps to complex hardware instructions).

Disadvantages. API's provide generic abstractions for game development that add a level of complexity to the task of making games. A developer, in order to make a game is now also tasked with understanding and mastering the chosen API, which for many cases comes with its own domain specific languages for various internal tasks. Moreover, in many cases, developers are also asked to learn and master other domains to effectively use the selected API, thus adding yet another layer of complexity. For example, when dealing with shaders, math is important in order to apply any form of visual effects, from basic linear algebra in vertex transformations to approximation of complex integrals for lighting computations.

These layers of complexity make the learning curve of such API's steep, further affecting the costs of game development.

3.4   Game Creation Systems

A game creation system [14] is an expression tool designed around the domain of video games. The goal of a game creation system is to make game development accessible also to developers with no (or little) knowledge of computer programming, by simply allowing them to click over buttons of a visual interface to define the entities of a game and their behaviors [12].

Game creation systems started to show off in the early'80s, when consoles and desktop stations started to become widespread, and was an exploratory parenthesis ahead of its time driven by the excessive low-level of alternative systems. ConstructionSet-Pinball, Garry Kitchen's GameMaker, and Adventure Construction Set (see Fig. 5) are examples of such systems.

Typically, a game creation system focuses on a single genre of games plus a restricted few *similar* sub genres. This is due to the fact that different genres share little logic. Therefore, expressing different game genres by means of just a

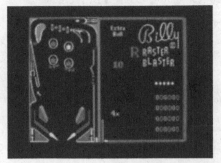

(a) ConstructionSet: Pinball (1983)

(b) Shoot-'Em-Up Construction Kit (1987)

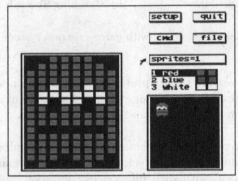

(c) Garry Kitchen's GameMaker (1985)

Fig. 5. Some game creation systems

visual interface (without the support of any programmable system) is difficult, if not impossible.

For adventure games we find: the inform language (1996), a text adventure language; Adventure Game Toolkit (1987), a program for adventure games development; RPG Maker (1995) and The Bard's Tale Construction Set (1991), softwares for creating role-playing-games; The 3D Gamemaker (2001), a software that allows users to make 3D FPS's and adventure games; Game-Maker (1991) and Indie game maker (2014), general purpose software tools for game development. These tools are mainly used by small groups of developers, sometimes even by single developers.

In Fig. 6 games made with some creation systems are presented. Nowadays game creation systems are used less when compared to the past. Among the most active creation systems we find RPG Maker and Indie Game Maker editor.

Advantages. By targeting specific game genres, game creation systems can provide a domain interface that allows developers to effectively build a game with no knowledge of computer programming. The design of such visual interfaces

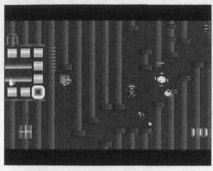

Office

"Chaos treads the halls of Bedlam; her work is evident everywhere..."

Slouching Towards Bedlam
An entry in the 9th Annual Interactive-Fiction Competition
Copyright 2003 by Star C. Foster and Daniel Ravipinto
[First time players should type 'about'. Credits are available via 'credits'.]
Release 1 / Serial number 030925 / Inform v6.21 Library 6/10

Office
A massive cedar desk, well-polished and worn, looks elegantly out-of-place among the chaos. Papers, files, and books cover nearly every flat surface in the room.

There is a phonograph on the table near the window.

A black cube on wheels sits near the door to the south.

(a) Pipemare (Game-Maker)   (b) Slouching Towards Bedlam (Inform 6)

Fig. 6. Games built with game creation systems

is meant to allow developers to fast prototype and test games, therefore reducing costs. Fast game prototyping, reduced game development costs, and domain interfaces are the main signifiant advantages of these tools.

Disadvantages. Different games implementing different genres share little logic (for example, how much can we recycle from a solitary game into a shooter game?). In order to deal with such differences, different tools (each targeting specific genres) with ad-hoc interfaces were developed. Such differences made learning these game creation systems relatively expensive: whenever a developer changes genres he would have had to learn, from the ground up, yet another system. This task is not only time consuming but also is expensive in terms of effort.

The same issues apply to the customization of games made with such tools. As games got more and more sophisticated, the necessity for more powerful and expressive game creation systems piled up. Game creation systems try to tackle the expressiveness limitations of their visual interface, by extending/augmenting game creation system with scripting facilities. Because of the lack of standardization of such scripting facilities and their poor integration in the system (game creation systems are not developed with scripting on mind), experienced developers prefer to choose more powerful and standard tools such as a game engine.

3.5   Game Engines

A game engine [8] is a specific tool designed to abstract the development process of a game and is used to develop games for different platforms such as consoles, desktop PCs, mobile phones, etc.

The goal of game engines is to provide a series of reusable abstractions that can be composed in order to provide an effective extension tool that allows the tackling of a variety of different scenarios. This composition property, coupled with a relatively low number of abstractions available, means that we can now effectively face a variety of problems in game design without having to resort to building everything from the ground up, or use a broad variety of different tools, one per specific scenario.

Moreover, with the raise of 3D games and the increasing computational power of hardware in the'90s, games complexity started to become higher and higher. Games started to implement features such as sophisticated artificial intelligence, complex rendering effects, or networking, to satisfy consumers' need that added yet a further layer of complexity to the task of developing video games. Since these complex features were difficult to implement with traditional tools (due to their limited abstraction capabilities) the necessity for more expressive tools with higher abstraction, and specifically targeted to the domain of games mechanisms, became relevant. For this purpose game engines were developed. Typically, a game engine provides several components, each of which is designed for dealing with specific game development tasks such as physics, levels editing, rendering, sound, AI, networking, localization, input, etc.

Game engines became very popular in the mid-1990s after the ground breaking titles Doom and Quake made their appearance. The success of Doom and Quake was so dramatic that other developers and companies wanted to reuse elements of such games for their titles, so Id Software (and later Epic Games's with the Unreal series) designed successive versions of their game codes with reuse and extensibility in mind: first the game engine is implemented (made of composable and programmable modules) then the game engine is used to implement the game.

Among the most well-knowen game engines we find OGRE, XNA, Blender, Unreal Engine, IdTech, and Source. In Fig. 7 a series of games built with some game engines are shown.

Game engines differ from each other based on the level of details provided to developers to control and customize [4]. We group such engines in the following two categories:

- **Low-level engines** are engines where a series of libraries are provided within some frameworks. These frameworks typically provide developers with basic games abstractions such as the game loop, contents loading facilities, etc. Typically, low-level game engines give the most flexibility and performance, but they are expensive to build and use, since the developer has to maintain, program, and connect each component used in the engine. Customization is possible by means of fully fledged, general purpose programming languages that are used not only to connect the components but also to define the logic of the game. XNA [34], Pygame [43], jMonkeyEngine [26], Löve [2], etc. belong to this group of engines.
- **High-level engines** are sophisticated game engines that come *ready out of the box*. The goal of such engines is to reduce the complexity of developing games by providing already made components that do not need developers to adapt them or connect them, since they are already connected and integrated in the

(a) Star Wars Jedi Knight: Jedi Academy (idTech3)

(b) Quake III Arena (idTech3)

(c) Torchlight II (OGRE)

(d) Magicka (XNA)

(e) Poisonville(jMonkeyEngine)

(f) Half-Life 2 (Source)

Fig. 7. Games built with custom engines

engine. Developers are only tasked to use such components and compose them, typically by means of a GUI, to build their games. Customization in high-level engines is possible, but by means of general purpose languages (GPL's). OGRE [40], Unreal Engine [21], Torque Game Engine [27], id Tech [38], etc. belong to this group of engines.

Particle Example - XNA/C#. We now show a complete solution to the "particle" example presented in Sect. 2.1 written in a low-level game engine. Precisely, we use for this sample XNA as game engine.

Listing 1.7. Particle written in XNA and C#

```
public class Particle
{
  Vector2 particle_position ,
          particle_velocity = Vector2.One * 100;
  Texture2D texture;
  public Particle(Texture2D texture)
    { this.texture = texture; }
  public void Update(float dt)
    { particle_position = particle_position +
                          particle_velocity * dt; }
  public void Draw(SpriteBatch sprite)
    { sprite.Draw(texture, particle_position, Color.
      ↪ White); }

}

public class MyGame : Game {
...
  Particle particle;
  protected override void LoadContent()
  {
    spriteBatch = new SpriteBatch(GraphicsDevice);
    particle = new Particle(Content.Load<Texture2D>("
      ↪ circ.png"));
  }

  protected override void Update(GameTime gameTime)
  {
    //Logic code goes here...
    particle.Update((float)gameTime.ElapsedGameTime.
      ↪ TotalSeconds);
    base.Update(gameTime);
  }
  protected override void Draw(GameTime gameTime)
  {
    //Drawing code goes here...
    GraphicsDevice.Clear(Color.CornflowerBlue);
    spriteBatch.Begin();
    particle.Draw(spriteBatch);
    spriteBatch.End();
    base.Draw(gameTime);
  }
}
```

Advantages. Game engines are a great result of applying software engineering techniques to game development, such as composability and resuability, for the definition of a series of abstractions all meant to reduce costs and to support developers in the definition of games and on a variety of game design problems like defining advanced AI, networking, content, etc.

Disadvantages. Despite their power, engines suffer from severe limitations. These limitations are different depending on the architecture of the engine: low-level and high-level.

Low-level engines lack game-specific facilities to create a game due to the fact that these engines only offer libraries meant for general usage (libraries are unaware of the specific context in which they are going to be used). Building games then requires writing large amounts of complex game specific code, such as a path finder, optimizations, AI, etc. implemented by means of GPL's.

High-level engines provide a large amount of existing components that are a potential fit for many games. Unfortunately, being able to effectively choose and use a high-level engine requires developers to read lots of documentations.

Games that do not fit the standard components implementation can still be implemented, but this requires customizing components. Typically, customizing such components is done by means of GPL's and requires large amount of complex game specific code.

3.6   Domain Specific Languages (Next Stage)

So far, specific problems in games have been tackled with more and more domain specific tools (DST's) such as Unity. The limits of such tools were made less dire with extensibility, usually by means of a general purpose language (GPL). However these GPL's lack the domain specific abstractions of games, leading therefore to highly complex code that is expensive to maintain and develop. Indeed, modern GPL's are particularly weak when dealing with properties typical of the domain of games such as: concurrency over shared resources among game entities, distributed code in networked games, efficient event handling, and time manipulation.

In order to continue our search for better abstractions it makes sense that we now focus on GPL's in order to augment our domain specific tools with domain specific languages (DSL's) [31]. A DSL is a specialized language [18], typically small and very expressive, aimed at solving only problems within the chosen domain through an optimal choice of operators, abstractions, and level of focus. Attention on DSL's has been getting higher and higher, since mapping all the requirements of games with game tools exclusively is difficult and expensive (this difficulty gets even higher when variations in the requirements occur often, requiring to break the careful mixture of GPL code and tool settings found so far). Research in game development is pushing nowadays towards the study of such DSL's in order to provide additional support over different game tools. By means of such DSL's, game tools (and game development in general) would benefit from the following properties:

Agility since DSL's are small and built ad-hoc to react to, and capture variations in, the domain;

Consistency domain concepts such as flow of time, optimization, etc. can be
expressed as first-class constructs in the domain language);

Productivity/Quality different layers of reusable abstractions built around
the domain allow developers to talk only in terms of the essential properties of
the domain, making therefore the resulting clear, readable, and maintainable.

In what follows we present an example of a DSL for games and discuss how
game tools would benefit from it.

3.6.1 Casanova: A Domain Specific Language for Game Development

The Casanova language [1] is an example of a domain specific language. Its goal
is to abstract the logic of games by means of a series of primitives and language
structures designed to capture properties shared among all applications in the
domain of games.

Being within a specific domain makes Casanova capable of expressing properties that are tightly related to the game domain such as time flow, awaits,
optimization, etc. As an immediate result the resulting Casanova code is similar
to how we think of a game from a mathematical perspective, see Sect. 2.1, where
the pure logics description of a game is not fuzzed by unrelated details such as
graphic effects, hardware oriented optimizations, etc.; indeed in Casanova developers are only tasked with designing the logic of the game whereas rendering,
defining the content, etc. must be provided by integration with existing game
tools. In the current release of the language the authors used Unity Editor for
visual editing and scene definition, and Casanova for defining the logic of the
game. Figure 8 shows an example game in Casanova and Unity editor.

The Casanova Model. The Casanova model follows the same philosophy as that
of the mathematical model presented in Sect. 2.1. In that model, a game was
made up of (i) a state, (ii) dynamics, and (iii) a starting point. Similarly, in
Casanova, a game is made up of entities (organized in a tree hierarchy and
where the world is marked as *world*) with (i) a series of fields, (ii) rules, and (iii)
a constructor.

Fields represent the fundamental attributes of an entity; just like in our
mathematical model, w_t is made up of the values of all fields for all entities
present in the game at time t.

A constructor returns an instance of its entity container; just like in our mathematical model, calling the constructor of the entity marked as world returns
the initial game state, that is w_0.

Rules, just like the dynamics in our mathematical model, are a block of
code, each acting on a subset of the entity fields called *domain*. The rules of a
game may feature suspensions; this means that suspensions depending on some
conditions, or temporal delays, interrupt the execution of the block of code,
which is resumed at a different time; the latter is a classification of code blocks
that are always run atomically and without any intermediate suspension.

In what follows we present our particle example and show how, using Casanova, the resulting code is not only close to the mathematical description but also compact and readable. We also provide an additional example implementing discrete dynamics. More sophisticated and brood samples of the Casanova language, including multiplayer, can be found at the following link https://github.com/vs-team/casanova-mk2/wiki/.

Particle Example - Casanova. We now show a complete solution to the "particle" example presented in Sect. 2.1 written in Casanova. A particle in Casanova becomes an entity containing fields (representing position and velocity) and dynamics with basic movements. Among the fields of the particle we find its visual properties (inherited from `VisualParticle`, which also includes the position of the particle). The dynamics of the particle are expressed by two rules: the first one applies velocity to the current position of the particle; and a second one that applies gravitational force to the velocity of the particle.

Listing 1.8. Particle written in Casanova

```
entity Particle = {
  inherit VisualParticle
  Velocity : Vector3

  rule Position = yield Position + Velocity * dt
  rule Velocity = yield Velocity + Vector3(0, -9.8, 0)

  Create() = {
    VisualParticle = VisualParticle.Find()
    Velocity = Vector3.zero
  }
}
```

Patrolling in Casanova. We now improve our particle by making it behave as a patrol moving through checkpoints. We did not show this example in the previous sections, since it would not have introduced any additional insight in our investigation, besides taking too many lines of code (while you are reading such code try to think how it would implemented, if possible also efficiently, in the Assembly language or in C++). We present this example to show how by promoting natural expressions of the domain as first-class constructs makes it possible for developers are not supposed to include further considerations, not related to the problem itself, in their reasoning. Typically, with general purpose tools or languages (as shown in the previous sections) it is hard to map domain-specific aspects "one-to-one" with language constructs.

In Casanova, the patrol becomes an entity containing fields (representing position, velocity, current animation, and the list of checkpoints) and dynamics with basic movements and checkpoints selection. Among the fields of the patrol we find its visual properties (inherited from `VisualBob`, which also stores the

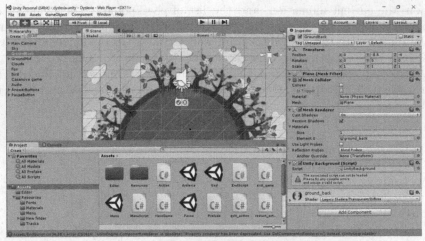

(a) Editing in the Unity Editor

```
193
194       entity Animal =
195       {
196           inherit UnityAnimal
197           Walk : bool
198           Sing : bool
199
200           WalkTexture       : string
201           WalkTextureFrames : int
202
203           SingTexture       : string
204           SingTextureFrames : int
205
206           Enter             : Vector3
207           Exit              : Vector3
208           Destination       : Vector3
209
210           rule Position = Position + Velocity * dt
211           rule Velocity =
212             wait 0.0f
213             if Vector3.Distance(Position, Destination) > 0.1f then
214               yield Destination - Position
215             else yield Vector3.zero
216
217
218
219           rule AnimationIndex, AnimationNumber, AnimalTexture =
220             yield 0, WalkTextureFrames, WalkTexture
221             wait Walk
222             while(Walk) do
223               for i in [0, WalkTextureFrames - 1] do
```

(b) Coding logic in VIsual Studio with the Casanova lanugage

Fig. 8. A Casanova/Unity project

position, the current animation, and the list of checkpoints). The behavior of the patrol is defined by only one rule, which for every checkpoint, after computing the direction to the next checkpoint and setting it as the current velocity, waits until the patrol reaches the checkpoint (`wait Vector3.Dot(dir0, c - Position) < 0.0f`). Once passed, the patrol stops, waits one second, and moves towards the next checkpoint. Once all checkpoints are reached the patrol starts again.

Listing 1.9. A patrol written in Casanova

```
worldEntity World = {
  inherit VisualBob
  Velocity : Vector3

  rule Position = yield Position + Velocity * dt

  rule Velocity, CurrentAnimation =
    for c in Checkpoints do
      let dir0 = c - Position
      yield dir0, BobAnimation.Walk
      wait Vector3.Dot(dir0, c - Position) < 0.0f
      yield Vector3.zero, BobAnimation.Idle
      wait 1.0f

  Create() = {
    UnityBob = UnityBob.Find()
    Velocity = Vector3.zero
  }
}
```

Advantages. Specific problems in games have been tackled with domain specific tools. Limits of such game tools were made less dire with extensibility, usually by means of a general purpose language (GPL). GPL's are languages designed to provide general abstractions for general purpose programming tasks. GPL's pay for their generality and flexibility with a lack of specific tools. In some very narrow scenarios, such as building concurrent distributed state machines, the general facilities can indeed be used to tackle the problem, but are awkward and cumbersome to use. This translates into verbosity, debuggin difficulties, reability, and maintainability.

DSL's for games, and DSL's in general, try to reduce such difficulties and costs by providing powerful abstractions built ad-hoc to tackle problems related to the domain of games. These abstractions allow developers to define complex games requiring limited effort, since these abstractions help to focus only on the the problem at hand, instead of "fighting the language". By using DSL's in games not only maintainability is achieved (filtering external considerations makes the code much more readable), but also expressiveness (few composeable abstractions are enough to express many complex behaviors).

Evidence of usage of DSL's in game tools can be found in important/widely used commercial engines (e.g. see *UnrealScript* [41] for Unreal Engine or *Galaxy script* for the Starcraft II editor [42]) and in research projects (e.g. the *SharpLudus software factory* [20], the *SGL* programming language [22]).

Disadvantages. DSL's are meant for domain specific usage. Their designs are meant to solve tasks within the specific application domain. Every DSL comes with its own philosophy and constructs, both tightly associated to the tackled domain (in a sense, DSL's are concrete languages). This translates into the fact that when dealing with different DSL's developers need to *literally* deal with different designs that require to be studied and mastered.

In Casanova, for example, developers need to first understand all the fundamental aspects of the language that are essential to effectively master it. Thus, in order efficiently use language, developers are supposed to become proficient with the following properties first, which are not common in other DSL's or GPL's: the rules system, the hierarchy of entities, the special constructs such as `wait` or `yield`, etc.

Moreover, DSLs do not enjoy the same share and investments as GPL's, although attention on DSL's for games is getting higher. Many are the realities where DSL's are developed and maintained by small groups of researchers. Unfortunately, this lack of investments make the quality of such DSL's not always comparable to the one of the GPL's (which are typically supported by big companies or communities), since a language, and its components (parser, lexer, back-end, optimizer, etc.), is very expensive to build, debug, and maintain (bugs at the compiler level are a big issue, since correct user programs might potentially exhibit wrong behaviors at run-time). Developers are left the task of continuously updating their DSL's runtimes and possibly to report bugs.

All these issues make developing games with such DSL's less ideal, and certainly less attractive in practice than it should/could potentially be.

3.7   Summary

Developing a game is an expensive and time consuming activity that needs to be kept in check especially for those developers with limited amount of resources, such as serious game developers. During the past years game development tools evolution included the previous tools philosophies and followed the language paradigms that were in vogue. This made game development tools evolve towards systems which game code is close to a high-level representation (see the mathematical representation of Sect. 2) and less close to a low-level representation, where considerations that have little to do with the game itself (such as hardware switches, algorithms optimization, etc.) are included. We believe that the work in this field is not yet mature enough to ignore further evolutions, and that investigating domain tools could be an interesting opportunity to further explore, seen that domain languages could help achieve the desired abstraction level for what concerns the game logic, while achieving at the same time high-levels of readability and compactness. This translates into code that is less expensive to build and maintain, and ultimately opens up new possibilities for experimentation without huge budgets and the backing of a large company.

References

1. Abbadi, M., Giacomo, F., Cortesi, A., Spronck, P., Costantini, G., Maggiore, G.: Casanova: a simple, high-performance language for game development. In: Göbel, S., Ma, M., Baalsrud Hauge, J., Oliveira, M.F., Wiemeyer, J., Wendel, V. (eds.) JCSG 2015. LNCS, vol. 9090, pp. 123–134. Springer, Heidelberg (2015). doi:10.1007/978-3-319-19126-3_11
2. Akinlaja, D.D.: LÖVE2d for Lua Game Programming. Packt Publishing Ltd, Olton (2013)
3. Amory, A., Naicker, K., Vincent, J., Adams, C.: The use of computer games as an educational tool: identification of appropriate game types and game elements. Br. J. Educ. Technol. **30**(4), 311–321 (1999)
4. Anderson, E.F., Engel, S., Comninos, P., McLoughlin, L.: The case for research in game engine architecture. In: Proceedings of the 2008 Conference on Future Play: Research, Play, Share, pp. 228–231. ACM (2008)
5. Atkinson, K.E.: An introduction to numerical analysis. Wiley, New York (2008)
6. Bancilhon, F.: Naive evaluation of recursively defined relations. In: Brodie, M.L., Mylopoulos, J. (eds.) On Knowledge Base Management Systems. Springer, New York (1986)
7. Berens, K., Howard, G.: The Rough Guide to Videogames. Rough Guides, London (2008)
8. Bishop, L., Eberly, D., Whitted, T., Finch, M., Shantz, M.: Designing a pc game engine. IEEE Comput. Graph. Appl. **1**, 46–53 (1998)
9. Blum, R.: Professional Assembly Language. Wiley, New York (2007)
10. Butcher, J.C.: The Numerical Analysis of Ordinary Differential Equations: Runge-Kutta and General Linear Methods. Wiley-Interscience, New York (1987)
11. Carter, P.A.: PC Assembly Language (2007). Lulu.com
12. Chamillard, A.: Introductory game creation: no programming required. ACM SIGCSE Bull. **38**, 515–519 (2006). ACM
13. Crawford, C.: Chris Crawford on Game Design. New Riders, San Francisco (2003)
14. Darby, J.: Awesome Game Creation: No Programming Required. Cengage Learning, Boston (2008)
15. Fabricatore, C.: Gameplay and game mechanics: a key to quality in videogames (2007)
16. Ferguson, E., Rockhold, B., Heck, B.: Video game development using xna game studio and c#. net. J. Comput. Sci. Coll. **23**(4), 186–188 (2008)
17. Fojdl, J., Brause, R.W.: The performance of approximating ordinarydifferential equations by neural nets. In: 20th IEEE International Conference on Tools with Artificial Intelligence, ICTAI 2008, vol. 2, pp. 457–464. IEEE (2008)
18. Fowler, M.: Domain-Specific Languages. Pearson Education, Boston (2010)
19. Furtado, A.W., Santos, A.L.: Using domain-specific modeling towards computer games development industrialization. In: The 6th OOPSLA Workshop on Domain-Specific Modeling (DSM 2006). Citeseer (2006)
20. Furtado, A.W.B., de Medeiros Santos, A.: Sharpludus: improving game development experience through software factories and domain-specific languages. Universidade Federal de Pernambuco (UFPE) Mestrado em Ciência da Computação centro de Informática (CIN) (2006)
21. Games, E.: Unreal engine 3. https://www.unrealengine.com/
22. Hastjarjanto, T., Jeuring, J., Leather, S.: A dsl for describing the artificial intelligence in real-time video games. In: Proceedings of the 3rd International Workshop on Games and Software Engineering: Engineering Computer Games to Enable Positive, Progressive Change, pp. 8–14. IEEE Press (2013)

23. Hudlicka, E.: Affective game engines: motivation and requirements. In: Proceedings of the 4th International Conference on Foundations of Digital Games, pp. 299–306. ACM (2009)
24. Kent, S.: The Ultimate History of Video Games: From Pong to Pokemon and Beyond.. The Story Behind The Craze That Touched Our Lives and Changed The World. Three Rivers Press, New York (2010)
25. Kushner, D.: Masters of Doom: How Two Guys Created an Empire and Transformed Pop Culture. Random House Incorporated, New York (2004)
26. Kusterer, R.: jmonkeyengine 3.0-develop professional 3d games for desktop, web, and mobile, all in the familiar java programming language (2013)
27. Lloyd, J.: The torque game engine. Game Devel. Mag **11**(8), 8–9 (2004)
28. Luna, F.: Introduction to 3D Game Programming with DirectX 10. Jones and Bartlett Publishers, Burlington (2008)
29. Maggiore, G., Costantini, G.: Friendly f# (fun with game programming) (2011)
30. Mens, T., Wermelinger, M., Ducasse, S., Demeyer, S., Hirschfeld, R., Jazayeri, M.: Challenges in software evolution. In: Eighth International Workshop on Principles of Software Evolution, pp. 13–22. IEEE (2005)
31. Mernik, M., Heering, J., Sloane, A.M.: When and how to develop domain-specific languages. ACM Comput. Surv. (CSUR) **37**(4), 316–344 (2005)
32. Morrison, M.: Beginning Game Programming. Pearson Higher Education, New York (2004)
33. Mycroft, A.: Programming language design and analysis motivated by hardware evolution. In: Nielson, H.R., Filé, G. (eds.) SAS 2007. LNCS, vol. 4634, pp. 18–33. Springer, Heidelberg (2007). doi:10.1007/978-3-540-74061-2_2
34. Petzold, C.: Microsoft XNA Framework Edition: Programming for Windows Phone 7. Microsoft Press, Redmond (2010)
35. Press, W.H.: Numerical Recipes: The Art of Scientific Computing, 3rd edn. Cambridge University Press, New York (2007)
36. Reich, C.: Simulation of imprecise ordinary differential equations using evolutionary algorithms. In: Proceedings of the 2000 ACM Symposium on Applied Computing, vol. 1, pp. 428–432. ACM (2000)
37. Shreiner, D., Bill The Khronos OpenGL ARB Working Group, et al.: OpenGL Programming Guide: The Official Guide To Learning OpenGL, versions 3.0 and 3.1. Pearson Education, Upper Saddle River (2009)
38. Smith, S.P., Trenholme, D.: Rapid prototyping a virtual fire drill environment using computer game technology. Fire Saf. J. **44**(4), 559–569 (2009)
39. Steuer, J.: Defining virtual reality: dimensions determining telepresence. J. Commun. **42**(4), 73–93 (1992)
40. Streeting, S., Johnstone, B.: Ogre-open source 3d graphics engine (2010). URL-http://www.ogre3d.org/. Accessed 26 Sep–Dec 2010
41. Sweeney, T., Hendriks, M.: Unrealscript Language Reference. Epic MegaGames Inc, Cary (1998)
42. Sweetser, P.: Teaching games level design using the starcraft ii editor. J. Learn. Des. **6**(2), 12–25 (2013)
43. Sweigart, A.: Making Games with Python & Pygame. CreateSpace, North Charleston (2012)
44. Van Roy, P., et al.: Programming paradigms for dummies: what every programmer should know. New Comput. Paradigms Comput. Music 104 (2009)

Serious Games Architectures and Engines

Heinrich Söbke[1(✉)] and Alexander Streicher[2]

[1] Bauhaus-Institute for Infrastructure Solutions (b.is), Bauhaus-Universität Weimar, Weimar, Germany
heinrich.soebke@uni-weimar.de
[2] Fraunhofer IOSB, Karlsruhe, Germany
alexander.streicher@iosb.fraunhofer.de

Abstract. The term *Serious Game* includes a wide, heterogeneous field of digital games with varying purposes and objectives and for a multitude of different application areas. All in common is the underlying software. This chapter gives an overview on the technical aspects of serious games including their software architectures and engines. As the general topic is manifold and the technical aspects of serious game software are quite comprehensive, this chapter covers the basic principles of and requirements for serious game software. It depicts selected software architectures and provides examples for game engines including a description of selected components.

Keywords: Serious games architecture · Game engine · Serious game development · Distributed architecture · Game component · Schema

1 Introduction

What are serious games and how can they be categorized? Schmidt et al. [1] suggest a categorization according to the purpose of the game: they follow the work of Connolly et al. [2] and classify the purposes of a game as *Attention*, *Motivation*, *Knowledge or skill acquisition*, *Process Support*, *Joy/Playfulness* and *Information*. Michael and Chen [3] identify eight categories as markets for serious games: *Military*, *government*, *education*, *corporate games*, *healthcare*, *politics*, *religion* and *art*. These are only two of the suggested categorizations – Djaouti et al. [4] present a literature review of serious games categorization in their work to develop their G/P/S model. This model divides a serious game into **G**ame aspects and serious aspects (**P**urpose and **S**cope). Another classification has been defined by Ratan and Ritterfeld [5]. Their proposed dimensions to classify serious games comprise *Primary Educational Content*, *Primary Learning Principles*, *Target Age Group* and *Game Platform*.

The amount and depth of all those classifications can be taken as an indicator for the great diversity in the field of serious games. Sophisticated distributed virtual training systems for military operations [6] are subsumed under this term as it is done for multiplayer online games [7], or for a simple gamified quiz app [8]. Software is a common component of all these games. This requires a non-trivial software development process. Such a process, the chosen software architecture and the employed software development

R. Dörner et al. (Eds.): Entertainment Computing and Serious Games, LNCS 9970, pp. 148–173, 2016.
DOI: 10.1007/978-3-319-46152-6_7

tools depend on the planned serious game. Obviously, neither a universal serious game template nor a universal, all-inclusive software architecture does exist yet. Nevertheless, in order to provide an orientation regarding the technical necessities for software architectures and engines in serious game development, this article discusses the following content: First, the specific needs of serious game development in contrast to the needs of game development and software development are identified. The following section on architectures introduces basic game architectures as well as distributed architectures, and it discusses approaches and standards for interoperability. Especially schemes for learning objects and serious games metadata can be considered as essential principles of interoperable architectures. The section about game engines presents a general overview and lists exemplary game engines. Afterwards, a selection of open research questions is followed by summarizing conclusion and further recommended readings.

2 Requirements to Software Development

Although serious games consist of a wide range of manifestations regarding purposes, game mechanisms and technical implementation, there may be a common core of prevalent requirements and characteristics of appropriate architectures and engines. In a first approach to gather further hints, we have a look at the development process. As systematic research about serious game development is rare, we have included game development in our literature review as well. Generally, serious games are a subset of digital games, which are a significant part and driving factor of the creative industries.

2.1 Game Development

It is common practice to describe game development by comparison to software development. This approach is followed by Murphy-Hill et al. [9]. They state that software development for digital games is not a well-researched topic yet. However, they identified tendencies and first important findings in the results of their survey: in game development, the requirements to the product are more unclear compared to conventional software development. Therefore, requirements often are subject to change during the development process. This finding is backed by the complex, non-deterministic and non-linear but iterative process of game design in order to develop working, fun-creating game mechanics. That is, if implemented game mechanics do not seem to work, changes have to be made in order to achieve the development goal [10]. Such a process requires agile development methods, which are in fact more prevalent in game development projects. Murphy-Hill et al. [9] consider the ability to communicate with non-engineers or domain experts as a key-skill of game developers and coin the term of "software cowboys" as one archetype of a successful game developer. Accordingly, Hagan et al. [11] point out, that the combination of people from different disciplines imposes specific importance on communication and team building: "effective collaboration requires a team that respects each other's contributions, communicates frequently and shares a similar conceptual model of the product and goals". Cooper and Scacchi [12] even underline that game development is a broad and comprising field, which leads to developers being narrowly skilled in probably only one game genre. For the field of online game development Morgan [13] postulates that "the commercial success of online gaming [..] has masked the technological inadequacies". He mentions missing standards for content sharing and non-given interoperability between games (Morgado [14] extends this deficit to virtual worlds) and unavailable model-driven development procedures. The proliferation of Minecraft [15] in educational and research contexts [16, 17] illustrates, that content sharing standards and interoperability can facilitate the use of games: gaming scenarios from a broad range of versatile contexts can easily be provided and deployed by the usage of a standardized platform.

Ampatzoglou and Stamelos [18] conducted a systematic literature review about research topics in game engineering. According to their findings, software development for games recently has become a more vital research field increasing year by year at a disproportionately higher rate compared to software engineering research in general. The thesis of a game development as an emerging and progressing field is supported by Prakash et al. [19]. Most prevalent topics are *requirements and specification, management* and *coding tools and techniques. Software architecture* and *software reuse* are among the less focused topics. Ampatzoglou and Stamelos [18] cite McShaffry [20], who found diverse criteria to "differentiate game software engineering from classical software engineering", and they conclude that games have a shorter-lifecycle as well as a shorter development period. Product maintenance consists mainly of bug fixing; therefore, no revenues are generated from maintenance releases. Nevertheless, sequels and extensions are considered as a kind of maintenance releases, which create revenues.

Another result of Murphy-Hill et al. [9] is that game development relies often on in-house tools in contrast to standard software. However, Wang and Nordmark [21] identify integration of third party components as one tendency in game development.

Blow [22] uses case studies to describe that game development becomes more complex as technical options progress. Kanode and Haddad [23] identify the combination of multiple and diverse kinds of assets like graphics, videos, code, sound effects as one challenge of game development in contrast to software development. Hagan et al. [11] add that innovation and speed to market are vital in game development.

2.2 Serious Game Development

Serious game development has – compared to plain game development – the additional burden of integrating the "serious" element into the game. This demand complicates the development process further as it removes degrees of freedom from the design process (see chapter "Processes and Models for Serious Game Design & Development" in this volume) in order to achieve a seamless integration of content and game [24].

Among the differences to conventional game development is that the hardware requirements should be rather low [3]. For example, educational application settings of serious games are often connected to schools where not always the most recent hardware is available. In addition, target systems and target groups may be more heterogeneous. The application setting of a serious game may comprise target groups that are not necessarily gamers. As the example of Social Network Games (SNGs) shows (cf. e.g. [25, 26] and chapter "Social Network Games"), hereby further requirements are imposed on the user interface design beyond digital game standards. Another characteristic of serious games is the necessity of more accurate simulation models. In conventional digital games, simulation models are optimized for entertainment purposes, in most serious games the simulation models are a significant part of the serious content and have to be close to reality.

Testing of serious games not only comprises play tests (in order to ensure fun creating game mechanics). Furthermore, validation steps must be included to test if the actual purpose of the game can be fulfilled. For this reason, monitoring functionality has to be integrated. One approach to accomplish this is the employment of third party tools through the support of standardized interfaces. The possibility to conduct *Learning Analytics* has become an impacting side-goal in serious game design [27, 28].

These additional requirements to design and implementation of serious games are often diametrically opposed to low budgets, and it is considered as one of the main contradiction in serious game development [29]. There are only few cases with exceptional high budgets, e.g. serious games for military training. The most prevalent attempt to face this dilemma is to reduce technical complexity of serious games [30, 31]. Authoring tools are a relevant contribution in this category. Lester et al. [32] define a list of requirement for the specific case of authoring tools for pedagogical agents. They request familiar user interface paradigms with standard editing features, support for author collaboration and rapid iteration and testing. In addition, different levels of experience should be accommodated as well as automation of complex and tedious tasks. Usage should be eased by templates and tutorials [32].

Between developers of commercial entertainment games it is controversially discussed, if in-house game engines or third-party game engines are preferable [33]. Whereas the creation of an own engine can free game developers from vendor-dependency, serious game development typically does not have the necessary budgets to develop an in-house game engine. Thus, this make-or-by-decision commonly is taken away from serious game development in favor of freely available or affordable engines.

In conclusion, serious game development is a complex task in a technically fast moving environment. Whereas commercial games can just focus on achieving a great portion of fun, the development of serious games also has to adhere to the integration of the "serious" goal. In addition to this increased difficulty, technological progress also boosts the capabilities of commercial entertainment games that can be considered as a benchmark for attractiveness of serious games. This tremendously complex task is faced by commonly low budgets. The lack of resources can be compensated at least partially by functionality and efficiency of the underlying software, tools and their compositions, i.e. architectures.

3   Architectures

In its basic form "software architecture deals with abstraction, decomposition and composition, and style and aesthetics" as stated by Kruchten in his 4+1 view model of architecture [34], which is depicted in Fig. 1.

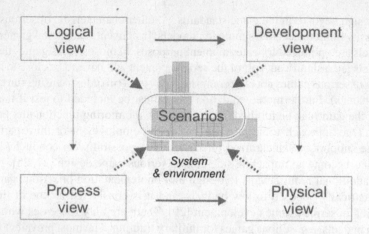

Fig. 1. 4+1 view model of architecture by Kruchten [34]

Kruchten [34] suggests four views of a software architecture to describe its model: (I) a logical view illustrates the object model, (II) a process view deals with concurrency and synchronization issues, (III) a physical view describes the "mapping of the software onto the hardware and reflects its distributed aspects" and (IV) a development view represents the software's static organization in its development environment". Bass et al. [35] add the concepts of components, their interfaces and their interrelated compositions.

The notion of software architecture as a composition of components becomes especially apparent in depictions of game engines, as shown in Fig. 2. Self-contained components with well-defined interfaces are arranged to build a game engine. This representation suggests that the views I and II of Kruchten's 4+1 model [34] are

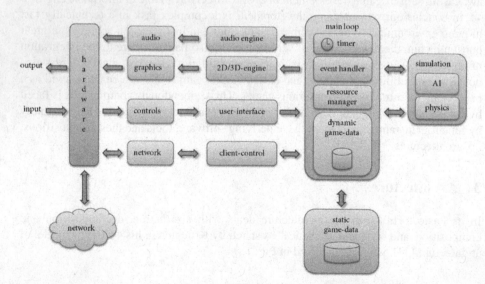

Fig. 2. Game engine: software architecture as a composition of components and interfaces [36]

handed by the game engine's architecture: object models have to follow the game engines' technical conventions and within their game loop they frame the handling of synchronization and concurrency issues. The views III and IV are applicable to game architecture itself: the distribution of components among the involved hardware is handled by the physical model. The development model describes the integrated components and libraries. Therefore, we differentiate between the architecture of a *game engine* and the architecture of a *game*. While we deal with the latter in this section, the first is handled in Sect. 4.

3.1   Game Architectures and Its Typical Components

Apart from game engines (software frameworks that provide basic services for game development in order to enable an efficient development process – cf. Sect. 4), there are further components, which are typically included in architectures for (serious) games. Hereafter we look at typical examples of serious games and describe their architectures, focusing on the aspects of the physical and the development view; each of the described exemplars illustrates typical facets. We use the platform categorization from Connolly et al. [2] which comprises *Mobile*, *Internet*, *PC* and *Console*. Non-digital games are excluded, because they do not require a software infrastructure. The category *Virtual World* is disregarded, as the results of Connolly et al. do not indicate significance in the past for the field of serious games (which probably may change with the raise of head-mounted virtual reality displays as *Oculus Rift* [37]). From a technical point of view, this distinction becomes - at least partially – obsolete. game development environments, which support multiple (target) platforms, are evolving (e.g. Unity [38]). However, a complete unification for all platforms will not take place: there is a continuous stream of emerging hardware devices, which facilitate new forms of gaming. Recent developments in this context are, for example, mobile devices, virtual reality displays or sensors. The emergence of new hardware devices leads to further developments of new architectures.

This section continues with a short overview on exemplary architectures for prevalent platforms. It shortly discusses sensors as architecture components and concludes with a paragraph about common components.

PC. *Mobility* is a city-builder game with the focus on traffic simulation [39, 40]. It has been released in 2000 and has been developed with the support of a German industrial and governmental consortium that contributed a budget of approximately € 500.000. Developed as an educational game and installed a million times, it also received popularity as an entertainment game [41]. Its architecture is simple: As a PC game it is installed on a Microsoft Windows-based computer. It does not require an internet connection. Regarding the development view, it is remarkable that it was developed without a dedicated game engine. The entire game has been created from scratch using a C++ programming environment. The monolithic simulation model has been defined beforehand; it comprises 112 relevant factors.

Minecraft [15] is an example of a widespread PC based game, which is used in educational contexts. It has been developed in Java and is able to run without a network connection. The multiplayer mode requires a network connection and a server that hosts a common virtual world.

Mobile Games. *JuraShooter StGB* [42] is a learning app for law students. It facilitates multiple response questions (MRQ) for learning and animates the answering process. From a physical view, there are three components: the app itself, a content management system and the *Apple Game Center* as a rudimentary assessment administration tool (see Fig. 3).

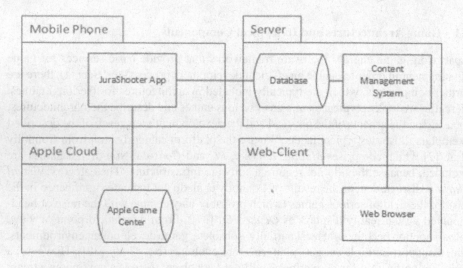

Fig. 3. Physical view of JuraShooter StGB

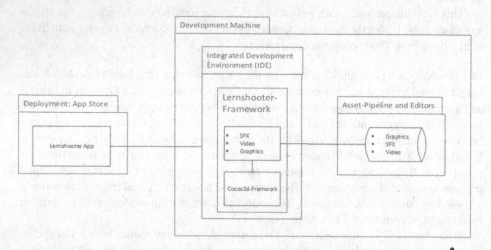

Fig. 4. Development view of the LernShooter architecture

The JuraShooter StGB has been developed using *Cocos2d* [43], an open source software development framework. The software structure of JuraShooter StGB is based on a framework called *LernShooter*: by supplying another set of graphics, video, sound effects (SFX) and content in the form of MRQs a new app can easily be created. This has been done various times (e.g. *KanalrattenShooter* [8]). Figure 4 depicts the development view of a new LernShooter app. Its content will be supplied by the content management system (see Fig. 3).

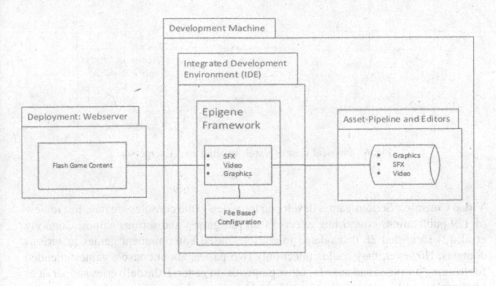

Fig. 5. Development view of a web-based game (Energetika)

Web-Based Games. Web-based Games are operable in a web browser. *Energetika* [44] is an example for a web-based serious game. It received attention, as it has been awarded the *Deutscher Computerspielpreis* (the most important award for digital games in Germany) in the category *Serious Game* in 2011. In that year the nuclear disaster of Fukushima led to a turnaround in Germany's energy policy. Energetika helps to illustrate characteristics and consequences of different energy sources. It is a simulation game about the energy supply for industrial nations, raising issues like carbon dioxide emissions and radioactive waste repositories. Its technical base is the proprietary, Adobe Flash-based framework *Epigene* [45]. The implemented simulation model is comprehensive and self-contained. It is not intended for subsequent extension. The attached database stores high scores of different categories. Among the categories are the energy mix and achievements (see Fig. 6). The deployment is managed via dedicated web servers (see Fig. 5).

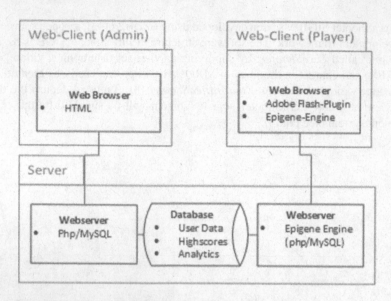

Fig. 6. Physical view of a web-based game (Energetika)

Video Console. Serious games developed for video game consoles are rare. In a review of 129 publications concerning effects of digital games and serious games, Connolly et al. [2] identified 26 that related to console-based entertainment games in serious contexts. However, they could collect only two papers about console games intended for learning purposes and none for other purposes. In general, the deliveries and services of consoles, which are specifically designed hardware devices for gaming, can also be provided by personal computers (PCs). PCs are by far more widespread than consoles and have no functional limitations compared to consoles. In general, console games do not differ significantly from PC games. However, console games make more use of additional sensory input devices, like the *Nintendo Wii Remote* or the *Microsoft Kinect*. Microsoft Kinect tracks the movements of the players, based on a range-camera. It can facilitate for instance sport simulation games [46]. The Wii Remote achieves a similar effect by using a combination of accelerometer and optical sensors.

Sensors as Architecture Components. As consoles and PCs are by and large functionally equivalent as deployment platforms, we focus on the aspect of sensors as components of serious games. An example of a serious game processing sensor data is the *Aiming Game*. It uses sensor-provided biofeedback by means of electroencephalography and electromyography to train emotion regulation [47]. The game *Letterbird* is an example for an exergame and intends to control the load of endurance training. It processes sensor data of the athlete (heartrate) and the training device (ergometer, pedal rate and resistance setting) [48]. In this context, Hardy et al. [49] have developed a *Framework for adaptive Serious Games for Health* (see Fig. 7). Besides pointing to sensors as an essential part of this framework, it is an example of components forming a system architecture. A kind of exergame, following the metaphor of an air puck, with an additional social dimension has been described by Maier et al. [50]. The experimental setup consists of two PCs, each equipped with a *Kinect* sensor and connected via local area network (LAN). Players' performances are balanced by an adaptation component. As a result, impaired patients can match up with non-impaired.

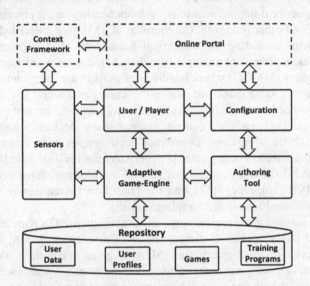

Fig. 7. *Framework for adaptive Serious Games for Health* derived from Hardy et al. [49]

In general, the integration of sensors opens further application areas for serious games. Among these are exergames, Games for Health (see chapter *Games for Health* in this volume), Pervasive Games (see chapter *Pervasive Games* in this volume) and embodied interaction (see chapter *Embodied Interaction in Play* in this volume). Regarding the architecture, it expands the physical view with hardware-based sensors and probably further game engine components. The development view is extended with drivers and programming interfaces.

Common Components. Summarizing the previous examples, a game engine (see Sect. 4) is an important part of the development view of almost any architecture of serious games. Commonly, web-based architectures include servers, which host the game itself and deliver it to the web browser. Additionally, they host authoring tools or content management systems as well as the databases with content, user data, sensory input data, etc. Another component used in professional web-based game development is a client-server-middleware handling request management. *SmartFoxServer* [51] is an example for such a middleware. Furthermore, to select an appropriate client/server model is crucial in case of highly frequented virtual worlds [14, 52].

3.2   Distributed Architectures

Distributed software architectures are widely applied to various kinds of application areas where software components are not just located on a single computer but on networked computer systems. Advantages of distributed architectures like shared use of resources (assets, code, logic blocks, etc.), openness, parallelism, scalability or transparency also apply for games. Examples of distributed software architectures are client-server, peer-to-peer or *n*-tier architectures (web applications are a prominent example for the latter). For further reference, Coulouris et al. [53] give a detailed overview of distributed systems, including the theoretical foundation of distributed algorithms. Regarding games, a prominent example of a distributed system are massively multi-player online games (MMOG) where hundreds of players are interconnected over the internet and play the same game instance in the same game world [54, 55]. Whereas first games have been completely monolithic, today's games are often modular and dynamic. They can load new game content, game states or mechanics from the internet and incorporate them at runtime. Distributed architectures with interoperable data models are needed to realize such games. In the broader field of distributed virtual reality environments and distributed simulations several architectures have been proposed, notably MASSIVE [56], DIVE [57], and the High Level Architecture (HLA) or its predecessor Distributed Interactive Simulation (DIS).

Whereas distributed game architectures are commonly used in popular commercial games, they are rarely applied to serious games. Carvalho et al. [58] introduce the concept of a service-oriented architecture (SOA) as an architectural model for serious games. In this model, the game components are distributed to various servers offering their services through web interfaces. The advantages are up-to-date components, automated detection of services and exchangeability of service providers in case of standardized interfaces. Furthermore, it removes special hardware requirements from clients as web browser access enables ubiquitous accessibility.

A distributed, multi-agent system has been presented by van Oijen et al. [59] in their CIGA middleware for intelligent virtual agents (IVAs). CIGA is a software architecture to connect multi-agent systems to game engines using ontologies as a design contract. The CIGA middleware negotiates between the physical layer of game engines and the cognitive layer of multi-agent systems (IVA).

Jepp et al. [60] describe an agent-based architecture for modular serious games. The framework strives to provide serious games with believable, emotional agents to help players learn skills and evaluate their performance. It is part of the TARGET platform helping learners to train competencies in game scenarios. The framework is interlinked with a game engine, a dialogue system and a narrative engine via a so-called translation engine handling synchronization and communication.

A distributed architecture for testing, training and simulation in the military domain is TENA by the U.S. Department of Defense (DoD) [61]. This extensive architecture focuses on interoperability for military test and training systems. At its core, the TNA middleware interconnects various TENA applications and tools for the management, monitoring, analysis, etc. of military assets. Via a gateway service, they can be linked with other DIS or HLA conformant simulators that provide real sensor data or data from live, virtual and constructive simulations (LVC) for the TENA environment.

Peirce et al. [62] present the ALIGN architecture to enable the adaptability of serious games in a minimal-invasively fashion. The ALIGN system architecture decouples the adaptation logic from the actual game without mitigating the game play. It is divided into four conceptual processes: the accumulation of context information about the game state; the interpretation of the current learner state; the search for matching intervention constraints; and a recommendation engine, which applies adaptation rules to the game. ALIGN is not included in the actual game but communicates with attached game engines via TCP/IP. It has been applied in the educational adventure game of the ELEKTRA project [62].

3.3   Data Models and Interoperability

While the software architecture specifies the structure of a software system and how data flows through it, the technical specification of the data itself (the schema) is also part of the overall system specification and the specification of the scenarios. This section focuses on the data schemas for interoperability. In the domain of Modeling and Simulation (M&S) exist various standards to describe virtual environments, e.g. the *Simulation Reference Markup Language* (SRML) [63, 64] or state-machine models like *State-Chart XML* (SCXML) [65].

Standards for technical data representation enable systems to be interoperable, that is to effectively exchange data and information. In sustainable IT environments the interoperability of data and processes is one of the core aspects for efficiency, responsiveness and cost reduction. This applies to serious games as well: Only when data schemas are interoperable with other serious games, true data exchange is effectively possible (e.g. data exchange on usage activity or content). Stănescu et al. [66] give an overview of the interoperability of serious games. They propose a *Serious Games Multidimensional Framework* (SG-MIF) to consider different levels of interoperability, regarding serious games components, their ecosystem and how to handle topics following the use of serious games [66].

For learning management systems (LMS) various data models and exchange formats have been proposed, notably the IEEE *Learning Object Metadata* LOM) [67] or the exchange format *Shareable Content Object Reference Model* (SCORM) [68]. The IEEE-LOM is a base schema to annotate learning resources with metadata. Annotated learning resources are called Learning Objects (LO). LOM was developed to facilitate the search, acquisition, exchange and use of LOs. It allows the specification of new application profiles with mixed element sets and references to other vocabularies. Whereas LOM specifies a schema for metadata annotation, SCORM makes use of it in its own LOM application profile: It provides a collection of standards for the communication and data exchange of LOs. SCORM includes a specification about packaging LOs for interchange between different LMSs. What sounds good in theory has its pitfalls in reality. A simple exchange of learning resources via SCORM proved to be difficult and far from "plug & learn". Simple, static data can be exchanged but dynamic content or learning settings cannot, because of the different learning concepts of the LMSs. For Intelligent Tutoring

Systems (ITS) and adaptive learning systems LOM is a key model for repurposing content or aligning it along adaptive learning pathways [69, 70]. The effective reusability and repurposing of learning objects offer the possibility of an efficient game development process. It enables the computer to personalize and adapt games to individual users by, e.g. rearranging content. The reusability of learning objects has already been demonstrated between web-based LMS and game-based LMS [71]. The data exchange between games and LMS has been shown in the <e-Adventure> platform by Torrente et al. [72]. It is a set of platforms for developing inexpensive, educational games, including an API for tracking and assessment. The API can transfer results of the game play to a learning management system (LMS), and thus, students' performances can be monitored and aggregated. Similarly, the API implemented by the <e-Adventure> platform follows the SCORM specifications [68], which eases integrations with LMS servers that adhere to this standard.

Further research has to be done to establish a commonly accepted metadata schema for serious games. LOM as an already accepted base schema, provides the foundation for such a schema. A taxonomy of educational games that is compatible to IEEE-LOM is presented by Silva et al. [73].

El Borji and Khadi [74] present an application profile of the IEEE LOM as the so-called *SG-LOM* for serious games (see Fig. 8). The intention is to use serious games as learning resources that are integrated into existing LMS. This metadata schema allows to exchange tracking and assessment data between serious games and LMS.

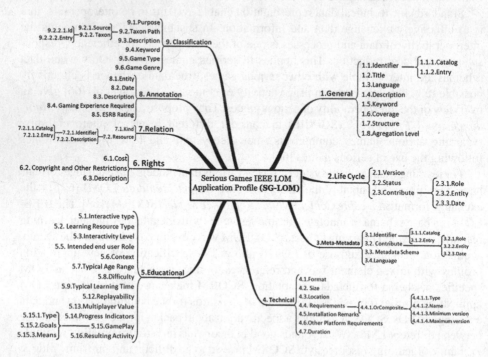

Fig. 8. Learning Object Model (LOM) application profile for serious games [74]

4   Engines

This section gives a short introduction to game engines in general. It describes the function of common core components, lists examples of popular game engines and presents methods how to categorize them.

4.1   Overview

In software engineering, the term *engine* is reserved for a self-contained software framework that processes input data into output data (input-process-output model). The applied processes as well as the input and output data can be described formally, e.g. using formal modeling standards like UML2 [75], State-Chart XML [65], etc., or using XML schema to define the data models. There are different kinds of software engines, e.g. simulation engines, search engines, inference engines, etc. An engine is a part of a software system; thus, a game engine is usually an essential part of game software. Engines offer services that free programmers from developing low-level algorithms, like algorithms for computer graphics and rendering or for user-adaptive non-player character (NPC) behavior, thus engines contribute to efficient game development. For example, a game engine often provides the service of visualizing 2D or 3D worlds. Rucker [76] describes the game development framework *Pop*, which has been developed for educational purposes. It documents basic requirements, processes in development and the usage of an elementary game engine.

In his description of the evolution of game engines, Gregory "reserve[s] the term 'game engine' for software that is extensible and can be used as the foundation for many different games without major modification" [77]. In a short definition Anderson et al. [78] identify reusable software components as game engines. They point out that different game genres require different game engines. Gregory supports this statement: a game genre often has specific requirements on a game engine. However, he admits that borders have blurred with the technical progress of game engines. Nowadays there are game engines that are capable of being applied to various genres. Resulting games may not achieve the quality of commercial games, but they deliver astonishingly acceptable player experiences [77].

Often a game engine provides multiple aspects that are included in game play. A set of aspects of digital games, which commonly are handled by game engines, are shown in Fig. 2. This figure also includes the main structure (i.e. architecture) of a typical game engine. A main control loop handles events and calls and coordinates various components of the engine. Often these components themselves are called "engines" as they handle a single aspect of the game engine. Therefore, the audio engine is responsible for providing an acoustical environment in the game.

Authoring environments for games (e.g. StoryTec, G-Flash, <e-Adventure> and SeGAE [72, 79–81]) differ from game engines: the game designer has to provide content to create a self-contained game. In contrast to an authoring environment a game engine provides just the base for a digital game – game designers have to design the game and programmers have to transform it into a working game using the game engine's services.

Game engines provide very powerful concepts. One challenge in game design is to use these concepts purposefully to provide immersive and engaging games. Usage of features which are not appropriately integrated in the game design concept (e.g. the narrative) may cause an unwanted distraction and may lead to "breaking the magic circle" [82]. In his discussion of physics in a game, Gregory points out that non-purposefully used physics features may distract the player from the intended game experience [67].

4.2   Selected Components

Although most functionalities of a game engine are provided unrecognized as transparent services to the game developers, it is reasonable to introduce some components in detail. This may be useful as they have to be developed or adapted to serious games (like personalization or adaptation); or the knowledge about their principles helps to understand the development process (as in the case of 2D/3D engines or physics engines).

2D/3D-Engine.   The *graphics engine* is a component on the view- or presentation-layer and handles all rendering of graphics, text and symbols (i.e. all visuals). Graphics are an important part of a game. Graphical effects and quality are often considered as to play a significant role in the playing experience. Almost every game engine includes a graphics engine. Functionalities of a graphics engine primarily comprise visualization of geometric objects and handling of textures. Additionally, visual effects like shading, transparency and reflections also belong to the capabilities of a graphics engine. Rendering is the process of creating an image from the 2D or 3D model. An introduction to the principles of a graphics engine is given in [20].

Artificial Intelligence (AI).   In order to provide challenging scenarios for players, AI is introduced into games. A common purpose of AI is to NPC. To challenge the player, the AI plans the reactions of the NPCs in real-time, according to the player's actions. The implementation of AI is demonstrated for example in the first-person-shooter *F.E.A.R.* [83] or in other fight games [84]. Recently, a main goal in the field of AI focusses on the design of more reasonable and believable AI behavior. Besides these extensions, Yannakakis, discusses three further areas of AI in games [85]: (1) *Player experience modeling* (PEM) adopts the game environment to the player's capabilities and preferences. It can provide an individualized and therefore intriguing game play. (2) *Procedural content generation* (PCG) deals with the automated generation of game elements, e.g. creation of new game levels. As content has not to be created manually, it reduces development costs. Furthermore, the created content can be adapted to the player (see chapter *Content generation for Serious Games* in this volume). Additionally, Yannakakis points out the capability of PCG to contribute to design solutions beyond human imagination. The last application area discussed is (3) *Massive-scale Game Data Mining*. It is used to optimize a game "around the player". Conventional algorithms can no longer handle the amount of available data ("Big Data"). This has led to the facilitation of data mining algorithms in games: Collaborative filtering, for example, searches for recurring patterns in interaction data of other human users. The data is matched to the user model of the current user to provide more human-like behaviors.

Commonly a game engine does not support the complete range of AI engines. Instead, AI engines are available as plugins. The *Unity* game engine for example [38] supports a limited set of AI technologies including algorithms for finite state machines, pathfinding and navigation. Additional plugins can be found in Unity's distribution platform *Asset Store*. For instance *RAIN for Unity* adds behavior trees to control the behavior, navigation, motion or animation [86].

Physics. Virtual worlds in games often include simulations of physics. Some genres, like shooter games, depend on it. In game development classical laws of mechanics are subsumed under the term *physics* [87]. Based on the concept of gravity (an object falls down) further phenomena like rigid bodies dynamics (an object is not deformed when external forces impact it) and collision detection (two objects partly overlap during their movement trajectories) are implemented by *physics engines*. Although a physics engine is often implemented as a separate software component, most game engines include them. Other game engines facilitate third party engines. For example, *PhysX*, an engine by NVIDIA that outsources calculations to the graphical processing unit (GPU) is used by *Unity* [88]. Physics engines allow the programmer to model a virtual world by means of configuration to avoid manual programming. As physics calculations are often computationally demanding, offline pre-calculations of movement sequences can be an appropriate optimization strategy [77].

4.3   Game Engine Examples

In literature, a few selection processes of game engines for serious contexts are documented. As already mentioned in Sect. 2.2, a relevant criterion is the ease of use. It should enable even domain experts, who are not experienced game developers, to create serious games and related tools [32]. Cowan and Kapralos [89] emphasize available budgets as a main difference between commercial and serious game development. They conducted a literature research to identify prevalent game engines and frameworks in the context of serious games. Their results indicate that mostly game engines produced for commercial entertainment settings are used for developing serious games. The ten top-most named game engines or frameworks identified (in combination with the keywords *simulator*, *serious game* and *educational game*) are, ordered by decreasing frequency: *Second Life, Unity* [38], *Unreal* [90], *Flash, XNA, Torque, OGRE, Game-Maker* [91], *StoryTec* and *OLIVE*.

In 2007 Marks et al. [92] describe the selection of a game engine as a well-tested foundation for simulated surgical training. Their main selection criteria have been inexpensiveness and popularity of the game engines. The final list of candidates consisted of *Unreal Engine, id Tech 4* and *Source Engine*. Examination criteria have been the availability of editing features, integration of further content and support of multiple users of the simulator.

As resources for serious game development are often are limited, the results of Rocha et al. [93] are relevant: In 2010 they evaluated the market of open source 3D game engines. Their sub-criteria have been: (a) recent stable version, (b) source code is available, (c) support for both operating systems, *Windows* and *Linux,* (d) not restricted to a specific game genre and (e) documentation is available and a lively community of users. They found the following game engines and tool kits: *Blender Game Engine* [94], *Crystal Space* [95], *Delta3D* [96], *Irrlicht* [97], *jMonkey Engine* [98], *Ogre3D* [99], *OpenSceneGraph* [100] and *Panda3D* [101]. These engines are discussed regarding the categories of graphics and non-graphics features, their development support and their organizational and technical maturity.

Petridis et al. [102] propose a framework for selecting game engines for serious games in high fidelity applications. Fidelity in their context refers to audiovisual and functional fidelity. Among the applied criteria are **audiovisual fidelity** (to enable immersion), **functional fidelity** (to support learning goals), **composability** (which relates to the reuse of existing components), **accessibility** (as serious games have to support inexperienced players, serious games should not require knowledge about standard game operations), **networking** (to enable multiple users to create a social context), and **heterogeneity** (i.e. multiplatform support). In order to validate this framework, they reduced a comprehensive list of game engines according to the criteria of wide usage, availability, modularity and innovative features. Finally they evaluated four game engines: *CryEngine* [103], Valve's *Source Engine*[1] [104], *Unreal* [90], and *Unity* [38]. These engines can be considered as a good match to the provided framework. However, it needs further refinement as the field progresses at a fast pace.

Table 1. Criteria for selecting game engines as proposed by Westhofen and Alexander [105]

Software	Development	Acquisition
Audiovisual display • Rendering • Animation • Sound • Streaming	Accessibility • Documentation • Support • Code access • Introduction effort	Accessibility • Licensing • Cost • System requirements
Functional display • Scripting • Supported AI • Physics Engine • Event handling		
Combinability • Component export/ import • Development tools		
Networking • Client-Server • Peer-to-Peer		
Heterogeneity • Multi-platform support		

---

[1] *Source Engine* has been discontinued in 2014. Its successor, *Source Engine 2,* has been announced [125].

Westhoven and Alexander [105] proposed a further methodological attempt to structure the selection process of game engines. They extended the framework of Petridis et al. [102] with aspects mentioned by Marks et al. [92] and Sarhan [106] (cf. Table 1) to select a game engine for a Virtual Reality (VR) application. They divided their criteria catalog into three categories: *software-related* criteria, which focus on the technical capabilities of the game engine; *development-related* criteria, which characterize requirements for the development process; and finally *acquisition-related* criteria. The latter categorie summarizes criteria which impact the provision of a game engine in a concrete development setting. In their case study they demonstrate that the proposed selection criteria have to be taylored to specific requirements. They evaluated *Unity* and *CryENGINE* as potential development platforms for their VR application.

Besides commercial game engines, there are specific educational game engines. These are mainly applied in contexts where the process of creating games itself is an educational measure. *GameMaker* [91] is a typical representative of this group. A more complete list of game making tools is maintained on Google Docs [107].

Another kind of game engines is specialized on browser games. These game engines mostly use HTML5 technology or provide browser-plugin support. *GameMaker,* for example, provides export to HTML5 besides other formats.

Seldom game engines are created from scratch by a game developer studio. The reasons for own developments are to support a specific genre and to reuse results for other games – as it has been done in the case of *CryEngine, SourceEngine* and *Unreal.* An remarkable attempt has been undertaken for SimCity 5 [108], because not only graphics but also the modeling of the simulation itself can be adapted: the underlying *GlassBox* engine, which has not been disclosed to the public, uses agent-based simulation and adheres to the *What You See Is What You Simulate Principle* [109, 110].

5 Research Questions (Starting Points for PhDs)

The most prominent research questions mostly concern the **efficient game development process**. As stated in Sect. 2, serious games require a huge development effort by design. Because of their multidisciplinary nature, their development could in fact cost more than business applications. Concepts for easy transferable – or even universally applicable – architectures, as well as supporting and flexible game engines are needed.

Before thinking about universally applicable architectures first steps towards commonly accepted **architecture blueprints** have to be devised. In software engineering, architecture blueprints are a proven tool in the efficient development of good and sustainable software products [111]. Standardization of architectures and data schemas could provide the community with interoperable data models and facilitate the data exchange between applications.

The integration of **emerging end user interfaces** into serious games is another reoccurring topic of research [14]. Such technologies could include cloud-based rendering (e.g. OTOY [112]) and virtual (e.g. Oculus Rift [37]) and augmented reality devices (e.g. Google Glasses). Data from other sources (e.g. Internet of

Things) and sensors (e.g. eye tracking devices, Xbox Kinect, etc.) could enable new fields of application of serious games.

In general, **arising gaming technologies** have to reviewed regarding to their facilitation of serious gaming (e.g. cloud gaming or computation offloading [113]).

Domain-specific game engines can increase the efficiency of development. An example is SimCity's *GlassBox* engine. It eases development by visualizing the simulation processes specific to city building games. The same principle can be used to **integrate further domain specific features** into game engines or integrated development environments (IDEs). A candidate could be the integration of learning analytics components and further supporting tools for educational games.

Model driven development decreases development efforts. Providing tools to generate games from models would ease the development process and probably lower the requirements to the technical knowledge of game designers and developers. **Authoring tools** ease game development in a similar way, but probably have a limited variability of resulting products.

Interoperability and data exchange has been identified as crucial for a widespread usage of serious game. However, it is not applied in practice at a reasonable rate. Among the reasons are technical limitations, which have to be eliminated.

6 Summary and Outlook

Serious game development is a highly complex and demanding process that relies on expert knowledge and software development experience. Currently available game engines and common architectures support the creation of decent serious games. However, there is potential for improvements.

There are some main challenges in serious game development: heterogeneous teams and a perpetual tendency of changing requirements. These issues are by far more specific to game development than to conventional software development. Commercial digital games provide a benchmark in terms of fun and entertainment. The need for "serious" content complicates game design. Development budgets are often comparatively small. Additional components like sensors and data have to be included in game architectures. Technical possibilities change at a fast pace.

The main contribution of architectures and game engines is to improve the efficiency of the development process. The quality of serious games in terms of resulting engagement level has to follow those of pure entertainment games. For this reason, there will always be a pressure to enhance the technical foundation of serious games. This technical foundation includes tools specific to the requirements of serious games (e.g. the integration of learning analytics in educational games).

Although in recent years the technical foundation has improved significantly, there is still great potential to enhance the efficiency of serious game development. Established principles of conventional software development have not yet been applied to serious games. Therefore, besides developing game specific technologies and algorithms, conventional software development can be used as a pool of inspiration and ideas to streamline serious game development.

Further Readings and Resources

Books

- **Gregory, J.** *Game Engine Architecture* **(2014).** A basic reading about the internals of game engines. It is one of the standard references for services offered by game engines and therein applied algorithms and principles [77].
- **Cooper, K.M.L., and Scacchi, W.** *Computer Games and Software Engineering* **(2015).** A recent collection of academic articles giving an overview about difficulties in software engineering for digital games. It serves as a starting point for a more theoretical approach to the topic [114].
- **McShaffry, M., Graham, D.** *Game Coding Complete* **(2012).** The fourth edition of a standard work in game development. It gives an overview of the (technical) challenges in game development and delivers recipes to master them. [20]
- **Hocking, J.** *Unity in Action: Multiplatform Game Development in C# with Unity 5* **(2015).** A well-written recent introduction into the currently leading game development tool. This book is an excellent resource in case a concrete initial implementation, based on the widespread game engine Unity, is intended [115].
- **Nystrom, B.** *Game Programming Patterns* **(2014).** A well-received book about the principles of game development. It covers specific patterns, which solve problems occurring specifically in game development. Thus, this book helps both to understand common game engines and game architectures and to design and implement proprietary ones [116].

Among further notable books are [54, 55, 117].

Websites

Gamasutra is a considerable online magazine about commercial digital game development. Among websites about technical aspects of game development are further **gamedev.net** [118] and **AIGameDev** [119]. A Q&A-platform about game development is provided by **StackExchange** [120].

Databases collecting information about game engines can be found on the websites **DevMaster** [121] and **HTML5 Game Engines** [122].

Conferences

All issues of commercial game development are addressed at the **Game Developers Conference (GDC).** It is the most renowned, mainly non-academic conference about development of digital games.

In the academic sector there are a few conferences dedicated to serious games, which allow discussions about their technical foundations. Among them are the **European Conference on Games Based Learning (EGBL)** and the **Joint Conference on Serious Games (JCSG).** Technical aspects of game development in general are handled for example by **IFIP International Conference on Entertainment Computing (ICEC)** and **Advances in Computer Entertainment Technology (ACE)**. Digital games in general are discussed at the renowned **DiGRA Conference** and **Foundations of Digital Games (FDG)**.

Mailing Lists

The **DiGRA-Mailing List** [123] is highly frequented and discusses all topics of digital games. Another relevant mailing list is maintained by the **IFIP Entertainment Computing Community** [124].

References

1. Schmidt, R., Emmerich, K., Schmidt, B.: Applied games – in search of a new definition. In: Chorianopoulos, K., Divitini, M., Hauge, J.B., Jaccheri, L., Malaka, R. (eds.) ICEC 2015. LNCS, vol. 9353, pp. 100–111. Springer, Heidelberg (2015)
2. Connolly, T.M., Boyle, E.A., MacArthur, E., Hainey, T., Boyle, J.M.: A systematic literature review of empirical evidence on computer games and serious games. Comput. Educ. **59**, 661–686 (2012)
3. Michael, D.R., Chen, S.L.: Serious Games: Games That Educate, Train, and Inform. Course Technology, Mason (2005)
4. Djaouti, D., Alvarez, J., Jessel, J.-P.: Classifying serious games: the G/P/S model. In: Felicia, P. (ed.) Handbook of Research on Improving Learning and Motivation Through Educational Games: Multidisciplinary Approaches, pp. 118–136. IGI Global, Hershey (2011)
5. Ratan, R., Ritterfeld, U.: Classifying serious games. In: Ritterfeld, U., Cody, M., Vorderer, P. (eds.) Serious Games: Mechanisms and Effects, pp. 10–22. Routledge, New York (2009)
6. Streicher, A., Szentes, D., Roller, W.: Scenario assistant for complex system configurations. IADIS Int. J. Comput. Sci. Inf. Syst. **9**, 38–52 (2014)
7. Reuter, C., Tregel, T., Mehm, F., Göbel, S., Steinmetz, R.: Rapid prototyping for multiplayer serious games. In: Busch, C. (ed.) Proceedings of the 8th European Conference on Games Based Learning, Reading, vol. 2, pp. 478–486 (2014)
8. Söbke, H., Chan, E., von Buttlar, R., Große-Wortmann, J., Londong, J.: Cat king's metamorphosis. In: Göbel, S., Wiemeyer, J. (eds.) GameDays 2014. LNCS, vol. 8395, pp. 12–22. Springer, Heidelberg (2014)
9. Murphy-Hill, E., Zimmermann, T., Nagappan, N.: Cowboys, ankle sprains, and keepers of quality: how is video game development different from software development? In: 36th International Conference on Software Engineering (ACM), pp. 1–11 (2014)
10. Fullerton, T.: Game Design Workshop: A Playcentric Approach to Creating Innovative Games. Morgan Kaufmann, Burlington (2008)
11. Osborne O'Hagan, A., Coleman, G., O'Connor, R.V.: Software development processes for games: a systematic literature review. In: Barafort, B., O'Connor, R.V., Poth, A., Messnarz, R. (eds.) EuroSPI 2014. CCIS, vol. 425, pp. 182–193. Springer, Heidelberg (2014)
12. Cooper, K.M.L., Scacchi, W.: Introducing computer games and software engineering. In: Cooper, K.M.L., Scacchi, W. (eds.) Computer Games and Software Engineering, pp. 1–27. Chapman and Hall/CRC, Boca Raton (2015)
13. Morgan, G.: Challenges of online game development: a review. Simul. Gaming **40**, 688–710 (2009)

14. Morgado, L.: Technology challenges of virtual worlds in education and training - research directions. In: 2013 5th International Conference on Games Virtual Worlds Serious Applications (VS-GAMES), pp. 1–5 (2013)
15. Mojang: Minecraft. https://minecraft.net/
16. Nebel, S., Schneider, S., Rey, G.D.: Mining learning and crafting scientific experiments: a literature review on the use of minecraft in education and research. J. Educ. Technol. Soc. **19**, 355–366 (2016)
17. Petrov, A.: Using minecraft in education: a qualitative study on benefits and challenges of game-based education (2014). https://tspace.library.utoronto.ca/bitstream/1807/67048/1/Petrov_Anton_201406_MT_MTRP.pdf
18. Ampatzoglou, A., Stamelos, I.: Software engineering research for computer games: a systematic review. Inf. Softw. Technol. **52**, 888–901 (2010)
19. Prakash, E., Brindle, G., Jones, K., Zhou, S., Chaudhari, N.S., Wong, K.-W.: Advances in games technology: software, models, and intelligence. Simul. Gaming **40**, 752–801 (2009)
20. McShaffry, M., Graham, D.: Game Coding Complete. Course Technology, Boston (2012)
21. Wang, A.I., Nordmark, N.: Software architectures and the creative processes in game development. In: Chorianopoulos, K., Divitini, M., Hauge, J.B., Jaccheri, L., Malaka, R. (eds.) ICEC 2015. LNCS, vol. 9353, pp. 272–285. Springer, Heidelberg (2015). doi: 10.1007/978-3-319-24589-8_21
22. Blow, J.: Game development: harder than you think. Queue **1**, 28–37 (2004)
23. Kanode, C.M., Haddad, H.M.: Software engineering challenges in game development. In: Sixth International Conference on Information Technology: New Generations, 2009, ITNG 2009, pp. 260–265. IEEE (2009)
24. Habgood, M.P.J., Ainsworth, S.E.: Motivating children to learn effectively: exploring the value of intrinsic integration in educational games. J. Learn. Sci. **20**, 169–206 (2011)
25. Fields, T.: Mobile and Social Game Design: Monetization Methods and Mechanics. A K Peters/CRC Press, Boca Raton (2014)
26. Kinder, K.: "You have a Farmville gift request": Thesen zum Erfolg von Social Casual Gaming auf Facebook. kommunikation@gesellschaft. 13, 19 pages (2012)
27. Khalil, M., Ebner, M.: Learning analytics: principles and constraints. In: Proceedings of World Conference on Educational Multimedia, Hypermedia and Telecommunications, pp. 1326–1336. Association for the Advancement of Computing in Education (AACE) (2015)
28. Serrano-Laguna, Á., Torrente, J., Moreno-Ger, P., Fernández-Manjón, B.: Tracing a little for big improvements: application of learning analytics and videogames for student assessment. Procedia Comput. Sci. **15**, 203–209 (2012)
29. Torrente, J., Mera, P.L., Moreno-Ger, P., Fernández-Manjón, B.: Coordinating heterogeneous game-based learning approaches in online learning environments. In: Pan, Z., Cheok, A.D., Müller, W., Rhalibi, A.E. (eds.) Transactions on Edutainment II. LNCS, vol. 5660, pp. 1–18. Springer, Heidelberg (2009)
30. Moreno-Ger, P., Torrente, J., Bustamante, J., Fernández-Galaz, C., Fernández-Manjón, B., Comas-Rengifo, M.D.: Application of a low-cost web-based simulation to improve students' practical skills in medical education. Int. J. Med. Inform. **79**, 459–467 (2010)
31. Warren, S.J., Jones, G.: Overcoming educational game development costs with lateral innovation: chalk house, the door, and broken window. J. Appl. Instr. Des. **4**, 51–63 (2012)
32. Lester, J., Mott, B., Rowe, J., Taylor, R.: Design principles for pedagogical agent authoring tools. In: Sottilare, R.A., Graesser, A.C., Hu, X., Brawner, K. (eds.) Design Recommendations for Intelligent Tutoring Systems Volume 3 Authoring Tools and Expert Modeling Techniques, pp. 151–160. U.S. Army Research Laboratory, Orlando, FL, USA (2015)

33. Hauser, D.D.: License an engine or create your own. Mak. Games **6**, 41–45 (2015)
34. Kruchten, P.B.: The 4+1 view model of architecture. IEEE Softw. **12**, 42–50 (1995)
35. Bass, L., Clements, P., Kazman, R.: Software Architecture in Practice. Addison Wesley, Boston (2003)
36. Masuch, M., Abbadi, M., Konert, J., Streicher, A., Söbke, H., Dey, R.: Lecture "Serious Game Technology". In: Dagstuhl GI Seminar 15283 on Entertainment Computing and Serious Games (2015)
37. Oculus VR LLC: Oculus. https://www.oculus.com/
38. Unity Technologies: Unity - Game Engine. https://unity3d.com/
39. Brannolte, U., Harder, R.J., Kraus, T.J.: Virtual city and traffic simulation game based on scientific models. In: Zupančič, B., Karba, R., and Blažič, S. (eds.) EUROSIM 2007: Proceedings of the 6th EUROSIM Congress on Modelling and Simulation, Ljubljana, Slovenia, 9–13 September 2007, vol. 1. Argesim (2007)
40. Glamus GmbH: Mobility - A city in motion! http://www.mobility-online.de
41. Schmitz, P.: CD-ROM-Kritik: mobility. c't Mag. für Comput. 252 (2000)
42. von Buttlar, R., Kurkowski, S., Schmidt, F.A., Pannicke, D.: Die Jagd nach dem Katzenkönig. In: Kaminski, W., Lorber, M. (eds.) Gamebased Learning: Clash of Realities 2012, pp. 201–214. Kopäd, München (2012)
43. cocos2d.org: Cocos2d (2008). http://cocos2d.org/
44. Takomat GmbH: Energetika. http://www.wir-ernten-was-wir-saeen.de/energiespiel/
45. Takomat GmbH: Good Games - takomat Games|Neue Lebensformen für Medien. http://www.takomat-games.com/en/games/good-games.html
46. Rare: Kinect Sports (2010)
47. Cederholm, H., Hilborn, O., Lindley, C., Sennersten, C., Eriksson, J.: The aiming game: using a game with biofeedback for training in emotion regulation. In: Copier, A., Kennedy, M., and Waern, H. (eds.) DiGRA 2011 - Proceedings of the 2011 DiGRA International Conference: Think Design Play. DiGRA/Utrecht School of the Arts (2011)
48. Hoffmann, K., Wiemeyer, J., Hardy, S., Göbel, S.: Personalized adaptive control of training load in exergames from a sport-scientific perspective. In: Göbel, S., Wiemeyer, J. (eds.) GameDays 2014. LNCS, vol. 8395, pp. 129–140. Springer, Heidelberg (2014)
49. Hardy, S., Dutz, T., Wiemeyer, J., Göbel, S., Steinmetz, R.: Framework for personalized and adaptive game-based training programs in health sport. Multimed. Tools Appl. **74**, 5289–5311 (2015)
50. Maier, M., Rubio Ballester, B., Duarte, E., Duff, A., Verschure, P.F.: Social integration of stroke patients through the multiplayer rehabilitation gaming system. In: Göbel, S., Wiemeyer, J. (eds.) GameDays 2014. LNCS, vol. 8395, pp. 100–114. Springer, Heidelberg (2014)
51. SmartFoxServer. http://www.smartfoxserver.com/
52. Street, S.: Massively multiplayer games using a distributed services approach. In: Alexander, T. (ed.) Massively Multiplayer Game Development, pp. 233–241. Charles River Media, Boston (2005)
53. Coulouris, G., Dollimore, J., Kindberg, T., Blair, G.: Distributed Systems: Concepts and Design. Pearson, Harlow (2011)
54. Hall, R., Novak, J.: Game Development Essentials: Online Game Development. Delmar, Clifton Park (2008)
55. Alexander, T. (ed.): Massively Multiplayer Game Development 2. Charles River Media, Newton Centre (2005)
56. Greenhalgh, C., Benford, S.: MASSIVE: a collaborative virtual environment for teleconferencing. ACM Trans. Comput. Interact. **2**, 239–261 (1995)

57. Frécon, E., Stenius, M.: DIVE: a scalable network architecture for distributed virtual environments. Distrib. Syst. Eng. **5**, 91–100 (1998)
58. Carvalho, M.B., Bellotti, F., Berta, R., De Gloria, A., Gazzarata, G., Hu, J., Kickmeier-Rust, M.: A case study on service-oriented architecture for serious games. Entertain. Comput. **6**, 1–10 (2015)
59. van Oijen, J., Vanhée, L., Dignum, F.: CIGA: a middleware for intelligent agents in virtual environments. In: Beer, M., Brom, C., Dignum, F., Soo, V.-W. (eds.) AEGS 2011. LNCS, vol. 7471, pp. 22–37. Springer, Heidelberg (2012)
60. Jepp, P., Fradinho, M., Pereira, J.M.: An agent framework for a modular serious game. In: 2nd International Conference on Games and Virtual Worlds for Serious Applications, VS-GAMES 2010, pp. 19–26 (2010)
61. Noseworthy, J.R.: The test and training enabling architecture (TENA) supporting the decentralized development of distributed applications and LVC simulations. In: 12th IEEE/ACM International Symposium on Distributed Simulation and Real-Time Applications, 2008, DS-RT 2008, pp. 259–268 (2008)
62. Peirce, N., Conlan, O., Wade, V.: Adaptive educational games: providing non-invasive personalised learning experiences. In: 2008 Second IEEE International Conference on Digital Game and Intelligent Toy Enhanced Learning, pp. 28–35. IEEE (2008)
63. Reichenthal, S.W.: The simulation reference markup language (SRML): a foundation for representing BOMs and supporting reuse. In: Proceedings Fall 2002 Simulation Interoperability Workshop, vol. 1, pp. 285–290 (2002)
64. Reichenthal, S.W.: SRML - Simulation Reference Markup Language. https://www.w3.org/TR/SRML/
65. Barnett, J., Akolkar, R., Auburn, R., Bodell, M., Burnett, D.C., Carter, J., McGlashan, S., Lager, T., Helbing, M., Hosn, R., Raman, T.V., Reifenrath, K., Rosenthal, N., Roxendal, J.: State Chart XML (SCXML): State machine notation for control abstraction. https://www.w3.org/TR/scxml/
66. Stănescu, I.A., Stefan, A., Kravcik, M., Lim, T., Bidarra, R.: Interoperability strategies for serious games development. In: Internet Learning, pp. 33–40. DigitalCommons@APUS (2013)
67. IEEE Learning Technology Standards Comittee: IEEE standard for learning object metadata. IEEE Stand. **1484**, 2004–2007 (2002)
68. ADLnet: SCORM. http://www.adlnet.org/scorm/
69. Henning, P.A., Heberle, F., Fuchs, K., Swertz, C., Schmölz, A., Forstner, A., Zielinski, A.: INTUITEL - intelligent tutoring interface for technology enhanced learning. International Workshop on Perspective Approaches for Learning Environment, 4 pp. (2014)
70. Szentes, D., Bargel, B.-A., Streicher, A., Roller, W.: Enhanced test evaluation for web based adaptive learning paths. In: 2011 7th International Conference on Next Generation Web Services Practices, pp. 352–356 (2011)
71. Minović, M., Milovanović, M., Starcevic, D.: Using learning objects in games. In: Lytras, M.D., Ordonez De Pablos, P., Ziderman, A., Roulstone, A., Maurer, H., Imber, J.B. (eds.) WSKS 2010. CCIS, vol. 111, pp. 297–305. Springer, Heidelberg (2010)
72. adelbla, Marchiori, E., EUCM-Developer, Martinez, Torrente, J., Moreno-Ger, P.: eAdventure (2015). http://sourceforge.net/projects/e-adventure/
73. Silva, J., Teixeira, F., de Jesus, E., Sá, V., Fernandes, C.T.: A taxonomy of educational games compatible with the LOM-IEEE data model. Proceedings of Interdisciplinary Studies in Computer Science, SCIENTIA, pp. 44–59 (2008)
74. El Borji, Y., Khaldi, M.: An IEEE LOM application profile to describe serious games «SG-LOM». Int. J. Comput. Appl. **86**, 1–8 (2014)

75. Object Management Group: Unified Modeling LanguageTM (UML®) Resource Page. http://www.uml.org/
76. Rucker, R.: Software Engineering and Computer Games. Addison-Wesley, Harlow (2003)
77. Gregory, J.: Game Engine Architecture. A K Peters/CRC Press, Boca Raton (2014)
78. Anderson, E.F., Engel, S., Comninos, P., McLoughlin, L.: The case for research in game engine architecture. In: Proceedings of 2008 Conference on Future Play: Research, Play, Share – Future, Play 2008, pp. 228–231 (2008)
79. Göbel, S., Salvatore, L., Konrad, R.: StoryTec: a digital storytelling platform for the authoring and experiencing of interactive and non-linear stories. In: International Conference on Automated Solutions for Cross Media Content and Multi-channel Distribution, 2008, AXMEDIS 2008, pp. 103–110 (2008)
80. Jumail, A., Rambli, D.R.A., Sulaiman, S.: G-Flash: an authoring tool for guided digital storytelling. In: 2011 IEEE Symposium on Computers Informatics (ISCI), pp. 396–401 (2011)
81. Yessad, A., Labat, J.M., Kermorvant, F.: SeGAE: a serious game authoring environment. In: Proceedings of 10th IEEE International Conference on Advanced Learning Technologies, ICALT 2010, pp. 538–540 (2010)
82. Huizinga, J.: Homo Ludens. Routledge & Kegan Paul, London, Boston, Henley (1949)
83. Orkin, J.: Three states and a plan: the AI of FEAR. In: Game Developer's Conference 2006, pp. 1–18 (2006)
84. Majchrzak, K., Quadflieg, J., Rudolph, G.: Advanced dynamic scripting for fighting game AI. In: Chorianopoulos, K., Divitini, M., Hauge, J.B., Jaccheri, L., Malaka, R. (eds.) ICEC 2015. LNCS, vol. 9353, pp. 86–99. Springer, Heidelberg (2015)
85. Yannakakis, G.N.: Game AI revisited. In: Proceedings of the 9th Conference on Computing Frontiers, pp. 285–292 (2012)
86. Rival Theory: RAIN AI for Unity (2014). https://www.assetstore.unity3d.com/en/#!/content/23569
87. Millington, I.: Game Physics Engine Development. Morgan Kaufmann Publishers, Amsterdam (2010)
88. Anthony: High-performance physics in Unity 5. http://blogs.unity3d.com/2014/07/08/high-performance-physics-in-unity-5/
89. Cowan, B., Kapralos, B.: A survey of frameworks and game engines for serious game development. In: 2014 IEEE 14th International Conference on Advanced Learning Technologies (ICALT), pp. 662–664 (2014)
90. Epic Games: Unreal Engine (2015). http://www.unrealengine.com/
91. YOYOGames: Gamemaker. http://www.yoyogames.com/gamemaker
92. Marks, S., Windsor, J., Wünsche, B.: Evaluation of game engines for simulated surgical training. In: Proceedings of the 5th International Conference on Computer Graphics and Interactive Techniques in Australia and Southeast Asia - GRAPHITE 2007, pp. 273–280. ACM, New York (2007)
93. Rocha, R., Araújo, R.: Selecting the best open source 3D games engines. In: Proceedings of Brazilian Symposium on Games and Digital Entertainment, Florianópolis, St. Catarina, pp. 333–336 (2010)
94. Blender. https://www.blender.org/
95. Crystal Space. http://www.crystalspace3d.org/main/Main_Page
96. Delta3d. http://www.delta3d.org/
97. Gebhardt, N., Stehno, C., Davidson, G., Celis, A.F., Hoschke, L., MacDonald, C., Zeilfelder, M., Nadrowski, P., Hilali, A., Wadsworth, D., Alten, T., Jam, Goewert, J.: Irrlicht 3D Engine. http://irrlicht.sourceforge.net/

98. jMonkeyEngine. http://jmonkeyengine.org/
99. OGRE (2001). http://www.ogre3d.org/
100. OpenSceneGraph. http://www.openscenegraph.org/
101. Walt Disney Imagineering Carnegie Mellon University: Panda3D. http://www.panda3d.org/
102. Petridis, P., Dunwell, I., Panzoli, D., Arnab, S., Protopsaltis, A., Hendrix, M., Freitas, S.: Game engines selection framework for high-fidelity serious applications. Int. J. Interact. Worlds **2012**, 1–19 (2012)
103. Crytek GmbH: CryEngine (2015). http://cryengine.com/
104. Valve: Source Engine (2014)
105. Westhoven, M., Alexander, T.: Towards a structured selection of game engines for virtual environments. In: Shumaker, R., Lackey, S. (eds.) VAMR 2015. LNCS, vol. 9179, pp. 142–152. Springer, Heidelberg (2015)
106. Sarhan, A.: The utilisation of games technology for environmental design education. Ph.D. thesis, University of Nottingham (2012)
107. Chen, M.D.: Game making tools round up. http://markdangerchen.net/2015/08/27/game-making-tools-round-up/
108. Electronic Arts Inc.: SimCity. www.simcity.com
109. Cifaldi, F.: Breaking down SimCity's Glassbox engine. http://www.gamasutra.com/view/news/164870/gdc_2012_breaking_down_simcitys_.php
110. Willmott, A.: Inside GlassBox. http://www.andrewwillmott.com/talks/inside-glassbox
111. Buschmann, F., Meunier, R., Rohnert, H., Sommerlad, P., Stal, M.: Pattern-Oriented Software Architecture: A System of Patterns, vol. 1. Wiley, Chichester (1996)
112. OTOY Inc.: OTOY. https://home.otoy.com/
113. Messaoudi, F., Simon, G., Ksentini, A.: Dissecting games engines: the case of Unity3D. In: 2015 International Workshop on Network and Systems Support for Games (NetGames), pp. 1–6 (2015)
114. Cooper, K.M.L., Scacchi, W. (eds.): Computer Games and Software Engineering. Chapman & Hall/CRC, Boca Raton (2015)
115. Hocking, J.: Unity in Action: Multiplatform Game Development in C# with Unity 5. Manning Publications, Shelter Island (2015)
116. Nystrom, B.: Game Programming Patterns. Genever Benning, Carrollton (2014)
117. Schuller, D.: C# Game Programming: For Serious Game Creation. Cengage Learning PTR, Boston (2010)
118. GameDevNet LLC: gamedev.net. http://gamedev.net
119. AiGameDev.com KG: AIGameDev.com. http://aigamedev.com
120. Stack Exchange Inc.: Game Development – Stackexchange. http://gamedev.stackexchange.com/
121. DevMaster LLC: Engines|DevNaster. http://devmaster.net/devdb/engines
122. clay games: HTML5 game engines - find which is right for you. https://html5gameengine.com/
123. Gamesnetwork list at listserv.uta.fi. https://listserv.uta.fi/archives/gamesnetwork.html
124. ICEC – mailing list of the IFIP entertainment computing community. http://listserver.tue.nl/mailman/listinfo/icec
125. Mahardy, M.: GDC 2015: Valve announces source 2 engine. http://www.ign.com/articles/2015/03/04/gdc-2015-valve-announces-source-2-engine

Content Generation for Serious Games

Rahul Dey[1,2(✉)] and Johannes Konert[3]

[1] Centre for Digital Entertainment, Bournemouth University, Poole, UK
[2] Sony Interactive Entertainment, Euro R&D, London, UK
rahul.dey@bournemouth.ac.uk
[3] Department VI Information Technology and Media,
Beuth University for Applied Sciences Berlin, Berlin, Germany
books@johannes-konert.de

Abstract. Content is a key component for successful computer games and it is also one of the most labour and time intensive tasks a game developer can face. As the scale of contemporary games increases, players come to expect higher standards of fidelity and immersion, thus increasing the need to create large amounts of content. This chapter focuses on the creation of content for serious games, particularly research that can aid designers and game developers in generating large amounts of content quickly and effectively. While game developers have had many tools and methods for creating content for standard computer games, this chapter will concentrate on the types of content specific to serious games.

1 Introduction

Serious games require a multitude of material to ensure that users are being satisfactorily informed. Such material is represented as *content*. Content itself can come in many different forms and this chapter will distinguish the difference between various types of content, focusing on categories specific to the field of serious games. This chapter defines *content* as any piece of data that a game loads and uses in the process of typical gameplay.

Section 2 of this chapter provides an overview of the types of content that can be created for both games and serious games, as well as summaries for content creation methods. Section 3 reviews the current state of the art in content related research for serious games along with real world examples. Section 4 presents a set of technical challenges that content creation methods can face during development and uses this information as a basis for offering potential research questions for new researchers in the field. The chapter concludes with Sect. 5 along with some predictions for future research. Section "Further Reading" offers the reader some further sources to consult that hold a wealth of relevant information for the processes of content creation although are not directly related to serious games.

© Springer International Publishing AG 2016
R. Dörner et al. (Eds.): Entertainment Computing and Serious Games, LNCS 9970, pp. 174–188, 2016.
DOI: 10.1007/978-3-319-46152-6_8

2 Concepts of Content Creation

2.1 Types of Content

Serious games tend to use much of the content types already in wide adoption for standard computer games. Typically a game consists of media that gives it a particular visual and aural aesthetic, as well as content specific to the game's mechanics. For example, *Call of Duty 4: Modern Warfare* [56], a first person shooter (FPS) game, contains artificial intelligence (AI) opponents to challenge the player (commonly known as *bots*). For real time game play, the AI for bots can be constructed from scripts developed by the game designers. These scripts are content as they would be packaged as data for the game.

A further example is a role-playing game (RPG), such as *The Elder Scrolls V: Skyrim*[52]. It consists of many different tasks and quests for the player to perform in order to further progress of the game's narrative. The game's developers have carefully designed quests for the game by determining tasks the player must perform (e.g. "retrieve an object from a location", "defend a character from bandits", etc.) to satisfy the quest's *victory conditions*. This information must be stored and utilised by the game, and is therefore content as well.

The visual and audio media that make up other parts of a game's content are typically known as *assets*. The types of visual assets required for a game depends on the type of game. For 2D games, images are handled using sets of textures. Textures are primarily used to represent visual data. For a game this data can be comprised of the player's avatar, objects within the environment, or icons for the user interface. Textures can be used in the same way for 3D games, where they are used to project detailed colours onto a wireframe mesh made of polygons.

Textures have a number of uses. They can be created by artists to approximate various rendering functionalities to save on computation times. Ambient occlusion [32] and lightmaps [3] are used to approximate self shadowing for lit objects and indirect lighting computations, respectively. Textures can also be used as inputs to algorithms. For example, rendering terrains can take a grayscale texture, called a *heightmap*, where each *texel* - texture element - contains a value between 0 and 1 to determine the height of a point of a vertex within a grid [34]. Thus providing a very artist friendly pipeline to develop complex terrain without having to interact with the mesh directly.

Individual images can also be packed into a single large texture called a *texture atlas* [24]. This is to increase efficiency and performance as it reduces the number of graphics state changes when rendering a scene of the game - i.e. it is much better to set one texture resource once for the duration of the frame, than it is to set multiple smaller textures every time a frame is rendered.

3D games make frequent use of *3D models* - typically a collection of polygons representing objects in a game world. Contemporary graphics hardware is optimized for processing millions of polygons within miniscule time constraints so models can be used for both small scale objects (e.g. characters, hand held items, etc.) as well as large scale objects (e.g. terrains and planets).

Modern GPU power and flexibility with writing GPU programs has meant that some games are rendering 3D objects without the use of polygons. Game objects are instead represented using *signed-distance fields (SDFs)* [10], which can provide several powerful functions for mesh editing, such as *constructive solid geometry (CSG)* [17]. These SDFs are then rendered typically with variants of the raymarching algorithm [45].

Beyond visual elements, most games also require an aural element to be a fully immersive experience for the player. Audio plays a major role in computer games as it can relay information about the atmosphere, provide feedback to player inputs, and can even give the game its own style, setting it apart from others in a similar genre.

Audio content can be split into two types: *sound effects* and *music*, both of which are usually required to create games. While music provides information about the mood of the current game situation and the style of the game, sound effects give the player feedback.

Furthermore, there are more esoteric elements of a game that can be considered as content, such as behaviours authored for non-playable characters (NPCs) that act as either friend or as opposition to the player. Many games consist of activities given to the player in order to progress through the game's narrative. They can be tasks given to a player, goals a player must meet and adverse scenarios that the player must find the solution to. Such elements are ideal for serious games particularly focused on training users to deal with numerous situations such as those described in [31].

2.2   Methods of Content Creation

Numerous methods for authoring content have been developed by many different game developers and all of them can be separated into the *Developer generated content (DC)* and *Procedurally generated content (PC)* where each of these categories attempts to fabricate various assets as described in Sect. 2.1. Additionally, the niche of *user-generated content (UGC)* in games is described as it allows new interaction formats and open task formats for deep learning in serious games as demanded from a pedagogical point of view.

2.2.1   Developer Content (DC)

During the game development process, the first set of content that ships with the game is usually tailor-made by the original developers. Teams of artists and designers collaborate to populate the game with content that can be consumed by the player. This batch of content is usually of very high quality as the developers have knowledge of the structure and design of their game, the constraints and limitations of their game engine, and possess the ability to create cohesive elements that fit with the overall style of their desired aesthetic. Furthermore, larger game studios have access to teams of quality assurance engineers (QA) who can provide near-immediate feedback on whether the content produced works on a functional level. Examples of this include: part of a level deemed too difficult for a player, or a 3D model that can be seen clipping through another piece of geometry in the game world negatively impacting on the player's sense of immersion.

In order to do well as a product, games also tend to be designed to "hook" the player early on. This particularly applies to mobile games where the retention rate of players tends to be lower for games that do not provide an interesting introduction [23]. Therefore, to satisfactorily pique the player's curiosity, it follows that the quality of the content should meet a minimum set of standards, such as eliminating unappealing graphical glitches, creating a steady difficulty curve, and developing some form of "fun factor". Developers strive for this and possess many methods to create content to meet these high standards. A good overview of such techniques can be found in [30].

2.2.2 Procedural Content (PC)

A large game (both serious and non-serious) requires a substantial amount of content in a number of domains. Producing the content required can be a long and arduous process. Therefore, it is prudent in many situations to make use of computational power to automate the content creation pipeline, either wholly or otherwise. Such content is produced algorithmically and is known as *procedural content generation (PCG)* which can be either fully automated or semi-automated.

As well as greatly reducing the iteration times, PCG allows for the creation of content that can build upon a baseline and produce a very large number of variations. Providing ample varied content ensures that the player does not have to play through the same scenarios, and in turn getting frustrated or bored at the repetition. Dynamically altering content during the game's run time also enables developers to save on memory requirements as they can simply create only the foundational content that is built upon by the procedural algorithm. For example, an artist could create a hull of a spaceship, the algorithm can then be applied to it that determines how big the wings are, if the ship has turrets, how many thrusters the ship has, and a multitude of other attributes. As the content becomes larger and more time-consuming to create, PCG begins to become a necessity as it can save a substantial amount of time and human effort.

PCG in its most basic form can be randomizing various attributes of a piece of content. [54] and similar games (known as "roguelikes"), made heavy use of random number generation to vary the placements of items in dungeons, the attributes associated with collected items, as well as the layouts of entire dungeons by assigning a number of entrances and exits to a room in a dungeon and where it led to. [36,37] also used randomization, although extended it by introducing a user-directed element with the difficulty increasing as the game progressed through its narrative. However, using a completely random function is often discouraged as determinism is an important property for the development of games. Deterministic random values ensure that validation and effective debugging of the game can be carried out without the game state changing from one run-through to the next.

Whilst random values can produce interesting results in certain development situations, more controllable functions have been developed for a number of different domains. These functions are termed *noise functions*. The cornerstone of noise that has seen use in many different domains is Perlin noise and Simplex noise [42]. The resulting noise value is an interpolation of other noise values based on pseudo-random gradient vectors on a grid (or simplex grid in the case of Simplex noise). These are the primary noise functions that are used when utilising random numbers for PCG, however other noise algorithms have also been created that possess qualities that make them useful for the generation of content such as textures [11,57].

PCG is not only limited to the creation and utility of different noise types, however. It can also use systems based on a set of rules or conditions that satisfy a set of constraints defined by the user. For example, the concept of grammars has been used to create content for games. A formal grammar consists of a set of axioms (or rules) that expands an initial state for a number of iterations. This has been expanded to computer graphics in the form of *shape grammars* [53]. An initial shape is transformed depending on a set of rules until a termination rule is reached. Such transformation rules can take make forms, and recently [33] has taken the approach to generate 3D models describing architecture procedurally.

Lindenmayer systems (or L-systems) [44], and its variants, are another form of grammar based algorithm that has been utilised to model plant growth, generate trees and foliage [55], as well as generating entire cities, including road layouts and building placements [41]. They work similarly to shape grammars, with starting states, rules and terminal states, but differ in one primary way: shape grammar rules are matched serially when a string of symbols is being evaluated, L-systems evaluate rules in parallel, i.e. all rules' effects that are found to match at each iteration are simultaneously executed. This enables L-systems to model the property of growth over a number of iterations.

A disadvantage of fully automated PCG is that it removes much of the control a manual user is accustomed to. By gathering direction from the user, procedural algorithms can be made even more powerful and flexible as it adapts around a user's requirements. For example, a level generator may be able to create a level for a game completely autonomously. However, it may differ from the game designer's original vision of how a level was meant to be. Instead the system could provide an intuitive set of input controls for the user to specify constraints (such as a primary path for the player to follow during the course of gameplay), and the algorithm would procedurally generate other level details whilst remaining aware of the designer's original intentions. While this form of *procedural assistance* adds some manual labour to content creation, it provides a balance between high-level user control and automation of more arduous tasks.

An oft-cited and highly researched form of procedural content that can be found in many games with a large outdoor game world is that of terrain generation. It can be generated with each type of PCG as described above and [50] provides an excellent survey of methods that can be used.

There are many examples of PCG systems that are robust enough to be used in the wild. While there are many examples for computer graphics, more esoteric elements related to gameplay can be created. *Elite* [4] used PCG to create galaxies that the player was free to explore, and more recently *No Man's Sky* [12] claims to be able to generate an entire universe - from high-level elements, such as galaxies and planets, to very low-level entities, such as plant-life and animals that are governed by the structure of the ecosystem of each planet. PCG has also been utilised to generate quests and can be seen with the *Radiant Story* system found in *The Elder Scrolls V: Skyrim* [52]. After the player has completed all available quests, the game begins to generate quests automatically. This offers players a near-limitless increase in game longevity and increases further immersion in the game world.

Various artificial intelligence (AI) methods have also been used to procedurally generate content such as game levels, many of which are described by [47] and a point has been reached where even a procedural content generator can be generated procedurally! [20].

2.2.3 User-Generated Content (UGC)

Especially Serious Games suffer from very limited budgets for creation, but face the challenge to align game story with the serious content properly to create a game flow and learn flow simultaneously. Based on the ideological foundations of the web 2.0 movement, the community of players and potential players could contribute to the game eco-system by creating and sharing content they created themselves. User-generated content ' "comprises various forms of media and creative works (written, audio, visual, and combined) created by Internet and technology users" ' [38, p. 17]. An example of successful commercial application of UGC in games is *Little Big Planet (LBP)* from Sony Entertainment [8]. Players earn more and more assets and creative tools during game play which allow the creation of own creative levels. These levels are shared, played, rated and recombined by the community of LBP players. One step further moved Electronic Arts with the game *Spore* [2]. From a set of basic components players create their own creatures. By crossover with other species new characteristics emerge. The Spore universe of creatures is continuously growing as players share their species online, download and populate others in their world(s) and re-combine them accordingly. Both examples show that the content creation and sharing interaction unleashes creative potential of players, leads to manifold new variations that game developers could not have foreseen and even procedural content would not have thought of. Thus, the game environment becomes more open and allows new deeper insights.

This potential of UGC to allow creative solutions and solutions to open-tasks leads to the attractiveness for Serious games. As Gee consternates [13], serious games lack a support for *deep learning*, which is relevance of the tasks, open-format tasks that allow multiple ways of solution, and emotional involvement of the player, to name some aspects of *deep learning*. From this pedagogical perspective UGC can be used either as an artifact (produced content as result of

working at a task) or as a new game asset that allows manifold new game variations and specializations (egŕnew levels) or personalization (and thus immersion)
for individual players with their own created content (personalized game worlds).
Only few serious game prototypes exist yet that utilize UGC for personalization
or even for tasks based on UGC; even less games have been evaluated in user
studies. One example shows that personalization of game worlds by social media
profile data and the possibility to inject UGC into the game can lead to higher
acceptance [22, p. 123–136] (and this could imply better learning outcomes). To
let this potential use of UGC be fruitful a pedagogical alignment of the UGC is
necessary (as stated in Sect. 3.4 below).

3   State of the Art

3.1   Scenario Generation

One of the uses for serious games is that of training skills, and effective training
requires varied and frequent training [5]. Therefore, scenarios, tasks and goals
are appropriate types of content to be generated for these games. Being able
to generate this allow users to be exposed to a multitude of different training
scenarios and fulfils the sought after experience requirement of effective training.

Scenarios can be made up of a sequence of different tasks meaning that each
scenario has a set of dependencies. Therefore, a rule-based system of PCG is
usually an appropriate method to use. [19] have used a scenario generator in
commercial flight simulators. They do so by decomposing complex scenarios for
a pilot into small, modular, FAA-approved tasks. A sequence of tasks is then
generated and validated against a set of heuristics to determine their suitability
as a scenario. This has been a successful venture, and is still used to train pilots.
[16] is a more generic framework that works in a similar way. They also offer
the ability to effectively validate their generated scenario. By modelling the
scenario as a *finite state machine* (FSM) they also offer the ability to effectively
validate the generated scenario. It provides a suite of tools to be able to identify
errors, such as states that are never executed or conflicting next states, as well
as permitting user interaction to further refine the scenario.

A demonstration of rule-based systems in practise can be found with the use
of grammars to generate scenarios. [28] generates situations for military training. They observe that current methods of content creation is time consuming
and manual. As such scenarios are reused with minor changes made to them to
provide variety to the user. Instead, they decided to use a variant of an *L-system*
known as a *functional L-system* [29]. Unlike a traditional L-system, a functional
L-system utilises *terminal functions* instead of terminal symbols. When a terminal function is reached when the algorithm is run, the function can call other
subroutines and thus allowing for more advanced behaviour. Firstly, they define
a scenario in terms of its constituent parts: objectives, baselines, augmentations
and vignettes. Objectives are the primary driver of a scenario as they define
what set of skills are to be trained by the simulator. Baselines are the simplest

form of an existing scenario and provides the foundation to build upon to create a newly generated scenario. Augmentations define properties of the starting state of the baseline. Vignettes are miniature subtasks that may occur during the course of a scenario (e.g. coming under fire, an object exploding, and other distractions). Their system takes a numeric complexity level as an input and each baseline, augmentation and vignette has a complexity value associated with it. During the generation phase, each complexity value is summed to ensure it is less than or equal to the desired complexity level. As the terminal functions can be executed during the rewriting process of the grammar, entities such as vignettes can be chained together to generate a more complex grammar than if a standard L-system was used. A significant advantage of this approach is that a complicated rule system can be created with fewer rules, as terminal functions postpone the resolution of initial requirements.

Planners are another example of a rule-based system that have been used for PCG. [43] has been designed for military simulations. It takes a metadata file containing situational information, mission tasks, available support information and more. The scenario is generated from this file and uses a planner to complete any missing information inferred from rules created with domain-specific information (in this case, military knowledge of battlefield situations). Some methods of scenario generation utilise a *Hierarchical Task Network* (HTN) planner [9]. HTN planners work by initially creating a high level overview plan from a start state and a goal state. They subsequently decompose each task in the plan into a set of subtasks until a set of primitive operators is reached that successfully spans from the initial to the goal state. [18] adopts this approach in order to generate scenarios for search and rescue operations, and train practitioners to find people trapped in collapsed buildings. They do this by using the *Simple Hierarchical Ordered Planner* (SHOP) variant of the HTN planner [35]. Rather than model the building with physically, they use a qualitative, common-sense approach to generate plausible scenarios. Using this data, the planner reasons about the situation and models how the internal components of the building will interact with each other - e.g. if a supporting structure has been sufficiently damage, it is reasonable to assume the ceiling being supported has collapsed. By building this plan a scenario is generated. However, a disadvantage of planner-based approaches is the determinism they exhibit. This removes their ability to generate a multitude of different plans when the same start and end goal are given as inputs. [18] compensates for this by introducing appropriate levels of randomization to the damage that the walls and supporting structures receive, thus resulting in the ability to generate multiple scenarios for the same building.

Scenario generation has also adapted some methods found in the artificial intelligence domain. [49] utilises knowledge gained from crowdsourcing in order to generate scenarios for a variety of applications. Data from the crowd is used for collecting data that can be used to generate a scenario, as well as validating and evaluating scenarios resulting from the system. This research makes use of a satisfiability solver to keep the scenario internally consistent and identify areas to modify. It uses the crowd database to add activities to the scenario, and finally adds details by using another crowdsourced database to ensure the result is coherent and realistic.

3.2   Terrain Generation

Terrain represents the large outdoor environments of games. While there has been much research done on this topic in the domains of computer games and computer graphics, there are some standout works affecting particular serious games such as flight and military simulators.

Realism is an important factor in the creation of terrain to maintain parity with what the user already knows, especially in a simulation environment. In [39], Parberry develops a method that utilises real world topological data to generate terrain. Typically, Perlin noise can be used to generate terrain. Parberry extends on this by allowing the user to download any piece of geographical height data they wish and then the method calculates the distribution of height values. This distribution is then used to bias some fractal Perlin noise in order to create realistic terrains. This work has recently been extended upon with the use of noise with an exponential distribution [40]. It was observed that the distributions of height values of real world landscapes are similar to an exponential distribution. Modifying the existing Perlin noise algorithm with a small change to account for this exponential factor yielded convincing results, where terrain was smoother overall yet sparsely adorned with cliffs and mountainous regions to indicate the concept of landmarks.

Terrain generation can be a fully automated process as outlined above, however this does not offer the user too much control over what they want the finished result of the environment to look like. A more controllable system is presented by [51]. Designed for military simulations, they separate the creation of an environment into a declarative task. Users do not need much experience in the creation of art assets so long as they have a general idea of what they want the final terrain to look like. A sketch-based tool is provided to create layers comprising the separate components of the terrain, including land, water, vegetation and urban placements. By providing this set of layers consisting of regions of approximate influence, the underlying generation system can infer the terrain model from this set of intuitive, yet powerful, inputs.

3.3   Adaptive Content

Procedural generation can be taken a step further in serious games by creating content that dynamically adapts to the user. Adaptivity has a number of advantages for serious games: it ensures that the player is not fatigued by the gameplay as it removes repetition, also it provides a better gauge of a player's individuals strengths and weaknesses which can be valuable when it comes to analysing results of an individual. Adaptivity is particularly useful for games designed to be therapeutic and useful to a person's self-development. For example [15,58] describe a serious game being used to help a user improve at conflict resolution in the form of a resource management game. The content is generated depending on the user's experience and progress through existing scenarios using a genetic algorithm. However, in order to be able to adapt to a player successfully, the underlying system should be able to model the player's experience to a satisfactory level. [48] presents a good survey on methods that can be used to model a player.

Adaptivity also plays a part in learning processes. For example, when a person is using a serious game to learn a new subject, quizzes could be used to test the player's knowledge. A low score would the player has not fully understood and thus the game can redo the lesson. This concept has been presented in [1]. Using a game to teach fractions, they maintain a "concept map" which determines whether the player has progressed far enough to be presented with a more complex set of equations to solve, thus procedurally generating new questions and adapting.

A framework for adaptive game worlds has been described and developed in [26,27]. It was observed that anything that doesn't make up the geometry of the game world can be as part of the gameplay and in doing so they can be decomposed into semantic descriptions. They procedurally generate descriptions that dictate the gameplay of a game and the framework has been set up in such a way that it can take into account multiple methods of modelling players and their experiences. They then use this data to adapt the state of the game world to satisfy constraints identified by their models.

3.4   Pedagogical Alignment

While commercial games tend to address a broad audience of potential players with a one-size-fits-all approach, serious games are designed for a smaller audience (one exception are the *games for change* which address a wide audience). This is necessary due to the integration of serious games into a specific context of learning. This is strongly the case for exergames (games for health) and educational games. The challenge of missing curriculum alignment, missing possibilities to configure and adapt games (by teachers) and missing technical adjustability are some factors identified by the EU GALA project[1] as reasons for the limited distribution of serious games in education [6, p. 24ff]. Within the EU project 80 days[2] a format was created to allow better sharing and re-distribution of game content. The format allows annotation of game scenes not only by their game and storytelling value, but also referencing of competency fields required for a game scene and competencies learned. The narrative game based learning objects (NGLOB) are described in an XML-format [14], but have not yet been widely used. Like for open educational resources (OER) an initiative has been started by the EU project Rage[3] to create a directory and eco-system of modular game-technology assets that allow faster reuse, especially in the educational context.

4   Research Questions

While there is a lot of literature on procedural content generation in general, research applied to serious games is somewhat sparse. This section discusses a

---

[1] http://www.galanoe.eu/index.php/documents/.

[2] http://www.eightydays.eu/.

[3] http://rageproject.eu/.

number of open questions that may be developed further. PCG has a number of challenges associated with it that can pose problems to novices of the field too. Much of this challenge comes from initial implementation of procedural algorithms and this leads to further potential avenues of research.

Effective debugging of procedural algorithms can be difficult as the inner workings of some techniques are hidden within a "black box". Providing methods to hone in on issues early on in the development phase will prove useful to many developers. Tools to help identify issues early can range from lower level, domain-specific utilities (e.g. contextual analysis on generated content or parsers for grammar-based systems) to more abstract concepts such as a language specifically designed to generate content for serious games.

If more procedural algorithms are being used, much of the control is handed over to the computer. As noted in [21], when the procedural generator is given the role of scenario designer, **scenario validation** can be extremely important when the game has been designed for sensitive situations. For example, any scenario in a serious game designed to aid recovery of post-traumatic stress disorder patients must be validated to ensure it does not contain any stimuli that can trigger a traumatic response. However, if an inordinate number of scenarios has been created it is cumbersome to manually validate each one in turn. Techniques that provide automated and accurate validation of content is open for research in this field and [46] provides a good overview of methods to this end. Some serious games already have methods for validation in place, however these are usually manual - investigating methods to integrate these validation tools into the content creation pipeline could be particularly fruitful.

At a more technical level, with the advent of **high-performance computing technology** such as *General Purpose GPU* (GPGPU) computing - there is a lot of scope for research in this area. Perhaps existing methods can be scaled up massively providing faster content generation, or richer simulations to maintain a user's sense of immersion. Recently, for example, a parallelizable L-system has been developed and ported to execute on GPU hardware [25]. This could be extended to other grammar based systems, potentially extending the complexity of situations generated in serious games, and therefore being closer to the real world.

Many current systems make use of qualitative reasoning models in order to generate their content. However, there is little research in using **physically based models** in order to generate content. Examples of this could entail modeling the collapse of a building physically and forming a plan for emergency rescue could be a more flexible solution than current methods - particularly as one can simply modify the building to generate entirely different plans. As serious games become better in terms of visual appeal, a more physically based model of problems may have a better impact in training users in real-world skills, as reality is simulated accurately.

In more abstract terms, it may be conducive to the wider field of serious games to identify specific types of content and construct a formal ontology. This could be used to help identify similarities in content used for sub-genres of serious and games, and if successful, could be used to help developers in designing novel procedural systems.

When user-generated content is part of the game concept, the quality and accuracy of the content has to be assessed. While for images and written text machine learning algorithms make progress to semantically analyze and categorize the content, little progress has been made in assessing the difficulty of created tasks or the quality of submitted solutions of users. Concepts that combine machine-based assessment and analysis with human-in-the-loop concepts like Peer Assessment [7] seem promising and need further investigation to unleash the potential of UGC in serious games. First prototypes have been investigated that show better acceptance from players and the potential for deep learning in serious games by integrating UGC [22].

5 Conclusions and the Future

As the scale of a contemporary game increases, so does the amount and standards of fidelity of its content. Therefore it is necessary to curb the time intensive nature of creating content. Some form of assisted content generation is ideal for helping serious game developers in realizing their game to the best of their ability in a reasonable amount of time. This can be helped with more research in the field of procedural generation or procedural assistance directly applied to serious games. However, it is very important to be wary of giving complete control to procedural systems as validation is an important step in ensuring content generation is context-aware.

Further Reading

- *Procedural Content Generation in Games: A Textbook and an Overview of Current Research* (http://pcgbook.com)
- *Texturing and Modelling: A Procedural Approach*, Ebert et al.
- *Artificial Intelligence: A Modern Approach*, Norvig
- *GPU Pro* series
- *GPU Gems* series (http://developer.nvidia.com/gpugems)

References

1. Andersen, E.: Optimizing adaptivity in educational games. In: Proceedings of the International Conference on the Foundations of Digital Games - FDG 2012, p. 279 (2012). http://dl.acm.org/citation.cfm?id=2282338.2282398
2. Electronic Arts: Spore (Computer Game) (2008)
3. Blow, J.: Implementing a texture caching system. Game Developers Magazine (1998)
4. Braben, D., Bell, I.: Elite (computer game) (1984)
5. Cannon-Bowers, J.A., Salas, E.: Team performance and training in complex environments: recent findings from applied research. Curr. Dir. Psychol. Sci. **7**, 83–87 (1998)

6. Connolly, T.M., Boyle, L., Hainey, T., Ger, P.M., Earp, J., Ott, M.: Report on the integration of SGs in educational processes. Technical report, Games and Learning Alliance (GALA) (2013)
7. Damon, W.: Peer education: the untapped potential. J. Appl. Dev. Psychol. 5(4), 331–343 (1984). http://linkinghub.elsevier.com/retrieve/pii/0193397384900066
8. Sony Computer Entertainment: Little Big Planet (computer game) (2008)
9. Erol, K., Hendler, J., Nau, D.S.: Htn planning: complexity and expressivity. In: Proceedings of AAAI 1994, pp. 1123–1128 (1994)
10. Frisken, S.F., Perry, R.N., Rockwood, A.P., Jones, T.R.: Adaptively sampled distance fields: a general representation of shape for computer graphics. In: Proceedings of the 27th Annual Conference on Computer Graphics and Interactive Techniques, pp. 249–254. ACM Press/Addison-Wesley Publishing Co. (2000)
11. Galerne, B., Lagae, A., Lefebvre, S., Drettakis, G.: Gabor noise by example. ACM Trans. Graph. (TOG) 31(4), 73 (2012)
12. Hello Games: No Man's Sky (computer game) (2016)
13. Gee, J.P.: Deep learning properties of good digital games. In: Ritterfeld, U., Cody, M.J., Vorderer, P. (eds.) Serious Games: Mechanisms and Effects, 1st edn, pp. 67–82. Routledge, New York (2009). Chap. 5
14. Göbel, S., Mehm, F., Radke, S., Steinmetz, R.: 80 days: adaptive digital storytelling for digital educational games. In: Cao, Y., Hannemann, A., Manjón, B.F., Göbel, S., Hockemeyer, C., Stefanakis, E. (eds.) Proceedings of the 2nd International Workshop on Story-Telling and Educational Games (STEG 2009), Aachen (2009)
15. Grappiolo, C., Cheong, Y.G., Togelius, J., Khaled, R., Yannakakis, G.N.: Towards player adaptivity in a serious game for conflict resolution. In: Proceedings 2011 3rd International Conferenceon Games and Virtual Worlds for Serious Applications, VS-Games 2011, pp. 192–198 (2011)
16. Hall, R.J.: Explanation-based scenario generation for reactive system models. Autom. Softw. Eng. 7(2), 157–177 (2000)
17. Hughes, J.F., Van Dam, A., Foley, J.D., Feiner, S.K.: Computer Graphics: Principles and Practice. Pearson Education, Essex (2013)
18. Hullett, K., Mateas, M.: Scenario generation for emergency rescue training games. In: Proceedings of the 4th International Conference on Foundations of Digital Games - FDG 2009, pp. 99–106 (2009)
19. Jentsch, F., Abbott, D., Bowers, C.: Do three easy tasks make one difficult one? Studying the perceived difficulty of simulation scenarios. In: Proceedings of the 10th International Symposium on Aviation Psychology, Columbus, OH, pp. 1295–1300 (1999)
20. Kerssemakers, M., Tuxen, J., Togelius, J., Yannakakis, G.N.: A procedural procedural content generator generator. In: IEEE Conference on Computational Intelligence and Games, pp. 335–341 (2012)
21. Khaled, R., Nelson, M.J., Barr, P.: Design metaphors for procedural content generation in games. In: Proceedings of the SIGCHI Conference on Human Factors in Computing Systems, pp. 1509–1518. ACM (2013)
22. Konert, J.: Interactive Multimedia Learning: Using Social Media for Peer Education in Single-Player Educational Games. Springer, Darmstadt (2014). http://www.springer.com/engineering/signals/book/978-3-319-10255-9
23. Leuva, C.: Mobile game retention: 16 reasons why gamers leave. http://www.apptentive.com/blog/mobile-game-retention-why-gamers-leave/
24. Lévy, B., Petitjean, S., Ray, N., Maillot, J.: Least squares conformal maps for automatic texture atlas generation. ACM Trans. Grap. (TOG) 21, 362–371 (2002). ACM

25. Lipp, M., Wonka, P., Wimmer, M.: Parallel generation of l-systems. In: Procced-dings of VMV, pp. 205–214. Citeseer (2009)

26. Lopes, R.: Scenario adaptivity in serious games. In: Proceedings of the Fifth International Conference on the Foundations of Digital Games, FDG 2010, pp. 268–270 (2010). http://portal.acm.org/citation.cfm?doid=1822348.1822389

27. Lopes, R., Bidarra, R.: A semantic generation framework for enabling adaptive game worlds. In: Proceedings of the 8th International Conference on Advances in Computer Entertainment Technology, pp. 6:1–6:8 (2011). http://doi.acm.org/10.1145/2071423.2071431

28. Martin, G., Hughes, C., Schatz, S., Nicholson, D.: The use of functional L-systems for scenario generation in serious games. In: Proceedings of the 2010 Workshop on Procedural Content Generation in Games, p. 6 (2010)

29. Marvie, J.E., Perret, J., Bouatouch, K.: The FL-system: a functional L-system for procedural geometric modeling. Vis. Comput. **21**(5), 329–339 (2005)

30. McShaffry, M.: Game Coding Complete. Cengage Learning, Boston (2012)

31. Michael, D.R., Chen, S.L.: Serious Games: Games that Educate, Train, and Inform. Muska & Lipman/Premier-Trade (2005)

32. Miller, G.: Efficient algorithms for local and global accessibility shading. In: Proceedings of the 21st Annual Conference on Computer Graphics and Interactive Techniques, pp. 319–326. ACM (1994)

33. Müller, P., Wonka, P., Haegler, S., Ulmer, A., Van Gool, L.: Procedural modeling of buildings. ACM Trans. Graph. (TOG) **25**(3), 614–623 (2006)

34. Musgrave, F.K., Kolb, C.E., Mace, R.S.: The synthesis and rendering of eroded fractal terrains. In: Proceedings of ACM SIGGRAPH Computer Graphics, pp. 41–50. ACM (1989)

35. Nau, D., Cao, Y., Lotem, A., Munoz-Avila, H.: Shop: simple hierarchical ordered planner. In: Proceedings of the 16th International Joint Conference on Artificial Intelligence, Vol. 2, pp. 968–973. Morgan Kaufmann Publishers Inc. (1999)

36. Blizzard North: Diablo (PC game) (1997)

37. Blizzard North: Diablo 2 (PC game) (2000)

38. OECD: Participative Web and User-Created Content. Technical report, OECD Publishing, Paris (2007)

39. Parberry, I.: Designer worlds: procedural generation of infinite terrain from real-world elevation data. J. Comput. Graph. Tech. (JCGT) **3**(1), 74–85 (2014). http://jcgt.org/published/0003/01/04/

40. Parberry, I.: Modeling real-world terrain with exponentially distributed noise. J. Comput. Graph. Tech. **4**(2), 1–9 (2015)

41. Parish, Y.I., Müller, P.: Procedural modeling of cities. In: Proceedings of the 28th Annual Conference on Computer Graphics and Interactive Techniques, pp. 301–308. ACM (2001)

42. Perlin, K.: Implementing improved perlin noise. In: Pharr, M. (ed.) GPU Gems, pp. 73–85. Addison-Wesley, Boston (2004)

43. Pfefferman, M.W.: A prototype architecture for an automated scenario generation system for combat simulations. Technical report, DTIC Document (1993)

44. Prusinkiewicz, P., Lindenmayer, A.: The Algorithmic Beauty of Plants. Springer Science & Business Media, Berlin (2012)

45. Quilez, I.: Rendering worlds with two triangles with raytracing on the GPU in 4096 bytes (2008)

46. Shaker, N., Smith, G., Yannakakis, G.N.: Evaluating content generators. In: Shaker, N., Togelius, J., Nelson, M.J. (eds.) Procedural Content Generation in Games: A Textbook and an Overview of Current Research. Springer, New York (2015)
47. Shaker, N., Togelius, J., Nelson, M.J.: Procedural Content Generation in Games: A Textbook and an Overview of Current Research. Springer, New York (2015)
48. Shaker, N., Togelius, J., Yannakakis, G.N.: The experience-driven perspective. In: Shaker, N., Togelius, J., Nelson, M.J. (eds.) Procedural Content Generation in Games: A Textbook and an Overview of Current Research. Springer, New York (2015)
49. Sina, S., Rosenfeld, A., Kraus, S.: Generating content for scenario-basedserious-games using crowdsourcing. In: Proceedings of the National Conference on Artificial Intelligence, vol. 1, pp. 522–529 (2014). http://www.scopus.com/inward/record.url?eid=2-s2.0-84908217049&partnerID=40&md5=93ca38f1bd0457e456ab8b180e5713c5
50. Smelik, R.M., De Kraker, K.J., Tutenel, T., Bidarra, R., Groenewegen, S.A.: A survey of procedural methods for terrain modelling. In: Proceedings of the CASA Workshop on 3D Advanced Media In Gaming And Simulation (3AMIGAS), pp. 25–34 (2009)
51. Smelik, R.M., Tutenel, T., De Kraker, K.J., Bidarra, R.: Declarative terrain modeling for military training games. Int. J. Comput. Games Technol. **2010**, 2 (2010)
52. Bethesda Softworks: The Elder Scrolls V: Skyrim (computer game) (2011)
53. Stiny, G.: Introduction to shape and shape grammars. Environ. plann. B **7**(3), 343–351 (1980)
54. Toy, M., Wichman, G., Arnold, K.: Rogue (computer game) (1980)
55. Interactive Data Visualization: Speedtree (1999)
56. Infinity Ward: Call of Duty 4: Modern Warfare (computer game) (2007)
57. Worley, S.: A cellular texture basis function. In: Proceedings of the 23rd Annual Conference on Computer Graphics and Interactive Techniques, pp. 291–294. ACM (1996)
58. Yannakakis, G.N., Togelius, J., Khaled, R., Jhala, A., Karpouzis, K., Paiva, A., Vasalou, A.: Siren: towards adaptive serious games for teaching conflict resolution. In: Proceedings of the 4th Europeen Conference on Games Based Learning ECGBL2010, Copenhagen, Denmark, p. 10 (2010). http://www.image.ntua.gr/papers/640.pdf

Games for Learning

Michaela Slussareff[1(✉)], Eelco Braad[2], Philip Wilkinson[3], and Björn Strååt[4]

[1] Institute of Information Science and Librarianship, Charles University in Prague,
Prague, Czech Republic
michaela.slussareff@ff.cuni.cz
[2] School of Communication, Media and IT, Hanze University of Applied Sciences,
Groningen, The Netherlands
e.p.braad@pl.hanze.nl
[3] Centre for Excellence in Media Practice, Bournemouth University, Poole, UK
pwilkinson@bournemouth.ac.uk
[4] Department of Computer and Systems Sciences, Stockholm University, Stockholm, Sweden
bjor-str@dsv.su.se

Abstract. This chapter discusses educational aspects and possibilities of serious games. For researchers as well as game designers we describe key learning theories to ground their work in theoretical framework. We draw on recent meta-reviews to offer an exhaustive inventory of known learning and affective outcomes in serious games, and to discuss assessment methods valuable not only for research but also for efficient serious game design. The implementation and design of serious games are outlined in separated sections. Different individual characteristics that seem to be strongly affecting process of learning with serious games (learning style, gender and age) are discussed with emphasis on game development.

Keywords: Digital game-based learning · Serious games · Serious game design · Learning theories

1 Introduction

To understand game as a specific and persuasive medium for learning is an approach with a rich history (See Chapter History of Serious Games). In recent years however, this approach has become increasingly sophisticated with the emergence of game-based learning as a research field, the development of digital technologies to support gaming, and the convergence of traditional theories of learning and games' design. Digital game-based learning (DGBL) becomes an important element in pedagogical discussion. Computer games shape the natural life and learning environment of nowadays' students and propose new tools and techniques for teaching, class interaction and home preparation of students.

In this chapter we will outline relevant aspects of serious games supporting a learning process. Under the term games for learning we refer to games specifically designed for learning as opposed to the use of games in learning - although many authors proved

R. Dörner et al. (Eds.): Entertainment Computing and Serious Games, LNCS 9970, pp. 189–211, 2016.
DOI: 10.1007/978-3-319-46152-6_9

positive results within use of commercial games (e.g. Charsky and Mims 2008; Chen and Yang 2013).

This chapter discuss different theories of learning as a theoretical framework for researching and designing serious games (Sect. 2), describes the classification of learning outcomes (Sect. 3), proposes how to assess the serious games learning outcomes (Sect. 4), outlines recent research results in the wide area of affective dimension of learning with serious games (Sect. 5), discusses important individual characteristics of players' (Sect. 6), principles for designing serious games for learning (Sect. 7) and proposes how to successfully implement serious games in learning curricula (Sect. 8).

2 Theories of Learning

A recent study that explored the relationship between theories of learning and game-based learning designs neatly justifies the attention we are giving to theories of learning. Wu et al.'s (2012) meta-analysis discovered that the majority of games-based learning approaches do not explicitly align with the one of the four key learning theory paradigms (behaviourism, cognitivism, constructivism, and humanism). This of course has implications for the study of these games as there needs to be a clear conception of 'learning' as design and evaluation methods will be linked to this conception.

Surrounding each theory is an assumption about what we understand by 'learning'. For instance behaviouristic theories focus on a change of behaviours whereas cognitivist theories focus on structuring - and restructuring - of mental schemas. Therefore, it is necessary to understand the pre-eminent philosophical assumptions regarding the nature of knowledge (epistemology) that inform key learning theories.

It is worth acknowledging the anguish of all theories is that they show us only the part of reality that we question. Learning - regardless of your epistemological position - is a complex process with potentially many internal or external factors. There is therefore a difficulty in reconciling these theories as each theory assumes not only a different understanding of 'learning' but a different perception on surrounding processes such as design and evaluation.

This chapter will cover the pre-eminent paradigms - behaviourism, cognitivism, constructivism, and connectivism. As discussed above, the epistemology of paradigm will be identified before identifying key theories of learning. In addition examples will be used to connect these theories of learning with games-based learning design and evaluation processes.

2.1 Behaviorism

Philosopher John Locke's (1697) argued that children can be considered children *tabula rasa* - or blank slates. He argues that the mind is born perfect yet empty of knowledge and that knowledge comes through the senses. Therefore, pedagogy can be viewed as the practice of transferring knowledge from the teacher - or teaching material - to the student. Behaviourism builds upon this empirical notion of knowledge as a universal set of observable or measurable stimuli. However, it focuses on knowledge as learned behaviours and learning, therefore, as the development of behaviours.

Behaviourism first emerged through the work of John B. Watson (1913), he argued that inner experiences are not observable and therefore not appropriate for laboratory experimentation. As a result Watson developed the *stimulus-response* model - a stimulus from the environment creates a response in an individual through formalising Ivan Pavlov's work looking at *classical-condition*. (Pavlov 1927). This *stimulus-response* model was directly applied to learning through the work of Edward Thorndike (1898) in his concept of the *law of effect* - a behaviour that is followed by pleasant consequences is likely to be repeated (Thorndike 1898). This notion was further developed by perhaps the most well known behaviourist B.F. Skinner. In Skinner's theory of *operant conditioning* (Skinner 1948).

The work of Skinner is perhaps the most evident in modern game-based learning approaches - and even general in entertainment games. In his discussion of *operant conditioning* he outlined *reinforcers, punishers,* and *reward-schedules. Reinforcers* refer to stimuli that encourage behaviour either by introducing *positive* stimulus or removing *negative* stimuli. *Punishers* are stimuli that are intended to weaken a behaviour. At this point it is worth considering the ease at which the idea of *reinforcers* and *punishers* can be applied to digital games. Games frequently reward behaviour in the form of in-game currency, power-ups, and points. Additionally, behaviour can consequently be punished through losing in-game currency, losing items, or player death.

Reward schedules refer to the time intervals of a given stimuli reward in relation to the intensity of the respondent behaviour, and the time taken for the behaviour to disappear after removal of the initial stimuli - referred to as the *response rate* and *extinction rate* respectively (Skinner 2015). Skinner identified that a *continuous reinforcement* in which behaviour is reinforced after every occurrence. This is common in the development of games-for-learning as it involves a simple mechanism - for every right answer, the player receives a reward. However, this reward schedule is identified as producing a *weak response rate* and *fast extinction rate*. Skinner of course identified other reward schedules (Skinner 2015) and for the purpose of games design we will focus on *variable ratio reinforcement* and *variable interval reinforcement.*

Variable ratio reinforcement refers to the reinforcement of a behaviour after a random number of occurrences. It has been identified that this creates a *strong response rate*, and *slow extinction rate*. This is supported by the problematic addictive nature of gambling. Furthermore, this approach of random reward intervals has been heavily adopted by video games to promote engagement (Hopson 2001; Nagle 2014; Sylvester 2013). For example, the random dropping of loot after killing enemy. Implementing this in learning games has been shown to create additional motivation and engagement (Howard-Jones 2011). In these instances players received a random reward for the correct behaviour - correctly answering a question - rather than.

In the case of *variable interval reinforcement,* given the 'correct' behaviour, reinforcement is given at a random time interval. This is a popular approach in the development of games generally - the random dropping of items or resources that can be collected (Farmville, Plants vs Zombies). MeTycoon (PlayGen 2013) is a game designed to teach players about different post-compulsory education pathways and employment options. Throughout the game rewards - in the form of items and new job opportunities - will float along the screen at random intervals. This is an example of the use of a *variable interval reinforcement* schedule to engage students in the learning game. It can be argued however, that this is not a behaviourist approach to learning, but rather a behaviourist approach to engage players in a learning game (Allsop 2013).

This is often a key criticism of behaviouristic approaches to learning, it focuses primarily on the engaging with learning activities - through rewards - rather than learning itself. Additionally, it's use in games-based-learning relies predominantly on extrinsic motivational factors (Ang et al. 2008). For these reasons, behaviouristic games designs are often well suited for the rote memorization of facts, or 'learning' that requires the repeated practice of mental processes.

2.2   Cognitivism

During the 1950s the startings of a revolution began as the behaviorist paradigm began to lose ground to the growing world-view of cognitivism. This shift captured by Noam Chomsky's work A Review of B.F. Skinner's *Verbal Behaviour* (1967). Chomsky argues that a limit had been reached for the behaviorist approach's ability to inform our understanding of linguistics. Along with other writing of the time (Miller 1956; Newell 1958; Neisser 1967), Chomsky's review of B.F Skinner's work was a key catalyst for the retroactively called cognitive-revolution (Pinker 2002).

Chomsky' began to frame the formation of language as an internal, functionalized mental process that follows a model of taking sensory input and providing an output (1972). Applied to learning, the cognitivist approach features a preeminence of this structural approach to knowledge combined with an information-processing model of learning. Preceding this cognitive revolution, Jean Piaget developed the notion of mental structures as *schema*, building blocks of intelligent behavior and a means of organising knowledge (Wadsworth 2004). Learning, then refers to the increasing number and complexity of these *schemata*.

In this instance learning is viewed as the *assimilation* and *accommodation* of mental *schema*. *Assimilation* is the process by which new knowledge is acquired and captured in an existing *schema* - *accommodation* is the modification of an existing *schema* to account for new information. In addition to the demarcated structuring of knowledge, two other conceptualisations are apparent from this simple introduction to Piaget's work. Firstly, knowledge units are internally constructed and secondly, these structured units are constructed with connection to other units.

A key contributor to cognitivist learning and instructional design Robert Gagne, developed this notion further (Gagne 1972) in the development of *situated learning*. Digital games are seen as an apt way to support situated learning as they are able simulate meaningful real-world contexts (Gee 2007; Lowrie 2015) and emphasize player agency and discovery (Gros 2006). The development of computers in the 1950s or 1960s had a significant influence on our conceptualisation of mind. *Information processing theory* models the human mind as a computer. For instance, when remember information sensory information first enters *sensory register* - for very short term storage; before then entering *working memory*, and finally being stored in *long-term memory* (Shiffrin 1970).

This cognitive understanding of memory follows the seminal work of George A. Miller. In his article The Magical Number Seven, Plus or Minus Two (1956) he postulates that our *working memory* has the capacity to store seven pieces of information (plus or minus 2). Along with theory of *cognitive load* - our brain's cognitive capacity is a function of the complexity of the process and the quantity of information (Sweller 1998) - has had profound implications for instructional design (Mayer 2001) and - of course - games based learning (Huang 2009).

Cognitive theories emphasize knowledge acquisition, mental structure construction, and information processing of individuals and the factors that would promote their active involvement (Ertmer and Newby 1993). Therefore learning through serious games emphasizes the context-dependent nature of knowledge where learning is promoted through *scaffolding* - additive learning based on previous learning - for task completion. At this point it is important to acknowledge the considerable conceptual overlap between cognitivist, and constructivist approaches - Piaget himself is considered a key contributor in both paradigms. Although both focus on learning as an structured internal process that actively constructs knowledge, constructivism focuses on this active construction.

2.3 Constructivism

As mentioned the conceptual lines between constructivism and cognitivism are blurry. This confusion is further confounded by the different positions that can be adopted within constructivism itself. Building on the work of John Dewey, Piaget is largely responsible for the notion of *cognitive constructivism* - the internal construction of knowledge structures - whereas Vygotsky's notion of *social constructivism* refers to the social construction of knowledge. That is knowledge and learning is socio-culturally situated and has meaning in relation to specific socio-cultural contexts. Additionally, Seymour Papert's (one of Piaget's students) notion of *constructionism* - the construction of an artefact as a pedagogic approach - adds further complexity.

The work of Piaget, Papert, and Vygotsky can be categorised under the umbrella term of constructivism and they have direct implications for games-based learning. Therefore, for posterity we will revisit Piaget's cognitive constructivism, followed by briefly discussing Seymour Papert's constructionism, and then finally finishing with Vygotsky's social constructivism. Note that these areas are often conflated, and there is little agreement in the way of universal boundaries or definitions for these paradigms. The categorisation we have adopted is designed primarily for comprehension and readability. The reader may note that with further investigation into this area slightly different categorised are offered, occasionally directly misconstruing the three areas.

In the early 20th century John Dewey advocated for a learner-centric approach in pedagogic practice, and a move away from repetitive, rote learning (Dewey 1938). This was the beginning of the constructivist approach in education - a position that priorities *active inquiry* and *reflection* in the learner. This approach has obvious overlap with *problem-based* and *experience-based (or experiential learning)* learning (Ultanir 2012; Dewey 1998). *Problem-based learning* is a popular approach in games-based learning

(Walker 2008; Reng 2011) due to opportunities for active inquiry, added meaning, and additional levels of engagement. Similarly, *experiential learning* is frequently used in game-based learning as games can add contextual meaning to the learning content (Whitton 2009; Li 2010).

Although not directly concerned with systematic approaches to education like Dewey, his work did lay the foundation for Piaget's constructivist approach. For Piaget the need for *accommodation* when current experience cannot be *assimilated* in existing *schema* is a key catalyst in learning (Piaget 1977; von Glaserfeld 1989). In addition he argued that learning is an active process informed by previous experience (Piaget 1953).

A seminal figure in the use of educational technology and student of Piaget, Papert argued that the most effective learning takes place during the active *construction* of a real or digital artefact (Papert 1991). He was one of the first to explore the role of software in education - inventing the now ubiquitous programming language logo (Papert 1980). Currently, researchers are now exploring this approach through the production of digital learning games as a learning process in its own right (Kafai 1995, 2006, 2009; Li 2010).

Piaget reflects Dewey's prioritisation of inquiry through the theory of *discovery learning*. According to Piaget *"Understanding is the process of discovery or re-construction by re-discovery"*. (Piaget 1973). *Discovery learning* focuses on independent - but teacher facilitated - inquiry based learning, often using problem-based approach. The initial theory was developed by Jerome Bruner (1951) - a key proponent of *social constructivism* - and is applicable to games-based learning (Dong 2012; Jong 1998). Again, proponents of games-based learning argue that games intrinsically follow an approach akin to *discovery learning* (Gee 2003; Prensky 2005).

2.3.1   Social Constructivism

Discovery learning as developed by Bruner extends *constructivist* thinking into a *social constructivist* paradigm as it highlights the potential need for a facilitator. When applied to educational games this is illustrated through the use of *intelligent tutoring systems* (Virvou 2002) and *personalised feedback* (Kickmeier-Rust 2008). A key concept developed by Bruner is that of *scaffolding* (Wood 1976) - it is the role of the educator to *scaffold* learning through providing guidance. In Bruner's words:

> *"[Scaffolding] refers to the steps taken to reduce the degrees of freedom in carrying out some task so that the child can concentrate on the difficult skill she is in the process of acquiring."*
> (Bruner 1978)

When applied to digital learning games this concept of *scaffolding* is illustrated through the limiting of player choice, signposting goals, and using dynamic-difficulty (Melero 2011). This notion of *scaffolding* has obvious parallels (and is frequently conflated with) with the work of key Lev Vygotsky. Vygotsky's *zone of proximal development* illustrates a learner's sphere of knowledge in relation to their potential knowledge should they be assisted by a *more knowledgeable other* (Vygotsky 1978). Vygotsky differs from Bruner and Piaget however, as he prioritised the role of the socio-cultural context in learning. He argued that knowledge is culturally created and situated and - counter to Piaget - models of cognitive learning are not culturally universal (Vygotsky 1978). Therefore, when applied to games-based learning social constructivists will prioritise the socio-cultural context that the games will be played in, and the role of the players peers or teacher (Foko 2008).

To summarise, social constructivism emphasizes the interactions between learning and social, cultural, historical, and institutional contexts (O'Loughlin 1992). Constructivism in serious games research and design stresses the interaction among players, games, and this socially situated context (Wu et al. 2012; Barab et al. 2009).

2.4 Humanism

Reflecting the emergence of cognitivism, humanism emerged in the 1950s as a counter to the reductionist nature of behaviourism largely due to the work of Abraham Maslow (Hoffman 1988; Carl Rogers 1969). Both humanistic proponents - like their constructivist counterparts - postulated a learner centricity when understanding learning. However, they adopt a holistic perspective on learning generally and attempt to account for the cognitive, physical, emotional and social l needs of the learner (Johnson 2014). To quote Rogers highlights the social constructivist-humanist similarities whilst illustrating this holistic approach:

> *"The facilitation of significant learning rests upon certain attitudinal qualities that exist in the personal relationship between facilitator and learner"*(Rogers 1990)

Maslow and Rogers argue that learning is a natural human desire for growth. Maslow refers to this as *self-actualizing* (1968), and Rogers described this as an instinct to move towards an individual's full-potential (Rogers 1969). When adopting this paradigm, education - and by extention games-based learning - becomes the facilitation of a learning experience that aligns with an innate human desire. For instance, Maslow's (1943) seminal work A Theory of Human Motivation he stratifies what he sees as basic, unconscious, human motivations to satisfy certain needs. This *hierarchy of needs* has implications for games based learning as it captures the emotional, self-esteem, and motivational needs of the learner. Through the development of affective computing (See Chap. 'x'), it has now become possible for educational game developers to create emotionally sensitive, responsive games (Wilkinson 2013).

Additionally, *rubber-banding* - the changing of difficulty - is frequently used as to not undermine a learner's confidence and manage levels of anxiety (Liu 2009). Motivation is of course, a key area of research (Wouters et al. 2013) and a core justification (Gee 2003; Prensky 2005) in game-based learning. From a survey exploring the use of digital games in a classroom context there are reportedly two primary reasons for the use of game-based learning. First, a belief that learning by doing through contextually meaningful simulations is an effective pedagogic approach and second, a desire to harness the motivational capacity of games (Groff 2010).

Relating this desire to create motivation, experience based learning opportunities back the humanistic paradigm of learning illustrates two key aspects - the assumption of intrinsic motivation in the learner, and the perceived supremacy of *experiential learning*. Maslow argues that effective learning takes place when learner is intrinsically motivated - after all of their baser needs are met - and the are no longer aware of the passing of time. This has considerable overlap with the notion of *flow* - the experience of 'effortless effort' - conceived by Csikszentmihalyi (1990).

Both Rogers and Maslow advocate for the importance of *experiential learning*. For instance, Rogers made a distinction between experiential, and cognitive learning referring to them as meaningful (real-world, applied knowledge) and meaningless (academic, abstracted knowledge) (Rogers 1968). Additionally, many games-based learning proponents - or game as educational tools generally - argue that games intrinsically follow Kolb's *experiential learning cycle* theory of *concrete experience, reflection, conceptualisation,* and *experimentation* (Kolb 2012; Gee 2007; Prensky 2005). Additionally there has been interest in the direct modelling of this experiential learning with game-based learning (Killi 2005; Ruben 2002).

Given the above information regarding different learning paradigms and subsequently theories of learning two things should be apparent. Firstly, there are multiple paradigms that are conceptually blurred, and that these paradigms may manifest themselves in different ways through game-based learning. As mentioned earlier, due to the lack of use of theories of learning in the design of games-based learning (Wu et al. 2012) it is perhaps worth considering games, not from the position of the theories that are informing their design, but their intended learning outcomes.

3   Learning Outcomes Classification

Learning with digital games and simulations needs to be viewed by special optic, they are dynamic systems of information representation that are in comparison to other media able to provide some additional representational aspects. In particular they can attribute sound and visual characteristics to specific details, portray inter-relations of its subsystems and simulate its behavior in various situations (Buchtová 2014). Through appealing audiovisual design and narrativity the players often feel immersed and emotionally attached to the presented theme. For this reason games might facilitate not only a knowledge acquisition but understanding of complex systems and phenomenons.

Wouters et al. (2009) proposed a model of four kinds of learning outcomes that games might have; cognitive learning outcomes (divided into knowledge and cognitive skills), motor skills (its acquisition and compilation), affective learning outcomes (divided into attitude and motivation) and communicative learning outcomes (communication, collaboration, negotiation). To the evaluation of games for learning Connolly et al. (2012) apply as well other important variables that includes motivational outcomes, interest and effort, as well as learners' preferences, perceptions and attitudes to games. We partly focus on those in the Sect. 5.

3.1   Cognitive Learning Outcomes

Cognitive learning outcomes are mostly understood as knowledge and cognitive skills (e.g. problem solving, decision making) gained through game-play. Those has been analyzed by many studies and in their meta-analyses Vogel et al. (2006), Wouters et al. (2009, 2013), Li (2009) proven that compared to traditional teaching practices (e.g.

passive treatment and classic lecture) facilitate interactive games higher cognitive gains. Moreover such knowledge tend to persist over long time (Sitzmann 2011).

The best results (and as well most studies) can be observed in science education as biology, physics and math. Huge amount of games and studies in this area corresponds with reality that the process of measuring learning outcomes in this area is well established and the outcomes can be well quantified and observed. Overall very positive outcomes were also measured within game-based language learning (Wouters et al. 2013). On the other hand only small number of studies comprehend as well social science games or simulations; they still show only mixed results in cognitive learning outcomes (Druckman and Ebner 2008).

3.2 Motor Skills

Recent reviews bear mixed but promising results in the area of motor skills development through serious games (Connolly et al. 2012; Wouters et al. 2009). Real-like simulators seem to help specialists in task performance, hand-eye coordination (Hogle et al. 2008; Stefanidis et al. 2008; Wouters et al. 2013), depth perception (Hogle et al. 2008) and visual search (Wouters et al. 2013). As well frequent video game players develop such skills faster but eventually do not perform better than non-video game players (Hogle et al. 2008).

3.3 Affective Outcomes

Affective outcomes belong to those worst measurable. They can be influenced by individual, social, cultural characteristics or situational feelings, moreover generally they are changing through time. As affective outcomes of serious games we often understand personal attitudes toward specific theme, and motivation to some action or learning itself. A valuable approach to affective domain made Krathwohl with his taxonomy containing five stages of affective outcomes in learning (Krathwohl et al. 1964). Educational practices mostly endeavor to deepen affective states from something what Krathwohl described as receiving - awareness of or sensitivity to existence of certain ideas, material, or phenomena and willingness to tolerate them - to characterization by value or value set - or likely acting consistently in accordance with the values the individual has internalized; the active element. From Wouters' et al. (2009) meta-review emerges that serious games facilitate attitudinal change, but individual characteristics needs to be taken in account. In research studies within the game use attitudes and motivation toward learning are often analyzed; a meta-analysis of gaming conducted by Vogel et al. (2006), reported better attitudes toward learning compared with those using traditional teaching methods.

3.4 Social Outcomes

While collaborative learning appears, social outcomes (e.g. communication, collaboration skills) often follow. As playing serious games is frequently individual activity, if the social learning is a desired outcome, training communication and collaboration should be an inherent part of instructional intervention (Wouters et al. 2009) (for more see Sect. 8). Other option is to implement Massive Multiplayer Online Games (MMOGs) or 3D graphical virtual reality games that reflect positive results in social interaction and communicational skills enhancements, tangibly science literacy (Steinkuehler and Duncan 2009), reading comprehension (Steinkuehler et al. 2010), collective information literacy (Martin and Steinkuehler 2010).

3.5 Complex Learning

Different internal and external conditions are necessary for each type of learning but not all of them are well explored and not a good quality instructional design is always being proposed. The example of well described application area is cognitive learning, there we can find some clear proposition for user experience design and interaction design. Instead for example attitudinal learning is mostly unexplored area where learner must be exposed to a credible role model or persuasive arguments whereas many (individual, social, cultural etc.) influences upon the process appear.

In our everyday life we deal with complex problems and complex tasks that demand involvement of different types of knowledge and skills. In the complex world we need complex learning outcomes. Playing a serious game is surely a complex task involving all layers of human capacities; players have to visually attend different locations on the screen (spatial abilities), coordinate this with mouse or joystick movement (hand-eye coordination), interpret verbal cues (cognitive activity), and solve problems that occur during the game play (problem solving, dealing with complex problems). Bogost (2007) proposes term "procedural rhetoric" to describe the specifics that medium of game incorporates in contrast to other mediums as book or movie. The theory argues that games can make strong claims about how complex systems or processes work, not simply through words or visuals but through the processes they embody and models they construct. Game rules, goals, feedback system, possible interactions etc. are all processes opening a new domain for persuasion. This kind of rhetoric can be highly efficient, maybe unconscious, thus Bogost explores its characteristics while used in politics, advertising and education. Learning within the environment of serious games might get different maybe more persuasive outlines than other learning possibilities.

Considering that still little is known about the cognitive processes that occur during serious gaming, Wouters et al. (2009) recommend more research in the area of effective and ineffective cognitive processes in learning with serious games.

4   Assessment of Serious Games

Although the up-to-date research responds with mixed results, while designing or using serious games, like with every other tool of education, we must be able to show that the necessary learning has occurred. As Plass et al. (2011) stated, when games are designed with the explicit goal of facilitating learning, game mechanics must go beyond making a game fun and engaging, they must engage players in meaningful learning activities. Therefore the very complex knowledge constructed by game-play is difficult to identify and measure by classic knowledge measurements used in schools and training classes (verbal or written knowledge tests and transfer tests). Promising outcomes brought some alternative measurements like ordered-tree techniques, hierarchical cluster analysis, relationship-judgment tests, concept maps, multidimensional scaling and network techniques for cognitive learning outcomes assessment (Wouters et al. 2011). For other than cognitive outcomes might be more appropriate the methods as essays, observation, psychometrics, physiological measurements etc.

One of the most appropriate approach is to make the most of the medium of game itself. Games can learn from the player's actions within the game and to customize its content or pace based on real time data as time required to complete the lesson; number of mistakes made; number of self-corrections made; and more (Chen and Michael 2005). Such build-in game assessment features are called assessment mechanics. They create a new layer above game mechanics and Salen and Zimmerman (2003) defined them as patterns of behavior or building blocks of diagnostic interactivity, which may be *"a single action or a set of interrelated actions that form the essential diagnostic activity that is repeated throughout a game"*. Thus the game can adapt to the player's behavior and to give the player the appropriate feedback. Players come to understand the connection between their in-game actions and the outcomes. Meanwhile, the teacher receives detailed assessment results to properly gauge the student's progress. In addition, the assessment engine leads the student through a series of reasoning questions exploring real motivation of players' actions and/or choices. Therefore teacher can better judge the students' understanding of the material being taught (Chen and Michael 2005).

5   Affective Dimension of Learning with Serious Games

In the affective dimension of learning we can find a wide variety of theoretical concepts describing combination of situational cognitive and emotional state determining involvement within topic. The mostly often used terms are motivation (e.g., Wouters et al. 2013), engagement (e.g., van Dijk 2010; Parchman et al. 2000), flow (e.g., Brom et al. 2014) and interest (e.g., Ritterfeld et al. 2009).

Educational treatments that provide contexts highly appealing learners' affective states were confirmed to have a great influence on (1) process of knowledge construction; (2) situational involvement within topic and (3) later involvement within topic and its related areas. In Isen et al. 1978 suggested that a positive emotional state improves recall, and positive emotions help as retrieval cues for long-term memory. In his research more positive emotions also resulted in readiness to invest more effort in learning tasks. Alternative approaches suggest, that emotions may impact knowledge acquisition in a positive way, for example by increasing learners' interest and motivation. (Hidi and Renninger 2006) proposes that emotional arousal might affect situational or individual interests, which directly influence attention and levels of learning. Active engagement of learners fosters higher levels of knowledge transfer and better integration of new knowledge with prior knowledge (Chi et al. 1994). In a study by Craig et al. (2004), it appears that learning gains might be positively related to state of flow and slight confusion, and negatively related to boredom. Moreover, Litman and Jimerson (2004) pinpoint positive emotional connections as determinant factors of future information seeking behavior.

Digital games are often associated with positive affective states and it became the foremost reason to serious games use in education (Garris et al. 2002; Malone 1981). Games generally provide a safe environment where fear of failure is minimized and curious behavior becomes a key to success. Game elements such as challenging tasks, narratives or perceptual changes might evoke curiosity and consequently motivate students to explore the game world and learn in an engaging way (Dickey 2011). Digital games also provide students with instant feedback on their actions, which helps them to remain in a psychological state of flow (Csikszentmihalyi 2008), wherein individuals become unaware of themselves, their physical environment and the passage of time. Their behavior is concentrated, goal-oriented, and associated with wider and deeper attention. All those qualities are also essential to curiosity. Indeed, even Kashdan and Roberts (2004) apply the model of flow to curiosity, employing the term "absorption" in that context.

However opinion spectrum in the question of positive emotional design within learning situations balances. In study of Um et al. (2012) multimedia educational programs with positive emotional design (arranged through color and shape design of multimedia materials) had a positive influence on comprehension and knowledge transfer, motivation toward learning and perceived difficulty of the task. On the other hand Richard Mayer in his cognitive load theory mentions problem of extraneous cognitive load (2001). In the context of cognitive load theory, emotional content as designed sounds, colors, shapes etc., is on the contrary typically understood as a source of extraneous cognitive load, and is considered a disturbing element for learning. Nonetheless, in their recent studies, Moreno and Mayer (2007) incorporated into the cognitive load theory some factors stimulating extraneous cognitive load but still having a motivational potential.

Positive effect of games on situational learning motivation was described in several meta-analytic studies (Ke 2008a; Wouters et al. 2011), nonetheless the latest meta-review of Wouters et al. (2013) provided mixed results; it did not show serious games as being more motivating than the instructional methods used in the comparison group but proved that serious games are more effective in learning gains and knowledge retention. Wouters et al. (2013) speculate classic design problems in serious games, i.e. lower decision control on game-play that is limited in sake of learning process regulation; problem of balancing entertainment and instructional design with a focus on learning. Last but not least problem stems from methods commonly used for the measurement of affective states (Wouters et al. 2013).

Emotional state is mostly monitored within class observations, direct questioning or questionnaires that may not always provide comprehensive data and largely lack the ability to capture inner emotional richness. Physiological or behavioral measures such as eye tracking or skin conductance seem to be more appropriate methods, because they can be collected during game play. Similar approach offer collection of in-game log-files that is even less invasive and discreet to the player.

6 Important Players' Individual Characteristics

Three big components need to be considered in the process of learning with serious games: game design (see Sect. 7), its application (educational treatment) (see Sect. 8) and a player(-learner)'s characteristics (see below).

As different people learn and process (convert, store, and retrieve) information differently, it is important to understand the characteristics predicting how learners will react on specific content, treatment and situations. Recently, most studies focus on learning styles, gender, age and game literacy.

6.1 Learning Style

Learning style is both a characteristic which indicates how a student learns and likes to learn, as well as an instructional strategy informing the cognition, context and content of learning (Keefe 1991). Previous studies have reported that students' learning performance could be improved if proper learning style dimensions are taken into consideration when developing adaptive learning systems (Hwang et al. 2013). One of the valuable theoretical approach to categorization of learning styles for serious game design was developed by Honey and Mumford (1982). They consider four types of learners: Activists, Theorists, Pragmatists, Reflectors. Activists learn by doing and they like to involve in new experiences; Theorists like to understand the theory behind the actions, they prefer to analyze and synthesise, to have clear models and concepts; Pragmatists need to be able to see how to put the learning into practice in the real world; and Reflectors learn by observing, they prefer to stand back and view experience from a number of different perspectives and to collect data (Honey and Mumford 1982).

Chong et al. (2005) studied relationship between learning styles and effectiveness of learning within computer games. Based on the study building upon the Honey and Mumford (1982) four types of learning styles he proposes categorization of genres appropriate for learners with specific learning styles. Activists took advantage of role-playing game and puzzle where they could use their brainstorming skills to solve problems. Theorists and reflectors preferred and benefited from strategy game, contradictory they did not learn well from role-play and puzzle game. Pragmatists showed great interest in puzzle game, but disliked role-playing game. Reflectors appreciated observing activities, feedback from others and coaching interviews.

6.2 Gender

There is a long-term persisted hypothesis that gender partly determines motivation to play games, specific genre interests, and learning outcomes within game-play. Cassell and Jenkins (1998) indicate that within video games, girls tend to show more situational interest in story development, relationships, and collaboration, whereas boys tend to prefer competition and aggression. Even though percentage of girl-gamers and boy-gamers is comparable, in average girls still spend less time by playing (e.g. Lee et al. 2009; McFarlane et al. 2002).

There have been recently a number of studies investigating the impact of gender on students' performance when using digital games. They describe some gender-determined styles while interacting with serious game and learning with it; Nelson (2007) found girls to be more effective in using guidance and Barab et al. (2007) claimed that girls wrote more in their online notebooks when completing quests, they as well engaged longer time in reflections about their work. Despite those differences most studies did not find any differences in learning outcomes while comparing male and female players (e.g. Barab et al. 2007; Dede et al. 2004; Joiner et al. 2011).

Some studies confirmed lower visual-spatial abilities in girls, but those seem to decrease with increasing duration of gameplay (Nietfeld et al. 2014), e.g. Feng et al. (2007) propose that playing action video games might reduce gender differences in attentional and spatial skills.

6.3   Age

Wouters et al. (2009) points out that elderly learners might have problem to discern between relevant and irrelevant information in the game while the young learners can keep up well without any instructional support. Nevertheless such characteristic is more likely connected with proficiency in playing games than the age group. Moreover those characteristics are being shifted rapidly in the gamers' population. For more see Chapter Heterogeneous groups.

7   Designing Serious Games for Learning

For an educational game to work effectively, the design of the game must incorporate the educational objectives and methods as well as motivational aspects from the field of game design (Connolly, et al. 2012). When games are designed with the explicit goal of facilitating learning, game mechanics must go beyond making a game fun and engaging, they must engage players in meaningful learning activities. The game mechanic becomes an integral part of the learning activity (Plass et al. 2011). In the past decade, research has focused on two topics: whether games can be effective learning tools at all and how games can increase motivation for learning. However, with mostly positive results in these two areas, the next question becomes how to combine principles from education and game design to provide effective methods and mechanisms for integrated educational game design. The question for educational games is not whether they can be useful for learning, but how games can best be designed to support learning (McLarty et al. 2012).

To ensure that an educational game is effective in helping the learner to achieve the learning goals, it is important to consider how the learning content is embedded into the game. Scholars from the field of game design and from the field of instructional design and pedagogy have approached this question from different perspectives (Ryan and Charsky 2013). One approach is to organise the learning content around the gameplay, interweaving or alternating the emphasis on learning and playing – this is called exogenous game design (Squire 2006). Another approach is to integrate the learning content directly in the gameplay, such that the mechanics, goals, and rewards within the game foster learning (e.g., Habgood 2010; Kelly et al. 2007) – we could label this as endogenous game design. A third option, following the constructivist approach and related to experiential learning, is to provide a narrative or environment for the player to explore and unfold the learning content as they go along (e.g., Barab et al. 2005). For example surprising or unexpected moments in the serious game's narrative yielded a higher level of deep knowledge without a decline in the reported engagement (van der Spek 2011). While these approaches are being explored in academia, practitioners report a wider range of approaches, processes and barriers in the design and development of educational games (Lim et al. 2013; Popescu et al. 2012; Ryan and Charsky 2013).

The endogenous or integrated approach to educational game design tries to reduce the discrepancy between design choice made from an educational perspective and those made from a motivational perspective, in order to design an effective and coherent learning tool. In a study on designing a game to teach basic arrhythmic (Habgood and Ainsworth 2011; Habgood 2010) compared two versions of the same game. Both games put the player in the role of a hero that has to combat various enemies in a medieval setting by selecting combat moves from a set of available options. However, in one version the arrhythmic is implemented extrinsically: enemies and combat moves are labelled with numbers, and a successful move is constituted by selecting a combat move with a number that divides the number on the enemy. In the other version, this relation is defined intrinsically by providing symbols that represent the numbers (e.g., the divisor five is represented by a five-fingered gauntlet combat move). They argue that the integrated design of the core mechanics of the game is critical to creating an effective educational game.

While the previous study remains inconclusive on the effectiveness of integrated game design, the need to combine insights from game design with those from instructional design receives wide support. Four leading questions from instructional design were proposed to structure the design of learning (Anderson and Krathwohl 2001): the learning question, the instruction question, the assessment question, and the alignment question. Using this tetrad as a pivotal point, several existing approaches, frameworks and insights were combined into the game-based learning framework (De Freitas and Van Staalduinen 2009). In this framework, learning, instruction, and assessment are positioned to align game elements within the game design to address context (e.g., learning objectives), pedagogy (e.g., feedback), learner specific (e.g., previous knowledge or experience), and representation (e.g., learning content).

The derivative question of how game elements can be used to support learning has received further attention. Recognising that game elements may overlap and that it is sometimes unclear which aspects of them or interrelations between them supports which learning effects, (Bedwell et al. 2012) defined an extensive taxonomy of game attributes related to learning. Rooting the collection in existing literature, this provides a valuable initial overview of possible game elements to include and how they affect learning. Whereas this approach takes on an in-depth perspective on educational game design, other classifications attempt to describe and compare games by their high-level traits (Heintz and Law 2015).

If we look at the interaction of a learner with an educational game, what matters is the activities that a player engages in: the gameplay or game activities as created through the game mechanics. The integration-oriented approach takes on the perspective that these activities need to be aligned with learning. The learning mechanics-game mechanics (LM/GM) model explores how this matching can be made effectively (Arnab et al. 2014). Such a model also supports the coming together of perspectives from domain experts, pedagogics, and game designers. Expanding the LM/GM model for serious games design, (Carvalho et al. 2015) used activity theory to discern between the layers of goal-oriented design. At the higher levels, with the goal of achieving the learning goals, the layers of instruction and learning define actions, tools, and goals for this purpose. At the instantiated level of gaming, again actions, tools, and goals are described to foster learning. By assessing these layers in a holistic perspectives, the elements at each level can be aligned to embed learning within gameplay effectively.

In addition to the mechanics of the game defining the game activities a player engages in, other aspects of the game design are relevant as well. To foster transfer, the transportation of in-game knowledge to applications in the real world, game designers need to consider the distance between these contexts. The taxonomy of transfer (Barnett and Ceci 2002) describes how what is to be transferred (e.g., procedures, skills, principles) relates to the context of acquiry and the context of application, and defines several dimensions of this contextual distance. For example, in the temporal dimension acquiry and application may be separated in time by a small or a large amount, or in the physical context dimension the separation may be defined by the environment. To address these concepts of near and far transfer, game designers may seek to increase congruence between contexts (Holbert and Wilensky 2006). When discussing integrated educational game design we have already addressed conceptual congruence. However, representational congruence seeks to align the game context with the transfer context visually and interactively as well.

Having discussed the specific design choices within educational games, it is important to emphasize that motivation and learning does not work the same for all people. In instructional design, much attention has been given to the differences in learning styles (Coffield et al. 2004; Peterson et al. 2009; for more see Sect. 6.1), and in game design the player's preference is widely discussed (Bartle 1996; Lessard 2015; Squire 2003). Some scholars have studied the implications of learning style for educational game design (Hwang et al. 2012) to personalize games. One important distinction that seeps through in educational game design is the goal orientation of the learner, distinguishing between performance-oriented and learning-oriented learners (Dweck 1986). Counterintuitively, performance-oriented learners underperform under stress, whereas a growth-oriented attitude leads to increased performance. This raises questions around the commonly adopted competition-based nature of many games, whereas cooperative goal structures have been shown to be more effective in promoting a positive learning attitude (Ke 2008a).

8 Instructional Design and Support

Game designers need as well consider the specific needs of teachers, parents, instructors or non-formal educational institutions who are responsible for implementation of serious games into their educational praxis or curricula.

Even though games are complex environments that do not require additional instructional support, in serious games is believed that some support to engage in relevant cognitive activities is essential (Wouters and Van Oostendorp 2013). In recent meta-analysis of instructional support in digital game-based learning Wouters and Van Oostendorp (2013) propose especially modeling (showing which information is important in order to solve a problem and how to solve a problem), modality (the use of the audio channel for verbal explanations to limit visual search) and feedback (information whether and/or why an answer is correct) as effective techniques to support learners in selecting relevant information. Mayer (2008) proposes 10 principles for efficient instructional design; specifically five principles for reducing extraneous processing: (1) coherence - for reducing extraneous material that could mislead students' cognitive efforts and thus limit their engagement in core learning material; (2) signaling - highlighting essential material to structure learning content; (3) redundancy - for reducing extraneous load by respecting cognitive load capacity of each sensory channel (visual and auditive memory); (4) spatial contiguity - placing text near to corresponding visuals; (5) temporal contiguity - presenting visuals with corresponding narration in the same time (voice-over); three principles for managing essential processing: (6) segmenting - assuring that visuals are presented in learner-paced segments; (7) pretraining - in key components; (8) modality - presenting words as spoken text rather than printed text; and two principles for fostering generative processing: (9) multimedia - presenting words and pictures rather than words alone; (10) personalization - using conversational style rather than formal style.

On the other hand the instructional support that would motivate learners to engage in the organization and integration of new information is more difficult. So far the best way is a reflection and debriefing session. Hays (2005) strongly recommends to include debriefing after the game. Debriefing is crucial and should be more than a simple recounting of the game. It should be a structured, guided, activity that brings meaning to the experience and fosters learning from that meaning. Debriefing gives the learners the opportunity to reflect on their experience with the game and understand how this experience supported the instructional objectives of the course or program of instruction.

9 Research Questions

Mayer (2011) proposed very nice outline for future research questions while he divided game research into three categories: a value-added approach, which questions how specific game features foster learning and motivation; a cognitive consequences approach, which investigates what people learn from serious games; and a media comparison approach, which investigates whether people learn better from serious games than from conventional media.

The future research in serious games for learning might focus on decomposing games and finding specific elements efficient in the process of learning. As well developing intelligent in-game assessment systems that help to evaluate players' activities and to adjust game walkthrough to the player's individual needs and learning path. Moreover so far not much is known about cognitive processes occurring while interacting with such complex systems as serious games. More experimental studies involving psychologists and digital engineers will be needed.

10   Conclusion and Outlook

In this chapter we attempted to describe all known important aspects of serious games influencing their capability to provide an efficient learning environment. Wide theoretical background was provided; behaviourism, cognitivism, constructivism, social constructivism and experience-based learning are theoretical approaches that offer an efficient framework for researching and designing serious games for specific learning purposes. Their concepts help us to assess educational outcomes and coverage of learning fundamentals identified by each of the theories.

The process of serious games assessment is an inseparable part of design and implementation. All discussed outcomes: cognitive learning, motor skills, affective and communicative - create very heterogeneous group that is furthermore often interconnected in complex learning outcomes. Assessment mechanics seem to be the most valuable approach today but as well other appropriate methods for qualitative assessment are discussed.

To ensure that an educational game is effective in helping the learner to achieve the learning goals, it is important to consider how the learning content is embedded into the game. In this perspective, while designing a serious game, we need to consider the learning question, the instruction question, the assessment question, and the alignment question. Some important rules for instructional design were as well described - principles for reducing extraneous processing, managing essential processing and fostering generative processing.

As the important questions for the future research in this area we consider decomposing games and finding specific elements efficient in the process of learning and exploring cognitive processes while interacting with environment of serious games.

Further Reading

- Video Games and Learning: Teaching and Participatory Culture in the Digital Age by Kurt Squire (Teachers College Press, 2011)
- Games, Learning, and Society: Learning in Doing: Social, Cognitive and Computational Perspectives by Constance Steinkuehler, Kurt Squire, Sasha Barab (Cambridge University Press, 2012)
- Persuasive Games: The Expressive Power of Videogames by Ian Bogost (The MIT Press, 2010)

- Values at Play in Digital Games by Mary Flanagan and Helen Nissenbaum (The MIT Press, 2014)

References

Anderson, L.W., Krathwohl, D.R.: A taxonomy for learning, teaching, and assessing: a revision of Bloom's taxonomy of educational objectives. Theory into Practice, Complete, xxix, p. 352 (2001). http://doi.org/10.1207/s15430421tip4104_2

Ang, C.S., Avni, E., Zaphiris, P.: Linking pedagogical theory of computer games to their usability. Int. J. E-Learning 7(3), 533–558 (2008). Merriam, S.: Association for the Advancement of Computing in Education (AACE), Chesapeake, VA

Arnab, S., Lim, T., Carvalho, M.B., Bellotti, F., de Freitas, S., Louchart, S., De Gloria, A., et al.: Mapping learning and game mechanics for serious games analysis. Br. J. Educ. Technol. (2014). http://doi.org/10.1111/bjet.12113

Barab, S., Thomas, M., Dodge, T., Carteaux, R., Tuzun, H.: Making learning fun: Quest Atlantis, a game without guns. Educ. Technol. Res. Dev. 53(1), 86–107 (2007). http://doi.org/10.1007/BF02504859

Barab, S., Scott, B., Siyahhan, S., Goldstone, R., Ingram-Goble, A., Zuiker, S., Warren, S.: Transformational play as a curricular scaffold: using videogames to support science education. J. Sci. Educ. Technol. 18(4), 305–320 (2009)

Barnett, S.M., Ceci, S.J.: When and where do we apply what we learn?: a taxonomy for far transfer. Psychol. Bull. 128(4), 612–637 (2002)

Bartle, R.: Hearts, clubs, diamonds, spades: players who suit MUDs. J. MUD Res. 1(1), 19 (1996)

Bedwell, W.L., Pavlas, D., Heyne, K., Lazzara, E.H., Salas, E.: Toward a taxonomy linking game attributes to learning: an empirical study. Simul. Gaming 43(6), 729–760 (2012). http://doi.org/10.1177/1046878112439444

Bogost, I.: Persuasive Games: The Expressive Power of Videogames. The MIT Press, Cambridge (2007)

Brom, C., Buchtová, M., Šisler, V., Děchtěrenko, F., Palme, R., Glenk, L.M.: Flow, social interaction anxiety and salivary cortisol responses in serious games: a quasi-experimental study. Comput. Educ. 79, 69–100 (2014)

Buchtová, M.: Information behavior and learning in the context of new media: digital games and simulations as complex systems for information representation (Unpublished dissertation). Charles University in Prague, Prague (2014)

Caffarella, R.: Learning in Adulthood: A Comprehensive Guide. Jossey-Bass, San Francisco (1999)

Carvalho, M.B., Bellotti, F., Berta, R., De Gloria, A., Sedano, C.I., Hauge, J.B., Rauterberg, M., et al.: An activity theory-based model for serious games analysis and conceptual design. Comput. Educ. 87, 166–181 (2015). http://doi.org/10.1016/j.compedu.2015.03.023

Cassell, J., Jenkins, H.: From Barbie to Mortal Kombat: Gender and Computer Games. MIT Press, Cambridge (1998)

Charsky, D., Mims, C.: Integrating commercial off-the-shelf video games into school curriculums. Techtrends Linking Res. Pract. Improve Learn. 52(5), 38–44 (2008). doi:10.1007/s11528-008-0195-0

Chen, H.H., Yang, T.C.: The impact of adventure video games on foreign language learning and the perceptions of learners. Interact. Learn. Environ. 21(2), 129–141 (2013). doi:10.1080/10494820.2012.705851

Chen, S., Michael, D.: Proof of learning: assessment in serious games (2005). http:// www.gamasutra.com/view/feature/2433/proof_of_learning_assessment_in_.php

Chi, M.T.H., Slotta, J.D., De Leeuw, N.: From things to processes: a theory of conceptual change for learning science concepts. Learn. Instr. **4**, 27–43 (1994)

Chong, Y., Wong, M., Thomson Fredrik, E.: The impact of learning styles on the effectiveness of digital games in education. In: Proceedings of the Symposium on Information Technology in Education, KDU College, Patailing Java, Malaysia (2005)

Coffield, F., Moseley, D., Hall, E., Ecclestone, K.: Learning styles and pedagogy in post-16 learning: a systematic and critical review. Learning and Skills Research Centre, 84 (2004). http://doi.org/10.1016/S0022-5371(81)90483-7

Connolly, T.M., Boyle, E.A., MacArthur, E., Hainey, T., Boyle, J.M.: A systematic literature review of empirical evidence on computer games an serious games. Comput. Educ. **59**(2), 661–686 (2012). doi:10.1016/j.compedu.2012.03.004

Craig, S.D., Graesser, A.C., Sullins, J., Gholson, B.: Affect and learning: an exploratory look into the role of affect in learning with AutoTutor. Learn. Media Technol. **29**, 241–250 (2004)

Csikszentmihalyi, M.: Flow: The Psychology of Optimal Experience. Harper Perennial Modern Classics (2008). ISBN 978-0061339202

Dede, C., Nelson, B., Ketelhut, D.J.: Design-based research on gender, class, race, and ethnicity in a multi-user virtual environment. Paper presented at the American educational research association, San Diego, CA (2004)

Dickey, M.D.: Murder on grimm isle: the impact of game narrative design in an educational game-based learning environment. Br. J. Educ. Technol. **42**, 456–469 (2011)

Druckman, D., Ebner, N.: Onstage or behind the scenes? Relative learning benefits of simulation role-play and design. Simul. Gaming **39**(4), 465–497 (2008)

Dweck, C.S.: Motivational processes affecting learning. Am. Psychol. **41**(10), 1040–1048 (1986). http://doi.org/10.1037/0003-066X.41.10.1040

Ertmer, P.A., Newby, T.J.: Behaviorism, cognitivism, constructivism: comparing critical features from an instructional design perspective. Perform. Improv. Q. **6**(4), 50–72 (1993)

Feng, J., Spence, I., Pratt, J.: Playing an action video game reduces gender differences in spatial cognition. Psychol. Sci. **18**(10), 850–855 (2007)

De Freitas, S., Van Staalduinen, J.-P.: A game based learning framework linking game design and learning outcomes. In: Learning to Play: Exploring the Future of Education with Video Games, pp. 1–37. http://sgiwiki.cueltd.co.uk/papers/Chapter_Staalduinen_Freitas_-_Final.pdf

Garris, R., Ahlers, R., Driskell, J.E.: Games, motivation, and learning: a research and practice model. Simul. Gaming **33**, 441–467 (2002)

Habgood, M.P.J.: The Effective Integration of Digital Games and Learning Content. Learning Sciences Research Institute, Doctor, July 2010. http://etheses.nottingham.ac.uk/385/

Habgood, M.P.J., Ainsworth, S.E.: Motivating children to learn effectively: exploring the value of intrinsic integration in educational games. J. Learn. Sci. **20**(2), 169–206 (2011). http:// doi.org/10.1080/10508406.2010.508029

Hays, R.T.: The Effectiveness of Instructional Games: A Literature Review and Discussion. Naval Air Warfare Center Training Systems Division Report, Orlando (2005)

Heintz, S., Law, E.L.: Game Elements-Attributes Model: A First Step towards a Structured Comparison of Educational Games (2015)

Hidi, S., Renninger, A.K.: The four-phase model of interest development. Educ. Psychol. **41**(2), 111–127 (2006)

Hogle, N.J., Widmann, W.D., Ude, A.O., Hardy, M.A., Fowler, D.L.: Does training novices to criteria and does rapid acquisition of skills on laparoscopic simulators have predictive validity or are we just playing video games? J. Surg. Educ. **65**(6), 431–435 (2008)

Holbert, N., Wilensky, U.: Representational congruence: connecting video game experiences to the design and use of formal representations. J. Res. Math. Educ. **37**(4), 297–312 (2006). http://doi.org/10.2307/30034852

Honey, P., Mumford, A.: Manual of Learning Styles London. Peter Honey, Maidenhead (1982)

Hwang, G.-J., Sung, H.-Y., Hung, C.-M., Huang, I., Tsai, C.-C.: Development of a personalized educational computer game based on students' learning styles. Educ. Technol. Res. Dev. **60**(4), 623–638 (2012). http://doi.org/10.1007/s11423-012-9241-x

Hwang, G.-J., Sung, H.-Y., Hung, C.-M., Huang, I.: A learning style perspective to investigate the necessity of developing adaptive learning systems. Educ. Technol. Soc. **16**(2), 188–197 (2013)

Isen, A.M., Shalker, T.E., Clark, M., Karp, L.: Affect, accessibility of material in memory, and behavior: a cognitive loop? J. Pers. Soc. Psychol. **36**, 1–12 (1978)

Joiner, R., Iacovides, J., Owen, M., Gavin, C., Clibbery, S., Darling, J., Drew, B.: Digital games, gender and learning in engineering: do females benefit as much as males? J. Sci. Educ. Technol. **20**(2), 178–185 (2011)

Kashdan, T.B., Roberts, J.E.: Trait and state curiosity in the genesis of intimacy: Differentiation from related constructs. J. Soc. Clin. Psychol. **23**(6), 792–816 (2004)

Keefe, J.W.: Learning style: Cognitive and thinking skills. National Association of Secondary School Principals, Reston, VA (1991)

Ke, F.: A case study of computer gaming for math: engaged learning for gameplay? Comput. Educ. **51**(4), 1609–1620 (2008a)

Ke, F.: Alternative goal structures for computer game-based learning. Int. J. Comput. Support. Collaborative Learn. **3**(4), 429–445 (2008b). http://doi.org/10.1007/s11412-008-9048-2

Keller, J.M.: Development and use of the ARCS model of instructional design. J. Instr. Dev. **10**(3), 2–10 (1987)

Kelly, H., Howell, K., Glinert, E., Holding, L., Swain, C., Burrowbridge, A., Roper, M.: How to build serious games. Commun. ACM **50**, 44 (2007). http://doi.org/10.1145/1272516.1272538

Klopfer, E.: Augmented Learning: Research and Design of Mobile Educational Games. The MIT Press, Cambridge (2008)

Krathwohl, D.R., Bloom, B.S., Masia, B.B.: Taxonomy of Educational Objectives: Handbook II: Affective Domain. David McKay Co., New York (1964)

Lee, S.-J., Bartolic, S., Vandewater, A.: Predicting children's media use in the USA: differences in cross-sectional and longitudinal analysis. Br. J. Dev. Psychol. **27**(1), 123–143 (2009)

Lessard, J.: Early Computer Game Genre Preferences (1980–1984) (2015)

Li, Q.: Digital game building: learning in a participatory culture. Educ. Res. **52**(4), 427–443 (2010). doi:10.1080/00131881.2010.524752

Lim, T., Suttie, N., Ritchie, J.M., Louchart, S., Aylett, R., Stănescu, I.A., Moreno-Ger, P., et al.: Strategies for effective digital games development and implementation. In: Cases on Digital Game-Based Learning: Methods, Models, and Strategies (2013). http://doi.org/10.4018/978-1-4666-2848-9.ch010

Litman, J.A., Jimerson, T.L.: The measurement of curiosity as a feeling of deprivation. J. Pers. Assess. **82**(2), 147–157 (2004)

Malone, T.W.: Toward a theory of intrinsically motivating instruction. Cogn. Sci. **5**, 333–369 (1981)

Martin, C., Steinkuehler, C.: Collective information literacy in massively multiplayer online games. E-Learning Digital Media **7**(4), 355–365 (2010)

Mayer, R.E.: Multimedia Learning. Cambridge University Press, New York (2001)

Mayer, R.E.: Applying the science of learning: evidence-based principles for the design of multimedia instruction. Am. Psychol. **63**(8), 760–769 (2008)

Mayer, R.E.: Multimedia learning and games. In: Tobias, S., Fletcher, J.D. (eds.) Computer Games and Instruction, pp. 281–305. Information Age, Charlotte (2011)

McFarlane A, Sparrowhawk A, Heald Y.: Report on the educational use of games (2002)

McLarty, K.L., Orr, A., Frey, P.M., Dolan, R.P., Vassileva, V., McVay, A., Mcclarty, K.L.: A Literature Review of Gaming in Education. Pearson (2012)

Moreno, R., Mayer, R.E.: Role of guidance, reflection, and interactivity in an agent-based multimedia game. J. Educ. Psychol. **97**(1), 117–128 (2005)

Moreno, R., Mayer, R.E.: Interactive multimodal learning environments. Educ. Psychol. Rev. **19**, 309–326 (2007)

Nietfeld, J.L., Shores, L.R., Hoffmann, K.F.: Self-regulation and gender within a game-based learning environment. J. Educ. Psychol. **106**(4), 961–973 (2014)

Nelson, B.C.: Exploring the use of individualized, reflective guidance in an educational multiuser virtual environment. J. Sci. Educ. Technol. **16**(1), 83–97 (2007)

O'Loughlin, M.: Rethinking science education: beyond piagetian constructivism toward a sociocultural model of teaching and learning. J. Res. Sci. Teach. **29**(8), 791–820 (1992)

Parchman, S.W., Ellis, J.A., Christinaz, D., Vogel, M.: An evaluation of three computer-based instructional strategies in basic electricity and electronic. Mil. Psychol. **12**, 73–87 (2000)

Peterson, E.R., Rayner, S.G., Armstrong, S.J.: Researching the psychology of cognitive style and learning style: is there really a future? Learn. Individ. Differ. **19**, 518–523 (2009). http://doi.org/10.1016/j.lindif.2009.06.003

Plass, J.L., Homer, B.D., Kinzer, C., Frye, J.M., Perlin, K.: Learning mechanics and assessment mechanics for games for learning. Institute for Games for Learning, NYU, White Paper 1/2011 (2011)

Popescu, M.-M., Roceanu, I., Earp, J., Ott, M., Moreno-Ger, P.: Aspects of serious games curriculum integration - a two-folded approach. In: 8th International Scientific Conference on eLearning and Software for Education, pp. 359–366 (2012). http://doi.org/10.5682/2066-026X-12-149

Ritterfeld, U., Shen, C., Wang, H., Nocera, L., Wong, W.L.: Multimodality and interactivity: connecting properties of serious games with educational outcomes. CyberPsychol. Behav. **12**, 691–697 (2009)

Russell, J.A.: Core affect and the psychological construction of emotion. Psychol. Rev. **110**, 145–172 (2003)

Ryan, W., Charsky, D.: Integrating serious content into serious games. In: Foundations of Digital Games (2013). http://www.fdg2013.org/program/papers/paper43_ryan_charsky.pdf

Salen, K., Zimmerman, E.: Rules of Play: Game Design Fundamentals. MIT Press, Cambridge (2003)

Sitzmann, T.: A meta-analytic examination of the instructional effectiveness of computer-based simulation games. Pers. Psychol. **64**, 489–528 (2011). doi:10.1111/j.1744-6570.2011.01190.x

Spires, H.A., Rowe, J.P., Mott, B.W., Lester, J.C.: Problem solving and game-based learning: effects of middle grade students' hypothesis testing strategies on learning outcomes. Educ. Comput. Res. **44**(4), 453–472 (2011)

Steinkuehler, C., Duncan, S.: Scientific habits of mind in virtual worlds. J. Sci. Educ. Technol. **17**(6), 530–543 (2009)

Steinkuehler, C., Compton-Lilly, C., King, E.: Reading in the context of online games. In: Proceedings of the Ninth International Conference of the Learning Sciences. Erlbaum, Mahwah (2010)

Stefanidis, D., Scerbo, M.W., Sechrist, C., Mostafavi, A., Heniford, B.T.: Can novices achieve automaticity during simulator training? Am. J. Surg. **195**(2), 210–213 (2008)

Squire, K.D.: Video games in education. Int. J. Intell. Simul. Gaming **2**, 49–62 (2003). http://doi.org/10.1145/950566.950583

Squire, K.D.: From content to context: videogames as designed experience. Educ. Res. **35**(8), 19–29 (2006). http://doi.org/10.3102/0013189X035008019

Um, E., Plass, J.L., Hayward, E.O., Homer, B.D.: Emotional design in multimedia learning. J. Educ. Psychol. **104**(2), 485–498 (2012)

van der Spek, E.D.: Experiments in serious game design a cognitive approach. SIKS Dissertation Series No. 2011-36 (2011)

van Dijk, V.: Learning the triage procedure: serious gaming based on guided discovery learning versus studying worked examples (Unpublished master's thesis). Universiteit Utrecht, Utrecht, The Netherlands (2010)

Vogel, J.J., Vogel, D.S., Cannon-Bowers, J., Bowers, C.A., Muse, K., Wright, M.: Computer gaming and interactive simulations for learning: a meta-analysis. J. Educ. Comput. Res. **34**(3), 229–243 (2006)

Wouters, P., Van der Spek, E.D., Van Oostendorp, H.: Current practices in serious game research: a review from a learning outcomes perspective. In: Connolly, T.M., Stansfield, M., Boyle, L. (eds.) Games-Based Learning Advancements for Multisensory Human Computer Interfaces: Techniques and Effective Practices, pp. 232–255. IGI Global, Hershey (2009)

Wouters, P., Spek, E., Oostendorp, H.: Measuring learning in serious games: a case study with structural assessment. Educ. Tech. Res. Dev. **59**(6), 741–763 (2011). doi:10.1007/s11423-010-9183-0

Wouters, P., van Nimwegen, C., van Oostendorp, H., van der Spek, E.D.: A meta-analysis of the cognitive and motivational effects of serious games. J. Educ. Psychol. (2013). doi:10.1037/a0031311

Wouters, P., Van Oostendorp, H.: A meta-analytic review of the role of instructional support in game-based learning. Comput. Educ. **60**, 412–425 (2013)

Wu, W., Hsiao, H., Wu, P., Lin, C., Huang, S.: Investigating the learning-theory foundations of game-based learning: a meta-analysis. J. Comput. Assist. Learn. **28**(3), 265–279 (2012)

Games for Health

Jan D. Smeddinck[✉]

Digital Media Lab, TZI, University of Bremen, Bremen, Germany
smeddinck@tzi.de

Abstract. Health is an elementary foundation of prosperous human life. Average human life expectancy has never been as long as it is today and medical advances have greatly improved overall population health. However, modern societies are burdened by new complications in the form of lifestyle diseases which arise due to various aspects of modern life, such as sedentary behavior. The pressure on public health systems is ever increasing with the emergence of further complex and expensive treatment options, and due to the complications resulting from demographic change. The technological advancements of the industrial and information age, the computational revolution in general, and video games for entertainment specifically contribute to the prevalence of some prevalent lifestyle-related health issues. At the same time, computing devices and interactive applications also play an important role in improving all areas of individual and public health. Recent research and early commercial releases deliver convincing evidence that playful applications and games for health in particular offer approaches that can help overcome the motivational barriers which often restrain successful health treatments or preventive actions and behavior. This chapter provides an overview of the arguments that motivate the application of play and game techniques for personal and public health. It summarizes the basic promises and challenges of games for health research and development, provides starting points regarding their design and implementation, illustrates selected aspects along the lines of exemplary applications, and hints at pressing open challenges as well as promising avenues for further research and developments. A selection of quality references for further reading is included in the last section.

Keywords: Serious games · Games for health · Exergames · Motion-based games · Health · Game design · Game user research

1 Introduction

Playful digital media applications for serious purposes in health, or *games for health* (GFH), have seen growing attention both in research and in industry, especially since ubiquitous connectivity and sensors have enabled a large number of promising use cases beyond mere information processing. Nowadays, games for health are created for a large variety of purposes ranging from the classic use cases in information processing and analysis, over individual and public education, to the active support of diagnostics or treatments [52].

R. Dörner et al. (Eds.): Entertainment Computing and Serious Games, LNCS 9970, pp. 212–264, 2016.
DOI: 10.1007/978-3-319-46152-6_10

In the area of physiotherapy, rehabilitation, and prevention (PRP) [136], for example, motion-based games for the support of existing treatments and exercises [119] have been explored for a wide range of target groups, such as older adults [10,39,53,149,155], people with Parkinson's disease [11,110,134], children with cerebral palsy [45,68,74], people in stroke recovery [6,29,38,156], and more [52], with many positive indications [62,72,102,124]. Other application scenarios cover a broad range from surgeon education [61], over public health information [47], to personal hygiene and nutrition [14], as well as cognition and mental health [7,10,51].

Independent of the specific application area, games for health offer three central pillars of potential [135] which also apply to serious games in general. Most prominently, they have the potential to (1) *motivate* players to perform tasks that they might otherwise be less motivated to perform by employing a playful, game-like, or fully game-style mixture of design, reward structures, game mechanics, and storytelling. However, due to their interactive nature, serious games can also offer (2) *guidance* and *feedback* regarding the task at hand that might otherwise not be available, thereby potentially improving task execution and minimizing the risk of mal-executions. Lastly, next to momentary feedback for guidance, serious games (e.g. for health) can also provide tools to support the (3) *analysis* of user performance over time, which can help with forming a more objective picture of individual progress.

In order to utilize these potentials, games for health need to be carefully designed to match the respective use case and target group. To this end, user-centered iterative design and participatory approaches are frequently applied. However, since iterative design usually targets average users from a larger group, and since the target groups of games for health are often composed of individuals with very heterogeneous abilities and needs, methods for personalization via adaptability and adaptivity are required if the use of the potentials is to be optimized (cf. also Streicher and Smeddinck on *Personalized and Adaptive Serious Games* in this volume). While adaptability and adaptivity [17] in the context of health applications are a topic that has been covered by research for many years, recent advancements in the mobility, ubiquitous availability, and inter-subjectivity of the analysis of sensor data and user performances allow for much more comprehensive and contextually grounded data analysis and user model construction. In turn, these developments facilitate more densely evidence-based and quantitatively stable decision-making.

Besides the potential of playful methods and games in health which motivates research and development, there is also considerable economic pressure that is visible in auspicious market estimations [124]. Despite the positive outlook, games for health developments are often held back by challenges such as the complexity of clinical validations, the need to compete with high-quality game productions, limited evaluation methods, regulatory hurdles, and limited acceptance of playfulness in professional and serious contexts. Due to the inter-disciplinarity in the research and development of games for health, which involve game designers, researchers, and professionals, as well as due to the dual role of players that are often patients with primary and secondary interests that differ both from those of regular gamers and between individuals, various complex and interdependent challenges arise. At the same time, a wide range of design and research methods have been tested in the context of games for health and some guidelines are beginning to emerge together with informative application examples.

The remainder of this chapter will provide detailed discussions of the topics that were summarized in this introduction and aims to leave the reader with an initial broad understanding of the state of the art, the central challenges, technical and methodological approaches, and avenues for future work, allowing for directed further reading and exploration of this comparatively young and yet broad and challenging research area.

1.1   Chapter Overview

This chapter is structured as follows:

Foundations of Games for Health. A summary of the foundations that support a further discussion of the topic, including the terminology, the relation to eHealth, the central promises of games for health, a brief discussion of theories of motivation that are closely tied to games for health and serious games as a whole, heterogeneity as a central challenge in the design, development, and evaluation of games for health, as well as an overview of considerations on types and classes of games for health.

Designing Games for Health. A discussion of important aspects of the design of games for health, such as the importance of user and expert involvement, the perspective on player abilities as resources, considering levels of gamification and the importance of stories, as well as general approaches to evaluations.

Games for Health Examples and Illustration. The section contains a summary of seminal work together with a discussion of the progression of three consecutive games for health projects that serves to illustrate practical challenges, approaches to these challenges, design and implementation strategies, intermediate evaluations, and the respective outcomes that occurred during the practical research and development of motion-based games for health projects.

Challenges with Designing and Researching GFH. A summary of common challenges that occur when researching, designing, and implementing games for health, ranging from interdisciplinary and multiple party interests, over heterogeneous target groups and the need for adaptability and adaptivity, to safety, practical integration, long-term situated evaluation, and ethics, data privacy, as well as regulatory concerns.

Current Trends and Open Research Questions. A brief outlook on promising avenues for currently breaking and future work.

Conclusion, Outlook, and Further Reading. This chapter closes with a general summary of the content and the outlook, together with a brief list of recommended related work for further reading and online resources that contain further information on the topic of games for health.

2   Foundations of Games for Health

Games and playful elements have been used for serious purposes in health even before the appearance of computer or video games. Examples range from colorful illustrations in eye-sight tests for children to analogies such as "holding one's arms up like branches of a tree", or "hopping like a frog" in kinesiatric therapy. The potential transfer from employing the motivational power of traditional (non-video) games and playful elements for health purposes to employing computer or video games instead has been recognized even in very early video game research literature. Crawford [35], for example, highlights physical or mental exercise as a secondary motivation to play games that is rooted in the evolutionary benefits of engaging in such exercises.

Since the early conceptual references, *games for health* has not been the only term used to describe the application of computer or video games for serious purposes related to health. An overview of common terminology, including definitions that this chapter relies upon and relating the most central terms to each other, thus lays the foundation for the following sections on *the foundations of games for health*. The central promises of games for health are covered in a separate section, as well as the foundations from motivational psychology that are frequently employed in serious games and general game research and design. The central challenges stemming from the heterogeneous abilities and needs of target groups of games for health, the interdisciplinary nature of games for health research, design, and development, as well as the interests of various parties involved with creating and using games for health are also discussed. Furthermore, general eHealth is discussed as a larger related context for games for health together with central approaches in GFH, a structure for the types and classes of GFH, and a gamification continuum to provide a further delimitation of GFH from related approaches.

2.1   Terminology

The *Games for Health Project*[1] defines *games for health* simply as "game technologies that improve health and the delivery of health care" [115]. GFH are sometimes referred to as *serious games for health*. Since the term *serious* is

---

[1] Games for Health Project: http://www.gamesforhealth.org/.

redundant, the addition can be abandoned. The term *health games* is used synonymously. Other less common terms that are used synonymously are *eHealth games* [34], *digital health games* [18,24], *healthy gaming* [25], and more. In order to avoid fragmentation of the field, it appears advisable to consider whether the term *games for health* may be used in future discourse. Other terms such as *exergames*, *fitness games*, *virtual rehabilitation*, *kinesiatric games*, *motion-based games for health*, *mental health games*, or *cognition games* are sometimes used synonymously, although they can arguably be seen to describe specific subclasses of GFH (here: different physical and mental health targets).

The terms *gamified health*, *health gamification*, or alternatively *gHealth* bring the aspect of *gamification* into the terminology and are not easily dismissed since they do arguably match the definition provided for GFH above. Since the debate on gamification and games is not the topic of this chapter, this text operates on the premise that both approaches reflect different angles of the same concept of using game technologies [44] to improve health and the delivery of health care: While gamified health highlights the underlying serious purpose and application as the origin to which gamification elements can be added to a variable degree, GFH highlights the motivational potential of fully fledged games which can encompass a certain range of serious health purposes.

While games for health can often also be *games for behavior change* [48,65] or *persuasive games* [111], those two classes encompass many other application areas. Moreover, GFH can also be non-persuasive and not tailored towards behavior change (as for example in many GFH that support the education or training of health care professionals [14]). There is, however, considerable overlap between *education* or *learning games* that target professional or public education in health related areas and *educational* or *learning games for health* that is difficult to avoid since the framing usually depends on the professional backgrounds of the researchers or game designers. It is therefore important to be aware of the various angles that different researchers, designers, developers, and GFH projects can take regarding the same core subject matter.

2.2 Background in eHealth

Games for health are rooted in both (serious) games and health information technology applications. The latter are also frequently referred to as *eHealth*. The eHealth field is currently growing rapidly, fueled by an increased connectivity of devices and services, as well as by growth in the areas of mobile devices and other affordable multi-sensor devices with access to powerful data processing. Mobile eHealth applications exist for a large range of application areas ranging from diagnostics, over education and information or health service localization and promotion, to activity tracking and the active support of treatments. Although the integration in widespread public health treatment is often still experimental [100], more than 31,000 applications were reportedly available on app markets by 2014 [97]. In an example of a rather developed eHealth market segment, a number of tracking platforms for exercising and fitness have been established (e.g.

Strava, RunTastic, RunKeeper, Nike Plus, MyFitnessPal, etc.) [88]. These applications support a wide range of different sports and health activities, but they usually do not incorporate specific health treatments and they are limited to the support of selected consumer tracking devices. However, many applications tailored to specific and often complex medical devices, such as robotic walking aids or exoskeletal hands for rehabilitation [116], are currently being researched and developed. The notable involvement in existing or upcoming eHealth platforms of all big players in digital technology, namely Apple, Google, and Microsoft [94] shows that eHealth is a considerable market.

While digital health applications are already being used by more than 30 % of all US adults [88], there is still a lack of clinical research, especially regarding the usage of the platforms that encompass multiple health related activities [21, 88]. Despite this widespread lack of clear scientific evidence, many consumers are willing to pay for existing applications, even in cases where manual data entry is required [94]. Due to the growing number of integrated sensors and their processing and connective capabilities, smartphones (and to a certain extent tablets and digital watches) are becoming the primary devices for eHealth platforms and their interfaces. This, of course, raises a need of ethical and lawful data storage and processing [118], which also applies to most GFH.

2.3   Promises of Games for Health

In the context of motion-based games for the support of physiotherapy, rehabilitation, and prevention, three central areas of potential benefits of employing game technology have been identified in a classification that arguably generalizes to motion-based games for health (MGH), GFH, and even serious games as a whole. These three "promises" are motivation, guidance, and analysis [103,135] (Fig. 1).

Motivation: Game technology enables entertaining and captivating experiences that can motivate players to perform actions, even if these actions are repetitive, strenuous, or straight out undesirable to a considerable extent. This is clearly evidenced by behaviors such as grinding in games, where players willingly accept long stretches of tiring and repetitive activities due to the promise of following rewards. In GFH this can mean, for example, that patients can be motivated to perform the often strenuous and repetitive exercises that are required for successful physiotherapy or rehabilitation. In the context of health professional education, games or a playful approach can motivate surgeons to perform a large number of simulator trials whilst staying focused despite being aware of the unreal nature of the procedure. A specific example of a GFH that makes use of a broad range of motivating game elements is Valedo [81].

Guidance: The interactive nature of digital applications paired with sensing and feedback modalities as well as analytic abilities allow for guiding the players regarding the quality and safety of their target activity performance. In the context of MGH this can mean that players are informed when they fail to assume the proper stance or pose during a physiotherapy exercise and that corrections can be offered, potentially avoiding mal-executions and injuries, especially in situations where no professional support would otherwise be available, such as in the frequent use case of exercising at home. The same principle can apply to a professional health game for surgeon training that could facilitate training with less (or without immediate) supervision. Specific examples can be found in the visual body representations with highlights and shapes outlining go-to positions or postures in the VirtualRehab Body [150] and Reflexion Health [1] systems.

Analysis: GFH are usually deployed on platforms with rich information processing capabilities and Internet connectivity, making data aggregation across sessions (and potentially also across different users) possible. Thus, the regular and prolonged usage of GFH allows for the objective analysis of the development of individuals with regard to specific game performances, and sometimes even regarding general abilities, which can be useful for individual users and professional personnel alike. In the context of motion-based games for the support of physiotherapy, for example, it is usually difficult for patients and therapists to gain an objective impression of patient performance and development between practice visits. MGH can deliver objective data for the time between practice visits, where therapists previously had to rely solely on patients' self-reports [148]. Users of professional learning GFH and their educators can likewise benefit from developmental overviews and grounded projections. Practical examples can be found in many patient and professional information interfaces for games for health and in personalized reports, such as the development reports targeting parents that are available in the game *Meister Cody* (transl.: Master Cody) by Kasaa Health, which focuses on children with dyscalculia [90,91].

Considering the wide scope of these promises, it is important to recognize that any specific GFH does not have to implement all of them to the full extent, since GFH are already successful in beating many baselines that are defined by the most common approaches to real-world situated health applications. For

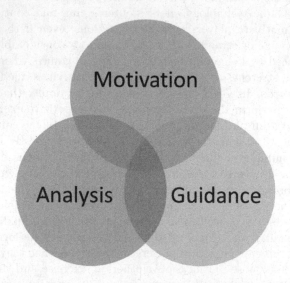

Fig. 1. Three central areas of potential benefits of GFH; after [103,135].

example, as Uzor et al. show [148], the current standard in many kinesiatric therapy applications for practicing at home is to provide patients with a sheet of paper with some instructive images and a description of how to perform exercises. It was shown that this practice leads to patients performing exercises in a suboptimal or even malicious manner, miscounting their repetitions, forgetting whole sets of exercises, misreporting to therapists, etc. [148]. It is clearly apparent that the potential in data recording and analysis of MGH offer opportunities for improvements regarding these problems. On a similar note, the inter-rater variance of movement quality judgements between therapists has been shown to be considerably high [114], meaning that different therapists, for reasons such as different schooling or professional foci, may judge the quality of a certain movement execution by a patient considerably differently. The objective data gathered by GFH and analyses based on such data have the potential to offer improvements with regard to such issues as well.

While these potential areas of benefit certainly validate research and development efforts in GFH, it is important to underline that the potentials are frequently abused to exaggerate the practical benefits of GFH and even to challenge the relevance of human health professionals. As the following sections regarding challenges of GFH will show, it is much more reasonable to approach research and development regarding GFH with an aim at augmenting the available palette of tools for supporting health and the delivery of health care. Health professionals will likely continue to play a central role in steering the general direction of treatments and in assuring the adequacy of using specific GFH with apt configurations. In any case, the research and development of GFH involves considerable challenges. In the context of the foundations of GFH, an awareness of the psychological basis of motivation and employing existing theories based on an understanding of the implications of widely varying individual abilities, needs, and the resulting game and exercise performance skills, is key to successful GFH projects.

2.4   Theories on Motivation and Games for Health

Related work in GFH references the same foundations that are frequently relied upon in general serious games and game user research. Perhaps most prominently, the theory of *flow* is used to explain how games can motivate players to become so engaged that they are apparently completely drawn 'out of their bodies' and 'into a play session' [36]. While flow theory encompasses analog play and many other activities that can induce the arguably highly intrinsically motivated state of flow that supports the execution of evolutionarily beneficial activities [36], it has been connected to digital games both by Csikszentmihalyi [37] and other authors (e.g. [32]). From a number of requirements that can facilitate a state of flow [36], the balance between the skills of a player and the challenges presented (by the game), is most frequently employed in order to illustrate the game design challenge of creating adequate tasks and exercises that match a given player at a given time.

Concerning GFH, Sinclair et al. [129] have presented the important argument that in motion-based applications for exercise and health, the balance between player skills and game challenges exceeds the traditional focus on digital game design and mechanics, and the balance between physical abilities of a player and the challenges presented plays an equally important role (see Fig. 2) [130]. It is also due to the interwoven nature of cognitive and physical activity in motion-based games for health that they are almost intrinsically of a dual-task nature [113]. Dual-tasks have been shown to be more beneficial than either cognitive or motor training alone [27]. The dual-flow approach to the balance of skills and challenges can be generalized to highlight the need to consider any physicality or otherwise expressed ability or skill that is directly linked to the effectiveness of an intended outcome of any GFH (not only motion-based) or serious game. For example, if mental skills are the serious focus in a GFH, the balance between player skill and presented challenges regarding these skills must be considered in addition to any balance of challenges and skills related to the playful or game elements employed in the GFH. Arguably, in many well integrated GFH there is an overlap between these two areas; however, both views are important angles of consideration during game design and for game user research in the context of games with serious purposes that are to be implemented in an effective manner while maintaining the motivating power of (adequately challenging) game play.

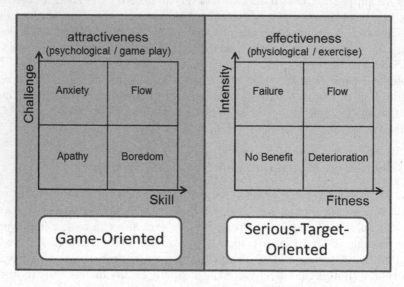

Fig. 2. The dual-flow model for exergames; a generalized adaptation of the model after Sinclair et al. [130].

In these terms, it is also apparent that this perspective can be connected to the three central promises of GFH, where motivation corresponds to attractiveness, and guidance and analysis are linked to effectiveness (momentary and prolonged).

As another approach on motivation, *self-determination theory* (SDT) [41] is increasingly being used in the context of games, serious games, and GFH. Summarizing in plain terms, SDT as a need satisfaction theory states that three basic human needs must be fulfilled in order to support intrinsic motivation via a self-determination motive: *competence* (the need to feel competent at things we do), *autonomy* (the need to feel free in our decisions and goal selection), and *relatedness* (the need to feel related and socially connected to other people). Rigby and Ryan [121,123] have convincingly established the application of SDT in games, while SDT has also been successfully employed in the context of sports/exercising and general health behavior motivation. It is therefore a very interesting tool in the context of GFH and MGH. Psychometric instruments constructed on the basis of SDT, such as the *intrinsic motivation inventory* [104] or the *player experience of need satisfaction* questionnaire [122] can not only supply game researchers and designers with validated measures of motivation, but also shed light on the subscales of motivation that often show additional telling trends under experimental manipulation [19,20,136] (Fig. 3).

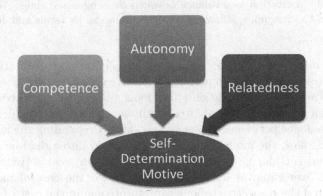

Fig. 3. Competence, autonomy, and relatedness needs satisfaction combined facilitate the self-determination motive. After Deci et al. [41].

While stemming from different schools, flow theory and SDT do recognize each other and research could benefit from the simultaneous use of both theories despite their similar foci. While SDT focuses mainly on the basic premises that shape a self-determination motive that enables intrinsic motivation in the first place, flow theory is mostly concerned with questions around how a momentary situation of very strong intrinsic motivation arises and how it can be maintained [139]. Thus, both approaches can make important contributions to dissecting the overall perception of motivation in research on GFH. Likewise, Denis and Jouvelot [42] have suggested a model that relies on SDT, however, they establish motivation in the context of games as a balance of challenge and skills in a manner akin to the application of flow theory in the context of games [32].

Drawing from the classification of motivational qualities into (a) *intrinsic motivation*, which relates to the push to act freely and on one's own volition,

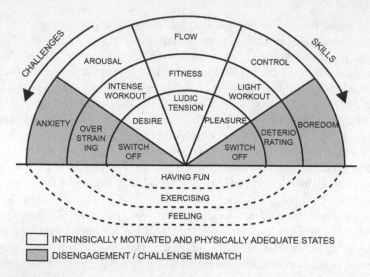

Fig. 4. Intrinsic motivation as a balance between challenges and skills. Adapted from learning games to exergames, following the original model by Denis and Jouvelot [42].

(b) *extrinsic motivation*, which relates to factors external to the activity itself, leading an actor to be willing to perform an activity, and (c), *amotivation*, which describes the absence of motivation [40], Denis and Jouvelot construct a model that suggests a central corridor of intrinsically motivated states which only arise in a state of balance between challenges and skills. Prepending the notion of the duality of dual-flow, the model can also be expanded into a dual-balance model where a second corridor is constructed around the physical activity (replacing learning with exercising, as indicated in Fig. 4), for the case of motion-based GFH, or around the respective serious target outcome in the case of other GFH or serious games.

A third prominent motivational theory that is employed in the context of serious games is *self-efficacy* [12]. Self-efficacy, or the extent of one's belief in one's own ability to complete tasks and reach goals, has been linked as a predictor to completing health related tasks and goals, and has also been used in the context of games [141]. While the construct is helpful in principle, it does not lend itself to comparative reasoning as readily as SDT, since it is recommended to construct customized measures for independent use cases [13]. However, since motivation and feedback play explicit roles in self-efficacy, it can provide insightful perspectives in GFH research and development.

While motivation is important, the challenge of researching and creating successful GFH exceeds the aspect of momentary or prolonged motivation to engage with activities that have some direct or indirect health benefit. The goal is often to *persuade* users into first starting a treatment or change, and to trigger lasting *behavior change*. Models and approaches from persuasive applications design [112] and behavior change [48] have been used in the context of serious games [14,147] and provide further background on these broader concerns. We do not provide a more detailed discussion of these approaches, since they are discussed in other chapters of this volume.

2.5   The Central Challenge of Games for Health

Due to heterogeneity on multiple levels, in addition to user and use case centered design, flexible yet efficient adaptability and adaptivity to create optimized experiences for groups or personalized experiences and outcomes for individuals, is the arguably most central challenge around GFH. It is also the reason why commercial mass market games can only rarely be used successfully as GFH. Typical monolithic and coarse difficulty settings like "easy", "medium", and "hard" do not allow for the required level of flexibility. This challenge stems from the strong differences in capabilities and needs of GFH users, which - in turn - result from a number of aspects.

Heterogeneous Application Areas. As argued above, GFH are being researched and developed for use in widely different application areas. Still, GFH often target multiple application scenarios within the same application area, which can require notable adjustments.

Heterogeneous Target Groups. Sometimes, application areas or scenarios are tied to a very specific demographic sub-group, such as people within a certain age range (young children, children, adolescents, young adults, or older adults [109], or frail older adults [55]), or people of a specific social, cultural, or economic status. Oftentimes, however, a GFH will be aiming to encompass multiple of these groups with the resulting requirement to allow for enough flexibility to cater to the respective abilities and needs of their individual members.

Heterogeneous Individuals. Even within specific target groups and sub-groups, individuals frequently have strongly different abilities and needs. For example, due to increasing variance in age-related afflictions and related physical and mental abilities, older adults of similar age can be very different from one another. In another example, strong differences e.g. in the range of motion of different players of a game for the support of therapy for Parkinson's disease patients were recorded and discussed (cf. Fig. 5 which illustrates differences in motion dynamics and range of motion in two players)[134].

Games have been shown to have the potential of positive impacts on *intergenerational acceptance* [146] and *social integration* [26,101]. Social interaction around games and multiplayer situations between members of heterogeneous target groups require careful consideration and often times additional flexibility, or even different approaches to adaptability and adaptivity altogether. This was reported, for example, in a study by Gerling et al. [56], which gives insight into how visible adaptations for balancing between two players of a local multiplayer game led to adverse results in homogeneous player pairs. Further results indicate that such adjustments are much more readily accepted in notably heterogeneous player pairs (in this case wheelchair users playing with non-wheelchair users; cf. Fig. 6).

Fig. 5. A series of images of participants in a study of motion-based games for the support of physiotherapy for Parkinson's disease patients [134]. One participant (left) shows a notably smaller range of motion, and less dynamic movement than the other (right).

Fig. 6. Two photos taken as part of a study of the impact of different levels of visibility of difficulty adjustments on player performance and experience with different results in dyads of players with more homogeneous abilities (right), compared to dyads of players with rather heterogeneous abilities (left).

Heterogeneous Interested Parties. In addition to the challenges mentioned above, a number of different parties act with different interests, needs and abilities in the larger ecosystems that GFH must function in. Next to the players or patients (a complex duality in and of itself), professionals, such as doctors, therapists, care givers, or professional educators, may interact with the games or with information and settings interfaces for the games. Family members and other relatives, such as parents, or other guardians of the core users are often involved. Lastly, game makers, developers, designers, artists, system administrators, and researchers (from a wide range of disciplines, such as game design, computer science, medical science, therapy, sports science, psychology, storytelling, etc.) are also part of the development and release ecosystem of GFH.

Drawn together, in many cases, GFH need to cater to very specific needs and abilities of their players due to a broad range of heterogeneous target groups which are themselves typically composed of people with considerable variance regarding abilities and needs in terms of both the interaction with the game and the interactions linked to the targeted serious outcome, as well as variance regarding prior knowledge, and expectations of games. Next to the impact of the application target, the social status, age, technological affinity, and further factors, such as the interests of many different user groups, must be considered when designing, implementing, and researching GFH. Even given a proper approach to design (cf. to Sect. 3 on designing games for health in this chapter), this leads to *manual adaptability* and *automated adaptivity* as central challenges (the chapter on *Personalized and Adaptive Serious Games* by Streicher and Smeddinck in this volume provides a detailed discussion).

2.6   Types and Classes of Games for Health

Considering the broad range of application scenarios and potential user groups, a structured approach to the types and classes of GFH is helpful to allow for a systematic discussion of design and development methods, as well as research efforts. One approach are grids with game characteristics, such as the summary presented by Rego et al. [119] for serious games for rehabilitation. They sample related work to retrieve characteristics such as application area (motor or cognitive), interaction technology (motion tracking, keyboard, etc.), as well as game interface, number of players, competitive or collaborative nature, game genre, adaptability (yes/no), progress monitoring, performance feedback, and portability. Other, more top-down approaches generate a structure along (usage) fields and areas of application (cf. Table 1) [52,125]. This taxonomy is especially helpful when planning the design of GFH or research about GFH, since it induces a conscious reflection about the potential interests in other usage fields and helps with clearly defining areas of application.

In combination, both approaches can inform decisions and help shape discourse. The layers of of *active* GFH (i.e. used to work on a specific health issue) or *supportive* GFH (employed for related serious targets around a specific health issue) could make a useful addition. Within a motion-based GFH category, reasonable sub-classes are *pervasive/location-based games* vs. *partial-body*, or *full-body motion-based games*. Sawyer and Smith's class of *assessment* should be read to explicitly include diagnostics [85,143], and a sub-class of *structural support* (memorizing medication schedules, playful day planning, etc.) could be added to the informatics area of application. While these taxonomy and classification

Table 1. A taxonomy for games for health as suggested by Sawyer and Smith [125].

Fields -> /Areas of application	Personal	Professional/ practice	Research Academia	Public health
Preventative	Exergaming stress	Patient communication	Data collection	Public health messaging
Therapeutic	Rehabilitainment disease management	Pain distraction cyber physiology disease management	Virtual humans	First responders
Assessment	Self-Ranking	Measurement	Inducement	Interface/Visualization
Educational	First aid medical information	Skills/Training	Recruitment	Management simulations
Informatics	Personal health records	Electronic health records	Visualization	Epidemiology

efforts can help shape a more grounded dialogue about GFH and hopefully support the transfer of findings, it is important to note that many GFH and GFH systems will represent a mixture of multiple classes, and that characteristics will be expressed to variable degrees.

3   Designing Games for Health

The usual steps of a design process as illustrated in the general context of serious games (please confer to the respective chapters in this volume) also form the basis of GFH design. However, as indicated in the preceding sections, GFH introduce challenging additional aspects that require consideration. During the design process, after having determined the target group and serious purpose, a reflection of the application area is helpful. Brox et al. [25] have structured this consideration into design for education, or persuasion, or exercising. Following the classes by Sawyer and Smith to discuss and determine primary and secondary targets would be another option.

3.1   The Importance of User and Expert Involvement

In addition to reviewing related literature, explorative methods, such as target group surveys, interviews, expert involvement, paper prototyping, or participatory design play an important role with GFH design, since these methods make requirements and challenges evident that designers and developers might otherwise overlook.

Participatory design workshops can deliver insights into unexpected target group preferences or whole alternative game concepts. For example, in a participatory design workshop that was carried out in the context of the project Adaptify while planning the development of games for the support of back pain

Fig. 7. The images show older adults during a participatory design workshop on motion-based games for health that was carried out as a formative measure in the currently ongoing project Adaptify [2]. The picture on the left shows participants composing own game screen designs and the picture on the right shows a final design. The study served the purpose of determining preferred game screen elements and approaches to embedding instructor figures and player characters.

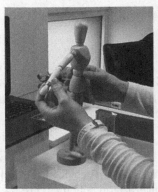 

Fig. 8. A participant enacting movement capability adjustments either on a physical or digital manikin during a series of two studies performed in the context of the project Adaptify. The study explored approaches to realizing efficient and well-integrated patient movement capability configurations for physiotherapists [138].

physiotherapy (see Fig. 7), older participants were found to largely avoid comparative score or ranking displays, while younger participants highlighted their importance when asked to compose their own game screens using a large number of pre-printed typical game assets and pens for the inclusion of own ideas. The same series of workshops also produced alternative approaches to interspersing play sessions with storytelling content that had not been considered by the project designers or researchers prior to the workshops.

In another example from the same project, therapists were involved in the early planning stage of an application for tablet devices for configuring motion-based games for health. Even before a first digital interactive prototype was produced, therapists were asked to enact movement capability configurations on a wooden figure in order to explore their bimanual interaction and how they comment on which aspects of the movement capability configurations are important to them (see Fig. 8). While a following study with an early interactive prototype (see Fig. 8) found that a mixture of direct manipulation of a 3D avatar with traditional input elements and clearly separated movement axes worked best for the therapists, the early involvement of the therapist led to the unexpected finding that the therapists highlighted the usefulness of such a tool for communicating with other therapists and with patients about movement capabilities and the development of individual patients [138].

As the game development progresses, and input from non-gaming experts becomes available, the involvement of gaming experts can help interpreting that information [59]. Following the application use case of MGH for older adults, Fig. 9 illustrates that non-gamer experts, such as doctors, therapists, and nurses, can provide valuable contributions with their insights into common age-related changes and impairments, giving recommendations that help designers implement beneficial movement-based game input, and supporting game developers

Fig. 9. The figure illustrates that non-gamer experts and gaming experts can both be involved to cover different aspects of GFH development (here with the example of motion-based games for health for older adults) [59].

throughout evaluation processes. Gamer experts, such as interaction and game designers, can also make valuable contributions by providing insights regarding enjoyable game mechanics, appropriate interaction schemes, etc.

3.2 Patient Abilities as Resources

Based on the model of digital games produced by Adams [5] and Fullerton et al. [49], related work has discussed the perspective that player resources can require special consideration with target groups such as older adults [58]. Similarly, with games for health, players may have limited attention spans, abilities, or special requirements that can be seen as a depletable resource in game design (see Fig. 10). This lens is often helpful when planning interactions around the serious target of the game. In a game for mental rehabilitation, for example, the duration for which a player can be very focused, can be seen as a resource that may be limited, changes over time, and may yet be a central target for change due to interacting with the game.

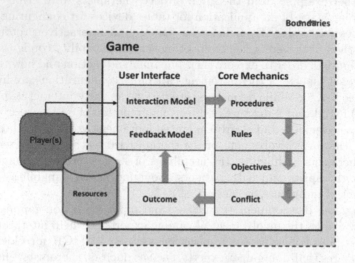

Fig. 10. An extended model of digital games after Fullerton et al. [49] and Adams [5] via [58].

3.3   Evaluation Criteria in Usability, User Experience, Playability, Player Experience, and Accessibility

Most importantly, next to traditional game user experience outcomes, the specific health outcomes of a GFH matter. This duality of target outcomes suggests that both should be considered in design and testing. As noted before, a theoretical approach to this end is presented by Sinclair et al. [130] with the dual-flow framework. This work suggests a split of the general concept of flow into psychological flow and physiological flow, which is relevant for any motion-based playful application. The physical fitness and abilities of any given user present a physiological counterpart to the aspect of skill (which would likely contain elements of hand-eye coordination, fine-grained muscle control, and reflexes with any sedentary game as well) and have to be balanced with the level of physical challenges that are presented by the game. If the challenges exceed the physical fitness or abilities of a player, there is an increased risk of overstraining and injury. If the challenges notably undercut the physical fitness or abilities of the player, there is a risk of deteriorative effects due to a lack of training intensity, or at least of a lack of an impact regarding the targeted health outcomes. This has to be considered in game design, implementation, and testing, but it also has to be taken into account by adaptive systems for motion-based GFH. Next to the temporal fluctuations, the general interpersonal difference in abilities also entail that accessibility plays an important role in the design of (motion-based) games for health. The question whether the game system at hand contains barriers that could prevent users from the target group from reaping the potential benefits of the application is even pre-conditional to the questions of playability and player experience that are commonly discussed in game design literature [135]. If the games are not accessible, any theoretical playability or player experience and any resulting motivation to be active or any resulting positive impact on health cannot come to fruition.

Given that aspects of accessibility are explicitly encompassed, user-centered design, repeated prototype testing and early pilot studies play an important role, if the complex challenges outlined in the preceding sections are to be tackled. GFH teams will benefit from following the classic user-centered design cycle [64] of analysis, design, implementation, and evaluation. However, it is important to point out that the iterations evolve around *multiple evaluative criteria* (see Fig. 11).

Usability matters in games, because they come with menus, settings, and controllers that are not necessarily part of the game design in terms of mechanics or aesthetics, yet are elementary for facilitating unhindered game play. It is thus useful to evaluate them with classic usability criteria such as efficiency, ease of use, performance, etc. Additionally, the *user experience* that is perceived by the players in the interactions with the application surrounding the core game is important. Unlike non-game applications, games, serious games, and GFH must be designed for a good player experience as well. *Player experience* results from the interaction with the core game, the game mechanics, the rewards, potential social interactions, etc. and is measured with different tools (see for example the

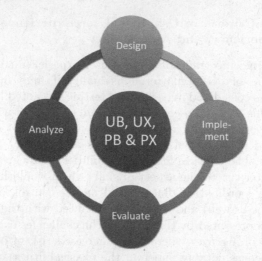

Fig. 11. The figure illustrates how user-centered iterative design in GFH revolves around the four cornerstones of usability (UB), user experience (UX), playability (PB), and player experience (PX).

section on *Theories on Motivation and Games for Health* in this chapter) than usability (e.g. SUS [23]) or user experience (e.g. [93]). As a fourth evaluative focus, *playability* regarding the interaction with the core game itself should be considered separately from the usability of the immediately surrounding interactions, and it is important to note that, while inefficiencies and challenges in use will only be tolerated to a certain level, they do not always exert a clearly negative impact as they would be from the perspective of usability, since challenge and inefficient behaviors are important elements of many games [139]. Lastly, it is also helpful to recall the different parties of interest introduced in the preceding sections, which should be considered separately with regard to how important usability (UB), user experience (UX), playability (PB), and player experience (PX) in a specific GFH are, or are likely to be, to them. This overview clearly illustrates the complexity of the iterative user-centered design approach with GFH. Given an awareness of these challenges, however, these considerations can help prioritize evaluations and design targets in GFH where both patients and therapists are important target groups. While playability and player experience are usually most important to the patients, the usability and user experience of the interactions surrounding the core game play are of usually most important to the therapists or other professionals.

Balancing Challenges and Ease of Use. When a game is reliably accessible, playability frames the next set of pre-conditional design criteria that resemble critical elements of usability. It is important to notice that classic criteria from usability often do play a role in games, for example in interfaces, but also concerning the game controls, although maximum efficiency and effectiveness (as exemplary aspects of usability) are usually not the focus of the core game mechanics [139]. To the contrary, since playful and/or game mechanics often evolve around purposefully challenging the user, they can oppose the judgement by such usability criteria. Games for health are interesting in this regard, since the serious purpose often results in designers having to find compromises between providing enjoyable game experiences and supporting the serious goals. Arguably, good GFH designs feature core mechanics that support the serious outcomes as directly as possible. However, such solutions cannot always be found and are often not cost-effective. Alternatively, approaches with a less direct integration of game mechanics and health-related activities, such as episodic game play or game narrative interwoven with temporally distinct episodes of health-related activities, also have the potential to support improved beneficial health outcomes compared to non-game-based interventions.

3.4 Levels of Gamification and the Importance of Story

As indicated in Sect. 2.2 on the relation of games for health to general eHealth applications, there is no clear line that separates playful eHealth applications from GFH. One can envision a continuous scale of gamification ranging from fully serious applications to fully entertaining games, where, depending on the point of origin, game elements or serious application elements are added or removed. The understanding of gamification is often limited to rewards that are not closely related to the remaining activities in an application. However, game mechanics, design aesthetics, and storytelling, as viable game elements for games for health, should all be considered during conceptualization and design. While the simple addition of a reward layer, such as the one illustrated in Fig. 12 in playful applications has been shown to provide measurable benefits [137], it can be expected that the introduction of a broader repertoire of game elements, if done in a harmonious fashion, can lead to more far-reaching positive impacts on game experience and both game and health related performance.

Evidence for this hypothesis can be found, for example, in a comparative study of different levels of visual fidelity about the impact on game experience and performance in a game to support physical activity in older adults (see Fig. 13). Notable differences only occurred when the visual fidelity was reduced to a level that made the micro-story that was inherent in the fishing scenario of the game disappear [132].

Given the complexity of GFH design and research, the sections in this chapter merely scratched the surface of the approaches and methods that have been discussed. Additional design and evaluation approaches are the topic in related work on games for health in general [16] and in related work on the various subclasses of GFH, such as motion-based games for health (or exergames) [108]. Many practical materials and more recent approaches and methods are shared and discussed in various online communities on GFH (see further reading below).

Fig. 12. The figure shows two examplary screenshots of a gamified information application for users of electro muscle stimulation training [137]. The screen on the left shows stimulation intensities of different body parts in the last training session compared to a reference session and date picker UI components for selecting the respective sessions. The right screen shows a reward screen with a gallery of achievement badges and a total score. Augmenting trainer discussions with small interaction sessions with such performance-oriented applications was shown to lead to improvements in some motivational measures.

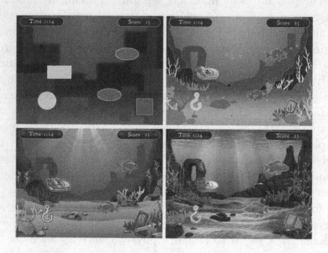

Fig. 13. Four levels of visual complexity of the same game, where the abstract version (top left) was shown to have inferior effects on player experience compared to the other versions.

4   Games for Health Examples and Illustration

In this chapter we do not present a survey of GFH with a strict sampling and analysis method, since such surveys have recently been produced with a range of foci. Ricciardi et al. [120] provide a survey of serious games in health professions, while Baranowski et al. [14] provide an overview of games with a focus on health-related behavior change, and Kato [83] reports on various examples of games in professional health care applications. Notably, all of these surveys report numerous positive indications.

4.1 Seminal Work

In order to name some specific projects for further reading, this section highlights GFH work of seminal character. This means that each project has considerable novelty (usually due to the serious target), features a convincing production quality, and is in the best case accompanied by research to supply evidence in favor of the approach. Validated with clinical trials, the games *Re-Mission* one and two, where players enter "their own bodies" to take on the fight against malicious cells, help improve drug administration adherence and indicators of cancer-related self-efficacy and knowledge in adolescents and young adults diagnosed with different types of cancers [84]. The playful VR experience *Snow World* [71,72], where patients visit a world full of shades of light blue and other colors associated with cold and imagery of snow and ice, has been shown to be a potentially viable adjunctive nonpharmacologic analgesia both in the context of wound treatment for burn victims and in dental pain control. The game *Relive* [47] focuses on cardiopulmonary resuscitation (CPR) training and puts players into a compelling space station scenario with a high production quality. It features competitive multiplayer and has been released as a free game on the distribution platform Steam where it competes with many commercial titles. In *Project:EVO*, a game created to detect and track the development of Alzheimer's disease, players play a flying race type of game, in order to improve cognitive control via interference processing [10]. In the creature-care game *Monster Manor*, children with type 1 diabetes are encouraged to take responsibility of controlling their own blood sugar levels, earning them upgrades and support items for a monster they take care of [82]. *Meister Cody* [90] is a game to support children with dyscalculia [91], which features diagnostics, rich adaptability, adaptivity, as well as therapist and parental information and control; it is currently undergoing a large-scale trial. As an example from the large subgroup of motion-based games for health, *Valedo* is a gaming system where two motion-sensors are attached to a patient's body in order to enable full-body control of a suite of well-designed mini games for the support of back pain movement exercises [81].

4.2 Motion-Based Games for Health

The following sections illustrate the evolution of motion-based games for health (MGH) in the exemplary therapeutic application area of physiotherapy, rehabilitation, and prevention (also sometimes referred to as kinesiatric games), along the lines for three quasi-consecutive projects that were carried out at the Digital Media Lab of the Center for Computing and Communication Technologies (TZI) of the University of Bremen, Germany, in cooperation with students, as well as partners from research and industry. The discussion in this chapter focuses on approaches to – and challenges in – the general design, implementation, and evaluation of these GFH. A separate discussion that focuses on the aspects of adaptability and adaptivity in each project can be found in Sect. 5.2 of the chapter on *Personalized and Adaptive Serious Games* in this volume.

A Brief History of Motion-based Games for Health. First historical examples of motion-based games for health (MGH) have been produced as early as the 1990s [89]. MGH have a close relation to exergames, which have an even longer history, reaching back to first exercise bicycle and dance mat games in the 1980s [126]. In a modern classification, exergames would likely be interpreted as a subclass of MGH with a loose medical focus on prevention. GFH experienced a first small surge with the introduction of first sensor and input devices for digital interactive systems for home use (i.e. the PC and gaming consoles with dance mats). A second surge was supported by recent improvements in sensor and interaction device technology due to low-cost and small scale sensors, sensor fusion, and increased processing power. This has enabled affordable consumer devices such as the EyeToy, the WiiMote, wearable fitness trackers, and the Kinect, which all augment the readily available technologies for motion-tracking, which in turn forms the basis of all motion-based games for health that aim to be truly interactive and make use of the three basics promises of MGH.

During the second surge over roughly the last ten years, games have been introduced to more and more application areas and target groups. While exergames had been created early on to focus on the young target audiences that were already accustomed to video games, and consumer releases for younger audiences are already commonplace and reach large international markets, different target groups have recently stood in the focus of a growing number of projects [14,83,120]. Positive indications have been found with GFH for a wide range of target groups, such as stroke patients, children with cerebral palsy, people with multiple sclerosis, or more general groups, like older adults (cf. to the introduction and the background sections of this chapter). This line of work can also be seen as a continuation of explorations of virtual reality (VR) applications in the respective application areas, such as hand function rehabilitation for people recovering from stroke [79]. As with other GFH, personalization through adaptability and adaptivity remains an important challenge, although promising advantages over traditional approaches, e.g. for instructing exercise executions, have already been demonstrated. In the case of exercise instructions, exercise executions at home were performed at a more adequate speed [148].

Project 1: WuppDi. *WuppDi*, the first project at the TZI Digital Media Lab at the University of Bremen targeting motion-based games for health focused on supporting physiotherapy for people with Parkinson's disease (PD) [11]. PD is a non-reversible progressive neurodegenerative condition that affects many motor-related functions with symptoms such as balance problems, rigidity, and tremor. Physiotherapy is an important element of the long-term treatment of the disease. However, the frequent exercising sessions are often perceived as boring, and the slowly reduced abilities over time can lead to frustration, endangering a continued treatment. It is apparent how the three areas of potential of GFH, motivation, guidance, and feedback, appear valuable in the context of PD. Since the patients were largely older adults and had little experience with video games, it was assumed that games would have to be designed specifically for the use case. This decision was supported by informal trials of commercially available motion-based games with members of the target group. The games were found to be mostly overstraining and confusing.

An *iterative user-centered design approach* was employed from the beginning, including therapists and patients in exploratory discussion rounds and early prototype testing. Figure 14 shows the start screen of the game suite with the final selection of mini games, which were all designed around the scenario of fairy tales. That scenario had been determined to have positive associations and to be motivating for most patients. A number of earlier prototypes were abandoned, some since they were found to be too fast, or require motion patterns that were too complex, some due to less expected factors, such as the perceived violence of smashing bugs in one prototype. Overall, the final prototypes were perceived to be fun and motivating by both patients and therapists. However, it was also found that no single game fit the abilities and needs of all patients during evaluation sessions and it was concluded that the games, which featured traditional difficulty selection via different levels of difficulty, could be improved by realizing more *flexible* (adaptable) and potentially (automatically) *adaptive* implementations. Patients were also found to require *close guidance*, even after detailed video instructions had been added to the game suite, and all feedback in the games was tuned to focus on positive advancements. The focus on exclusively *positive feedback* was chosen since patients often lacked confidence and could be demotivated by negative feedback (e.g. "You Lose!"), although such feedback is a common element in regular video games.

Fig. 14. The game selection screen and screenshots of all five final prototypes in the WuppDi suite of games for the support of physiotherapy for PD patients.

The common and familiar theme of fairy tales was noted to reduce anxiety in some patients and attempts at hiding unnecessarily visible technical equipment (e.g. dangling connector cables) also appeared to reduce aversions towards interacting with the applications. Next to the need for personalization, shortcomings in tracking accuracy, accessibility, and playability for some patients were also identified as avenues for further improvements. Follow-up studies employing the WuppDi games informed the following projects by investigating the impact of various factors and manipulations on player performance and experience. The studies included topics such as adaptability with calibration and adaptivity via threshold heuristics [134], visual complexity [132], the role of rhythm and timing [95], rewards and achievements [142], and cooperative multiplayer effects [67].

Project 2: Spiel Dich Fit und Gesund. On the basis of the lessons from the WuppDi project, and given the strong positive response expressed not only by PD patients, their relatives, and therapists, but also through notable public interest and requests by therapists for similar programs for other target groups, the project *Spiel Dich fit und gesund* (SDF), which translates roughly to "play to become fit and healthy", was set up to focus on exploring the use of MGH for older adults. Gerontologists and social care workers had suggested that games similar to those that they had seen as part of the WuppDi suite of games for people with PD could work well for general movement motivation with older adults. Thus, a suite of games was envisioned around the cornerstones of supporting motivation to improve upper body movement, flexibility, and balance, as well as exploring general movement motivation, cognitive training, and MGH with a strong musical, or rhythm and timing component. The possibility to personalize the games to individual users was also an integral part of the concept.

Older Adult Gamers. In opposition to the common assumption that computer or video games do not play a role in the day to day life of older adults, research has shown that many older adults do play games [78], although their preferences differ from those of younger target groups. Video games had even been considered for potential cognitive training benefits for older adults as early as 1983 [154]. Furthermore, recent research indicates that older adults have a strong interest in games that they credit with a reasonable potential of helping with improving their physical and mental well-being [109,134]. This encompasses so-called "mind training" games, such as quizzes or mathematical puzzles, but increasingly also motion-based implementations, for example of known games, such as bowling [45]. Depending on the individual implementation and use case, such games or playful activities have been shown to have both cognitive [7] and physical [86] benefits. It can also be assumed that younger players will come to expect to continue to be able to play sedentary and motion-based games that work adequately for them as they age. Even today, video games as a market are often underestimated and in some markets, as many as 20 % of the regular gamers are older than 50 years of age [28], with the average age being 35 years and the largest market segment by age being the gamers of age 35+ with 36 % (US market data from 2012/2013) [46]. Such developments, together with the fact that the older adult population is notably impacted by modern sedentary lifestyle, provide good reason to suggest the exploration of MGH for the target group of older adults.

Perpetual User-Centered Iterative Design for MGH. Since related work and the prior project had underlined the importance of user-centered iterative design in the context of MGH, SDF was designed around that approach from the start. The project aimed for continuous iterative testing alongside the project development to start as soon as interactive prototypes were available. The continuous brief iterative testing was flanked by selective, more quantitative evaluations and comparative studies around specific questions that arose during the development.

Since SDF targeted the implementation of prototypes around three topic areas, namely *movement activation, cognitive training,* and *music, rhythm, and timing guided movement dual-tasks,* the first year of the project started with early brainstorming and conceptualization sessions together with experts from social support services for older adults and experts from a game development studio. These initial planning steps involved the creation of persona to facilitate a guided discussion and pre-evaluation of various design approaches and concepts, as well as discussions around topics such as the movement patterns that were to be implemented, the settings or scenarios in which the players should be placed, and potential game concepts which could serve to connect both of the prior aspects. Early on, group interviews with attendees of various older adult meeting centers, including the center staff, were conducted to gather more information regarding target group preferences regarding suggestions for game world scenarios, their musical taste, favored types of games, exercising, and preferences regarding potential visual styles for the game prototypes. The outcomes were largely in agreement with related work on similar sets of preferences [78,109].

In these early explorations and throughout the iterative process of the SDF project it was regularly challenging to find groups with balanced numbers of male and female participants. While this largely represents the gender proportions present in older adult populations, differences in interests and motivation of the gender groups should still be considered if the target group definition does not explicitly exclude either them. In summary, and not separating by gender, the results hinted at "familiar scenarios", such as a garden or a shopping mall being frequently selected over more exotic ones. The importance of popular songs stood out regarding musical tastes, although later on, music that was not well-known also turned out to be accepted. Members of the target group mostly favored classic board or card games, and those that played computer or video games also most often reported to be playing digital versions of such classics or games of a very similar nature. Participants were split regarding exercising with some being regularly active and a larger portion not being active, although many said that they had been regularly active in the past. After showing members of the target group pictures of different levels of visual complexity to determine target design styles the responses were mixed.

Since the fidelity of the visual design has a large impact on the resource allocation in a game development project, the topic was selected for a detailed study that was performed to gain a more nuanced understanding of the preferences and needs of the target group with regard to visual complexity. Because it was not clear how the deterioration of vision ability with increasing age would combine with preferences of the members of the target group and the general setup of standing two to three meters away from a large screen for projecting game content, the comparative within-subjects design study referenced in Fig. 13 was setup to compare different levels of visual complexity on a continuum from completely abstract (only clear and simple shapes) to very detailed (almost photorealistic). In brief, regarding player experience, manipulating the presence or absence of a micro-story (compare the "abstract" version of the game to the other versions shown in Fig. 13) was shown to have an impact on the player experience, but strong differences in player experience or performance between three levels of visual complexity that all carried the micro-story of a fishing game were not detected [132]. For the SDF project these results led to the preference of a reduced complexity visual style as a cost-efficient approach. While the study on visual complexity was carried out with modified versions of non-SDF prototypes, the first SDF prototypes of movement activating games set in a garden scenario were tested early on with older adults in social meetup facilities, to allow for pre- and post-play discussions. Further early trials were conducted in public spaces, such as malls, which allowed for a broad exposure, testing the reactions of heterogeneous "walk-in subjects". Requests by a number of physiotherapists who showed great interest in the approach of MGH led to the more formal definition of the support of their application scenarios with the target group of older adults as a development target for SDF in order to determine the applicability in the context of physiotherapy, rehabilitation, and prevention.

After initial user feedback and observations (both collected following loosely structured protocols) were integrated to improve the initial prototypes, regular bi-weekly testing sessions with roughly two to five participants per test run were started in cooperation with a large physiotherapy practice to accompany the further development and fine-tuning. Player feedback was collected with single-sheet questionnaire featuring smiley scales (regarding the game experience and the experience of performing the exercises) for brevity and clarity. Therapist feedback on their impression of interacting with the system, as well as their evaluation of the way that the respective patients interacted with the system, was also collected with a questionnaire accompanying each test session. The first major development cycle was rounded up by interviews and discussion rounds with therapists regarding their requests for settings and parameters to make the games adaptable to individual users, leading to the user-centric parameters *range of motion, speed, accuracy, endurance, cognitive complexity*, and *resilience* being targeted for settings interfaces with a threshold-based mapping onto game variables.

In addition to the continued iterative testing, the games were also employed in a first exploratory evaluation in a nursing home. While most patients were aware of the connection between their body movements and actions by a player character on screen after a thorough introduction, they still required close

Fig. 15. A screenshot of the game Sterntaler which was employed for the study of adaptability and adaptivity in MGH for PD patients [134].

guidance or direct physical support and in many cases tracking was complicated by obstructive devices, such as wheelchairs or walking aids, or by limitations in the tracking of less pronounced movements. These findings are in line with the limitations encountered by other researchers when attempting to employ MGH with frail older adults [54]. Due to the challenges encountered in this exploratory trial, the target group for SDF was limited to not include frail older adults.

The approach to adaptability and adaptivity in SDF was informed by a further study based on the WuppDi (cf. Sect. 4.2) project where three PD patients were observed during multiple consecutive sessions of play over the course of three weeks (Fig. 15). The study setup featured a calibration- and settings-based original set of three parameters (*range of motion*, *accuracy*, and *speed*) that was adjusted between sessions following a threshold-based rubberbanding heuristic with predefined upper limits that were based on individual calibration. This approach was found to work well in increasing the range of motion whilst maintaining good player experience measures. Clarifications were found to be helpful with regard to the impact on scoring and therapists remarked that the set of parameters was rather limited, leading to the extended parameter set employed in SDF. In further adjustments of the principle for prolonged use in SDF the single pre-calibrated development targets were replaced with a milestone system that enabled therapists to set development milestones with target values for all parameter settings for either individual players or groups of players. The heuristic employed in SDF then facilitated automatic adaptation as long as the performance was found to remain in pre-configured acceptable boundaries around the current interpolated performance target at any given point in time.

With first prototypes of a settings and configuration interface for therapists at hand, usability focused testing helped with resolving general design challenges. A small study with therapists confirmed the adequate breadth, understandability, and flexibility of the chosen user-centered parameter set. Since movement capability configurations were deemed important by the therapists, a special grid-based settings interface was implemented that allowed therapists to configure

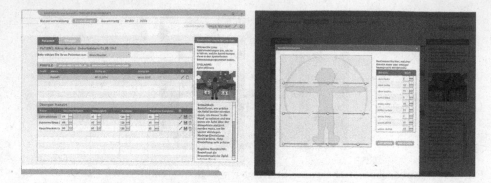

Fig. 16. Screenshots from the configuration interface for therapists designed in the context of the SDF project. Left: Settings are performed per player/per group on separate controls for speed, accuracy, etc. Right: A custom grid-based component that allows for configuring range of motion via active or inactive motion-target zones.

intensities of activation (ranging from full activation to complete deactivation) of zones for the placement of interactive targets in the game (see Fig. 16).

Next to the subsequent introduction of more game prototypes from the second and third development target areas, which were tested in social meetup facilities for older adults and in public spaces, further dedicated studies investigated the *impact of modality and delay of audio instructions*, especially in the games focused on rhythm and timing, the *optimal activation time for motion-based interactions with hover activated buttons* for the target group, and the *preference and impact on player experience and performance of different modalities for instructing dance movements* in a rhythm and timing game. The latter included a comparison of instructions between dance moves shown by (a) an instructor character that was similar in visual style to the player character (the player character is not shown in the figure), (b) instructions shown by icons approaching an "action zone" akin to popular dance games in the tradition of Dance Dance Revolution, and (c) a mixture of both approaches (see Fig. 17).

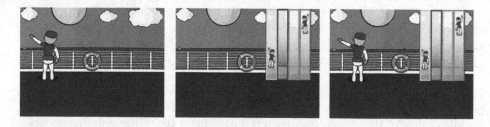

Fig. 17. Screenshots of the dancing game from the rhythm and timing development target in SDF showing the different experiment conditions (left to right: a, b, c) for motion instructions.

While quantitative results on game experience and performance showed no consistent differences, observations and player comments indicated that the participants were able to play with all three modalities. However, the overlay version (b) required more introduction and training than the instructor character version (a) and while the overlay version was eventually used by some participants to foresee the coming actions, many participants had troubles with understanding the instructions indicated by the icons, thinking, for example, that poses should be held indefinitely. The version with both displays (c) was confusing to some participants, which led to SDF adopting the instructor character for the continuing development.

Additional parallel studies that were carried out alongside the principal development of SDF investigated the impact of different *interaction modalities for range of motion* and other movement related capability adjustments (leading to the selection of the grid-based method over a more classic windows-icons-mouse-pointer components based interface or motion-based input), *reactions to being informed or not informed about automated difficulty adjustments* (leading to the decision to spare attempts at avoiding any mention or visibility of the adjustments), and the *impact of different modalities for presenting movement instructions* comparing a virtual character to video based and real human instructor based instructions [140], with the latter study underpinning the adoption of a virtual instructor for SDF, since the resulting performance was found to be significantly improved over the performance achieved with a video instructor, while there were no clear and consistent differences on the experiential measures aside from a greater ease of understanding and preference of the human instructor.

The last major development and evaluation cycle included further implementations of the interaction work-flow surrounding the core games (game menus, pausing the game, etc.), validating the acceptance of intermittent non motion-based quizzes that were implemented to ensure breaks between sessions of more physically intense gameplay in order to avoid overstraining, as well as prototype finalizations and polishing (including, for example, visual notifications and guides if players left the trackable space in front of the sensor device). In a final study, the suite of movement activating games was employed in situated use over a period of five weeks in individual therapy sessions in a large physiotherapy practice. The study compared the usage and impact on performance, experience, and on upper body flexibility and balance indicators, of (a) the suite of games with purely manual settings with (b) the suite with semi-automatic difficulty adjustments, and (c) classic therapy interventions without the games [136]. Findings indicated that using the games benefitted the perception of *autonomy* and *presence* expressed as need satisfaction components, while the classic therapy sessions showed higher *tension-pressure* and *effort-importance* with all measures being positively related to intrinsic motivation. While no significant differences were found on these measures regarding the two versions of the game suite, automatic adjustments were preferred by the therapists, and the game groups showed significantly increased functional reach compared to classic treatment [136]. For SDF these findings were interpreted to support the integration

Fig. 18. Screenshots of two games that were part of the final SDF suite, a photo of a player interacting with a third game from the suite, and a screenshot of the range of motion configuration component of the therapist configuration interface.

of semi-automatic adaptivity, since it was not found to have notable negative impacts on the player experience while therapists indicated a preference for automated support in adjusting the games to the individual patients (following the semi-automatic miltestone-based pattern with threshold-limited linearly interpolated game parameter settings that is mentioned above and detailed in the chapter on *Personalized and Adaptive Serious Games* in this volume) (Fig. 18).

Project 3: Adaptify. SDF had demonstrated, along with simultaneously developing related work, further aspects of the applicability of MGH in the context of physiotherapy, rehabilitation, and prevention. The games were largely tailored to motivate movements of broad characteristic classes, such as picking apples from a tree (broad movements at medium or high, self-controlled speed), catching locusts (slow movements that require more accuracy) or striking balancing poses with stretched out arms (very slow, highly controlled, endurance poses). Many physiotherapy treatment programs can incorporate such elements, but many exercises that therapists regularly work with were not explicitly present in those games. The SDF games were also limited to a suite of mini games that were very accessible but did not aim to provide a lot of alternation over time and all games relied on a direct player-body to player-character mapping as the core mechanism. While semi-automatic adaptivity was present, it required the initial configuration of milestones and no direct relation to the content, duration, or progression of traditional physiotherapy treatment programs was given. Lastly, the optical tracking from the front limited the number of exercises that could be reliably and accurately detected. The subsequent project *Adaptify* [2] is currently en-route targeting these potential points for improvements, along the design and implementation of a new series of prototypes for motion-based games for health. Three MGH are being created, focusing on (1) the modular extensibility to multiple exercises, (2) the implementation of more complex game mechanics and elements of storytelling, as well as (3) generative content for improved alternation in game play experiences. Adaptify targets adaptivity both with regard to the personalization of therapeutic exercise programs, expressed in series of exercising sessions (which are composed of sets of established therapeutic exercises) over time, as well as in user capability and needs modeling, which can facilitate the automatic generation of customized exercises, guidance, and feedback.

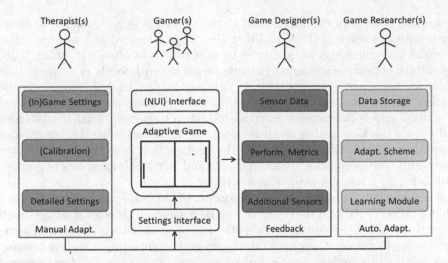

Fig. 19. Modular components of the general engineering model for the project Adaptify.

Figure 19 shows the complexity of a project such as Adaptify that takes a modular approach to the iterative user-centered design of MGH and the surrounding ecosystem that is designed to support multiple MGH and future expansions with additional exercises. The project also focuses on adaptability and adaptivity that encompasses overarching therapy goals and includes the design and inclusion of a sensor mat (see Fig. 23) to augment the vision-based full-body tracking, in order to support a broader selection of exercises including many exercises that are performed whilst kneeling or lying down and which are central to the main use case of chronic lower back afflictions. The project focus on supporting physiotherapy was determined based on experiences and findings in the prior projects, and also since physiotherapy presents a considerable section of the health market, where increases in demand put notable pressure on individual therapists, practices, and the system as a whole.

Games for Health in Physiotherapy. Taking Germany as an example, although the number of practicing physiotherapists in in the country has more than doubled since 2000 (data from 2000 to 2011), many therapy practices are operating at capacity limits. Expenses of public health insurances on physiotherapeutic services have almost doubled from about 0.9 billion Euros in 1993 to 1.8 billion Euros in 1999 [60]. The gross expenses have since increased to 2.9 billion Euros in 2005 [3] and reached 4.4 billion Euros in 2015 [4]. Opportunities for saving costs are in great demand and therapy guidelines already implement a larger proportion of self-directed and at home exercising. Dynamic and "hands-off" exercises in which the patient is not actively guided by a therapist are growing in importance and the clinical indications of such approaches are positive [144]. In the context of reduced supervision, achieving a high and constant quality of treatments is a major challenge. Next to the challenge that therapists, in many ways, mirror aspects of the school that they were educated in, and that inter-therapist agreement e.g. in quality of motion ratings is often not strong [114], the self-dependent adherence of patients to exercise protocols is an important factor for therapeutic success [144]. In this context, unchecked increases in the number of prescribed exercises can lead to reduced compliance [66]. Individual behavioral and socioeconomic factors are known to present further challenges and even a life threatening diagnosis does not necessarily increase compliance (e.g. in cardiac rehabilitation [77]). Further factors that have been found to correlate with non-compliance are self-reported and factual barriers, lack of positive feedback, and a sense of helplessness [131].

Improvements in compliance in the context of physiotherapy, prevention, and rehabilitation (PRP), on the opposite, can be a achieved through strategies such as (a) the frequent encouragement of patients, (b) stimulus control, such as wearing training clothing, (c) cognitive strategies such as directing attention towards the thoughts of a patient before, during, and after exercising, (d) time oriented and flexible personalized goals from session to session and for the month, (e) codes of conduct between patients and therapists regarding long-term goals, (f) including family members, (g) increased interactions with therapists and consistent binding of therapists to patients, (h) goal oriented clubs, (i) increased feedback regarding progress, (j) self-directed goals [77]. Furthermore it has been shown that written exercise instructions with illustrations led to increased compliance rates compared to purely verbal instruction for back pain exercises [127]. In this light, and considering the potential of MGH to provide, e.g., positive feedback, clear and self-directed goals, encouraging guidance, and immediate feedback, as well as a reliable and objective overview of the individual progress, strongly suggest further explorations of MGH in the context of PRP, especially for usage scenarios where patients would otherwise perform exercises without immediate professional oversight by a therapist.

In summary, MGH for the support of PRP have seen increasing attention in research and development over the past years and GFH have also been explored for many other application scenarios ranging from specific maladies to general fitness. First validated MGH are beginning to enter the market and the basic promises of GFH are beginning to show real outcomes with broad audiences. What is mostly missing are approaches to more overarching treatments, such as protocols for data exchange not only concerning the health status of individual patients, but also the MGH history and achievements. While aggregating information from multiple GFH is extremely promising, and first GFH are beginning to make use of game delivery and platforms that feature mechanisms for performance data aggregation and exchange [47], there are a number of challenges that remain with the developing ambitious GFH. We will discuss a selection of prominent challenges in the following section.

5   Challenges with Designing and Researching GFH

While helpful design techniques and research approaches are available for GFH, as illustrated above, a number of central challenges with researching, creating, and evaluating GFH still remain. The following sections build on prior work [133] and summarize challenges, adding additional aspects to those areas that have already been mentioned in the prior sections, and discussing a number of additional aspects that have only been touched implicitly in the remainder of this chapter (namely truly user-centered design, sensing and tracking, practical integration, safety and clinical validation, ethics, data privacy, and regulations).

5.1   Interdisciplinarity and Multiple Party Interests

As noted before, the field of GFH is highly interdisciplinary, with contributions from many fields of work with numerous respective sub-fields, including *research* with the fields of human-computer interaction, game user research, game studies, psychology, medicine, health sciences, and more; *engineering*, with subfields such as graphics engines, networking, multi-sensor devices, etc.; *design*, with game design, game asset design, user interface (UI) and UX design, sound design, etc.; and *health*, with therapy, nursing, pharmacology, etc. and many others, which may or may not be actively involved. In addition, besides the patients or players, multiple parties may interact with GFH or the surrounding projects and become stakeholders with their own interests and impact, such as (a) health professionals, care-givers or medical staff, who use the applications in their line of work, (b) guardians or relatives of patients who are interested in the well-being, safety, and progress, (c) the researchers, designers, health professionals, and engineers involved with creating the GFH, and (d) even co-players or bystanders who are not directly involved with using the GFH for any serious purpose. Next to careful user-centered iterative research and design as noted above, acknowledging the interdisciplinarity of GFH, and proactively analyzing projects with regards to potential interest groups can be helpful. Assuming different lenses of reflection, such as investigator-specific, project-specific, and external factors [87] related aspects of interdisciplinarity can help to avoid neglecting important angles.

5.2   Truly User-Centered Iterative Design

Approaching the conceptualization and design of GFH around multiple party interests serves to illustrate a common misconception with *user-centered design*: Encompassing a single user group often is not sufficient. This is aggravated by the fact that test or evaluation candidates have to be swapped out frequently if shortcomings are to be detected reliably, since users frequently adapt to existing problems more swiftly than those problems can be detected and fixed across iterative design and evaluation cycles. Thus, if evaluation participants are frequently changing, it would perhaps be more adequate to speak of *user-group centered design*. This, of course, implies the insight that GFH, at the beginning of an interaction with a new player, are always optimized for a certain sample group mean, indicating that there is still room (and often the need) to optimize the game further for individual users. Thus, while user-centered design and participatory methods are important, they often leave room for further improvements. As the next section will discuss in more detail, manual adaptability and automatic adaptivity play an important role in further optimizing GFH for individual players. Yet again, testing adaptable and adaptive systems in an iterative manner is complicated, since multiple game sessions are usually necessary in order to gain any reliable evidence regarding the quality of the adaptation approaches. Approaches range from simulating users with automated actors or recordings, over collecting group-based information to provide a reasonable initial setup, to the continuous development of the adaptability and adaptivity of a game as a service after an initial release.

5.3 Heterogeneity and a Broad Range of Serious Goals: The Need for Adaptability and Adaptivity

In addition to multiple party interests, the central challenge of adaptability and adaptivity results from the highly variable individual abilities and needs of patients even within specific target groups and within the individuals themselves, due to complex change over time. While GFH have great potential in terms of health applications, education, or behavioral change, an efficient personalization [62] and customization to groups and individuals is clearly a requirement. Despite notable setbacks and disappointments since the early beginnings of adaptive software [75], the area has made great progress, and many commercial and mass-market applications nowadays have adaptive features. It is therefore not surprising that adaptive elements are increasingly being explored for usage within games, be it for personalization regarding a single player, or for balancing between multiple players [57,107]. Adaptive techniques in the context of games have been shown to have the potential to improve game experiences [9] and are being discussed intensively especially in the context of motion-based games for health [6,119], due to the complexity of body-based input [70,73,134,136] and the related physiological health targets. While *implicit* game performance data and physiological data play a self-evident role in measurements to perform adaptation in GFH, psychological data and *explicit* user feedback can complement that information both as feedback data for "on-line" adaptive mechanisms [98] and for determining presets [96]. Methods that are based on user-centered feedback measurements also offer great potential for efficient generalizations and transfer from one GFH application to another, since the outcome measures are not relating to aspects of the game, but to aspects of the player [69].

The Role of Machine Learning and Data Analysis in Games for Health. In many cases, due to the multivariate and nonlinear nature of measures and settings in GFH, heuristics that are fully defined during development become hard to employ efficiently and may not be the optimal choice. Methods from artificial intelligence, machine learning, and statistical data analysis, both with a frequentist and Bayesian background, are not only employed in the larger context of GFH development for research and evaluations, as well as for learning about application scenarios etc.; they can also be employed for dynamic difficulty adjustments [76] and other kinds of adaptivity in GFH [62]. Examples range from the heuristic analysis of facial expressions in order to determine the emotional status of the players [63], over the usage of Bayesian methods for overcoming cold-start problems [157], the usage of support vector machines for classifying emotional states based on physiological player data (see discussion in the chapter in *Affective Computing* in this volume) such as galvanic skin response and body temperature [30], reinforcement learning for determining challenge sensitive actions [8], and genetic algorithms for difficulty adjustments in platform games [153], to neural networks for games for the support of rehabilitation [15], and implementations featuring components of recommender systems [105]. Furthermore, the construction of dynamic user models [92] for supporting the continued optimization of adaptive components can be helpful during development and after deployment [106], especially when complex multivariate fluctuations of player preconditions are closely tied to the potential serious outcomes, as for example in the application area of depression prevention [80]. Furthermore, games with online functions and account management, and games with large player numbers can allow for a continuous adaptation to individual players whilst also adapting the parameters of the underlying models themselves [99].

5.4 Sensing and Tracking

GFH frequently rely on special sensing and tracking devices, be it for direct player input and control, for performance, action execution quality, or player health status estimation, or to provide data for performance measures for adaptivity. Next to costs and maintenance, accuracy, and reliability can often be challenging to achieve and maintain, although the increasing ability of affordable and durable consumer (multi)sensor devices such as optical body trackers or wearables with motion-tracking capabilities are easing some of these challenges. For example, the Kinect depth-camera based skeleton tracking has been shown to provide comparable performance to professional optical tracking systems [31,50], with some limitations due to the fixed tracking angle, yet some advantages in terms of ease of use and calibration drift.

In some areas, the integration with professional medical devices, services, and medical data management have to be considered early in the process, since they can otherwise grow very expensive to implement. As examples like Snow-World [72], where a virtual reality display was required to be submerged under water during burn treatment, show, additional and highly unusual requirements regarding hardware can occur with GFH. Early explorations investigating the context for later situated use [136] of the GFH in a targeted domain can help with foreseeing the requirements and early tests of sensing and tracking hardware often lead to additional analysis methods, or modes, or to switching to alternative hardware.

One aspect that is frequently overlooked is the strong likelihood that sensing and tracking not only present challenges in accuracy, reliability, and calibration drift, any given combination of sensors will also not capture all information that is relevant to determining the full objective state of a complex game-player ecosystem. This strongly implies the perspective of augmenting the toolset for professionals instead of replacing professionals in GFH, as not to lose the flexibility and ability of embodied judgement provided by human professionals.

Lastly, when discussing sensing and tracking, it should be mentioned that actuation also plays an important role in GFH. Especially with motion-based games, exploring additional actuation channels in addition to the traditional non-tactile audio-visual feedback provided by computing and gaming systems can be beneficial. While the SDF project mentioned above, for example, gained notable benefits in tracking reliability due to employing the advanced depth-image based tracking of the Kinect device compared to the difference image and color-blob tracking employed in most prototypes from the WuppDi project, the latter required players to hold sticks with bright-colored markers in their hands and this tactile aspect of the interaction was missed by some testing participants who got to experience both systems.

5.5   Practical Integration

The aforementioned potential special requirements with regard to the environmental compatibility of hardware represent one important consideration regarding practical integration. GFH only make for a worthwhile pursuit if they can eventually be used in the targeted application scenarios. In many cases this means practices or clinics, where next to special requirements (e.g. with regard to hygiene or electromagnetic shielding), the efficient integration into existing procedures is usually key. Experience from projects about MGH for the support of physiotherapy, rehabilitation, and prevention at the University of Bremen with deployments at multiple therapy practices have produced the expert guideline that roughly two minutes per patient are the maximum time for adjustments and calibrations in settings interfaces such as those pictured in Fig. 20 that therapists will tolerate on a regular basis, since the usual treatment blocks last for only 20 min in total. Furthermore, manual configuration should always be optional, although clinic and practice leaders found it important to be able not only to make customized treatment plans for groups or personalized treatment plans for individuals, but also to be able to customize the whole GFH system to encompass some of their respective branding as well as their own treatment approaches or patterns.

In home or unsupervised usage scenarios, the setup has to be manageable for novice users and spatial requirements can quickly become limiting, especially with full-body based input. Lastly, acceptance is an important factor, and due to the multiple interest groups unusually difficult to achieve equally well in all relevant groups for GFH. With health professionals, for example, it has proven important to clearly develop and position GFH as augmentations and not as

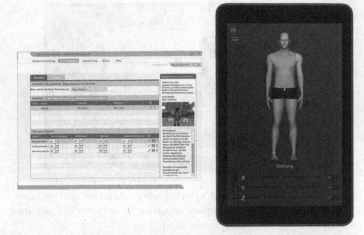

Fig. 20. Studies with physiotherapists in the context of the projects Spiel Dich Fit and Adaptiv have indicated that the time required to successfully interact with therapist configuration interfaces for motion-based games for health for individual players should be kept smaller than two minutes per patient. Accordingly, more efficient interaction modalities for mobile devices (right) are being explored as an alterternative or augmentation to classical windows, mouse, icons, and pointer (WIMP; components highlighted with color markings) interfaces on stationary or laptop devices (full classic WIMP interface on the left).

potential replacements for the very health professionals who would oversee their use with patients.

5.6   Safety and Clinical Validation

Both with supervised and unsupervised usage in healthcare environments and at home, safety plays an important role and can be challenging to guarantee to the required extent. MGH carry a risk of overexertion and the ties to health applications mean that special health implications may be present with many players. Even under supervision, patients have been observed to perform beyond their usual limits, which can be beneficial and is part of the motivation to employ games in health applications, but also carries the danger of both physically and mentally overstraining players. Clear information and instructions regarding proper usage (Fig. 21, for example, shows frequent embedded video demonstrations of how a movement exercise should be performed in *sPortal*, an experimental modification of the game Portal 2 that was employed for a study about motion-based game inputs for existing high quality commercial games [152]) and potential dangers are important issues to be considered in the creation of MGH. Furthermore, the implementation of heuristics for detecting dangerous states and forced breaks or usage limits can be required. It has to be taken into consideration that unnecessary interruptions due to false-positives can have

Fig. 21. A screenshot from the project sPortal where detailed instructions are delivered via integrated video during gameplay in order to achieve correct executions of movement patterns without breaking immersion [152].

very negative impacts on the player experience in such cases. Next to careful testing and cautious recommendation for usage scenarios that should only include tested contexts, the numerous laws and regulations that might apply to the interdisciplinary application should be researched early in order to facilitate implementations that respect these requirements.

For GFH respecting existing regulations will often mean that clinical trials must eventually be pursued. While some clinical investigations of GFH have been published [7, 10, 22, 117] and a larger number is currently underway, the number is still very limited compared to the number of GFH that have been developed and discussed publicly or published. The often prohibitive costs of clinical trials are one reason, as is the duration that clinical trials require not only for the execution, but also in planning with complex ethics approvals and pre-studies for endpoint investigation to facilitate effect size estimations. These aspects quickly sum up to multiple years of planning and preparation. In the light of the usual speed of operations in the game development world, this aspect represents a further point for frictions in the interdisciplinary field of GFH.

5.7   Evaluation Methods and Long Term Use

Not only are clinical or any reliable studies of GFH challenging to setup, due to the hard-to-control environments that situated use of GFH usually entails, due to the complications around acquiring participants for health-related studies, and due to the complexity of human-subject research with heterogeneous subjects, but validated research tools are also often not readily available, since tools are originally made either for the investigation of health aspects, or for the investigation of game user experience, yet not for a combination. This means that tools are frequently challenged to include potentially conflicting sub-scales and tradeoffs (e.g. regarding the importance of efficiency and effectiveness). Furthermore, research methods may feel intrusive to the players, interfering with positive game experiences and also with health-related outcomes. While some validated game user research questionnaires have been successfully used in recent GFH studies (such as the player experience of needs satisfaction (PENS) questionnaire [122]), personality or player types also play an important role [112], and health related endpoints (typically dependent variables in studies) are usually most important in clinical terms. These require domain knowledge for the application use case. The combination of multiple research instruments further complicates setups and analyses, and can quickly lead to survey fatigue and overstrained study participants. It is therefore not surprising that clinical studies or other controlled medium- to long term preclinical studies of GFH are still rare. In this light, the careful piloting of studies, expert advice in selecting measurements and target endpoints, as well as a limitation in the implemented features of a GFH and in the number of study conditions can be strategies to approach the aforementioned challenges.

5.8   Ethics, Data Privacy, and Regulations

As noted above with regard to safety, laws and regulations play a much more critical role in many GFH when compared to games that are produced primarily for entertainment. With patient data, data privacy becomes much more sensitive than regular game performance data and even seemingly non-medical information (such as a purely game mechanics oriented game performance measures) can carry medical implications. This poses challenges when aiming to capitalize on the promises of guidance and feedback in GFH (as discussed above), and also concerning learning for adaptivity across individual users and use cases, since such aspects typically entail the transfer of player-patient data via the Internet and the storage of said data on remote servers.

With regards to promises of benefits, claims regarding medical or therapeutic effectiveness and potency require the cautious use of specific legal terms and phrasing, and beyond adhering to regulations as required by law, it should be a general concern to produce ethical GFH, which may in many cases mean limitations beyond what is required by law. For example, while games for positive health behavior change can make use of persuasive techniques, the users should not be coerced into act in ways they would normally not approve of [65] and creators of GFH should keep in mind that the data gathered from players interacting with these games often has the potential to be a unique identifier for a given user, akin to a fingerprint, since it stems from physiological origins.

6   Current Trends and Open Research Questions

In summary it can be said that, while a large number of research and development projects on GFH have been completed or are currently underway, the challenges around researching, designing, implementing, and using GFH in practice are still considerable and there is a lot of room for research and technical innovation in the field. At the same time, it should also be highlighted again

Fig. 22. Screenshots from prototypes of a collection of small movement and cognition stimulating GFH around familiar scenarios, such as a cruise ship (with a dancing game), a shopping mall (with a calculation game shown in the top right and an item matching game in the bottom right), or a garden (with an apple picking game) that were produced for the project Spiel Dich fit.

that GFH do not necessarily have to compete with the highest quality commercial games for entertainment, since they often rather compete with the existing alternative applications regarding the serious health target [149]. However, the pursuit of a higher production quality, of moving beyond mere (collections of) mini games (see Fig. 22 for an example collection of small motion-based GFH from the project Spiel Dich Fit that feature micro stories due to being set in different vivid scenarios) into the domain of storytelling and more complex overarching game mechanics for improved motivation and longer adherence is one of the trends that is currently occurring, after first GFH and MGH products have started to take hold in the broader (health) consumer market.

Figure 23 shows the exemplary approach of the project *sPortal* [152], which investigated a control layer abstraction to turn existing first-person games into motion-based games [151]. In some cases, studies have shown greater benefits in well-produced games without explicit serious focus than the benefits achieved with explicit serious games (e.g. neurocognitive benefits from playing *Portal 2* compared to *Luminosity*, a game designed specifically for cognitive training [128]). With most GFH, however, the specifics of the targeted health aspects likely make the usage of existing high quality games without large modifications unreasonable, even if considerations about copyrights are put aside. As indicated in the section on sensing and tracking, hardware devices, especially with (multiple) sensing abilities are major drivers of GFH development. This trend will likely continue with new GFH being developed for existing medical or therapeutics devices (such as the gait rehabilitation harness shown in Fig. 23), other devices becoming affordable enough for larger health market applications (as for

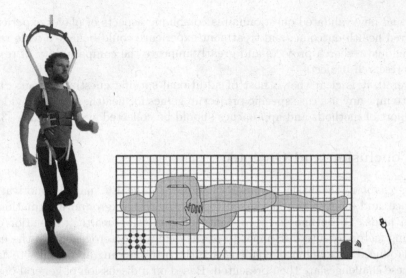

Fig. 23. Left: The project sPortal explored a motion-rehabilitation harness suspension together with motion tracking for walking in virtual worlds that could be employed in GFH. Right: Early concept draft from the context of the project Adaptify of an affordable sensor mat to support motion tracking of complex exercises that could not be tracked fully adequately with optical motion sensing alone.

example with pressure sensitive mats, as developed in the project Adaptify for MGH that feature exercises where ground contact points matter; cf. Fig. 23 on the right; other examples of similar mats from related research efforts are also available [145]), and new devices being developed or brought into medical or therapeutic use specifically for coupling with GFH.

From the point of view of medical and health research, next to questions relating to the given health target, general effects from health and medical research are increasingly investigated with regard to their applicability with GFH, such as the prevalence and impact of placebo effects [43]. Sensor fusion, mixed sources of evidence, and the continuous integration into user and user-group models contain numerous open ends for future research that can serve both game control, difficulty- and health-target-related challenge adjustments, as well as potential health analysis. From a health psychological point of view, the aspect of competitive and cooperative multiplayer in the context of different GFH application areas requires further study, since the aspect of relatedness bears great promise with regard to increasing motivation, whilst people show specific and culturally influenced interplay in the context of health. On a similar note, the impact of different approaches to balancing and finding tradeoffs between playfulness and seriousness in terms of framing, presentation, and interaction with patients as well as with health professionals, has yet to be explored systematically. Intercultural research and research between different socio-economic groups is also still rare. Many existing research methods still require validation for use with

GFH, and new validated questionnaires combining aspects of player experience, perceived health outcome, and treatment experience could benefit a wide range of individual research projects and greatly improve the comparability of results across research projects.

Overall, it is clear that a host of additional specific questions awaits those who attempt any use case specific project in games for health, and that evidence in support of methods and approaches should be collected systematically [33].

7   Conclusion and Outlook

In this chapter, the basic promises of games for health, namely motivation, guidance, and analysis, are discussed together with background information on related fields. To outline the complexity of games for health, the major contributing factors of interdisciplinarity of the field and heterogeneity of the users are introduced. A number of challenges with corresponding approaches to tackling these challenges are then presented. Based on a discussion of general design principles, research and design of GFH is illustrated along the lines of several motion-based games for the support of physiotherapy, rehabilitation, and prevention. These projects, together with the overview of seminal works show that, despite the considerable challenges, GFH are a worthy area of investigation with great potential to improve health applications in many areas and to benefit from the considerable size of the health market. Recent trends are discussed together with suggested topics for much needed further research. Progress in technical developments and research will likely facilitate the much more ubiquitous deployment of games for health over the next years, if advancements in personalization can be implemented together with reasonable integration into existing health application procedures, and if the regulatory frameworks evolve to facilitate GFH to enter health applications with as little friction as necessary. In tight coupling with non-game applications and with data exchange between multiple platforms, GFH stand to play an important role in the movement towards a more quantified and personalized overall approach to health. Due to the possibility of aggregating much more detailed and comprehensive information about the development of individual abilities, needs, and maladies over time, this looming shift has the potential to empower individuals and to – in turn – inform the rapid improvement of GFH and related health applications in the near future.

Acknowledgments. I would like to thank Stefan Göbel and Jenny Cramer for supporting the writing of this chapter. The non-external projects mentioned in this text were in part supported and in part spearheaded by the research staff and students at the *Digital Media Lab* at the *University of Bremen* as well as members of the *Interaction Lab* at the *University of Saskatchewan*. Marc Herrlich, Markus Krause, and Rainer Malaka are invaluable collaborators in this line of work. The projects were also supported by the consortium partners of the projects *Spiel Dich Fit* and *Adaptify*, as well as by the German Parkinson's association (*Deutsche Parkinson Vereinigung*) Bremen. Funding was provided by the *Klaus Tschira Stiftung*, the *GRAND NCE*, as well as by the *Federal Ministry of Education and Research, Germany* (BMBF).

Further Reading

- Beale I.L.: *Video Games for Health: Principles and Strategies for Design and Evaluation*. Nova Science Publishers (2011).
  The book focuses on the transfer of lessons from learning theory and technology to support procedures for the evaluation of the efficacy of (mostly educational) health games and their design components.
- Göbel S., Wiemeyer J. *Games for Training, Education, Health and Sports*: 4th International Conference on Serious Games, GameDays 2014, Darmstadt, Germany, April 1–5, 2014. Proceedings. Springer (2014).
  This is a proceedings volume which covers a wide range of fields with roughly half of the chapters focussing on topics that are directly related to games for health, while the other half focuses mostly on educational games.
- Ma M., Jain L.C., Anderson P.: *Virtual, Augmented Reality and Serious Games for Healthcare 1*. Springer Science & Business (2014).
  This book covers applications and games for health largely from the angle of the virtual reality and virtual rehabilitation communities. Many practical developments from a broad range of medical application areas are discussed.
- Primack B.A., Carroll M.V., McNamara M., et al.: *Role of Video Games in Improving Health-Related Outcomes: A Systematic Review*. American Journal of Preventive Medicine 42:630–638 (2012).
  This review paper provides a concise overview of recent work in the area of games for health together with a discussion of signs for aggregating evidence of their role in improving health-related outcomes.
- Bauman, E.B.: *Game-Based Teaching and Simulation in Nursing and Health Care*. Springer Publishing Company, New York (2012).
  This book provides theory and practical guidelines for the application of game-based teaching / learning and simulations in healthcare.

Online Resources.
http://www.ebgd.be/
http://gamesforhealth.org/
http://www.cdgr.ucsb.edu/db/
http://gameswithpurpose.org/
http://www.seriousgamesdirectory.com/proj/health-care-medical/
http://www.fitness-gaming.com

References

1. http://reflexionhealth.com/
2. https://adaptify.de/
3. Der Heilmittelmarkt in Deutschland - Januar bis Dezember 2005. Der Heilmittelmarkt in Deutschland, Apr 2006. http://www.gkv-heilmittel.de/media/dokumente/his_statistiken/2005_04/HIS-Bericht-Bund_200504.pdf
4. Heilmittel-Schnellinformation - Januar bis Dezember 2015. Der Heilmittelmarkt in Deutschland, Apr 2016. http://www.gkv-heilmittel.de/media/dokumente/his_statistiken/2005_04/HIS-Bericht-Bund_200504.pdf

5. Adams, E.: Fundamentals of Game Design. New Riders, Berkeley (2010)
6. Alankus, G., Proffitt, R., Kelleher, C., Engsberg, J.: Stroke therapy through motion-based games?: A case study. Therapy, pp. 219–226 (2010)
7. Anderson-Hanley, C., Arciero, P.J., Brickman, A.M., Nimon, J.P., Okuma, N., Westen, S.C., Merz, M.E., Pence, B.D., Woods, J.A., Kramer, A.F., et al.: Exergaming and older adult cognition. Am. J. Prev. Med. **42**(2), 109–119 (2012)
8. Andrade, G., Ramalho, G., Santana, H., Corruble, V.: Extending reinforcement learning to provide dynamic game balancing. In: Proceedings of the Workshop on Reasoning, Representation, and Learning in Computer Games, 19th International Joint Conference on Artificial Intelligence (IJCAI), pp. 7–12 (2005)
9. Andrade, G., Ramalho, G., Gomes, A.S., Corruble, V.: Dynamic game balancing: an evaluation of user satisfaction. In: AIIDE 2006, pp. 3–8 (2006)
10. Anguera, J.A., Boccanfuso, J., Rintoul, J.L., Al-Hashimi, O., Faraji, F., Janowich, J., Kong, E., Larraburo, Y., Rolle, C., Johnston, E., et al.: Video game training enhances cognitive control in older adults. Nature **501**(7465), 97–101 (2013)
11. Assad, O., et al.: Motion-based games for parkinson's disease patients. In: Anacleto, J.C., Fels, S., Graham, N., Kapralos, B., Saif El-Nasr, M., Stanley, K. (eds.) ICEC 2011. LNCS, vol. 6972, pp. 47–58. Springer, Heidelberg (2011). doi:10. 1007/978-3-642-24500-8_6
12. Bandura, A.: Self-efficacy mechanism in human agency. Am. Psychol. **37**(2), 122–147 (1982)
13. Bandura, A.: Guide for constructing self-efficacy scales. Self-efficacy Beliefs Adolesc. **5**, 307–337 (2006)
14. Baranowski, T., Buday, R., Thompson, D.I., Baranowski, J.: Playing for real: video games and stories for health-related behavior change. Am. J. Prev. Med. **34**(1), 74–82 (2008)
15. Barzilay, O., Wolf, A.: Adaptive rehabilitation games. J. Electromyogr. Kinesiol. (official journal of the International Society of Electrophysiological Kinesiology) **23**(1), 182–189 (2013). pMID: 23141481
16. Beale, I.L.: Video Games for Health: Principles and Strategies for Design and Evaluation. Nova Science Publishers, New York (2011)
17. Benyon, D.: Adaptive systems: a solution to usability problems. User Model. User Adap. Inter. **3**(1), 65–87 (1993)
18. Berkowitz, L., McCarthy, C.: Innovation with Information Technologies in Healthcare. Springer Science & Business Media, New York (2012)
19. Birk, M., Mandryk, R.L.: Control your game-self: effects of controller type on enjoyment, motivation, and personality in game. In: Proceedings of the SIGCHI Conference on Human Factors in Computing Systems, CHI 2013, pp. 685–694. ACM (2013)
20. Birk, M.V., Mandryk, R.L., Miller, M.K., Gerling, K.M.: How self-esteem shapes our interactions with play technologies. In: Proceedings of the 2015 Annual Symposium on Computer-Human Interaction in Play, CHI PLAY 2015, pp. 35–45. ACM (2015)
21. Black, A.D., Car, J., Pagliari, C., Anandan, C., Cresswell, K., Bokun, T., McKinstry, B., Procter, R., Majeed, A., Sheikh, A.: The impact of ehealth on the quality and safety of health care: a systematic overview. PLoS Med **8**(1), e1000387 (2011)
22. Bredl, K., Bösche, W.: Serious Games and Virtual Worlds in Education, Professional Development, and Healthcare. IGI Global, Hershey (2013)
23. Brooke, J.: SUS: A "Quick and Dirty" Usability Scale, pp. 189–194. Taylor & Francis, London (1996)

24. Brooks, A.L., Brahnam, S., Jain, L.C.: Technologies of Inclusive Well-Being: Serious Games, Alternative Realities, and Play Therapy. Springer, New York (2014)
25. Brox, E., Fernandez-Luque, L., Tollefsen, T.: Healthy gaming video game design to promote health. Appl. Clin. Inf. 2(2), 128–142 (2011)
26. Brox, E., Hernandez, J.E.G.: Exergames for elderly: Social exergames to persuade seniors to increase physical activity. In: 2011 5th International Conference on Pervasive Computing Technologies for Healthcare (PervasiveHealth), pp. 546–549 (2011)
27. Bruin, E., Schoene, D., Pichierri, G., Smith, S.: Use of virtual reality technique for the training of motor control in the elderly. Z. Gerontol. Geriatr. 43(4), 229–234 (2010)
28. Bundesverband Interaktive Unterhaltungssoftware e.V. (2013). http://goo.gl/ge2ht2
29. Burke, J.W., McNeill, M.D.J., Charles, D.K., Morrow, P.J., Crosbie, J.H., McDonough, S.M.: Optimising engagement for stroke rehabilitation using serious games. Visual Comput. 25(12), 1085–1099 (2009)
30. Chanel, G., Rebetez, C., Betrancourt, M., Pun, T.: Boredom, engagement and anxiety as indicators for adaptation to difficulty in games. In: Proceedings of the 12th International Conference on Entertainment and Media in the Ubiquitous Era, MindTrek 2008, pp. 13–17. ACM (2008)
31. Chang, C.Y., Lange, B., Zhang, M., Koenig, S., Requejo, P., Somboon, N., Sawchuk, A.A., Rizzo, A.A.: Towards pervasive physical rehabilitation using Microsoft Kinect. In: 2012 6th International Conference on Pervasive Computing Technologies for Healthcare (PervasiveHealth), pp. 159–162. IEEE (2012)
32. Chen, J.: Flow in games (and everything else). Commun. ACM 50(4), 31–34 (2007)
33. Cheng, J., Putnam, C., Rusch, D.C.: Towards efficacy-centered game design patterns for brain injury rehabilitation: A data-driven approach. In: Proceedings of the 17th International ACM SIGACCESS Conference on Computers & Accessibility, ASSETS 2015, pp. 291–299. ACM (2015)
34. Ciaramitaro, B.L.: Mobile Technology Consumption: Opportunities and Challenges: Opportunities and Challenges. IGI Global, Hershey (2011)
35. Crawford, C.: The Art of Computer Game Design. Osborne/McGraw-Hill, Berkeley (1984)
36. Csikszentmihalyi, M.: Flow: The Psychology of Optimal Experience. Harper & Row, New York (1990)
37. Csikszentmihalyi, M., Abuhamdeh, S., Nakamura, J.: Flow Flow and the Foundations of Positive Psychology, pp. 227–238. Springer, Heidelberg (2014)
38. Curtis, J., Ruijs, L., de Vries, M., Winters, R., Martens, J.B.: Rehabilitation of handwriting skills in stroke patients using interactive games: a pilot study. In: Proceedings of the 27th International Conference Extended Abstracts on Human Factors in Computing Systems. pp. 3931–3936. ACM (2009)
39. De Schutter, B., Vanden Abeele, V.: Designing meaningful play within the psychosocial context of older adults. In: Proceedings of the 3rd International Conference on Fun and Games, pp. 84–93 (2010)
40. Deci, E.L.: Effects of externally mediated rewards on intrinsic motivation. J. Pers. Soc. Psychol. 18(1), 105–115 (1971)
41. Deci, E.L., Ryan, R.M.: The "what" and "why" of goal pursuits: Human needs and the self-determination of behavior. Psychol. Inq. 11(4), 227–268 (2000)

42. Denis, G., Jouvelot, P.: Motivation-driven educational game design: Applying best practices to music education. In: Proceedings of the 2005 ACM SIGCHI International Conference on Advances in Computer Entertainment Technology, ACE 2005, pp. 462–465. ACM (2005)

43. Denisova, A., Cairns, P.: The placebo effect in digital games: phantom perception of adaptive artificial intelligence. In: Proceedings of the 2015 Annual Symposium on Computer-Human Interaction in Play, pp. 23–33. ACM (2015)

44. Deterding, S., Dixon, D., Khaled, R., Nacke, L.: From game design elements to gamefulness: defining "gamification". In: Proceedings of the 15th International Academic MindTrek Conference: Envisioning Future Media Environments, MindTrek 2011, pp. 9–15. ACM (2011)

45. Deutsch, J.E., Borbely, M., Filler, J., Huhn, K., Guarrera-Bowlby, P.: Use of a low-cost, commercially available gaming console (wii) for rehabilitation of an adolescent with cerebral palsy. Phy. Ther. 88(10), 1196–1207 (2008)

46. Entertainment Software Association (ESA): Essential Facts About theComputer and Video Game Industry 2013 (2013). https://igea.wpengine.com/wp-content/uploads/2013/06/ESA_EF_2013.pdf

47. Federico Semeraro, A.F.: Relive: a serious game to learn how to save lives. Resuscitation 85(7), e109–e110 (2014)

48. Fogg, B.: A behavior model for persuasive design. In: Proceedings of the 4th International Conference on Persuasive Technology, Persuasive 2009, pp. 40:1–40:7. ACM (2009)

49. Fullerton, T., Swain, C., Hoffman, S.: Game Design Workshop: Designing, Prototyping, and Playtesting Games. Focal Press, Waltham (2004)

50. Galna, B., Barry, G., Jackson, D., Mhiripiri, D., Olivier, P., Rochester, L.: Accuracy of the microsoft kinect sensor for measuring movement in people with parkinson's disease. Gait Posture 39(4), 1062–1068 (2014)

51. Gao, Y., Mandryk, R.L.: The acute cognitive benefits of casual exergame play, pp. 1863–1872 (2012)

52. Gekker, A.: Health games. In: Ma, M., Oliveira, M.F., Hauge, J.B., Duin, H., Thoben, K.-D. (eds.) SGDA 2012. LNCS, vol. 7528, pp. 13–30. Springer, Heidelberg (2012). doi:10.1007/978-3-642-33687-4_2

53. Gerling, K.M., Livingston, I.J., Nacke, L.E., Mandryk, R.L.: Full-body motion-based game interaction for older adults. In: Proceedings of the 30th International Conference on Human Factors in Computing Systems, CHI 2012, pp. 1873–1882 (2012)

54. Gerling, K.: Motion-based video games for older adults in long-term care. Ph.D. thesis, University of Saskatchewan, May 2014

55. Gerling, K., Schulte, F., Masuch, M.: Designing and evaluating digital games for frail elderly persons. In: International Conference on Advances in Computer Entertainment Technology (ACE 2011), pp. 62:1–62:8. ACM (2011)

56. Gerling, K.M., Mandryk, R.L., Miller, M., Kalyn, M.R., Birk, M., Smeddinck, J.D.: Designing wheelchair-based movement games. ACM Trans. Access. Comput. 6(2), 6:1–6:23 (2015)

57. Gerling, K.M., Miller, M., Mandryk, R.L., Birk, M., Smeddinck, J.: Effects of balancing for physical abilities on player performance, experience and self-esteem in exergames. In: CHI 2014: Proceedings of the 2014 CHI Conference on Human Factors in Computing Systems, pp. 2201–2210 (2014)

58. Gerling, K.M., Schulte, F.P., Smeddinck, J., Masuch, M.: Game design for older adults: effects of age-related changes on structural elements of digital games. In: Herrlich, M., Malaka, R., Masuch, M. (eds.) ICEC 2012. LNCS, pp. 235–242. Springer, Heidelberg (2012). doi:10.1007/978-3-642-33542-6_20

59. Gerling, K.M., Smeddinck, J.: Involving users and experts in motion-based game design for older adults. In: Proceedings of the CHI Game User Research Workshop (2013)

60. Gesundheitsberichterstattung des Bundes (2006). http://www.gbe-bund.de/gbe10/abrechnung.prc_abr_test_logon?p_uid=gasts&p_aid=&p_knoten=FID&p_sprache=D&p_suchstring=10791::Physiotherapie

61. Giannotti, D., Patrizi, G., Di Rocco, G., Vestri, A.R., Semproni, C.P., Fiengo, L., Pontone, S., Palazzini, G., Redler, A.: Play to become a surgeon: Impact of nintendo wii training on laparoscopic skills. PLoS ONE 8(2), e57372 (2013)

62. Göbel, S., Hardy, S., Wendel, V., Mehm, F., Steinmetz, R.: Serious games for health: personalized exergames. In: Proceedings of the International Conference on Multimedia, MM 2010, pp. 1663–1666. ACM, aCM ID: 1874316 (2010)

63. Grafsgaard, J.F., Wiggins, J.B., Boyer, K.E., Wiebe, E.N., Lester, J.C.: Automatically recognizing facial expression: predicting engagement and frustration. In: Proceedings of the 6th International Conference on Educational Data Mining, pp. 43–50 (2013)

64. Hartson, R., Pyla, P.: The UX Book: Process and Guidelines for Ensuring a Quality User Experience, 1st edn. Morgan Kaufmann, San Diego (2012)

65. Hekler, E.B., Klasnja, P., Froehlich, J.E., Buman, M.P.: Mind the theoretical gap: interpreting, using, and developing behavioral theory in hci research. In: Proceedings of the SIGCHI Conference on Human Factors in Computing Systems, pp. 3307–3316. ACM (2013)

66. Henry, K.D., Rosemond, C., Eckert, L.B.: Effect of number of home exercises on compliance and performance in adults over 65 years of age. Phys Ther. 79(3), 270–277 (1999). pMID: 10078770

67. Hermann, R., Herrlich, M., Wenig, D., Smeddinck, J., Malaka, R.: Strong and loose cooperation in exergames for older adults with parkinson s disease. In: Boll, S., Maaß, S., Malaka, R. (eds.) Mensch & Computer Workshopband, pp. 249–254. Oldenbourg Verlag, Munich (2013)

68. Hernandez, H.A., Graham, T.C., Fehlings, D., Switzer, L., Ye, Z., Bellay, Q., Hamza, M.A., Savery, C., Stach, T.: Design of an exergaming station for children with cerebral palsy. In: Proceedings of the 2012 ACM Annual Conference on Human Factors in Computing Systems, pp. 2619–2628 (2012)

69. Hocine, N., Gouaich, A., Di Loreto, I., Joab, M.: Motivation based difficulty adaptation for therapeutic games. In: 2011 IEEE 1st International Conference on Serious Games and Applications for Health (SeGAH), pp. 1–8 (2011)

70. Hocine, N., Gouaïch, A., Cerri, S.A.: Dynamic difficulty adaptation in serious games for motor rehabilitation. In: Göbel, S., Wiemeyer, J. (eds.) GameDays 2014. LNCS, pp. 115–128. Springer, Heidelberg (2014). doi:10.1007/978-3-319-05972-3_13

71. Hoffman, H.G., Garcia-Palacios, A., Patterson, D.R., Jensen, M., Furness, T., Ammons, W.F.: The effectiveness of virtual reality for dental pain control: a case study. Cyber Psychol. Behav. 4(4), 527–535 (2001)

72. Hoffman, H.G., Patterson, D.R., Seibel, E., Soltani, M., Jewett-Leahy, L., Sharar, S.R.: Virtual reality pain control during burn wound debridement in the hydrotank. Clin. J. Pain 24(4), 299–304 (2008)

73. Hoffmann, K., Wiemeyer, J., Hardy, S., Göbel, S.: Personalized adaptive control of training load in exergames from a sport-scientific perspective. In: Göbel, S., Wiemeyer, J. (eds.) GameDays 2014. LNCS, pp. 129–140. Springer, Heidelberg (2014). doi:10.1007/978-3-319-05972-3_14

74. Holt, R., Weightman, A., Gallagher, J., Preston, N., Levesley, M., Mon-Williams, M., Bhakta, B.: A system in the wild: deploying a two player arm rehabilitation system for children with cerebral palsy in a school environment. J. Usability Stud. 8(4), 111–126 (2013)

75. Horvitz, E., Breese, J., Heckerman, D., Hovel, D., Rommelse, K.: The lumiere project: Bayesian user modeling for inferring the goals and needs of software users. In: Proceedings of the fourteenth Conference on Uncertainty in Artificial Intelligence, pp. 256–265 (1998)

76. Hunicke, R.: The case for dynamic difficulty adjustment in games. In: Proceedings of the 2005 ACM SIGCHI International Conference on Advances in Computer Entertainment Technology, pp. 429–433 (2005)

77. Ice, R.: Long-term compliance. Phy. Ther. 65(12), 1832–1839. (1985). pMID: 3906687

78. Ijsselsteijn, W., Nap, H., de Kort, Y., Poels, K.: Digital game design for elderly users. In: Proceedings of the 2007 Conference on Future Play, pp. 17–22 (2007)

79. Jack, D., Boian, R., Merians, A.S., Tremaine, M., Burdea, G.C., Adamovich, S.V., Recce, M., Poizner, H.: Virtual reality-enhanced stroke rehabilitation. IEEE Trans. Neural Syst. Rehabil. Eng. 9(3), 308–318 (2001)

80. Janssen, C.P., Van Rijn, H., Van Liempd, G., Van der Pompe, G.: User modeling for training recommendation in a depression prevention game. In: Proceedings of the First NSVKI Student Conference, pp. 29–35 (2007)

81. Jarske, H., Kolehmainen, H.: Valedo(r)motion-terapialaitteiston hyväksyminen ja käyttökelpoisuus tullinkulman työterveydessä (2013)

82. Kamel Boulos, M.N., Gammon, S., Dixon, M.C., MacRury, S.M., Fergusson, M.J., Miranda Rodrigues, F., Mourinho Baptista, T., Yang, S.P.: Digital games for type 1 and type 2 diabetes: underpinning theory with three illustrative examples. JMIR Ser. Games 3(1), e3 (2015)

83. Kato, P.M.: Video games in health care: closing the gap. Rev. Gen. Psychol. 14, 113–121 (2010)

84. Kato, P.M., Cole, S.W., Bradlyn, A.S., Pollock, B.H.: A video game improves behavioral outcomes in adolescents and young adults with cancer: a randomized trial. Pediatrics 122(2), 305–317 (2008). pMID: 18676516

85. Kayama, H., Okamoto, K., Nishiguchi, S., Nagai, K., Yamada, M., Aoyama, T.: Concept software based on kinect for assessing dual-task ability of elderly people. Games Health J. 1(5), 348–352 (2012)

86. Kempermann, G., Fabel, K., Ehninger, D., Babu, H., Leal-Galicia, P., Garthe, A., Wolf, S.A.: Why and how physical activity promotes experience-induced brain plasticity. Front. Neurosci. 4, 189 (2010). pMID: 21151782PMCID: PMC3000002

87. Kessel, F., Rosenfield, P., Anderson, N.: Interdisciplinary Research. Oxford University Press, New York (2008)

88. Kratzke, C., Cox, C.: Smartphone technology and apps: rapidly changing health promotion. Int. Electron. J. Health Educ. 15, 72 (2012)

89. Krichevets, A.N., Sirotkina, E.B., Yevsevicheva, I.V., Zeldin, L.M.: Computer games as a means of movement rehabilitation. Disabil. Rehabil. 17(2), 100–105 (1995)

90. Kuhn, J.T., Holling, H., Raddatz, J., Dobel, C.: Meister CODY: ein computergestützter Test und Training für Kinder mit Dyskalkulie (2015)

91. Kuhn, J.T., Raddatz, J., Holling, H., Dobel, C.: Dyskalkulie vs. re-chenschwäche: basisnumerische verarbeitung in der grundschule. Lernen Lernstörungen **2**(4), 229–247 (2013)

92. Langley, P.: User modeling in adaptive interface. In: Kay, J. (ed.) UM99 User Modeling. CICMS, pp. 357–370. Springer, Heidelberg (1999). doi:10.1007/978-3-7091-2490-1_48

93. Laugwitz, B., Held, T., Schrepp, M.: Construction and evaluation of a user experience questionnaire. In: Holzinger, A. (ed.) USAB 2008. LNCS, vol. 5298, pp. 63–76. Springer, Heidelberg (2008). doi:10.1007/978-3-540-89350-9_6

94. Leijdekkers, P., Gay, V.: User adoption of mobile apps for chronic disease management: a case study based on myFitnessCompanion®. In: Donnelly, M., Paggetti, C., Nugent, C., Mokhtari, M. (eds.) ICOST 2012. LNCS, pp. 42–49. Springer, Heidelberg (2012). doi:10.1007/978-3-642-30779-9_6

95. Lilla, D., Herrlich, M., Malaka, R., Krannich, D.: The influence of music on player performance in exergames for parkinson's patients. In: Herrlich, M., Malaka, R., Masuch, M. (eds.) ICEC 2012. LNCS, pp. 433–436. Springer, Heidelberg (2012). doi:10.1007/978-3-642-33542-6_46

96. Lindley, C.A., Sennersten, C.C.: Game play schemas: from player analysis to adaptive game mechanics. In: Proceedings of the 2006 International Conference on Game Research and Development, pp. 47–53 (2006)

97. Lister, C., West, J.H., Cannon, B., Sax, T., Brodegard, D.: Just a fad? gamification in health and fitness apps. JMIR Serious Games **2**(2), e9 (2014)

98. Liu, C., Agrawal, P., Sarkar, N., Chen, S.: Dynamic difficulty adjustment in computer games through real-time anxiety-based affective feedback. Int. J. Hum. Comput. Interact. **25**(6), 506–529 (2009)

99. Lomas, D., Patel, K., Forlizzi, J.L., Koedinger, K.R.: Optimizing challenge in an educational game using large-scale design experiments. In: Proceedings of the SIGCHI Conference on Human Factors in Computing Systems, CHI 2013, pp. 89–98. ACM (2013)

100. Luxton, D.D., McCann, R.A., Bush, N.E., Mishkind, M.C., Reger, G.M.: mhealth for mental health: Integrating smartphone technology in behavioral healthcare. Prof. Psychol. Res. Pract. **42**(6), 505–512 (2011)

101. Maier, M., Rubio Ballester, B., Duarte, E., Duff, A., Verschure, P.F.M.J.: Social integration of stroke patients through the multiplayer rehabilitation gaming system. In: Göbel, S., Wiemeyer, J. (eds.) GameDays 2014. LNCS, pp. 100–114. Springer, Heidelberg (2014). doi:10.1007/978-3-319-05972-3_12

102. Malaka, R.: How computer games can improve your health and fitness. In: Göbel, S., Wiemeyer, J. (eds.) GameDays 2014. LNCS, pp. 1–7. Springer, Heidelberg (2014). doi:10.1007/978-3-319-05972-3_1

103. Malaka, R., Herrlich, M., Smeddinck, J.: Anticipation in Motion-based Games for Health. Lecture Notes in Computer Science. Springer, Heidelberg (2016) (accepted)

104. McAuley, E., Duncan, T., Tammen, V.V.: Psychometric properties of the intrinsic motivation inventory in a competitive sport setting: a confirmatory factor analysis. Res. Q. Exerc. Sport **60**(1), 48–58 (1989). pMID: 2489825

105. Medler, B.: Using recommendation systems to adapt game-play. Int. J. Gaming Comput. Mediat. Simul. **1**(3), 68–80 (2009)

106. Missura, O., Gärtner, T.: Player modeling for intelligent difficulty adjustment. In: Gama, J., Costa, V.S., Jorge, A.M., Brazdil, P.B. (eds.) DS 2009. LNCS (LNAI), pp. 197–211. Springer, Heidelberg (2009). doi:10.1007/978-3-642-04747-3_17

107. Mueller, F., Vetere, F., Gibbs, M., Edge, D., Agamanolis, S., Sheridan, J., Heer, J.: Balancing exertion experiences. In: Proceedings of the 2012 ACM Annual Conference on Human Factors in Computing Systems, pp. 1853–1862 (2012)

108. Mueller, F., Gibbs, M.R., Vetere, F., Edge, D.: Supporting the creative game design process with exertion cards. pp. 2211–2220. ACM Press (2014)

109. Nap, H., de Kort, Y., IJsselsteijn, W.: Senior gamers: preferences, motivations and needs. Gerontechnology 8, 247–262 (2009)

110. Natbony, L.R., Zimmer, A., Ivanco, L.S., Studenski, S.A., Jain, S.: Perceptions of a videogame-based dance exercise program among individuals with parkinson's disease. Games Health J. 2(4), 235–239 (2013)

111. Oinas-Kukkonen, H., Harjumaa, M.: Persuasive systems design: Key issues, process model, and system features. Commun. Assoc. Inform. Syst. 24(1), 28 (2009)

112. Orji, R., Mandryk, R.L., Vassileva, J., Gerling, K.M.: Tailoring persuasive health games to gamer type. In: Proceedings of the SIGCHI Conference on Human Factors in Computing Systems, CHI 2013, pp. 2467–2476. ACM (2013)

113. Pichierri, G., Wolf, P., Murer, K., de Bruin, E.D.: Cognitive and cognitive-motor interventions affecting physical functioning: a systematic review. BMC Geriatr. 11(1), 29 (2011)

114. Pomeroy, V.M., Pramanik, A., Sykes, L., Richards, J., Hill, E.: Agreement between physiotherapists on quality of movement rated via videotape. Clin. Rehabil. 17(3), 264–272 (2003)

115. Portland Pharmaceuticals, G.f.H.P.: Games for health project

116. Prange, G.B., Jannink, M.J.A., Groothuis-Oudshoorn, C.G.M., Hermens, H.J., IJzerman, M.J.: Systematic review of the effect of robot-aided therapy on recovery of the hemiparetic arm after stroke. J. Rehabil. Res. Dev. 43(2), 171 (2006)

117. Primack, B.A., Carroll, M.V., McNamara, M., Klem, M.L., King, B., Rich, M., Chan, C.W., Nayak, S.: Role of video games in improving health-related outcomes: a systematic review. Am. J. Prev. Med. 42(6), 630–638 (2012)

118. Privacy Rights Clearinghouse: fact sheet 39: mobile health and fitness apps: What are the privacy risks? (2014). https://www.privacyrights.org/mobile-health-and-fitness-apps-what-are-privacy-risks

119. Rego, P., Moreira, P., Reis, L.: Serious games for rehabilitation: a survey and a classification towards a taxonomy. In: 2010 5th Iberian Conference on Information Systems and Technologies (CISTI), pp. 1–6, June 2010

120. Ricciardi, F., De Paolis, L.T., Ricciardi, F., De Paolis, L.T.: A comprehensive review of serious games in health professions. Int. J. Comput. Games Technol. 2014, e787968 (2014)

121. Rigby, S.: Glued to Games: How Video Games Draw Us In and Hold Us Spellbound. Praeger, Santa Barbara (2011)

122. Rigby, S., Ryan, R.: The Player Experience of Need Satisfac-tion(PENS): an applied model and methodology for understanding key components of the player experience (2007)

123. Ryan, R.M., Rigby, C.S., Przybylski, A.: The motivational pull of video games: a self-determination theory approach. Motiv. Emot. 30(4), 344–360 (2006)

124. García Sánchez, R., Thin, A.G., Baalsrud Hauge, J., Fiucci, G., Nabeth, T., Rudnianski, M., Luccini, A.M., Star, K.: Value propositions for serious games in health and well-being. In: Ma, M., Oliveira, M.F., Hauge, J.B., Duin, H., Thoben, K.-D. (eds.) SGDA 2012. LNCS, pp. 150–157. Springer, Heidelberg (2012). doi:10.1007/978-3-642-33687-4_12

125. Sawyer, B., Smith, P.: Serious games taxonomy (2008)

126. Schneider, G.: Exergames. Ph.D. thesis, Uniwien (2008)

127. Schneiders, A.G., Zusman, M., Singer, K.P.: Exercise therapy compliance in acute low back pain patients. Manual Ther. **3**(3), 147–152 (1998)

128. Shute, V.J., Ventura, M., Ke, F.: The power of play: the effects of portal 2 and lumosity on cognitive and noncognitive skills. Comput. Educ. **80**, 58–67 (2015)

129. Sinclair, J., Hingston, P., Masek, M.: Considerations for the design of exergames. In: Proceedings of the 5th International Conference on Computer Graphics and Interactive Techniques in Australia and Southeast Asia, GRAPHITE 2007, pp. 289–295. ACM, aCM ID: 1321313 (2007)

130. Sinclair, J., Hingston, P., Masek, M.: Exergame development using the dual flow model. In: Proceedings of the Sixth Australasian Conference on Interactive Entertainment, IE 2009, pp. 11:1–11:7. ACM (2009)

131. Sluijs, E.M., Kok, G.J., van der Zee, J.: Correlates of exercise compliance in physical therapy. Phy. Ther. **73**(11), 771–782 (1993). pMID: 8234458

132. Smeddinck, J., Gerling, K.M., Tiemkeo, S.: Visual complexity, player experience, performance and physical exertion in motion-based games for older adults. In: Proceedings of the 15th International ACM SIGACCESS Conference on Computers and Accessibility, ASSETS 2013, pp. 25:1–25:8. ACM (2013)

133. Smeddinck, J., Herrlich, M., Krause, M., Gerling, K., Malaka, R.: Did they really like the game? - challenges in evaluating exergames with older adults. In: Proceedings of the CHI Game User Research Workshop (2012)

134. Smeddinck, J., Siegel, S., Herrlich, M.: Adaptive difficulty in exergames for parkinson's disease patients. In: Proceedings of the 2013 Graphics Interface Conference, GI 2013, pp. 141–148. Canadian Information Processing Society (2013)

135. Smeddinck, J.D., Gerling, K.M., Malaka, R.: Anpassbare computerspiele für senioren. Informatik-Spektrum **37**(6), 575–579 (2014)

136. Smeddinck, J.D., Herrlich, M., Malaka, R.: Exergames for physiotherapy and rehabilitation: a medium-term situated study of motivational aspects and impact on functional reach. In: Proceedings of CHI 2015, pp. 4143–4146. ACM (2015)

137. Smeddinck, J.D., Herrlich, M., Roll, M., Malaka, R.: Motivational effects of a gamified training analysis interface. In: Mensch & Computer 2014-Workshopband, pp. 397–404 (2014)

138. Smeddinck, J.D., Hey, J., Runge, N., Herrlich, M., Jacobsen, C., Wolters, J., Malaka, R.: Movitouch: mobile movement capability configurations. In: Proceedings of the 17th International ACM SIGACCESS Conference on Computers & Accessibility, ASSETS 2015, pp. 389–390. ACM (2015)

139. Smeddinck, J.D., Mandryk, R., Birk, M., Gerling, K., Barsilowski, D., Malaka, R.: How to present game difficulty choices? exploring the impact on player experience. In: Proceedings of the 34th Annual ACM Conference on Human Factors in Computing Systems, CHI 2016. ACM (2016, inpress)

140. Smeddinck, J.D., Voges, J., Herrlich, M., Malaka, R.: Comparing modalities for kinesiatric exercise instruction. In: CHI 2014 Extended Abstracts on Human Factors in Computing Systems, CHI EA 2014, pp. 2377–2382. ACM (2014)

141. Song, H., Peng, W., Lee, K.M.: Promoting exercise self-efficacy with an exergame. J. Health Commun. **16**(2), 148–162 (2011). pMID: 21213171

142. Springer, M., Herrlich, M., Krannich, D., Malaka, R.: Achievements in Exergames for Parkinson's Patients. Oldenbourg Verlag, Munich (2012)

143. Staiano, A.E., Calvert, S.L.: The promise of exergames as tools to measure physical health. Entertain. Comput. **2**(1), 17–21 (2011)

144. Stenström, C., Arge, B., Sundbom, A.: Home exercise and compliance in inflammatory rheumatic diseases-a prospective clinical trial. J. Rheumatol. **24**(3), 470–476 (1997). pMID: 9058651
145. Sundholm, M., Cheng, J., Zhou, B., Sethi, A., Lukowicz, P.: Smart-mat: Recognizing and counting gym exercises with low-cost resistive pressure sensing matrix. In: Proceedings of the 2014 ACM International Joint Conference on Pervasive and Ubiquitous Computing, UbiComp 2014, pp. 373–382. ACM (2014)
146. Theng, Y.L., Chua, P.H., Pham, T.P.: Wii as entertainment and socialisation aids for mental and social health of the elderly. In: Proceedings of the 2012 ACM Annual Conference Extended Abstracts on Human Factors in Computing Systems Extended Abstracts, pp. 691–702. ACM (2012)
147. Thompson, D.: Designing serious video games for health behavior change: current status and future directions. J. Diab. Sci. Technol. **6**(4), 807–811 (2012). pMID: 22920806PMCID: PMC3440151
148. Uzor, S., Baillie, L.: Exploring & designing tools to enhance falls rehabilitation in the home. In: Proceedings of the SIGCHI Conference on Human Factors in Computing Systems, CHI 2013, pp. 1233–1242. ACM (2013)
149. Uzor, S., Baillie, L.: Investigating the long-term use of exergames in the home with elderly fallers, pp. 2813–2822. ACM Press (2014)
150. VirtualRehab: VirtualRehab - Virtual rehabilitation through gaming, Sep 2014
151. Walther-Franks, B., Wenig, D., Smeddinck, J., Malaka, R.: Exercise my game: turning off-the-shelf games into exergames. In: Anacleto, J.C., Clua, E.W.G., Silva, F.S.C., Fels, S., Yang, H.S. (eds.) ICEC 2013. LNCS, pp. 126–131. Springer, Heidelberg (2013). doi:10.1007/978-3-642-41106-9_15
152. Walther-Franks, B., Wenig, D., Smeddinck, J., Malaka, R.: Sportal: a first-person videogame turned exergame. In: Boll, S., Maaß, S., Malaka, R. (eds.) Mensch & Computer 2013 - Workshopband, pp. 539–542. Oldenbourg Verlag, Munich (2013)
153. Watcharasatharpornpong, N., Kotrajaras, V.: Automatic level difficulty adjustment in platform games using genetic algorithm based methodology. Department of Computer Engineering, Faculty of Engineering, Chulalongkorn University. (Cited: October 14, 2010) (2010)
154. Weisman, S.: Computer games for the frail elderly. Gerontologist **23**(4), 361–363 (1983)
155. Wiemeyer, J., Kliem, A.: Serious games in prevention and rehabilitation-a new panacea for elderly people? Eur. Rev. Aging Phys. Act. **9**(1), 41–50 (2011)
156. Yavuzer, G., Senel, A., Atay, M.B., Stam, H.J.: Playstation eyetoy games" improve upper extremity-related motor functioning in subacute stroke: a randomized controlled clinical trial. Eur. J. Phys. Rehabil. Med. **44**(3), 237–244 (2008). pMID: 18469735
157. Zigoris, P., Zhang, Y.: Bayesian adaptive user profiling with explicit & implicit feedback. In: Proceedings of the 15th ACM international conference on Information and Knowledge Management, CIKM 2006, pp. 397–404. ACM (2006)

Serious Games Evaluation: Processes, Models, and Concepts

Katharina Emmerich[1](✉) and Mareike Bockholt[2](✉)

[1] Entertainment Computing Group, University of Duisburg-Essen,
Forsthausweg 2, 47057 Duisburg, Germany
katharina.emmerich@uni-due.de
[2] Graph Theory and Complex Network Analysis Group,
University of Kaiserslautern, Gottlieb-Daimler-Straße 48,
67663 Kaiserslautern, Germany
mareike.bockholt@cs.uni-kl.de

Abstract. Serious games are developed with the goal of having a certain impact on players which goes beyond mere entertainment. This purpose-driven design is immanent to serious games and can be stated as the key characteristic that distinguishes serious games from other digital games. Hence, verifying that a serious game has the intended effect on the players needs to be an essential part in the development process. This and the following chapters are therefore dedicated to give a guidance how evaluation procedures can be planned and realized. The main focus is on aspects which are particularly distinctive to the evaluation of serious games, while methods and principles related to the evaluation of digital games in general will not be covered in detail. The structure of this chapter is as follows: After emphasizing the specific importance of evaluation for serious games, we describe a set of challenges which might occur in this context. In order to enable the reader to face these challenges, we present a framework of evaluation-driven design which offers guidance in the evaluation process. Other models which address different challenges are described before three examples of commendably evaluated serious games are discussed. These examples are intended to demonstrate how the presented abstract models can be applied in concrete evaluation procedures.

1 Introduction

This chapter gives comprehensive information about the evaluation of serious games. Each serious game is supposed to fulfil a certain purpose beyond mere entertainment. However, in order to ensure that this goal is achieved, it has to be tested in form of experiments and user tests. This process is called evaluation. Without evaluation, there is no evidence that the purpose of the game is achieved. Ideally, a serious game is evaluated with members from the target group in a comprehensive evaluation process. There are several criteria for a well-conducted and informative evaluation, as well as a range of challenges and problems that have to be met.

© Springer International Publishing AG 2016
R. Dörner et al. (Eds.): Entertainment Computing and Serious Games, LNCS 9970, pp. 265–283, 2016.
DOI: 10.1007/978-3-319-46152-6_11

Serious games are often used in new contexts as a medium of intervention, and in many cases there are little to no existing successful examples for orientation. Thus, as there are few proven strategies or approaches to be guided by, the design and development of serious games is often based on literature, theories and to some part on intuition and personal experience (see also the chapter about game design in this book). Although this is a reasonable approach, it raises the need to test and confirm the underlying assumptions afterwards. However, the process of proving the effectiveness of a serious game is in general more involved than the evaluation of a commercial entertainment game, as a serious game needs to be especially evaluated with respect to its "serious" purpose. In the following, we will thus concentrate on the evaluation of the effectiveness of serious games in regard to their purposes, not on mere usability testing or the assessment of general player experience issues (e.g. fun), which is also a part of evaluation. Those aspects are interesting to study as well, but they are not serious games specific, thus techniques and methods from game design and evaluation in general can be applied easily and read about in other books (e.g. see [36, 39, 44] in the further readings sections). Here, evaluation is discussed in terms of its characteristics and specialities regarding the serious games context.

1.1   Overview

In order to approach the topic, this chapter is structured into four main parts: First, Sect. 2 declares the importance of comprehensive evaluation processes in general. Section 3 then emphasizes its complexity by pointing out characteristic challenges and problems related to the evaluation of serious games. Based on that, a framework for serious games evaluation is proposed in Sect. 4, which is supposed to provide guidance for the planning and realization of evaluations during and after the design process of a serious game. Finally, some examples of successfully conducted studies are presented in Sect. 5 and discussed with respect to the introduced framework of evaluation-driven design. The chapter concludes with a short summary and a selection of further reading regarding the topic of evaluation.

2   Importance of Evaluation

The idea of using digital games for purposes like learning, health promotion and persuasion is not new and has evolved into an extensive field of research. During the last decades, more and more serious games and applications have been developed and the endeavours to prove their effectiveness were high. Literature reviews show that there are several studies implying the benefit of serious games in general [3, 6, 25] or regarding different aspects, for instance as a tool to support learning processes or to induce health-related behaviour changes [4, 7, 9, 11, 26]. However, these reviews also indicate that there are even more studies and serious games which were not that successful due to sundry reasons. The question arises what makes a good evaluation and whether the results are worth the effort, i.e., why evaluation is important at all.

The overall goal of evaluation is to prove the game's effectiveness and suitability with respect to its designated purpose and application context. The purpose is thereby always in the center of investigation. Reliable results are supposed to lend credence to serious games, to convince diverse stakeholders and to inform future design approaches. Game researchers can learn more about the relationships between game design elements and the resulting player experience and thus gain insights into the impact of games in general. Additionally, researchers as well as developers are supposed to gain experience from both successful and failed game concepts and may thus improve in designing effective serious games [19]. Moreover, evidences of the effectiveness of serious games are necessary to convince the users of serious games themselves, as they have to believe and trust in their capability. Michael and Chen state that "[t]rainers and educators need to know whether or not the player has actually learned the content of the serious game" [22]. They thus underline the need of evaluation in order to gain a better acceptance of the games and to be competitive compared to established non-gaming interventions and programs. Those who have to support the use of serious games in their field of work, for instance teachers, physicians and other intermediaries, have to be convinced of their positive effect, because otherwise they will simply not recommend to use them [5,19]. Mayer et al. [21] mention two main reasons to conduct a structured and reproducible evaluation: accountability and responsibility. Accountability refers to the fact that users "have the right to know what they are actually buying, using or playing" [p. 234] and that they have to be convinced of the effectiveness of serious games. Responsibility, on the other hand, refers to developers and advocates of serious games and their duty to critically question the effects and consequences their games may have, especially in case of vulnerable target groups.

Furthermore, researchers and practitioners also emphasize the importance of evaluation for the commercial success and the growth of the serious games industry [2,10]. Successfully evaluated serious games can help to advance the dissemination and to optimize the image of serious games while at the same time adhering to the concept of responsibility. Without proper evaluation, the establishment of serious games as considered interventions is not possible, or as Kevin Corti, Managing Director from *PIXELearning*, puts it: Serious games "will not grow as an industry unless the learning experience is definable, quantifiable, and measurable. Assessment is the future of Serious Games." (quoted from Chen and Michael [2]). Summarizing these aspects, there are four different main groups of stakeholders that benefit from structured evaluations as shown in Fig. 1: serious games developers, researchers, intermediaries as well as the users. Overall, serious games evaluation is important for underlining the potential of serious games in various application fields and extending the effort in serious game development, research and application.

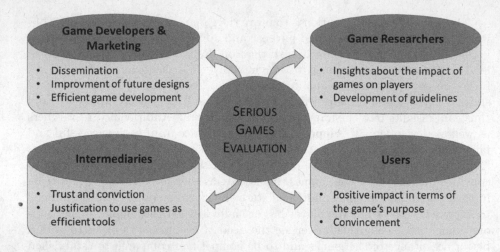

Fig. 1. Stakeholders and their advantages of serious games evaluation.

3   Challenges of Evaluation

As there are only few examples of comprehensively evaluated serious games, the question arises of what challenges and problems are there making evaluation an ambitious task. Most evaluation processes follow the same general structure: The study design is planned and set up, then participants are recruited and divided into different experimental groups. Normally, there are at least two groups, one that is provided with the serious game, called the *treatment* group, and one that does not use the game, called the *control* group. Of all groups, several data before, in the middle of and after the experiment needs to be logged and evaluated. Finally, this data is analyzed in terms of the purpose of the game and conclusions about its effectiveness are derived. However, Mayer et al. declare that "we lack an overarching methodology" [21]. According to them, the main problem is that there is a lack of comprehensive frameworks, theories, operationalized models, validated measurement methods, proper research designs, and generic tools for unobtrusive data gathering [21]. Hence, challenges appear all along the process of evaluation and can be further be classified into the following categories:

Recruitment of participants. Recruitment is often a time-consuming task, especially in the case of sensitive and vulnerable target groups like patients, children or disabled persons. If participants are already burdened with illness or complicated circumstances, which is true for many serious games for health, an experimental study is an additional strain. It is hard to find suitable volunteers and the risk of dropouts is high. However, a representative sample is important: Without a significant number of subjects a proper statistical analysis is not possible or will lead to results with just small effect sizes. Furthermore, it might occur that the recruited participants bring along different prerequisites, i.e., their previous knowledge or experiences with other games are different. This can have an impact on the evaluation results and should be considered. If for example a serious game for learning is evaluated and learning through a serious game instead of conventional methods is a completely new experience for the participants, their attention for the game and also for the material to be conveyed might increase. In this case, the evaluation of the game will likely yield better results in the sense that the knowledge or skills of the participants have improved than if the participants are used to the application of games for learning. For the recruitment, it is therefore recommended to either choose a group of participants which is a representative sample for the intended target group of the game with regard to their prerequisites, or to determine their prerequisites beforehand and take them into account in the analysis and interpretation of the results.

Operationalization. Even if a representative sample and number of participants is achieved, the most sophisticated questions are what exactly has to be measured and how this can be done. Starting from the overall purpose of a serious game and the underlying theories, it has to be defined which concrete measurable aspects best reflect the game's purpose. This process is called operationalization. For instance, if the game's purpose is to support pupils in learning vocabulary, the number of recalled words after playing the game compared to their prior state of knowledge could be measured by a common vocabulary test. In other cases, the operationalization is much more ambiguous, for example if an increase of well-being is striven for. As operationalization and assessment are such complex processes, another full chapter goes into detail regarding this subject in this book.

Choice of measurement methods. Closely related to the issue of operationalization is the choice of measuring instruments. There are many different types of these instruments like questionnaires, physiological measures and observations, which all have different advantages and disadvantages regarding objectivity, validity and clarity. Hence, it is recommended to combine several kinds of methods to gain comprehensive insights into the effects of the game [1].

Design of control group conditions. Apart from methods of measurement, there are several more decisions to be made regarding the experimental design that can be challenging. One of those is the choice of an appropriate control group. Most serious games are supposed to be applied in contexts in which other (non-game) interventions with similar purposes already exist. In those cases, the evaluation of a serious game does not only have to aim at verifying a general intended effect of the game, but also has to take into account a comparison with existing solutions in order to answer the question of whether the game is better than established non-game alternatives. Girard et al. [9] propose to use at least two control groups instead of one: one group that receives no training at all, and one that receives a training with comparable contents as the game, but built on a different method, for example pencil and paper or classic teaching situations. Besides, it is also possible to create different versions of the game to identify the impact of single game elements. In any case, if the treatment of the control group is incomparable to the serious games intervention, the results are incomparable and a badly chosen control group condition makes claims of effectiveness impossible.

Consideration of time-dependent effects. Another challenge related to the experimental design is timing. While it is already demanding to conduct a sound study with one point of measurement, most serious games would benefit from long-term assessment: Experiments in which participants are playing the game only once or for a short period of time, allow suggestions about short-term effects of the game, but do not take into account any wear-out effects. Due to its novelty, the game may attract more attention than established alternatives, but the resulting motivation to play it and to deal with the content might decrease after a while, impeding the impact of the game. Especially evaluation processes for games that are supposed to support long-term motivation of players should include this aspect as well.

Reach of effects. Besides considerations of time, it is also challenging to assess the reach of serious games effects in terms of the transfer to real-life contexts. Ideally, serious games evaluation includes both direct effects that playing the game has on players and subsequent effects that influence their future behavior in everyday life [9]. While this aspect is somehow interwoven with long-term effects, it does not describe effects over time, but rather defines on which level the effectiveness of a serious game is evaluated.

Processing of results. Finally, the evaluation of serious games bears the challenge to draw conclusions from results and meaningfully deploy them to improve the game. Evaluation does not terminate at the point that data is collected, but should lead to a process of revision to make the game more effective and appealing.

In sum, the result of an evaluation process should be data that is characterized by generalizability and validity [29]. To achieve this, we need a more structured way for evaluating serious games, hence in the following section we will present a framework of evaluation-driven design which is supposed to support the design of a proper and comprehensive evaluation process.

4   Evaluation Frameworks

The previous section contains a description of challenges that appear during an evaluation process and need to be handled. The following section is dedicated to the question of how to face these challenges. Because of the great variety of serious games regarding their background, purpose, or target audience, it is impossible to give concrete instructions for the evaluation procedure of every serious game, but it is possible to provide a set of guidelines and models which are general and abstract enough to be valid for the complete spectrum of serious games. For the specific evaluation procedure, guidelines and suggestions need to be derived carefully. They offer a useful standardization of evaluation procedures.

The section is structured into two parts: The first part contains the *framework of evaluation-driven design*, the second part contains a selection of further models and frameworks proposed by other researchers which are of use for evaluation procedures.

The framework of evaluation-driven design embeds the evaluation and design process into the general structure of scientific working and can be considered as a "step towards a science of game-based learning" and serious games [27]. It offers guidance to when to evaluate, how to plan the evaluation process, and which questions need to be answered beforehand. Other existing models and existing frameworks either fall in one of the two categories of *when* and *what* can be evaluated. Models and frameworks of both categories are presented in the second part of the section in order to give additional guidance for an evaluation process. Models and frameworks which are not of specific use for the evaluation of serious games, but are valid in other areas and might be considered for the evaluation of serious games, are not explicitly mentioned. For those general methods, a list of references is given in the section for further reading at the end of this chapter.

4.1   Framework of Evaluation-Driven Design

The framework of evaluation-driven design offers guidance in the planning and realization of the evaluation of a serious game. It particularly highlights the role of evaluation during the design and development process which is why it is called framework of evaluation-driven design.

An illustration of the proposed framework is shown in Fig. 2, the next sections will describe the overall structure and the single components of the framework. The framework is intended to contextualize the well-known phases of a game development and evaluation process, set them in relation to each other and emphasize the similarity of the game development process with scientific processes. Therefore, the framework consists of mainly three phases: the preparation phase, the design phase and the evaluation phase, where the design and the evaluation phase are closely interlinked with each other and are iterated as often as necessary. It is clearly to see (and also intended) that neither of the elements is formulated in a detailed manner because each of the elements is a broad topic itself which needs elaboration and reflection. For the process of game design for example, there has been done a lot of research and practical studies which yielded a great variety of theories, models, guidelines, and best practices (see for example the chapter about game design in this book). This is intentionally not addressed in the present framework, but included implicitly on a high and abstract level because the framework is intended to model the whole process of designing and evaluating a serious game.

Preparation Phase. The preparation phase is in the beginning of every serious game project and starts with stating the problem which should be solved. The reason for investing effort and resources into the development of a serious game is that a problem exists which is to be remedied by the serious game. This might concern the society as a whole, or it might only concern a particular group of people, for example patients with a particular illness, students of a specific

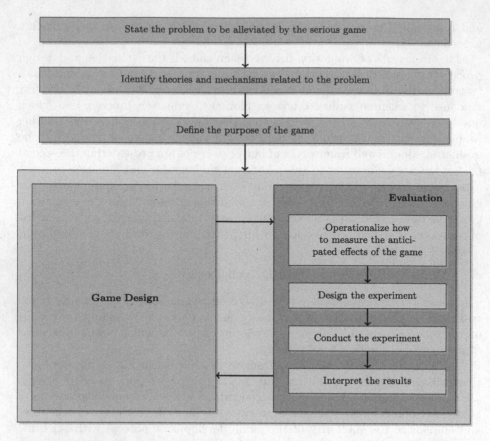

Fig. 2. The proposed serious game evaluation framework for evaluation-driven design.

grade, elderly people, etc. Such aspects of the current situation which should be improved by applying the serious game are for example:

○ the percentage of the population which suffers from obesity is too high (and should be reduced)
○ the awareness in society about human exploitation in third world countries is too low (and should be increased)
○ the knowledge of cancer patients about their disease is too little (and should be increased)

In order to contribute to an improvement of the situation, the next step is to identify the theory behind the problem which is necessary to tackle the problem by a game. This means that we need to identify the reasons why the problem exists at all, the underlying processes or mechanisms, which factors contribute to the problem, etc. Furthermore, it needs to be analysed which of these factors can be changed by a game at all. For the example of obesity, possible reasons might be an insufficient amount of physical activity or poor nutrition habits. But also the influence of lacking motivation, the social environment, or genetic predisposition might be considered. There is no doubt that in most cases it is impossible to identify all contributing factors and their relations to each other, but having identified at least one which is then addressed in the serious game is essential for the development and also for the evaluation of the game. Furthermore, the context of the game in which it will be applied, needs to be considered. It might be helpful to answer the following questions: (i) Why do other methods which have been used before did not work sufficiently to solve the problem? (ii) What is significantly different in a game than in previously applied methods? (iii) Is there an aspect that can be supported by a serious game in coordination with a traditional method? (iv) Is there an aspect which can even be treated better by a serious game than by other means?

Otherwise, a serious game will not be more successful than traditional methods. Having analysed the conventional methods and their effects has another advantage: the effects of the conventional methods set a lower bound on the effects of the serious game in order to rate the quality (or appropriateness) of the serious game: The measured effects of the serious game should be significantly larger than the traditional methods.

The next step is the definition of the purpose of the serious game. Based on the factors which contribute to the stated problem, the purpose of the serious game can be defined. The purpose of a serious game is to influence the identified factor which again has an impact on the situation and might solve the stated problem. The defined purpose is later the criterion by which the serious game is evaluated. Therefore, it is important that the purpose of the game can be operationalized, otherwise a proper evaluation is hardly possible. If it cannot be measured whether the serious game fulfils its designated purpose because the purpose can not be operationalized and measured, it is questionable whether this game should be called a serious game in the stricter sense.

Iterative Process of Games Design and Evaluation. The two other components, game design and game evaluation, build on the preparation phase and are tightly linked to each other. This means that the game is designed in an incremental way such that already at early stages of development, a prototype can be used for testing. Results from such an early evaluation will be taken into account in the next design step which results in another prototype which can be evaluated, etc. Hence, the results of an evaluation phase need to be usable in the game design in the sense that the feedback from the evaluation allows to draw conclusions which can be used to improve the game. The evaluation phase itself contains three main steps and is highly dependent on the results of the preparation phase. Depending on the defined purpose of the game, it needs to be analysed how the desired effect of the game can be measured in order to verify that the game fulfils its designated purpose. This is a great challenge in the evaluation procedure. This is the reason why a full chapter of this book is dedicated to the question of how to operationalize anticipated effects and elaborates on the existing methods of measuring concepts as motivation, fun, learning effects, behavioral changes, etc. However, the step of operationalization is facilitated by a carefully and thoroughly performed preparation phase. The next step is then the design of an experiment which tests whether the game has the intended impact on the players. The design of an experiment should follow general scientific standards and contains a great amount of challenges itself for example the treatment of the control group or the recruitment of participants. Therefore, experimental design is discussed in another chapter in this book. The interpretation of the experiment results should be done carefully and with the appropriate methods. The results from the evaluation cycle then serve as input for the design process in order to adapt the chosen design. In the ideal case, this incremental, iterative and integrated design and evaluation process allows to develop a serious game which can be shown to have a significant impact on the players. However, this framework only focuses on the impact of a game related to the defined purpose of the game because the designated purpose is the quality which distinguishes serious games from other games. It should nevertheless taken into account that the serious game is also a good game which is fun to play, engages the player, etc.

Summarizing, the proposal of the present framework is mainly intended to highlight the following recommendations for evaluation: (i) evaluation should be an integral element of the development of serious games and be present in all stages of development and should be even considered before the game design starts, (ii) evaluation and design should be two processes in the game development which benefit and are dependent of each other, (iii) the development of serious games should follow the general process of scientific working, and (iv) the evaluation and development of serious games should be centered on the intended purpose of the game—therefore, a clearly defined purpose is a necessary prerequisite for evaluation.

4.2   Further Evaluation Frameworks and Models

The previously described framework of evaluation-driven design integrates evaluation and design into a process model, other existing frameworks or models of evaluation address other aspects of evaluation. In general, all existing models can be categorized along two dimensions: the time point of evaluation (when to evaluate), and the content of evaluation (what to evaluate).

When to evaluate. As pointed out in Sect. 3, timing is one of the challenges in the process of evaluation: when in the development and deployment should the evaluation phase(s) take place? In literature, there is usually the distinction between summative and formative evaluation. Formative evaluation takes place during the development of the game and is supposed to yield results which can be incorporated in the further development, while summative evaluation is carried out after the development phase and assesses the quality of the end product and its best use. Still, time-dependent effects—measuring long-term effects or short-term effects for example— need to be considered. Therefore, there are several models which are concerned with the time point of evaluation and integrate the phase of evaluation in the design process. These models and frameworks can be found in the chapter about game design in this book, of particular interest are the classic *ADDIE* model [24] and the *Simulation-Games Instructional Systems Design Model* [17]. Both models contain at least one cycle meaning that several development stages are (intended to be) iterated which emphasizes that game development is not a sequential process, but rather each development stage is repeated several times such that the game improves in every iteration.

What to evaluate There exist many models that are concerned with the content of evaluation from which two are presented in the following: the model of Kirkpatrick [18], and the framework of Mitgutsch and Alvarado [23]. These are not redundant, but both valuable additional tools for the evaluation of serious games and address different challenges of evaluation.

Kirkpatrick's Model of Four Levels of Evaluation. Particularly for the evaluation of serious games, it is a difference whether only the quality of the game is evaluated or whether its effectiveness regarding its purpose is evaluated. This dimension might be summarized by the question of *what* exactly is intended to be measured, and can be quantified by Kirkpatrick's model of *four levels of evaluation* [18]. He developed his model for the evaluation of training programs in companies, but it is also applicable for the evaluation of serious games. In his model, evaluation can take place on the level of reaction, of learning, of behaviour, or of results.

The lowest level, the level of reactions, assesses whether a participant liked the training and therefore, applied to the area of serious games, measures the player's satisfaction with the game experience and evaluates the quality of the game mechanics, graphics, etc. However, a positive result in the evaluation on the reaction level does not necessarily imply that the desired outcome of the game has occurred. Therefore, the next level—the level of learning—tests to which extent participants "change attitudes, improve knowledge, and/or increase skill as a result of attending the program" [18]. Hence, evaluation on the second level assesses the short-time effectiveness of the game. Yet, having understood the pure contents of the game and being able to apply them in the context of the game does not mean that the players are able to transfer the acquired attitudes, knowledge, or skills in their normal environment. This is assessed on the level of behavior which evaluates "the degree to which learners have changed their behaviour outside of the learning environment because of their participation in the learning activities." [18]. Also for serious games, evaluation of the third level measures to which extent the players can apply the acquired skills outside of the game environment or to which extent the achieved change of attitude or condition are preserved in the long run. The last level—the level of results—measures the actual effect the participation in the training/game has in the larger context, i.e. in the institution or organization where it is deployed. For the field of serious games, evaluation on this level measures the long-term impact of the game on the whole target group. It is clear that the evaluation becomes harder to realize with increasing level, but the results become more interesting.

Kirkpatrick's model of *four levels of evaluation* is a valuable tool for planning and designing an evaluation process. In order to choose appropriate methods for the evaluation, it is necessary to know on which level the evaluation is supposed to take place. For each level, other tools and methods are appropriate. This also holds for the challenges of time-dependent effects and the reach of effects described in Sect. 3.

Serious Game Design Assessment Framework. A totally different approach to an evaluation model is presented by Mitgutsch and Alvarado with their *Serious Game Design Assessment Framework* [23]. They emphasize that evaluation of a serious game should always be with respect to a clearly articulated purpose which is also pointed out in Sects. 2 and 3.

They notice that serious games are often assessed in terms of quality of their content, and not in terms of their intention-based design. In order to allow a structured discussion about the different elements of game design and to assess their cohesiveness as well as their coherence in relation to the purpose of the game, Mitgutsch and Alvarado propose a *Serious Game Design Assessment Framework* (see Fig. 3). It identifies six essential components of serious game design among which the purpose of the game should be the driving force for the design of the remaining elements. Besides the purpose of the game, the elements of the framework are *(i)* content & information, *(ii)* game mechanics, *(iii)* fiction & narrative, *(iv)* aesthetics & graphics, and *(v)* framing, of which all should reflect the purpose of the game. How these elements are related to each other has

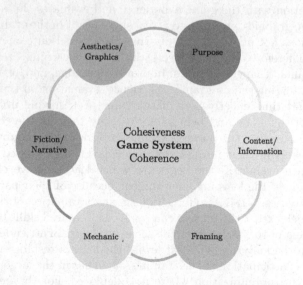

Fig. 3. Serious game design assessment framework, proposed by Mitgutsch and Alvarado [23].

an impact on the coherence and the cohesiveness of the game which is important for the game play experience since the game is perceived as one system by the player and not as single components. Their main contribution is the development of a questionnaire by which a given serious game can be analysed with respect to the identified components, their relation to each other, and their connection to the purpose of the game.

With this questionnaire at hand, a systematic and purpose-driven evaluation of a given serious game is possible. The authors deliver a well-thought decomposition of the elements of game design with a particular focus on the intended impact of the game which is essential for the design of serious games. However, this method of evaluation is not bale to measure whether the serious game is effective with regard to its designated purpose, but it might serve as a base for a discussion—as the authors also state it—and is raising attention to the fact that the intended impact should be in the focus of the design process of a serious game.

5   Examples of Commendable Serious Games Evaluation

After having introduced a general framework for serious games evaluation, this section presents practical examples of commendably evaluated serious games and discusses them in terms of the aforementioned framework. Though evaluation is a substantial part in the serious games development process, there are to date only few reported studies about full-fledged serious games that have successfully been evaluated in structured and comprehensive evaluation processes. Among these are the games *Re-Mission*, *SnowWorld* and *Frequency 1550*.

5.1   Re-Mission

One well-known example is the game *Re-Mission* by *HopeLab* for children and adolescents suffering from cancer [30]. In this third-person shooter-like game, the player controls a little nanobot inside the human body and uses different weapons related to cancer treatment, e.g. chemotherapy and radiotherapy, to destroy cancer cells and manage treatment side effects. The overall purpose of *Re-Mission* is to increase patients' well-being by inducing health-related behavioral change: The basic idea is to achieve a better treatment compliance due to an enhancement in knowledge and understanding regarding the disease and its treatment. Furthermore, the act of fighting against cancer in a digital environment was supposed to increase the patients' beliefs that they are able to influence their recovery and thus their feeling of cancer-specific self-efficacy. Hence, the purpose of the game was explicitly defined based on the problem of non-compliance and suffering of patients, and with respect to psychological determinants of behavior as well as related theories [30]. This is in accord with the preparation phase of the proposed serious games evaluation process.

Accordingly, the effectiveness of *Re-Mission* was then tested in a broadly conceived study [16] with 375 young cancer patients in the United States, Canada, and Australia, focusing on health-related behavior changes, but additionally also evaluating fun and success as a digital game in general. Researchers faced the challenge of assessing a very vulnerable target group by extending the duration and draw area of the experiment in order to obtain a reasonable sample size. The long-term formal experiment was conducted for over two years and it included two evaluation conditions: One group of patients played *Re-Mission* over a period of three months, while the control group was given a comparable but not cancer-related digital game (*Indiana Jones and the Emperor's Tomb*), which is based on similar game mechanics and perspective. While this control group condition was a good choice to prove whether the gaming experience as such has an effect on compliance, another control group would have been beneficial in order to compare the game against alternative intervention methods such as a knowledge-providing text.

The focus of outcome measurements was on medication adherence, self-efficacy, cancer-related knowledge, feelings of control and stress level. Those variables were operationalized in several ways and assessed at three time points (baseline, after one month, after three months) by various measures ranging from subjective self-reports (questionnaires and scales) to objective control mechanics regarding adherence (blood tests and electronic pill-monitoring devices) and time spent playing the game (data logging). This multidimensional measurement approach combined with the long-term character of the experiment allowed for a comprehensive data analysis leading to informed results regarding the impact and appeal of *Re-Mission*. Consequently, besides just confirming the intended positive effect on medical adherence and knowledge, researchers were also able to gain valuable insights into the processes by which the game influences players [16,30]: Contrary to prior assumptions, the observed behavioral changes are mainly associated with an increase of self-efficacy, and can hardly be explained by knowledge acquisition and experiences made in the game world. Hence, motivational and emotional components were more influential than expected and should be considered intensely in future work on serious games for behavioral change.

5.2   SnowWorld

Another interesting example of a comprehensively evaluated serious game is *SnowWorld* developed by Hunter Hoffman and Dave Patterson at the University of Washington in cooperation with *Firsthand Technology*, a company focused on serious games and virtual environments[1]. In *SnowWorld*, the player becomes immersed in a virtual reality (VR) setting of an icy canyon using a head-mounted display and earphones. By using VR technology, the distraction from everything happening in the real world is high. The users are enveloped by the cold and chilly atmosphere inside the gameworld and are able to interact with it by navigating and throwing snowballs. This effect is the fundamental serious' mechanic

---

[1] http://www.firsthand.com/services/pain.html.

of the game, as it's purpose is to distract burn victims from painful procedures like daily wound caring and physical therapy in order to reduce feelings of pain. Thus, the game addresses the problem of severe pain during treatment and uses theories of distraction and attention as well as knowledge about brain functions related to pain in order to serve the purpose of pain relief. Based on these thorough considerations beforehand, the effectiveness of *SnowWorld* could be confirmed in a wide variety of studies with different focus groups, including pediatric and adult burn patients, e.g. [8,13,28], military patients with combat-related burn injuries, e.g. [20], as well as healthy volunteers who agreed to pain stimulating procedures [14,31]. In all studies, the use of the VR system and *SnowWorld* significantly reduced pain during painful treatment (up to 41 % of subjective pain relief and 50 % or greater reductions in pain-related brain activity), thereby strongly confirming its effectiveness both regarding subjective feelings of pain and objective assessments of pain-related brain activity (see [12] for a summarizing overview). Moreover, the development and evaluation process of *SnowWorld* is especially interesting in the context of serious games evaluation, as it demonstrates the advantages of several evaluation cycles. Due to repeated phases of (re-)developing and testing instead of conducting one big experiment at the end of the development process, the design of the game has been optimized and the underlying processes that lead to pain relief have been revealed to a great extent. The general system design allowed for several variations of different game and system parameters, which was used by researchers to test the influence of single design elements such as the level of presence and interactivity [31] and the VR display quality [14] (which both turned out to be important impact factors influencing pain relief). The wide variety of studies with different focal points concerning *SnowWorld* provides great insights into the functionality of the game and underlines the value of an iterative evaluation process as suggested by our framework.

5.3   Frequency 1550

The proper evaluation of serious games for health like *Re-Mission* and *Snow-World* is especially important as they are supposed to positively influence the players' health and well-being without harming sensitive target groups, and this promise has to be proven. However, evaluation is also relevant in other application areas. One example of a serious game for learning which was evaluated in a comprehensive study is *Frequency 1550* by the *Waag Society*[2]. *Frequency 1550* is a location-based mobile educational game about the medieval city of Amsterdam designed for pupils in secondary school [15]. Its purpose is to convey knowledge about the history of places in an interactive way and to overcome a possible lack of motivation of pupils. Although the game had already won an award as the world's most innovative e-learning application due to it's design, researchers were aware of the fact that its effectiveness was still to be proven, hence they conducted a study with 458 pupils in Amsterdam [15]. Half of the participants

---

[2] http://freq1550.waag.org/.

played the game while exploring the city of Amsterdam during one school day while the other half learned the same educational content in a project-based lesson series in the classroom without the game, forming a reasonable control group. Measurement included engagement, motivation for history in general and the topic of Middle Ages in particular as well as knowledge of medieval Amsterdam. Results of the knowledge test that was conducted after the lessons demonstrate that *Frequency 1550* significantly increased learning outcomes compared to the control condition (with about 24 % more questions answered correctly), while topic-related motivation did not differ. Furthermore, the examination of possible influencing variables revealed that the prior knowledge level and level of education did moderate the effect. Hence, researchers were able to show an advantage of their game regarding learning outcomes compared to a non-gaming alternative, although long-term effects remain unclear.

In all those examples, interdisciplinary teams managed to successfully develop serious games based on grounded theory and to finally prove their efficacy in a proper evaluation process. However, many other serious games lack evidence of success due to minor or inconclusive evaluation activities or have not even been evaluated at all [6,9,11]. Moreover, in general there are still many open questions left and the empirical basis regarding the success of serious games is still far from being conclusive. In order to strengthen the trust in serious games and to help the industry grow, more studies are needed following a comprehensive evaluation approach. Therefore we introduced our framework of evaluation-driven design which offers guidance for future research activities.

6   Conclusion

This chapter gave an introduction into the evaluation of serious games focused on general evaluation procedures and models. We outlined the importance of evaluation during and after the design process and highlighted characteristic challenges that have to be met when the effectiveness of a serious game is to be tested. The framework of evaluation-driven design presented here comprises theories as well as practical experiences regarding the evaluation of serious games and is thus supposed to give guidance for all those who want to design, develop or research serious games, as evaluation is important to all these areas. The framework describes the important steps of the design and evaluation process and thereby highlights aspects that have to be considered like the definition and operationalization of the game's purpose as well as the iterative cycle between design process and evaluation.

While this chapter is supposed to introduce the evaluation process in general and to point out what has to be taken into account while planning and conducting a serious game study, certain aspects are just broached without going into detail. After gaining insight into the evaluation process, we recommend to continue with the following chapters about operationalization and experimental design to deepen the knowledge about serious games evaluation. Those chapters may answer questions that remain unanswered here and go into more detail regarding single steps of the evaluation process. Moreover, we compiled the following list of further reading on related topics, that may be worth taking a closer look.

References

1. Baranowski, T.: Measurement method bias in games for health research. Games Health J. **3**(4), 193–194 (2014)
2. Chen, S., Michael, D.: Proof of learning: assessment in serious games (2005). http://www.gamasutra.com/features/20051019/chen_01.shtml
3. Chin, J., Dukes, R., Gamson, W.: Assessment in simulation and gaming: a review of the last 40 years. Simul. Gaming **40**(4), 553–568 (2009)
4. Coleman, J.S., Livingston, S.A., Fennessey, G.M., Edwards, K.J., Kidder, S.J.: The hopkins games program: conclusions from seven years of research. Educ. Res. **2**(8), 3–7 (1973)
5. Connolly, T., Stansfield, M., Hainey, T.: Towards the development of a games-based learning evaluation framework. In: Games-Based Learning Advancements for Multi-Sensory Human Computer Interfaces: Techniques and Effective Practices. IGI Global, Hershey (2009)
6. Connolly, T.M., Boyle, E.A., MacArthur, E., Hainey, T., Boyle, J.M.: A systematic literature review of empirical evidence on computer games and serious games. Comput. Educ. **59**(2), 661–686 (2012)
7. DeSmet, A., van Ryckeghem, D., Compernolle, S., Baranowski, T., Thompson, D., Crombez, G., Poels, K., van Lippevelde, W., Bastiaensens, S., van Cleemput, K., Vandebosch, H., de Bourdeaudhuij, I.: A meta-analysis of serious digital games for healthy lifestyle promotion. Prev. Med. **69**, 95–107 (2014)
8. Faber, A.W., Patterson, D.R., Bremer, M.: Repeated use of immersive virtual reality therapy to control pain during wound dressing changes in pediatric and adult burn patients. J. Burn Care Res. **34**(5), 563–568 (2013)
9. Girard, C., Ecalle, J., Magnan, A.: Serious games as new educational tools: how effective are they? a meta-analysis of recent studies. J. Comput. Assist. Learn. **29**(3), 207–219 (2013)
10. Göbel, S., Gutjahr, M., Hardy, S.: Evaluation of serious games. In: Bredl, K., Bösche, W. (eds.) Serious Games and Virtual Worlds in Education, Professional Development, and Healthcare, pp. 105–115. IGI Global, Hershey (2013)
11. Hainey, T., Connolly, T.: Evaluating games-based learning. Int. J. Virtual Per. Learn. Environ. (IJVPLE) **1**(1), 57–71 (2010)
12. Hoffman, H.G., Chambers, G.T., Meyer, W.J., Arceneaux, L.L., Russell, W.J., Seibel, E.J., Richards, T.L., Sharar, S.R., Patterson, D.R.: Virtual reality as an adjunctive non-pharmacologic analgesic for acute burn pain during medical procedures. Ann. Behav. Med. **41**(2), 183–191 (2011)
13. Hoffman, H.G., Patterson, D.R., Seibel, E., Soltani, M., Jewett-Leahy, L., Sharar, S.R.: Virtual reality pain control during burn wound debridement in the hydrotank. Clin. J. Pain **24**(4), 299–304 (2008)
14. Hoffman, H.G., Seibel, E.J., Richards, T.L., Furness, T.A., Patterson, D.R., Sharar, S.R.: Virtual reality helmet display quality influences the magnitude of virtual reality analgesia. J. Pain **7**(11), 843–850 (2006)
15. Huizenga, J., Admiraal, W., Akkerman, S., Dam, G.T.: Mobile game-based learning in secondary education: engagement, motivation and learning in a mobile city game. J. Comput. Assist. Learn. **25**(4), 332–344 (2009)

16. Kato, P.M., Cole, S.W., Bradlyn, A.S., Pollock, B.H.: A video game improves behavioral outcomes in adolescents and young adults with cancer: a randomized trial. Pediatrics **122**(2), e305–e317 (2008)

17. Kirkley, S.E., Tomblin, S., Kirkley, J.: Instructional design authoring support for the development of serious games and mixed reality training. In: Proceedings of the Interservice/Industry Training, Simulation and Education Conference (I/ITSEC) (2005)

18. Kirkpatrick, D.L., Kirkpatrick, J.D.: Evaluating Training Programs: The Four Levels, 3rd edn. Berrett-Koehler Publishers, San Francisco (2006)

19. Loh, C.S., Sheng, Y., Ifenthaler, D.: Serious games analytics: theoretical framework. In: Loh, C.S., Sheng, Y., Ifenthaler, D. (eds.) Serious Games Analytics: Methodologies for Performance Measurement, Assessment, and Improvement. Advances in Game-Based Learning, pp. 3–29. Springer International Publishing, Cham (2015)

20. Maani, C.V., Hoffman, H.G., Morrow, M., Maiers, A., Gaylord, K., McGhee, L.L., DeSocio, P.A.: Virtual reality pain control during burn wound debridement of combat-related burn injuries using robot-like arm mounted VR goggles. J. Trauma: Injury, Infection Crit. Care **71**(supplement), 125–130 (2011)

21. Mayer, I.: Towards a comprehensive methodology for the research and evaluation of serious games. Procedia Comput. Sci. **15**, 233–247 (2012)

22. Michael, D.R., Chen, S.: Serious Games: Games That Educate, Train and Inform. Course Technology PTR, Boston (2005)

23. Mitgutsch, K., Alvarado, N.: Purposeful by design?: a serious game design assessment framework. In: Proceedings of the International Conference on the Foundations of Digital Games, FDG 2012, New York, NY, USA, pp. 121–128. ACM (2012)

24. Molenda, M.: In search of the elusive ADDIE model. Perform. Improv. **42**(5), 34–36 (2003)

25. O'Neil, H.F., Wainess, R., Baker, E.L.: Classification of learning outcomes: evidence from the computer games literature. Curriculum J. **16**(4), 455–474 (2005)

26. Papastergiou, M.: Exploring the potential of computer and video games for health and physical education: a literature review. Comput. Educ. **53**(3), 603–622 (2009)

27. Sanchez, A., Cannon-Bowers, J.A., Bowers, C.: Establishing a science of game based learning. In: Sanchez, A., Cannon-Bowers, J.A., Bowers, C. (eds.) Serious Game Design and Development: Technologies for Training and Learning, pp. 290–304. IGI Global, Hershey (2010)

28. Schmitt, Y.S., Hoffman, H.G., Blough, D.K., Patterson, D.R., Jensen, M.P., Soltani, M., Carrougher, G.J., Nakamura, D., Sharar, S.R.: A randomized, controlled trial of immersive virtual reality analgesia, during physical therapy for pediatric burn injuries. Burns: J. Int. Soc. Burn Injuries **37**(1), 61–68 (2011)

29. Shapiro, M.A., Peña, J.: Generalizability and validity in digital game research. In: Ritterfeld, U., Cody, M.J., Vorderer, P. (eds.) Serious Games: Mechanisms and Effects, pp. 389–403. Routledge, New York (2009)

30. Tate, R., Haritatos, J., Cole, S.: HopeLab's approach to re-mission. Int. J. Learn. Media **1**(1), 29–35 (2009)

31. Wender, R., Hoffman, H.G., Hunner, H.H., Seibel, E.J., Patterson, D.R., Sharar, S.R.: Interactivity influences the magnitude of virtual reality analgesia. J. Cyber Ther. Rehabil. **2**(1), 27–33 (2009)

Further Reading

32. Abt, C.C.: Serious Games. University Press of America, Lanham (1987)
33. Ainsworth, S.: Evaluation methods for learning environments. In: A Tutorial for the 11th International Conference on Artificial Intelligence Education, Amsterdam. www.psychology.nottingham.ac.uk/staff/Shaaron.Ainsworth/Evaluationtutorial. ppt
34. All, A., Castellar, E.P.N., Van Looy, J.: Towards a conceptual framework for assessing the effectiveness of digital game-based learning. Comput. Educ. **88**, 29–37 (2015)
35. Bellotti, F., Kapralos, B., Lee, K., Moreno-Ger, P., Berta, R.: Assessment in and of serious games: an overview. Adv. Hum. Comput. Interact. **2013** (2013). Article no. 1
36. Bernhaupt, R. (ed.): Evaluating User Experience in Games: Concepts and Methods. Human-Computer Interaction Series. Springer, London and New York (2010)
37. Bredl, K., Bösche, W. (eds.): Serious Games and Virtual Worlds in Education. Professional Development, and Healthcare. Premier reference source, Information Science Reference, Hershey (2013)
38. Dondi, C., Moretti, M.: A methodological proposal for learning games selection and quality assessment. Br. J. Educ. Technol. **38**(3), 502–512 (2007). http://dx.doi.org/10.1111/j.1467-8535.2007.00713.x
39. El-Nasr, M.S., Drachen, A., Canossa, A. (eds.): Game Analytics: Maximizing the Value of Player Data. Springer, London and New York (2013)
40. Göbel, S., Gutjahr, M., Steinmetz, R.: What makes a good serious game - conceptual approach towards a metadata format for the description and evaluation of serious games. In: Gouscous, D., Meimaris, M. (eds.) 5th European Conference on Games Based Learning, pp. 202–210. Academic Conferences Limited, Reading (2011)
41. Law, E.L.-C., Kickmeier-Rust, M.D., Albert, D., Holzinger, A.: Challenges in the development and evaluation of immersive digital educational games. In: Holzinger, A. (ed.) USAB 2008. LNCS, pp. 19–30. Springer, Heidelberg (2008). doi:10.1007/978-3-540-89350-9_2
42. Loh, C.S., Sheng, Y., Ifenthaler, D.: Serious Games Analytics: Methodologiesfor Performance Measurement, Assessment, and Improvement. Advances in Game-Based Learning. Springer International Publishing, Cham (2015)
43. Mayer, I., Bekebrede, G., Harteveld, C., Warmelink, H., Zhou, Q., Ruijven, T., Lo, J., Kortmann, R., Wenzler, I.: The research and evaluation of serious games: toward a comprehensive methodology. Br. J. Educ. Technol. **45**(3), 502–527 (2014)
44. Schultz, C.P., Bryant, R.: Game Testing All in One, 2nd edn. Mercury Learning & Information, Dulles (2011)
45. Serrano, Á., Marchiori, E.J., Blanco, Á.D., Torrente, J., Fernández-Manjón, B.: A framework to improve evaluation in educational games. In: Global Engineering Education Conference (EDUCON), pp. 1–8. IEEE (2012)

The Experimental Method as an Evaluation Tool in Serious Games Research and Development

Nataliya V. Bogacheva[✉]

Pedagogics and Medical Psychology Department, Faculty of Higher Nursing Training,
Psychology and Social Work, Sechenov First Moscow State Medical University,
8-2 Trubetskaya street, Moscow 119991, Russia
bogacheva.nataly@gmail.com

Abstract. This chapter aims to provide the reader with basic knowledge about the experiment as a general method that can be applied towards serious games research and evaluation. It explains the main terms and rules of the experimental design, as well as points out the main risks and difficulties to avoid. The chapter also explains the differences in possible conclusions between true experiments, quasi-experiments, and correlational studies.

Keywords: Experiment · Experimental design · Variables · Validity · Biases · Samples · Quasi-experiment · Correlational study

1 Introduction

Serious games are commonly defined as games, "designed for a primary purpose other than pure entertainment" [5]. In this chapter, we are not going to discuss whether this definition is good or not, but it definitely brings up an evaluation problem, specific for all serious games. If the game has some "serious" purpose, then in must not only be entertaining as any other game, but also effective in some definite area. With different types of serious games, developed for various purposes, such as post-traumatic and post-stroke physical rehabilitation [36, 39], therapy of phobias [8, 54], autism treatment [56], cognitive training [4, 52], cognitive disability treatment [48], pain and stress management [6, 13, 55], training programs for surgeons, odonatologists, nurses and other specialists [45], pedagogical and educational reasons [16, 17, 23], business training [7], sports [46], military purposes [17, 32], global project planning [38], racing car design [2] and even research of protein sequences in biology [25] possible outcomes indicate the games effectiveness in different ways. In all these games, one can measure different parameters and there are different criteria of effectiveness, so there is no common receipt for serious game evaluation. In general, while developing or researching a serious game, we eventually face such questions, as "Does this serious game really work? Does the game fulfil its purpose?" There are even more questions that are important: "Does this serious game work as it was supposed to? Is this serious game more effective than some other instrument for the same purpose? Which one of two (or more) serious games, designed for the same purpose works better?" and so on. The final question might be as global as "Why do we actually are making this game?"

© Springer International Publishing AG 2016
R. Dörner et al. (Eds.): Entertainment Computing and Serious Games, LNCS 9970, pp. 284–305, 2016.
DOI: 10.1007/978-3-319-46152-6_12

With entertaining games (games, designed for entertaining purposes in the first place), we can say the game is "effective" if many people buy it, play it and give positive reviews on it. Predicting game success in advance can be difficult, but at least the parameters of the success are rather obvious [33, 34]. With serious games, the effect is sometimes neither obvious nor rapid – and many people are prone to under- or over-estimating this rather new and sometimes even exotic educational, training, awareness raising and treatment tool [37, 53]. Here comes one more reason for evaluation in serious games development: it is the way to acquire strong evidence about the effectiveness of the game. First, it can tell the game developers whether they are doing right and second, it helps to convince doctors, psychologists, teachers, parents and other reference groups that this particular serious game and serious games in general are useful (and worth paying for).

When we say that the use of a serious game leads to an improvement (cognitive learning, motor skills development, awareness raising, collaboration, pain reduction, etc.) we suppose that the relationship between the game and its effect is causal (also called "cause and effect"). When we want to check causality between some factors, the most relevant method is *an experiment*.

1.1 What Is an Experiment?

While most people have some basic ideas about what an "experimental method" is, the definitions of this term may vary greatly. Merriam-Webster online dictionary explains the experiment as "an operation or procedure carried out under controlled conditions in order to discover an unknown effect or law, to test or establish a hypothesis, or to illustrate a known law" [20]. This definition is broad and does not give us much information about the method, except the idea that the conditions of our experimental study must be controlled. This is how the experiment differs from another important research method - the observation. The observation, on the contrary, generally implies that there is no interference with the observable reality.

Another common definition [14] gives us a more concrete idea of what an experiment is: "an orderly procedure carried out with the goal of verifying, refuting, or establishing the validity of a hypothesis." This suggests that (1) we should have a hypothesis that requires some verification before setting up an experiment; (2) this is the procedure that follows some predesigned order; (3) the definition brings up an important concept – the *validity*. It will be discussed in paragraph 4 of this chapter. The experiment is used when we need to find or prove that there is a causal connection between something – and it is the only scientifically approved method, that can test causality. The simplest example of a causal connection in the field of serious games design is the suggestion that playing a certain serious game really leads to an increase in some skill or knowledge. In the social sciences and psychology, causal connections between factors are known to be the most difficult to set up and the experiment is the only method that provides the researcher with required arguments for this [1]. To specify the possibility of causal interpretations, three rules of the causal conclusion can be introduced: (1) variable X changes before variable Y; (2) the linkage between the variables is consequential; (3) there is no other possible explanation for the causal relationship between X and Y [30].

The third definition to discuss states that an experiment is "a systematic research study in which the investigator directly varies some factor (or factors), holds all other factors constant and observes the results of the variation" [24]. This definition includes the idea of the "controlled conditions" from the first definition and uses the terms "factor" and "variation". Those concepts lead us towards another important term that requires further discussion – the *variable* (see Sect. 3 of this chapter).

While the first two definitions relate to experiments in general, the third definition describes the so-called "controlled" or "laboratory" experiment – the experimental design with the most controlled conditions, where the researcher tries to manipulate or control as many factors as possible. Another type of the experiment that usually occurs in practice is a "field experiment". In this type of the experiment, the researcher manipulates some parts of the reality outside the laboratory, for example, when the educational serious game is being researched while already introduced into the educational process. The researcher still controls as many factors as possible, without disturbing the educational process. However, the situation is by far not as controllable as in a laboratory experiment, thus field experiments need a lot of caution to avoid confounds.

2   Experiment as a Scientific Method

2.1   The Rules of the Scientific Thinking

All the experiments in every scientific field more or less share the same rules of scientific thinking. First, all the scientists and sciences assume that events around us have a causal effect. Scientific methods help to discover these causes. These two rules of thinking are known as *determinism* and *discoverability*. Without these two assumptions, no science would be possible. Second, all the sciences are based on so-called *paradigms*. The term "paradigm" was intensively developed in the works of T. Kuhn. According to him, a paradigm in science is a set of "universally recognized scientific achievements that for a time provide model problems and solutions to a community of practitioners" [31]. The paradigm includes the ways scientists are required to build up their theories and to use empirical methods to prove those theories true. Although another famous philosopher of science, K. Popper argues with Kuhn's idea that a "normal" scientist is usually bound to use the paradigm in his works [41], it is impossible to build scientific knowledge without following some shared rules.

While paradigms in particular sciences seem to shift in a rather fast pace (a serious games related example: S. de Freitas and F. Liarokapis suggest that the extensive use of serious games for learning can lead to a paradigm shift in education [15]), the basic rules of scientific thinking in general stay rather constant.

C.J. Goodwin [24] summarizes them into five statements: (**1**) scientific knowledge must be *objective* (free from the scientists expectations and other biases); (**2**) scientific knowledge must be *data-driven*; (**3**) scientific conclusions are *never absolute*, but tentative; (**4**) sciences ask empirical questions, which means that these questions can be answered through *empirical research* and (**5**) scientific theories *can be disproven*. The last point represents K. Popper's concept of falsifiability of theories – a theory can be considered a scientific one only if it is at least hypothetically possible to falsify that theory [42]. In this case, "falsification" does not refer to any kind of fraud. Instead, it means that a theory is open for possible disproof. What is more, methodological implications from the famous K. Gödel's incompleteness theorems state that in every formal system (and every science is a formal system) there are statements that cannot be proven within this system [12], so scientific knowledge is always incomplete and open for further development.

As it was mentioned above, scientific theories use empirical data as a resource for development, growth, and possible falsification. The relationship between theoretical and empirical knowledge is built by deductive and inductive thinking. Through induction, we reason numerous events (e.g. the results of the experiments) into general theories, while through deduction we state some theoretically based hypotheses about the events (results) that would possibly occur. At this point, we face real difficulties, as the theories and the reality do not use identical elements.

2.2 Theoretical and Experimental Hypotheses

For example, one wants to develop a serious game for a medical purpose such as distracting a child patient from pain and discomfort at the dentist's (Dutch scientists developed a game with this underlying idea [6]). Discussing the possibilities to develop the game, the authors suggest that the key point to relaxation (a required state of patient) is immersion. However, immersion (as well as relaxation itself) is not something from the objective reality. It is a hypothetical construct, which belongs to the theoretical level of science. You can measure someone's heart rate to see if the person is relaxed or not. You can run an IQ test to find out something about the intelligence of the student or use an academic test to measure his or her knowledge in a certain area, but this is all possible only because we have some theory about what relaxation, intelligence and knowledge are. Psychological laws, concepts, and terms belong to the theoretical level of thinking. Heart rate, true or false answers, and behavior patterns happen in the reality. The link between those two worlds sometimes seems obvious, and we jump from one level to another without much thinking.

However, it is more difficult, when we plan an experiment. First, we need to develop a hypothesis, based on our theory (a simple definition for a theory is "an existing knowledge that scientists use to explain and predict events" [24]). When we suggest that the use of a serious game leads to an improvement (cognitive learning, motor skill development, awareness raising, collaboration, pain reduction, etc.) we suppose that the relationship between the game and its effect is causal. As mentioned above, when we need to check causality between some factors, the most relevant method is an experiment.

A link between the theory and the research is the hypothesis, "a reasoned prediction about some empirical result that should occur under certain circumstances" [24]. Another definition for a hypothesis, retrieved from the online dictionary is: "a tentative assumption made in order to draw out and test its logical or empirical consequences" [26]. With both these definitions, we can see that a hypothesis is a statement and not a question. An empirical question usually precedes the hypothesis, but we need a theoretical background to make a hypothesis. And we need the hypothesis to conduct an experiment. Hypotheses, however, can differ. If we suggest that a particular serious game raises human awareness of ecological problems, we have a causal hypothesis, a hypothesis that predicts a cause and effect relationship. This hypothesis is a theoretical one and uses theoretical terms, like "awareness". To conduct an empirical study, we will need to transform this hypothesis into an experimental one, where we establish the empirical evidence for ecological awareness.

On the other hand, a hypothesis can be formulated like "people, who play our serious game have higher awareness about ecological problems" – a theoretical hypothesis as well, which is not causal, but correlational, a hypothesis about a connection. The linkage, however, says nothing about cause and effect relationship. Such hypotheses are proved through so-called correlational studies. For example, we found out that higher use of the serious game coexists with higher knowledge of ecological problems. Then there will be at least two possible explanation. The first one is that our serious game develops ecology-oriented thinking (something that we really want to prove as the game developers) and the second one is that people, who already are anxious about ecology, are more likely to play our ecology-oriented game. Maybe, they think they can learn from it. One of the explanations, or both of them, or none of them can be true, but we are unable to prove it empirically before we conduct an experiment. Well, actually, we can provide strong theoretical reasons to promote the explanation that we think is more liable (and/or desirable) but there will always be a possibility for counter arguments.

Nevertheless, even if we have a causal hypothesis, there is still a lot of work to be done before we can conduct an experiment. As the world of theories and the world of objective reality merge in the experimental study, we need to "translate" our hypothesis into the terms of measurable parameters. This process is called *operationalization* and the parameters that substitute theoretical constructs are *variables*.

3 Variables

3.1 Dependent and Independent Variables

A *variable* is an operationalized parameter or attribute of an object. Wikipedia describes the process of operationalization as "a process of defining the measurement of a phenomenon that is not directly measurable, though its existence is indicated by other phenomena" [40]. We can suggest that a serious game increases the users' knowledge in some field, but to prove this in an experiment we initially need to operationalize this knowledge or, in other words, find some measurable attribute, that represents the knowledge. For example, we can measure someone's knowledge with an academic test. We can operationalize this knowledge in terms of behavior – for example, we suggest that ecology-oriented person will not ignore a kicked down trash can. Therefore, we can organize this condition and see what is happening… In this example, we showed that the same concept from the hypothesis can be operationalized in different ways. Almost the same theoretical hypotheses can be possible proven by very different (in the terms of variables) experiments.

As the name states, variables do vary, or, in other words, have levels. For example, with the academic test, we do not usually use the exact test scores. More often, we subdivide the group into subgroups, like "those who successfully passed the test" or "those who did not pass the test" (two levels of the variable "academic knowledge"); "those who scored low", "those who scored medium", "those who scored high" (three levels of the variable) and so on. Playing a serious game can be operationalized with variable levels: "played the game" and "did not play the game" (two levels) or "played a short amount of time", "played a lot of time", and "did not play the game" (three levels). This seems obvious, but we must be extremely accurate with variables levels operationalization. We cannot voluntary assign users, who play 10 h a week to "played a lot of time" group without theoretical or statistical explanation, why this is "a lot of time" and not "a moderate amount of time". The operationalization is also needed to transfer the collected data (scores and measures) into the variable's levels.

In every experimental study, we meet at least two types of variables: *dependent* and *independent*. In a correlational study, instead, the variables are equal to each other, so there are no dependent or independent variables.

Independent variable is the variable that we can control directly. J.S. Goodwin describes the independent variable as "the factor of interest to the experimenter, the one that is being studied to see if it will influence behavior" [24]. This definition, however, includes so-called *subject variables*. A subject variable is a variable that differentiates subjects from one another, but it exists prior to our research. Gender, age, intelligence, sometimes – educational level are all subject variables. The research, where we cannot influence independent variables directly and use subject variables instead is a quasi-experiment. This research scheme will be discussed at the end of this chapter.

The independent variable must have two or more levels. The two-level variable is called bivalent and a variable with more than two levels – a multivalent [30]. In general, we need to pick as many experimental groups (of participants), as there are levels of the independent variable. If we have more than one variable, we need enough groups to test each level of each variable separately. For example, with two bivalent independent variables we need at least four groups to cover all possible combinations of variables' levels, etc. This type of experimental design is called between-group design. In serious games research, we sometimes prefer to expose the same group of participants to different levels of the independent variable. This design is called within-subjects experimental design. Both types of the experiments are further discussed in Sect. 6 of this chapter.

According to J.S. Goodwin [24], there are three main types of independent variables in psychology and social science experiments: (1) *Situational variables* – the different environmental features, that the participants encounter; (2) *Task variables*, which occur when participants are asked to complete different tasks and (3) *Instructional variables*, where the participants are asked to perform the same task in different ways or under different circumstances like different payment for solving tasks. We can meet all these types of independent variables in serious games research. For example, in the Dutch research of game-based cognitive control training for elders [52], the independent variable had two levels: one group of the participants used video games for their training, while people from the other group were watching documental films and were completing quizzes. This is the example of the task independent variable.

If one of the independent variable's level is a zero level (the participants in one of the experimental groups receive no treatment, do not play the serious game, etc.), the group, receiving this zero level independent variable is called the *control group*, opposed to other, *experimental groups*. Depending on the hypothesis you want to check and the empirical question you want to answer, the control group may appear or may not appear in your experimental design. For example, if you want to compare two different serious games, developed for the same purpose – then you have two experimental groups. However, if you want to compare future surgeons who played the training serious game with their fellow students, who did not – there are an experimental group and a control group.

The variables that are influenced by the levels of our independent variables are called *dependent variables*. J.S. Goodwin [24] describes these variables as "those behaviors that are the measured outcomes of experiments". We do not manipulate the dependent variables directly, but we can measure them if they are properly operationalized. The experimental hypothesis usually includes our assumption about the behavior of the dependent variable. For example, we assume that our participants' test performance in history would raise after they played our educational serious game. The test score is the dependent variable. The hypothesis, though, can be either confirmed or denied.

It is possible to measure several dependent variables in the same experiment. One independent variable may influence more than one dependent variable. However, such experiments require more complex statistical analysis [22] on further stages of the research, as simple statistical procedures, commonly used in experimental research, ignore interactions between the variables [27].

3.2   Other Types of Variables in the Experimental Research

While we only need independent and dependent variables to imagine an experiment, in the real experiment, we can never separate them from many other factors. When we deal with people of certain age, background, personalities, experience we can never ignore the fact that there are many variables, influencing their behavior and responses. The variables, which can influence the results of the experiment and therefore must be controlled are known as *extraneous variables*. Extraneous variables, that have not been properly controlled and appear alongside the independent variable's levels are called *confounding variables*. These variables give us an alternative explanation for the relationship between the independent and the dependent variable and therefore limit our possibility to verify the causal relationship. In digital game research, the participant's gender is generally a confounding variable, as in general population men are more likely to play video games in their everyday lives, comparing to the women, and there are age differences between male and female gamers as well [18]. This means, that if we experiment with a serious game, designed for young adults, we are more likely to have male participants with more video games experience, comparing to the female participants of the same age. The gaming experience, as well as gender specified differences in spatial thinking, working memory, etc. can influence the results of serious game training as well if we do not control those parameters [28].

The most obvious way to control extraneous variables is to hold them fixed. Such variables are called *control variables* or constants [35]. It might seem that we need to control as many variables as possible, but with too many constants, our experimental condition becomes extremely artificial. We can get a clear causal relationship between the variables in the laboratory with many constants, but that condition would be artificial and impossible in the real world where no one holds control variables fixed. With the serious games research, that point is crucial, as we develop them mostly for practical reasons. Therefore, control variables are very important, you should not try to maximize the number of them if you do not want to get the result only applicable in a laboratory.

Such variables as age, educational level of the participants, their psychological characteristics, IQ level, gender and many others can deeply influence the experimental results, but if we use them as control variables, we can end up with the results, adequate only for, e.g. highly intelligent male participants age from 25 to 30. This condition is certainly not generalized.

Another way to deal with such variables is *randomization*. In this case, participants with different levels of uncontrolled variables are randomly assigned to different groups. With large enough groups, the possible side effects of different variables would compensate each other with no significant impact on the main experimental effect. If the groups are rather small, however, it is statistically possible that one group will differ greatly from another – for example, the participants from one group might be older or there might be significantly more female or male participants in one of them. In this case, the randomization is still possible, but with some constraints to make the groups equal. For example, the male and female participants are assigned to groups at random but we keep the number of them equal in each group. In our example from van Muijden and al. study [52] the groups are randomized, but equal by age, level of education, IQ, and psychological state. These variables are rather general random variables for most of the studies in psychological and social research, but you might want to consult a specialist in the particular area you develop your serious game for to find what is important for your research.

Alongside with variables, that appear due to participants differences, there are also variables inside the experimental design, which provide some additional circumstances. When the researcher does not recognize such variables or does not properly control other variables, the experimental results are influenced by *biases*.

3.3 Biases

In general, we say that someone's viewpoint is biased when a person views things from a partial perspective and refuses to consider alternative points of view. In a scientific research framework we speak about biases when the research or the researcher's conclusions are incorrect due to some inner mistakes, intentional or not. There are different biases that may occur during the experimental evaluation process, but most of them can be subdivided into several groups:

- *Sampling biases* - occur when our sample does not match the referencing population. General population and samples are discussed further in the chapter, but in short, the sample we use must adequately represent the population or target group we are referring to. If we design a serious game for schoolchildren, we should not base our evaluation on adults and vice versa.

- **Selection biases** - occur when for some intentional or unintentional reasons the control and the experimental groups in a between-group experimental design are different. Accurate randomization and variables control could help with these biases.
- **Response biases** - self-selection of the respondents according to some implicit variables. Some people are more willing to take part in the research, while the others are not. These participants might not represent the general population.
- **Performance biases** – occur when participants from one group behave differently due to some reasons. Sometimes performance biases occur due to inequality in the experimenter behavior (for example, more attention towards the experimental group). In a critical article about entertaining video games related cognitive training T. Shubert and T. Strobach [47] suggest that commitment to training and motivational state might affect the results of the experimental study and artificially enhance the experimental effect. Another example of the performance bias is the placebo effect. The participants from the experimental group under certain condition believe that might perform better and they really do, but not because of our treatment or playing the game. Such performance biases can be avoided with a blind experiment – a scheme, where the participants do not know, which group they belong to. In the double-blind experiment neither participants nor the experimenter knows where the participants do belong to. Thus, these schemes require more efforts and resources to conduct.

4   Validity and Reliability

Avoiding biases is an important problem of the experimental research. There are two other concepts that a researcher must keep in mind when conducting any type of the empirical research: *validity* and *reliability*.

The word *"valid"* is defined as a synonym to "justifiable" and "logically correct" [50], while *"reliability"* means "the extent to which an experiment, test, or measuring procedure yields the same results on repeated trials" [44], a synonym for *repeatability*. So, an experiment is considered reliable, if anyone can repeat it, using the same variables and matching population. As for the validity, J.C. Goodwin [24] suggests four types of validity in an experimental design.

1. **Statistical validity** – is determined by accurate and adequate use of statistical methods. The threats to this type of validity are wrong analysis tactics and deliberate analysis, where the researcher describes only the results that match his or her experimental hypothesis.
2. **Construct validity** – is determined by the accurate and adequate operationalization of independent and dependent variables. In psychology and social sciences, the use of some constructs inevitably threatens construct validity of the research. For example, one of the most controversial topics in modern cyberpsychology is the relationship between violent digital games and aggression. The research group under the leadership of C. Anderson [10] sees the violent video games as the proved source of aggressive behavior and thoughts in children and adults, while other researchers, including C. Ferguson [21] point out that Anderson's methods of aggression

measurement lack the construct validity and this is a shortcoming to the whole experimental research's conclusion. However, sometimes it is equally difficult to prove both the construct validity and the lack of the construct validity of the research, mostly due to ethical reasons. It is very difficult to maintain ethics in true experiments dealing with aggression, violence, discrimination, etc. The researchers need either to perform correlational studies instead or find some non-obvious and ethical ways to operationalize those important parameters. For example, in C. Anderson and K. Dill research [3] aggression was operationalized through "noise blast", a noxious blast of white noise with changeable intensity and duration. Participants, who used longer and more intense noise blast, than the others, were supposed to be more aggressive and violent. Though the linkage between the noise punishment and real aggression is arguable, the experiment itself shows a creative way to operationalize a difficult concept.

3. *External validity* – is the degree to which research findings can be applied out of the experimental sample. Most of the time for obvious reasons we deal with samples that do not resemble the general population. The most acquirable and willing participants for many researchers are students, but the question is whether we can distribute their results to people of different age or background. Aside from their age, students are likely to have higher mean intelligence than the rest of their contemporaries and on certain faculties, they might have specifics abilities and psychological characteristics as well [30]. This means that there are numerous risks for external validity when we use students' samples. Response biases also threaten this type of the validity alongside with mistreatment of such confounding variables as gender.

4. *Ecological validity* belongs to external validity but relates not to the samples, but to the experimental environments. Many laboratory experiments while being perfectly reliable often lack this type of validity. J.C. Goodwin also points out that historical context influence the external validity of classical experimental research as well, as they might not be valid in modern society [24]. D. King, P. Delfabbro and M. Griffiths point out that playing digital games at home or in the laboratory is a very different experience for the player [29]. Besides the environment, laboratory experiments are usually time-bound while some of digital games effects require a lot of time to develop, so we might fail to prove our serious game works due to lack of time or participants being nervous. On the other hand, a serious game that worked in a laboratory with few distractions might not work in a crowded classroom with old and slow computers or with smartphones instead of 10" tablets.

5. *Internal validity* – apparently the most important type of the validity. It qualifies the complete experimental research as being valid. An experiment is internally valid if its methodology is adequate and confounding variables properly controlled.

Different types of validity apply to different types of experiments. Internal validity should be evaluated in every experimental research, regardless of its type. The same could be applied to the statistical validity, as the use of statistical analysis is common for the experimental research. External validity is important for the experiments with broad and practical conclusions, while construct validity is crucial for experiments with a highly theoretical background [30].

5   The Verification of a Statistical Hypothesis

5.1   H1 and H0 Hypotheses

Earlier in this chapter, we discussed that the connection between the independent and dependent variables forms our experimental hypothesis. In the research design, the experimental hypothesis stands between the theoretical hypothesis level and the statistical hypotheses level. We have already discussed the nature of theoretical hypotheses. As for statistical hypotheses level, we require it when we use inferential statistical methods (we use inferential statistics when we want to make interferences about the population while working with our samples; to describe the characteristics of our sample we use descriptive statistics) to prove that the differences between some groups of variables are statistically significant. In the experimental setting, we usually need to prove that there is a difference between dependent variables levels in an experimental and control conditions. In the other words, we need to prove that our independent variable really affects the dependent one though the methods of inferential statistics. Most of these tests are based on null hypothesis significance testing. The null hypothesis (often referred as H0 for short) states that the levels of the independent variable have no effect on the dependent variable level [34]. In our example with the ecologically oriented serious game, the H0 hypothesis says that people who played the game and those who did not will have just the same levels of ecological consciousness. Even if the results are slightly different in numbers, it does not mean anything, as they are insignificant. The opposite of the null hypothesis is the alternative hypothesis, also known as the H1. The H1 hypothesis suggests that there are significant differences between the levels of dependent variable, affected and unaffected by the manipulations with the dependent variable. If we reject H0 hypothesis and accept the H1 hypothesis, we state that there is *a significant experimental effect*.

However, any conclusions on the statistical hypotheses are only made with a certain confidence degree – thus, there is always a probability for a mistake. In fact, there are two different types of the mistakes, occurring while operating the statistical hypotheses.

If we falsely reject the H0 hypothesis, when it was true, we face the Type I error. If we falsely reject the H1 hypothesis, we face the Type II error. In psychology, we usually set the confidence interval for Type I error as 0.05. This means, that the chance to reject the H0 hypothesis falsely is 5 %. With confidence interval equal to 0.01, this chance is reduced to 1 %. This level usually depends on the sample size (with relatively small samples 0.05 confidence interval is more common, while with large samples 0.01 interval is more accurate).

5.2   Basic Inferential Statistical Methods

Talking about inferential statistics in general, we cannot avoid discussing some of its methods. There are not so many serious games studies, involving multivariate analysis, structural modeling, and other advanced statistics methods, so we relegate this part to further reading [22]. On the other hand, such methods as ANOVA or

Student's T-test appear in many studies, including experimental research (for formulas see [35] or any other textbook in statistics).

There are two types of data that can be gathered through the research: quantitative (deals with numbers, measures something) and qualitative (describes something, but does not measure it). In the experimental research, we usually deal with quantitative data, but some qualitative data can be obtained as well. Gender, nationality, preferences are qualitative characteristics of people, while their reaction time, IQ score or heart rate are quantitative. At the same time, there are different types of data inside those groups. Thus, qualitative data can be measured by a nominal scale or by an ordinal scale. Quantitative scales are either interval or ratio (with the statistics being mostly the same).

Gender is an example of a nominal scale. The only thing that you can do is to count the number of people with each gender. The same rule applies to nationality, skin or hair color, etc. "gamer" and "non-gamer" also belong to nominal scale, while the amount of time spent in games is not. The only inferential statistics procedures, applicable for nominal data is Chi-square. If you know, that among gamers there are 59 % males and 41 % females [18] and you have a sample of 40 gamers, 13 males, and 27 females among them, you can use Chi-square to evaluate, whether you sample reflects the general gamers population or not (the answers will be "no" with confidence interval around 0.004).

If you ask your participants to rate your serious game with such parameters as entertainment, difficulty or immersion and ask them to use a five-item Likert-like scale (e.g., 1 stands for a completely boring game while 5 stands for a very interesting game), you gather ordinal data. You can never measure the amount of interest between 4 and 5 points on this scale, and you cannot say for sure that a person, who rated the game with 5 received more positive emotions than a person, who rated it with 4. Thus if you want to compare two games or two groups, you can do it, using *Mann-Whitney U test,* and if you want to see, how the scores changed, for example on the first and the last level of difficulty, you can use *Wilcoxon matched-pairs signed-ranks test*. Note, that those two tests show the difference between groups or conditions, either separate like two different groups (Mann-Whitney) or related like the same group on different stages of the game (Wilcoxon). If you want to see how subjective entertainment is linked to subjective immersion, use non-parametric correlation test (*Spearman rank-order correlation coefficient* seems to be the most common). If you have three or more levels of the variable to compare, there *is Kruskal-Wallis test*. Note that it only tells you that there is a significant difference somewhere between the groups, but it does not mean that all of them differ significantly from one another.

In the experiment, we are more likely to use parametric statistics. Those methods can be applied towards interval or ratio scales only. Temperature is an example of interval scale data (every single °C is equal, so you can say that +10°C is 5°C warmer, then +5°C, but it does not mean that it feels twice as warm) [35]. Time is an example of ratio scale data, as 20 s are twice as long as 10 s, etc. With such scales, you can use *Student's T-test for dependent or independent samples* for two-level variables and one-way *ANOVA* for multivalent variables. Note that you will still need Bonferroni's or Scheffe's method to compare separate groups, after ANOVA showed that there are significant differences. For correlational research, *Pearson's correlation coefficient* is the most common. Note also, that you are not supposed to use parametric statistics if your data is not normally distributed (does not have that well-known "bell" shape and/or specific mean and standard deviation parameters; it can be checked with Kolmogorov-Smirnov test). Additional correction is also needed if the measurement has different dispersion in the groups you compare. This might happen with relatively small or ungeneralized samples, but you still can use non-parametric statistics.

6 The Participants in an Experiment

6.1 Sampling and Sample Sizes

As it was described earlier in this chapter, the recruitment of the participants is an extremely important part of the experimental research. Adequate sampling influences the external validity of the research and helps to avoid many types of biases.

In a perfect experiment, we would be able to access and test an unlimited number of participants. Of course, this is impossible. In the real world, we can only access samples, more or less representative. A representative sample is a sample that is formed out of the general population and copies its general internal structure.

J.C. Goodwin [24] points out that the psychologists often use a so-called *convenience sample.* A convenience sample can be recruited by different ways – for some studies they can be students, while for other research you might need to place ads in the newspapers or use a so-called "snowball" sampling. Although convenience samples are very common in the experimental studies, these samples often lack the external validity and are prone to sampling and response biases.

Simple random sampling – participants are drawn from some general population at random, usually with the help of random numbers generator. While this type of sampling is sometimes used for survey studies, especially in sociology, there is also a statistical chance for biases.

Stratified sampling – unlike the random sample, stratified sample represents the adequate proportions of important subgroups in the population. It is important to plan this type of sampling relying on those factors that can influence the results of the research.

Cluster sampling – is used when it is impossible to acquire a complete list of individuals to run a random or stratified sampling. With a cluster sampling, a few of relatively identical groups are selected, like school classes or students. Cluster sampling can be combined with stratified sampling for better results.

It is worth to remember, that experimental research design requires a number of identical groups, determined by the number and levels of independent variables. Therefore, not only we need to create a more or less representative sample, but to divide it into equal groups as well. With a big enough sample a random assignment will do, with a procedure of block randomization used to ensure that every group gets an equal number of participants (in each block a participant is assigned to each condition). However, if there are only a few participants, randomization possibly leads to biases. In this situation, matching is a preferred alternative for randomization. Matching means that the experimenters choose matching variables and pick up pairs/triplets/etc. of participants with the nearest scores in these variables. One participant from each pair will belong to one group, while the second one – to the other one.

As for the general amount of the participants, there is always "the more the better rule", as the bigger sample usually tends to be more representative and we are more likely to get statistically significant results.

To give a more precise answer to the question "How many participants do we need?" we need to introduce the concept of experimental effect. The experimental effect in the population, the preferred statistical method, confidence interval and the sample size form the power of the research. In a good research, we try to achieve the power of at least 0.80 with a confidence interval level of 0.05. With the medium population effect, we will need at least 64 participants in each group (if we use Student's T-test for independent samples) or 33 participants in each group (if we use Student's T-test for dependent samples) [30]. With stronger effects, smaller samples are required, but we do not face such effects on a regular basis. Anyway, if the size of the effect is known, it is possible to use one of the numerous online calculators to evaluate the required sample.

6.2 Considering Ethics

Serious games are developed for people and the experiments we conduct involve people. That means that research ethics in serious game research is basically the same as in psychological and social science research.

APA Code of Ethics [19] states five general principles, applicable to all the fields of psychology. There are (A) Beneficence and Nonmaleficence; (B) Fidelity and Responsibility; (C) Integrity; (D) Justice and (E) Respect for People's Rights and Dignity. Applied towards the experimental research paradigm, these rules can be summarized as follows: the researcher must respect the participants' wellbeing and the participation in the experiment must be physically and psychologically harmless, until the participant knowingly and willingly accepts the risk, if any. No force or threats are allowed to involve or keep the participant in the experiment. People must be allowed to discontinue their participation at any time if they want to.

The researcher is responsible for every possible outcome of the experiment as well as for the accuracy, honesty, and truthfulness of his research and scientific conclusions. In the research that involves digital games in general and serious games in particular, the participants tend to be less suspicious about the possible effects and side-effects and thus more prone to them, so the researcher takes the responsibility for the psychological outcomes. The experimenter needs to respect dignity and worth of all people and the rights of individuals, including privacy, and confidentiality. This means that the results of any experimental research should not involve any personal data of the participants without their informed consent.

A written informed consent might be useful for both the experimenter and the participant. Some experiments require the experimenter to actively hide the aim of the study or to withhold some principal information, but this must be done in the least harmful way. An ethic committee must be consulted and must approve the research plan to avoid harmful effects.

7 Experimental Designs

7.1 Between-Groups and Within-Subjects Experiments

There are two main types of the experimental designs: between-subjects design where we compare different groups of participants and within-subjects design, where the same participants are tested more than once. In both variants, there can be one or more than one independent variable with two or more levels in it. In the simplest case, however, there is a single independent variable with two levels in it.

Between-groups designs are necessary when certain levels of the independent variable give the participants some experience that would influence further research with other levels of the variable. In the serious game testing, this might be important if participants receive plot or strategy-related information, which can influence their further gameplay tactics. The main advantage of this scheme is that all the participants are so-called "naive subjects" with no previous experience with our game. The main disadvantages are the large amount of the participants required and the problem of the equivalent groups, which was discussed in the section about samples [24].

Within-subject design requires fewer participants than the between-groups scheme. The group equality is not a problem, due to the self-equality of all the participants. In this type of the experimental design, each participant meets all levels of the independent variable so that we can measure how his condition or knowledge changes. In cases other than experimental plus zero condition (bivalent independent variable) we need to keep in mind that there might be different types of sequence effects, which appear through trials. Speaking about the sequence effects, we mean that the order in which different experimental conditions are presented may influence the outcome of the research. Apart from practice and fatigue effects, this involves many other possible factors. For example, if we want to compare two educational serious games and we also have a boring online lecture as a control condition. If the order in which we present those three conditions in always the same, one of the games might benefit not because it is more effective, but because it contrasts the lecture. At the same time the lecture might lose some of its effectiveness simply because the participants are too aroused to concentrate after all those games.

With more than two levels of the independent variable, we need to use counterbalancing schemes to apply all possible sequences of variable level for at least once. Complete counterbalancing is possible for 3 or 4 conditions as there are six and twenty-four sequences respectively, but for more levels of the independent variable partial counterbalancing is needed. These schemes can be represented with the use of a balanced Latin square. A Latin square is a way to ensure that every condition of the study occurs equally often, precedes and follows every other condition exactly once.

An example of a balanced Latin square with 4 conditions is, as follows (different letters represent different conditions):

A B D C
B C A D
C D B A
D A C B

Other counterbalancing technics, such as reverse counterbalancing are also possible, though it seems rather hard to introduce a serious game experiment, requiring those experimental designs.

7.2   Examples of the Real Experimental Schemes in Serious Games Studies

Let's discuss a couple of real examples of experimental schemes.

The first one is the experiment from J. van Muidjen and colleagues' study of cognitive control in elderly people [52]. The study aimed first, to show that cognitive training games can improve cognitive control functions and second, to compare training with games to training with documentaries and quizzes. In this study, both experimental designs are applied in different parts of the research, due to multiple dependable variables. In the experiment, there were two independent groups of participants (the between-group scheme; bivalent variable) and controlled randomization was used to form the groups out of the general population, with groups being equal in age, educational level, IQ, and cognitive heath scores. There were two levels of the independent variable – the game condition and the documentary film condition. There were a pretest and posttest with nine cognitive tests (the scores form dependable variables). As the tests could interfere with each other results, the scheme was introduced to counterbalance the battery across the participants (like in within-subjects design). While the statistical hypothesis examined the differences between the groups in terms of test scores, the discussion and the final conclusion were made in terms of cognitive controls theory.

The second example is retrieved from the E.D. van der Spek's dissertation [51]. The author describes a variety of experiments held on different stages of a training serious game development. In one of the experiments three independent variable level were introduced (with no cues, auditory cues or visual cues). As the researcher used between-group scheme, there were three groups, with two balanced extraneous variables – gender and gaming experience of the participants. There were four dependent parameters to measure – three learning tests and an engagement questionnaire with pretest and posttest made. The research is especially interesting due to the results, which were unpredicted by the researcher and led to the experimental hypothesis rejection (though, alternative explanations were made out of the theoretical background).

8   If an Experiment Cannot Be Conducted

8.1   Quasi-Experiment

The quasi-experiment occurs, when instead of usual, manipulated independent variable we use a so-called *subject variable* [24]. Subject variables are already existing characteristics of the individuals, participating in the study. Gender, age, culture, level of intelligence, personality attributes and so on can be used as subject variables. For sure, we cannot manipulate sex or personality of our participants. Instead, we can select people with different levels of these variables into different groups to compare, if their reaction towards our serious game would be the same or not.

Alongside with the quasi-experimental scheme above, D.T. Campbell [11] introduces two more variants of the quasi-experimental design. One of these schemes is a between-group comparison without group randomization. The second one is the quasi-experimental scheme with a single group, where experimental condition changes might blend with a time factor.

In general, quasi-experiment shares most of the true experiment's advantages but has lesser control over any additional variables and influences. This means, that we should be especially accurate with extraneous variables on the one hand and that sometimes we will not be able to prove a causal hypothesis for sure on the other hand, as less control leads to the possibility of alternative explanations. Some quasi-experimental schemes, though, have better ecological validity than true experiments.

Quasi-experimental schemes sometimes can involve numerous groups and conditions. For example, in the flow and anxiety research in serious games [9] participated six different groups and there were five different conditions as well. A true experiment with such amount of variable levels would require enormous efforts. The authors introduce their research as an exploratory study, which means that the discussed problem is not clearly defined. In this case, the quasi-experimental scheme is more reasonable, as the research itself is not intended to prove causalities. Instead, it searches for relationships and succeeds. Please note, that quasi-experimental scheme still requires a lot of variable control, with pre- and posttest, different sampling technics and many efforts to manage equal timing for different groups and participants.

8.2   Correlational Study

While quasi-experiments (with some additional reservations and strict control schemes) can still be used to verify a causal hypothesis, the correlational study only shows the positive or negative linkage between certain parameters. Due to its simplicity, correlational studies are very common in psychology and social sciences. M.L. Raulin [43] notices that in the experimental design correlations of demographical variables are often used to point out possible confounding variables to enhance the control.

The correlational study requires to be mentioned in the experimental design chapter due to the fact that sometimes people tend to discuss correlations in the term of cause and effect. Such assumptions are methodologically wrong and considered to be non-scientific, as not only we cannot determine which variable precede the other, but also we cannot exclude the possibility of the third variable that is linked to both variables or causes their correlation in some other way.

In a validation study of serious games for clinical assessments [49], different correlational coefficients were used to obtain as much data as possible with different types of scales. While the authors use Mann-Whitney test as well, correlations are more important in this particular study, as it aims to find linkage between cognitive assessments and serious games. One of the goals is described as "develop a method for predicting the presence of delirium, using serious game". As the correlation describes that some variables coexist with each other, it can support such a notion, though it does not show why this happens.

9 Conclusions

The chapter discusses the use of the experimental methodology in serious games research. The main advantage of the experimental method, that it does not share with any other empirical methods in modern science, is the possibility to testify causal hypotheses according to an approved scientific paradigm. This means, that the only way to prove empirically that a serious game causes some changes in the users knowledge, skills or awareness is to conduct an experiment within one the discussed schemes. The advantages and disadvantages of between-groups and within-subjects experimental designs are mentioned alongside with some real life examples of experimental serious games research, retrieved from scientific publications. The chapter encourages the readers to use experiments in their own research projects and helps them to understand the terminology of experimental research. It also points out some general mistakes, that students should avoid while practicing in serious games evaluation.

While scientifically the experiment is one of the best evaluation tools, it is also one of the most labor- and time-consuming ones. Without proper control of the variables, the researcher can overlook the serious game's effect. What is more important (as it will be Type I error), the experimental research, influenced by biases, leads to a poor evaluation of the serious game. Faulty experiments (and "cause-and-effect" conclusions based on the wrong methods) cannot only damage the particular researcher's reputation but the reputation of the serious games in general.

Many serious games are developed to help vulnerable groups of people, such as children and adults with disabilities, people with phobias, medical patients, elders with dementia, etc., so it is very important to foresee not only the positive effects but also the negative once. This means that experiments with people playing serious games must maintain the highest ethical standards and that is why the researcher needs to work together with an ethical committee.

You need to remember that before starting the experiment, you need to pass the whole way from theoretical background to the experimental hypothesis. Evaluation through the experiment is sometimes a very long process, and you will probably need more than one experiment to prove your hypotheses. You also need to find suitable statistical methods for your research and you need to understand how these methods work to avoid misinterpretations. If researchers are unfamiliar with these methods a cooperation with experts from psychology or Human Computer Interaction is recommended. However, the evidence of your serious game effectiveness obtained through the adequate experiment absolutely worth the efforts.

Further Reading

For more experiments on serious games, see:

- Van der Spek, E.D.: Experiments in Serious Game Design: a Cognitive Approach. Utrecht University Repository (Dissertation). Utrecht University, Utrecht (2011)

For deeper knowledge about experimental and other research types in social sciences and psychology, as well as for common statistical procedures see:

- Kantowitz, B.H., Roediger, H.L.III, Elmes, D.G.: Experimental Psychology. Wadsworth, Belmont (2009)
- Martin D.W.: Doing Psychology Experiments. Thompson Higher Education, Belmont (2008)
- Goodwin C.J. Research in Psychology: Methods and Design. Wiley, Danvers (2010)

To learn about online experiments' possibility, see:

- Reips, U.-D.: Standards for Internet-based Experimenting. In: Experimental Psychology. 49(9), 243–256 (2002)
- Reips, U.-D., Krantz, J.H.: Conducting True Experiments on the Web. In: Gosling, S., Johnson, J. (eds.) Advanced Methods for Conducting Online Behavioral Research, pp. 193–216. American Psychological Association, Washington DC (2010)

For basic knowledge about latent variables (variables, which can only be discovered through statistical procedures, very common in psychology and social sciences) see:

- Bollen, K.A.: Latent Variables in Psychology and the Social Sciences. In: Annu. Rev. Psychol. 53, 605–634 (2002)

For advanced knowledge in statistical methods (multivariate analysis of variance, multiple regression, etc.), see:

- Foster J., Barkus, E., Yavorsky, C.: Understanding and Using Advanced Statistics: A Practical Guide for Students. SAGE Puclications, London, Thousand Oaks, New Delhi (2006)

References

1. Adams, K.A., Lawrence, E.K.: Research Methods, Statistics and Applications. SAGE Publications, London (2014)
2. Adejumobi, B., Franck, N., Janzen, M.: Designing and testing a racing car serious game module. In: Ma, M., Oliveira, M.F., Baalsrud Hauge, J. (eds.) SGDA 2014. LNCS, vol. 8778, pp. 192–198. Springer, Heidelberg (2014)
3. Anderson, C.A., Dill, K.E.: Video games and aggressive thoughts, feelings, and behavior in the laboratory and in life. J. Person. Soc. Psychol. **78**(4), 772–790 (2000)

4. Anguera, J.A., Boccanfuso, J., Rintoul, J.L., Al-Hashimi, O., Faraji, F., Janowich, J., Kong, E., Larraburo, Y., Rolle, C., Johnston, E., Gazzaley, A.: Video game training enhances cognitive control in older adults. Nature **501**, 97–101 (2013)
5. Baek, Y., Ko, R., Marsh, T. (eds.): Trends and Applications of Serious Gaming and Social Media. Gaming Media and Social Effects. Springer, New York (2014)
6. Bidarra, R., Gambon, D., Kooij, R., Nagel, D., Schutjes, M., Tziouvara, I.: Gaming at the Dentist's–serious game design for pain and discomfort distraction. In: Schouten, B., Fedtke, S., Bekker, T., Schijven, M., Gekker, A. (eds.) Games for Health 2013. Proceeding of the 3rd Conference on Gaming and Playful Interaction in Healthcare, pp. 207–215. Springer, Heidelberg (2013)
7. Boinodiris, P., Fingar, P.: Serious Games for Business: Using Gamification to Fully Engage Customers, Employees and Partners. Meghan-Kiffer Press, Tampa (2014)
8. Botella, C., Breton-Lópeza, J., Queroa, S., Bañosh, R.M., García-Palaciosa, A., Zaragozac, I., Alcanizc, M.: Treating cockroach phobia using a serious game on a mobile phone and augmented reality exposure: a single case study. Comput. Hum. Behav. **27**(1), 217–227 (2011). Current Research Topics in Cognitive Load Theory. Third International Cognitive Load Theory Conference
9. Brom, C., Buchtová, M., Šisler, V., Děchtěrenko, F., Palme, R., Glenk, L.M.: Flow, social interaction anxiety and salivary cortisol responses in serious games: a quasi-experimntal study. Comput. Educ. **79**, 69–100 (2014)
10. Bushman, B.J., Anderson, C.: Violent video games and hostile expectations: a test of the general aggression model. Pers. Soc. Psychol. Bull. **28**(12), 1679–1686 (2002)
11. Campbell, D.T., Cook, D.T.: Quasy-Experimental Design and Analysis Issues for Field Setting. Rand McNally, Chicago (1979)
12. Casti, J.L.: Reality Rules, Picturing the World in Mathematics–The Fundamentals, vol. I. Wiley, New York (1997)
13. Choo, A., Tong, X., Gromala, D., Hollander, A.: Virtual reality and mobius floe: cognitive distraction as non-pharmacological analgesic for pain management. In: Schouten, B., Fedtke, S., Schijven, M., Vosmeer, M., Gekker, A. (eds.) Games for Health 2014 Proceeding of the 4th conference on gaming and playful interaction in healthcare, pp. 8–12. Springer Fachmedien Wiesbaden, Heidelberg (2014)
14. Adams, K.A.: Cram101 Textbooks Reviews, Just the facts101 Textbook Key Facts: Research Methods, Statistics, and Applications. Content Technologies (2014). http://cram101.com
15. De Freitas, S., Liarokapis, F.: Serious games: a new paradigm for education? In: Ma, M., Oikonomou, A., Jain, L.C. (eds.) Serious Games and Edutainment Applications, pp. 9–23. Springer, London (2011)
16. De Gloria, A., Bellotti, F., Berta, R.: Serious games for education and training. Int. J. Serious Games. **1**(1). http://dx.doi.org/10.17083/ijsg.v1i1.11
17. Djaouti, D., Alvarez, J., Jessel, J., Rampnoux, O.: Origins of Serious Games. In: Ma, M., Oikonomou, A., Jain, L.C. (eds.) Serious Games and Edutainment Applications, pp. 25–43. Springer, London (2011)
18. Essential facts about the computer and video game industry. 2016 Sales, Demographic and Usage Data. ESA (2016). http://www.essentialfacts.theesa.com/Essential-Facts-2016.pdf
19. Ethical Principles of Psychologisys and Code of Conduct. APA (2010). http://www.apa.org/ethics/code/
20. Experiment. In: Merriam-Webster.com. Merriam-Webster. http://www.merriam-webster.com/dictionary/experiment

21. Ferguson, C., Kilburn, J.: Much ado about nothing: the misestimation and overinterpretation of violent video game effects in eastern and western nations: a comment on Anderson, et al. Psychol. Bull. **136**(2), 174–178 (2010)

22. Foster, J., Barkus, E., Yavorsky, C.: Understanding and Using Advanced Statistics: A Practical Guide for Students. SAGE Puclications, London, Thousand Oaks (2006)

23. Girard, C., Ecalle, J., Magnan, A.: Serious games as new educational tools: how effective are they? a meta-analysis of recent studies. J. Comput. Assist. Learn. **29**(3), 207–219 (2013)

24. Goodwin, C.J.: Research in Psychology Methods and Design. Wiley, New York (2010)

25. Hess, M., Wiemeyer, J., Hamacher, K., Goesele, M.: Serious games for solving protein sequence alignments - combining citizen science and gaming. In: Göbel, S., Wiemeyer, J. (eds.) GameDays 2014. LNCS, vol. 8395, pp. 175–185. Springer, Heidelberg (2014)

26. Hypothesis. In: Merriam-Webster.com. Merriam-Webster. http://www.merriam-webster.com/dictionary/hypothesis

27. Kantowitz, B.H., Roediger, H.L., Elmes, D.G.: Experimental Psychlogy, vol. III. Wadsworth, Belmont (2009)

28. Kaufman, S.B.: Sex differences in mental rotation and spatial visualization ability: can they be accounted for by differences in working memory capacity? Intelligence **35**, 211–223 (2007)

29. King, D.L., Delfabbro, P., Griffiths, M.D.: The psychological study of video game players: methodological challenges and practical advice. Int. J. Mental Health Addict. **7**(4), 555–562 (2009)

30. Kornilova, T.V.: Experimental Psychology. Jurajt, Moscow (2014). (in Russian)

31. Kuhn, T.S.: The Structure of Scientific Revolutions. International Encyclopedia of United Science, vol. 2. The University of Chicago Press, Chicago (1962)

32. Lim, C., Jung, H.: A study on the military serious game. Adv. Sci. Technol. Lett. **39**, 73–77 (2013). Proceedings. SERSC 2013

33. Marchand, A., Hennig-Thurau, T.: Value creation in the video game industry: industry economics, consumer benefits, and research opportunities. J. Interact. Market. **27**, 141–157 (2013)

34. Marsden, J.: The essential checklist for making an awesome video game, According to Futurlab (2013). http://indiegames.com/2013/07/the_essential_checklist_for_ma_1.html

35. Martin, D.W.: Doing Psychology Experiments. Thompson Higher Education, Belmont (2008)

36. Martins, T., Araújo, M., Carvalho, V., Soares, F., Torrão, L.: PhysioVinci – a first approach on a physical rehabilitation game. In: Ma, M., Oliveira, M.F., Baalsrud Hauge, J. (eds.) SGDA 2014. LNCS, vol. 8778, pp. 1–9. Springer, Heidelberg (2014)

37. Martin-SanJosé, J.-F., Juan, M.-C., Segui, I., Garcia-Garcia, I.: The effects of computer-based games and collaboration in large groups vs collaboration in pair or traditional methods. Comput. Educ. **87**, 42–54 (2015)

38. Mayer, I., Zhou, Q., Keijser, X., Abspoel, L.: Gaming the future of the ocean: the marine spatial planning challenge 2050. In: Ma, M., Oliveira, M.F., Baalsrud Hauge, J. (eds.) SGDA 2014. LNCS, vol. 8778, pp. 150–162. Springer, Heidelberg (2014)

39. Omelina, L., Jansen, B., Bonnechère, B., Van Sint Jan, S., Cornelis, J.: Serious games for physical rehabilitation: designing highly configurable and adaptable games. In: Proceeding 9th International Conference on Disability, Virtual Reality and Associated Technologies Laval, France, 10–12 September 2012 (ICDVRAT 2012), pp. 195–201. ICDVRAT (2012)

40. Operationalization. Wikipedia. https://en.wikipedia.org/wiki/Operationalization

41. Popper, K.: Normal Science and its Dangers. In: Lakatos, I., Musgrave, A. (eds.) Criticism and the Growth of Knowledge, pp. 51–58. Cambridge University Press, Cambridge (1970)

42. Popper, K.: The Logic of Scientific Discovery. Routledge, London (2002)
43. Raulin, M.L., Graziano, A.M.: Quasi-experiments and correlational studies. In: Colman, A.M. (ed.) Companion Encyclopedia of Psychology, vol. 2, pp. 1124–1141. Routledge, London (1994)
44. Reliability. In: Merriam-Webster.com. Merriam-Webster. http://www.merriam-webster.com/dictionary/reliability
45. Ricciardi, F., De Paolis, L.T.: A Comprehensive review of serious games in health professions. Int. J. Comput. Games Technol. (2014). http://dx.doi.org/10.1155/2014/787968
46. Senevirathne, S.G., Kodagoda, M., Kadle, V., Haake, S.J., Senior, T., Heller, B.W.: Application of serious games to sports, health and exercise. In: Proceedings of the 6th SLIIT Research Symposium, Sri Lanka, vol. 4, pp. 6–9 (2011)
47. Shubert, T., Strobach, T.: Video game experience optimized executive control skills—on false positives and false negatives: reply to boot and simons. Acta Psychol. **141**, 278–280 (2012)
48. Tomé, R.M., Pereira, J.M., Oliveira, M.: Using serious games for cognitive disabilities. In: Ma, M., Oliveira, M.F., Baalsrud Hauge, J. (eds.) SGDA 2014. LNCS, vol. 8778, pp. 34–47. Springer, Heidelberg (2014)
49. Tong, T., Chignell, M., Tierney, M.C., Masella, C.: A Serious game for clinical assessment of cognitive status: validation study. JMIR Serious Games **4**(1), e7 (2016). doi:10.2196/games.5006
50. Validity. In: Merriam-Webster.com. Merriam-Webster. http://www.merriam-webster.com/dictionary/validity
51. Van der Spek, E.D.: Experiments in serious game design: a cognitive approach. Utrecht University Repository (Dissertation). Utrecht University, Utrecht (2011)
52. Van Muijden, J., Band, G.P.H., Hommel, B.: Online games training aging brains: limited transfer to cognitive control functions. Front. Hum. Neurosci. **6**, 221 (2012). doi:10.3389/fnhum.2012.00221
53. Wouters, P., van Nimwegen, C., van Oostendorp, H., van der Spek, E.D.: A meta-analysis of the cognitive and motivational effects of serious games. J. Educ. Psychol. **105**, 249 (2013). doi:10.1037/a0031311
54. Wrzesien, M., Alcañiz, M., Botella, C., Burkhardt, J.-M., Lopez, J.B., Ortega, A.R.: A pilot evaluation of a therapeutic game applied to small animal phobia treatment. In: Ma, M., Oliveira, M.F., Baalsrud Hauge, J. (eds.) SGDA 2014. LNCS, vol. 8778, pp. 10–20. Springer, Heidelberg (2014)
55. Yoo, K., Ahn, J., Lee, W.: A design of the stress relief game based on autonomic nervous system. In: Park, J.H., Jeong, Y.-S., Park, S.O., Chen, H.-C. (eds.) EMC 2012. LNEE, vol. 181, pp. 371–376. Springer, Heidelberg (2012)
56. Zakari, H.M., Ma, M., Simmons, D.: A review of serious games for children with autism spectrum disorders (ASD). In: Ma, M., Oliveira, M.F., Baalsrud Hauge, J. (eds.) SGDA 2014. LNCS, vol. 8778, pp. 93–106. Springer, Heidelberg (2014)

Operationalization and Measurement of Evaluation Constructs

Katharina Emmerich[1]($\boxtimes$), Natalya Bogacheva[2], Mareike Bockholt[3],
and Viktor Wendel[4]

[1] Entertainment Computing Group, University of Duisburg-Essen,
Duisburg, Germany
katharina.emmerich@uni-due.de
[2] Moscow State University, Moscow, Russia
bogacheva.nataly@gmail.com
[3] Graph Theory and Complex Network Analysis Group, TU Kaiserslautern,
Kaiserslautern, Germany
mareike.bockholt@cs.uni-kl.de
[4] Multimedia Communications Lab, TU Darmstadt, Darmstadt, Germany
viktor.wendel@kom.tu-darmstadt.de

Abstract. This chapter deals with the operationalization and measurement of evaluation constructs, an important and challenging part of the serious games evaluation process. Hereby, advices will be given on what has to be measured and how to quantify an abstract concept. Thus, the chapter makes two main contributions. First, general data gathering methods are described and discussed in terms of advantages and disadvantages. Second, main psychological concepts and evaluation constructs relevant in the context of serious games, as well as their theoretical foundations, are introduced. In order to support the reader on planning future serious game evaluations, a list and description of concrete techniques and questionnaires addressing concepts like motivation, player experience, learning outcomes, health, well-being, and attitudes are compiled.

Keywords: Operationalization · Measurement methods · Player experience · Psychological constructs · Evaluation

1 Introduction: What Is Operationalization?

This chapter covers an important part of the serious games evaluation process, namely the operationalization of evaluation constructs. Operationalization is a substantial aspect of quantitative research and generally referred to as the process of defining how to quantify a phenomenon or concept which itself is not directly measurable. This applies to basic psychological constructs as for example motivation, well-being, and emotions, but also to seemingly more concrete concepts like health, intelligence, or learning progress. Though we all have some kind of understanding of all these constructs, we cannot tell a direct and distinct

© Springer International Publishing AG 2016
R. Dörner et al. (Eds.): Entertainment Computing and Serious Games, LNCS 9970, pp. 306–331, 2016.
DOI: 10.1007/978-3-319-46152-6_13

way to quantitatively measure them. This is a great issue regarding the evaluation of serious games: Serious games are supposed to serve a certain purpose besides mere entertainment, but this purpose is mostly described in terms of such rather fuzzy concepts. This is where operationalization comes in.

Operationalization is based on the assumption that an abstract construct under examination can be inferred from its observable effects. For instance, if a serious game is supposed to address the player's attitude towards junk food, we cannot directly measure this attitude after a playing session, because an attitude itself is neither observable nor directly graspable by existing measuring tools. However, there are several indicators that are supposed to be closely related to attitudes and thus allow for drawing conclusions. Regarding the given example, players may be asked some questions about their opinion on junk food ("To what extent do you agree that junk food is unhealthy?"). In this case, the questions constitute the operational definition of a person's attitude towards junk food. But asking questions is not the only possibility to operationalize it. Attitudes are often also reflected by behavior. Hence, it could also be observed whether (and how often) a person consumes junk food in a certain period of time after playing the game. The number of times someone eats junk food in one month is another operationalization of one's attitude towards it.

1.1   The Challenge of Operationalization

As the example of attitude towards junk food illustrates, the process of operationalization is complex and ambiguous. Hence, the biggest challenge and the goal is to ensure that the construct is measured in a way that is "as accurate a representation of the construct as possible" [44]. Landers et al. [44] describe this issue with regard to classical test theory and explain that an operational definition is composed of two parts: a true score, meaning the correct inference to the construct, and an error score, meaning the proportion of mis-measurement of the construct. The challenge of operationalization is thus to minimize error scores by finding proper measurement approaches.

One strategy to reduce misleading results is to apply multilayered measures. If, for instance, the player's perceived autonomy should be assessed, instead of using just one single item like "I felt autonomous while playing the game", error score minimization can be achieved by asking for agreement on multiple statements, for example "the game provides me with interesting options and choices" and "I experienced a lot of freedom in the game" (cf. [61]). Moreover, different measurement methods like questionnaires and observations can be combined in order to check correlations and confirm results.

However, finding appropriate operational definitions remains challenging. Therefore, this chapter is supposed to provide assistance for the process of operationalization by addressing the core question on how evaluation constructs can be quantified. In the context of digital games and serious games, there are many constructs which are repeatedly under investigation, like motivation, player experience, learning outcomes, well-being and concepts regarding attitudes and personality traits. Accordingly, researchers already made experiences with different approaches and in some cases already developed validated measurements. Those will also be discussed in the chapter in order to gather information, exchange experiences and give advise for future operationalization processes.

1.2 Overview

The chapter is divided into three main parts. First, general data gathering methods are introduced to give an overview of available means to assess data. Related characteristics, advantages, and disadvantages are shortly discussed. Subsequently, different constructs that are relevant in the context of serious games evaluation are addressed, as it is important to understand those constructs to be able to derive concrete operationalizations. Those constructs are motivation, player experience, learning outcomes, health and well-being, and attitudes. For each construct, common ways to operationalize them are presented. Finally, the chapter concludes with a summary of concrete method implementations, mainly standardized questionnaires and psychological test procedures, that are currently used in game research to assess the concepts discussed before. This list is not exhaustive, but provides a helpful starting point for the planning and conducting of evaluation in terms of operationalization.

2   User-Centered Data Gathering Methods

The main goal of serious games evaluation is to prove whether a game fulfills its designated purpose. Serious games are applied in very different contexts and thus can serve manifold purposes. However, they are always supposed to somehow influence the players by addressing their knowledge, emotions, attitudes, or behavior. This implies that the evaluation process should reasonably focus on user-centered data gathering methods. As the name indicates, those methods put the user in the center of the evaluation process. There are several core ideas that stand behind this methodology: First, the goal is to optimize the product (the game) to make it convenient for the users. Second, the game has to be evaluated from the users point of view (and not from the developers' one) to ensure that optimization is done in the right way. To put it in the simplest possible way, the developers know how their serious game is supposed to work but the players do not. Third, to achieve points one and two data has to be gathered directly from the users to validate hypotheses, while it needs to be done in a way that will not harm or interfere the players' gaming experience.

In this part of the chapter, we discuss the general methods that can be used to gather user-centered data while developing and evaluating a serious game. While the methods are generally all the same throughout different user-centered designs, their configurations differ according to the application field and the current stage of the game development process [7].

2.1 Types of Measurement Methods

Measurement methods that are applicable to evaluate serious games are diverse. Most of them can be assigned to one of the four main categories: self-reports, physiological measures, gameplay metrics, and observations.

Self-reports. Self-report measurements directly ask the players to answer concrete questions or to freely give their opinion on certain aspects. Hence, resulting data is always subjective. Common forms are questionnaires, focus group discussions, and interviews. The last two methods mainly result in qualitative data, as they allow for free (and long) answers. Focus groups are usually used at early stages of the development and evaluation process and help to investigate the general acceptance and opinions of players on the game.

The data gathered from interviews is quite similar, though questions are more focused on the individual. Gill et al. [27] differentiate three major types of interviews: structured, semi-structured, and unstructured. A structured interview is a verbalized questionnaire with predetermined questions and usually a set of possible answers. On the opposite, unstructured interviews do not strictly follow a predefined plan, but are adapted to the situation and previous answers. These interviews can last unlimited amount of time and, although they do not require much organization, the do require a lot of skill from the interviewer to make results useful. Semi-structured interviews are more common in most sciences and have the advantages of both other types. They do have a structure (a number of key questions, outlining important areas of the research), but they are also flexible enough to discover some essentially new data if the dialog goes that way. Semi-structured interviews also require more skill than fully structured ones, as well as more time and general efforts.

Standardized questionnaires, in contrast, consist of carefully selected items and provide quantitative data related to an abstract construct, and are thus most interesting in the context of operationalization. In general, a questionnaire is an instrument to quantify player-related constructs like feelings and thoughts. Unlike interviews, they are usually used if data from numerous participants has to be gathered with relatively small efforts. As it can be extracted from the name, questionnaires are made of questions or statements that participants are required to agree or to disagree with. The questions can be either closed or open-ended. Closed questions can be answered by "yes" or "no" or by choosing a response from several given alternatives. Open-ended questions require broader answers. The participants need to add something to the answers or create it by themselves. Open-ended questions can be more informative in some way, and in some studies they are shown to provide more valid data [43]. However, they are much more difficult to analyze and to be used in statistical calculations, as answers are not standardized.

Many questionnaires, especially those that use statements as their items, use interval scales (or Likert scales) to evaluate participant agreement or disagreement with the statement. Scales usually consist of an odd number of points (to have a neutral answer in the middle) [30], ranging in meaning from "Strongly

Disagree" to "Strongly Agree". Likert scales usually have from five to nine points; lónger scales give the participants better opportunity to specify their attitude to the statement, but too many variants can be confusing. The same rule can be applied to the number of answers of closed questions – there should be enough answers to cover all possible or at least common alternatives, but not too many to make participants insecure.

Depending upon what data should be assessed, either already existing questionnaires made by some other scientists can be used, or an own questionnaire with a unique set of questions has to be developed. Once a questionnaire is compiled and proven to be valid and reliable, it is rather easy and convenient to use, but the development of a new questionnaire is difficult and complex. Unlike an interview, which allows to control the data gathering process and to change the pace and the manner to get information, the questionnaire is used as it is. Hence, it has to be easy to understand and well-conceived. One of the most important problems while creating a questionnaire is the actual wording. You cannot explain or reframe the questions during use, if the participant does not understand it, so the question or the statement must be as simple as possible. Characteristics of the target group have to be considered before creating the questionnaire: If the users of the serious game are going to be children or teenagers, probably a different language should be used compared to older participants. Moreover, if the question is quite simple for a psychologist or computer-science specialist, it is not necessarily understandable for a common user with no scientific background. This is the reason why pilot studies are needed before using new questionnaires on large groups of people. Goodwin et al. [30] give seven guidelines on phrasing good questionnaire items: They advise to prefer simplicity over complexity, to use complete sentences instead of some short phrase, to avoid any abbreviations that are not completely universal, to avoid slang and jargon, to avoid negatively phrased questions, and to make questions as balanced as possible, without favoring one position and without giving the participant any clues on the desired answer. This will help avoiding bias and making the results more objective.

Furthermore, questionnaires for evaluation purposes should be based on theories and conceptual frameworks regarding the construct under investigation (like the ones discussed in the second part of this chapter) in order to make proper interpretation possible. Most of the questionnaires are designed to measure more than one characteristic or parameter of a certain construct. Single scale questionnaires are also possible, but rare in psychological and related research because the reality that stands behind complex behaviors or attitudes is usually too complex to be described by a single latent variable.

Physiological Measures and Biometrics. Another approach to assess player data is to measure physical reactions of the player while playing the game. Based on the assumption that the processing of any stimuli (so also during play) always provokes physical reactions, those so-called biometrics [53] are used to draw conclusions about psychological phenomena [40]. This data is objective in contrast to self-report measures, but psychophysiological data is sensitive to noise (for instance, facial EMG measurement can be confounded by related muscle activity such as speaking) and mostly ambiguous with regard to interpretation: Most relations between certain psychological states and physiological outcomes are not one-to-one but many-to-one relations, turning the interpretation of data into a challenging task [40,67]. There are various ways to assess physical reactions. The currently most common ones are shortly described in the following:

- Skin conductance: The electrodermal activity (EDA) can be assessed with sensors attached to the fingers. It is supposed to be related to arousal and stress [40].
- Cardiac activity: An electrocardiogram (ECG) or a peripheral pulse oximeter can be used to measure heart rate and pulse. These biometrics are indicators for arousal, attention, or stress [40].
- Electrical activity of facial muscles: Facial electromyography (EMG) measures facial expressions by means of the electrical activation of facial muscles. This data gives information about the valence and arousal of emotional reactions [40,53,58].
- Brain activity: Brain waves are measured by electroencephalography (EEG) and allow for deriving cognitive processes, the degree of attention and the use of mental resources [40,53].
- Respiration: The rate or depth of breathing provides an indication of relaxation, stress, or negative emotions [50].
- Eye movement: In order to investigate which elements are recognized, focused and paid attention to by the player, eye tracking systems can be used to record viewing direction and movement of gaze [53].

Gameplay Metrics. Gameplay metrics provide information about the interaction between the player and the game in terms of numerical data [53]. Compared to the other types of measurement, this method gathers data from the game system and not directly from the player. While playing, the player's in-game behavior is automatically tracked by the system and related to certain game events or locations (for instance, by time-stamps and labels). Results allow conclusions about the player experience as they offer insights into how people are actually playing the games under examination [53] (p. 50). The events and behavior that are relevant for the evaluation process differ with respect to the purpose of the game. Typical game metrics for example quantify how many times the player performs a certain action. However, this behavioral data does not inform about the reasons why players are acting the way they do. Thus, gameplay metrics are often used in combination with other methods to gain additional insights about the course of the game session and relevant events and actions. A proper visualization of gameplay data can reveal patterns of player behavior that otherwise would have been undetected. Hence, metrics are supposed to be highly relevant to serious games evaluation and can be applied in diverse contexts (see for instance [48] for further details).

Observations. Besides asking players directly, measuring their physiological reactions or assessing their in-game behavior, researchers might also gain valuable insights by simply observing players during play. In fact, observations are not that easy to conduct and to analyze properly, but nevertheless often used in games research. Body language, gestures, interactions, facial expressions as well as verbal communication are supposed to be rich data sources for evaluating player experience [50]. Especially video recording assesses many details that have to be edited and coded based on a predefined scheme, which mostly is a time-consuming process. In order to account for validity and reliability, observation plans and coding methods have to be tested and differences between observers have to be considered (inter-rater reliability). Often observation is focused on a few specific aspects in order to facilitate the process and to support the evaluation of other measures [50].

2.2   Advantages, Disadvantages and Challenges of Methods

The aforementioned general methods of data gathering for evaluating serious games all feature certain advantages, disadvantages and challenges. They mainly differ regarding aspects of objectivity, immediacy of measurement, obtrusiveness and gameplay interference, as well as effort and costs of conduction and data analysis. Table 1 gives an overview of those differences.

While data assessed by questionnaires and any other form of self-report is always more or less subjective, the other methods provide more objective data. In the case of observation, objectivity depends on the existence and quality of an observation scheme and whether game sessions are recorded or directly processed by present observers. Observer bias (different observers interpret occurring events differently) or ambiguous observation categories might harm objectivity. Gameplay metrics and physiological measures, in contrast, are hardly manipulable and thus, most objective. The advantage of objectivity

Table 1. Overview of the characteristics and differences of main measurement method types regarding objectivity, immediacy, interference and effort/cost.

	Objectivity of data	Immediacy of measurement	Interference of gameplay	Effort/Cost
Self-reports	subjective	post-hoc	no interference	low costs, easy processing
Observation	objective but prone to observer bias	immediate	possibly interfering	high effort in processing if not automated
Gameplay metrics	objective	immediate	no interference	implementation effort, low assessment costs
Psycho-physiological measures	objective	immediate	possibly interfering	high effort, huge datasets, tools needed

is that data is not blurred by personal sensitivities or social effects (like social desirability) and hence more reliable. However, objective data provides only limited insights regarding a person's thoughts, feelings and reasons to act the way that was detected. At this point, subjective data helps to find explanations and relations between observable behavior, physiological reactions, and psychological processes.

Another aspect that distinguishes self-reports from the other methods is the immediacy of the measurement. Questionnaires and interviews are obtained after the gaming session, thus participants have to rate the experience retrospectively. Hence, results may be influenced by memory effects, for instance primacy and recency effects, as the first and the last events of the session are recalled better than the rest of the experience. However, asking questions while participants play the game would interrupt the game flow and severely influence the experience. Post-hoc tests at least do not interfere with the gameplay. Observations, gameplay metrics, and physiological measures enable immediate assessment of data while players are interacting with the game. While data collection via metrics is unapparent for participants and thus not distracting, observations and physiological measures are not in any case unobtrusive. If the observation is not covert, the feeling of being observed might influence the behavior of players, and the attachment of measurement tools to the body might also have impact. That shows that the degree of interference depends on the way measures are applied in those cases.

Finally, methods differ regarding effort and costs of their implementation and analysis of data. Self-reports, especially questionnaires are rather easy to apply and provide clear scoring schemes. The effort of observations is variable: if observers are taking notes during the gameplay session, the assessment of data takes more time for researchers, while the use of video recording reduces personnel expenditure. However, the evaluation process of observational data is very time-consuming, as the whole video material has to be coded regarding predefined aspects. The implementation of gameplay metrics demands technical expertise and additional costs during the game development process, but once they are implemented the assessment is very easy. Psychophysiological measurements are most expensive and demanding. Some techniques require complex and expensive equipment and have to be applied by trained experimenters [40]. Their usage is time-consuming and the datasets provided by them are very extensive.

3   Evaluation Constructs and Their Operationalization

The core of each serious game is its purpose. A well-designed game is based on a theoretical ground related to this purpose. If the goal is to enhance the motivation to physically exercise, game mechanics and content should be designed with respect to theories of intrinsic and extrinsic motivation, self-efficacy, personal needs as well as self-determination. If, on the other hand, the game is supposed to impart knowledge, learning principles and theories of knowledge creation should be considered. Those considerations are not only relevant during the game development process, but may also substantially influence the evaluation: Depending on the respective theories, the evaluation has to be designed with the knowledge of the corresponding theories in mind. In this context, the proper operationalizsation of theoretical constructs is one of the main challenges. Hence, this section introduces main constructs that are relevant in the context of serious games evaluation, as it is important to understand those constructs to be able to derive concrete operationalizations. It is shown how the methods described in Sect. 2 can be applied to this constructs in order to prove a serious game's effectiveness. While the first two sub-chapters deal with rather generic concepts that do apply to any kind of digital game, namely motivation and player experience, the other three refer to more specific concepts particularly relevant for the design and evaluation of serious games: learning outcomes, health and well-being, as well as attitudes.

3.1 Motivation, Player Models and Personality Traits

Often motivation is the core argument when deciding to use a serious game instead of other forms of educational tools or information material. It is commonly believed that games are highly motivating and a pleasant experience [25]. Diverse game mechanics like progress visualization, immediate feedback, rewards, and challenges constantly motivate the player to engage in the game and to master it [16,24]. Hence, the willingness of users to play games voluntarily is seen as vehicle to start the involvement of the targeted audience regarding a certain topic. A typical example is the use of digital games in schools to provide educational material in an innovative and motivating way. Furthermore, there are also some serious games that explicitly serve the purpose of fostering motivation at the core, for instance games that are supposed to enhance physical activity of players in general without referring to specific movement patterns or rehabilitation programs.

In any case, motivation is a relevant part of serious games evaluation, hence the question arises how this construct can be operationalized in order to measure it. In general, motivation is seen as a theoretical construct describing the active pursuit of an (individually) positively rated target state [59]. It can be distinguished between *intrinsic* and *extrinsic* motivation, which refers to the source of motivation. While extrinsic motivation emerges from external rewards and impact factors (for instance, if someone is paid for doing something), intrinsic motivation describes the individual, inherent willingness to do something that is rated as interesting or enjoyable [60]. Digital games are supposed to particularly trigger the latter form.

In the context of serious games evaluation, motivation can be seen from mainly two different points of view: It is both an antecedent of playing, because only persons who are motivated are supposed to decide to start (and keep) playing a certain game [21], as well as a part of the player experience itself, as game events and features can increase or decrease motivation. Moreover, the perceived motivational qualities of the game and the current motivational level of a player will probably influence the way the game is perceived and rated.

Accordingly, if the motivation of players should be measured, these two facets of player motivation have to be distinguished.

General Motivation to Play a Certain Game: Player Models. Regarding the general motivation to choose and start playing a certain digital game, diverse motives for playing have been researched and assembled into so-called *player models*, which classify players in terms of the main reasons why they play games. Popular player models are Bartle's player taxonomy [3,4], Yee's model of player motivation [73] and the BrainHex model [52]. Bartle more or less laid the foundation of player models in his early work by defining four main player categories based on the analysis of multi-user dungeon games [3]: *achievers, explorers, socializers*, and *killers*. The player types are characterized by different main interests and playing styles. For example, achievers are trying to master all game challenges and seek for success, while explorers like to immerse in the game world and explore it without focusing on the main goals. Yee [73] proposes three main categories of player motivation, namely achievement, immersion, and social. The BrainHex model differentiates further sub-categories, resulting in seven player types. However, the idea behind all those player taxonomies is the same. While such player categories are non-exclusive and simplify the construct of motivation to some degree, they provide a first understanding as to how motivation influences a player. And – even more important in terms of the topic of this chapter – they significantly help to operationalize the construct of player motivation. Based on those theories, questionnaires have been developed in which participants are asked to rate different game experiences and events, which are internally related to one or more of the defined player types. This way, it is possible to measure a player's general motivation to play digital games. Measuring player motivation in terms of player types may reveal different effects of the game on different groups of players and can thus be part of serious games evaluation.

There are also some more general methods to assess more generic player personality traits, which may also be interesting for investigating a game's effect on certain target groups. While a detailed discussion of general psychological models of personality traits is beyond the scope of this chapter, we suggest the very popular model of the Big Five personlity traits [57] as a starting point if you are interested in investigating such aspects. The Big Five is a five factor model describing five main dimensions of personality, namely *openness to experience, conscientiousness, extraversion, agreeableness*, and *neuroticism*, which are established in psychological research and applied to diverse research fields, also to digital games. Here, too, the common form of operationalization is using a questionnaire. There are many different versions and inventories, for instance the short 10 Item Big Five Inventory (BFI-10) [57].

The Perceived Motivational Quality of a Game. As described above, besides general models of player motivation, which try to explain why players prefer certain kinds of games and show certain playing styles, another interesting aspect regarding the construct of motivation is the actually perceived motivational quality of a game. In this context, a basic theory of motivation, namely the *self-determination theory* (SDT), has been applied to games by Ryan et al. [61]: SDT comprises main factors that are supposed to facilitate or undermine motivation, focusing especially on intrinsic motivation. Those factors are based on the psychological needs for *autonomy, competence,* and *relatedness*. According to the application of SDT to digital games by Ryan et al. [61], a player's intrinsic motivation is supported by

- perceived autonomy: a sense of own volition and freedom of choice;
- perceived competence: appropriate challenges and the sense of efficacy;
- perceived presence: a sense of actually being within the game world;
- intuitive controls;
- and perceived relatedness: the feeling of being connected with others.

In order to measure need satisfaction, the *Player Experience of Need Satisfaction (PENS)* questionnaire was developed [61], taking into account the aforementioned dimensions of player needs and experiences by integrating them as sub-scales. Based on the same idea, the Intrinsic Motivation Inventory (IMI) [51] can be used to assess dimensions of the intrinsic motivation related to a game. Based on grounded theory, those measures are supposed to be valid operationalizations of the motivation construct and thus offer possibilities to evaluate serious games in terms of motivational aspects.

3.2 Facets of Player Experience

Game user research is concerned with the user experience of players, often called game experience or player experience. Though there is no sole definition of player experience, the ISO standard definition of user experience allows for approximation: It defines user experience as "a person's perceptions and responses that result from the use or anticipated use of a product, system or service" (ISO Norm 9241) and thereby matches the conception of most researchers and practitioners [45]. In contrast to usability, which is focused on functionality and ease of use, the user experience is a psychological construct and primarily comprises the feelings, thoughts, and reactions of the user [6]. Accordingly, regarding digital games it can be specified as the individual, context-sensitive experience in terms of cognitions, emotions, and physical responses emerging from the interaction between a player and a game system [6]. In short, it deals with the direct effect that the game has on its players and thus is highly relevant in the context of serious games. The definition above underlines the complexity of player experience, as it comprises several concepts and research focuses from the fields of cognition, motivation, emotion and attention [14]. In order to be able to assess the player experience of a game, current research models (for instance [69]) break it down into single, more tangible sub-dimensions. The most prevalent and investigated sub-components are

- *fun,*
- *flow,*
- *immersion,*
- *presence,* and
- *social presence*

and will therefore be shortly introduced in the following.

Fun. Fun and flow are both concepts which are long-since established in game research. The evocation of fun, which means an intense and positively valenced emotion, is commonly seen as the main objective of entertainment games; it is commonly accepted that it is also a main element of serious games. However, fun is a rather fuzzy concept without clear definition and hardly to grasp or measure as such [22,35]. Therefore, researchers have established diverse theories about the emergence and manifestations of fun. For instance, Koster [42] relates fun to brain functionalities and learning processes and attributes feelings of joy to the relief resulting from mastering new patterns. Though this might be one aspect of fun, it does not account for individual preferences and differences. Lazzaro [46], in contrast, underlines the emotional facets of fun and proposed four basic types, called Four Keys, that lead to an enjoyable experience: *hard fun, easy fun, altered states* and the *people factor. Hard fun* arouses from meaningful challenges and a feeling of success and pride. On the other hand, *easy fun* is attributed to the investigation of interesting stimuli like a story, a game world or ambiguous details and is thus linked to surprise and curiosity. *Altered states* stands for the potential of games to arouse different emotions and to let people feel something new or different (also including the aspect of distraction). Finally, the *people factor* emphasizes that also the interaction with other players may lead to enjoyment. In a similar way, Dillon [17] connects fun to certain emotions and instincts, but goes a bit more into detail by differentiating six basic emotions and eleven related instincts (*6-11 framework*). These three representative examples of fun theories illustrate well that fun is not a single emotion but comprises several feelings as well as cognitive processes and can be induced in manifold ways. Hence, it should be considered as a multidimensional factor during evaluation.

Flow. A related concept, which is comparable to the idea of hard fun, is flow. Based on the research of Csikszentmihalyi, flow can be seen as a desirable effect in games, as it describes a mental state of total engagement [13] resulting from a proper balance of challenge and individual skills. The flow experience is characterized by an altered sense of time and a loss of self-consciousness due to a narrow focus on the game. Sweetser and Wyeth [68] transferred this general idea of flow to digital games and developed the *GameFlow model* for evaluating player enjoyment. For that purpose, they synthesized current game evaluation heuristics from the field of usability with those from the field of user experience research. They merged different heuristics (each focusing on single game elements such as the interface, the gameplay or the mechanics) into one comprehensive model of player enjoyment. As result, they suggest eight interrelated core elements of *GameFlow*, namely

- concentration,
- challenge,
- skills,
- control,
- clear goals,
- feedback,
- immersion, and
- social interaction.

For each of those elements, they comprised a set of criteria for player enjoyment derived from game design heuristics. It is assumed that a game which supports all those criteria is most enjoyable [68].

Immersion and Presence. The constructs *immersion* and *presence* are often considered in game user research, as they describe the process of projecting one's thoughts into the game world and to immerse in the virtual environment and story. However, both terms are not uniformly defined, but often mixed up and sometimes even used synonymously [20].

Slater [65] presents an approach to disambiguate the concepts and defines *immersion* as the objective quality of an interactive system to deliver sensory cues to the human sensory system. That is to say, a system is more immersive if it occupies large parts of a person's perception. For instance, a system containing a head-mounted display and earphones shields a person's visual and auditory senses from stimuli of the real world and thus features higher immersion than an ordinary monitor display. *Presence*, in contrast, is described as the feeling of actually being in the virtual world, being part of it, interacting with it and perceiving it as real. It can be seen as a result of immersion, because high immersion is supposed to support higher feeling of presence [65].

As immersion and presence are both concepts that are not only important for games, but also in the larger context of virtual environments and tele-presence, a lot of approaches to operationalize and measure them can be found in the literature. As with the assessment of motivation and other facets of player experience, questionnaires are the commonly used methods to measure aspects related to presence and immersion. One example that has also been applied to games is the *Igroup Presence Questionnaire* (IPQ) [34]. It is used to assess the degree of presence, on four dimensions: *general presence, spatial presence, involvement* and *experienced realism*. Another popular questionnaire addressing presence is the *Presence Questionnaire (PQ)* by Witmer et al. [72]. Furthermore, it might also be interesting to assess individual differences of players regarding their interest and capability to immerse into a virtual world. For this purpose, the *Immersive Tendencies Questionnaire* (ITQ) [71] was developed, which includes questions regarding the general tendency of a person to immerse.

Social Presence. Besides the common concept of presence described above, which is mainly related to the physical gameworld, Takatalo et al. [70] argue that there is also the feeling of *social presence*, accounting for socially meaningful contexts of digital games. That social meaning does not only apply to multiplayer games, but more generally describes the feeling of being in a socially meaningful world (for instance elicited by non-player characters). The social presence construct is further divided into three components by Takatalo et al. [70]: *Social richness, social realism* and *co-presence*. With social richness they describe the degree to which a game is assigned certain social attributes such as being familiar or personal. Social realism refers to the similarity of in-game objects, events and behaviors with the ones the player is familiar to from the real world. Co-presence is defined as the sensation of being together and interacting with other persons (players or non-player characters) inside the game world.

Similarly, Biocca et al. [8] also elaborated on social presence and define it as the degree to which two (or more) persons are aware of each other (co-presence) and feel psychologically and behaviorally involved. Based on this concept, de Kort and colleagues [15] developed a self-report measure to assess social presence in digital games. The result is the *Social Presence in Gaming Questionnaire* (SPGQ) with three sub-scales: *Psychological Involvement – Empathy, Psychological Involvement – Negative Feelings*, and *Behavioral Engagement*. During the development of the questionnaire, de Kort et al. found that – in contrast to the concepts described above – co-presence should not be seen as a separate dimension, but that it instead relates to aspects of awareness and behavioral involvement, resulting in a scale the authors call behavioral engagement. Furthermore, the dimension psychological involvement was separated into empathy and negative feelings, thus accounting for positive and negative affect and feelings provoked by another social entity.

Another questionnaire that was recently developed and that tries to assess the relation between players in terms of social presence and related concepts is the *Competitive and Cooperative Presence in Gaming* scale (CCPIG) [33]. As the name indicates, it differentiates between competitive and cooperative gaming scenarios and is meant to be applied in multiplayer games. It assesses competitive social presence on the two dimensions awareness and engagement, while cooperative social presence is divided into perceived team cohesion and team involvement. Hence, if the interaction of players and their feelings related to each other have to investigated, this questionnaire is supposed to provide valuable insights and a proper operationalization of social presence.

Comprehensive Models of Player Experience. The aforementioned sub-dimensions of the player experience are not exclusive and do not represent all possible aspects. There is no consensus which dimensions constitute the overall player experience, but there are some comprehensive models that go even further into detail and distinguish some more dimensions. The purpose of those models is to gain a better understanding of player experience as a whole and also to make it measurable by defining sub-dimensions and concrete characteristics.

Accordingly, the two models described in the following both serve as the theoretical background for respective questionnaires that were developed to assess player experience as a comprehensive construct in experiments.

The first example is the *Presence-Involvement-Flow Framework (PIFF)* by Takatalo et al. [69]. It comprise all main aspects mentioned in different prior approaches and is built around the main constructs *presence, involvement* and *flow* (as its name already indicates). *Presence* is supposed to describe the intensity and extensity of the experience, and is subdivided into the concepts of physical presence and social presence, which in turn are subdivided into further subcomponents (quality of interaction, physical presence, attention, role engagement, co-presence and emotional arousal). *Involvement* is composed of the two factors importance and interest and describes the personal value (valence) and meaning (relevance) of the experience. Finally, seven subcomponents are related to the concept of flow: challenge, competence, playfulness, control, hedonic valence, impressiveness and enjoyment. Overall, this dimension is supposed to mainly describe the quality of player experience. This multidimensional model is based on literature review and a series of validating studies. The associated questionnaire is the Experimental Virtual Environment Experience Questionnaire-Game Pitk (EVEQ-GP), which is a very long questionnaire containing 180 items related to all of the sub-dimensions of the PIFF.

Another comprehensive model of player experience is the *Game Experience Model* by Poels et al. [56]. It is the result of a study based on focus group discussions and subsequent expert meetings, which were then combined with theoretical considerations. It defines nine main dimensions of player experience, namely enjoyment, flow, imaginative immersion, sensory immersion (comparable to our notion of presence), suspense, competence, negative affect, control, and social presence. The self-report scale belonging to this model of player experience is the *Game Experience Questionnaire* (GEQ) [36], which consists of a couple of questions for each of the eight dimensions *competence, sensory and imaginative immersion, flow, tension, challenge, negative affect* and *positive affect*. If the game under investigation is a multiplayer game or contains social entities, the GEQ is often combined with the SPQG (cf. section about social presence above). During the development of this questionnaire, the nine primary categories were further adapted: control is no dimension on its own anymore, and was integrated into the remaining ones.

In contrast to those comprehensive models, which define the constituents of player experience on a content-related level, Nacke et al. [53] have formulated the *Gameplay Experience Model*, which is a framework for the assessment of player experience and thus presents a more abstract view. The model emphasizes the importance of considering two taxonomical dimensions of gameplay, namely abstraction and time, and divides both of them into three layers resulting in a two-dimensional, three-layer gameplay experience model. The dimension of abstraction consists of the layers *Game System, Player* and *Context*. The game system itself is the most concrete layer and includes the apparent features of the game such as mechanics, interface and content. The player interacts with this system and constitutes a more abstract layer, as the individual experience consisting of thoughts and feelings is not entirely externally visible. Finally, the most abstract layer of the gameplay experience is the current context, as it does not only refer to the contemporary interaction but also includes prior experiences, memories, knowledge and anticipated consequences. According to Nacke et al., all three layers include complex processes and interact with each other, thereby determining the experience. The second dimension accounts for the fact that those processes are not static but may change as a function of time due to different contexts, player attributes or changes in the game system. Accordingly, the three layers of time in this model are past, present and future. The *Gameplay Experience Model* is especially informative for the evaluation of games, because it points out that the dimensions of time as well as the three components *game system*, *player*, and *context* have to be considered in order to obtain a comprehensive impression of the experience. Applied to serious games, this underlines that evaluation approaches should not only focus on the player, but also on the context in which the game is used, as well as on possible time effects [53].

Summarized, the concept of player experience and its sub-components provide the basis of game user research in general, and thus should be considered in the evaluation process of serious games as well. Though aspects like fun, flow, immersion, presence, and involvement are often just indirectly associated with the purpose or desired outcome of a serious game, insights regarding the experience of players are supposed to explain their reactions to the game and may also give reasons for unexpected outcomes.

3.3 Learning Outcomes

After having discussed the more general constructs regarding motivation and player experience, this section focuses on a concrete purpose that many serious games are supposed to serve: learning. It addresses the question of how the efficacy of learning games can be evaluated, i.e. how the learning outcome of a serious game can be measured. To test whether the players learn what they are supposed to learn is not an easy task, since learning is a complex process, which is hard to assess and quantify. The research field in psychology that is concerned with the objective measurement of mental capabilities offers a broad range of theories and results. A broad overview of psychometrics for measuring human abilities, also in educational contexts, as well as its underlying models and theories can be found in Kline [41]. A general introduction into the different fields of psychological assessment is provided by Goldstein [29].

The term *learning* does not only contain the acquisition of simple facts, but also the acquisition of other cognitive skills. For instance, Connolly [12] mentions several possible learning outcomes for game-based learning:

- the improvement in knowledge acquisition which might be procedural, declarative, or general knowledge,
- the formation of meta-cognitive strategies,
- and the improvement in the formation of skills.

Accordingly, it has to be stated clearly what learning outcomes are intended by game designers in order to be able to find appropriate operationalizations.

The classical experiment design for evaluating the learning outcome of a serious game is the pre-post-test-design [10,19]. In this experimental design, participants are randomly divided into two groups of which the one is going to play the serious game of interest (treatment group), and the other will be taught by another comparable instruction technique (control group). The skills of each participant are tested before and after playing the game (or after getting the different instructions, respectively). This technique aims at measuring the acquisition of skills by measuring the difference of skills before and after playing the game. In order to analyze whether the knowledge gain is caused by the game and not by other reasons, the players knowledge gain is compared with the knowledge gain of the participants in the control group. The treatment of the control group is crucial for measuring a learning effect and has to be selected carefully and well-conceived [28]. For instance, the basic learning content should be similar in both groups to ensure that theoretically both groups have the same possibilities to access and acquire knowledge about it. Detailed information about experiment design will not be discussed here, but can be found in the chapter about experimental design in this book. In general, designing questions or tasks for the pre-test and the post-test is challenging. Theoretical background for test development can be found in Guilford [32]. Depending on which skill improvement is aimed at in the game, there are standardized and validated tests that might be appropriate to use. In the context of general educational assessment, there are for example the Collegiate Assessment of Academic Proficiency (CAAP)[1], the Collegiate Learning Assessment (CLA)[2], or the ETS Proficiency Profile[3]. Those tests are based on core skill areas and knowledge and supposed to help institutions to assess the general skill level of their students.

Additionally, it is important to be aware of the evaluation model of Kirkpatrick [39], which states that evaluation can take place on four different levels. An evaluation can measure whether the players liked the game (reaction level), to which extent the players improved their skills through playing the game, and can apply them in the game environment (level of learning), whether the players are able to transfer the gained skills outside the game environment (level of behavior), and how playing the game had an effect on the system in which the game was deployed (level of results). Hence, each of the levels needs to be evaluated in a different way.

There are several metà-studies of evaluations of serious games regarding learning [11,28,54]. The study of O'Neil et al. for example reviews all peer-reviewed papers in which learning outcomes in video games for adults are evaluated by quantitative and/or qualitative methods [54]. O'Neil et al. found that out of the 19 available studies, only three evaluated learning outcomes on level three or four of Kirkpatrick's model. Girard et al. [28] present a survey of the

---

[1] http://www.act.org/content/act/en.html.
[2] http://cae.org/participating-institutions/cla-references.
[3] https://www.ets.org/proficiencyprofile/about.

effectiveness of serious games for learning and conclude that the majority of analyzed games is evaluated by a classical pre-post-test-design of which some include a second post-test in order to measure long-term effects.

While the previous paragraphs describe experiment designs in order to evaluate the learning efficacy of a serious game, the following paragraph presents methods which can be used to concretely operationalize learning and effectively measure the learning outcome of a game. Maki [49] classifies the methods by which the learning outcome of students can be measured into two categories: direct and indirect methods. Direct methods ask students to "represent or demonstrate their learning or produce work so that observers can assess how well students' work or responses fit institution or program-level expectations". As examples for direct methods she mentions responses to questions, interactions within group problem solving, or observable performances. This also includes all kind of (standardized) tests of the particular skill, the players' performance in the game or – if in an educational context – their grades in assignments or exams, which follow the use of the serious game. Bellotti lists several tools for measuring players' game performance [5]. However, Chin et al. note that the usage of exam grades as assessment data is often not a good idea since assessment and grading are driven by conflicting motives [11]. While these methods take place after playing the game, there are also direct methods which take place during the game play and which give further insights. These include think-aloud-protocols, observations of the player by the instructor or video-recordings.

Indirect methods capture students' perceptions of their learning and include all measures in which the players are asked for their perceived learning outcome. Maki [49] mentions inventories, surveys, questionnaires, interviews, and focus group meetings as examples. It is clear that the players' self-reports of their learning efficacy are subjective and might over- or underestimate their actual learning performance. Nevertheless, accompanied by results of direct methods, indirect methods give valuable insights into the students' learning process, interpretations, and perceptions in order to improve the learning process and increase the learning outcome. Maki [49] is a good source for more information of direct and indirect methods as well as for an overview of standardized tests.

The described assessment methods either take place at the end of the learning process (and are summarized by summative evaluation methods) or are implemented and presented throughout the entire learning process (formative evaluation methods) [62]. Formative evaluation can give valuable insights in the players' learning process, however, it is desirable that the assessment methods do not disrupt the game flow. For this reason, assessment methods are incorporated in the game environment in a way that the game experience is not affected. Assessment methods which are "virtually invisible" for the player are called *stealth assessment* by Shute et al. [64]. An overview of embedded assessment in learning games and how game log data can be used for analyzing the learning process of a player can be found in the work of Plass et al. [55], Shute et al. [64], and Loh et al. [47]. Stealth assessment is particularly useful in the assessment of serious games for learning since assessment can be part of the game experience and allows to give feedback to the user while playing in order to improve the learning process and increase the learning outcome.

3.4 Health and Well-Being

Besides learning, the promotion of health and well-being is one of the biggest application fields of serious games [26]. According to the World Health Organization, *health* is defined as a state of "complete physical, mental and social well-being and not merely the absence of disease or infirmity" [9] (p. 365). Serious games that somehow address the physical or mental health of players or health-related behavior are commonly called serious games for health or shortly health games (cf. the chapter on serious games for health in this book for a comprehensive overview and discussion of characteristics, design approaches and challenges). There are many aspects beside the purpose that differentiate those games from other serious games, like particularly sensitive target groups, specific risks and concerns as well as the involvement of various health-related disciplines. Furthermore, there is a special demand for verifiable effects: It has to be ensured that the game does not have any negative side effects like overstrain, and is at least as effective as any alternate intervention, because otherwise health or recovery may be at risk, especially in case of ill target groups. The goals of serious games for health are manifold and include many different approaches and purposes that are pursued by the games. They may:

- promote movement and physical exercise by giving reason, motivation and/or instructions,
- promote adherence to medical treatment such as the intake of pills by giving information and/or changing attitudes,
- promote healthy behavior like the abandonment of drugs and deleterious food,
- reduce negative thoughts and feelings and improve stress management in various situations (psychological components of health),
- provide knowledge about a disease or health-related issues, or
- support other medical interventions and procedures, e.g. distract from pain or frightening situations.

Depending on these goals the measures that are appropriate to evaluate the effectiveness of the game have to be chosen. As health as such is a highly complex construct impossible to assess directly, the main challenge is to identify sensible indicators of health and find ways to assess those. This will allow for drawing conclusions about how the game effects a player's state. Hence, the main question is what can be measured. As the change of attitudes, which is one of many possibly intended effects of health games, will also be discussed in the following section, this section will mainly focus on the assessment of physical attributes and indicators of health on the one hand, and of perceived well-being on the other.

Indicators of Physical Health and Healthy Behavior. As physical health is inherently related to bodily responses and physiological reactions, it is standing to reason to use physiological measurement methods like the ones described in Sect. 2.1 to assess health indicators and to investigate the effectiveness of a health game. Similar to games for learning, a pre-post-test-design should be applied in most cases, in order to prove that the game affects the players' health. One sub-category of serious games for health are so-called exertion games or fitness games. Their purpose is to motivate players to physically exercise or to show increased physical activity in order to improve their overall constitution. To operationalize health improvement in those cases, classical medical tests to test stamina and resilience, like stress electrocardiograms (electrodes are attached to the participant's upper body and an ECG is recorded while he or she is riding an exercise bicycle). Furthermore, reaction tests can be applied or indicators like weight and the body-mass-index can be easily assessed.

Some serious games also serve the purpose of increasing medical adherence. Often, the intake of medicine (or its denial) can be tracked by blood analysis or saliva tests. In those cases, the specific indicators related to the medication should be identified and measured (see the popular evaluation of the serious game Re-Mission for children diagnosed with cancer for an example [38]). Of course self-report measures can be used for assessing adherence as well, though it has to be considered that participants may lie if they feel that they did not behave the way they should. See [23] for some guideline to the design of self-report measures regarding medical adherence.

If the serious game is meant to complement medical treatment, that is to say used as a therapy instrument, researchers may use standard evaluation methods, design features and measurement instruments of new medical therapies to prove the game's clinical impact. This was for instance done during the evaluation of the game Re-Mission [38], which is an interesting example of a comprehensive evaluation.

Besides direct physiological measures, game metrics also offer good opportunities to evaluate health games in some cases. If a serious game addresses a very specific part of physical health, its efficacy is best to be measured by assessing a player's performance on a given task over a certain period of time and check the results for significant improvements. For instance, if a game is supposed to improve a person's manual fine motor skills after being handicapped by stroke by training small and precise movements of the fingers/hand, then the accuracy and speed of participants should be tracked by the gaming system.

Indicators of Well-Being. Apart from direct physical consequences, games for health can also focus on improving a person's perceived health and well-being. Well-being is a complex and blurry concept. According to Dodge et al. [18], who considered and analyzed different approaches towards well-being, the term well-being describes a state in which "individuals have the psychological, social and physical resources they need to meet a particular psychological, social and/or physical challenge" (p.230). As this is very difficult to operationalize in terms of objective measures, aspects of well-being are often assessed by self-reports (see e.g. [37] for an overview).

One construct that is closely related to well-being in the case of ill persons is self-efficacy towards the disease [38]. It describes the feeling of being able to cope with the current situation and the perception of having a chance to overcome the situation. A high perceived self-efficacy is assumed to be beneficial for recovery and thus can be addressed by health games as well, like in the game Re-Mission [38]. Self-efficacy is also often operationalized by using questionnaires. In this context, Bandura proposes a guide for constructing self-efficacy scales related to certain situations [2].

Stress. Finally, two aspects that are quite similar and both related to physical health and psychological well-being, are stress and anxiety. Those concepts are relevant to serious games for health as well, as their purpose can also be to reduce stress (or at least not to increase it). An established questionnaire for assessing stress is the *State-Trait-Anxiety Inventory* (STAI) [66], which is supposed to measure both trait and state anxiety and thus is considered to be an indicator for distress. Moreover, stress has been shown to be related to several physiological processes as well and thus can also be measured by psycho-physiological measurement methods. Here, blood pressure, heart rate, heart rate variability (HRV), skin conductance, cortisol measures as well as the pupil diameter have been used to detect stress levels in several studies [63].

3.5   Attitudes

Attitudes are the last evaluation construct that should shortly be discussed here, as some serious games also aim at changing attitudes of the players and their related behavior. An attitude in general is the evaluation of persons, objects or ideas with favor or disfavor [1]. Attitudes can mainly result from cognitive, affective or behavioral processes and thus are supposed to be modifiable to some degree by offering new cognitive, emotional or behavioral input [1]. However, the operationalization of attitudes is challenging, because they are very individual and subjective. Sometimes, people tend to hide their real attitude towards something if they feel some social pressure or discomfort. Hence, self-reports as well as observations can be applied but are prone to bias and social desirability effects.

As attitudes are an important object under investigation in the broad field of social psychology, researchers have invented more creative techniques to assess attitudes, which can also be applied to serious games evaluation. Those methods are projective, as they are indirect measures and participants are not aware that their attitude is measured. One classical test is the *Implicit Association Test* (IAT) [31]. Broadly speaken, in this test participants have to rate two different concepts (e.g. "junk food" and "vegetables") regarding a certain attribute (e.g. "pleasant"). Then the time they need to react is measured and indicates whether participants think the concepts fit the attribute or not. The whole setting of the IAT, which is too extensive to be described here, is described in [31] and worth a consideration if attitudes should be measured.

4   Summary of Concrete Measurement Methods

To conclude this chapter about operationalization and measurement methods, we present an overview of all the concrete questionnaires mentioned in the text

Table 2. Overview of taxonomies and questionnaires discussed in this chapter, which can be used to assess different evaluation constructs.

Evaluation construct	Name of questionnaire	Sub-dimensions/ Concepts	References
Player experience	Experimental Virtual Environment Experience Questionnaire-Game Pitk (EVEQ-GP)	Presence, Involvement, Flow	Takatalo et al. [69]
Player experience	Game Experience Questionnaire (GEQ)	Competence, Sensory and Imaginative Immersion, Flow, Tension, Challenge, Negative Affect, Positive Affect	IJsselsteijn et al. [36]
Flow	GameFlow Model Heuristics	Concentration, Challenge, Skills, Control, Clear Goals, Feedback, Immersion, Social Interaction	Sweetser and Wyeth [68]
Presence	Igroup Presence Questionnaire (IPQ)	general presence, spatial presence, involvement, experienced realism	Igroup Presence Consortium [34]
Presence	Presence Questionnaire (PQ)	ooehm	Witmer et al. [72]
Immersion presence	Immersive Tendencies Questionnaire (ITQ)	Focus, Involvement, Emotion, Games	UQO Cyberpsychology Lab [71]
Social presence	Competitive and Cooperative Presence in Gaming scale (CCPIG)	competitive social presence (awareness, engagement), cooperative social presence (perceived team cohesion, team involvement)	Hudson et al. [33]
Social presence	Social Presence in Gaming Questionnaire (SPGQ)	Psychological Involvement – Empathy, Psychological Involvement – Negative Feelings, Behavioral Engagement	De Kort et al. [15]
Personality	Big Five Inventory (short) (BFI-10)	Openness to experiences, Conscientiousness, Extraversion, Agreeableness, Neuroticism	Rammstedt et al. [57]
Player taxonomy	Bartle's Player Taxonomy	Achievers, Explorers, Socializers, Killers	Bartle [3,4]
Player taxonomy	Yee's Player Taxonomy	Achievement, Immersion, Social	Yee [73]
Player taxonomy	BrainHex	Seeker, Survivor, Daredevil, Master- mind, Conqueror, Socialiser, Achiever	Nacke et al. [52]
Stress/ Anxiety	State-Trait-Anxiety Inventory	State Anxiety, Trait Anxiety	Spielberger [66]

before and assume this collection to be useful for the planning and conduction of future evaluations of serious games or games in general (see Table 2). Moreover, a short list of further reading recommendations is provided.

References

1. Aronson, E., Wilson, T.D., Akert, R.M.: Social Psychology, 7th edn. Pearson, Boston (2010). Global edn
2. Bandura, A.: Guide for constructing self-efficacy scales. In: Pajares, F., Urdan, T.C. (eds.) Self-Efficacy Beliefs of Adolescents, pp. 307–337. Information Age Publishing, Charlotte (2006)
3. Bartle, R.: Hearts, clubs, diamonds, spades: players who suit muds. J. Virtual Environ. **1**(1) (1996). http://mud.co.uk/richard/hcds.htm
4. Bartle, R.A.: Designing Virtual Worlds. New Riders Pub., Indianapolis (2004)
5. Bellotti, F., Kapralos, B., Lee, K., Moreno-Ger, P., Berta, R.: Assessment in and of serious games: an overview. Adv. Hum. Comput. Interact. **2013**, 1–11 (2013)
6. Bernhaupt, R. (ed.): Evaluating User Experience in Games: Concepts and Methods. Human-Computer Interaction Series. Springer, London, New York (2010)
7. Bernhaupt, R.: User experience evaluation in entertainment. In: Bernhaupt, R. (ed.) Evaluating User Experience in Games. Human-ComputerInteraction Series, pp. 3–7. Springer, London, New York (2010)
8. Biocca, F., Harms, C., Burgoon, J.: Towards a more robust theory and measure of social presence: Review and suggested criteria. Presence Teleoper. Virtual Environ. **12**(5), 456–480 (2003)
9. Bircher, J., Kuruvilla, S.: Defining health by addressing individual, social, and environmental determinants: new opportunities for health care and public health. J. Public Health Policy **35**(3), 363–386 (2014). http://www.palgrave-journals.com/jphp/journal/v35/n3/pdf/jphp.201419a.pdf
10. Campbell, D.T., Stanley, J.C., Gage, N.L.: Experimental and Quasi-Experimental Designs for Research. Ravenio books, New York (2015)
11. Chin, J., Dukes, R., Gamson, W.: Assessment in simulation and gaming a review of the last 40 years. Simul. Gaming **40**(4), 553–568 (2009)
12. Connolly, T., Stansfield, M., Hainey, T.: Towards the development of a games-based learning evaluation framework. In: Games-Based Learning Advancements for Multisensory Human Computer Interfaces: Techniques and Effective Practices (2009)
13. Csikszentmihalyi, M.: Flow: The Psychology of Optimal Experience. Harper Perennial, New York (1990)
14. De Kort, Y.A.W., Ijsselsteijn, W.A.: People, places, and play: player experience in a socio-spatial context. Comput. Entertain. **6**(2), 18 (2008)
15. De Kort, Y.A.W., Ijsselsteijn, W.A., Poels, K.: Digital games as social presence technology: development of the social presence in gaming questionnaire (SPGQ). In: Proceedings of the 10th Annual International Workshop on Presence, pp. 195–203 (2007)
16. Dignan, A.: Game frame: Using Games as a Strategy for Success. Free Press, New York (2011). 1st free press hardcover edn
17. Dillon, R.: On The Way to Fun: An Emotion-Based Approach to Successful Game Design. A K Peters, Natick (2010)
18. Dodge, R., Daly, A., Huyton, J., Sanders, L.: The challenge of defining wellbeing. Int. J. Wellbeing **2**(3), 222–235 (2012)
19. Dugard, P., Todman, J.: Analysis of pre-test-post-test control group designs in educational research. Educ. Psychol. **15**(2), 181–198 (1995)

20. Ermi, L., Mäyrä, F.: Fundamental components of the gameplay experience: Analysing immersion. In: DiGRA 2005, Proceedings of the 2005 DiGRA International Conference: Changing Views: Worlds in Play (2005). http://www.digra.org/wp-content/uploads/digital-library/06276.41516.pdf

21. Fernandez, A.: Fun experience with digital games: a model proposition. In: Leino, O., Wirman, H., Fernandez, A. (eds.) Extending Experiences, pp. 181–190. Lapland University Press, Rovaniemi (2008)

22. Ferrara, J.: Playful Design: Creating Game Experiences in Everyday Interfaces. Rosenfeld Media, Brooklyn (2012)

23. Garfield, S., Clifford, S., Eliasson, L., Barber, N., Willson, A.: Suitability of measures of self-reported medication adherence for routine clinical use: a systematic review. BMC Med. Res. Methodol. **11**, 149 (2011)

24. Garris, R., Ahlers, R., Driskell, J.E.: Games, motivation, and learning: a research and practice model. Simul. Gaming **33**(4), 441–467 (2002)

25. Gee, J.P.: What video games have to teach us about learning and literacy. Comput. Entertain. **1**(1), 20 (2003)

26. Gekker, A.: Health games. In: Ma, M., Oliveira, M.F., Baalsrud Hauge, J. (eds.) SGDA 2014. LNCS, vol. 8778, pp. 13–30. Springer, Heidelberg (2012). doi:10.1007/978-3-642-33687-4_2

27. Gill, P., Stewart, K., Treasure, E., Chadwick, B.: Methods of data collection in qualitative research: interviews and focus groups. Br. Dent. J. **204**(6), 291–295 (2008)

28. Girard, C., Ecalle, J., Magnan, A.: Serious games as new educational tools: how effective are they? a meta-analysis of recent studies. J. Comput. Assist. Learn. **29**(3), 207–219 (2013)

29. Goldstein, G., Hersen, M.: Handbook of Psychological Assessment. Elsevier, Hoboken (2000)

30. Goodwin, C.J., Goodwin, K.A.: Research in Psychology: Methods and Design, 7th edn. Wiley, Hoboken (2012)

31. Greenwald, A.G., McGhee, D.E., Schwartz, J.L.: Measuring individual differences in implicit cognition: the implicit association test. J. Person. Soc. Psychol. **74**(6), 1464–1480 (1998)

32. Guilford, J.P.: Psychometric Methods, 2nd edn. McGraw-Hill, New York (1954)

33. Hudson, M., Cairns, P.: Measuring social presence in team-based digital games. In: Riva, G., Waterworth, J., Murray, D. (eds.) Interacting with Presence: HCI and the Sense of Presence in Computer-Mediated Environments. DE GRUYTER OPEN, Warsaw, Poland (2014)

34. Igroup Project Consortium: Igroup presence questionnaire (ipq)

35. IJsselsteijn, W., de Kort, Y., Poels, K., Jurgelionis, A., Bellotti, F: Characterising and measuring user experiences in digital games. In: ACE 2007 International Conference on Advances in Computer Entertainment Technology, Workshop 'Methods for Evaluating Games - How to measure Usability and User Experience in Games' (2007)

36. Ijsselsteijn, W.A., De Kort, Y.A.W., Poels, K.: The game experience questionnaire: Development of a self-report measure to assess the psychological impact of digital games. Manuscript in preparation

37. Kahneman, D., Krueger, A.B.: Developments in the measurement of subjective well-being. J. Econ. Perspect. **20**(1), 3–24 (2006)

38. Kato, P.M., Cole, S.W., Bradlyn, A.S., Pollock, B.H.: A video game improves behavioral outcomes in adolescents and young adults with cancer: a randomized trial. Pediatrics **122**(2), e305–e317 (2008). 18676516

39. Kirkpatrick, D.L.: Evaluating Training Programs. Tata McGraw-Hill Education, San Francisco (1975)
40. Kivikangas, J.M., Chanel, G., Cowley, B., Ekman, I., Salminen, M., Järvelä, S., Ravaja, N.: A review of the use of psychophysiological methods in game research. J. Gaming Virtual World **3**(3), 181–199 (2011)
41. Kline, P.: Psychometrics and Psychology. Academy Press, Washington, D.C. (1979)
42. Koster, R.: A Theory of Fun for Game Design, 2nd edn. O'Reilly Media Inc., Sebastopol (2014)
43. Krosnick, J.A., Presser, S.: Question and questionnaire design. In: Marsden, P.V. (ed.) Handbook of Survey Research. Emerald Group Publishing, Bingley (2010)
44. Landers, R.N., Bauer, K.N.: Quantitative methods and analyses for the study of players and their behaviour. In: Lankoski, P., Björk, S. (eds.) Game Research Methods, pp. 151–174. ETC Press, Pittsburgh (2015)
45. Law, E.L.C., Roto, V., Hassenzahl, M., Vermeeren, A.P., Kort, J.: Understanding, scoping and defining user experience. In: Olsen, D.R., Arthur, R.B., Hinckley, K., Morris, M.R., Hudson, S., Greenberg, S. (eds.) The SIGCHI Conference, p. 719 (2009)
46. Lazzaro, N.: Why we play games: Four keys to more emotion without story (2004)
47. Loh, C.S., Anantachai, A., Byun, J., Lenox, J.: Assessing what players learned in serious games: in situ data collection, information trails, and quantitative analysis. In: 10th International Conference on Computer Games: AI, Animation, Mobile, Educational & Serious Games (CGAMES 2007), pp. 25–28 (2007)
48. Loh, C.S., Sheng, Y., Ifenthaler, D. (eds.): Serious Games Analytics: Methodologies for Performance Measurement, Assessment, and Improvement. Springer, Heidelberg (2015)
49. Maki, P.L.: Assessing for Learning: Building a Sustainable Commitment Across the Institution. Stylus Publishing, LLC, Menlo Park (2012)
50. Mandryk, R.L., Inkpen, K.M.: Physiological indicators for the evaluation of co-located collaborative play. In: Herbsleb, J., Olson, G. (eds.) The 2004 ACM Conference, p. 102 (2004)
51. McAuley, E., Duncan, T., Tammen, V.V.: Psychometric properties of the intrinsic motivation inventory in a competitive sport setting: a confirmatory factor analysis. Res. Q. Exerc. Sport **60**(1), 48–58 (1989)
52. Nacke, L.E., Bateman, C., Mandryk, R.L.: BrainHex: preliminary results from a neurobiological gamer typology survey. In: Anacleto, J.C., Fels, S., Graham, N., Kapralos, B., Saif El-Nasr, M., Stanley, K. (eds.) ICEC 2011. LNCS, vol. 6972, pp. 288–293. Springer, Heidelberg (2011). doi:10.1007/978-3-642-24500-8_31
53. Nacke, L.E.: Affective ludology: scientific measurement of user experience in interactive entertainment, Blekinge Institute of Technology doctoral dissertation series, vol. 2009: 04. School of Computing, Blekinge Institute of Technology, Karlskrona (2010)
54. O'Neil, H.F., Wainess, R., Baker, E.L.: Classification of learning outcomes: evidence from the computer games literature. Cirriculum J. **16**(4), 455–474 (2005)
55. Plass, J.L., Homer, B.D., Kinzer, C.K., Chang, Y.K., Frye, J., Kaczetow, W., Isbister, K., Perlin, K.: Metrics in simulations and games for learning. In: El-Nasr, M.S., Drachen, A., Canossa, A. (eds.) Game Analytics, pp. 697–729. Springer, Heidelberg (2013)
56. Poels, K., de Kort, Y., Ijsselsteijn, W.: It is always a lot of fun! In: Kapralos, B., Katchabaw, M., Rajnovich, J. (eds.) The 2007 Conference, p. 83 (2007)
57. Rammstedt, B., Kemper, C.J., Klein, M.C., Beierlein, C., Kovaleva, A.: A short scale for assessing the big five dimensions of personality

58. Ravaja, N., Saari, T., Turpeinen, M., Laarni, J., Salminen, M., Kivikangas, M.: Spatial presence and emotions during video game playing: does it matter with whom you play? Presence Teleoper. Virtual Environ. 15(4), 381–392 (2006)
59. Rheinberg, F.: Motivation, Kohlhammer-Urban-Taschenbücher, vol. 555. Kohlhammer, Stuttgart, 7, aktualisierte aufl. edn. (2008)
60. Ryan, D.: Intrinsic and extrinsic motivations: classic definitions and new directions. Contemp. Educ. Psychol. 25(1), 54–67 (2000)
61. Ryan, R.M., Rigby, C.S., Przybylski, A.: The motivational pull of video games: a self-determination theory approach. Motiv. Emot. 30(4), 344–360 (2006)
62. Sadler, D.: Formative assessment and the design of instructional systems. Instr. Sci. 18(2), 119–144 (1989). http://dx.doi.org/10.1007/BF00117714
63. Sano, A., Picard, R.W.: Stress recognition using wearable sensors and mobile phones. In: 2013 Humaine Association Conference on Affective Computing and Intelligent Interaction (ACII), pp. 671–676 (2013)
64. Shute, V.J., Ventura, M., Bauer, M., Zapata-Rivera, D.: Melding the power of serious games and embedded assessment to monitor and foster learning. Serious Games Mech. Effects 2, 295–321 (2009)
65. Slater, M.: A note on presence terminology. Presence Connect 3(3), 1–5 (2003)
66. Spielberger, C.D.: State-trait anxiety inventory. In: Weiner, I.B., Craighead, W.E. (eds.) The Corsini Encyclopedia of Psychology. Wiley, Hoboken (2010)
67. Strube, M.J., Newman, L.C.: Psychometrics. In: Cacioppo, J., Tassinary, L.G., Berntson, G.G. (eds.) The Handbook of Psychophysiology, pp. 789–811. Cambridge University Press, Cambridge (2007)
68. Sweetser, P., Wyeth, P.: Gameflow: a model for evaluating player enjoyment in games. Comput. Entertain. 3(3), 3 (2005)
69. Takatalo, J., Häkkinen, J., Kaistinen, J., Nyman, G.: Presence, involvement, and flow in digital games. In: Bernhaupt, R. (ed.) Evaluating User Experience in Games, pp. 23–46. Human-Computer Interaction Series, Springer, London, New York (2010)
70. Takatalo, J., Häkkinen, J., Komulainen, J., Särkelä, H., Nyman, G.: Involvement and presence in digital gaming. In: Mørch, A., Morgan, K., Bratteteig, T., Ghosh, G., Svanaes, D. (eds.) The 4th Nordic Conference, pp. 393–396 (2006)
71. UQO Cyberpsychology Lab: Immersive tendencies questionnaire (itq) (2004)
72. Witmer, B.G., Singer, M.J.: Measuring presence in virtual environments: a presence questionnaire. Presence Teleoper. Virtual Environ. 7(3), 225–240 (1998)
73. Yee, N.: Motivations for play in online games. Cyberpsychol. Behav. 9(6), 772–775 (2006). The impact of the Internet, multimedia and virtual reality on behavior and society

Personalized and Adaptive Serious Games

Alexander Streicher[1](✉) and Jan D. Smeddinck[2]

[1] Fraunhofer IOSB, Karlsruhe, Germany
alexander.streicher@iosb.fraunhofer.de
[2] Digital Media Lab, TZI, University of Bremen, Bremen, Germany
smeddinck@tzi.de

Abstract. Personalization and adaptivity can promote motivated usage, increased user acceptance, and user identification in serious games. This applies to heterogeneous user groups in particular, since they can benefit from customized experiences that respond to the individual traits of the players. In the context of games, adaptivity describes the automatic adaptation of game elements, i.e., of content, user interfaces, game mechanics, game difficulty, etc., to customize or personalize the interactive experience. Adaptation processes follow an adaptive cycle, changing a deployed system to the needs of its users. They can work with various techniques ranging from simple threshold-based parameter adjustment heuristics to complex evolving user models that are continuously updated over time. This chapter provides readers with an understanding of the motivation behind using adaptive techniques in serious games and presents the core challenges around designing and implementing such systems. Examples of how adaptability and adaptivity may be put into practice in specific application scenarios, such as motion-based games for health, or personalized learning games, are presented to illustrate approaches to the aforementioned challenges. We close with a discussion of the major open questions and avenues for future work.

Keywords: Adaptivity · Educational learning games · Games for health · Intelligent tutoring systems · ITS · AI

1 Introduction

Serious games can be wearing for the users when activities are repetitive or redundant, or when the games present an imbalance of challenge relative to the skill level of the players. An example for educational games is when a player already has reliable knowledge on a certain topic, e.g., relativity theory, yet still has to complete a whole introductory level on this topic. This could be streneous for the user and could lead to impatience with the game. An adaptive game, however, can react to the player and the respective individual prior experience or background by offering context-adaptive modifications, e.g., in the present example a shortcut to skip the introductory level.

Personalized and adaptive serious games offer great opportunities for a large range of potential application areas, since they can promote motivated usage,

© Springer International Publishing AG 2016
R. Dörner et al. (Eds.): Entertainment Computing and Serious Games, LNCS 9970, pp. 332–377, 2016.
DOI: 10.1007/978-3-319-46152-6_14

user acceptance, and user identification within and outside of the games. Potential application areas range from general learning games to games for health, training, and games for specific target groups such as children with dyslexia or people with Parkinson's disease. Examples for motion-based serious games for health are the so-called exergames, such as *ErgoActive* and *BalanceFit* for prevention and rehabilitation [38]. Their promise lies in motivating players to perform exercises that might otherwise be perceived as dull, repetitive, strenuous, etc. However, since personal differences with regard to physical and gaming abilities vary notably amongst the players, especially with specific heterogeneous target groups as mentioned above, providing a personalized experience is crucial in order to facilitate achieving the targeted positive outcomes.

Personalized *learning* games, as a further example, could offer all learners from a heterogeneous user group the possibility to make progress in a motivating and rewarding manner, and offer increased chances and a more equal basis regarding individual preparation for standardized expected learning outcomes, such as passing an exam. The following often cited anonymous[1] quote which underlines the necessity for qualified individualized assessment when it comes to heterogeneity is in-line with the basic promise of adaptive e-learning:

> *Everybody is a genius. But if you judge a fish by its ability to climb a tree, it will live its whole life believing that it is stupid. (Anonymous (see Footnote 1))*

In predefined, static (software) systems, an extensive adaptation to individual user potentials and needs is typically not possible, because these systems can only act within their predefined limits. Therefore, when talking about personalized and adaptive games, one often thinks of games which actually can adapt - or be adapted - beyond a limited set of predefined settings through an intelligently acting engine. At this point, reference is often made to intelligent games and Artificial Intelligence (AI). However, despite remarkable progress in AI in recent years, as evidenced by projects such as the Human Brain Project [57] and prominent advances in deep learning with neural networks [53], adding adaptivity or personalization features to serious games in a fully automated manner (e.g., automatically producing adequate content for an individual player of a learning game without employing predefined manually selected sets or parametrized collections) is not yet easily feasible.

The building blocks of modern artificial intelligence, such as machine learning and data mining techniques are, however, beginning to play an important role in the development of adaptive and personalized serious games, since the digital nature of serious games allows for recording and analyzing usage data. The possibility to monitor interactions is the foundation of new research fields like game analytics or, in the educational context, learning analytics and educational data mining. Furthermore, such data could be used to synthesize objective

---

[1] Whilst this "But if you judge a fish..." saying is often quoted as originating from famous physicist Albert Einstein, there is no substantive evidence that Einstein really made this statement [68].

information about the state and progress of a user regarding the serious aim of a game (e.g., progress on English vocabulary while exercising).

In order to allow these potential benefits to unfold, players must remain engaged over prolonged periods of time. This requires adequate game user experience design which must match the player type, play style, and preferences of as many users as possible. In addition to this requirement, which can also be stated for general game development, serious games must consider the success of the desired serious outcome, which requires further careful balancing. In many cases, user-centered iterative design and a small number of predefined difficulty modes for manual adaptation (such as "easy", "medium" and "hard") do not provide enough flexibility. Additional manual settings can be made available, via settings interfaces, to allow for a more personalized experience. However, players do not always want to interact with manual settings and they may interfere with the player experience by, e.g., breaking the magic circle [46]. Automatic adaptivity can reduce the potential negative impact of extensive manual adaptability options by automatically tuning games to optimize and personalize game experiences as well as to personalize interactions regarding the serious outcome.

For instance, digital game-based learning systems could utilize the learners' intrinsic motivation for interaction and learning to keep them motivated and to ultimately increase the learning outcome. Dynamic adaptive systems can help with achieving these goals by adapting the educational games to the knowledge level, skill, and experience of the users. Techniques for personalization can adjust the content and interaction schemes of virtual environments to make them more attractive to the users. Digital game-based learning systems must consider the heterogeneity of the users and their varying knowledge levels, cultural backgrounds, usage surroundings, skills, etc. In a well-defined and controlled environment, the interaction schemes could be very homogeneous and modeled in a deterministic fashion. For learning games this is usually not the case, because everyone tends to learn differently. In the real world, one-to-one tutoring or well-guided group learning that respect the heterogeneous properties of groups of learners and individual learners can arguably produce the best educational outcomes. Thus, targeting to replicate the customization and personalization present in these antetype scenarios in the development of serious games appears a reasonable pursuit. Moving towards that goal, however, requires advanced adaptable and adaptive techniques, since the optimal setup cannot be determined prior to situated use.

For the example of adaptive digital game-based learning systems is that in current systems, little or no concepts for adaptivity of educational techniques and content to the learners' needs exist. Didactic adaptivity needs didactic models based on learning theories, e.g., behaviorism, constructivism, cognitivism, etc. [96]. For *Intelligent Tutoring Systems* (ITS) such models have already been created [96]. Ideally, these models would be designed in a generic, interoperable way to allow for transfer to other ITS. The transfer of mature ITS models to virtual environments seems to be the next logical step when thinking about adaptive game systems [40, 92].

However, the development of such adaptive, or partially (automatically) adaptive and partially (manually) adaptable systems is not trivial, as the approach comes with a broad range of challenges. In the remainder of this chapter we will provide a more detailed overview on the general objectives of adaptivity based on initial terms and definitions, together with a discussion of the main challenges. These challenges encompass, but are not limited to, cold-start problems and co-adaptation. General approaches to implementations as well as two implementation scenarios (game-based learning and games for health) are presented to provide a structured discussion of specific implementation challenges. We will close with an overview of the most pressing open research questions and indicate directions for future work.

1.1 Chapter Overview

This chapter is structured as follows.

Introduction. The introduction (Sect. 1) gives a short overview on basic adaptivity principles and defines the scope and objectives. Furthermore, to differentiate the scope of dynamic artificial adaptivity, the introduction also includes some remarks on the broadly used term *Artificial Intelligence* (AI).

State-of-the-Art. Section 2 on the state-of-the-art provides the reader with starting points on the topic in general as well as with references to distinct work and current research topics.

Adaptation. Section 3 introduces the general principles of adaptation towards personalized and adaptive serious games. This includes a clarification on the terms personalization, customization, adaptation, and adaptivity. Secondly, we differentiate between the concepts behind each of these terms and bring them into an alignment with the general topic of this chapter.

Games for Health. A manifestation of the adaptation concepts is provided along the example of adaptive motion-based games for health (Sect. 4).

Application Examples. Subsequently, applications of some of the presented methods, principles and techniques are presented in examplary use-cases from learning games and games for health (Sect. 5).

Challenges. Personalization and adaptivity in games is a young research area that is difficult to aptly define due to the large number of involved disciplines. Accordingly, the sections on technical challenges (Sect. 6) and research questions (Sect. 7) mark directions for future research.

Conclusion. This chapter finishes with a conclusion (Sect. 8) and gives recommendations for further reading (Sect. "Further Reading").

1.2 Scope of this Chapter

This chapter aims at providing readers with an initial understanding of the motivation of using adaptive techniques in serious games, and of the core challenges that designing and implementing such systems entails. Examples illustrate how adaptability and adaptivity may be realized in more specific application scenarios, and major open challenges and paths for future work are presented. Dynamic adaptivity involves multiple disciplines ranging from initial game design over software design and engineering to topics from artificial intelligence or modeling tasks and up to aspects of game evaluation. Because of this multiplicity and interdisciplinarity, only a subset of the disciplines involved can be presented here. More details can be found in the remaining chapters of this book and in the recommended literature (*cf.* Sect. "Further Reading").

1.3   Remarks on AI

The term *Artificial Intelligence* (AI) [76] is widely used, but the interpretations of what exactly artificial intelligence means differ considerably. In the gaming industry, AI has been stretched to a popular marketing term, encompassing anything from simple if-then-else rules to advanced self-learning models. Nevertheless, AI techniques are commonly used in computer simulations and games; typical examples are pathfinding and planning [59,76]. Behavior trees have become very popular to model the behavior of *Non-Player Characters* (NPCs) as seen in the high profile video games *Halo 2, Bioshock,* and *Spore.* In serious games, however, the goal is to facilitate gameplay that optimally assists the users in their endeavors for training, learning, etc. - and AI offers promising approaches to this end. Regarding the aspect of NPC behavior, for example, AI driven NPCs could be designed to produce more human behaviors, either in cooperative or in competing ways, with the goal of allowing players to more naturally relate to these artificial agents. In an educational context, this could mean that the program attempts to mimic a tutor to provide individualized learning assistance. The same is true for serious games in general where intelligent, artificial, cooperative players (e.g., NPCs) mimic supporting peers to achieve a common task. Of course, this is still an emerging field of research. Truly human-alike behavior for games falls under the umbrella of *Strong AI* or *Artificial General Intelligence* (AGI). Strong AI aims at establishing systems which, in their behavior, cannot be differentiated from humans, i.e., a perfect mimicry in the sense of a solution to the Turing test [76]. "Intelligent" NPCs, as a potential direct embodiment of the role of a human tutor outside of the realm of serious games, are an element that can occur in a wide variety of serious games, and they can heavily benefit from AI techniques [40,45,87,96]. However, numerous other elements of serious games (e.g., training intensity, prediction of difficulty parameters, complexity of a given task, etc.) could arguably also benefit from the wide array of AI techniques. This does not necessarily encompass the full range of AGI techniques, but could factor in advanced AI techniques which are less symbolic and complex, such as automatically learned probabilistic models (e.g., dynamic Bayesian networks) or natural language understanding (as an extension of basic natural language processing) [76]. Since related work is often vague in describing the role and extent of AI techniques that are used to implement adaptivity and personalization in serious games, future work should direct effort towards (1) applying modern AI or AGI technologies like cognitive architectures [54] in the context of personalized adaptive serious games; (2) being very specific about the term AI; (3) clearly stating which technologies are implemented and if they reasonably match the understanding of intelligent behavior.

2 State of the Art

Adaptivity and personalization have long been an active topic for applications which target heterogeneous user groups. With the advent of the *World Wide Web* Brusilovsky laid the foundation for adaptive and user model-based interfaces in his work on adaptive hypermedia [16]. He described how adaptive hypermedia systems can build a model of the user and apply it to adapt to that user. Adaptation could be the personalization of content to the user's knowledge and goals or the recommendation of links to other hypermedia pages which promise to be most relevant to the user [16]. This concept has been driven forward ever since, for instance in the development of adaptive e-learning systems, so-called *Intelligent Tutoring Systems* (ITS) [96]. It is a logical step to transfer the established models and principles from ITS to serious games. Lopes and Bidarra (2011) give a thorough overview on techniques for adaptivity in games and simulations [55]. They surveyed the research on adaptivity in general and discussed the main challenges. In their paper they concluded that, among other methods, procedural content generation and semantic modeling were promising research directions [55].

In a broader view, adaptivity for games for entertainment is often masked behind the term *Artificial Intelligence* (AI). However, the term AI is often somewhat overstretched as a pure marketing term, as noted above (*cf.* Sect. 1.3). Nevertheless, games for entertainment and serious games have at least one goal in common: to motivate the user to play the game in a given session - and to motivate to continue playing the game for prolonged periods. AI always played a role in games [17] and the listing of all AI techniques that have been used in the context of games is far beyond the scope of this chapter and subject to further reading (*cf.* Sect. "Further Reading"). In 2007, the webpage *aigamedev.com* by A. Champandard listed prominent examples for influential AI in games. These include (1) *Sim City* as an example for complex simulations; (2) *The Sims* as an example for emotional modeling; (3) *Creatures* showing the first application of machine learning in games; (4) *Halo* for intelligent behavior of enemies with behavior trees; (5) *F.E.A.R.* for an implementation of AI planning for context-sensitive behavior; and (6) the strategy game *Black & White* which uses Belief-Desire-Intention (BDI) modeling inspired by cognitive science research as well as machine learning techniques like decision trees and neural networks. Another game AI example can be seen in the cooperative first-person shooter video game *Left 4 Dead*. The game intensity in *Left 4 Dead* is adapted following psychological models for increased tension and surprising moments. Other titles employ heuristics to optimize the difficulty settings for the individual players, for instance in the survival horror game *Resident Evil 5* where a sub-range of a more fine-grained difficulty selection is determined through the manual difficulty choice of the players. The exact setting on the subscale, which affects multiple aspects of game difficulty, is dynamic and based on the player performance. Such techniques are most commonly referred to as dynamic difficulty adjustment or dynamic game difficulty balancing.

Dynamic Difficulty Adjustment (DDA) is the automatic adaptation of the difficulty level to the current level of the user, based on predefined general parameter ranges, or according to a user model. DDA is predominantly used in entertainment games to increase the difficulty of the game along with the increasing capabilities of the player. A commonly used manifestation of the DDA balancing technique is *rubber banding* [69] which artificially boosts the possibilities (as expressed in game resources) of players to increase their performance when the actual performance drops below a certain threshold. Rubber banding is often used in racing games, a popular example being Nintendo's *Mario Kart*. In the case of *Mario Kart*, DDA has arguably helped making the game very inviting for novice players, but the very visible boosts provided to trailing players and NPCs can potentially harm the experience of advanced players, since weaker players receive advantages that may be perceived as being unfair [35].

DDA has also been implemented in the context of learning games. For game-based intelligent tutoring systems, DDA has been employed by Howell and Veale (2006) [45]. Their game-based ITS for learning linguistic abilities was designed to attempt to keep learners immersed in the game, in a state of flow, by dynamically adjusting the difficulty level, while at the same time respecting educational constraints to achieve learning targets. This balancing of serious games has also been studied by Kickmeier-Rust and Albert (2012) in their work on adaptive educational games [52]. Their report emphasizes the importance of creating an "educational game AI" which dynamically balances educational serious games to "achieve superior gaming experience and educational gains" [52].

Further examples for adaptive game balancing in other research projects have been shown in the EU projects ELEKTRA and *80 Days* [37,71]. ELEKTRA focuses on assessment and adaptation in a 3D adventure game: NPCs give educational and motivational guidance by providing students with situation-adaptive problem solving support [51]. The goal of the project was to utilize the advantages of computer games and their design principles to achieve adaptive educational games. People from various disciplines worked together, including pedagogy, cognitive science, neuroscience, and computer science. The project developed a methodology for designing educational games that was applied to a 3D adventure game demonstrator to teach physics, more precisely optics. This methodology led to the development of an adaptive engine [71] which uses the outcomes of evaluating the learner's performance by applying Bloom's taxonomy [15]. The results are stored in a learner model which reflects the skill level of the learners. A further example for adaptive guidance is the *Prime Climb* game by Conati and Maske (2009) [20]. Their study showed the educational effectiveness of a pedagogic virtual agent, embodied as a magician NPC in the game world, for a mathematics learning game.

In the *80 Days* project concepts for adaptive, interactive storytelling were developed to teach students geography. Göbel et al. (2010) introduce the concept of *Narrative Game-based Learning Objects* (NGLOBs) to dynamically adjust narratives for adventure-like, story-based educational games [39]. An implementation of adaptive, interactive storytelling with NGLOBs has been shown in the EU project *80 Days* [39]. Another popular example for an interactive story is the digital interactive fiction game *Façade* by Mateas and Stern (2005) [58]. Façade makes use of *Natural Language Processing* (NLP) to allow the player to naturally interact with a couple which invited the player to their home for a cocktail party. The combination of an NLP interface and a broad spectrum of possible story outcomes positively influences the game experience and immersion. Whereas the technical aspects of the game have been received well, the drama aspects have received mixed reviews [61].

An often cited example for an effective serious game is the DARPA-funded *Tactical Language and Cultural Training System* (TLCTS) [50] for the US military. However, as TLCTS is a combination of an adaptive ITS component for skill development (the *Skill Builder*) and two games, only the ITS component shows adaptive behavior [50].

The dynamic adjustment of game mechanics or content is another field of research. Niehaus and Riedl (2009) present an approach to customize scenarios by dynamically inserting or removing events from a scenario that relate to learning objectives [63].

A major problem arises when the player first starts a game and the system has no information on the user yet. A commonly used approach for the initial phase of adaptation is stereotyping or classification [96]. At the beginning, the system utilizes questionnaires, or very early player performance observations, to classify the knowledge or skill level of the users. Based on the results the system can map the learner to predefined class-stereotypes, like "beginner", "intermediate" or "expert". This form of personalization is mostly applied to static games with predefined learning pathways for each stereotype and does not consider adaptation based on current learning contexts. An example for stereotyping in serious games is *S.C.R.U.B.* which aims at teaching microbiology concepts to university students [56].

On the technical side various software architectures and middlewares support the development of adaptive serious games [21, 66, 67, 71]. The ALIGN system architecture by Peirce et al. (2008) presents a way how to noninvasively introduce adaptivity to games [71]. It has been applied in the educational adventure game of the ELEKTRA project. The ALIGN system architecture can decouple the adaptation logic from the actual game without mitigating the gameplay. It is divided into four conceptual processes: the accumulation of context information about the game state; the interpretation of the current learner state; the search for matching intervention constraints; and a recommendation engine, which applies the adaptation rules to the game. Further architecture examples are the distributed architecture for testing, training and simulation in the military domain, TENA [66], or the CIGA middleware for distributed intelligent virtual agents [67]. The extensive software architecture of TENA [66] focuses on interoperability for military test and training systems. The U.S. Department of Defense (DoD) uses TENA for distributed testing and training. At its core, the TENA middleware interconnects various applications and tools for the management, monitoring, analysis, etc., of military assets. Via a gateway service they can be linked with other conformant simulators that provide real sensor data or data from live, virtual and constructive simulations (LVC) for the TENA environment. The CIGA [67] middleware is an architecture to connect multi-agent systems to game engines using ontologies as a design contract. It negotiates between the game engine on the physical layer and the multi-agent system on the cognitive layer [67].

Most game engines come with built-in artificial intelligence (AI) procedures for common problems such as pathfinding and NPC behavior. But since game engines have a generic characteristic to allow the creation of a variety of different game types for different genres, the AI in such game engines is often not tailored towards specific needs in serious games. When additional AI functionality is needed, various game AI middlewares exist to incorporate specific AI functions to existing games. Examples range from more sophisticated path planning algorithms for massive amounts of NPC steering, to dynamically extendable models like behavior trees for intelligence-akin behavior, or to machines learning algorithms to learn human-like behavior. However, AI packages for use in terms of adaptivity and personalization in *serious* games development are not yet commonly available.

3   General Principles of Adaptation

This section introduces the general principles of personalized and adaptive serious games. The general objectives of adaptivity are discussed, i.e., why one may want to make a game adaptive at all. The section includes clarifications regarding the understanding of the differentiation between the varying terms around *adaptation*, i.e., adaptivity, adaptation, personalization, and customization. In a broader view and in general applications these terms are often used as synonyms to describe the user-centered adjustments of systems; but in the context of this chapter, with its discussions of the core principles of adaptation, we employ more nuanced definitions and differentiations. We discuss several approaches to adaptability and adaptivity and introduce concepts for the dimensions of adaptation. Since adaptation is an ongoing process we describe the adaptive cycle and one possible manifestation of this model for adaptive serious games. Related to that is the question when and how to start an adaptive cycle; this is discussed in the sections on the cold-start problem and on co-adaptation.

3.1   Objectives of Adaptivity

Adequately matching challenges presented in a game with the capabilities and needs of its players is a prerequisite to good player experience. Furthermore, the "serious" purpose of a serious game must be taken into account, i.e., the desired successful outcome of playing a serious game, such as achieving individual learning or health goals. This challenge has been discussed in an early work which stood at the beginning of a field that is now called game user research [23].

Since then, game user researchers have connected such game-related considerations to candidate psychological models, mostly from motivational and behavioral psychology, including *flow* by Csikszentmihalyi [24], *Behavior Change* by Fogg [32], and *Self-Determination Theory* (SDT) by Deci [27]. As a needs-satisfaction model, SDT explains (intrinsic) motivation based on pre-conditions that lie in a range of needs that must be satisfied, namely competence, autonomy, and relatedness. Rigby and Ryan provide a detailed argument how video games have managed to fulfill these needs better and better during the last 30 years of video game history [73]. Due to their common relation to motivation SDT and flow do have similarities, although SDT is arguably concerned with conditions that enable intrinsic motivation to arise while flow is more concerned with conditions that enable sustained periods of intrinsically motivated actions [86]. In the remainder of this section, we will focus on how these theoretical models relate to adaptability and adaptivity in serious games.

Flow theory by Csikszentmihalyi [24] is one of the most prominently cited theories that discusses the psychological foundations of motivation. It introduces so-called enabling factors, such as a balance of challenges and skills. According to Csikszentmihalyi, flow is a state of being fully "in the zone" that can occur when one is engaging in an activity that may have very positive effects. As an underlying reason, he discusses an enjoyment that may be explained by evolutionary benefits of performing activities that trigger the state of flow, which in turn leads to increased motivation to repeatedly perform an activity [24].

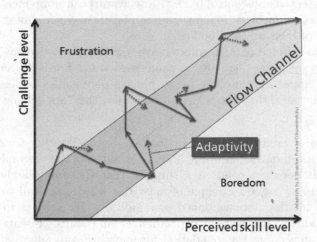

Fig. 1. The Flow model (based on Csikszentmihalyi [24]). Adaptivity (dotted arrow-lines) can support keeping the user's interaction route through the game (arrow-lines) in the flow channel between perceived skill and challenge level.

Flow theory has been connected both to games (by Csikszentmihalyi himself and also by Chen [18]) and also explicitly to serious games (e.g., by Ritterfeld et al. [74]). This connection can easily be understood when considering the conditions under which flow can occur: Csikszentmihalyi argues that there are nine preconditions that need to be present in order to attain a state of flow when performing an activity. The most prominent precondition is an optimal balance of risk of failure (i.e., "challenge", as mentioned above; which may translate to risk of losing a game life, level, or an entire game when considering flow in games) and the chance to attaining a goal (i.e., "skill", which in games may mean winning some points, a level, a bonus, or the whole game). A visual representation of this balance can be seen in Fig. 1, which also highlights that this balance is subject to change over time due to the developing, deteriorating, or temporarily boosted or hindered level of skill of each individual player. This is an early indicator of the need for a dynamic level of challenge (e.g., adaptive difficulty) in games. While increasing levels of challenge are usually achieved by pre-defined game progression to a certain extent, this is rarely optimal with regard to the actual skill development of any specific individual (since user-centered design optimizes game experiences for groups of users). Returning to remaining prerequisites for flow according to Chen, the activity must also

– lead to or present clear goals (e.g., "save at least five bees", "open the door by solving a puzzle"),
– give immediate feedback (e.g., "the door opens given the right pass-code"),
– action and awareness must merge (e.g., no need to look at the controller in order to move),
– concentration on the task at hand (e.g., little to no interruption, for example with non-matching menus, of the actual game content),
– a sense of potential and control (e.g., "I [my avatar] can jump incredibly far"),
– a loss of self-consciousness (in many games, players may get almost fully transported "out of their physical bodies"),
– a sense of time altered (e.g., in games players often only notice how much time they actually spent on them after a game session has finished), and
– the activity appearing autotelic (most players play games because they like to and not because they are told to, or because they are getting paid to do so) [24].

More examples of conditions in games that can be facilitating factors for flow have been discussed in related work [22, 89]. Considering the preconditions mentioned above it does not come as a surprise that Csikszentmihalyi explicitly relates to games as a good example of activities which can lead to flow experiences. While all the aforementioned preconditions are subject to differences between individuals, the balance of challenges and skills presents a tangible model which can serve as the foundation for approaches to adaptivity in games and serious games [74]. The complex nature of the challenge of balancing a game so that it does not only manage to capture some players sometimes but most of the players most of the time also delivers a good explanation for the presence of manual difficulty choices, such as those presented in settings menus, in many - and even in very early - video games.

The ultimate goal of an adaptive educational game is to support players in achieving progress towards individual learning goals. Since technical measurement methods for the direct and effective assessment of knowledge gain in the human brain are not available [2,14], the evaluation of learning efficiency has to be done indirectly by assessment tests or other forms of interaction or data analysis processes. The idea behind adaptive educational games is that the users experience an increased flow resulting in an increased game immersion, which in turn positively increases the user's intrinsic motivation to interact, play and learn - and ultimately to produce an increased learning outcome.

Oftentimes the ingrained purpose of serious games is not just to perform a specific activity (often repeatedly), but also to have a lasting effect on the players' traits or behavior. A prominent model for behavioral change is the *Fogg Behavior Model* (FBM) (Fig. 2). The FBM has been developed in relation to general interactive media and stems from research on persuasive design [32]. In comparison to flow and other motivational theories, which discuss the motivational support, the FBM and related skill development theories discuss the enabling factors of ability. The FBM states further factors that are not considered in the flow model, framing a broader view that is necessary to explain the arguably broader outcome of behavioral change (as opposed to explaining momentary motivation, which is tackled by the flow model).

In the larger picture of serious games, it is interesting to notice that it will likely be desirable to induce phases of serious game interaction that are not spent in a state of flow in order to allow for self-aware reflection (for example after completing an exercise in a motion-based game for health). Reflection can play an important role when learning to complete complex tasks or exercises [7,30] and it can also play a key role in behavioral change.

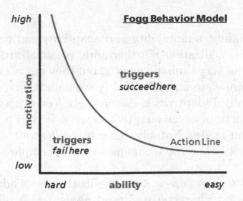

Fig. 2. An illustration of the action line of the *Fogg Behavior Model* (FBM); it conveys the principle that certain amounts of motivation and ability to change behavior are required in order to allow provided triggers for change to succeed [32].

3.2 Personalization and Adaptivity

Since the terms personalization and adaptivity, as well as customization and adaptability are used differently and sometimes interchangeably, it is important to provide an understanding of how the terms are used in the context of this chapter. Regarding their general meaning, we define the terms as specified in Table 1.

Table 1. Our definitions of the various adaptation terms.

Concept	Definition
Adaptability	The fact that a system is not fixed, but can be changed (to the needs of users, to changing environmental contexts, etc.; changes are usually understood to be performed manually)
Customization	The act of changing a system to the needs of a user group or individual user (manually or automatically; may can be done by the group itself or by the user him- or herself, but may also be done by third parties; often related to the appearance or content of the given system)
Personalization	The act of changing a system to the needs of a specific individual user (often automatic but does not have to be, i.e., can be understood as a specific form of customization with a focus on individuality; personalization is also often related to appearance or content)
Adaptivity	The fact that a system is not fixed, but dynamically changes over time (to adjust to the needs of users or an individual user, or to adjust to changing environmental contexts, etc.; typically happens automatically; often related to settings and parameters present in the given system)

In this understanding, adaptability and adaptivity can be means to achieve customization or personalization. Furthermore, personalization and adaptivity can at times be used in very similar contexts, but they make a different emphasis: the change to accommodate an individual (personalization), or the change that happens automatically (adaptivity). Accordingly, constructions such as automatic personalization or personal adaptivity can be formed to describe the same concept from different angles. Notably, these terms describe apparent properties of systems and do not define the techniques that are employed to achieve these ends.

In the context of serious games, a personalized game is adapted to the learners' individual situation, characteristics, and needs, i.e., it offers a personalized experience. The psychological background is that personalized content can cause a significantly higher engagement and a more in-depth cognitive elaboration (in-depth information processing) [72,90].

As indicated in the definitions above (Table 1), **personalization** can either be achieved manually or automatically by adapting the content, appearance, or any other aspect of the system. Different users have different preferences and many computer games offer the possibility for adjustment, e.g., brightness level, sound volume or input devices settings on the technical side, and on the content-side, for instance, difficulty levels, or game character or avatar profiles. Adaptivity, on the other hand, means the automatic adjustment of game software over time, be it either technical parameters or on the content-level. Technical adaptivity can, for example, be realized through the automatic setup of a game to best fit the user's surroundings.

Adaptivity of serious games content can mean the dynamic adjustment of learning paths, the dynamic creation of personalized game content with e.g., procedural generation or user- or task-centered recommendations. Adaptivity of content is typically achieved by applying techniques from the field of AI. It is important to notice that adaptivity typically involves a temporal component, i.e., the adaptive systems evolve over time by adjusting their internal parameters given acquired data from former states. This concept results in the adaptive cycle where each cycle refines the system [91]. The mechanisms behind the refinement process could be manifold and typically often arise from the field of AI since the system employs some form of optimization.

Customization is another term that is frequently used in the context of serious games and while it is sometimes used interchangeably with the term personalization, there is a subtle difference. In many cases where personalization relates to automatically individualized experiences (alas to adaptivity as mentioned above), meaning that a system is configured or adjusted implicitly without interaction by the user, customization relates to manual, explicit adjustments and choices made by the users to optimize their experience (alas employing adaptability as mentioned above). Furthermore, customization is not necessarily tailored towards the needs of individual players, but it may also target specific player groups or other user groups in the ecosystem around serious games.

Lastly, it is important to realize that many systems will employ designs that mix elements of adaptivity and adaptability, so users may have a say in the adjustments considered by the adaptive system, or the selection of choices made available in an interface for adaptability may have been produced dynamically with adaptive components. We will provide a more detailed discussion of the dimensions of adaptive systems in Sect. 3.5

3.3   Approaches to Adaptability

When designing and implementing adaptable serious games, meaning games that allow for manual adjustments, the focus lies on achieving a good usability and the user experience in the user interaction with the settings interfaces for explicit manual adjustments. This means that typical desirable goals like efficiency and effectiveness as key elements of usability [42] play a role while the experience of interacting with the adjustment options should also be enjoyable (which is a key component of user experience [42]).

In order to achieve these goals, methods from interaction design, such as iterative user-centered [5] or participatory [78] design play an increasingly important role in the development of settings interfaces and settings integration for serious games [84]. As a first step, the parameters that will be presented to the players must be isolated. In regular games monolithic one-dimensional difficulty settings are often employed (such as "easy", "medium" and "hard"), although the parameters typically map to a number of game variables (such as amount of energy, number of opponents, power-ups, etc.). Serious games should take considerable measures to optimize the match between the heterogeneous capabilities and needs of the players, and the content and challenges that are presented. Settings interfaces in this area often present more fine-grained parameters for tuning, in order to provide a more direct influence on the resulting game experience. A detailed example of such a development will be presented below in the section on the motion-based games for health (*cf.* Chap. 4).

Furthermore, the game developers need to decide whether to use player-based or game-based parametrization.

Game-centric parametrization means that settings are made per-game and the parameters typically represent aspects of the specific game. The level of abstraction can vary from terms as general and abstract as simply "difficulty" to specific descriptions of ingame, deep-influencing parameters (e.g., "amount of health" of a player character).

Player-centric parametrization means that settings are made on a per-user basis. In such scenarios, the parameters typically relate to the psychophysiological abilities and needs of a user (e.g., "range of motion" in a motion-based game for health). This model is frequently used when a suite of rather small ("mini" or "casual" style) games are employed as a suite targeting a serious purpose since the settings can be transferred from one small game to the other without additional configuration overhead. However, in such cases, an additional technical challenge arises in the mapping from the general per-user settings to the specific game parameters in the different games. Such mappings are often not linear, may be difficult to generalize across user populations, and generally require careful testing and balancing.

Mixed methods, where, e.g., settings are made on player-centric parameters while still being made per game are also possible, as are group-based settings.

3.4 Approaches to Adaptivity

When designing adaptive serious games, meaning games that automatically adjust to the player abilities and needs, the focus lies on a good playability and player experience, and it can be argued - perhaps somewhat counter-intuitively - that getting these aspects right is even more important than it is in the case of purely adaptable games. While many aspects of computation are inherently about automation [79], if the automation does not respect the intentions of the user, or even comes to hinder them, the most basic principles of usability and user experience can easily be violated. This has been discussed more extensively in the general literature on human-computer interaction, especially along the challenges with early embodied conversational agents. One prominent example of such an agent is the notorious "Clippy" which was present in some versions of Microsoft Word and led to numerous problems especially with more advanced users [60]. The same principles do, however, also apply to (serious) games, even though a playful setting may potentially render players more accepting of inefficiencies. While many adaptive systems are designed to address these concerns by implementing some form of explicit preliminary, live, or retroactive interaction with the automated system, which we will discuss in detail in the section on the dimensions of adaptation (*cf.* Sect. 3.5), all adaptive systems in the context of serious games are at least partially automated. This means that they must implement some form of *performance evaluation* in order to measure or estimate the impact of the current parameter settings on the player performance. Adaptive systems must also implement some form of an *adjustment mechanism* that adjusts the parameter settings depending on the outcome of the performance evaluation [1].

The exact realization of such an automated optimization process can take many forms and the adjustments does not have to be limited to tuning existing parameters. As examples from, e.g., learning games show, additionally prepared or generated content can be a means for adjustment next to more traditional approaches, such as heuristics or machine-learning techniques for tuning game variables.

One of the most common forms of adaptivity in games is heuristics-based adaptivity for dynamic game difficulty balancing, i.e., *Dynamic Difficulty Adjustment* (DDA). As illustrated in Fig. 3, the difficulty is either increased or decreased, depending on the player performance, which can be measured on one or multiple variables. If the performance is below a certain threshold, indicating that the game may be too hard, the difficulty is decreased. Otherwise, if the performance is above a certain threshold, indicating that the game is currently too easy, the difficulty is increased.

Adjustments can be performed on the basis of a single parameter, or with a direct influence on multiple variables. The variable game parameter mappings are usually determined and fine-tuned with iterative testing. The same applies to the thresholds, which can be either discrete, fuzzy, or quasi-continuous. Depending on the amount of adjustments and type of the parameters that are adjusted, the difficulty settings can be either visible or more or less invisible. This is closely linked to one of the largest challenges with straight-forward dynamic difficulty adjustment: Since the goal of the adaptive system is to notably impact player performance or experience, the adjustments usually lead to notable changes in the game, which in turn lead to a resulting difficulty that deviates around the current theoretically "optimal" settings for any given player. This effect is called rubber banding [69] and it can be perceived as annoying, or even unfair, especially when it affects other player or non-player entities in games, e.g., a computer-controlled opponent in a car racing game. A frequently referenced example for this rubber

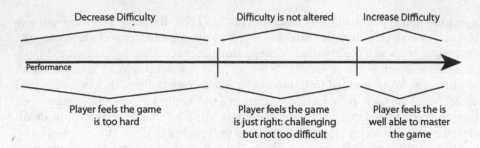

Fig. 3. Difficulty adjustment based on performance. The thick arrow indicates a possible range of performance from low to high. Three sections on the range of performance determine whether difficulty for the player should be increased, decreased, or left unchanged.

banding effect is the *Mario Kart* series. Despite the notable challenges, more subtle adjustments, such as slightly supporting the user with aiming (which is widely used in first-person shooters on gaming consoles) [93], or more readily available supply of resources (e.g., health packs) [47], have been shown to be successful in improving the overall game experience or performance.

Figure 3 has a resemblance to the flow model that shows very clearly how the approach of dynamic difficulty adjustments in games directly aims at addressing the prerequisite of presenting an adequate balance of challenges relative to the skills of an individual user. This connection has been discussed by Chen [18], who not only underlines the connection between DDA and flow but also remarks on the potential challenges when control is taken away from the player in fully automated systems. Chen [18] suggests a system where manual game difficulty choices are available, but integrated as credible choices in the game world, in order to avoid "breaking the magic circle" of a game [86]. Embedded difficulty choices have been shown to increase users perceived autonomy compared to fully automated DDA [86].

Since user skills are not a constant, both adaptable and adaptive systems face further challenges, as both users and the game undergo complex changes over time. Various forms of user models [31] have been explored to aggregate and estimate changes in players over time [19,49]. Machine-learning techniques, such as self-organizing maps [28], decision trees [94], neural networks [12,95] or reinforcement learning [6], have been employed to facilitate more complex optimizations or general decision making especially for many-to-many and nonlinear parameter mappings.

Next, we will discuss the multidimensional aspects of adaptivity and user involvement and the multiple layers of skill-influencing factors.

3.5   Dimensions of Adaptation

Making a system adaptive is a specific form of automation where the system takes over individual actions or larger activities that would otherwise have to be handled manually. In many cases, this opens possibilities for more fine-grained, frequent, or complex operations than what would have been possible with manual control. On the other hand, as mentioned above, getting automation "right" is crucial in order to avoid negative impacts on the usability, user experience, or the intended serious goals of a system. Related work from automation has framed such considerations in ways that are relevant to the development of adaptive serious games. Parasuraman, Sheridan and Wickens [70] have produced a model of types and levels of automation that describes the general process of designing and implementing automation systems (Fig. 4).

1. The model begins with the question of "What should be automated?", which in the case of serious games can range from general "difficulty settings", over specific challenging aspects, such as the required range of motion in a game for therapy, up to very complex aspects such assemblies of learning materials.
2. The next step "identify types of automation" is split into four types, all of which are frequently present in parallel in adaptive serious games, highlighting the complexity of these types of adaptive systems.
3. The model then suggests a decision on the level of automation that can range from fully automatic execution without informing the user about changes or offering options to influence the actions taken by the adaptive systems, to a system that offers a range of alternative suggestions for adjustments that the user must manually choose from (see 4 for a summary of levels of automation).
4. In the next step, the model suggests a primary evaluation based on performance criteria that are closely linked to usability in terms of interaction design.
5. Depending on these criteria, an initial selection of types and levels of automation is made which is then evaluated for secondary criteria, such as reliability and outcome-related costs, leading to a final selection of types and levels of automation.

We propose an adaptation of the model in order to make it fit for adaptive serious games. In this light, the first decision would be phrased as "Which aspects of the serious game should be adaptive?". Again, it could be a single parameter that influences difficulty, such as the maximum speed in a racing game, or more complex aspects, such as the content or the game mechanics. The layer of types of automation can be related directly to the basic components of adaptive games by Fullerton et al. [34]: Information acquisition and information analysis are components of the *performance evaluation*. Decision and action selection, as well as action implementation, are parts of the *adjustment mechanism*. Notably, some aspects of these steps are usually fixed or thresholded in the design phase of a game while some flexibility remains which then gives room to adaptive change during use.

Due to the importance of player experience as a prerequisite for successful outcomes regarding the serious intent, the level of automation requires further consideration. Under closer observation, the scale suggested by Sheridan [79] mixes multiple aspects of automation that should be discussed separately,

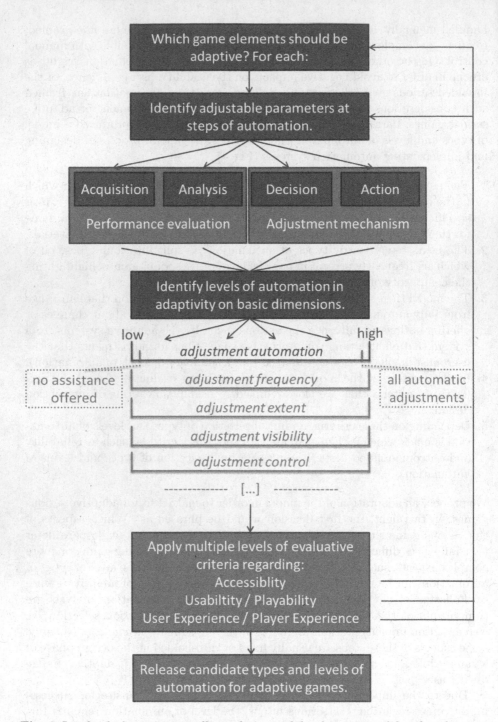

Fig. 4. Levels of adaptation as well as a design and development workflow for adaptive systems in the context of serious games.

although - in most cases - they are interrelated. One dimension is the basic level of automation, which can range from fully automatic to fully manual. Additional aspects are the frequency with which adjustments are made (which can range from constantly to never), the extent of changes that are made (which can range from a single, non-central element of the experience to encompassing the whole interaction experience), the visibility or explicitness [35] of changes that are made (which can range from completely invisible, not notable, to full visible, or salient), and also the aspect of user control over the changes that are made (which can range from no control at all to full manual control over every step, as indicated by Sheridan [79]). Other aspects which represent similar dimensions for design choices are (1) long-termedness; (2) target user group size; (3) game variable granularity; (4) explicitness of user feedback as it is provided by the user; (5) implicitness of the feedback data taken into account for adaptivity; (6) explorativeness of the adaptive system; (7) parameter complexity, and (8) the system's inherentness regarding the feedback.

While there are likely more aspects that become evident when designing for a specific use-case, this shows that any system must take a carefully designed position or subspace in a very complex, high-dimensional design space of adaptive systems. Additional complications are added with complex application areas such as serious games. This has implications not only for the design, implementation, and testing of adaptive systems, but also for any research on them, since these aspects can influence the outcomes of studies on the functioning or the acceptance of adaptive systems.

Following with the next step of the model, the usability-centric criteria presented in the general model on automation must be augmented with more specific criteria forming a notion of playability and player experience. In many use-cases of serious games, criteria from accessibility would also play a more important role. Lastly, outcomes with regard to the serious intent of the game must become part of the primary evaluative criteria.

The secondary outcome criteria should be augmented with evaluations of ecological applicability and validity, meaning that it must be clear whether the solution can effectively be applied in real usage contexts (and not only in laboratory tests), and whether the optimizations still function with regard to the primary goals.

Given the complexity of adaptive systems in the context of serious games, arriving at a near optimal system is likely to require multiple system design iterations based both on primary and secondary evaluative criteria. In this light, it also becomes clear how this model is a detailed realization of a general iterative design model (typically a cycle of analysis, design, implementation, and evaluation), as for instance presented by Hartson et al. [42].

3.6   The Adaptive Cycle

The grounding principle of evolving adaptation is the general cycle of adaptive change, or "Panarchy" as Gunderson and Holling describe it [41]. Panarchy is a

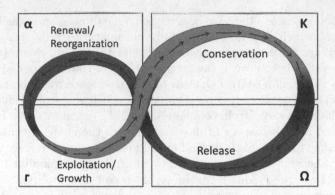

Fig. 5. The Adaptive Cycle by Gunderson [41]; temporal changes in a system iteratively proceed through the phases of reorganization, growth, conservation and release.

cycle of adaptive change, proceeding through "forward-loop" stages of exploitation, consolidation and predictability, followed by "back-loop" phases of novel recombination and reorganization (Fig. 5). The principle of adaptive management alone is inherent to almost all human and natural systems where decisions have been made iteratively using feedback acquired from observations. A famous technical application of an adaptive cycle is seen in the Kalman Filter and its derivatives [76]. This algorithm has prediction and update steps to refine estimates of unknown variables based on a set of noisy or inaccurate measurements observed over time. An example would be to determine the exact position of a moving object, e.g., a vehicle, when observing its movement.

The Panarchy principle can also be found in a 4-phased adaptive cycle for software systems. A typical 4-phased adaptive cycle consists of the acquisition and processing phases of capturing and analysis, to the phases of selection and presentation of new or modified (adapted) content (Fig. 6). Shute et al. [80] present such a 4-phased adaptive cycle for adaptive educational systems which also includes a learner model. Without loss of generality, this model can also be adapted to serious games in general; the learner model then becomes a user model without didactic and pedagogical concepts and it can also be related to *performance analysis* (capture and analyze) and an *adjustment mechanism* (select and present) as the general components of any adaptive game discussed above.

Before implementing each phase the general goals of the targeted adaptive system must be well-defined. One design pattern is to start with the outcome, i.e., the presentation phase, and proceed backwards to the selection, analysis, and capturing phases. A clear understanding of the expected output is oftentimes helpful in defining the input and the processes.

The first phase captures the interaction data of the users. For games this could include the mouse click positions, performance data, identifier names of selected game objects, or other interaction events like starting or stopping the game, or technical data like changes in network connection bandwidth.

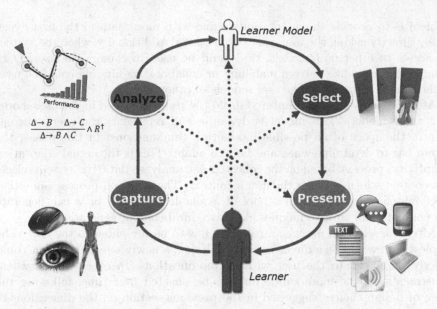

Fig. 6. 4-process adaptive cycle for adaptive learning systems (based on [80]); the dynamic system is updated through the phases capture, analyze, select and present.

With additional sensor or input devices, more data can be captured, for example, the loudness of the surroundings can be determined using a microphone; or with an eye-gaze tracker the eye fixations regarding specific objects in a game can be recorded [52]. Other possible suitable types of data include speech, gesture, posture, or haptic data. Of course, not everything which can be captured is necessary for the adaptation process. The nature of the captured data has to be specified in the early phases of the software design process. Regarding data reduction and data economy, one has to keep in mind privacy or ethical constraints when implementing data acquisition methods [29], although by implementing anonymization techniques or reduced personalization components the problems can be mitigated [8].

The second phase is the analysis of the captured data. In this the phase, the actual "intelligence" happens, i.e., an adaptation engine must attempt to "read" the captured data to infer the user's state or performance. This process can include qualitative or quantitative analysis techniques, analysis of cognitive or non-cognitive variables, machine learning, data mining, or other techniques from artificial intelligence. For well-defined domains, Bayesian networks could be used to probabilistically infer a cognitive state from observed (non-cognitive) variables [76]. The deduced information is then stored in the user model as the basis for the selection phase. After multiple interaction cycles, the analysis typically improves (higher precision) since (historic) data already stored in the user model can be used in addition to any data from the current interaction. Initially, a system can only act on the captured data of the first run. One strategy to this cold-start problem is to provide the adaptation engine with more data in the first cycle, i.e., by directly asking the user a set of questions. Additionally, when the system has access to other user models, this could be used to classify the user. Data mining techniques like pattern matching or collaborative filtering could be used to find similar patterns in the user models of other users.

After an analysis of the captured data, the result is stored in the user model (or learner model). This model is dynamic and represents the user's current state in the space of all possible interaction combinations. In this phase, the system has to determine when and how to adapt. This is the actual adaptation (adaptivity) process: based on the collected and analyzed data, the system selects that content which best fits the user's context. The selection process can either select matching content from a pool of available resources, or it can generate new content, e.g., with techniques like procedural content generation [55].

After the selection process, a response has to be presented to the user. The simplest case would be a direct presentation, i.e., a newly selected content could directly be shown to the user without modifications. In other cases, system adjustments can be more subtle, or can be enacted over time, following the range of design choices suggested in the previous section on the dimensions of adaptation (Sect. 3.5).

3.7   When, What and How to Adapt

This section discusses the main challenges which arise when asking when, what, and how to adapt. Answers to these questions concern multiple disciplines, i.e., game design, software engineering, cognitive science, pedagogy, evaluation methodologies, etc. An adaptive system typically evolves over time [41, 80]. This temporal aspect is reflected in the adaptive cycle where each cycle refines the system one step closer to be personalized to the user's needs (*cf.* previous Sect. 3.6 and Figs. 5 and 6). Each of the following questions can be mapped to the 4-phased adaptive cycle, although some of the questions involve more than one phase.

When to adapt, is a key question of adaptivity, because adaptivity must be justified at each and every step when a user is playing an adaptive game. An adaptive software system must have some kind of reaction model which determines when to start the adaptation process. For an adaptive serious game, the measure could be a decrease in motivation (e.g., captured indirectly through a number of unsuccessful repetitions); or when their assessed effectiveness is below a certain threshold (e.g., learning progress measured by questionnaires). Hence, the software must constantly measure the current state of the user to be able to react to deviations which hinder the user to reach the targeted goals. In the 4-phased adaptive cycle this is done in the selection process after the system has analyzed to observed interaction data.

What to adapt concerns the question which media, game mechanics, rules, assets, etc. can be designed and utilized in an adaptive way. This involves game design aspects, for example, modularized content which can be realigned in a dynamic fashion and which can sometimes exist independent of context, i.e., stand-alone. For games, the content often cannot directly be divided into atomic parts because of narrative constraints. Breaking up the storyline typically also breaks the narrative coherence and, therefore, has negative impacts on immersion. A comprehensive overview on game elements that could be adapted is given by Lopes and Bidarra [55]. They list examples for commercial games and academic research along the dimensions game worlds, mechanics, AI or NPC, narratives, and scenarios or quests.

How to adapt involves the mechanics behind the adaptation, i.e., the possibilities given by the underlying software architecture or by techniques from Artificial Intelligence. In the 4-phased adaptive cycle this question typically concerns the presentation phase, but with strong entailment of the result of the previous selection phase.

3.8 Cold-Start Problem

Two challenges that frequently arise with adaptive systems are cold-start and co-adaptation. Cold-start is known as a common challenge from machine learning and describes the problem of making first predictions in the absence of a proper amount of data. This problem is prevalent in adaptive serious games, since systems are usually designed to adapt to individual players, who, at one point in time, are all new users for whom no performance data have been recorded. A common approach to this challenge is, first of all, to assure careful user-centered iterative design and balancing, creating a game that works comparatively well for an average population. This can be augmented by

- calibration procedures;
- models that require manual settings before first play sessions;
- taking into account the performance and development of user groups that are very similar to the new user (similarity can be determined by prior tests, questionnaires, or very early performance data);
- taking into account established models of development based on the application use-case (e.g., a typical rehabilitation curve after a prosthetic implant with motion-based games for the support of rehabilitation); or simply
- refraining from any adaptivity until enough data has been captured to inform the model in order to avoid maladaptations.

3.9 Co-Adaptation

The challenge of co-adaptation can be explained well in relation to the problem of rubber banding [69]. In real prolonged use of any serious game, the player capabilities and needs are not only complex and multivariate, they also change (adapt) over time in a nonlinear fashion; the user adapts to changes in the adaptive system. This can lead to situations where a system adapts settings in a specific way and the user adapts to handle these settings even though they are not objectively optimal, and in worst-case scenarios may even lead to harmful interactions. One way to tackle co-adaptation are careful user-centered iterative design cycles. It is important that test groups are frequently changed so that problems can be found. This way, testers do not have enough interaction-time with the system to adjust to the problems before the design problems have been detected and fixed. Since the most common motivation for using adaptivity in serious games is an optimization of the experience with regard to individual users, manual means to interfere with changes made through the adaptive system, or to correct them, can also avoid malicious co-adaptation. However, this challenge remains elusive, and controlling for problems with co-adaptation requires detailed observations of both the system and the user behavior, both during formative iterative testing and during more summative evaluations and studies.

4   Adaptive Motion-based Games for Health

The need for adaptivity is frequently discussed in the context of *Motion-based Games for Health* (**MGH**). This section will provide some background to explain why that notion is frequently discussed and we will outline a number of major design concerns and challenges with implementing adaptability and adaptivity functionality for MGH.

Games for Health (**GFH**) are one of the major categories of serious games. The class encompasses a number of sub-classes, such as games for health education of professionals or the public, games for tracking general health behavior, or games for practical health applications [77]. One common class of health applications in serious games are motion-based games for health (MGH).

4.1   Adapting to the Players

As detailed in the chapter on games for health in this book, MGH bear the potential to motivate people to perform movements and exercises that would otherwise be perceived as strenuous or repetitive, they offer the potential to provide feedback regarding the quality of motion execution especially in the absence of a human professional (e.g., when executing physiotherapy exercises at home), and they offer the potential to gather objective information concerning the medium- to long-term development of the users. Adaptability and adaptivity are important aspects of MGH due to the often very heterogeneous abilities and needs even within specific application areas. MGH have been developed for a range of application areas such as children with cerebral palsy [43], people in stroke recovery [4,44], people with multiple sclerosis [65], or people with Parkinson's disease [82]. In a game designed to support the rehabilitation of stroke patients, for example, it may be necessary to facilitate game play while a player is unable to employ a specific limb. It may, in fact, even be the target of the serious game to support training of a largely non-functional limb.

With GFH it is also very apparent that the abilities and needs of an individual player are not fixed over time, but instead fluctuate constantly. Recognizing the

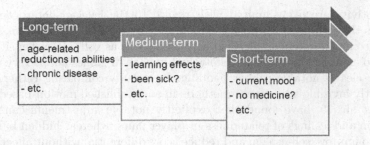

Fig. 7. Three temporal categories of individually changing differences that affect player abilities and needs in the context of GFH.

following three general temporal classes of fluctuation can help designers with structured considerations [83]:

- *Long-term developments*, such as age-related limitations [36], state of fitness, chronic disease, etc., form an underlying base influence on the abilities and needs of an individual.
- However, they are also influenced by *medium-term trends* such as learning effects, a temporary sickness, environmental factors such as season and weather, etc.
- Lastly, *short-term influences* such as the current mood, potentially forgotten medication, etc. can also play a considerable role.

Figure 7 outlines a visual summary of these aspects. While similar aspects also play a role in other application areas of serious games, MGH make for a comprehensible concrete example.

4.2 Adapting to Many Stakeholders

The considerations mentioned so far are framed by considerations of the player as an individual. However, GFH typically have multiple stakeholders, and modern GFH are designed with multiple stakeholders in mind. Beyond the players, whom the primary outcomes are usually targeting, doctors, therapists or other caregivers, family members, guardians or other third parties that are closely related to the player are involved in the larger context of GFH. Adaptive functions may be employed with regard to their interests as well [81]. For example, personalized reports based of GFH performance may be tailored for parents of a child with cerebral palsy who regularly uses a GFH. Further parties are also interested in the interaction with GFH or their subsystems, such as developers and researchers, and the design of some GFH is beginning to take the interests of these groups into account. Additional challenges arise when GFH feature a multi-player mode. Adaptive functions can have a strong impact on the balancing and the perception of the balancing by the players, which in turn may interfere with the player experience [35]. While in many cases, it will simply be suggested to avoid adaptivity in multiplayer settings, games without strong adaptability and adaptivity are likely limited with regard to the level of heterogeneity of co-players they support. Notably, balancing in the form of, for instance, "handicaps" is common in analog physical activities (such as golf). However, it is reasonable to expect measurable psychological impacts if games adapt very visibly, e.g., with clearly notable rubber banding. In a study comparing rather visible with mostly invisible adjustment methods in an established motion-based game, Gerling et al. [35] have found that explicitly notable adjustments can reduce self-esteem and feelings of relatedness in player pairs, whereas hidden balancing appears to improve self-esteem and reduce score differential without affecting the game outcome. It is also important to keep in mind that non-competitive multiplayer settings will likely result in different patterns of technique acceptance and resulting game experience [93] and adaptive techniques may, for example, be less intrusive when the player roles are not symmetrical.

4.3   Adapting to Further Context and Devices

There are various further aspects that can be important surrounding the usage of adaptive systems. Examples are the need to adequately serve potential multiplayer situations, or the context of gameplay, i.e., where it is played, how much space is needed, whether it happens at home or in a professional context, such as a physiotherapy practice. In order to control for such impacts the possible target environments can be modeled and simulated beforehand. However, this is still an area in need of further research. The same goes for additional sensor or control devices, which again hints at the complexity of adapting adequately in real gaming situations - even if "simple" heuristics are used. These challenges support the need for medium- to long-term studies and for studies that make ecological validity a primary target.

Drawn together these aspects explain why commercial movement-based games cannot simply be used for most serious health applications. Commercial products lack matching design, target-group orientation (e.g., Xbox Kinect, Playstation Move, EyeToy or Wii titles), and adaptability and adaptivity that is tailored towards supporting a good game experience while also supporting the targeted serious outcomes.

5   Application Examples

In the following, examples for the application of the described adaptation principles of this chapter are presented. This includes a digital learning game for image interpretation as well as games for health with a focus on kinesiatrics.

5.1   Lost Earth 2307 - Learning Game for Image Interpretation

The serious game *Lost Earth 2307* (LE) is a digital learning game for education and training in image interpretation. The game is part of ongoing research projects to find solutions for an effective and lasting knowledge transfer in professional image interpretation. One element of the approach is to introduce adaptive concepts to match the requirements of heterogeneous user groups and the additional requirement of efficient training at the workplace. *Lost Earth 2307* was developed by the Fraunhofer Institute of Optronics, System Technologies and Image Exploitation IOSB for the *Air Force Training Center for Image Reconnaissance* (AZAALw) of the German Armed Forces [33].

The application domain of this game is image interpretation for reconnaissance, i.e., the identification and analysis of structures and objects by experts (image interpreters) according to a given task. The image data could be optical, radar, infrared, hyperspectral, etc. Radar image interpretation, for example, is used in search and rescue operations to find missing earthquake victims. However, peculiar effects of the radar imaging technology (e.g., compression of distances by the foreshortening effect, or ghosting artifacts for moving objects) make it hard for non-experts to interpret the resulting image data, hence expert knowledge and experience is needed and people have to be trained [75]. Education and training facilities have to handle very heterogeneous groups of students varying in age, education, and technical background. The target group of LE consists of students, mainly from the Generation Y, which are eager to play and are going to be trained as image interpreters.

Lost Earth 2307 (Fig. 8) is a *4X* strategy game (4X as in eXplore, eXpand, eXploit, and eXterminate) for training purposes. The explorative and exploiting characteristics are mirrored in its game mechanics and are congruent with the job description of an image interpreter. This encompasses the systematic identification of all kinds of objects in challenging image data from various sensor types.

The rationale for adaptivity is, besides the effective knowledge transfer by personalized learning and recommendations for heterogeneous user groups, the introduction of an intelligent tutoring agent which allows gaining advantages by interlinking multiple software products for learning. Since this game is part of a digital ecosystem of learning management systems, computer simulators and serious games, the goal is to have an intelligent tutoring component for adaptivity which can be attached to each learning system and which allows for data interoperability to facilitate learning and training between multiple software products [88]. Intelligent game-based learning systems are typically not designed in interoperable ways. For adaptive serious games and adaptive simulations in image interpretation the intelligent tutoring component is designed as an external software system which follows commonly used interoperability standards for data acquisition and information exchange. The solution approach is the development of an adaptive interoperable tutoring agent, called *"E-Learning AI"* (ELAI) which consists of multiple game engine adapters, a standardized communication layer and an external intelligent tutoring agent which interprets the collected data to adjust the game or simulation mechanics [88]. The interoperability lays in the communication layer and its data format. Interlinking various computer simulation systems and serious games can be done by using general purpose

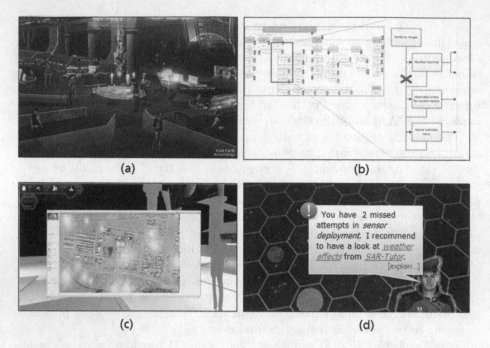

(a)   (b)

(c)   (d)

Fig. 8. Serious game *Lost Earth 2307* for image interpretation training; (a) Bridge scene for mission tasking; (b) adaptive storyboard pathways (the red X indicates elimination of a formerly optional, now mandatory path); (c) dynamic difficulty adjustment with image modifications; (d) virtual agent with help and recommendations. (Colour figure online)

communication architectures and protocols, for instance, the *High Level Architecture* (HLA) for distributed simulation systems interoperability. Additionally, by using standardized data specifications like the *Extended API* (xAPI; also *Tin Can API*) [3] and *Activity Streams* [64], the interlinked systems not only gain a common, learning-affine data exchange language (for intra-communication), but they can also be integrated in networks of other learning systems which use xAPI or *Activity Streams* (for inter-communication).

The adaptive aspects developed for *Lost Earth 2307* are (1) dynamic adaptation of storyboard pathways that are achieved by dynamically modifying the underlying state-transition-models (e.g., eliminating crossings with optional paths to retain only mandatory pathways); (2) modification of imagery content in the sense of *Dynamic Difficulty Adjustment* (DDA) (e.g., dynamically inserting simple effects like clouds or, in the radar case, partial blurring, to make the identification of objects more difficult); and (3) dynamic injection of an *Intelligent Virtual Agent* (IVA) [88] which gives context-sensitive guidance by providing help- and learning material which fits best (i.e., is most relevant) to the current working context of the user [87]. Figure 8 b–d outline these aspects. Considering the problematic outcomes of overly active or intrusive IVAs (like "Clippy" [60]), the ELAI IVA must be actively triggered by the users to provide context-related help and learning recommendations [87].

5.2   Motion-based Games for Health

The following sections discuss the adaptability and adaptivity of three consecutive projects on motion-based games for health. In this chapter we only include brief general introductions to the projects in order to provide sufficient background to contextualize our coverage of the aspects regarding presonalization and adaptivity that are relevant to this chapter and are discussed in more detail. A broader introduction and a more general discussion of the projects is available in Sect. 4.2 of the chapter on *Games for Health* in this volume.

WuppDi! - Motion-Based Games for People with Parkinson's. The *WuppDi! suite* of games for patients with Parkinson's disease (PD) [9] was developed following a user-centered, iterative approach, targeting a collection of games that could support regular physiotherapy sessions for PD patients by offering an alternative source of motivation. The suite features five games that are controlled by hand or arm movements and implement wide motor action with a focus on upper body activation and control. For details on the *WuppDi! suite* see the chapter on games for health in this volume.

Although the game prototypes were repeatedly adjusted to be easier to use and understand, and despite the fact that difficulty choices were available (as classic options or changes in levels), early evaluations suggested that the games were not able to fully cover for the very heterogeneous abilities and needs of individual users from the target group. As a result the game *Sterntaler* (Fig. 9) was augmented with an adaptive system based on heuristic DDA [82].

Details regarding the calibration of *Range of Motion* (ROM), the adaptivity module and the results of a first evaluation can be found in Smeddinck et al. [82]. In brief, while the calibration focuses on ROM, the game was changed to be adaptive with regard to three aspects: ROM, accuracy, and speed (Fig. 10).

Fig. 9. Game *Sterntaler*. The hand cursor is controlled by a person standing in front of a screen or display. Players have to collect streaks of stars that mirror therapeutically helpful motion.

Fig. 10. Three adjustment mechanisms employed in the adaptive version of Sterntaler: speed, accuracy, and range of motion (left to right).

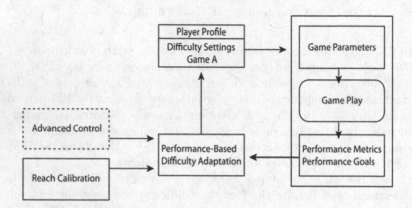

Fig. 11. Schematic overview of a game architecture with mixed adaptability and adaptivity. Elements for advanced control allow for manual adjustments, while reach calibration and performance-based difficulty adaptation implement automated adjustments.

Figure 11 shows an extension of the general model with a performance evaluation and a difficulty adjustment mechanism component mentioned above, by introducing system boundaries, configuration, and calibration. A study of the adaptive components was performed with three participants over a course of five sessions [82].

The results were promising in that the participants managed to reach the calibrated target ROM thresholds almost without exception during the study period. They also accepted the games and were not irritated by the updated adjustment mechanisms. However, some challenges became more clear and additional challenges also became evident. The visibility of adjustments, for example, proved to be potentially problematic, even though this was a singleplayer situation (and not a competitive multiplayer where obvious differences can be much more problematic). Some questions also arose around the scoring. Remarks by the participants in different directions indicated that the question whether scoring should be adjusted to reflect the current internal difficulty level requires further study. Lastly, even with only three participants, the detailed analysis underlined the existence of extreme interpersonal differences and even the same person could perform very differently with one arm compared to the another, or perform differently from day to day, for example due to variations in medication [82].

Spiel Dich Fit - Activating Motion-Based Games for Older Adults. Following up on the *WuppDi!* project, the project *Spiel Dich Fit* (SDF) aimed at integrating a broader number of options for adaptability and more advanced semi-automatic adaptivity. A suite of MGH was developed implementing activating movement games for older adults and for explorative use in physiotherapy, prevention, and rehabilitation [84]. Accordingly, a configuration tool for therapists was developed alongside the games (Fig. 12). Both elements were developed with a user-centered iterative design process featuring multiple formative exploratory studies and continuous evaluations.

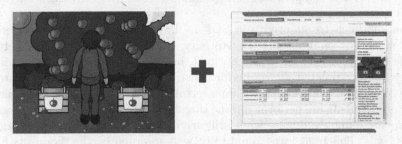

Fig. 12. Settings tool that allows therapists to perform detailed manual adaptations.

The project was followed by a medium-term study of the situated use of the games and settings interface in a physiotherapy practice over the course of five weeks [84]. The player performance, functional development, and experience have been compared, as well as the therapist experience between a group working with activating movement games in a garden setting with a manual settings interface. The study included a group of therapists and participants working with the same games and interface, but with added semi-automatic adaptivity, and a control group that performed traditional physiotherapy exercises without MGH. Initial results showed mixed impacts on experiential measures while the physiological measure of functional reach increased significantly more in both games groups than it did in the traditional therapy group over the course of five weeks [84].

With regard to adaptability, the settings interface allowed the therapists to perform personalized settings for range of motion (by active game screen zones; Fig. 12), required speed, motion accuracy, endurance (level duration) and complexity (amount of active objects) for each level. These settings were subject to a pre-study with ten therapists and were evaluated as being "easily understandable", "useful for making meaningful adjustments", and "allowing for efficient configurations". Since therapists are likely to be able to make informed decisions about the physical abilities much more so than about specific game performance abilities of their patients, the decision was made to express options for manual adaptation as parameters that relate to the player abilities (such as at what speed a person can or should move) and not to specific ingame variables (e.g., how many apples per minute should appear on a tree to be picked by the player). However, this does result in the need for a translation of the difficulty settings that were performed by therapists into difficulty adjustments of actual ingame variables. In SDF, these were achieved via the linear mapping of thresholded variable ranges to normalized difficulty parameters from the interface. Since the project did not encompass extended user models or a heavy focus on translatable settings, the therapists supplied settings per player per game. An additional layer of translation would be necessary to achieve the most efficient way of providing settings; only once per player; which could then be transformed into normalized parameters for a potentially broad number of games. This method was found to be preferred by the therapists, but it requires extensive balancing and would likely benefit from complex adaptive techniques that exceeded the scope of the project.

The approach to adaptivity in SDF is illustrated in Fig. 13. It featured a mixed model for semi-automatic adaptivity. In that approach, manual settings provide keyframes between which optimal, but manually determined candidate settings are interpolated. Player performance is then allowed to fluctuate around the target level of performance within a certain threshold (Fig. 14). Dynamic difficulty adjustments are performed if the thresholds are violated in order to assure an adequate game experience while still driving the player towards the targeted serious goals. This model was found to be well-accepted by the therapists in the study and allowed for steady performance increases without notable frustration among the patients [84].

While the medium-term study showed promising effects with non-frail older adults, and the options for adaptability were found to be telling and easy to use for therapists, the semi-automatic adaptivity did not lead to large differences between the two game groups (i.e., compared to purely manual settings). The mixed model with difficulty parameters, that where oriented around the physiological abilities of each player and which where configured on a per player per game basis, requires at least semi-regular active involvement by therapists.

Fig. 13. (Left to right) Screenshots of the games from *Spiel Dich Fit* employed in the medium-term study; apple picking and catching locusts; balancing with butterflies (with a player from the target group); the settings interface for controlling adaptations and adaptivity.

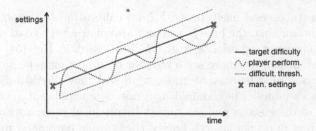

Fig. 14. Adaptivity approach in the *Spiel Dich Fit* project by dynamic difficulty adjustment.

Additionally, automatic adjustments in some cases quickly reached thresholds that did not respect the abilites and needs of all members of the target population, so that notably suboptimal situations did occur. The following project *Adaptify* was thus designed to tackle these potential areas for improvements.

Adaptify - Personalized Playful Programs in Therapy for Chronic Lower-Back Pain. The project *Adaptify* focuses on improvements in adaptability and adaptivity in GFH. The objectives are to a focus on (1) low-friction applicability in real world situated use; (2) sensor augmentation with pressure sensitive mats in addition to optical skeleton tracking; and (3) to establish a commercially competitive production quality for a new generation of GFH for lower back pain afflictions. The main goals in this regard are far-reaching yet highly efficient options for manual settings, fast onboarding of new users, and powerful automatic adaptivity that results in less frequent need of manual therapist adjustments. To these ends, player models are built that are supported by a rich multi-sensor data image of the psychophysiological state of the players. These models are augmented with models of typical developments during treatment and aggregated developments of clustered groups that allow for similarity-based adaptivity.

First results regarding manual adaptations show promise in using body-based and user-centric settings on tablet devices. This approach can produce further benefits by offering visual support for communication about patient abilities and development between therapists and patients, or between therapists and other therapists [85].

There is a considerable complexity in the endeavor of creating an advanced adaptive MGH as outlined for the *Adaptify* project. Next to well-designed manual adaptation, reliable performance data must be collected, the system must allow for player or patient feedback to be taken into account, and modules for data storage, analysis, and action strategies must be realized for the automatic adaptation. Notably, a considerable amount of effort in research and development around adaptive GFH is not concerned with the games themselves, but with various aspects of the surrounding ecosystem. Manual adaptation requires not only a detailed yet functional and effective selection of parameters that translate into ingame settings, and likely benefits from calibration to support therapists in their decision making, the interfaces must also offer a very good usability and at least adequate user experience (e.g., *cf.* illustration in Fig. 15). When manual settings are presented, there are a number of important aspects to consider: The parameters should be easy to understand and they should relate to meaningful ingame variables. They should also not be encumbering (i.e., a limited total number of dimensions and possibly a hierarchical presentation with more advanced settings in deeper layers). Lastly, the optimal parameter mapping from the therapist interface to ingame settings is often not linear. Typically, because of ease-of-use and intuitive adjustment possibilities the therapist interface provides access to linearly scaling and normalized setting parameters. However, these linear settings must be mapped to nonlinear ingame parameters. Advanced systems for adaptability and adaptivity can make use of modular architectures to make portions of such solutions re-usable, since they are expensive upon first implementation.

Fig. 15. Therapist interacting with an early concept of an updated settings interface for motion-based games for health in the project Adaptify.

Therapists involved with the project reported that a configuration and settings process should not take longer than two minutes per patient. Additionally, therapists reported that they are not likely to find the time to perform weekly adjustments for each individual patient. Adaptive systems that partially automate the settings are thus called for, but they require rich feedback from (multiple) sensors with matching data analysis and performance metrics that are not trivial. Next to extensive data storage and adequate and tested adaptation schemes, machine learning and data mining are more likely to play an integral role the larger the involved data sets or the more complex the involved parameter spaces grow.

6   Technical Challenges

Various technical challenges exist which hinder adaptive games and adaptive concepts from easy spreading to other (game) engines, software applications, or to other domains or application areas. Some of these challenges are presented in the following. The technical challenges for personalization and adaptation of games with a focus on serious games are oriented around the core technical concepts of this chapter, i.e., data or content interoperability, modularization of content (e.g., splitting game episodes or scenes into smaller atomic chunks for flexible reorganization), as well as technical measurement of the players' intrinsic (e.g., learning) states or physical capabilities.

One key challenge in personalization and adaptation is the interoperability of data. The usage of commonly used standards for data representation enables systems to effectively exchange data and information. Re-using established adaptation and personalization strategies or modules only becomes possible when the implemented data schemata are interoperable (e.g., allowing data exchange on usage activity or content) with other serious games. Interoperable content can enable game engines to use content from other engines and incorporate it into their own settings. Interoperable data on usage activities can facilitate game analytics and provide the grounds for a broader and deeper understanding of player behavior beyond the limitations of one single engine [88]. In the learning domain, the *Experience API* (xAPI; also *Tin Can API*) specification provides an approach to effective and flexible data-transfer between different kinds of systems, e.g., between *Learning Management Systems* (LMS) and game engines or computer simulators. The xAPI makes use of the *Activity Streams* data format which is also being used for tracking activities in social networks, e.g., by Facebook, Google+ and others.

A further challenge, which is related to interoperability, is the modularization of content. This is still an active field of research and raises multiple technical challenges, for example how to (automatically) decontextualize content into stand-alone chunks, and how to semantically annotate those in a standardized interoperable fashion. The adaptation of games along personalized, individual pathways is only possible with modularized content, i.e., content which can be realigned and is not tightly integrated. Modularization at the same time facilitates effective interoperability. When content is modularized into smaller components (modules, building blocks, bits, etc.), application programming interfaces for exchanging information about such components, their handling, as well as for their(re-)combination must be considered. Existing metadata standards could be used as base schemata and be adapted for modularization of game content. An example of such a metadata base schema for the educational domain is the *IEEE Learning Object Model* (LOM) which has a built-in flexibility through a specification of application profiles for specific contexts [48].

Furthermore, it is still unclear how to technically measure the current immersion level of a player without breaking that very immersion, as asking players to respond to surveys would. The information on the current level of attention of the player is crucial for the adaptivity engine to automatically react and adapt the game. Of course, there are models from the cognitive sciences which can provide information about the cognitive state of the players (or learners) after monitoring them. Technical sensory devices could provide the system with data on the physiological state of the users [62]. *Human Computer Interfaces* (HCI), in particular *Brain Computer Interfaces* (BCI) could provide some insight in what kind of (cognitive) states the users of serious games are. The aforementioned techniques are just beginning to be employed for these purposes, yet such explorations appear worthwhile in order to investigate the neurophysiological basis for player engagement and for achieving the respective serious outcomes.

7   Research Questions

A general research question for personalized and adaptive (learning) games concerns the actual effects of such games – positive or negative. Especially for adaptive serious games: what is the long-term learning outcome? Measuring the short-term effects of games is doable and can provide the researcher with valuable information to optimize the feedback-loop. Medium- to long term evaluations, however, are complex and expensive. A further research question is how to assess the individual effects of different adaptive components within a broader setting. Generalizing results, i.e., inferring from single measurements to global statements, becomes more complex the more components are at interplay.

A further crucial question with adaptivity is when to adapt to the user. Decision making in this regard could include the measurement of immersion or other cognitive states. As noted before, user acceptance of both manual and automatic adjustments needs to be taken into consideration. Models like the *Technology Acceptance Model* (TAM) [26,97] could assist in gaining information on this matter. The TAM by Davis [26] lists factors which influence the perceived usefulness and perceived usability of a technological system, and it offers a model of how these aspects affect the acceptance by the users.

Another venue of open research questions is prediction and anticipation. The most common current approaches with heuristics-based DDA are reactive. This means that they react when a problematic configuration is detected through implicit or explicit feedback, indicating that the current settings are relatively suboptimal. By integrating user and world models, the impact of supposed adaptations can be estimated, theoretically allowing for a smaller number of suboptimal situations. Figure 16 outlines a typical cycle of adaptive gameplay: Some serious game is played and leads to a certain player experience. That experience or player performance are measured and an adjustment mechanism alters the game to keep the experience or performance in desired bounds. Such a process can be augmented with a predictive anticipatory loop before the actual adjustments are performed (as illustrated by the box with red outline in Fig. 16). To determine how different candidate adaptations would likely impact resulting play, experience, and performance, and to select the most viable candidate settings, such loops are typically run in simulations against user and world models. Depending on the player reactions following a choice and enaction of changes,

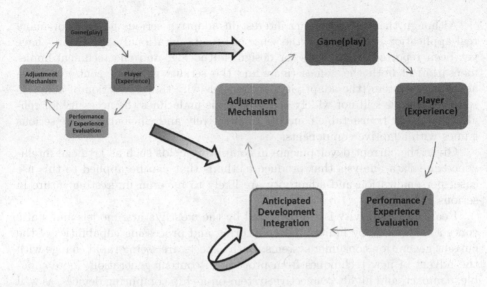

Fig. 16. Reactive adaptive systems can potentially be extended to prevent maladaptations by introducing a predictive anticipatory loop; it simulates various settings candidates and the likely effects on the player experience and performance to identify the most optimal adjustments.

world and user models can be adjusted. Due to the complexity of the required models, such anticipatory approaches are not yet commonly used in research prototypes or commercial serious games. However, in terms of general predictive personalization, such techniques have the potential to largely avoid maladaptations, making this area a very interesting spot for future research.

8 Summary and Outlook

Since the topic of personalized and adaptive serious games is highly multi-disciplinary, this chapter focuses on selected general principles, models, and techniques which are relevant in the eyes of the authors. Regarding the targeted audience of this book (doctoral students and topic-affine scientists) this chapter provides the readers with a solid basis for further investigations on the topic of adaptivity for serious games.

We discuss the general principles of adaptation in detail together with the objectives of adaptivity, common challenges, and discuss approaches to tackling these challenges. We include a process model of the adaptive cycle as a general framework for adaptivity. The central challenges of the cold-start problem and co-adaptation are discussed in relation to adaptivity and personalization. Furthermore, we discuss the basics for adaptivity in learning games, and games for health, in particular in motion-based games for health. Since the challenge of heterogeneous user groups is especially pronounced in the health area, personalization and adaptation are of high relevance for this domain.

Although there is a growing interest in adaptive serious games, not many real application examples - in the sense of broad operational application - have yet been reported. High costs for design, authoring, and the technical implementation of both the games (including the serious game elements) and the adaptation system (the adaptivity) are reasons why the production of adaptive serious games is still not widely observed. This underlines the necessity for reliable and easily transferable concepts to effectively and efficiently create serious games with adaptive components.

Given the current developments in computing fields such as artificial intelligence and data analysis that produce methods that can be applied to this use case, personalization and adaptivity are likely to have an interesting future in serious games.

Real-time adaptivity is still hindered by the mostly static models and static content, as well as by limited data capturing and processing capabilities of the current generation consumer systems. Both aspects are seeing rapid change with the advent of new techniques from procedural content generation, more capable, compact, and highly connective system-on-a-chip computing devices, as well as with capable and affordable sensor devices for context tracking, like gesture recognition (e.g., Xbox Kinect, Playstation Move, etc.) or eye tracking devices (e.g., EyeX, Eye Tribe Tracker Pro, etc.). With online adaptive content generation and real interoperability of data, models, and content, an adaptive game could modify not only the game mechanics to match the user's needs, but also edit, generate or collect new content which better fits the current situation of the user. In regard to interoperability, some strong foundations are already laid by the *Linked Open Data* (LOD) [13] initiative, or, in the educational context, by the *Open Educational Resources* (OER) [10,25] initiative.

Whereas this chapter mostly focuses on adaptivity in respect to the human operator, future work is going to include adaptivity in respect to production processes and the simulation or game itself. The latter aspect introduces self-learning and self-adapting systems, which have not been included in this chapter. A driving force behind adaptive serious games is the promise that companies and institutions can reduce the costs for repeated updates and customizations. For instance, a serious game for the training of specific logistics processes could not only personalize the training program to the human operators but also self-adapt to changing logistics requirements and processes. While such solutions will likely require prior breakthroughs in the underlying fields of computer science, current approaches to adaptivity and personalization in games already show promising results and given the rapidly broadening range of application scenarios for serious games, with widely different users, methods to effectively and efficiently increase player experience and performance with regard to the targeted serious outcomes are highly sought-after.

Further Reading

- Van Eck, Richard. 2007. Building Artificially Intelligent Learning Games. In Games and Simulations in Online Learning: Research and Development Frameworks, edited by David Gibson, Clark Aldrich, and Marc Prensky, 271–307. Hershey, PA, USA: IGI Global [92].
  This book chapter describes how to construct intelligent learning games based on theories and technologies in education, instructional design, artificial intelligence, and cognitive psychology.
- Millington, Ian, and Funge, John. 2009. Artificial Intelligence for Games. CRC Press [59].
  This book on game A.I. development explains numerous A.I. examples from real games in detail. Furthermore it introduces many techniques little used by game developers today which could also be advantageous for adaptive games.
- Ritterfeld, U., Cody, M., and Vorderer, P. 2009. Serious Games: Mechanisms and Effects. Defence Management Journal. Volume 12 [74].
  This book gives a general academic overview on the mechanisms and effects of serious games which should be considered when designing concepts for adaptive games.
- Bakkes, S., Tan, C. T., and Pisan, Y. 2012. Personalised gaming. In Proceedings of The 8th Australasian Conference on Interactive Entertainment Playing the System [11].
  This conference paper addresses multiple aspects regarding the motivation for personalized gaming, supported by an extensive overview of the scientific literature.
- Zarraonandía, T., Díaz, P., and Aedo, I. 2016. Modeling Games for Adaptive and Personalized Learning. In The Future of Ubiquitous Learning: Learning Designs for Emerging Pedagogies. Springer Berlin Heidelberg [98].
  This book section deals with the inter-disciplinary challenges when designing adaptive educational games, and it presents a conceptual model for flexible game designs.

References

1. Adams, E.: Fundamentals of Game Design. New Riders, San Francisco (2010)
2. Adams, R., Comley, R., Ghoreyshi, M.: The potential of the BCI for accessible and smart e-learning. In: Stephanidis, C. (ed.) UAHCI 2009. LNCS, vol. 5615, pp. 467–476. Springer, Berlin, Heidelberg (2009)
3. Advanced Distributed Learning (ADL): Experience API (xAPI) Specification, Version 1.0.1. Technical report, Advanced Distributed Learning (ADL) Initiative, U.S. Department of Defense (2013)
4. Alankus, G., Proffitt, R., Kelleher, C., Engsberg, J.: Stroke therapy through motion-based games: a case study. In: ASSETS 2010, pp. 219–226 (2010)
5. Allen, B.: Information Tasks: Toward a User-Centered Approach to Information Systems, 1st edn. Academic Press Inc., Orlando (1996)

6. Andrade, G., Ramalho, G., Santana, H., Corruble, V.: Extending reinforcement learning to provide dynamic game balancing. In: 19th International Joint Conference on Artificial Intelligence, Proceedings of the Workshopon Reasoning, Representation, and Learning in Computer Games, (IJCAI), pp. 7–12 (2005)
7. Antle, A.N., Bevans, A., Tanenbaum, J., Seaborn, K., Wang, S.: Futura: design for collaborative learning and game play on a multi-touch digital tabletop. In: Proceedings of the Fifth International Conference on Tangible, Embedded, and Embodied Interaction, TEI 2011, pp. 93–100. ACM, New York (2011)
8. Anwar, M.M., Greer, J., Brooks, C.A.: Privacy enhanced personalization in e-learning. In: Proceedings of the 2006 International Conference on Privacy Security and Trust Bridge the Gap Between PST Technologies and Business Services PST 2006, p. 1 (2006)
9. Assad, O., et al.: Motion-based games for parkinson's disease patients. In: Anacleto, J.C., Fels, S., Graham, N., Kapralos, B., Saif El-Nasr, M., Stanley, K. (eds.) ICEC 2011. LNCS, vol. 6972, pp. 47–58. Springer, Heidelberg (2011). doi:10.1007/978-3-642-24500-8_6
10. Atkins, D.E., Brown, J.S., Hammond, A.L.: A Review of the Open Educational Resources (OER) Movement: Achievements, Challenges, and New Opportunities. Creative Common, Mountain View (2007)
11. Bakkes, S., Tan, C.T., Pisan, Y.: Personalised gaming. In: Proceedings of the 8th Australasian Conference on Interactive Entertainment Playing the System -IE 2012, pp. 1–10. ACM, New York (2012)
12. Barzilay, O., Wolf, A.: Adaptive rehabilitation games. J. Electromyogr. Kinesiol. Official J. Int. Soc. Electrophysiol. Kinesiol. **23**(1), 182–189 (2013)
13. Bauer, F., Kaltenböck, M.: Linked Open Data: The Essentials. Edition-mono/monochrom, Vienna (2011)
14. Blakemore, S.J., Frith, U.: The learning brain: lessons for education: aprécis. Dev. Sci. **8**(6), 459–465 (2005)
15. Bloom, B.S.: Taxonomy of Educational Objectives, vol. 16. Longmans, Green, New York (1956)
16. Brusilovsky, P.: Methods and techniques of adaptive hypermedia. User Model. User-Adapt. Interact. J. Personalization Res. **6**(2–3), 87–129 (1996)
17. Champandard, A.J.: Top 10 most influential AI games (2007). http://aigamedev.com/open/highlights/top-ai-games/
18. Chen, J.: Flow in games (and everything else). Commun. ACM **50**(4), 31–34 (2007)
19. Chiou, A., Wong, K.W.: Player adaptive entertainment computing (PAEC): mechanism to model user satisfaction by using neuro linguistic programming(NLP) techniques. In: IEEE Symposium On Computational Intelligence and Games, CIG 2008, pp. 343–349 (2008)
20. Conati, C., Manske, M.: Evaluating adaptive feedback in an educational computer game. In: Ruttkay, Z., Kipp, M., Nijholt, A., Vilhjálmsson, H.H. (eds.) IVA 2009. LNCS (LNAI), pp. 146–158. Springer, Heidelberg (2009). doi:10.1007/978-3-642-04380-2_18
21. Corne, B.: Making existing educational games adaptive using AOP. Master thesis, Vrije Universiteit Brussel (2013). http://wise.vub.ac.be/content/making-existing-educational-games-adaptive-using-aop
22. Cowley, B., Charles, D., Black, M., Hickey, R.: Toward an understanding of flow in video games. Comput. Entertainment (CIE) **6**(2), 1–27 (2008)
23. Crawford, C.: The Art of Computer Game Design. Osborne/McGraw-Hill, New York (1984)

24. Csikszentmihalyi, M.: Flow: The Psychology of Optimal Experience. Harper & Row, New York (1990)
25. D'Aquin, M., Adamou, A., Dietze, S.: Assessing the educational linked data landscape. In: ACM Web Science 2013 (2013)
26. Davis, F.D.: A technology acceptance model for empirically testing new end-user information systems: theory and results. Ph.D. thesis (1985)
27. Deci, E.L., Eghrari, H., Patrick, B.C., Leone, D.R.: Facilitating internalization: the self-determination theory perspective. J. Person. **62**(1), 119–142 (1994)
28. Drachen, A., Canossa, A., Yannakakis, G.N.: Player modeling using self-organization in Tomb Raider: underworld. In: IEEE Symposium on Computational Intelligence and Games, CIG 2009, pp. 1–8 (2009)
29. El-Khatib, K., Korba, L., Xu, Y., Yee, G.: Privacy and security in e-learning. Int. J. Distance Educ. Technol. **1**(4), 1–19 (2003)
30. Eliëns, A., Ruttkay, Z.: Record, replay & reflect - a framework for understanding (serious) game play. In: Proceedings of Euromedia, vol. 9 (2008)
31. Fischer, G.: User modeling in human-computer interaction. User Model. User-Adapt. Interact. **11**, 65–86 (2001)
32. Fogg, B.J.: A behavior model for persuasive design. In: Proceedings of the 4th International Conference on Persuasive Technology, Persuasive 2009, pp. 40: 1–40: 7. ACM, New York (2009)
33. Fraunhofer, I.: Lost Earth 2307 (2016). http://www.iosb.fraunhofer.de/servlet/is/58015/
34. Fullerton, T., Swain, C., Hoffman, S.: Game Design Workshop: Designing, Prototyping, and Playtesting Games. Focal Press, Waltham (2004)
35. Gerling, K.M., Miller, M., Mandryk, R.L., Birk, M.V., Smeddinck, J.D.: Effects of balancing for physical abilities on player performance, experience and self-esteem in exer games. In: Proceedings of the 32nd Annual ACM Conference on Human Factors in Computing Systems, CHI 2014, pp. 2201–2210. ACM, New York (2014)
36. Gerling, K.M., Schulte, F.P., Smeddinck, J., Masuch, M.: Game design for older adults: effects of age-related changes on structural elements of digital games. In: Herrlich, M., Malaka, R., Masuch, M. (eds.) ICEC 2012. LNCS, vol. 7522, pp. 235–242. Springer, Heidelberg (2012). doi:10.1007/978-3-642-33542-6_20
37. Göbel, S., Mehm, F., Radke, S., Steinmetz, R.: 80days: adaptive digital storytelling for digital educational games. In: Proceedings of the 2nd International Workshop on Story-Telling and Educational Games (STEG 2009), vol. 498 (2009)
38. Göbel, S., Hardy, S., Wendel, V., Mehm, F., Steinmetz, R.: Serious games for health: personalized exer games. In: Proceedings of the International Conference on Multimedia, MM 2010, NY, USA, pp. 1663–1666 (2010)
39. Göbel, S., Wendel, V., Ritter, C., Steinmetz, R.: Personalized, adaptive digital educational games using narrative game-based learning objects. In: Zhang, X., Zhong, S., Pan, Z., Wong, K., Yun, R. (eds.) Edutainment 2010. LNCS, vol. 6249, pp. 438–445. Springer, Heidelberg (2010). doi:10.1007/978-3-642-14533-9_45
40. Gómez-Martín, M.A., Gómez-Martín, P.P., González-Calero, P.A.: Game-driven intelligent tutoring systems. In: Rauterberg, M. (ed.) ICEC 2004. LNCS, vol. 3166, pp. 108–113. Springer, Heidelberg (2004). doi:10.1007/978-3-540-28643-1_14
41. Gunderson, L.H., Holling, C.S.: Panarchy: Understanding Transformations in Systems of Humans and Nature. Island Press, Washington (2002)
42. Hartson, R., Pyla, P.: The UX Book: Process and Guidelines for Ensuring a Quality User Experience, 1st edn. Morgan Kaufmann, Burlington (2012)

43. Hernandez, H.A., Graham, T.C., Fehlings, D., Switzer, L., Ye, Z., Bellay, Q., Hamza, M.A., Savery, C., Stach, T.: Design of an exer gaming station for children with cerebral palsy. In: Proceedings of the 2012 ACM Annual Conference on Human Factors in Computing Systems, pp. 2619–2628 (2012)
44. Hocine, N., Gouaïch, A., Cerri, S.A.: Dynamic difficulty adaptation in serious games for motor rehabilitation. In: Göbel, S., Wiemeyer, J. (eds.) GameDays 2014. LNCS, vol. 8395, pp. 115–128. Springer, Heidelberg (2014). doi:10.1007/978-3-319-05972-3_13
45. Howell, S., Veale, T.: Dynamic difficulty adjustment in game-based intelligent tutoring systems. In: Cgames 2006 Proceedings of the 9th International Conferenceon Computer Games Artificial Intelligence and Mobile Systems, pp. 201–204 (2006)
46. Huizinga, J.: Homo ludens: proeve eener bepaling van hetspel-element der cultuur. Amsterdam University Press, Amsterdam (2008)
47. Hunicke, R.: The case for dynamic difficulty adjustment in games. In:Proceedings of the 2005 ACM SIGCHI International Conference on Advances in Computer Entertainment Technology, ACE 2005, pp. 429–433. ACM, New York (2005)
48. IEEE Learning Technology Standards Committee: IEEE standard for learning object metadata. IEEE Stand. **1484**(1), 2004–2007 (2002)
49. Janssen, C.P., Van Rijn, H., Van Liempd, G., der Pompe, G.: User modeling for training recommendation in a depression prevention game. In: Proceedings of the First NSVKI Student Conference, pp. 29–35 (2007)
50. Johnson, W.L., Wang, N., Wu, S.: Experience with serious games for learning foreign languages and cultures. In: Proceedings of the SimTecT Conference(2007)
51. Kickmeier-Rust, M.D., Albert, D.: Educationally adaptive: balancing serious games. Int. J. Comput. Sci. Sport **11**, 15–28 (2012)
52. Kickmeier-Rust, M.D., Hillemann, E., Albert, D.: Tracking the UFO's paths: using eye-tracking for the evaluation of serious games. In: Shumaker, R. (ed.) VMR 2011. LNCS, vol. 6773, pp. 315–324. Springer, Heidelberg (2011). doi:10.1007/978-3-642-22021-0_35
53. Krizhevsky, A., Sutskever, I., Hinton, G.E.: Image Net Classification with Deep Convolutional Neural Networks. In: Advances in Neural Information Processing Systems, pp. 1–9 (2012)
54. Langley, P., Laird, J.E., Rogers, S.: Cognitive architectures: Research issues and challenges. Cogn. Syst. Res. **10**(2), 141–160 (2009)
55. Lopes, R., Bidarra, R.: Adaptivity challenges in games and simulations: a survey. IEEE Trans. Comput. Intell. AI Games **3**(2), 85–99 (2011)
56. Magerko, B.: Adaptation in digital games. Computer **41**(6), 87–89 (2008)
57. Markram, H., Meier, K., Lippert, T., Grillner, S., Frackowiak, R., Dehaene, S., Knoll, A., Sompolinsky, H., Verstreken, K., DeFelipe, J., Grant, S., Changeux, J.P., Saria, A.: Introducing the human brain project. Procedia Comput. Sci. **7**, 39–42 (2011)
58. Mateas, M., Stern, A.: Build it to understand it: ludology meets narratology in game design space. In: DiGRA Conference Vancouver BC, pp. 16–20 (2005)
59. Millington, I., Funge, J.: Artificial Intelligence for Games. CRC Press, Boston (2009)
60. Murphy-Hill, E., Murphy, G.C.: Recommendation delivery. In: Robillard, M.P., Maalej, W., Walker, R.J., Zimmermann, T. (eds.) Recommendation Systems in Software Engineering, pp. 223–242. Springer, Berlin, Heidelberg (2014)
61. Murray, M.: Façade review (2005). http://brasslantern.org/reviews/graphic/facademurray.html

62. Nacke, L.: Affective ludology: scientific measurement of user experience in interactive entertainment Technology, p. 327 (2009)
63. Niehaus, J., Riedl, M.O.: Scenario adaptation: an approach to customizing computer-based training games and simulations. In: Proceedings of the AIED2009 Workshop on Intelligent Educational Games, vol. 3, pp. 89–98 (2009)
64. Niemann, K., Scheffel, M., Wolpers, M.: An overview of usage data formats for recommendations in TEL. In: CEUR Workshop Proceedings, vol. 896, pp. 95–100 (2012)
65. Nilsagård, Y.E., Forsberg, A.S., von Koch, L.: Balance exercise for persons with multiple sclerosis using wii games: a randomised, controlled multi-centre study. Multiple Sclerosis J. 19(2), 209–216 (2013)
66. Noseworthy, J.R.: The test and training enabling architecture (TENA) supporting the decentralized development of distributed applications and lvc simulations. In: 12th IEEE/ACM International Symposium on Distributed Simulation and Real-Time Applications, DS-RT 2008, pp. 259–268 (2008)
67. Oijen, J., Vanhée, L., Dignum, F.: CIGA: a middleware for intelligent agents in virtual environments. In: Beer, M., Brom, C., Dignum, F., Soo, V.-W. (eds.) AEGS 2011. LNCS (LNAI), vol. 7471, pp. 22–37. Springer, Heidelberg (2012). doi:10.1007/978-3-642-32326-3_2
68. O'Toole, G.: QuoteInvestigator.com: Did einstein really saythat? (2013). http://quoteinvestigator.com/2013/04/06/fish-climb/
69. Pagulayan, R.J., Keeker, K., Fuller, T., Wixon, D., Romero, R.L., Gunn, D.V.: User-centered design in games. In: The Human-Computer Interaction Handbook: Fundamentals, Evolving Technologies and Emerging Applications, pp. 795–824 (2012)
70. Parasuraman, R., Sheridan, T.B., Wickens, C.D.: A model for types and levels of human interaction with automation. IEEE Trans. Syst. Man Cybern. Part A Syst. Hum. Publ. IEEE Syst. Man Cybern. Soc. 30(3), 286–297 (2000)
71. Peirce, N., Conlan, O., Wade, V.: Adaptive educational games: providing non-invasive personalised learning experiences. In: 2008 Second IEEE International Conference on Digital Game and Intelligent Toy Enhanced Learning, pp. 28–35. IEEE (2008)
72. Petty, R.E., Cacioppo, J.T.: Issue involvement can increase or decrease persuasion by enhancing message-relevant cognitive responses. J. Person. Soc. Psychol. 37(10), 1915–1926 (1979)
73. Rigby, S., Ryan, R.: Glued to Games: How Video Games Draw Us in and Hold Us Spell bound. Praeger, Westport (2011)
74. Ritterfeld, U., Cody, M., Vorderer, P.: Serious Games: Mechanisms and Effects, vol. 12. Routledge, Abingdon (2009)
75. Roller, W., Berger, A., Szentes, D.: Technology based training for radar image interpreters. In: 2013 6th International Conference on Recent Advances inSpace Technologies (RAST), pp. 1173–1177. IEEE (2013)
76. Russell, S.J., Norvig, P.: Artificial Intelligence: A Modern Approach, 3rd edn. Prentice Hall, Upper Saddle River (2009)
77. Sawyer, B.: From cells to cell processors: the integration of health and videogames. IEEE Comput. Graph. Appl. 28(6), 83–85 (2008)
78. Schuler, D., Namioka, A.: Participatory Design: Principles and Practices. CRC Press, Boston (1993)
79. Sheridan, T.B.: Rumination on Automation, 1998. Ann. Rev. Control 25, 89–97 (2001)

80. Shute, V., Zapata-Rivera, D.: Adaptive educational systems. Adapt. Technol. Train. Educ. **7**(1), 1–35 (2012)
81. Smeddinck, J., Herrlich, M., Krause, M., Gerling, K., Malaka, R.: Did they really like the game? - challenges in evaluating exergames with older adults. In: CHI Workshop on Game User Research: Exploring Methodologies, Austin, Texas, USA (2012)
82. Smeddinck, J., Siegel, S., Herrlich, M.: Adaptive difficulty in exer games for parkinson's disease patients. In: Proceedings of Graphics Interface 2013, Regina, SK, Canada (2013)
83. Smeddinck, J.D., Gerling, K.M., Malaka, R.: Anpassbare Computerspiele fÃijr Senioren. Informatik-Spektrum **37**(6), 575–579 (2014)
84. Smeddinck, J.D., Herrlich, M., Malaka, R.: Exergames for physiotherapy and rehabilitation: a medium-term situated study of motivational aspects and impact on functional reach. In: Proceedings of the 33rd Annual ACMConference on Human Factors in Computing Systems, CHI 2015, pp. 4143–4146. ACM, New York (2015)
85. Smeddinck, J.D., Hey, J., Runge, N., Herrlich, M., Jacobsen, C., Wolters, J., Malaka, R.: MoviTouch: mobile movement capability configurations. In: Proceedings of the 17th International ACM SIGACCESS Conference on Computers & Accessibility, ASSETS 2015, pp. 389–390. ACM, New York (2015)
86. Smeddinck, J.D., Mandryk, R., Birk, M., Gerling, K., Barsilowski, D., Malaka, R.: How to present game difficulty choices? exploring the impact on player experience. In: Proceedings of the 34th Annual ACM Conference on Human Factors in Computing Systems, CHI 2016. ACM, New York (2016)
87. Streicher, A., Dambier, N., Roller, W.: Task-centered selection of learning material. Int. J. Comput. Inf. Syst. Ind. Manage. Appl. **4**, 267–274 (2012)
88. Streicher, A., Roller, W.: Towards an inter operable adaptive tutoring agent for simulations and serious games. In: Abraham, A.P., dos Reis, A.P., Roth, J. (eds.) International Conference on Theory and Practice in Modern Computing, MCCSIS 2015, pp. 194–197. IADIS Press, Las Palmas (2015)
89. Sweetser, P., Wyeth, P.: Gameflow: a model for evaluating player enjoyment in games. Comput. Entertainment **3**, 1–24 (2005)
90. Teng, C.I.: Customization, immersion satisfaction, and online gamer loyalty. Comput. Hum. Behav. **26**(6), 1547–1554 (2010)
91. Torrente, J., Moreno-Ger, P., Fernandez-Manjon, B.: Learning models for the integration of adaptive educational games in virtual learning environments. In: Pan, Z., Zhang, X., Rhalibi, A., Woo, W., Li, Y. (eds.) Edutainment 2008. LNCS, vol. 5093, pp. 463–474. Springer, Heidelberg (2008). doi:10.1007/978-3-540-69736-7_50
92. Van Eck, R.: Building artificially intelligent learning games. In: Gibson, D., Aldrich, C., Prensky, M. (eds.) Games and Simulations in Online Learning: Research and Development Frameworks, pp. 271–307. IGI Global, Hershey (2007)
93. Vicencio-Moreira, R., Mandryk, R.L., Gutwin, C., Bateman, S.: The effectiveness (or lack thereof) of aim-assist techniques in first-person shooter games. In: Proceedings of the 32nd Annual ACM Conference on Human Factors in Computing Systems, CHI 2014, pp. 937–946. ACM, New York (2014)
94. Walonoski, J.A., Heffernan, N.T.: Detection and analysis of off-task gaming behavior in intelligent tutoring systems. In: Ikeda, M., Ashley, K.D., Chan, T.-W. (eds.) ITS 2006. LNCS, vol. 4053, pp. 382–391. Springer, Heidelberg (2006). doi:10.1007/11774303_38
95. Wong, K.: Adaptive computer game system using artificial neural networks. In: Neural Information Processing, pp. 675–682 (2008)

96. Woolf, B.P.: Building Intelligent Interactive Tutors. Morgan Kaufmann, Burlington (2009)
97. Yusoff, A., Crowder, R., Gilbert, L.: Validation of serious games attributes using the technology acceptance model. In: 2010 Second International Conference on Games and Virtual Worlds for Serious Applications, pp. 45–51, March 2010
98. Zarraonandía, T., Díaz, P., Aedo, I.: Modeling games for adaptive and personalized learning. In: Gros, B., Kinshuk, K., Maina, M. (eds.) The Future of Ubiquitous Learning, pp. 217–239. Springer, Berlin (2016)

Embodied Interaction in Play: Body-Based and Natural Interaction in Games

Bernhard Maurer[✉]

Center for Human-Computer Interaction, University of Salzburg, Salzburg, Austria
bernhard.maurer@sbg.ac.at

Abstract. This chapter describes embodied interaction as a stance towards interaction design for games. It aims at informing game developers with bridging concepts between gameplay and different interaction paradigms that incorporate and focus on the human body (i.e., body-based, natural and tangible interaction). It highlights challenges, potentials and pitfalls of physical interactions and discusses the role of the human mind-body relation as a fundamental concept towards serious game interaction design. This chapter underlines *embodied interaction in play* as a promising perspective for game developers, that puts emphasize on the notion of humans as social and physical creatures with sentient bodies and highlights the relevance of this perspective for serious game interaction design as well as research in the field. One of the main challenges for researchers in this field will be to create meaningful interactions that internalize these concepts as integral parts of how serious games achieve their impact.

Keywords: Body-based interaction · Natural interaction · Embodied interaction · Interaction design · Game design · Tangible interaction · Serious games

1 Introduction

Traditional digital games often rely on visual on-screen feedback and are built around controller-based input. However, in recent years new technologies emerged that enabled game designers to utilize a more natural way of interaction, e.g., incorporating the human body as an interaction modality or using tangible interfaces for digital manipulation and game input. These new technologies also lead to new design spaces for serious games around using the players body as a means of input as well as designing with and around physical qualities. This notion of *natural interaction* [57] presents new design practices, that are deeply rooted in cognitive and perceptual assumptions about humans and are thus more close to how humans actually interact with their environment.

As human bodies are so fundamental to how a people experience themselves and their surroundings [30, 50], leveraging from body-based and physical interactions is a good opportunity for creating natural and immersive interactions.

© Springer International Publishing AG 2016
R. Dörner et al. (Eds.): Entertainment Computing and Serious Games, LNCS 9970, pp. 378–401, 2016.
DOI: 10.1007/978-3-319-46152-6_15

New technologies enable tracking the player's body, detecting hand gestures or recognizing eye movements via eye tracking, which can all be used as game interaction modalities. This new form of multimodality also brings the opportunity to design games around interactions with or via an avatar (i.e., virtual representations of the player's body) where a player's real body controls a virtual representation. This presents design opportunities, e.g., around deliberately changing and adapting the player body's digital representation in order to induce or change attitudes and behaviours of that person. Furthermore, embodied digital representations of physical artifacts, or tangible interfaces enable interactions that potentially foster sensorial stimulations, which purely digital interactions do not afford. However, these new forms of possible game interactions and experiences also require new design strategies and metaphors.

The human body and its senses are a natural means of interaction, as humans reason and form consciousness based on their bodily experiences and physical surroundings [34]. Thus, it is fundamental for serious game developers to understand how and why this human body-mind relation influences interaction, in order to incorporate a player's body successfully into a game's interaction design.

This chapter starts with a short overview on the concept of embodied interaction (Sect. 2), then focuses on the design challenges and technical peculiarities that emerge when dealing with and designing around body-based interactions (Sect. 3). We further illustrate design strategies that aim at using the human body as a resource for game interaction design towards creating immersive physical and body-based interactions (Sects. 4 and 5). As a theoretical grounding for utilizing and emphasizing the human mind-body relationship in game interaction design, we reflect on the concept of sensorimotor couplings (Sect. 6). The chapter closes with examples of existing serious games that already incorporate the human body and senses (Sect. 7).

This chapter aims at informing developers of serious games how to leverage from these interaction paradigms in order to create new game experiences that put emphasis on the relation between the human body and mind.

2 Embodied Interaction - Away from the Screen into the Real World

The idea of embodied interaction has been introduced by Paul Dourish [19] as a stance towards interaction design. This perspective focuses on designing interactions that are meaningful for humans as social creatures with sentient bodies. Other research around "tangible computing" within the field of HCI focuses on exploring how the interface can be moved *away from the screen into the real world* (i.e., interacting with physical artifacts that are computationally augmented). Further, the field of "social computing" (as coined by Dourish) on the other hand aims at incorporating sociological perspectives into the design of interactions and interfaces. This means that designers have to be aware of the fact that everyday interactions and systems are embedded in systems of social meaning. One aspect that these two research streams - tangible and social computing share - is a common foundation in the utilization of *embodiments*. In that regard, embodiment does not only mean physical reality, but rather, the way that physical and social phenomena unfold in the real world and influence the way we interact [19].

Embodied interaction also puts emphasis on the meaning of the human body, as people interact with their surrounding social and physical world *through* their bodies. Research by Klemmer et al. describes a perspective of *embodied engagement* towards interaction design which focuses on the relation of human "thought (mind) and action (body)" to explain how those factors "co-produce learning and reasoning" [34]. Games are also often based on a certain social setting and can be defined as a "situated collaborative practice" [55]. This social and situated nature of gaming is strongly rooted in other people's physical presence [21]. Hence, body-based and natural interactions can be a direct way to incorporate these social and physical qualities in game-based interactions.

This notion of designing with the human body in mind as well as emphasizing social and physical qualities can be promising for game interaction design in order to create new interaction paradigms and game experiences. Especially natural and body-based interactions bear much potential for game interaction design for serious games that harvest from this potential and relation of human mind and body.

2.1 Body-Based Interaction - The Player's Body as a Design Resource

Within recent years, new technologies that can track the player's body based on, e.g., 3D depth cameras (like Microsoft Kinect [6] or Leap Motion [5]) enable game designers to relate the physical world of the human body to the game world and to utilize it for interaction purposes. These technologies detect the players body, do motion analysis and extract a certain number of joints per player. These transformation of the physical human body into a digital counterpart (i.e., the avatar) can then be used to map for instance, certain functions to specific body parts (the body becomes the controller). However, the resulting new design spaces also introduces new design challenges on how to incorporate movement and the players body itself into engaging play experiences. In that regard, Mueller et al. describe a variety of guidelines and design opportunities that put the human body in the center of interaction and entertainment [46]:

Movement-based Interaction Requiring Special Forms of Feedback

– **Embracing ambiguity**: As usually no two body movements are exactly the same, this often results in inaccurate sensor data. Mueller et al. describe this as a chance for designers rather than a constraint and encourage game designers to "know the limits of your sensors, and use these limits as a design resource" [46, p. 4]. Based on that, they argue that one should design in a way that gives players' actions room for individual differences as well as work with potential sensor errors without drawing the player's attention to it. This means that a game should avoid mechanics that require completely precise controls of body movements and focus more on being liberal and adaptive to the user's individual movements.

- **The cognitive load of movement-based interactions**: Body movements can be demanding and result in high cognitive loads, e.g., when new movements are being learned. Mueller et al. point out that designers should not overload the players with too much feedback [46]. In that regard, *feedback* can be understood in a quite general way, meaning that it can range from being visual (e.g., via points or on-screen indicators), tactile feedback provided by potential wearable interfaces, etc. When learning new movements in a game, players initially focus on the feedback on this new movement itself, rather than focusing on other potentially more difficult interactions within the same game. Hence, Mueller et al. advice game designers to first provide "feedback on the movement itself without too much worrying about scores, multipliers etc." [46, p. 4]. Based on that, they argue that it is beneficial to provide a variety of different feedback channels and let the player choose which ones they want to engage with in order to loosen the cognitive load that engaging with all of them simultaneously would require.

Challenges of movement-based games

- **Special mappings of body movements**: When a player's body movements are digitalized it allows a variety of new mappings between input movement and actual outcome or digital representation. Mueller et al. state that for instance "Wii Tennis maps every simple up-down arm movement into a successful tennis serve, fueling the player's fantasy of being a successful and accomplished tennis player" [46, p. 6]. A resulting strategy for designers can be to map movements in non-linear ways to digital in-game outcomes and feedback, in order to create a certain kind of *amplification* of the players input (e.g., making the movements look better than they actually were).
- **The body as a way to support self expression**: The body is a primary means of human to human communication. Playing a movement-based game can thus be a good source of social interaction and self expression. Mueller et al. propose to allow players to perform their input movements in a unique and special way in order to foster this aspect of self expression within a games interactions, e.g., offering opportunities for secondary movements that do not directly relate to the actual goal of the game - like lifting the guitar in guitar hero [46].

These guidelines are good examples of how the specifics and individual differences of body-based interactions can be incorporated within game interactions. We argue that they can substantially improve movement and body-based game interactions and create engaging game designs beyond what would be possible with conventional graphical and controller-based user interfaces.

2.2 Full-Body Interaction and Learning

Humans as social creatures strongly rely on body movements and other people's bodily presence as a part of learning and collaboration. Malinverni et al. [38] investigated the impact of full-body interaction during collaborative learning processes, and showed that body movement has a highly significant impact on how people perceive collaboration in small groups. They further point out how full-body interaction can be beneficial for constructing a positive social space for collaborative learning as the usage of embodied resources for social communication and social cognition is an important aspect of learning [38].

However, the human body and its movements is prone to individual differences. These human factors and individual differences also influence how a player engages in full-body game interaction and respective learning processes. Mizobata et al. investigated three of these human factors related to full-body game interaction: "motivation to succeed (achiever vs. casual player), motivation to move (mover vs. non-mover), and game expertise (gamer vs. non-gamer)" [45, p. 1]. Their results suggest three main properties of a body-based game that affect players' engagement which are, the *level of cognitive challenge*, *level of physical challenge* and *level of realistic interaction* [45].

Utilizing body-based interactions in games for learning can be a substantial factor on how a game achieves its impact on the learning outcome of the player. However, the mentioned individual differences of every human body as well as individual player preferences have to be considered when designing such a game in order to be engaging for the player.

3 Design Challenges and Issues Related to Body-Based Interactions

Tracking technologies used for natural and body-based interactions introduce several technical challenges as well as design considerations. In order to incorporate a player's body into a game's interaction design, developers have to be aware of these limitations and challenges to find appropriate strategies and workarounds to deal with them.

3.1 Mapping of Player Action and Outcome

A game has to effectively communicate the relation between action (i.e., player input) and outcome (i.e., different forms of feedback e.g., visual, tactile,...) to the player. This relation of input and output is especially crucial in body-based interactions where *embodied metaphors* play an important role towards how a user might experience and understand such mappings of action and outcome. These mappings are individually different and are based on former physical and mental experiences of a player (see also Sect. 4). A game relying on body-based interactions has to successfully inform the player of the outcome of his/her actions (e.g., changes in the gameworld) in order to assure a connection between the user input and the game space with all its representations (e.g., a player's avatar). This is also important in avatar interactions where the player's body is mapped to a digital representation or counterpart. If in such a scenario the connection between the player's actions and in-game outcome is blurry or unclear to the player (e.g., player movement not mapped accurately to the avatar) the avatar player connection can potentially break. However, even if not a main design goal in general, this connection can also be intentionally be challenged or "broken" in order to enable new kinds of interactions and experiences for the player (see Sect. 6.3).

In body-based interactions the player often does not have a physical connection to an interface compared to typical controller-based game interactions. This creates the challenge of designing for accurate and understandable feedback modalities and strategies. Different sensors and actuators enable developers to provide feedback on specific body-parts and movements, thus, creating new information channels for the player beyond what traditional controller-based inputs would convey.

3.2 Limitations of Body-Based Interactions - Dealing with Unintended Inputs

In body-based and natural interaction (e.g., gaze-based input) it can be difficult to detect if at a giving moment the user actually interacts with the system intentionally. Otherwise, every user movement could be interpreted as an interaction, which is not always the case. In order to incorporate the user's body successfully into game-based interactions, the game has to distinguish between movements related to intentional inputs from the player and unintentional player movement detected by the sensing technology. This issue is often framed as the *Midas Touch Problem* (e.g., within research by Schwarz et al. [53]) which especially vision-based interfaces like Microsoft Kinect [6] suffer from.

One main aspect such vision-based interfaces often share is their "always on" nature, so everything a user does in front of the interface may be interpreted as an interaction with the system [33]. This makes it harder to actually interpret the user's intended actions. One way to deal with this technical issue is to utilize additional sensors and merge their information together to make it easier for a system to determine whether to pay attention to a user's interaction or whether to ignore them. For instance, Schwarz et al. propose an approach based on a combination of facial features, body pose and motion to approximate a user's intention to interact with a giving system [53]. Their approach calculates an "intention-to-interact metric" based on a collection of binary classifiers that use body pose, motion and gaze of the user. This metric is then used to determine the likelihood that a user intends to interact with an interface. Such a system could be especially helpful in multi-user settings to distinct between user's and in order to decide when to pay attention to specific users and their movements or when to ignore them.

The challenges around dealing with unintended inputs in body-based interactions also relates to a general design issue, which is, designing for a definite

Table 1. A selection of different sensor types, specific example devices and their corresponding tracking data.

Sensor type	Sensor	Exemplary tracking data
Vision-based	Leap motion [5]	Hand gestures and movements
Vision-based	Kinect [6]	Body movement, hand gesture, facial expression
Vision-based	Eye trackers, e.g., [9]	Eye movement, gaze direction, gaze saccades
Wearable	Smartwatches, e.g., [1]	Activity data, heart rate, locations
Wearable	Fitness band, e.g., [3]	Activity data, heart rate, sitting time

beginning and end of an interaction with a system or game. Sensing and defining these definite boundaries of an interaction is the core of the mentioned midas touch problem and a general issue and research topic within the field.

In sum, the challenge of tracking a user's body-based inputs and movements accurately is an integral topic and limiting factor in body-based and natural interactions. Existing tracking technologies often rely on vision- and camera-based sensors, enabling to track a user's hand-gestures or full-body movements, incorporate eye-movements or in general enable the usage of contact-free interactions. Further, also sensing based on wearable technology or fusing the data of multiple types of sensors can lead to more accurate and insightful user data as well as new interaction opportunities (e.g., [53]).

Table 1 shows a selection of various sensor types that represent enabling technologies for embodied interactions at the moment, and illustrates the sensor's tracking data accordingly.

Sensing technologies enabling body-based interactions are manifold, with Microsoft Kinect being probably the most used and prominent in recent research activities (see also Sect. 7).

4   Tangible Interaction and User Interfaces

Besides the human body as a resource for game interaction designs, also the incorporation of tangible and embedded interaction is an emerging topic within research and industry. As a further alternative to graphical interfaces the field of tangible interaction explores user interfaces that relate to a certain tangibility and materiality of an interface, physical embodiments and representations of digital data, as well as embedding a user interface in real world space and context [26,27].

Li et al., for instance, propose a tangible table-top game that aims at supporting the treatment of children with Cerebral Palsy (i.e., permanent movement disorders). Their game enables patients to interact with the game by directly manipulating physical objects, which in turn "encourages the children with Cerebral Palsy to make desired movements" [37, p. 10]. They argue that "physical interaction, motivated and constrained by the design of tangible interfaces, offers enormous potential for occupational and physical therapy where patients need to practice specific and repetitive movements" [37, p. 1].

The basic thinking behind tangible interaction design is to have some kind of physical representation or embodiment of digital data or interacting with digital things via physical artifacts. This interweaving of the physical and digital world has resulted in a variety of projects and approaches around e.g., collaborative interaction via tabletops [31] or digitally augmented board games [12,49]. The physical artifacts or tangible user interfaces (also referred to as TUIs) used for interaction are often based on a variety of sensors (e.g., bend, pressure, touch, etc.) in order to make everyday objects interactive or augment them with computational properties. Within the last years, easy to use, cheap and widely available toolkits for electronics and embedded technologies (e.g., Arduino [2] or Phidgets [8], etc.) resulted in a range of projects and products around making interaction with digital things more physical.

As tangible artifacts present the opportunity to be both, physical as well as social, they can potentially be incorporated into the user's everyday life. This is especially relevant to serious game design, as this incorporation into a user's everyday bodily practices can reach a point where the user perceives a physical artifact as a natural extension of themselves ("they act through it rather than on it"; [34, p. 4]). If a game can achieve such a level of integration into everyday practices and routines, also the level of immersion, engagement and related impact (regarding the overall goal of the game) will potentially be different.

Another fundamental concept of embodied interaction design (detailed in Sect. 2) and in particular the thinking behind tangible interfaces is the usage of *embodied metaphors*.

Embodied Metaphors: Tangible user interfaces are often more likely to be easy to understand when they are based on natural mappings and metaphors (e.g., their physical form). Bakker et al. highlight how tangible interaction and embodied metaphors can support learning by physical activity and manipulating physical objects [11]. Metaphorical mappings are promoted within the field of tangible and embodied interaction research, however, these metaphors are difficult to identify and implement. What the physical form of an artifact means for the individual user, is a matter of, e.g., finding the right form language for the tangible interface. As these mappings are prone to individual differences, the ideas and intentions of a designer of a tangible artifact, and what mapping and mental associations, e.g., the physical form of that artifact creates for the user, can widely differ. In that regard, Bakker et al. introduce a people-centered approach to the design of tangibles based on embodied metaphors. In their work, they found out how such embodied metaphors are actually an unconscious application of "embodied schemata" [11] (i.e., recurring patterns of bodily or sensori-motor experiences [30]) based on former individual experiences of the user. Hence, in order to apply the right metaphors and tangibles in a game's interaction design, these individual mental mappings of movement, action and outcome have to be understood and applied (e.g., through close user involvement in the design phase of a game).

Tangible interfaces for games have the advantage of creating a link between the physical and digital world (i.e., based on a natural mapping or metaphor). By giving something a physical representation or digital embodiment and using this as a design resource for game interactions, designers can create natural interactions that go beyond conventional controller-based game interaction.

5   Utilizing Natural Interaction Paradigms

Besides bodily movements and tangible interactions, also other natural inter-action modalities, for instance gaze-based input, are used in commercial games (e.g., [9]) as well as within research (e.g., [35,39]). Different tracking strategies and technologies apply to different modes of interaction, depending on what "body feature" to track and what kind of input to be used: For instance, using hand tracking for recognizing gestures [62], full-body interaction or eye-tracking to incorporate gaze based interaction for analyzing user behavior [47].

Natural interaction paradigms can provide an alternative way for making games accessible to people that cannot interact with games via conventional controller-based input. Gaze-based interaction, for instance, can be an especially interesting input modality in therapy or rehab, as it enables, e.g., people with impairments to participate in the playing experience. As an example for how gaze-based interaction can be incorporated in games, Istance et al. [28] investigated how to use gaze as an input modality for people with motor impairments that want to participate in Word of Warcraft, and map certain in-game tasks to specific gaze interactions. Furthermore, Vickers et al. [58] investigated the use of eye gaze for interaction in World of Warcraft towards enabling interaction for impaired users. In an experiment that mapped keyboard functions to areas of the screen to be activated via the gaze-based input, they showed that gaze control can be effective as an input modality but that task completion times are longer.

Gaze is also a social quality that is deeply rooted in interpersonal communi-cation and provides certain qualities that differentiates it from other interaction modalities: eyes are fast, always-on, potentially reveal a player's attention and are contact free [63]. Especially in co-located gaming, the physical presence of another person can be an interesting source for game interaction designs around incor-porating new interaction paradigms. A player's experience in co-located play is often directly related to social interaction with another person (e.g., via the game as a shared interaction space). In such a scenario, gaze can be a natural means of human-human collaboration and communication. Research also indicates that eye contact relates to higher levels of co-presence [13] and that utilizing such non-verbal human behaviour can support collaborative interaction [56].

Also in remote or physically constraining settings where typical human face-to-face qualities (e.g., the human gaze) are not possible, incorporating these non-verbal qualities into game interactions can have positive effects on social pres-ence [35] or interacting collaboratively with another person [39]. For instance, Maurer et al. [39] show how in a co-located setting an onlooking person can assist the player via a "shared gaze" approach (i.e., visualizing the gaze point

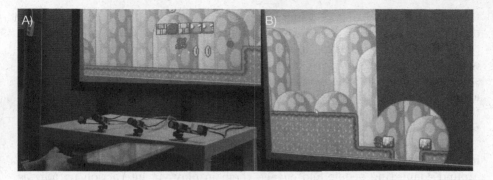

Fig. 1. Different visualizations and representations of a co-located onlooker's gaze as a means to assist the player. (A) Gaze as an abstract point visualization; (B) gaze point as a flashlight metaphor.

of the onlooker within the game). In their research, they use an onlooker's gaze as a natural means of spatial referencing and give the onlooker's gaze changing embodied representations within the game in order to explore different mappings of gaze and visual representation within the game (see Fig. 1). In a study, they observed positive effects on behavioral engagement and empathy as well as on the overall game experience for both, the player as well as the assisting onlooker. This illustrates, how a gaze-based interaction concept as a means of collaboration and non-verbal communication, can change a social gaming setting for the better (i.e., by turning an observers gaze tangible through representing it visually on the screen and thereby transforming it into a new tool for in-game communication) [39]. Further, this shows how utilizing a social quality (i.e., human gaze) and giving it an embodiment and representation within a game, can change gameplay experience towards creating new forms of non-verbal interaction between cooperating humans.

By applying this new form of collaborative interaction, they found out that the co-located nature of the game setting, as well as the fact that another person can observe and assist the player results in similar game experiences for both, the player and the observing person. They provide an explanation based on the perspective of *embodied simulation* [14] and refer to the fact that humans create meaning by dynamically constructing mental experiences according to the perceived scene. Seeing and understanding another human being (e.g., watching a player playing a game) means to some extend simulating their experiences [39]. Body-based and natural interaction paradigms can be a new way of fostering such processes besides other input modalities (e.g., typical controller-based input), as they are closely related to how the human mind creates meaning. Natural interaction paradigms like gaze-based input, can thus be used to design games around *distributed cognition* [18], where multiple people share and collaborate via an in-game task based on natural human-human communication (e.g., gaze-based augmentations of a game setting as a shared resource and interaction space).

From the standpoint of game interaction design, similar interaction paradigms around creating a social setting based on natural communication can create design opportunities "in-between" being an active player and a passive onlooker (i.e., having varying levels of player/audience engagement within the same game) [20,39]. When looking at serious games that are applied in specific areas in rehab and therapy, this can be a valuable source for new game designs (e.g., around integrating audience members into a game based on different interfaces, roles and varying levels of player engagement).

This perspective on co-located games and play, as being a collaborative activity and sense-making process, promises much design potential for serious games around connecting people and engage them in play via interaction paradigms based on natural human-human communication. In that sense, a game itself can act as a means to create a coupling e.g., between two co-located persons and can thus be understood as a kind of *relational* or mediatory artifact [41] mediating the communication between humans. Hence, body-based and natural interaction paradigms for games have the potential to put emphasis on the human mind as a substantial aspect on how games create impact and meaning, and are thus an important factor for designers of serious games to focus on.

6 Sensorimotor Couplings

A human's body and its movement are substantial factors of how a human perceives and makes sense of the world and its surroundings [30]. Sensorimotor-couplings are an integral part of this perspective on the human body and its learning and sense-making process [16]. The perspective of sensorimotor couplings describes how the human senses influence cognition and action [18]. A sensorimotor coupling is the coupling or integration of the sensory system and motor system of the human body and describes how the human senses influence cognition and action (see Fig. 2).

In that regard, Van Dijk et al. describe how the social and the sensorimotor aspects of embodied interactions are part of "one integrated sense-making process" [18, p. 1]. They further see cognition as a continuous process of social coordination and highlight the role of physical artifacts as "mediating objects"

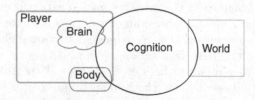

Fig. 2. Schematic of the human sensorimotor loop and embodied cognition perspective. Cognition is formed based on interactions between the human brain, body and world the human is situated in (meaning both the physical and social environment), after Van Dijk et al. [18].

in the way people deal with each other in the context of a situated practice" [18]. Emphasizing this notion is especially important for game designs that aim at incorporating the player's body and senses successfully. Games, either purely digital or based on some kind of physical interaction, are one way to address the social as well as the sensorimotor level of peoples interactions. Hence, utilizing and deliberately incorporating socio-sensorimotor couplings into a game's interaction design is a way to explore new design opportunities and understand a user's behaviour [18] (see also Sects. 5 and 7.3 for examples).

The meaning of embodied interactions is created in situ, through situated social positioning and sensorimotor coupling, hence, also challenging the viability of designer-chosen mappings of body-based interactions [18]. In that regard Van Dijk et al. further see the coupling of interactive technology directly to the human socio-sensorimotor loop itself, as a crucial challenge to address in embodied interaction design. Several concepts and strategies around body-based and natural interaction fostering ways to establish and use such couplings exist.

Based on the theoretical concepts mentioned in this chapter thus far, we propose and illustrate potential design strategies and leverage points that are based on creating and utilizing sensorimotor couplings for game interactions:

- Designing around and fostering a (socio-) sensorimotor loop e.g., via body-based game interactions.
- Utilizing embodied representations, i.e., giving something a bodily representation and meaning (e.g., by making internal body state visible/perceivable for the player). For instance, a player's movements could be directly/indirectly mapped to a digital counterpart e.g., an avatar.
- Deliberately using and intervening in this sensorimotor loop (i.e., mapping between cognition and action) to enable new game experiences.

These strategies emphasize the role of the human mind-body relation and aim at being a starting point for the design of body-based interaction in games that create and utilize rich sensorimotor loops.

6.1   The Human Body as an Input Resource for Game Interaction

Game interactions built around social and physical qualities are a way to create embodied representations in order to work with sensorimotor couplings within a game's design. However, enabling a coupling between a game, an avatar as a digital (mediating) artifact and the body movements of a player is a big design challenge. Physical and body-based interactions are fundamentally different from other interaction paradigms (e.g., controller-based game input) and present many opportunities in utilizing the human body as a resource for game interaction design. Klemmer et al. [34] describe five themes of how our human body matters in interaction and propose *thinking through doing, performance, visibility, risk* and *thick practice* as the main themes from the perspective of interaction design.

Thinking through doing: Physical action is an important component of human cognition. The act of "physical interaction in the world facilitates cognitive development" [34, p. 2]. Especially spatial cognitive abilities are built around locomotor experiences, thus, highlighting the fact that "humans learn about the world and its properties by interacting within it" [34, p. 2]. Further, also gestures and non-verbal communication characteristics play a large role in how humans interact with each other. Research has shown that gesturing decreases cognitive load [23]. Hence, Klemmer et al. argue that a system constraining this aspect of physically doing something, e.g., limiting the gestural abilities of a person via a controller-based interaction concept, is likely to influence and even hinder a user to think and communicate.

Performance: Physical artifacts used for interaction can be perceived as a natural extension of the user's body. Hence, tangible interfaces also offer to the human body a certain appeal of being part of a *skillful performance* and also offer benefits around rich physicality of interaction (e.g., addressing additional feedback channels of an input device). Further, the notion of the human as a *daily performer* of complex learned skills, puts emphasize on how interactive systems require to be tightly integrated into these performative practices of everyday use and practice. For instance, Klemmer et al. describe how the hands of a person relate to the development of action-centered skills and consequently the human motor memory, which can be facilitated via tangible interfaces that engage the body for interaction.

As an example of how typical game interfaces function as a bodily extensions and form practices that are grounded in physical mappings and representations, Klemmer et al. state:

"To date, computer game controllers have been the most commercially successful example of such interfaces. Players of flight simulators increase their 'grip' on the simulation using two-handed joystick plus throttle controllers; driving simulator players use foot pedals and table mounted wheels with force feedback to improve their vehicle control. The success of games and game controllers suggests that rich physical input devices may provide benefit in other domains as well [34, p. 5]."

Visibility: Body-based and tangible interaction and its inherent ability to be a practice that is made visible to (co-located) onlookers, is an important aspect of why such interactions often result in being a situated practice (e.g., through performance of the activity itself). This is what body-based and tangible interfaces substantially differentiates from typical graphical user interfaces. The visibility of physical actions for instance, facilitates social coordination and collaboration which can be an important factor of how serious games could be built around peripheral participation (e.g., by finding ways to include players with constrained movement capabilities).

Risk: This aspect of physical interactions focuses on how physical action is characterized by a sense of risk. In that regard, physical interactions are again fundamentally different from interactions via digital artifacts. Physical action requires some kind of commitment and often results in permanent consequences (e.g., choosing the "wrong" action in a social setting), whereas digital interactions are characterized by things like *undo/redo* and general reversibility of actions. This permanency and notion of direct consequence is an inherent characteristic of physical interactions. Hence, the potentially resulting sense of risk in physical interactions is an important aspect to consider for game interaction design. Some players could be hesitant to even interact via body-based interactions in a serious game, because the human body itself is a source of individual insecurities and a factor that can present a sense of vulnerability due to other co-located humans. However, physical interactions can also be used to deliberately change and create a social setting in order to diminish the sense of risk based on social bondings related to physical proximity of other persons.

The sense of risk is closely intertwined with engagement and attention of a human [34]. In turn, increasing the amount of risk and consequences of a game can influence engagement of player's. The Painstation [44], an arcade implementation of pong working with pain feedback, might be an extreme example.

Thick practice: Body-based and tangible interactions offer the ability to be deeply rooted in the *real world*. This relates to Weiser's notion of designing for "embodied virtuality" rather than "virtual reality" [59], which means that we should aim for designing interactions that *are* the real world instead of simulating it. In that regard, Klemmer et al. argue that interaction designers should integrate and combine the physical and digital world very carefully - "leaving the physical world alone to the extent possible"- in order to be more closely to the actual human practices grounded in interacting with the physical world [34, p. 8].

These themes are important factors to consider and show how body-based and natural interactions are fundamentally different to other interaction modalities. The perspective of these themes show how the act of interacting itself can be a *reflective practice* closely intertwined with human learning. Hence, incorporating these perspectives into serious game interactions can benefit the overall goal and impact of such a game.

Sensorimotor couplings are based on the mind constantly perceiving and adapting to the current body movements and surroundings. This sensorimotor loop can in turn be used to enable such reflective interactions or create new gaming experiences. For instance, Won et al. [60] propose to actually intervene in this loop between perception and action in order to leverage the digital amplification of input that games provide (e.g., creating large impact and consequence on the game environment from small body movements and player actions; see also Sect. 7.3).

This example further illustrates how the human body can be a design resource for interaction design applied to serious gaming, and how different mappings between real world and virtual world, are a promising design opportunity body-based and natural interactions offer to game designers.

6.2   Utilizing Avatars in Body-Based Interactions

Avatars are digital counterparts or representations of the player in the digital game world [48]. For instance, this can take the form of Mario being the player's digital counterpart in Super Mario bros. On the other hand, an avatar can also mean having a virtual representation of your own body (e.g., in a virtual reality setting) close to real life with real body movements accurately mapped to a digital avatar [10]. This range from realistic to unrealistic mappings is a promising source for avatar-based interactions in serious games.

Motion and body sensing, allow a player's body characteristics to be isomorphically mapped to a game space (e.g., an avatar), hence, making body-based interaction inherently "asymmetric" (i.e., due to individual body and movement differences). This is an opportunity to let people interact with a representation and mapping they are usually not familiar with (e.g., by interacting via a body representation that is different to their physical self). This can be utilized in terms of giving a person another body or role, by letting them perceive new things in order to induce behaviour change [61] e.g., by creating empathy. For instance, a body-based game could give a player different avatars and deliberately change their real body mapped to an avatar, thus, changing their own body perception and attitudes towards it by letting them experience another body.

Especially within field of virtual reality (VR) a lot of research has been done on the topic of human-avatar interactions and letting people experience another body (e.g., [10,32,65]). For instance, by changing the characteristics of a person's avatar (i.e., in that case a virtual representation of the user's body) the issue of body image disturbance (BID) as a primary feature of eating disorders was addressed [51]. Also the social aspects of body-based interactions were researched by assigning people specific roles within a virtual social setting, thus, letting them experience another body which can potentially change their attitudes. Further, also aspects like arbitrary gender representations in avatar-represented virtual reality group settings [36] or whether embodying a "dissimilar self" in virtual reality would impact anxiety in public speaking situations [10], have been investigated. The connection between self-perception and avatar-body representation can also positively influence our level of immersion, if the body and user tracking is incorporated in a proper way [17]. These examples illustrate the importance and potential of using avatars towards intentionally changing embodied representations of a user's body in game-based interactions.

6.3   Body-Based Interactions Enabling Reflective Interactions

One way of stimulating body perception and performance is by providing an opportunity to interact with digital representations of real-world things (e.g., avatars or other embodiments). Games are a means to create such bodily interactions that raise awareness in people for their own body and senses and create new game experiences (e.g., enabling somaesthetic reflections through interactive artifacts). For instance, games can be a way to give a physical body a digital (embodied) representation to interact with in a playful way. This perspective

of enabling somaesthetic reflections refers to work based on Richard Shusterman [54] who coined the term *somaesthetics* as a way of seeing the body as the
primary means of human perception.

Adopting this stance towards interaction design renders *somaesthetic design*
as a way to focus on making people more aware of their own bodily experiences [25]. Regarding game interaction design, this perspective can be utilized
to design games as interactive systems that enable such somaesthetic reflections
(i.e., let the user systematically reflect on their bodily perception by letting them
playfully interact embodied interactions) contributing to a different, potentially
better, body perception and self-awareness. This could be used by designers of
serious games in rehab or therapy in order to enable interactions around self
perception and body movements, e.g., for dementia patients that suffer from
continuously declining mental and physical capabilities that drastically change
their self and body perception. By interacting with a game that is based on using
their own body as an input modality, patients could be supported in finding new
ways of engaging with their (digital) environments, hence, are able to transform
these environments through their own body interactions. This can in turn help
patients regain a sense of impact and meaning of their own actions, thus, potentially changing their self-perception for the better and inducing new behaviours.
Related research in the field of therapy has been done by Zalapa et al. [64] who
investigated how tangible interactions can be used to enable body-awareness for
children with autism during sensory therapies.

7   Body-Based Interaction in Rehab and Therapy

Body-based interactions in games are often used as a strategy during rehab
and therapy e.g., to engage people with constrained movement capabilities in
playful interactions. A variety of examples from different application domains
of body-based interaction in serious games within therapy and rehab exist:
For instance, body-based games are used for stroke recovery [7], maintaining
a dementia patients mental abilities [24,43] or pain therapy [60]. Further, also
physical treatment and therapy uses serious games for instance for rehab after
spinal cord injury [4] or rehab after replacement surgery [40].

The following illustrates several examples and application domains of serious
games and body-based interaction in rehab and therapy ranging from exergames,
addressing mental and cognitive issues to utilizing different avatar-body mappings for changing a user's self-perception.

7.1   Exergames

A main objective of rehabilitation and therapeutical exercises is improving a
patient's motor functions and maintaining physical skills (e.g., [22,52]). However,
as most rehabilitation exercises are repetitive (e.g., performing the same motion
multiple times), the result is that patients are often not motivated to perform
these exercises after the initial treatment. Research in a that direction explores

how to incorporate games and playful interactions in a rehabilitation process and combine them with exercises the patient can for instance do from at home without the need for a therapist [40].

Games applied in therapy and rehab could be an important factor towards motivating and engaging a patient. Such games are often referred to as *exergames* and often aim at improving aspects like exercise accuracy or motivation. Designing games around such repetitive therapy exercises combined with proper feedback to engage the patient in a fun way can improve the patient's motivation to perform these exercises [15]. By interweaving typical game elements like challenge, progression, competition, rubber banding, etc. with a rehabilitation exercise can result in an exergame that motivates the patient, reacts to her/his progression (by constantly getting harder based on, e.g., tracking improvement of movement capabilities) and provides proper feedback (e.g., if the exercise is executed in the right way). When a game-based approach achieves to address these aspects, the game itself can become an intermediary, hence, being an information channel between the patient and the therapist. This fills a common gap that occurs within rehabilitation where patients do not perform exercises supervised by a therapist but exercising from at home [40]. The therapist here is often only teaching them how to perform the exercises initially. Thus, a game should be designed in a way that it can be a somehow "intelligent actor" in order to replace certain aspects only a therapist could provide or filling the information gap between this exercising at home and together with a therapist.

In that regard, a crucial aspect of all exergames is the need to provide adequate feedback to the player in order to prevent a patient from learning wrong movements that would result in long term problems. Typically, there is no physical connection to an interface during body-based interaction, like a player would have when giving input via a game controller. In that sense, the motion and body tracking applied in such games needs to be combined with additional feedback channels e.g., visual on-screen feedback to inform the patient on correct/incorrect movements. Other feedback strategies could also incorporate haptic on-body feedback (e.g., wearing a wristband that vibrates and informs the patient in that way). With such a feedback strategy based on wearable devices a game could convey feedback exactly on that part of the body the visual feedback relates to.

A further advantage of incorporating body-based game interaction in an exergame is the ability to focus on specific body parts for training purposes. For instance, a serious game aiming at maintaining physical skills of patients with upper limb disabilities, could focus on amplifying and training the body-parts and movements the patient is still capable of doing.

7.2 Embodied Interaction for Addressing Mental and Cognitive Issues

Besides the physical effects of movement-based and exertion based serious games, there is a growing body of research around investigations of the therapeutic value of games and play for cognitive and mental well being (e.g., [7, 24, 43]).

In that regard, McCallum et al. review and discuss the effects of existing commercial games on dementia-related conditions [42]. They conclude that even if many existing games were developed primarily for entertainment purposes, they are being used for health purposes as well, thus, acquiring the characteristics of serious games. Consequently, they also state that dementia games do have an effect on cognitive impaired people. However, they further see longterm effects and transferability into daily activities of these effects as open questions for future research. Other early work in the field aims at utilizing body-based interaction within therapy related to stroke recovery, e.g., by following a virtual reality based approach that presents the patient with a variety of rehabilitation exercises [29]. Another related project by Microsoft Research [7] aims at improving the upper-limb motor functions of patients that are currently recovering from a stroke. They developed a Kinect-based system that recognizes and interprets the user's gestures to assess their rehabilitation progress and adjust the level of difficulty for following therapy exercises accordingly.

What these examples have in common is that they use games and playful interactions as a kind of sandbox where body-based interactions take place and meaningful interactions for the user are triggered. They aim at providing appropriate feedback to the patient, and are personalized as well as adaptive to the individual user's progress and mental state.

As the human body is a crucial factor in how we perceive ourselves and surroundings in order to learn and reason, body-based interaction can be a valuable source when dealing with mental and cognitive issues in rehab and therapy. The stance towards the body as a design resource illustrated in this chapter, can be pursued to design games for people suffering from dementia or a general a state of decreasing physical and mental abilities. The nature of this disease often results in losing a sense of self and identity based on the shifting perceptions of the patient's own body. Embodied interaction combined with games and play can potentially address these issues. By letting a person suffering from dementia playfully interact with a digital body representation via, e.g., body movements or gestures, a new way of engaging with the (digital) world and transforming it through action and construction can be provided. This results in a potentially better awareness for the patient's own body and its capabilities. Furthermore, such interactions also present an opportunity to regain a sense of impact of peoples' actions.

7.3   Flexible Avatar-Body Mappings

A digital game's ability to enable large impact from small interactions (i.e., *amplification of input* - doing complex in-game things with the press of a button) can be a valuable design approach when applying a game to a challenging context like rehabilitation or therapy. Especially, in body-based interaction there is potential in combining these aspects of digital amplification with serious games applied in rehab. Won et al. for instance show, how augmenting the movements of a patient while interacting with an avatar can have positive effects during rehab and therapy exercises [60]. Their work describes how different mappings of patient movements to an avatar (i.e., leg movements mapped in a one-to-one manner or with 1.5x increased movements) resulted in higher motivation and more positive perception of the patient's body capabilities during pain therapy. Hence, they argue for more flexible avatar-body mapping for dealing with similar issues in therapy. This can also be a way of creating and using the digital amplification of input games typically provide and leverage from this for serious game interaction designs.

Especially in virtual reality, which partially replaces the sensory information from the physical world, users may also replace their sense of presence in the physical realm or their own physical body [60]. Based on this perspective of presence, Won et al. argue for utilizing the potentials of "flexible mappings" of the human body to an avatar for therapy purposes. They describe the ability to "change the relationship between a participants appearance and/or actions in the physical world, and the appearance and actions that this participant perceives virtually" [60, p. 1] as a promising source for VR in therapy. Utilizing this flexibility of virtual reality allows for more radical interventions during therapy (e.g., based on creating avatars with differing movements to the patient's own).

8   Conclusion

Embodied interaction is a perspective that focuses on humans as physical and social creatures. This stance puts emphasis on the meaning of the human body as a resource for interaction design. This notion of designing with and around social and physical contextual qualities can also be applied to the field of serious game design in order to create new paradigms of interaction and game experiences. Especially, within the field of serious game interaction design, this notion of creating interactions that are meaningful to the player because his/her body is incorporated, allows for new game experiences beyond purely physical or digital play.

The concepts mentioned in this chapter aim at informing researchers and designers within the field of serious games with theoretical perspectives and bridging concepts towards different interaction paradigms that incorporate and focus on the human body as a design resource (i.e., body-based, natural and tangible interaction). By following the concepts illustrated in this chapter (i.e., embodied simulation, sensorimotor couplings, etc.), games can be transformed into useful *mediatory artifacts*, e.g., in co-located settings or in rehab and therapy as a communicator between patient and therapist.

The main concept of utilizing embodied interaction in play is based on either transferring something physical (e.g., the player's body) into the digital world or giving something a physical body or representation (e.g., using tangible representations of digital data). However, tangible and body-based interactions are fundamentally different to conventional controller-based game input. For instance, the utilization of different body-avatar mappings for game interaction can support, but also deliberately intervene in a player's sensorimotor loop. Such interventions can be an important resource for game interactions that let the player experience the own body in new and unfamiliar ways (e.g., in order to induce change in attitude or behaviour). Such physical and body-based interaction are especially promising for creating serious games for rehab or therapy.

Natural and body-based interaction towards embodied interaction in play, bares much potential for creating gaming experiences around physical and social context qualities. Designing with theories of human cognition in mind allows developers of serious games to create impact in unconventional ways based on utilizing new interaction paradigms that are deeply rooted in how humans perceive their world. Body-based game interactions can be a way of how the act of interaction itself can become a reflective practice that game designers should harvest from. The main challenge for researchers in this field will be to create meaningful interactions that internalize these concepts as integral parts of how serious games achieve their impact.

Further Readings and Theoretical Grounding

To get a more thorough understanding of the theoretical concepts and perspectives mentioned in this chapter, the following list is suggested as a starting point for further readings:

Embodied Interaction: Dourish, P.: Where the action is: the foundations of embodied interaction. MIT press (2004) [19];

Somaesthetics: Shusterman, R.: Body consciousness: A philosophy of mindfulness and somaesthetics. Cambridge University Press (2008) [54];

Human body-mind relation: Bergen, B.K.: Louder than words: The new science of how the mind makes meaning. Basic Books (2012) [14];
Pfeifer, R., Bongard, J.: How the body shapes the way we think: a new view of intelligence. MIT press (2006) [50];

Tangible Interaction: Hornecker et al.: Getting a grip on tangible interaction: a framework on physical space and social interaction [26];
Ishii et al.: Tangible bits: towards seamless interfaces between people, bits and atoms [27].

References

1. Android wear. https://www.android.com/wear/
2. Arduino microcontroller. http://www.arduino.cc
3. Fitbit - activity tracker. http://www.fitbit.com
4. Jewel mine. http://ict.usc.edu/prototypes/jewel-mine/
5. Leap motion. https://www.leapmotion.com
6. Microsoft kinect. https://developer.microsoft.com/en-us/windows/kinect
7. Microsoft research: stroke recovery with kinect. http://research.microsoft.com/en-us/projects/stroke-recovery-with-kinect/
8. Phidgets - products for usb sensing and control. http://www.phidgets.com
9. Tobii eye tracking enabled games. http://www.tobii.com/xperience/apps/

10. Aymerich-Franch, L., Kizilcec, R.F., Bailenson, J.N.: The relationship between virtual self similarity and social anxiety. Front. Hum. Neurosci. **8**, 944 (2014)
11. Bakker, S., Antle, A.N., Van Den Hoven, E.: Embodied metaphors in tangible interaction design. Pers. Ubiquit. Comput. **16**(4), 433–449 (2012)
12. Bakker, S., Vorstenbosch, D., van den Hoven, E., Hollemans, G., Bergman, T.: Weathergods: tangible interaction in a digital tabletop game. In: Proceedings of the 1st International Conference on Tangible and Embedded Interaction, TEI 2007, New York, NY, USA, pp. 151–152. ACM (2007). http://doi.acm.org/10.1145/1226969.1227000
13. Bente, G., Eschenburg, F., Aelker, L.: Effects of simulated gaze on social presence, person perception and personality attribution in avatar-mediated communication. In: Presence 2007: Proceedings of the 10th Annual International Workshop on Presence, 25–27 October 2007, Barcelona, Spain, pp. 207–214 (2007)
14. Bergen, B.K.: Louder Than Words: The New Science of How the Mind Makes Meaning. Basic Books, New York (2012)
15. Chang, Y.J., Chen, S.F., Huang, J.D.: A kinect-based system for physical rehabilitation: a pilot study for young adults with motor disabilities. Res. Dev. Disabil. **32**(6), 2566–2570 (2011)
16. Clark, A.: Being There: Putting Brain, Body, and World Together Again. MIT press, Cambridge (1998)
17. Cummings, J.J., Bailenson, J.N.: How immersive is enough? a meta-analysis of the effect of immersive technology on user presence. Media Psychol. (ahead-of-print) **19**, 1–38 (2015)
18. van Dijk, J., van der Lugt, R., Hummels, C.: Beyond distributed representation: embodied cognition design supporting socio-sensorimotor couplings. In: Proceedings of the 8th International Conference on Tangible, Embedded and Embodied Interaction, pp. 181–188. ACM (2014)
19. Dourish, P.: Where the Action Is: The Foundations of Embodied Interaction. MIT press, Cambridge (2004)
20. Downs, J., Vetere, F., Howard, S., Loughnan, S., Smith, W.: Audience experience in social videogaming: effects of turn expectation and game physicality. In: Proceedings of the 32nd Annual ACM Conference on Human Factors in Computing Systems, pp. 3473–3482. ACM (2014)
21. Gajadhar, B.J., De Kort, Y., IJsselsteijn, W.A.: Rules of engagement: influence of co-player presence on player involvement in digital games. Int. J. Gaming Computer-Mediated Simul. (IJGCMS) **1**(3), 14–27 (2009)
22. Gerling, K., Livingston, I., Nacke, L., Mandryk, R.: Full-body motion-based game interaction for older adults. In: Proceedings of the SIGCHI Conference on Human Factors in Computing Systems, CHI 2012, New York, NY, USA, pp. 1873–1882. ACM (2012). http://doi.acm.org/10.1145/2207676.2208324
23. Goldin-Meadow, S., Nusbaum, H., Kelly, S.D., Wagner, S.: Explaining math: gesturing lightens the load. Psychol. Sci. **12**(6), 516–522 (2001)
24. He, G.F., Park, J.W., Kang, S.K., Jung, S.T.: Development of gesture recognition-based serious games. In: 2012 IEEE-EMBS International Conference on Biomedical and Health Informatics (BHI), pp. 922–925. IEEE (2012)
25. Höök, K., Ståhl, A., Jonsson, M., Mercurio, J., Karlsson, A., Banka Johnson, E.C.: Somaethetic design. Interactions **22**, 26–33 (2015). http://dx.doi.org/10.1145/2770888
26. Hornecker, E., Buur, J.: Getting a grip on tangible interaction: a framework on physical space and social interaction. In: Proceedings of the SIGCHI Conference on Human Factors in Computing Systems, pp. 437–446. ACM (2006)

27. Ishii, H., Ullmer, B.: Tangible bits: towards seamless interfaces between people, bits and atoms. In: Proceedings of the ACM SIGCHI Conference on Human Factors in Computing Systems, pp. 234–241. ACM (1997)

28. Istance, H., Vickers, S., Hyrskykari, A.: Gaze-based interaction with massively multiplayer on-line games. In: CHI 2009 Extended Abstracts on Human Factors in Computing Systems, pp. 4381–4386. ACM (2009)

29. Jack, D., Boian, R., Merians, A., Adamovich, S.V., Tremaine, M., Recce, M., Burdea, G.C., Poizner, H.: A virtual reality-based exercise program for stroke rehabilitation. In: Proceedings of the Fourth International ACM Conference on Assistive Technologies, pp. 56–63. ACM (2000)

30. Johnson, M.: The Body in the Mind: The Bodily Basis of Meaning, Imagination, and Reason. University of Chicago Press, Chicago (2013)

31. Jordà, S., Kaltenbrunner, M., Geiger, G., Alonso, M.: The reactable: a tangible tabletop musical instrument and collaborative workbench. In: ACM SIGGRAPH 2006 Sketches, SIGGRAPH 2006, New York, NY, USA. ACM (2006). http://doi.acm.org/10.1145/1179849.1179963

32. Kipp, M., Gebhard, P.: IGaze: studying reactive gaze behavior in semi-immersive human-avatar interactions. In: Prendinger, H., Lester, J., Ishizuka, M. (eds.) IVA 2008. LNCS (LNAI), vol. 5208, pp. 191–199. Springer, Heidelberg (2008). doi:10.1007/978-3-540-85483-8_19

33. Kjeldsen, R., Hartman, J.: Design issues for vision-based computer interaction systems. In: Proceedings of the 2001 Workshop on Perceptive User Interfaces, pp. 1–8. ACM (2001)

34. Klemmer, S.R., Hartmann, B., Takayama, L.: How bodies matter: five themes for interaction design. In: Proceedings of the 6th Conference on Designing Interactive Systems, pp. 140–149. ACM (2006)

35. Lankes, M., Mirlacher, T., Wagner, S., Hochleitner, W.: Whom are you looking for?: the effects of different player representation relations on the presence in gaze-based games. In: Proceedings of the First ACM SIGCHI Annual Symposium on Computer-Human Interaction in Play, pp. 171–179. ACM (2014)

36. Lee, J.E.R., Nass, C.I., Bailenson, J.N.: Does the mask govern the mind?: effects of arbitrary gender representation on quantitative task performance in avatar-represented virtual groups. Cyberpsychology Behav. Soc. Netw. 17(4), 248–254 (2014)

37. Li, Y., Fontijn, W., Markopoulos, P.: A tangible tabletop game supporting therapy of children with cerebral palsy. In: Markopoulos, P., Ruyter, B., IJsselsteijn, W., Rowland, D. (eds.) Fun and Games 2008. LNCS, pp. 182–193. Springer, Heidelberg (2008). doi:10.1007/978-3-540-88322-7_18

38. Malinverni, L., Burguès, N.P.: The medium matters: the impact of full-body interaction on the socio-affective aspects of collaboration. In: Proceedings of the 14th International Conference on Interaction Design and Children, IDC 2015, New York, NY, USA, pp. 89–98. ACM (2015). http://doi.acm.org/10.1145/2771839.2771849

39. Maurer, B., Aslan, I., Wuchse, M., Neureiter, K., Tscheligi, M.: Gaze-based onlooker integration: exploring the in-between of active player and passive spectator in co-located gaming. In: Proceedings of the 2015 Annual Symposium on Computer-Human Interaction in Play, CHI PLAY 2015, NewYork, NY, USA, pp. 163–173. ACM (2015). http://doi.acm.org/10.1145/2793107.2793126

40. Maurer, B., Bergner, F., Kober, P., Baumgartner, R.: Improving rehabilitation process after total knee replacement surgery through visual feedback and enhanced communication in a serious game. In: Proceedings of the 30th ACM International Conference on Design of Communication, pp. 355–356. ACM (2012)

41. Maurer, B., Gärtner, M., Wuchse, M., Meschtscherjakov, A., Tscheligi, M.: Utilizing a digital game as a mediatory artifact for social persuasion to prevent speeding. In: Meschtscherjakov, A., Ruyter, B., Fuchsberger, V., Murer, M., Tscheligi, M. (eds.) PERSUASIVE 2016. LNCS, pp. 199–210. Springer, Heidelberg (2016). doi:10.1007/978-3-319-31510-2_17

42. McCallum, S., Boletsis, C.: Dementia games: a literature review of dementia-related serious games. In: Ma, M., Oliveira, M.F., Petersen, S., Hauge, J.B. (eds.) SGDA 2013. LNCS, vol. 8101, pp. 15–27. Springer, Heidelberg (2013). doi:10.1007/978-3-642-40790-1_2

43. McCallum, S., Boletsis, C.: A taxonomy of serious games for dementia. In: Schouten, B., Fedtke, S., Bekker, T., Schijven, M., Gekker, A. (eds.) Games for Health, pp. 219–232. Springer Fachmedien Wiesbaden, Wiesbaden (2013)

44. Morawe, V., Reiff, T.: PainStation. Ars Electronica (2002)

45. Mizobata, R., Silpasuwanchai, C., Ren, X.: Only for casual players?: investigating player differences in full-body game interaction. In: Proceedings of the Second International Symposium of Chinese CHI, Chinese CHI 2014, New York, NY, USA, pp. 57–65. ACM (2014). http://doi.acm.org/10.1145/2592235.2592244

46. Mueller, F., Isbister, K., Mueller, F., Isbister, K.: Movement-based game guidelines. ACM, New York (2014)

47. Nacke, L.E., Stellmach, S., Sasse, D., Lindley, C.A.: Gameplay experience in a gaze interaction game. In: Proceedings of 5th Conference on Communication by Gaze Interaction - COGAIN 2009, pp. 49–54. The COGAIN Association (2009)

48. Nowak, K.L., Rauh, C.: The influence of the avatar on online perceptions of anthropomorphism, androgyny, credibility, homophily, and attraction. J. Computer-Mediated Commun. 11(1), 153–178 (2005)

49. Peitz, J., Eriksson, D., Björk, S.: Augmented board games: enhancing board games with electronics. In: Proceedings of DiGRA 2005 Conference: Changing Views-Worlds in Play (2005)

50. Pfeifer, R., Bongard, J.: How the Body Shapes the Way We Think: A New View of Intelligence. MIT press, Cambridge (2006)

51. Purvis, C.K., Jones, M., Bailey, J.O., Bailenson, J., Taylor, C.B.: Developing a novel measure of body satisfaction using virtual reality. PloS one 10(10), e0140158 (2015)

52. Schönauer, C., Pintaric, T., Kaufmann, H.: Full body interaction for serious games in motor rehabilitation. In: Proceedings of the 2nd Augmented Human International Conference, AH 2011, pp. 4:1–4:8, New York, NY, USA. ACM (2011). http://doi.acm.org/10.1145/1959826.1959830

53. Schwarz, J., Marais, C.C., Leyvand, T., Hudson, S.E., Mankoff, J.: Combining body pose, gaze, and gesture to determine intention to interact in vision-based interfaces. In: Proceedings of the 32nd Annual ACM Conference on Human Factors in Computing Systems, CHI 2014, New York, NY, USA, pp. 3443–3452. ACM (2014). http://doi.acm.org/10.1145/2556288.2556989

54. Shusterman, R.: Body consciousness: a philosophy of mindfulness and somaesthetics. Cambridge University Press, Cambridge (2008)

55. Sjöblom, B.: Gaming as a situated collaborative practice. Human IT 9(3), 128–165 (2008)

56. Steptoe, W., Wolff, R., Murgia, A., Guimaraes, E., Rae, J., Sharkey, P., Roberts, D., Steed, A.: Eye-tracking for avatar eye-gaze and interactional analysis in immersive collaborative virtual environments. In: Proceedings of the 2008 ACM Conference on Computer Supported Cooperative Work, pp. 197–200. ACM (2008)

57. Valli, A.: The design of natural interaction. Multimedia Tools Appl. **38**(3), 295–305 (2008)
58. Vickers, S., Istance, H., Hyrskykari, A., Ali, N., Bates, R.: Keeping an eye on the game: eye gaze interaction with massively multiplayer online games and virtual communities for motor impaired users (2008)
59. Weiser, M., Brown, J.S.: The coming age of calm technology. In: Beyond Calculation, pp. 75–85. Springer (1997)
60. Won, A.S., Tataru, C.A., Cojocaru, C.M., Krane, E.J., Bailenson, J.N., Niswonger, S., Golianu, B.: Two virtual reality pilot studies for the treatment of pediatric crps. Pain Med. **16**, 1644–1647 (2015)
61. Yee, N., Bailenson, J.: The proteus effect: the effect of transformed self-representation on behavior. Hum. Commun. Res. **33**(3), 271–290 (2007). http://dx.doi.org/10.1111/j.1468-2958.2007.00299.x
62. Yin, Y., Davis, R.: Toward natural interaction in the real world: real-time gesture recognition. In: International Conference on Multimodal Interfaces and the Workshop on Machine Learning for Multimodal Interaction, ICMI-MLMI 2010, New York, NY, USA, pp. 15:1–15:8. ACM (2010). http://doi.acm.org/10.1145/1891903.1891924
63. Zain, N.H.B.M., Jaafar, A.: Integrating digital games based learning environments with eye gaze-based interaction. In: 2011 International Conference on Pattern Analysis and Intelligent Robotics (ICPAIR), vol. 2, pp. 222–227. IEEE (2011)
64. Zalapa, R., Tentori, M.: Movement-based and tangible interactions to offer body awareness to children with autism. In: Urzaiz, G., Ochoa, S.F., Bravo, J., Chen, L.L., Oliveira, J. (eds.) UCAmI 2013. LNCS, vol. 8276, pp. 127–134. Springer, Heidelberg (2013)
65. Zhang, H., Fricker, D., Smith, T.G., Yu, C.: Real-time adaptive behaviors in multimodal human-avatar interactions. In: International Conference on Multimodal Interfaces and the Workshop on Machine Learning for Multimodal Interaction, ICMI-MLMI 2010, New York, NY, USA, pp. 4:1–4:8. ACM (2010). http://doi.acm.org/10.1145/1891903.1891909

Affective Computing in Games

Benjamin Guthier[1]([✉]), Ralf Dörner[2], and Hector P. Martinez[3]

[1] Department of Computer Science IV, University of Mannheim,
A5, 6, 68131 Mannheim, Germany
guthier@informatik.uni-mannheim.de
[2] Department Design, Computer Science, Media,
RheinMain University of Applied Sciences, Unter den Eichen 5,
65195 Wiesbaden, Germany
ralf.doerner@hs-rm.de
[3] Center for Computer Games Research, IT University of Copenhagen,
Rued Langgaards Vej 7, 2300 Copenhagen S, Denmark
hpma@itu.dk

Abstract. Being able to automatically recognize and interpret the affective state of the player can have various benefits in a Serious Game. The difficulty and pace of a learning game could be adapted, or the quality of the interaction between the player and the game could be improved – just to name two examples. This Chapter aims to give an introduction to Affective Computing with the goal of helping developers to incorporate the player's affective data into the games. Suitable psychological models of emotion and personality are described, and a multitude of sensors as well as methods to recognize affect are discussed in detail. The Chapter ends with a number examples where human affect is utilized in Serious Games.

Keywords: Affective Computing · Serious Game · Emotion · Affect detection · Sensors · Physiological data · Facial expressions · Speech

1 Introduction

One of the earliest mentions of the term *Affective Computing* can be found in the book by Picard [137]. It describes the ability of a computing device to recognize, interpret and simulate human affective states. Most commonly, the considered affective state is emotion, but mood and personality are also used. At first glance, uniting computing with emotion seems far-fetched and contradictory. However, emotion plays a crucial role in rational decision making by humans. When the space of possibilities is large and knowledge is incomplete and fuzzy, emotions serve as a filter that quickly label desirable and undesirable outcomes. The slow process of rational decision making then only has to be applied to those options that appear promising. From this consideration, it can be said that true intelligence requires the use of emotion. It can thus also be said that in order to make computers smart, they need to be able to utilize emotion as well.

© Springer International Publishing AG 2016
R. Dörner et al. (Eds.): Entertainment Computing and Serious Games, LNCS 9970, pp. 402–441, 2016.
DOI: 10.1007/978-3-319-46152-6_16

Affective computing has been applied to many different domains. Prominent among them is the field of computer-based learning. A good teacher is capable of recognizing the emotional state of a learner. This allows the teacher to adapt the speed and difficulty of the learning material based on whether the student is currently overwhelmed, highly focused or bored. Additionally, a skilled teacher knows how to influence the affect of a student in a way that improves their learning. Affective computing has the potential of bringing this skill into the domain of Serious Games for learning so that similar results could be achieved by a virtual tutor in a game. Another broad area is that of human-computer interaction. Whenever humans communicate with each other, they express emotion and react to the expressions they perceive. Although these processes are mostly subconscious, interactions may appear artificial if such clues are misplaced or entirely missing. In Serious Games that feature conversational agents, or are based on interactive storytelling with rich emotional content, interactions between the player and the game can be made more natural with the use of Affective Computing. Some Serious Games even specifically target the emotion of the players. Examples are games for emotion regulation, games that help with depression or ones with the goal of improving social behavior or changing attitudes. The benefit of applying Affective Computing here is immediately obvious. In a slightly different vein, the affect of the player can be harnessed to measure the user experience of a game. The user's emotion while playing may give more objective and real-time feedback than using a questionnaire. This sort of quantitative evaluation is essential for user-centered game design.

When discussing "affect" in the context of Serious Games or in general, it needs to be clarified what exactly is meant by the term. There are a number of different concepts that affect is composed of, like emotion, mood, personality, needs and subjective well-being. In the context of this Chapter, emotion is the most relevant one, followed by personality and mood. Despite its fuzzy meaning in colloquial use, emotion is defined distinctly in psychology. Emotion is a physiological reaction to events that are deemed relevant to the needs and goals of an individual [73]. An emotion starts quickly, only lasts for a short duration of time (e.g., 5 to 60 min) and is very specific to an external event that caused it. A related concept is that of a mood. Oftentimes the same terms are used to describe an emotion or a mood. However, moods can last for several days and are more diffuse, i.e., they are not triggered by a specific event. Personality is an even longer lasting pattern of behavior that also influences the range and frequency of emotions that a person experiences. It has been shown that after a certain age, the personality of a person remains constant even over periods of many years [149].

For each specific type of affect, there exist different models in psychology. In a Serious Game, these models can be used to create a digital representation of affect. On a broad scale, such representations can be classified into discrete and dimensional models. A discrete model represents an emotion or personality by labels from predefined lists. For emotion, such keywords could be "anger", "joy", or "sadness", and for personality, it could be "outgoing" or "risk-taking".

Oftentimes more practical in a computing context are the dimensional models. One example is the model of the so-called Big Five personality traits. According to this theory, someone's personality can be described by five numbers that signify to what extent each of the five personality traits applies to a person. Similar models exist for emotion as well.

After defining the concepts of emotion and personality, the next important question when incorporating them into a Serious Game is: How can we measure the player's affective state? Since humans actively or subconsciously express affect in many different ways, there are also countless different approaches to detect signals of affect. They all begin with sensors that gather data about various aspects of the human subject. For example, a camera can be used to detect the facial expressions of a person or their posture, and a microphone can be used to record the person's voice. The text they type could be another data source for affect recognition. There also exist many different sensors that record physiological data like the heart rate, the respiration rate, brain activity or sweating, to name a few. The choice of which of these sensor to use depends on factors such as the type of affect to detect, the desired availability of sensor data, and how much interference with the gameplay can be tolerated. While game designers should have convincing reasons for sticking 20 electrodes onto the player's scalp to measure brain activity, a wrist band that measures the heart rate or a camera that records the face might be much more tolerable. No matter by which kind of sensor the data is recorded, it then needs to be processed to extract meaningful features from the signal. Machine learning techniques like neural networks or hidden Markov models can then be used to interpret the feature values and to detect the player's affective state.

The rest of this Chapter is structured as follows. The next Section gives psychological definitions of emotion, mood and personality, and describes models in which they can be represented. They form the basis for the subsequent sections. Section 3 is the main part of this Chapter. It discusses the methods for obtaining affective data from the player of a Serious Game. It begins with general considerations about the data path from sensor to affect, and then presents in more detail various modalities and corresponding techniques that can be harnessed for affect detection. In Sect. 4, some examples of how Affective Computing has been used in existing Serious Games are given. Section 5 concludes the Chapter.

2   Psychological Models of Affect

Before going into the details of how human affect can be recognized and used in a Serious Game, this Section gives an overview of existing definitions and models of affect. In particular, emotion and personality are discussed here, since they are the affective states that are considered most often in this context. Both emotion and personality have been researched for decades and they are well understood in the field of psychology. Understanding the established psychological models helps developers to create computational models that can represent affect in software.

2.1   Models of Emotions

Human emotion is an inseparable part of human intelligence. It influences almost every aspect of our daily lives, including seemingly purely rational processes like decision making. In situations with uncertainty or where there is a large number of choices, pure logic reasoning is unfeasible due to the size of the possibility space. It takes too long to process every alternative and all variables. Emotions serve to filter out undesirable outcomes and to pre-select and label a smaller number of options that are then further processed by rational thinking [115].

In Human-Computer Interaction (HCI), emotions have been considered for over a decade. They are a major influence on how we interact with computer software like Serious Games. This influence goes beyond being happy to win a game or being frustrated when software is not working as expected. Emotions influence every aspect of the interaction [15]. As such, emotions are important to consider during the use of a Serious Game. If a Serious Game was aware of the emotional state of its player, it could guide the player towards positive emotions that are more beneficial for achieving its "serious" goal. The challenge level of the game could be adjusted based on emotions of anxiety or boredom, and the motivation to use a Serious Game for health purposes could be increased. In order to operationalize emotions for Serious Games, this section discusses different models of emotion from a psychology and a Human-Computer Interaction perspective.

In everyday speech, the term *emotion* is used in a broad and fuzzy sense. However, in the field of psychology, the term is defined in a much more specific manner. Despite the large number of differing definitions of emotion, many agree that emotion is a reaction to events that are deemed relevant to the needs and goals of an individual [73]. Examples for such emotions would be the fear of physical harm or the pride of one's own accomplishments. Emotions encompass affective, cognitive, physiological and behavioral components. They bring feelings of pleasure, displeasure or arousal (affective), guide the attention towards relevant stimuli (cognitive), adjust the autonomic nervous system to the arousing conditions (physiological) and lead to expressive behavior and specific action tendencies (behavioral) [73]. Emotions are further characterized by a rapid onset, a short duration, and little control over their occurrence or the appraisal of an event. These features are universal across all cultures [42].

The concepts of mood, sentiments and personality are related to emotion, but have distinct definitions. In order to define what emotions are, it may help to outline what they are not. While emotions are short in duration, intense, focused on an inducing event and have a high behavioral impact, moods typically have lower intensities, last longer, have a more diffuse origin and a lower impact on a person's behavior [155]. There exist a variety of different emotions whereas moods are unspecific and usually reduced to being positive or negative [178]. When certain emotions are experienced frequently, they can result in a change of a person's mood. Vice-versa, the mood that a person is in defines which type of emotions this person is likely to experience [53]. This is important to consider in a Serious Game where the current mood of a player may limit the range of beneficial emotional states that the player can be guided into. It is also more difficult to influence a player's overall mood than their specific emotion.

In contrast to emotions that are states of an individual, sentiments are perceived properties of an object or an event. They correspond more with the common notion of an opinion. A sentiment is the expectation of an emotion that will be experienced when the object or event is encountered. Even though sentiments can change over time, they are a largely persistent attribute of an object [53]. It may be the goal of a Serious Game to alter the player's sentiment towards an external entity. This could be the sentiment towards a medical treatment procedure or a certain product.

Personality will be discussed in more detail in the next Section. Personality is a very long-lasting trait of a person that has no focus on any specific event or entity. Compared to immediate emotion, personality has a lower impact on someone's behavior. However, similar to moods, personality shapes the kind of emotions that are likely to be experienced [155]. In a Serious Game, personality plays a more passive role. The personality of a player can be measured, but it cannot be influenced significantly. It may also be important to incorporate personality patterns when creating virtual agents with synthesized emotions.

The most straightforward way to represent emotions computationally is to assign labels to discrete categories of emotions. The underlying assumption is that there exist such distinct categories and that they are consistent across all humans. The most commonly agreed upon list of basic emotions consists of: anger, disgust, fear, joy, sadness and surprise. Sometimes, more labels like contempt, shame, guilt, embarrassment or awe are added [43,139]. While the insight that such basic emotions exist is an important finding in psychology, reducing a computational model of emotion to a small number of discrete categories may often be an over-generalization from an HCI point of view. Discrete emotion labels do not take into account the possible causes of emotion, mixed emotions or the variety of emotions in the same category [135]. For example, the anger experienced when performing poorly in a Serious Game greatly differs from the anger towards a person in an argument.

Dimensional models of emotion provide a more flexible computational representation than discrete classes. In a dimensional model, each emotion is represented as a point in a multi-dimensional coordinate system. Even though opinions about the exact number and interpretation of the dimensions vary, there is also a commonly agreed upon basis. The most fundamental model consists of the two dimensions of valence and arousal. The valence dimension distinguishes between pleasant and unpleasant emotions. It is the most intuitively interpretable dimension. The second dimension is arousal, and it denotes the amount of physiological change that the emotion causes in a person. This includes reactions like increased heartbeat, rate of breathing or sweating. For example, being excited is represented as value pair with positive valence and positive arousal, while being depressed corresponds to negative valence and negative arousal [151]. Examples of emotions and their valence and arousal values are given in Fig. 1.

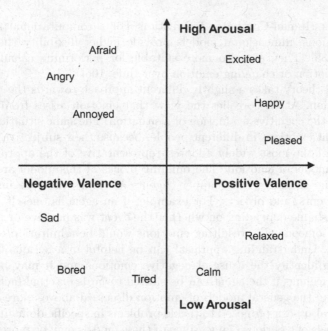

Fig. 1. Emotion can be represented by two values for valence and arousal. The coordinates of some example emotions in the two-dimensional model are illustrated here.

It is also common to add a third dimension, dominance, to the model. High dominance is characterized by the feeling of being in control and exerting influence over others and one's surrounding. Negative dominance on the other hand is the feeling of weakness and submission to external influences [106]. In a game, an emotion with high dominance may be experienced when the player performs better than other virtual or real players. The feeling of being lost when playing a game for the first time is an example of negative dominance. One advantage of the model of pleasantness, arousal and dominance (PAD) is that its original author also developed a linear mapping between the PAD emotion coordinates and personality traits [105]. This can be used when synthesizing virtual agents with a personality. The mapping can help to generate the PAD values of emotions that an agent with a given personality is most likely to experience.

Further dimensions than the three mentioned above have been proposed in the literature. For example, the fourth dimension of unpredictability may be considered. It expresses the novelty of the emotion eliciting stimulus versus the feeling of expectedness and familiarity. In this dimension, mainly surprise is distinguished from all of the other emotions. It has been found that unpredictability is less expressive than the three dimensions discussed so far, accounting for the lowest amount of variability [51]. For practical purposes, it is thus recommendable to focus on the first three dimensions.

While there is an ongoing controversy in psychology over whether discrete or dimensional models better reflect the true nature of emotions [61], the situation is different in Human-Computer Interaction. For a computational representation of emotions, dimensional models provide higher flexibility than discrete categories [135]. They are also more suitable for performing calculations like averaging emotion or changing emotion over time [106].

Appraisal theory takes a slightly different approach towards the representation of emotion. At its core lies the view that emotion arises from appraisal, that is, from the cognitive evaluation of a situation. The same situation can thus evoke different emotions in different people, because their subjective evaluation differs. One of the most widely adopted representative of the appraisal theory is the OCC model of emotion. The building blocks of this model are events as interpretations of things that happen, agents as things that are instrumental to causing events, and objects. For example, if an agent is oneself, one might feel pride or shame depending on whether the event was positive or negative. If the agent is someone else, resulting emotions would be admiration or reproach instead [126]. Understanding appraisal can be helpful in a Serious Game as it may allow to identify the cause of negative emotions and it may be easier to dissolve bad feelings if the agent can be shifted towards external factors.

Other than the general models of emotion discussed above, more specialized models have also been proposed to tackle problems in specific domains. Depending on the goals of a Serious Game, some of these models may be more applicable than a general one. For example in the context of e-learning software, the emotion categories of interest, engagement, confusion, frustration, boredom, hopefulness, satisfaction and disappointment have been used. These emotions have an impact on the effectiveness of learning. There also exists a mapping of these discrete, learning-specific labels into the two-dimensional emotion space [160].

In the context of adjusting the difficulty of a game based on the player's experience, the emotions of boredom, engagement and anxiety are of relevance [26,146]. If a game is too easy or too hard, a player will get bored or anxious, respectively. Only if the level of difficulty is appropriate, players will feel engaged in their task. A related term is that of *achievement emotion*. Such an emotion can be experienced during a competence-based activity like studying or sports, or it is focused towards the outcome of such an activity like success or failure. Examples for achievement emotion are the joy that arises from the feeling of being good at what one is doing or the boredom of performing a task without a perceived intrinsic value [132].

2.2   Personality Traits

Personality is commonly viewed as a defining attribute of someone's character and behavior. For example, when someone has an "outgoing personality", they are social and enjoy the company of other people, or someone may be "short-tempered", which means that they are quick to anger. More formally, personality is defined as a pattern of behavior, affect, and cognition that is consistent over long time spans. It defines a person's predisposition to experience certain emotions [149]. Personality develops until the age of 25–30 and then remains relatively stable even over intervals of decades [30]. This is in stark contrast to emotional episodes which have a much shorter duration. Due to this long term stability, it is not to be expected that a player's personality changes or can be influenced during the interaction with a Serious Game. However, as will be discussed later, there exist many methods to measure the player's personality so that the game can be adapted accordingly.

A major application area for models of personality in Serious Games is the synthesis of virtual agents with believable personalities. An example are conversational agents which react to the user in a way that is consistent with a realistic personality pattern [41,55]. In another example, synthesized personality is used to increase the realism of a Serious Game that simulations emergency evacuation scenarios [54]. Once a personality for an agent is defined, the personality values can also be used to synthesize emotions that are likely to be experienced by the agent [105].

In everyday communication, someone's personality can be described as having or not having any of a large number of possible personality traits [2]. Cattell et al. were among the first to operationalize the multitude of personality traits [22]. They were able to extract 16 meaningful personality factors like warmth, reasoning and emotional stability that describe personality and can be measured using a standardized questionnaire. These personality factors formed the basis for the Big Five personality traits that are the most widely used model of personality today [122]. It is a dimensional model that represents personality as a point in a five-dimensional space. The five dimensions are openness, conscientiousness, extraversion, agreeableness, and neuroticism. They can be remembered by the acronym OCEAN. Openness to experience and to new ideas describes a person's flexibility of thought, intellect and educational aptitude. Conscientiousness is the will to achieve, to be organized and having a high self-discipline. An extraverted person is outgoing and seeks the company of others. The amount of someone's agreeableness relates to their ability to get along with others and to be considerate of others' interests. And finally, neuroticism is a tendency towards negative affect, vulnerability and is the opposite of emotional stability. The opposites of each factor, i.e., the traits corresponding to negative values, can be defined accordingly.

The "Big" in the Big Five model does not imply the greatness of this model, but denotes that the five traits are very broad categories. In many practical applications, reducing personality to just five values is too coarse-scale. An alternative approach is to break the traits down further into a tree hierarchy where the topmost level consists of the original Big Five traits [130]. On the second level of the hierarchy, the Big Five traits are refined into a larger number of strongly related, more specific personality traits. Examples for second level traits are religiosity, thriftiness (not wasting resources on self-gratification), and risk-taking. A mixture of these traits creates the narrow and specific behaviors which form the lowest level of the hierarchy. It has been shown that complex behaviors like alcohol consumption, grade point averages or participation in sports can be predicted from the traits on the higher levels of the hierarchy [130]. This is useful when synthesizing the behavior of a virtual agent based on their assigned personality traits.

3   Capturing and Analyzing Data for Affective Computing in Games

After discussing the psychological models of affect that allow us to represent emotion and personality computationally, the next question is how to actually measure these affective states of a player while playing. One source of affective data are physiological signals such as the heart beat or electrical signals from the nervous system that can be obtained with various sensing technologies. Another information source are observations of the position, shape, orientation and size of the human body and its parts. Examples could be the position of the hands, facial expressions or the pupil diameter. In addition, utterances of the user via voice or text can serve as a starting point for extracting information about the players' affective states. This Section is organized according to the different sources of information. It begins with a brief examination of the process that is used to retrieve information needed for Affective Computing from relevant data.

3.1   From User Data to Affective State

Affect detection is the subject of many research efforts [19,184,185]. The text that was typed in by users during a game can serve as one possible starting point for the affect detection process. In this case, the information is readily available in the computer memory for further processing. Usually, however, some effort is needed to gather data, and various sensing technologies need to be employed. Characteristics of these sensors are the topic of the first subsection. The next subsection deals with the question of how the data can be processed and analyzed once it becomes available. Next, potential goals of this analysis are discussed that have some significance for Serious Games (e.g. the stress level of users or their mood). Finally, today's challenges in this process from data gathering to providing information are discussed briefly.

Sensor Characteristics. Affective Computing usually relies on sensors. When using Affective Computing in games, a first important task is to assess if a certain sensing technology can be used for a certain game and to select the most suitable sensors. Since there is no such thing as an optimal sensing technology, these decisions need to be made for each individual game.

One important criterion for comparing sensing technologies is the extent to which the sensing affects the player. Drilling a hole into the user's skull and placing an electrode on the brain to measure its activity would be on one end of the spectrum. Observing users with a camera without them even noticing would be on the other end. An important question here is not only whether a sensing technology is invasive or not, but also whether it is perceived as obtrusive. The need to wear a specific helmet or specific gloves may distract or even hinder users during gameplay. Players might also simply not accept obtrusive sensors. For instance, if electrodes are stuck on the face in order to sense facial expressions, users might feel uncomfortable in social situations or refuse to wear them, because they are worried about looking stupid. The advent of wireless technologies that eliminate the need for cables has been an important step towards less obtrusiveness. Sensors also tend to become more lightweight. Moreover, wearable sensing technology becomes more commonplace. An example would be joggers that use smart watches, wrist bands or chest belts to measure physiological data. There is an ongoing trend that users are willing to tolerate more types of sensing technologies which is advantageous for Affective Computing. In this context, it is also important to address security or privacy concerns. An optical sensor such as a webcam, for instance, could have a mechanical cover that allows the player to make sure that no image can be used.

There are many other criteria for assessing sensing technology. Typical questions could be: Is a sensor reliable? Is it affected by noise or changing environment conditions? What is the update rate? Is the sensor robust? How often does it need to be calibrated? How cumbersome is the calibration process? What is the energy consumption of the sensor? How much bandwidth is needed to relay the sensor's signal? Is the sensor capable of pre-processing data? The importance of all these criteria and the answers to these questions in an individual use case thus need to be evaluated before using Affective Computing in games.

Processing of Sensor Data. In general, psychological concepts such as emotion cannot be directly observed from sensor data. This is especially true if the data is noisy or context-sensitive. One important context is the individual player – there is a large variability of sensor data that can be obtained from different individuals. Culture also provides an important context. For instance, there are many variations of how to express emotion in different cultures. While laughter could convey happiness in one culture, it could also convey insecurity in another. The crossing of the middle finger and the index finger indicates a positive attitude in some cultures (e.g. in Canada it means "good luck") while it shows a negative attitude in other cultures (e.g. in Germany it indicates that a promise will be broken).

Usually, some sophisticated signal processing techniques, e.g., for removing noise or detecting patterns, are used to process the sensor data. Moreover, the data needs to be analyzed and interpreted. This can be accomplished with machine learning techniques. In Affective Computing, techniques such as neural networks [120], fuzzy logic [100], cepstrum analysis [27], dynamic time warping [113], discrete wavelet transform [112], fractal dimension [95], higher order crossings [136], or hidden Markov modeling [118] have been used successfully. One technique can be used for multiple purposes. For instance, Support Vector Machines make it possible to determine stress [165] or anxiety and boredom [93]. These techniques and their application to Affective Computing are a field of current research.

This research has reached a stage where not only single sensing systems are examined in isolation, but the fusion of several sensor data streams is explored. This results in an additional layer of complexity in the interpretation of the sensor data. Obviously, the combination of different pieces of information potentially provides more detailed and more accurate results. It can also lead to a more continuous availability of information about affective states as different information sources can compensate for errors or lack of data in one source. Indeed, advantages of multimodal detection are described in the literature. Anliker et al. describe how they use information about temperature, physical activity, blood pressure and oxygen saturation, heart rate, and electrical activity of the heart [3]. Moreover, devices exist that combine several sensors in one device. Smart watches combine gyroscopic sensors, acceleration sensors and sensors for measuring the heart rate. The ProComp infiniti system by Thought Technology Ltd. is an example of a commercial product that offers multiple channels where a multitude of sensors with different sampling rates can be flexibly attached to one device [168]. This device can then either record data or transmit it to a connected computer in real-time using a fiber-optic cable. On the software side, libraries are provided to access and process the sensor signals. Specifically for gaming, frameworks such as the one by Nogueira et al. have been developed that combine the processing of raw sensor data from various sources, its interpretation and user profiling [121]. The results of this processing can then be linked to the game logic.

Outcome. From a game developer's perspective, what can be expected as the outcome of the data processing? It could be information that still needs to be interpreted in the game such as context information (e.g., the player is sitting, walking or running). More often, information concerning the emotions of the player is provided directly. There is no universally accepted definition of emotion [67]. Literature such as handbooks or survey articles [32,33,87] from the area of psychology, neuroscience, or affective sciences give an overview of this topic. The most simple form is to use a list of discrete emotion categories for providing information about emotion of the player to the game logic. One of the first proposals by the psychologist Ekman was to distinguish six universal emotions: happiness, surprise, anger, disgust, fear, and sadness [25].

This approach has been refined by representing emotion in a multidimensional space. In the original work, Russell used a two-dimensional space with valence and arousal as axes [151]. Initially, a circumplex model with 28 words that describe different points in the valence/arousal space was used. Other models like a simplified one with only 12 core emotions [183] have been defined based on this initial model. Several works are available in the literature on this topic [28,51,58,59,138,145,152,158]. In this body of work, the dimensional description is shown to be more expressive than discrete models. By adding dominance as a dimension, the PAD model describes the emotional state with the three dimensions pleasantness, arousal and dominance [107].

Emotions are a complex phenomenon and an individual might have several emotions simultaneously [108]. In order to cover mixed emotions, new models are necessary [20,179]. A more recent approach to model mixed emotion is to use emotion profiles instead of emotion labels [110]. Emotion profiles consist of a collection of emotion labels that have a certain probability associated with them.

Besides information about emotional states, Affective Computing can also make other pieces of information available to a game developer. Mood or personality traits of a player can be assessed by integrating and evaluating the information about single emotions over a time frame. Moreover, game developers might be interested in the degree of relaxation or stress that a player is experiencing. In a similar way, information about the player's cognitive workload might be valuable for assessing the strain that a certain task imposes on a player's cognitive system [127].

Challenges. A variety of research challenges are present in the area of affect detection [39]. First, the underlying sensing technology poses research questions: How can sensors become less obtrusive or non-invasive in the first place? How can sensor noise be reduced and weak signals still be detected? How can the energy consumption of the sensors be lowered and sensing solutions with good scalability be found?

Second, the processing of sensor data should become more sophisticated. This includes research towards better data analysis techniques. Moreover, how to fuse information from different sources best is still an open question. This is particularly true for combining sensor data about the physical environment or the semantic context on the one hand and sensor data that stems directly from the body on the other. Here, top-down and bottom-up approaches need to be combined.

Third, the process of drawing conclusions from sensor data is not easy to generalize. Although being exposed to identical situations, different people may react with different emotions. Also, the same individual may react to the same stimuli differently at different times. Measurements between individuals cannot be compared easily. For instance, the pulse of a human being depends on age and physical fitness but also on the current stress level of a situation. A challenge here is to normalize the sensor data in order to facilitate a general interpretation. It is also an open question how to generalize the affect detection process across different contexts and cultures.

Fourth, samples of affective data are often obtained from laboratory experiments which are difficult to conduct. How can we find a ground truth to determine if our affect detection process identified the correct result? Asking people about their emotions might not be a valid approach to finding a ground truth as it is doubtful whether a test user's statements about their feelings are in alignment with their actual feelings [135]. Even if several observers are used in an experimental set-up to increase objectivity, the inter-observer agreement is often found to be low [39]. For testing Affective Computing systems, it proves difficult to elicit certain emotions in test subjects reliably. This becomes a problem for play testing where an affective computer game should react appropriately for all emotional states of the player. It is also cumbersome to collect training data for machine learning together with ground truth. A first step is to provide databases with test data which can be quite helpful in new research endeavors. Examples for such databases can be found in [8, 76, 79].

Fifth, most research results have been obtained in laboratory settings where the context (e.g. environmental conditions) can be controlled. Can these findings be transferred to real-world conditions? Some research, e.g., [37], specifically deals with Affective Computing in the field. Also, the ACM's International Conference on Multimodal Interaction has put forward several research challenges for "emotion detection in the wild".

3.2   Sensing Physiological Data

The emotional state of an individual is often connected to physiological responses of the body, like of the heart, the skin or the brain [143,177]. These responses can be automatic and difficult to manipulate by an individual. While facial expressions can be controlled willingly and people can feign emotions such as surprise or happiness, physiological signals that are emitted by their body are perceived to reflect people's affect more honestly. Using physiological data as a source for Affective Computing has the advantage that emotion can be identified continuously and without interruptions in contrast to using questionnaires. As the necessary sensing technology becomes non-invasive and even mobile and wearable [89], physiological data is gaining popularity as a basis for Affective Computing. This section is organized according to the different body parts that emit physiological signals. It discusses suitable measurements for Affective Computing and according sensor technology.

Heart. Electrical signals caused by contraction and depolarization in the heart muscle can serve as an information source about the heart's activity. An electrocardiogram (ECG) is an established way to record these electrical signals. By analyzing them, different characteristics of a heartbeat like the P-wave, T-wave and the QRS-complex can be distinguished. The heart rate variability (HRV) can also be derived. It measures the intervals between heartbeats and examines changes in duration. This analysis of electric signals can not only be accomplished in the time domain, but spectral methods like Fourier analysis can be used as well. The high-frequency band is associated with the parasympathetic parts of the autonomic nervous system (i.e., the branch of the mostly unconsciously acting peripheral nervous system that has a dampening effect and is reacting slowly) while the low frequency bands are associated with the sympathetic parts (i.e., the branch that allows quick responses to mobilize the body, sometimes labeled the "fight or flight system").

The ECG uses electrodes as sensors that can be placed on both arms and the left leg, or on the chest of the player. Mobile versions also exist in form of a chest strap that has two integrated electrodes or as smart shirts with integrated electrodes [96]. These mobile versions often offer less information. Less obtrusive or even contact-less ECG is a current area of research [94,111]. Seismocardiography (SCG) which is also named ballistocardiography (BCG) uses small body movements caused by contractions of the heart muscle to measure heart activity. Here, only an inertial sensor needs to be used which results in a simple set-up and less power consumption [21]. Non-contact measurements use technology such as Doppler radars [175] or thermal infrared imaging [131] to sense heartbeats.

HR and HRV have shown to serve as a reliable basis for emotion recognition [18,68] as they can be used to identify basic dimensions such as valence and arousal [116,144]. The HRV is ordered and rhythmic in states of positive valence, and it follows the breathing rhythm (respiratory sinus arrhythmia). In emotional states with negative valence such as sadness, anxiety or anger, the HRV is rather chaotic. This can also be expressed as cardiac coherence [170]. HRV increases with arousal and the pulse rate itself is high when pleasant stimuli are present [17]. Spectral analysis of HRV power spectra can reveal states of relaxation or stress, and thus can be used to detect mental workload in real-time [64]. HRV tends to decrease with an increase in mental effort, stress, and frustration [18]. Using machine learning, these emotional states and workload changes can be identified automatically.

The blood volume pulse (BVP) is linked to the heart rate and can be used for emotion or mental stress recognition. It can be measured by two electrodes that are placed on a finger. Alternatively, Photoplethysmography (PPG) using a pulse oximeter can be employed. This means that the light absorption through the skin is measured which reveals information about the BVP and oxygen saturation of the blood. PPG can be performed with a clip attached to a finger or an ear lobe, but there are also contact-less variants using a low-cost webcam [166].

Brain. Electroencephalography (EEG) records variations of the voltage on the scalp which are an indicator of the electrical activity of the brain. While there is rather expensive equipment for EEG available for medical applications, low cost EEG solutions exist for brain computer interface applications such as the EPOC+ and INSIGHT devices [48]. These wireless devices can be worn like a cap or a diadem. They support between 5 and 14 EEG channels. For comparison, devices for medical applications typically feature more than 250 EEG channels. Still, the manufacturer claims that these devices are able to detect facial expressions as well as emotional states such as instantaneous excitement, long term excitement, stress, engagement, relaxation, interest, meditation, frustration and focus.

Functional near infrared spectroscopy (fNIRS) is another non-invasive technology that works based on the analysis of infrared light absorption. These devices can be worn as a cap where the light emitters and light sensors are integrated. The fNIRS technology has been successfully used to implement brain-computer interfaces [6,49]. There are other methods from radiology to detect brain activity, such as Positron Emission Tomography (PET) or Magnetoencephalography (MEG). However, they are not used in the context of Serious Games.

An EEG can serve as a basis for recording data about valence and arousal for two-dimensional emotion analysis [65]. There is also plenty of literature available on how EEG data can be used to detect mental states such as fatigue [172] or negative emotions due to events such as software not behaving according to the user's expectations ("error-related negativity") [176].

Skin. Emotion and mood are correlated with skin temperature which can be measured easily. However, variations in emotional states are reflected with a significant delay, and external factors like the level of activity, time of day, place of measurement and changing environmental conditions have an influence on skin temperature. This makes it difficult to attribute a change in skin temperature to a single factor. Measuring the electrodermal activity (EDA) – which is also called galvanic skin response (GSR) – is a more responsive and robust technique [13]. It is based on the fact that sweat glands are connected to the sympathetic nervous system. In certain situations, ducts in the skin fill with sweat, making the skin more conductive. This change in electrical resistance can be measured with low-cost sensors. Usually two sensors are needed that are either attached to a hand (e.g. the palm and index finger of the non-dominant hand) or a foot. In an exosomatic measure, a small current is used to determine the electric resistance or the skin impedance. Endosomatic measures work without current and determine differences in electric potential. Besides environmental conditions (e.g., humidity, temperature) and context conditions (e.g., time since the last hand wash, type of soap used), the level of skin conductance also depends on the individual. Thus, measured values need to be normalized to compare them between individuals. For this purpose, minimum and maximum values are recorded over some time. Preferably, the person is in a relaxed state to obtain a minimum value that can serve as a baseline.

The skin conductance level (SCL) is the tonic level of the skin's electrical conductivity. If a person is exposed to a stimulus, the SCL reacts slowly within 10 s to several minutes. To detect reactions to stimuli with a shorter latency of one to four seconds, the phasic change in electrical conductivity can be analyzed. Such a change is called the skin conductance response (SCR). However, these phasic changes can also occur in the absence of an intentionally provided stimulus (non-specific SCRs or NS-SCRs).

A low level of skin conductivity is an indicator for a low arousal level [17]. In addition, EDA can also be used to sense emotion awareness [180], the level of trust [85], stress [88] or cognitive load [162]. Some studies found weak relations between EDA and emotion difficult to interpret. While most studies found that skin conductance increases with task difficulty, others found the opposite. This seeming contradiction was explained by the task difficulty in the latter case not being caused by a higher challenge but by being more tedious [66]. EDA has also been used to distinguish between a stress condition and a cognitive load condition [159].

Respiration. Respiration leads to body movements that can be detected by strain gauges, accelerometers, pressure sensors, microphones, nasal airflow sensors, or impedance plethysmography [111]. Such sensors can be integrated into clothing. For instance, a capacitive sensor can be hidden in a shirt [78]. Changes in emotion can lead to a change in respiration patterns [63]. For example, when people become calm, their breathing slows down, whereas the respiration rate raises with excitement. Irregular respiration is an indicator of valence.

Peripheral Nervous System. Information about the peripheral nervous system can be derived from muscular activity. This activity can be measured by an electromyograph where needle electrodes are inserted into the skin. As a non-invasive alternative, accelerometers can be used to measure microvibrations of the muscle. This information reveals the level of activity of a person. Ravaja et al. analyzed the activity of facial muscles to detect positive and negative emotions during gameplay [148].

3.3   Observing the Body

In addition to *sensing physiological data* from the body, information for Affective Computing can also be gathered by *observing* the body's posture and its movements. While the first part of this section looks at the body as a whole, the second and third part single out the face and the eyes, respectively, as specific body parts to observe.

Body Posture and Movements. Motion capturing is a technique where magnetic, inertial, mechanical or optical sensors are used to measure the motion of a person. A popular technique is making a person wear a suit with specific markers that can be easily spotted with computer vision algorithms. By observing the person with a camera, the imagery can be analyzed and the body posture can be reconstructed using a skeleton model. Beside the 3D position of different body parts, it is also possible to measure the angle of joints (goniometry). Alternatively, markerless optical systems are available where no special equipment needs to be worn. For example, Microsoft's Kinect game controller captures a 3D representation of a person which then serves as the basis for a markerless motion capturing system.

Humans are able to express emotion with their body, for example through the way they walk. Humans are able read body language not only from other humans but also from avatars [134]. There exists a whole body of literature that focuses on reading body language automatically [74,184].

Facial Expressions. Facial expressions convey emotions. The strong connection between the expression on a person's face and the emotion they are feeling has been studied rigorously in the past. Arguably one of the most noteworthy publications on this matter is the one by Ekman [44]. Ekman argues that this connection is so strong, that having a distinctive facial expression is a defining requirement for basic emotions. At the same time, facial expressions that arise due to an emotion use facial muscles that cannot be controlled deliberately. So facial expressions and emotion are mutually influencing each other. This is the reason why the vast majority of vision-based approaches to detect emotion focuses on faces.

Facial expressions have been used in applications of marketing, tutoring systems and pain research. In marketing, automatic recognition of facial expressions has been used to determine whether a customer in a store requires assistance, and to tailor specific services like recommendations to them [161]. Emotions also influence the viewing behavior of advertisement on the Internet. Whether a viewer will continue watching an advertisement video or skip forward to different content, can be predicted from the amount of joy and surprise they are experiencing while watching. These emotions can be determined automatically from their facial expression [167].

A good teacher recognizes the emotional state a student is in and adapts the teaching methods accordingly. If the student is highly engaged in the learning process, the teacher might present increasingly challenging problems. If the student is in a negative emotional state like frustration, however, the teacher may slow down and offer more help and explanations or give emotional support. The goal is to always keep the learner in the zone of proximal development, and emotions indicate to what degree this goal is met. So detecting emotion is highly relevant for educational games and facial expression recognition has been successfully used in a learning context [4,7,38,71].

When a person is experiencing immediate pain, for example while executing a certain motion, this pain will most likely be reflected in their facial expression. It has been shown that the experienced level of pain can be predicted from facial expressions [141]. Automatic systems even achieve a better accuracy at distinguishing real pain from a faked expression of pain than an untrained human observer [92]. This is a promising result that can be utilized in Serious Games for health. In a health game, the expression on the face of the player can be used to detect when they are exerting themselves or are experiencing pain, so that the game can be adapted accordingly.

It should be noted that even though facial expressions are most often used to detect emotion, there are also accounts in which they have been used to infer personality traits. Nonverbal cues in a person's face when they are talking give away information about their levels of extraversion and agreeableness [10]. If a Serious Game features a conversational agent, the facial expressions of the agent influence how players perceive its simulated personality [75].

A powerful tool that is often used when working with facial expressions is the Facial Action Coding System (FACS) [45]. It defines a list of 46 so-called Action Units (AU) like "cheek raiser" or "inner brow raiser" that roughly correspond to the facial muscles. Every expression a human face can take on can be described as a combination of these action units and corresponding intensities. This allows a trained coder to objectively label facial expressions, which is an important first step of building an automatic recognition system. The mapping between the occurrence of AUs in an expression and the emotion that is being expressed is also well understood [44]. One shortcoming of FACS is that it has been defined for still images that capture the moment when the expression is the most intense. It is thus not easily applicable to videos where expressions change over time. Especially for subtle expressions or emotions that are expressed as a timed interplay of action units, it is important to also capture the dynamics of a facial expression in order to recognize it [1].

There are a number of additional challenges to consider when detecting emotion based on facial expressions. The same facial expression embedded in a different scene with different bodily gestures may convey very different emotions. So in order to correctly interpret a facial expression, automatic systems and human observers alike require hints in the form of background knowledge and context [5]. There is also the challenge of obtaining realistic image or video samples of expressed emotion. Getting actors to pose facial expressions that are associated with certain emotions on demand is an unsatisfactory solution. A real smile differs greatly from a fake, posed smile in terms of the facial geometry and the timing at which the facial actions are performed [29,174]. This is also true for other expressions in general. Posed expressions are created in different parts of the brain and use different facial muscles than genuine ones. While spontaneous facial expressions are smooth, symmetric and consistent, acted ones are typically less smooth and have more variable dynamics. Some facial muscles that are involved in certain emotions cannot even be controlled deliberately [46].

To provide a basis for the development of emotion recognition systems based on facial expressions, databases of sample expressions have been proposed [57, 97,173]. The largest fraction of samples in these databases consists of short video clips of a frontal view of posed facial expressions that were recorded in a lab environment. They contain subjects from a large age range, various ethnic groups and both genders. The video clips are annotated with action units and labels of the six basic emotions [184]. Due to the difficulty of eliciting natural emotions in a lab setting, only few databases exist that show spontaneously occurring emotion. The samples contained in the databases by [104,171] are recordings of subjects watching video clips where the clips were chosen so that they elicit particular emotions in the viewers.

Once the decision has been made to incorporate facial expression recognition into a Serious Game, the fastest way to get started is to use an appropriate software for the task. The computer expression recognition toolbox (CERT) [91] is a freely available toolkit for detecting facial expressions in real-time. It is capable of detecting 19 different action units from FACS and can also detect their intensity. It does so by detecting and tracking 10 facial features like the corners of the eyes and mouth or the tip of the nose. These features are the input to a support vector machine for each AU. An additional module detects 3D head rotations as well as six basic emotions.

The discussion of the image processing techniques that enable computers to detect facial features and to recognize facial expressions is out of scope of this Chapter. The interested reader is advised to continue reading the great overview articles that have been published on this topic [128,153,169].

Eye Tracking. Eye tracking is a technique for detecting the direction in which a person is looking and for measuring the time the eye is focusing on a certain area [11]. Usually, an optical sensor is used to observe the eye's movement. Alternatively, electrodes placed above and below the eye can be used to obtain information on the eye's movement in an electrooculogram (EOG). Eye tracking is able to reveal information on what a person pays attention to. From the average duration of a fixation, conclusions can be drawn on the mental workload.

Mental workload can also be measured based on pupil diameter and pupillary response [182]. Bradley et al. have also used information about the pupil to measure emotional arousal [14].

3.4 Analyzing Voice

In addition to *what* someone is saying, the way *how* it is said also plays an important role in communication. The characteristics of someone's voice and the way they talk is influenced by the emotion that the person is experiencing at the time. For example, varying the pitch of the voice while speaking is used to produce intonation. If a person is depressed, their intonation will generally be rather flat. The voice of someone who is excited, on the other hand, contains much more variation in pitch. Humans are good at picking up on such subtle variations in speech. These variations can also be used by a computer to detect emotion from speech. Compared to facial expressions, emotions are not expressed as clearly in voice. In general, it can be said that the arousal dimension of an experienced emotion has the strongest impact on speech. High arousal emotions like anger and joy can be distinguished from neutral emotional states. However, the valence is much harder to estimate, i.e., it is more difficult to distinguish between positive and negative emotions [81,123].

Emotion recognition from speech has been used in a variety of applications where the human voice is involved. In applications where a user communicates directly with the computer, recognition of affect makes the interaction more satisfactory [156]. In automatic tutoring systems with voice-based human-computer interaction, the student's emotion can be predicted in an effort to adapt and to improve their learning performance. This is directly applicable to educational Serious Games [90]. In the context of interactive storytelling, a computer tells a story that the player can interact with – ideally also by talking to the computer. Since stories are rich with emotional content, emotion recognition from speech can be used to make this interaction more realistic [23]. These findings are also applicable to communication-based Serious Games, for example for improving social behavior and changing attitudes. Work has also been done on the detection of attributes such as depression [52] or stress [62] from speech. The latter can be useful in games for emergency training where stress management plays an important role.

In a slightly different context, [69] used a computer game to elicit specific emotions from players while they were experiencing winning and losing situations in the game. The voices of the players were then recorded after such events of success and failure and later manually analyzed for their emotional content. While this is not an example for the use of automatic emotion recognition, it is a good indicator that games do target the player's emotions and that these emotions are recognizable from their speech.

The starting point for research on emotion detection from speech, just like for the other modalities that have been discussed, is a database of labeled samples on which recognition algorithms can be trained. Such a database should ideally contain a large number of high quality recordings of utterances by different people with varying emotional content. The contained emotion should also be annotated. El Ayadi et al. discuss a number of challenges to be addressed when building an emotional speech database [47]. The most straightforward way to obtain speech samples that contain emotion is by recording trained actors as they perform them. The resulting emotion is more intense and clean than it would be in a realistic case, which makes it difficult to generalize the trained detectors to realistic scenarios. Also, the context in which acted utterances are produced is artificial and the linguistic content, i.e. *what* is being said, becomes meaningless for emotion detection. As opposed to the acted emotions, realistic voice samples contain background noise, and some emotions are expressed much more often than others. Labeling emotion in realistic recordings is also highly subjective and prone to disagreement. Privacy, legal and moral issues may arise as well. In [77], it was found that automatic emotion recognition systems perform similarly well as subjective listening tests. The majority of databases they surveyed only contained around five basic emotions and more than half of the databases consisted of acted emotions.

In an attempt to obtain speech samples with real emotions, Lee and Narayanan used recordings of the voice of humans that interact with a call center's automatic dialog system on the phone [82]. This approach yields samples with neutral or negative emotions like anger and frustration. Similarly, [69] used a computer game to get players into positive and negative emotional states when they were experiencing situations that were conducive or detrimental to their success in the game. The players were then recorded as they commented on their chances of winning the level.

A set of suitable features needs to be extracted from the speech samples in the database, so that a machine learning algorithm can be trained. The features need to represent aspects of the recorded voice that are relevant to the application of emotion detection. Features that are extracted from a sample as a whole are called *global features*. One example for a global feature is the fundamental frequency (pitch) of the voice over time and statistics thereof like the average, standard deviation or range. Emotions like fear and anger produce a tremor in the voice that can be detected from variations in the pitch. Another example is the so-called *voice quality*, which can be described with words like tense, harsh, whisper or breathy. Furthermore, the rate of speech, patterns of intonation, irregularities in voicing and the existence and duration of pauses can be used as global features [31].

As discussed in [47], global features fail to capture the dynamics of the speech signal, and information about the time of occurrence of a feature is lost. Since only a small number of global features is calculated for an entire sample, classification based on global features is typically fast. In contrast to the global features, *local features* are obtained by splitting the signal into short segments with durations in the order of 10 ms, and extracting features for each segment individually. This leads to a significantly larger number of samples that can be used for training. Classifiers like Support Vector Machines and Hidden Markov models are well-suited for processing such large amounts of samples.

The most common class of local features are spectral features. The short segments are transformed into the frequency domain using the Fast Fourier Transform (FFT). This gives information about the frequencies that are contained in the segment and their respective energies. The frequency spectrum after computing the FFT consists of evenly spaced frequency intervals (e.g., 10 Hz). However, humans do not perceive pitch to be linear; it is perceived in a logarithmic way. This means that the step from 1 kHz to 2 kHz appears to be as large as the step from 2 kHz to 4 kHz. This is reflected in a scale called mel-frequency, which is perceptually uniform and thus well suited for representing features of the human voice [34]. The energy spectrum of mel-frequencies that is obtained in such a way can then be transformed back by computing the inverse FFT. Since the signal was modified in the frequency domain, the resulting signal is not identical to the original speech segment. This representation where the inverse of the frequency spectrum is calculated is referred to as *cepstrum* (an anagram of "spectrum"). The coefficients that are calculated like this are the Mel-Frequency Cepstrum Coefficients (MFCC), which are the most widely employed local feature for emotion recognition from voice [124].

There are many more local features like the coefficients of linear predictive coding (LPC) (for example in [154]), but their discussion is out of scope of this article. It is also a viable approach to use linguistic features in addition to acoustic ones [83]. It is possible to segment words from the speech samples, so that text-based features can be extracted from the textual representation and be used for emotion detection. This is described in more detail in the section on text analysis.

Once features have been extracted from the recorded voice, mostly well-known classifiers have been used on these features to recognize emotion. The Hidden Markov model (HMM) is arguably the most commonly used machine learning technique for speech processing. The features are used as observations that indicate the hidden state which the model is in. One HMM is then trained for each emotion to be detected. HMMs, due to their underlying Markov processes, are well suited to model the temporal structure of the features [84,123]

Gaussian mixture models (GMM) are another popular type of classifiers that is used in emotion recognition from speech. The features are assumed to be drawn from a probability distribution that is modeled as a combination of normal distributions. One GMM is used to model this probability distribution for each emotion to detect. Since the probability distribution of the features is now (assumed to be) known, the probability of a feature vector belonging to one of the emotion classes can be calculated directly, and the emotion with the highest likelihood is chosen. Because of the assumption that the input observations are independent random variables, Gaussian mixture models do not capture the temporal structure of speech samples well. They are best suited for global, time-independent features [16].

Other popular techniques for classifying emotion from speech include Support Vector Machines [156] or Artificial Neural Networks [119]. Only few approaches use a combination of several classifiers in an effort to improve the recognition accuracy [98,157]. More details about the machine learning approaches that are used for emotion detection can be found in [72].

3.5   Analyzing Text

When people communicate with others through written text, e.g., when making a post to a social network or in a text-based chat room, they communicate more than just plain information. In many cases, written text also conveys information about the writer's feelings, or they intend to achieve a certain emotional reaction in the reader [103]. Subtleties in writing can be picked up on and used to infer the writer's affective state. The automatic detection of affective states like emotion, mood or personality from text is an application of the broader field of natural language processing. Many of the existing techniques in the field have recently been applied to the emerging field of affect detection from text [70].

The premise for the detection of affect from text is the availability of text written by the subject under consideration. In a Serious Game, this subject is the player. If the game features a conversational agent that the player interacts with by typing text, then access to their written text is immediate and straightforward [38]. However, even in the absence of directly typed player input, text samples may be obtainable. It is becoming more and more popular for games to have access to the player's account on social networks to post updates on the player's achievements. The textual information on social networks is a rich source of affective data. There are numerous recent approaches that utilize the posts made on the social network Twitter to detect emotions [60,109], moods [35], personality [142], and sentiments [129]. Furthermore, features from Facebook profiles have been used to predict personality [56], and blog texts can be analyzed to infer mood states [86].

The techniques for detecting affect from text can be divided into two broad categories: keyword-based and learning-based [70]. Both techniques begin by preprocessing the text. This step is similar in both cases. Keyword-based approaches then use dictionaries of words with predetermined affect values and search for occurrences of these keywords in the text. Learning-based approaches require a corpus of training data with known affect. Features are then extracted from the training text and used to train a classifier or a regression function.

The main goal of preprocessing is to eliminate variation in text that is unrelated to the detection problem while keeping the relevant information intact. Spelling errors are one example of such unrelated variation that can be partially alleviated by spell-checking algorithms. Converting all text into lowercase and segmenting sentences and word-boundaries based on punctuation and special characters is another example [60,129]. Based on the assumption that stop words like "a", "the", "on" contain little information about affect, they can be removed from the text as well [12]. The last step of preprocessing is to normalize language-specific features. In the case of English text, contractions like "you're" are expanded into "you are", and suffixes are stripped to unify grammatical variations of a word into a single concept [140]. Preprocessing is always a trade-off between removing irrelevant noise from text and over-generalization, so a critical evaluation is necessary.

Keyword-based approaches use extensive dictionaries of words, bigrams or general n-grams, i.e., sequences of n words. Each word is associated with a certain affective state like a mood label or a point in a dimensional emotion model. One example of such a dictionary is the profile of mood states, which is a list of adjectives that can be mapped directly onto a six-dimensional mood vector [12]. After preprocessing, the text is searched for keywords and the affective state of the text is determined as an average of the values assigned to the found keywords. This approach of detecting affect from text has a number of limitations. For some keywords, their affective connotation can be ambiguous. The word "accident" for example mostly describes an undesirable situation. However, it may also be used figuratively as in the case of a "happy accident" when something positive happens unexpectedly. Searching for the presence of keywords also disregards the linguistic structure and the context in which the keywords are used. For example, a "Happy Meal" is more likely referring to fast food than an actual emotional state. And lastly, keyword-based approaches fail in the absence of keywords. If none of the keywords are contained in a piece of text, no statement about its affective content can be made [163].

Learning-based approaches overcome some of these limitations. Instead of preassigned affective values, the relationship between words and affect are learned from examples. Depending on the choice of textual features, this also makes it possible to measure affect from texts that do not contain affective keywords. The basis for using machine learning to detect affect from text is a data set of text samples that are labeled with ground truth affect. Such data sets can be created by annotating them manually or existing data sets that have been made available can be used (see [117] for instance). Depending on the domain, there may be other useful sources of ground truth data. It has been shown that the emotional hashtags attached to messages sent on Twitter, e.g., "#happy" are an accurate indicator of the sender's actual emotion [60,109].

A decision then needs to be made regarding which features to extract from the text. Unigrams, bigrams [109] or general n-grams [129] are popular features. They are binary features that indicate whether a certain sequence of n words is contained in the text or not. A "bag of words" is a feature of a piece of text where all the unigrams contained therein and their multiplicity is recorded. It can be viewed as an extension to binary unigram features [86]. Dictionaries of features can either be derived from the text itself, or existing dictionaries like WordNet Affect can be used [164]. In addition to these, emoticons may be considered as features if the text stems from a social network or an informal chat [60]. However, features are not limited to simple word counts. They can also be made up of more advanced linguistic statistics as in the case of the Linguistic Inquiry and Word Count toolkit [133]. It contains a dictionary of words that are sorted into a hierarchy of categories like emotion words, family members or pronouns. The occurrence of words is counted for all categories the word belongs to. It additionally captures statistical information like the number of words per sentence, the length of words, the use of negation and so on. Especially in the case of using social networks to detect persistent patterns of affect like personality, statistical information that is derived from a user's profile, e.g., the number of posts per day or the number of friends and followers, can be used as features as well [56,125,142].

The last step of learning-based approaches is the choice and training of a machine learning algorithm so that it can then be used on new text for classification or to predict affective information by regression. Among the commonly used classification techniques are Support Vector Machines [24,86,163], Decision Trees [24,142] and Naïve Bayes classification [24,129]. The former two also have variants that perform regression rather than classification, which is useful when dimensional models are used to represent emotion or personality. The Waikato Environment for Knowledge Analysis (Weka) is a toolkit that implements many common machine learning techniques for natural language processing like the ones mentioned above. It allows users to quickly experiment with different algorithms and choose the ones that achieve the best results [181].

4   Exploiting Affective Computing for Games

For designers and developers of Serious Games, methodologies from Affective Computing are of interest for several reasons. First, these methodologies offer novel possibilities to evaluate a digital game. For example, Mandryk et al. suggest psychophysiological techniques to evaluate user experience in an entertainment context [102]. Drachen et al. use the heart rate and electrodermal activity to propose a technique for evaluating player experience [40]. In contrast to other techniques such as interviews or questionnaires, physiological signals can be used during gameplay without interrupting it. Results gathered may also be more objective and able to provide a more quantitative understanding. Having meaningful evaluation techniques is highly relevant, as evaluation is a key step in user-centered design in general and in game development in particular.

Second, Affective Computing can be used as input for adaptation. Research shows that it is feasible to model the emotional state of a player during interactive gameplay continuously [101]. For example, the 3D digital game Lost in the Dark [9] uses information from an EEG, facial expressions and head motion to detect the level of excitement and engagement of a player in a game. As a response to the current affective state of the player, the music, colors, lighting, difficulty of the level and other game elements are altered. This in turn elicits emotions in the player that can be detected in a next cycle. Thus, a closed loop for an adaptation process is achieved.

Third, methodologies from Affective Computing can be used as a basis for novel interaction techniques that the player willfully uses to achieve gaming goals. This can lead to novel game mechanics. For instance, a "Star Wars" inspired game could be conceived where the player needs to let go of all negative emotion in order to become one with the force and succeed in gameplay. As another example, facial expressions can be used as an interaction method. Lankes et al. showed that this natural interaction method is easy to learn and provides a good user experience [80].

Fourth, methodologies from Affective Computing can be used to put the player in a certain emotional state, as this might be desirable from a game design point of view. As shown in [36], users do not always notice how their physiological signals affect the game. Care thus needs to be taken that the player understands the mechanisms of this kind of novel interaction technique.

Fifth, Affective Computing can provide tools for research. This encompasses research in game usability [99], models to detect certain affective states such as fatigue during gameplay [150] as well as media research in general [147].

In the following Sections, we discuss three case studies where techniques from Affective Computing have been successfully applied to the field of gaming. In particular, they have been employed with the intention of: Sect. 4.1 evaluating the player experience during gameplay, Sect. 4.2 adapting the difficulty of a game to the player's current emotion, and Sect. 4.3 changing the player's emotional state into a more beneficial one.

4.1 Evaluating Player Experience

It is clear that having fun while playing a game is strongly tied to the emotions that are experienced during gameplay. However, how exactly experiences such as immersion or flow are related to measurable psychophysiological responses is not yet fully understood. Such an understanding would make it possible to continuously and objectively measure the player experience from physiological signals. This capability would be an invaluable evaluation tool for game designers.

One step towards this goal is made by Nacke and Lindley [114]. They present the results of an experiment with 25 participants, playing three different levels of the first-person shooter Half-Life 2 for up to ten minutes each. The three levels were specifically designed to elicit the gameplay experiences of boredom, immersion and flow. The level that targets boredom for example has a repetitive structure with easy opponents, no surprises and no particular winning conditions. The level to induce immersion on the other hand features a complex environment that encourages exploration. It contains much variety in textures, models, lighting and animation, and the player is rewarded with new weapons and ammunition upon reaching goals. The third level is meant to put the player into a state of flow. It consists of continuous combat which starts out with only easy opponents, but gets more and more challenging over time.

Each of the participants played all three levels one after another. After each level, they were given a game experience questionnaire to fill out. The questionnaire evaluates seven dimensions of player experience, including flow, challenge, positive affect and immersion. Each dimension was assessed by five items that were rated on a five-point agreement scale. The results of the questionnaire allow for a subjective evaluation of the players' experience during gameplay.

As an additional objective evaluation, the players' emotional state was assessed continuously by using psychophysiological measurements. By using facial electromyography (EMG), the activity of three facial muscles on the cheek, around the eye and on the brow was measured. These muscles are known to indicate positive and negative emotion. Additionally, electrodermal activity was measured, which is directly related to sweating and indicates arousal. With these two techniques, emotional valence and arousal could be measured directly as the players played the levels.

After evaluating the data gathered during the experiment, it was found that the cheek muscle, which indicates positive emotion, indeed showed significantly increased activity while playing the level that was designed to achieve a state of flow. For this level, the electrodermal activity was also significantly higher than for the other levels. This is in line with the questionnaire data that shows that the flow level was perceived as the most challenging one. Looking at the two-dimensional model of emotion, positive valence with high arousal as it was measured during gameplay of this level signalizes that the emotion of joy was experienced. While there is still more research to be done, this result is a promising first step towards an objective evaluation of fun in a game.

4.2 Affective Computing for Adaptation

The information that Affective Computing techniques provide about the emotional state of a player can be used to adapt various aspects of the game. Chanel et al. have shown that the states of boredom and anxiety correspond to a game that is too easy or too hard, respectively, and that the difficulty level of the game can be adjusted accordingly to maintain the player's engagement in the game [26]. In their work, a Tetris game is used where the difficulty level corresponds to the speed of the falling blocks. While not being a Serious Game per se, their findings can easily be generalized to different genres. Maintaining a state of flow in the player is desirable for Serious Games in order to keep the users playing so that the game's goals can be achieved.

In order to not interrupt the game flow, the player's emotional state is assessed by physiological sensors that measure skin conductance, pulse, respiration rate and skin temperature. Additionally, 19 electrodes attached to the skull collect EEG data. Features are extracted from the acquired data, which are then used to classify the player's emotional state into boredom, engagement and anxiety. In a two-dimensional pleasantness-arousal model of emotion, both boredom and anxiety are located on the side of negative pleasantness, with boredom being characterized by low arousal and anxiety by high arousal. Engagement can be found in the quadrant of high pleasantness and high arousal where emotions like joy are found. In addition to the physiological data, for the purpose of evaluation, a questionnaire was used in the experiments, consisting of 30 questions about emotion and engagement that are rated on a seven-point Likert scale.

The extent to which the emotional state of the player can be measured was evaluated in an experiment with 20 participants. Based on a few preliminary games, the difficulty levels which a player would find easy, medium and hard were determined for each player individually. In the experiment itself, the players then played six sessions of five minutes each where the difficulty level for each session was a random permutation of the three settings, each played twice. During the gameplay, the players' physiological data was collected and the questionnaire had to be answered after each session. From the evaluation of the collected physiological and questionnaire data, it was found that less pleasure and interest was experienced while playing the easy and the hard difficulty level compared to the medium difficulty. The measured arousal of the player increased with increasing difficulty. These results are in line with the three expected emotional states. The easy difficulty leads to low pleasantness and low valence (boredom) while the hard difficulty setting induced low pleasantness and high arousal (anxiety). Playing the game on the level that matched the player's skill resulted in high pleasantness and high arousal which is identified as engagement or joy.

The study demonstrated that the level of difficulty does indeed influence the emotional state that the players experience during gameplay, and that this emotional state can be measured from physiological signals. Physiological signals can thus be used as input to adapt the difficulty of a game, so that the desirable state of flow can be maintained.

4.3   Influencing Player Emotion

There are also Serious Games that specifically target the affective state of the player. For example, the objective of the game could be to improve the emotion regulation capabilities of the player to assist the treatment of mental disorders. In such a situation, Affective Computing can bring many benefits to the game. The emotional state of the player can be measured, the game can be adapted based on this state and direct feedback can be given to the players who can then change their behavior accordingly.

One such example that influences the emotion of the player in order to treat mental disorders is the Playmancer project [50]. It is an EU project that consists of a multidisciplinary team of clinicians and engineers. Playmancer itself is a game platform that is based on Unity which simplifies the development of Serious Games. It is capable of handling multimodal user input through mouse, keyboard, speech, facial expressions and various physiological signals. The Serious Game that was created by the Playmancer developers is called "Islands". It consists of three islands where different activities with varying difficulty must be performed. The overall goal of the game is to assist in the treatment of patients with eating disorders and gambling addictions, in parallel to more traditional treatment approaches. The challenges on the islands are tailored to impulse control and managing negative emotions like frustration and anger. With the immediate biofeedback given by the game, the players learn to control their negative emotions and delay or avoid impulsive behaviors.

The game uses the various input devices to continually update a model of the player's emotional state. In the Playmancer architecture, there is a speech recognition module included which allows for a natural interaction with the game. In addition to recognizing *what* is said, this module also considers *how* it is said. Features from the spoken utterances are used to recognize the emotional states of anger, boredom and a neutral state. Additionally, the platform is capable of detecting emotion from facial expressions of the player, as well as from a number of physiological signals like skin conductance, heart rate, and respiration rate.

Based on the player's emotional state, the game adapts its difficulty. If negative emotions like anger are detected, the game is made more difficult as a form of negative reinforcement to avoid such a behavior. For example, more obstacles are preventing the player from reaching their goal, or fish in the game are harder to catch. The game then directs the player avatar to a relaxing area to calm down, which in turn makes the game easier again. In this manner, the players learn to regulate their emotions towards more positive ones even when faced with frustrating situations.

The usability and usefulness of the game was tested by a group of 24 patients with eating disorders or gambling addictions and 14 healthy control subjects. They played the game for 20 min once a week over the course of 12–14 weeks. It was found that the patients feel comfortable playing the Serious Game. The game was able to trigger strong emotional reactions, which occurred more intensely in the patients than in the control group. Over the course of the study, the patients learned to cope with negative emotions and to manage their stress level more effectively.

5 Conclusions

This Chapter discussed, how the methods of Affective Computing can be utilized in a Serious Game. This was illustrated in three case studies where emotion recognition is employed during gameplay. The detected emotional state of the player then forms the basis for an evaluation of the player experience during gameplay, or an adaptation of the difficulty level of the game. In another example, the recognized affect serves as a form of biofeedback to help the player avoid negative emotions.

Emotion has been identified as a central concept in Affective Computing in general, and in the context of Serious Games in particular. The most obvious way to represent emotion computationally is as labels for a limited number of discrete emotion categories. This classification scheme is easy to implement, but may be too general to be useful. In practice, representing an emotion as a point in a multidimensional space is more beneficial in a computing context as this offers more flexibility. The three-dimensions of pleasantness, arousal and dominance have proven to be a useful model. As a complementary approach, appraisal models are preferred in certain domains due to their capability of offering insights into the circumstances which gave rise to an emotion.

Apart from emotion, the personality of a player can be measured and used as input for game adaptation, or models of personality like the Big Five can be used to create virtual characters with synthesized personality profiles. Since personality is known to be stable over many years, it is not expected that the player's personality can be influenced significantly by a Serious Game.

When Affective Computing is used in a game, the developers need to make a decision about which sensors to employ to measure affect. Obtrusive sensors like electrodes that are attached to the body typically offer a wider range of reliable data. Physiological data obtained in this manner includes the heart rate, brain activity, sweating, the respiration rate and muscular activity. However, if the users of the game are unwilling to tolerate such sensors, contact-less devices might be preferable. Webcams and microphones can observe the body posture, gestures, facial expressions, and speech. Either way, the captured sensor data must be processed and machine learning techniques are used to detect affect. In this way, it is possible to recognize the user's emotion, mood and personality, and the cognitive workload and the stress level can be assessed.

The field of Affective Computing in the context of games is still in its infancy. As such, there remain many open challenges that deserve more attention in research. A major hindrance when transferring an Affective Serious Game from the lab to the home is the lack of unobtrusive sensors. So far, the most reliable ways to detect affect are also the most obtrusive ones. In a similar vein, it is also questionable how well an affect recognition system that was built under ideal lab conditions can be generalized to people's homes where measurement conditions differ greatly and the people whose affect is measured are not the ones on which the system was trained. Overall, the implemented prototypes of Serious Games that use Affective Computing seem very promising. The combination of gaming and affect has the potential to improve the effectiveness of Serious Games, and it opens up many interesting new avenues for research.

Readings

– Scott Brave and Clifford Nass. Emotion in human–computer interaction. In *Human-Computer Interaction*, pp. 53–67. CRC Press, 2003

This article is the fourth chapter of a book on Human-Computer Interaction (HCI), and it describes the role of emotion in this context. It gives a motivation of why emotion is important in HCI, and describes methods to measure affect from various sources. The information provided in the article can be applied directly to Serious Games.

– Georgios N Yannakakis and Ana Paiva. Emotion in games. In *Handbook on Affective Computing*, pp. 459–471. Oxford University Press, 2014

This article is Chap. 34 of a book on Affective Computing. It specifically discusses emotion in the context of games and makes a strong point for the connection between Affective Computing and gaming. Methods to adapt a game to the player's affect and expressing emotion in a game are described. In the end of the article, a list of open research questions in the field is given.

– M Lewis, JM Haviland-Jones, and LF Barrett. *Handbook of Emotions*. Guilford Press, 2010

This book contains a very thorough review of many aspects of emotion from a psychologist's point of view. It is currently in its third edition. It describes the psychophysiology, the vocal, and the facial expression of emotion. These concepts form the basis for the automatic recognition of emotion through sensors.

References

1. Ambadar, Z., Schooler, J.W., Cohn, J.F.: Deciphering the enigmatic face - the importance of facial dynamics in interpreting subtle facial expressions. Psychol. Sci. **16**(5), 403–410 (2005)
2. Anderson, N.H.: Likableness ratings of 555 personality-trait words. J. Pers. Soc. Psychol. **9**(3), 272 (1968)
3. Anliker, U., Ward, J.A., Lukowicz, P., Tröster, G., Dolveck, F., Baer, M., Keita, F., Schenker, E.B., Catarsi, F., Coluccini, L., et al.: AMON: a wearable multiparameter medical monitoring and alert system. IEEE Trans. Inf. Technol. Biomed. **8**(4), 415–427 (2004)
4. Arroyo, I., Cooper, D.G., Burleson, W., Woolf, B.P., Muldner, K., Christopherson, R.: Emotion sensors go to school. In: Proceedings of AIED, vol. 200, pp. 17–24 (2009)
5. Aviezer, H., Hassin, R.R., Ryan, J., Grady, C., Susskind, J., Anderson, A., Moscovitch, M., Bentin, S.: Angry, disgusted, or afraid? Studies on the malleability of emotion perception. Psychol. Sci. **19**(7), 724–732 (2008)
6. Ayaz, H., Shewokis, P.A., Bunce, S., Onaral, B.: An optical brain computer interface for environmental control. In: International Conference on Engineering in Medicine and Biology Society (EMBC), pp. 6327–6330 (2011)
7. Bartlett, M.S., Littlewort, G., Fasel, I., Movellan, J.R.: Real time face detection and facial expression recognition: development and applications to human computer interaction. In: Proceedings of Computer Vision and Pattern Recognition Workshop, vol. 5, p. 53 (2003)
8. Baveye, Y., Dellandrea, E., Chamaret, C., Chen, L.: Liris-accede: a video database for affective content analysis. IEEE Trans. Affect. Comput. **6**(1), 43–55 (2015)
9. Bernays, R., Mone, J., Yau, P., Murcia, M., Gonzalez-Sanchez, J., Chavez-Echeagaray, M.E., Christopherson, R., Atkinson, R.: Lost in the dark: emotion adaption. In: Adjunct Proceedings of the 25th Annual ACM Symposium on User Interface Software and Technology (UIST), pp. 79–80 (2012). doi:10.1145/2380296.2380331, ISBN 978-1-4503-1582-1
10. Biel, J.-I., Teijeiro-Mosquera, L., Gatica-Perez, D.: Facetube: predicting personality from facial expressions of emotion in online conversational video. In: Proceedings of the 14th ACM International Conference on Multimodal Interaction, pp. 53–56 (2012)
11. Bojko, A.: Eye Tracking the User Experience. Rosenfeld Media, Brooklyn (2013)
12. Bollen, J., Pepe, A., Mao, H.: Modeling public mood and emotion: twitter sentiment and socio-economic phenomena. In: Proceedings of ICWSM, vol. 11, pp. 450–453 (2009)
13. Boucsein, W.: Electrodermal Activity. Springer Science & Business Media, Berlin (2012)
14. Bradley, M.M., Miccoli, L., Escrig, M.A., Lang, P.J.: The pupil as a measure of emotional arousal and autonomic activation. Psychophysiology **45**(4), 602–607 (2008)
15. Brave, S., Nass, C.: Emotion in human-computer interaction. In: Jacko, J.A., Sears, A. (eds.) Human-Computer Interaction, pp. 53–67. CRC Press, Boca Raton (2003)
16. Breazeal, C., Aryananda, L.: Recognition of affective communicative intent in robot-directed speech. Auton. Robots **12**(1), 83–104 (2002)

17. Brouwer, A.-M., Van Wouwe, N., Muehl, C., Van Erp, J., Toet, A.: Perceiving blocks of emotional pictures, sounds: effects on physiological variables. Front. Hum. Neurosci. **7**, 1–10 (2013). Article 295, ISSN 1662–5161
18. Cacioppo, J.T., Tassinary, L.G., Berntson, G.G.: Handbook of Psychophysiology. Cambridge University Press, Cambridge (2007)
19. Calvo, R.A., D'Mello, S.: Affect detection: an interdisciplinary review of models, methods, and their applications. IEEE Trans. Affect. Comput. **1**(1), 18–37 (2010)
20. Carrera, P., Oceja, L.: Drawing mixed emotions: sequential or simultaneous experiences? Cogn. Emot. **21**(2), 422–441 (2007)
21. Castiglioni, P., Faini, A., Parati, G., Di Rienzo, M.: Wearable seismocardiography. In: 2007 29th Annual International Conference of the IEEE Engineering in Medicine, Biology Society, pp. 3954–3957, August 2007. doi:10.1109/IEMBS. 2007.4353199
22. Cattell, R.B., Eber, H.W., Tatsuoka, M.M.: Handbook for the Sixteen Personality Factor Questionnaire (16 PF), in Clinical, Educational, Industrial, and Research Psychology, for use with all forms of the Test. Institute for Personality and Ability Testing, Champaign (1970)
23. Cavazza, M., Pizzi, D., Charles, F., Vogt, T., André, E.: Emotional input for character-based interactive storytelling. In: Proceedings of the International Conference on Autonomous Agents and Multiagent Systems, vol. 1, pp. 313–320 (2009)
24. Chaffar, S., Inkpen, D.: Using a heterogeneous dataset for emotion analysis in text. In: Butz, C., Lingras, P. (eds.) AI 2011. LNCS (LNAI), vol. 6657, pp. 62–67. Springer, Heidelberg (2011). doi:10.1007/978-3-642-21043-3_8
25. Chanel, G., Kronegg, J., Grandjean, D., Pun, T.: Emotion assessment: arousal evaluation using EEG's and peripheral physiological signals. In: Gunsel, B., Jain, A.K., Tekalp, A.M., Sankur, B. (eds.) MRCS 2006. LNCS, vol. 4105, pp. 530–537. Springer, Heidelberg (2006). doi:10.1007/11848035_70
26. Chanel, G., Rebetez, C., Bétrancourt, M., Pun, T.: Emotion assessment from physiological signals for adaptation of game difficulty. IEEE Trans. Syst. Man Cybern. Part A Syst. Hum. **41**(6), 1052–1063 (2011)
27. Childers, D.G., Skinner, D.P., Kemerait, R.C.: The cepstrum: a guide to processing. Proc. IEEE **65**(10), 1428–1443 (1977)
28. Christie, I.C., Friedman, B.H.: Autonomic specificity of discrete emotion and dimensions of affective space: a multivariate approach. Int. J. Psychophysiol. **51**(2), 143–153 (2004)
29. Cohn, J.F., Schmidt, K.L.: The timing of facial motion in posed and spontaneous smiles. Int. J. Wavelets Multiresolut. Inf. Process. **2**(02), 121–132 (2004)
30. Costa Jr., P.T., McCrae, R.R.: Set like plaster? Evidence for the stability of adult personality. In: Heatherton, T., Weinberger, J. (eds.) Can Personality Change?, pp. 21–40. American Psychological Association, Washington, D.C (1994)
31. Cowie, R., Douglas-Cowie, E., Tsapatsoulis, N., Votsis, G., Kollias, S., Fellenz, W., Taylor, J.G.: Emotion recognition in human-computer interaction. IEEE Sig. Process. Mag. **18**(1), 32–80 (2001)
32. Dalgleish, T., Dunn, B.D., Mobbs, D.: Affective neuroscience: past, present, and future. Emot. Rev. **1**(4), 355–368 (2009)
33. Davidson, R.J., Scherer, K.R., Goldsmith, H.: Handbook of Affective Sciences. Oxford University Press, Oxford (2003)
34. Davis, S.B., Mermelstein, P.: Comparison of parametric representations for monosyllabic word recognition in continuously spoken sentences. IEEE Trans. Acoust. Speech Sig. Process. **28**(4), 357–366 (1980)

35. De Choudhury, M.C.S., Gamon, M.: Not all moods are created equal! Exploring human emotional states in social media. In: Proceedings of the ICWSM (2012)
36. Dekker, A., Champion, E.: Please biofeed the zombies: enhancing the gameplay and display of a horror game using biofeedback. In: Proceedings of DiGRA, pp. 550–558 (2007)
37. Dhall, A., Goecke, R., Lucey, S., Gedeon, T.: Static facial expression analysis in tough conditions: data, evaluation protocol and benchmark. In: IEEE International Conference on Computer Vision Workshops (ICCV Workshops), pp. 2106–2112 (2011)
38. D'Mello, S., Graesser, A.: Autotutor and affective autotutor: learning by talking with cognitively and emotionally intelligent computers that talk back. ACM Trans. Interact. Intell. Syst. (TiiS) 2(4), 23 (2012)
39. D'Mello, S.K., Kory, J.: A review and meta-analysis of multimodal affect detection systems. ACM Comput. Surv. 47(3), February 2015. doi:10.1145/2682899, ISSN 0360-0300
40. Drachen, A., Nacke, L.E., Yannakakis, G., Lee Pedersen, A.: Correlation between heart rate, electrodermal activity and player experience in first-person shooter games. In: Proceedings of the 5th ACM SIGGRAPH Symposium on Video Games, pp. 49–54 (2010)
41. Egges, A., Kshirsagar, S., Magnenat-Thalmann, N.: A model for personality and emotion simulation. In: Palade, V., Howlett, R.J., Jain, L. (eds.) KES 2003. LNCS (LNAI), vol. 2773, pp. 453–461. Springer, Heidelberg (2003). doi:10.1007/978-3-540-45224-9_63
42. Ekman, P.: An argument for basic emotions. Cogn. Emot. 6(3–4), 169–200 (1992a)
43. Ekman, P.: Are there basic emotions? Psychol. Rev. 99(3), 550–553 (1992b)
44. Ekman, P.: Facial expression and emotion. Am. Psychol. 48(4), 384 (1993)
45. Ekman, P., Friesen, W.V.: Facial Action Coding System: A Technique for the Measurement of Facial Movement. Consulting Psychologists Press, Stanford University, Palo Alto (1978)
46. Ekman, P., Rosenberg, E.L.: What the Face Reveals: Basic and Applied Studies of Spontaneous Expression Using the Facial Action Coding System (FACS). Oxford University Press, Oxford (1997)
47. El Ayadi, M., Kamel, M.S., Karray, F.: Survey on speech emotion recognition: features, classification schemes, and databases. Pattern Recogn. 44(3), 572–587 (2011)
48. Emotiv.Emotiv (2016). http://emotiv.com. Accessed 26 May 2016
49. Fazli, S., Mehnert, J., Steinbrink, J., Curio, G., Villringer, A., Müller, K.-R., Blankertz, B.: Enhanced performance by a hybrid NIRS-EEG brain computer interface. Neuroimage 59(1), 519–529 (2012)
50. Fernández-Aranda, F., Jiménez-Murcia, S., Santamaría, J.J., Gunnard, K., Soto, A., Kalapanidas, E., Bults, R.G.A., Davarakis, C., Ganchev, T., Granero, R.: Video games as a complementary therapy tool in mental disorders: PlayMancer, a European multicentre study. J. Ment. Health 21(4), 364–374 (2012)
51. Fontaine, J.R.J., Scherer, K.R., Roesch, E.B., Ellsworth, P.C.: The world of emotions is not two-dimensional. Psychol. Sci. 18(12), 1050–1057 (2007)
52. France, D.J., Shiavi, R.G., Silverman, S., Silverman, M., Wilkes, M.: Acoustical properties of speech as indicators of depression, suicidal risk. IEEE Trans. Biomed. Eng. 47(7), 829–837 (2000)
53. Frijda, N.H.: Varieties of affect: emotions and episodes, moods, and sentiments. In: Ekman, P., Davison, R. (eds.) The Nature of Emotions: Fundamental Questions, pp. 197–202. Oxford University Press, Oxford (1994)

54. García-García, C., Larios-Rosillo, V., Luga, H.: Agent behaviour modeling using personality profile characterization for emergency evacuation serious games. In: Plemenos, D., Miaoulis, G. (eds.) Intelligent Computer Graphics 2012. Studies in Computational Intelligence, vol. 441, pp. 107–128. Springer, Heidelberg (2013)
55. Gebhard, P., Kipp, K.H.: Are computer-generated emotions and moods plausible to humans? In: Gratch, J., Young, M., Aylett, R., Ballin, D., Olivier, P. (eds.) IVA 2006. LNCS (LNAI), vol. 4133, pp. 343–356. Springer, Heidelberg (2006). doi:10.1007/11821830_28
56. Golbeck, J., Robles, C., Turner, K.: Predicting personality with social media. In: Proceedings of CHI 2011 Extended Abstracts on Human Factors in Computing Systems, pp. 253–262 (2011)
57. Gunes, H., Piccardi, M.: A bimodal face and body gesture database for automatic analysis of human nonverbal affective behavior. In: International Conference on Pattern Recognition (ICPR), vol. 1, pp. 1148–1153 (2006)
58. Gunes, H., Schuller, B.: Categorical and dimensional affect analysis in continuous input: current trends and future directions. Image Vis. Comput. 31(2), 120–136 (2013)
59. Gunes, H., Schuller, B., Pantic, M., Cowie, R.: Emotion representation, analysis, synthesis in continuous space: a survey. In: IEEE International Conference on Automatic Face & Gesture Recognition and Workshops, pp. 827–834 (2011)
60. Guthier, B., Alharthi, R., Abaalkhail, R., El Saddik, A.: Detection and visualization of emotions in an affect-aware city. In: Proceedings of the 1st International Workshop on Emerging Multimedia Applications and Services for Smart Cities, pp. 23–28 (2014)
61. Hamann, S.: Mapping discrete and dimensional emotions onto the brain: controversies and consensus. Trends Cogn. Sci. 16(9), 458–466 (2012)
62. Hansen, J.H.L., Cairns, D.A.: Icarus: Source generator based real-time recognition of speech in noisy stressful and lombard effect environments. Speech Commun. 16(4), 391–422 (1995)
63. Homma, I., Masaoka, Y.: Breathing rhythms and emotions. Exp. Physiol. 93(9), 1011–1021 (2008)
64. Hoover, A., Singh, A., Fishel-Brown, S., Muth, E.: Real-time detection of workload changes using heart rate variability. Biomed. Sig. Process. Control 7(4), 333–341 (2012)
65. Horlings, R., Datcu, D., Rothkrantz, L.J.M.: Emotion recognition using brain activity. In: Proceedings of the 9th International Conference on Computer Systems and Technologies and Workshop for PhD Students in Computing, p. 6 (2008)
66. Ikehara, C.S., Crosby, M.E.: Assessing cognitive load with physiological sensors. In: Proceedings of the Hawaii International Conference on System Sciences (HICSS), p. 295a (2005)
67. Izard, C.E., et al.: Special section: on defining emotion. Emot. Rev. 2(4), 363–385 (2010)
68. Jerritta, S., Murugappan, M., Nagarajan, R., Wan, K.: Physiological signals based human emotion recognition: a review. In: IEEE International Colloquium on Signal Processing and its Applications (CSPA), pp. 410–415 (2011)
69. Johnstone, T., van Reekum, C.M., Hird, K., Kirsner, K., Scherer, K.R.: Affective speech elicited with a computer game. Emotion 5(4), 513 (2005)
70. Kao, E.C.-C., Liu, C.-C., Yang, T.-H., Hsieh, C.-T., Soo, V.-W.: Towards text-based emotion detection a survey and possible improvements. In: International Conference on Information Management and Engineering, ICIME 2009, pp. 70–74 (2009)

71. Kapoor, A., Picard, R.W.: Multimodal affect recognition in learning environments. In: Proceedings of the 13th Annual ACM International Conference on Multimedia, pp. 677–682 (2005)
72. Kirk, M.: Thoughtful Machine Learning: A Test-Driven Approach. O'Reilly Media Inc., California (2014)
73. Kleinginna Jr., P.R., Kleinginna, A.M.: A categorized list of emotion definitions, with suggestions for a consensual definition. Motiv. Emot. **5**(4), 345–379 (1981)
74. Kleinsmith, A., Bianchi-Berthouze, N., Steed, A.: Automatic recognition of non-acted affective postures. IEEE Trans. Syst. Man Cybern. Part B Cybern. **41**(4), 1027–1038 (2011)
75. Knutson, B.: Facial expressions of emotion influence interpersonal trait inferences. J. Nonverbal Behav. **20**(3), 165–182 (1996)
76. Koelstra, S., Mühl, C., Soleymani, M., Lee, J.-S., Yazdani, A., Ebrahimi, T., Pun, T., Nijholt, A., Patras, I.: Deap: a database for emotion analysis; using physiological signals. IEEE Trans. Affect. Comput. **3**(1), 18–31 (2012)
77. Koolagudi, S.G., Rao, K.S.: Emotion recognition from speech: a review. Int. J. Speech Technol. **15**(2), 99–117 (2012)
78. Kundu, S.K., Kumagai, S., Sasaki, M.: A wearable capacitive sensor for monitoring human respiratory rate. Japan. J. Appl. Phys. **52**(4S), 04CL05 (2013)
79. Lang, P.J., Bradley, M.M., Cuthbert, B.N.: International affective picture system (IAPS): Affective ratings of pictures and instruction manual. Technical report A-8 (2008)
80. Lankes, M., Riegler, S., Weiss, A., Mirlacher, T., Pirker, M., Tscheligi, M.: Facial expressions as game input with different emotional feedback conditions. In: Proceedings of the 2008 International Conference on Advances in Computer Entertainment Technology, pp. 253–256 (2008)
81. Laukka, P., Juslin, P., Bresin, R.: A dimensional approach to vocal expression of emotion. Cogn. Emot. **19**(5), 633–653 (2005)
82. Lee, C.M., Narayanan, S.S.: Toward detecting emotions in spoken dialogs. IEEE Trans. Speech Audio Process. **13**(2), 293–303 (2005)
83. Lee, C.M., Narayanan, S.S., Pieraccini, R.: Combining acoustic and language information for emotion recognition. In: Proceedings of INTERSPEECH (2002)
84. Lee, C.M., Yildirim, S., Bulut, M., Kazemzadeh, A., Busso, C., Deng, Z., Lee, S., Narayanan, S.: Emotion recognition based on phoneme classes. In: Proceedings of Interspeech, pp. 205–211 (2004)
85. Leichtenstern, K., Bee, N., André, E., Berkmüller, U., Wagner, J.: Physiological measurement of trust-related behavior in trust-neutral and trust-critical situations. In: Wakeman, I., Gudes, E., Jensen, C.D., Crampton, J. (eds.) IFIPTM 2011. IAICT, vol. 358, pp. 165–172. Springer, Heidelberg (2011). doi:10.1007/978-3-642-22200-9_14
86. Leshed, G., Kaye, J.J.: Understanding how bloggers feel: recognizing affect in blog posts. In: Proceedings of CHI 2006 Extended Abstracts on Human Factors in Computing Systems, pp. 1019–1024 (2006)
87. Lewis, M., Haviland-Jones, J.M., Barrett, L.F.: Handbook of Emotions. Guilford Press, New York City (2010)
88. Liapis, A., Katsanos, C., Sotiropoulos, D., Xenos, M., Karousos, N.: Recognizing emotions in human computer interaction: studying stress using skin conductance. In: Abascal, J., Barbosa, S., Fetter, M., Gross, T., Palanque, P., Winckler, M. (eds.) INTERACT 2015. LNCS, vol. 9296, pp. 255–262. Springer, Heidelberg (2015). doi:10.1007/978-3-319-22701-6_18

89. Lisetti, C.L., Nasoz, F.: Using noninvasive wearable computers to recognize human emotions from physiological signals. EURASIP J. Adv. Sig. Process. **2004**(11), 1–16 (2004)

90. Litman, D.J., Forbes-Riley, K.: Predicting student emotions in computer-human tutoring dialogues. In: Proceedings of the 42nd Annual Meeting on Association for Computational Linguistics, p. 351 (2004)

91. Littlewort, G., Whitehill, J., Wu,T., Fasel, I., Frank, M., Movellan, J., Bartlett, M.: The computer expression recognition toolbox (CERT). In: IEEE International Conference on Automatic Face & Gesture Recognition and Workshops, pp. 298–305 (2011)

92. Littlewort, G.C., Bartlett, M.S., Lee, K.: Automatic coding of facial expressions displayed during posed and genuine pain. Image Vis. Comput. **27**(12), 1797–1803 (2009)

93. Liu, C., Rani, P., Sarkar, N.: An empirical study of machine learning techniques for affect recognition in human-robot interaction. In: IEEE/RSJ International Conference on Intelligent Robots and Systems (IROS), pp. 2662–2667 (2005)

94. Liu, X., Zheng, Y., Phyu, M.W., Zhao, B., Je, M., Yuan, X.: Multiple functional ECG signal is processing for wearable applications of long-term cardiac monitoring. IEEE Trans. Biomed. Eng. **58**(2), 380–389 (2011)

95. Liu, Y., Sourina, O., Nguyen, M.K.: Real-time EEG-based human emotion recognition and visualization. In: 2010 International Conference on Cyberworlds (CW), pp. 262–269 (2010)

96. López, G., Custodio, V., Moreno, J.I.: Lobin: E-textile and wireless-sensor-network-based platform for healthcare monitoring in future hospital environments. IEEE Trans. Inf. Technol. Biomed. **14**(6), 1446–1458 (2010)

97. Lucey, P., Cohn, J.F., Kanade, T., Saragih, J., Ambadar, Z., Matthews, I.: The extended cohn-kanade dataset (ck+): a complete dataset for action unit and emotion-specified expression.In: IEEE Conference on Computer Vision and Pattern Recognition Workshops (CVPRW), pp. 94–101 (2010)

98. Lugger, M., Janoir, M.-E., et al.: Combining classifiers with diverse feature sets for robust speaker independent emotion recognition. In: 2009 17th European Signal Processing Conference, pp. 1225–1229 (2009)

99. Mandryk, R.L.: Physiological measures for game evaluation. In: Lazzaro, M. (ed.) Game usability,: Advice from the experts for advancing the player experience, pp. 207–235. Morgan Kaufmann, Burlington (2008)

100. Mandryk, R.L., Atkins, M.S.: A fuzzy physiological approach for continuously modeling emotion during interaction with play technologies. Int. J. Hum. Comput. Stud. **65**(4), 329–347 (2007)

101. Mandryk, R.L., Atkins, M.S., Inkpen, K.M.: A continuous and objective evaluation of emotional experience with interactive play environments. In: Proceedings of the SIGCHI Conference on Human Factors in Computing Systems, pp. 1027–1036 (2006)

102. Mandryk, R.L., Inkpen, K.M., Calvert, T.W.: Using psychophysiological techniques to measure user experience with entertainment technologies. Behav. Inf. Technol. **25**(2), 141–158 (2006)

103. Marwick, A.E., et al.: I tweet honestly, I tweet passionately: twitter users, context collapse, and the imagined audience. New Media Soc. **13**(1), 114–133 (2011)

104. McDuff, D., El Kaliouby, R., Senechal, T., Amr, M., Cohn, J.F., Picard, R.: Affectiva-MIT facial expression dataset (AM-FED): naturalistic and spontaneous facial expressions collected "in-the-wild". In: IEEE Conference on Computer Vision and Pattern Recognition Workshops (CVPRW), pp. 881–888 (2013)

105. Mehrabian, A.: Analysis of the big-five personality factors in terms of the PAD temperament model. Aust. J. Psychol. **48**(2), 86–92 (1996a)
106. Mehrabian, A.: Pleasure-arousal-dominance: a general framework for describing and measuring individual differences in temperament. Curr. Psychol. **14**(4), 261–292 (1996b)
107. Mehrabian, A.: Comparison of the PAD and PANAS as models for describing emotions and for differentiating anxiety from depression. J. Psychopathol. Behav. Assess. **19**(4), 331–357 (1997)
108. Miyamoto, Y., Uchida, Y., Ellsworth, P.C.: Culture, mixed emotions: co-occurrence of positive and negative emotions in Japan and the United States. Emotion **10**(3), 404 (2010)
109. Mohammad, S.M.: #Emotional tweets. In: Proceedings of the Sixth International Workshop on Semantic Evaluation, pp. 246–255 (2012)
110. Mower, E., Matarić, M.J., Narayanan, S.: A framework for automatic human emotion classification using emotion profiles. IEEE Trans. Audio Speech Lang. Process. **19**(5), 1057–1070 (2011)
111. Mundt, C.W., Montgomery, K.N., Udoh, U.E., Barker, V.N., Thonier, G.C., Tellier, A.M., Ricks, R.D., Darling, R.B., Cagle, Y.D., Cabrol, N.A., et al.: A multiparameter wearable physiologic monitoring system for space and terrestrial applications. IEEE Trans. Inf. Technol. Biomed. **9**(3), 382–391 (2005)
112. Murugappan, M., Ramachandran, N., Sazali, Y., et al.: Classification of human emotion from EEG using discrete wavelet transform. J. Biomed. Sci. Eng. **3**(04), 390 (2010)
113. Myers, C.S., Rabiner, L.R.: A comparative study of several dynamic time-warping algorithms for connected-word recognition. Bell Syst. Tech. J. **60**(7), 1389–1409 (1981)
114. Nacke, L., Lindley, C.A.: Flow and immersion in first-person shooters: measuring the player's gameplay experience. In: Proceedings of the 2008 Conference on Future Play: Research, Play, Share (Future Play 2008), pp. 81–88. ACM, New York (2008). http://dx.doi.org/10.1145/1496984.1496998
115. Naqvi, N., Shiv, B., Bechara, A.: The role of emotion in decision making a cognitive neuroscience perspective. Current Directions in Psychological Science **15**(5), 260–264 (2006)
116. Neumann, S.A., Waldstein, S.R.: Similar patterns of cardiovascular response during emotional activation as a function of affective valence and arousal and gender. J. Psychosom. Res. **50**(5), 245–253 (2001)
117. Neviarouskaya, A., Prendinger, H., Ishizuka, M.: Compositionality principle in recognition of fine-grained emotions from text. In: Proceedings of ICWSM (2009)
118. Newberg, L.A.: Error statistics of hidden Markov model and hidden Boltzmann model results. BMC Bioinform. **10**(1), 1 (2009)
119. Nicholson, J., Takahashi, K., Nakatsu, R.: Emotion recognition in speech using neural networks. Neural Comput. Appl. **9**(4), 290–296 (2000)
120. Nicolaou, M.A., Gunes, H., Pantic, M.: Continuous prediction of spontaneous affect from multiple cues, modalities in valence-arousal space. IEEE Trans. Affect. Comput. **2**(2), 92–105 (2011)
121. Pedro Alves Nogueira: Rui Amaral Rodrigues, Eugénio C Oliveira, and Lennart E Nacke. Understanding and shaping players' affective experiences in digital games. In AIIDE, Guided emotional state regulation (2013)
122. Norman, W.T.: Toward an adequate taxonomy of personality attributes: replicated factor structure in peer nomination personality ratings. J. Abnorm. Soc. Psychol. **66**(6), 574 (1963)

123. Nwe, T.L., Foo, S.W., De Silva, L.C.: Speech emotion recognition using hidden Markov models. Speech Commun. **41**(4), 603–623 (2003)

124. Oppenheim, A.V., Schafer, R.W.: From frequency to quefrency: a history of the cepstrum. IEEE Sig. Process. Mag. **21**(5), 95–106 (2004)

125. Ortigosa, A., Carro, R.M., Quiroga, J.I.: Predicting user personality by mining social interactions in facebook. Journal of Computer and System Sciences **80**(1), 57–71 (2014)

126. Ortony, A., Clore, G.L., Collins, A.: The Cognitive Structure of Emotions. Cambridge University Press, Cambridge (1990)

127. Paas, F.G.W.C., Van Merriënboer, J.J.G.: Instructional control of cognitive load in the training of complex cognitive tasks. Educ. Psychol. Rev. **6**(4), 351–371 (1994)

128. Pantic, M., Bartlett, M.S.: Machine Analysis of Facial Expressions. I-Tech Education and Publishing, Vienna (2007)

129. Parikh, R., Movassate, M.: Sentiment analysis of user-generated twitter updates using various classification techniques. CS224N Final Report, pp. 1–18 (2009)

130. Paunonen, S.V., Haddock, G., Forsterling, F., Keinonen, M.: Broad versus narrow personality measures and the prediction of behaviour across cultures. Eur. J. Pers. **17**(6), 413–433 (2003)

131. Pavlidis, I., Dowdall, J., Sun, N., Puri, C., Fei, J., Garbey, M.: Interacting with human physiology. Comput. Vis. Image Underst. **108**(1), 150–170 (2007)

132. Pekrun, R., Stephens, E.J.: Achievement emotions: a control-value approach. Soc. Pers. Psychol. Compass **4**(4), 238–255 (2010)

133. Pennebaker, J.W., Francis, M.E., Booth, R.J.: Linguistic inquiry, word count: LIWC 2001. Mahwah: Lawrence Erlbaum Associates, vol. 71 no. 2001 (2001)

134. Perrinet, J., Olivier, A.-H., Pettré, J.: Walk with me: interactions in emotional walking situations, a pilot study. In: Proceedings of the ACM Symposium on Applied Perception, pp. 59–66 (2013)

135. Peter, C., Herbon, A.: Emotion representation and physiology assignments in digital systems. Interact. Comput. **18**(2), 139–170 (2006)

136. Petrantonakis, P.C., Hadjileontiadis, L.J.: Emotion recognition from EEG using higher order crossings. IEEE Trans. Inf. Technol. Biomed. **14**(2), 186–197 (2010)

137. Picard, R.W.: Affective Computing. MIT press, Cambridge (1997)

138. Picard, R.W., Vyzas, E., Healey, J.: Toward machine emotional intelligence: analysis of affective physiological state. IEEE Trans. Pattern Anal. Mach. Intell. **23**(10), 1175–1191 (2001)

139. Plutchik, R.: A general psychoevolutionary theory of emotion. In: Plutchik, R., Kellerman, H. (eds.) Theories of Emotion, vol. 1, pp. 3–31. Academic press, Cambridge (1980)

140. Porter, M.F.: An algorithm for suffix stripping. Program **14**(3), 130–137 (1980)

141. Prkachin, K.M., Solomon, P.E.: The structure, reliability and validity of pain expression: evidence from patients with shoulder pain. Pain **139**(2), 267–274 (2008)

142. Quercia, D., Kosinski, M., Stillwell, D., Crowcroft, J.: Our twitter profiles, our selves: predicting personality with twitter. In: IEEE International Conference on Privacy, Security, Risk and Trust (PASSAT) and Social Computing (SocialCom), pp. 180–185 (2011)

143. Quigley, K.S., Barrett, L.F.: Is there consistency and specificity of autonomic changes during emotional episodes? Guidance from the conceptual act theory and psychophysiology. Biol. Psychol. **98**, 82–94 (2014)

144. Rainville, P., Bechara, A., Naqvi, N., Damasio, A.R.: Basic emotions are associated with distinct patterns of cardiorespiratory activity. Int. J. Psychophysiol. **61**(1), 5–18 (2006)

145. Ramirez, G.A., Baltrušaitis, T., Morency, L.-P.: Modeling latent discriminative dynamic of multi-dimensional affective signals. In: D'Mello, S., Graesser, A., Schuller, B., Martin, J.-C. (eds.) ACII 2011. LNCS, vol. 6975, pp. 396–406. Springer, Heidelberg (2011). doi:10.1007/978-3-642-24571-8_51

146. Rani, P., Sarkar, N., Liu, C.: Maintaining optimal challenge in computer games through real-time physiological feedback. In: Proceedings of the 11th International Conference on Human Computer Interaction, pp. 184–192 (2005)

147. Ravaja, N.: Contributions of psychophysiology to media research: review and recommendations. Media Psychol. **6**(2), 193–235 (2004)

148. Ravaja, N., Turpeinen, M., Saari, T., Puttonen, S., Keltikangas-Järvinen, L.: The psychophysiology of James Bond: phasic emotional responses to violent video game events. Emotion **8**(1), 114 (2008)

149. Revelle, W., Scherer, K.R.: Personality and emotion. In: Scherer, K., Sander, D. (eds.) Oxford Companion to Emotion and the Affective Sciences, pp. 304–306. Oxford University Press, OXford (2009)

150. Ruan, S., Chen, L., Sun, J., Chen, G.: Study on the change of physiological signals during playing body-controlled games. In: Proceedings of the International Conference on Advances in Computer Enterntainment Technology, pp. 349–352 (2009)

151. Russell, J.A.: A circumplex model of affect. J. Pers. Soc. Psychol. **39**(6), 1161 (1980)

152. Russell, J.A.: Core affect and the psychological construction of emotion. Psychol. Rev. **110**(1), 145 (2003)

153. Sandbach, G., Zafeiriou, S., Pantic, M., Yin, L.: Static and dynamic 3D facial expression recognition: a comprehensive survey. Image Vis. Comput. **30**(10), 683–697 (2012)

154. Schafer, R.W., Rabiner, L.R.: Digital representations of speech signals. Proc. IEEE **63**(4), 662–667 (1975)

155. Scherer, K.R.: What are emotions? And how can they be measured? Soc. Sci. Inf. **44**(4), 695–729 (2005)

156. Schuller, B., Rigoll, G., Lang, M.: Speech emotion recognition combining acoustic features and linguistic information in a hybrid support vector machine-belief network architecture. In: IEEE International Conference on Acoustics, Speech, and Signal Processing (ICASSP), vol. 1, p. I-577 (2004)

157. Schuller, B., Lang, M., Rigoll, G.: Robust acoustic speech emotion recognition by ensembles of classifiers. Fortschritte der Akustik **31**(1), 329 (2005)

158. Schuller, B., Valster, M., Eyben, F., Cowie, R., Pantic, M.: AVCE 2012: the continuous audio/visual emotion challenge. In: Proceedings of the 14th ACM International Conference on Multimodal Interaction, pp. 449–456 (2012)

159. Setz, C., Arnrich, B., Schumm, J., La Marca, R., Troster, G., Ehlert, U.: Discriminating stress from cognitive load using a wearable EDA device. IEEE Trans. Inf. Technol. Biomed. **14**(2), 410–417 (2010)

160. Shen, L., Wang, M., Shen, R.: Affective e-learning: using emotional data to improve learning in pervasive learning environment. J. Educ. Technol. Soc. **12**(2), 176–189 (2009)

161. Shergill, G.S., Sarrafzadeh, A., Diegel, O., Shekar, A.: Computerized sales assistants: the application of computer technology to measure consumer interest-a conceptual framework. J. Electron. Commer. Res. **9**(2), 176–191 (2008)

162. Shi, Y., Ruiz, N., Taib, R., Choi, E., Chen, F.: Galvanic skin response (GSR) as an index of cognitive load. In: Proceedings of CHI 2007 Extended Abstracts on Human Factors in Computing Systems, pp. 2651–2656 (2007)
163. Shivhare, S.N., Khethawat, S.: Emotion detection from text. Comput. Sci. Inf. Technol. **5**, 371–377 (2012)
164. Strapparava, C., Valitutti, A., et al.: WordNet Affect: an affective extension of WordNet. In: Proceedings of LREC, vol. 4, pp. 1083–1086 (2004)
165. Sun, F.-T., Kuo, C., Cheng, H.-T., Buthpitiya, S., Collins, P., Griss, M.: Activity-aware mental stress detection using physiological sensors. In: Gris, M., Yang, G. (eds.) MobiCASE 2010. LNICSSITE, vol. 76, pp. 211–230. Springer, Heidelberg (2012). doi:10.1007/978-3-642-29336-8_12
166. Sun, Y., Hu, S., Azorin-Peris, V., Kalawsky, R., Greenwald, S.: Noncontact imaging photoplethysmography to effectively access pulse rate variability. J. Biomed. Optics **18**(6), 1–9 (2013). Article 061205
167. Teixeira, T., Wedel, M., Pieters, R.: Emotion-induced engagement in internet video advertisements. J. Mark. Res. **49**(2), 144–159 (2012)
168. Thought Technology Ltd.Procomp infiniti system (2016). http://thoughttechnology.com/index.php/hardware.html. Accessed 26 May 2016
169. Tian, Y., Kanade, T., Cohn, J.F.: Facial expression recognition. In: Li, S.Z., Jain, A.K. (eds.) Handbook of Face Recognition, pp. 487–519. Springer, London (2011)
170. Tiller, W.A., McCraty, R., Atkinson, M.: Cardiac coherence: a new, noninvasive measure of autonomic nervous system order. Altern. Ther. Health Med. **2**(1), 52–65 (1996)
171. Toole, A.J., Harms, J., Snow, S.L., Hurst, D.R., Pappas, M.R., Ayyad, J.H.: Hervé Abdi, A.: video database of moving faces, people. IEEE Trans. Pattern Anal. Mach. Intell. **27**(5), 812–816 (2005)
172. Trejo, L.J., Knuth, K., Prado, R., Rosipal, R., Kubitz, K., Kochavi, R., Matthews, B., Zhang, Y.: EEG-based estimation of mental fatigue: convergent evidence for a three-state model. In: Schmorrow, D.D., Reeves, L.M. (eds.) FAC 2007. LNCS (LNAI), vol. 4565, pp. 201–211. Springer, Heidelberg (2007). doi:10.1007/978-3-540-73216-7_23
173. Valstar, M., Pantic, M.: Induced disgust, happiness, surprise: an addition to the MMI facial expression database. In: Proceedings of International Workshop on EMOTION (satellite of LREC): Corpora for Research on Emotion and Affect, p. 65 (2010)
174. Valstar, M.F., Gunes, H., Pantic, M.: How to distinguish posed from spontaneous smiles using geometric features. In: Proceedings of the International Conference on Multimodal Interfaces, pp. 38–45 (2007)
175. Vasu, V., Heneghan, C., Arumugam, T., Sezer, S.: Signal processing methods for non-contact cardiac detection using doppler radar. In: 2010 IEEE Workshop on Signal Processing Systems (SIPS), pp. 368–373 (2010)
176. Vi, C., Subramanian, S.: Detecting error-related negativity for interaction design. In: Proceedings of the SIGCHI Conference on Human Factors in Computing Systems, pp. 493–502 (2012)
177. Wache, J.: The secret language of our body: affect and personality recognition using physiological signals. In: Proceedings of the 16th International Conference on Multimodal Interaction, pp. 389–393 (2014)
178. Watson, D., Tellegen, A.: Toward a consensual structure of mood. Psychol. Bull. **98**(2), 219 (1985)
179. Weigert, A.J.: Mixed Emotions: Certain Steps Toward Understanding Ambivalence. SUNY Press, New York (1991)

180. Westerink, J.H.D.M., Van Den Broek, E.L., Schut, M.H., Van Herk, J., Tuinen-breijer, K.: Computing emotion awareness through galvanic skin response and facial electromyography. In: Probing Experience, pp. 149–162. Springer (2008)

181. Witten, I.H., Frank, E., Mining, D.: Practical Machine Learning Tools and Tech-niques. Morgan Kaufmann, Burlington (2005)

182. Xu, J., Wang, Y., Chen, F., Choi, H., Li, G., Chen, S., Hussain, S.: Pupillary response based cognitive workload index under luminance and emotional changes. In: Proceedings of CHI 2011 Extended Abstracts on Human Factors in Computing Systems, pp. 1627–1632 (2011)

183. Yik, M., Russell, J.A., Steiger, J.H.: A 12-point circumplex structure of core affect. Emotion 11(4), 705 (2011)

184. Zeng, Z., Pantic, M., Roisman, G., Huang, T.S., et al.: A survey of affect recog-nition methods: audio, visual, and spontaneous expressions. IEEE Trans. Pattern Anal. Mach. Intell. 31(1), 39–58 (2009)

185. Zhou, F., Xingda, Q., Jiao, J.R., Helander, M.G.: Emotion prediction from physio-logical signals: a comparison study between visual and auditory elicitors. Interact. Comput. 26(3), 285–302 (2014)

Social Network Games

Johannes Konert[1]([✉]), Heinrich Söbke[2], and Viktor Wendel[3]

[1] Department VI Information Technology and Media,
Beuth University for Applied Sciences Berlin, Berlin, Germany
books@johannes-konert.de
[2] Bauhaus-Institute for Infrastructure Solutions (b.is),
Bauhaus-Universität Weimar, Weimar, Germany
heinrich.soebke@uni-weimar.de
[3] Multimedia Communications Lab, Technische Universität Darmstadt,
Darmstadt, Germany
viktor.wendel@kom.tu-darmstadt.de

Abstract. Based on the emerging popularity of social network services like Facebook, Online Social Network (OSNs) have found an increasing playership in the last years. Their proliferation is supported by an easy accessibility which enables even non-gamers to make use of these games. A main characteristic of these games is the utilization of already existing networks of social ties. At least in theory these foster communities of interest, which are considered a vivid source of learning. Summarizing these facts and considering the comparably low efforts for development of such games makes Social Network Games (SNGs) a remarkable instrument for serious games, especially educational games. For this reason we describe in this chapter unique characteristics of SNGs. Underlying theoretical models and concepts are presented. Example cases illustrate potential usages. The bridge to pedagogical and didactic use is illustrated by connecting theories from both worlds and naming best practice examples. Furthermore, specific aspects in the design and development of SNGs are discussed. Examples are establishment of deep learning and critical issues as monetarization strategies of developers or toxic behavior of players.

Keywords: Social network game · Game design · Game development

1 Introduction

1.1 Relevance for Serious Games Researchers

Social Network Games (SNGs) are the type of games played most often (31 %) by frequent gamers in the US in 2014 [25, p. 5]. Since 2012, the market for social games raised continuously by about 16 % each year and is forecasted to reach USD 17.4 billion worldwide in 2019 [88]. Most interesting about this development is the regular daily use of social games. 50 % of all Americans with online connection play daily [74]. A Facebook-based study reports most of such social

© Springer International Publishing AG 2016
R. Dörner et al. (Eds.): Entertainment Computing and Serious Games, LNCS 9970, pp. 442–474, 2016.
DOI: 10.1007/978-3-319-46152-6_17

game sessions last about 15 to 30 min [34]. Social games are preferably played on mobile devices (35 % of the US gamers mentioned before) and rather with others (multiplayer) than alone in [25, p. 7].

The growing market, regular use combined with the multiplayer aspects make SNGs an attractive and relevant research field as it opens new didactic possibilities for serious purposes. It is well known that playing (and learning) with peers in a group reduces drop-out rates and increases knowledge exchange within the group [16]. The challenge is to connect the right people within a community of interest with the same (learning) goals [52]. The social network structure behind SNGs lowers the barrier to interact even with community-members to which only weak-ties exist, but which are a great source of (new) knowledge [36]. Beside the beneficial network structure supporting SNGs, characteristics of such games allow new pedagogical concepts in the field of *Games for Learning* [35]. Fullan and Langworthy [29, p. 6] define *deep learning* in serious games as the support to develop skills "that prepare all learners to be life-long creative, connected, and collaborative problem solvers". Consequently, characteristics, like the continuous (endless) gameplay and the chance to allow players the exchange of user-generated game content to solve problems (game quests) collaboratively, make OSNs a valuable aspect of serious games research.

1.2   Chapter Structure

The chapter is organized in five subsequent sections, which cover aspects of SNG development as follows: Sect. 2: *Characteristics and Foundations* will introduce major terms related to use and development of SNGs. Furthermore, it provides insight into the characteristics of SNGs and the beneficial as well as problematic consequences they cause. The section closes with a deep view into the technical and pedagogical foundations (Sect. 2.4) worth to know before *researching serious social network games*. Section 3: *Case Studies* highlights some prototypes and use of SNGs, Social Media, or OSNs for serious purposes. The studies provide insight, e.g., into different types of social networks evolving in dependency of the SNG type, use of user-generated content *for serious purposes*, use of SNGs as games *with a purpose*, and closes with famous examples from non-serious contexts. Section 4: *Challenges in SNG Design and Development* is dedicated to cutting edge research challenges in the field of SNGs. This section can be used as a starting point to find open research questions and challenges already identified by the serious games' and SNGs' community. Aspects like content quality, peer matchmaking, assessment, or toxic behavior are addressed. An introduction to the findings and characteristics in each of these fields is given as well as a (incomplete) list of research aspects worth to be worked on for a doctoral degree. Section 5: *Conclusion and Outlook* summarizes what has been introduced in this chapter about SNGs and what the future might bring for this young specialization field of serious games research.

2   Characteristics and Foundations

2.1   Definitions

Social is the base term for most subsequently defined terms, but at the same
time is the one nearly impossible to define unambiguous. Social science has
manifold different theories about what *social* is (or means) [21, cf. p. 23ff]. For
the course of the chapter we refer to social behavior as interaction of individuals (humans) in a network to satisfy their individual needs while respecting
the differences and needs of others (concept of co-existence) [21, p. 25]. The
emphasis is put on *inter*action and the *co*-existence of all participants.

A Social Network is a representation of individuals as nodes (vertices) connected by relationship between two of the individuals (edges). Such relationships can be any observable directed or undirected relation or state (e.g.,
friendship as undirected mutual, or send-a-letter-to as directed relation).
Thus, "individuals are, as it were, tied to one another by invisible bonds
which are knitted together into a criss-cross mesh of connections, much as a
fishing net (. . .)" [75, p. 109].

An Online Social Network (OSN) is a *Social Network* with individuals (vertices) represented by, e.g., distinct accounts or profiles of web applications
and their inter-dependencies (edges) are represented as electronically stored
links, e.g., in databases, tables or files remembering the type of interdependency and which two individuals are connected (e.g., a friendship established
in an web application like Facebook) [31, cf.]. Synonyms are *Social Networking Service, Social Network Service*, or *Social Network Site (SNS)*.

A Social Graph is the representation of a Social Network or OSN in a
mathematical form as graph G with vertices V and edges E defined as
$G = (V, E), E = (v_i, v_j)$ with $v_i, v_j \in V$ [19, cf.].

Social Media is ". . . a group of Internet-based applications that build on the
ideological and technological foundations of Web 2.0, and that allow the
creation and exchange of User Generated Content" [44, p. 61].

A Social Game is a game played by more than one individual. The oldest
referenced social game is the wooden board game *Senet*, dated to 3100 B.C.
in Egypt [66]. Today, the term *social game* is widely used as a shortcut for
Social Network Game (SNG), defined in the following.

A Social Network Game (SNG) is literally a social game using an OSN
as its basis. Precisely the term should be Online Social Network Game to
underline the digital nature of such games, but the prefix *online* was ignored
consequently. The use of OSNs as its basis is a too broad definition to work
with. Nearly every video game today (mobile or social) satisfies this criterion
and is a SNG in this sense. As SNGs emerged from casual games that were
deployed on OSNs around 2008 [56], first definitions and use of the term were
not scientific, but driven by the game industry.

Over time, scientific discussion and definition of characteristics emerged (see
Sect. 2.2). Based on these characteristics, a more distinctive definition can be
given. A Social Network Game (SNG) "is a video game satisfying the criteria

of *asynchronous play, casual multiplayer, coopetition*[1], and *beneficial social media interaction*" [47, p. 36].

A Social Serious Game "is a serious game satisfying all criteria mandatory for a social [network[2]] game" [47, p. 52] as stated above for the term Social Network Game. In difference to this, a *Serious Social Game* is a narrower defined sub-category of games that need to fulfill as well criteria of stickiness. These criteria include the support for co-creation and persistence of user-generated content as well as creation of a social network of players around the game [47, p. 36–38,51f].

2.2   Characteristics of Social Network Games and the Benefits for Serious Games

The tremendous success of commercial SNGs is caused—among others—by unique features which have been completely new in the field of gaming when these SNGs emerged. High accessibility is such a characteristic: "What constitutes a SNG is determined more by technical aspects of how it is accessed and distributed" [93]. SNGs are mostly seamlessly embedded in OSNs which are operable via web-browser and do not require especially powerful hardware. Therefore any person who is capable of accessing an OSN is a potential user of the SNG. This differs from conventional gaming, where playing requires possibly long-winded installation efforts. A low entry-barrier enables casual game play and opens SNGs to a group of players, who are not typical gamers ('casual gamers', cf. [10,13]). SNGs predominantly offer asynchronous game mechanics, which further lower the requirements: SNGs can be used regardless of time and space. On the other side, the life-cycle of a SNG is clearly defined. When a developer shuts down the server, there is no chance to keep playing a difference to locally installed games (This happended to the SNGs The Sims Social and SimCity Social on facebook in 2013[3]).

From a game developer's point of view the client-server architecture of SNGs shows remarkable characteristics. The game can be developed continuously: there is no need for explicit update procedures, the player is supplied with a current version. This enables game developers to ship early and adjust their games according to the feedback and the behavior of the players [58]. Players preferences can be measured just by logging the client requests on the servers. Metrics become an important means of game development [64]. Furthermore, such an architecture enables developers to deploy different versions of the game to different groups of players and to monitor the success of each version (so called A/B-Testing [30]). Similar approaches for personal computer or console based

---

[1] *coopetition* is a word combination of cooperation and competition to express the duality of cooperative game-play and competition for standings (like high-scores or resources).

[2] Authors' note: word *network* inserted.

[3] http://thenextweb.com/facebook/2013/04/15/ea-shuts-down-more-facebook-games-goodbye-the-sims-social-simcity-social-and-pet-society/.

games are received much more skeptically: when SimCity 5 has been released in 2013 with the requirement of an internet connection, very contrary discussions have taken place [62]. Although the game play is casual and short-cycled, the games are designed in order to keep players engaged. The retention rate is an important metric of an SNG and influences the game design [27, p. 64] [45]. So players should be kept engaged over a long period of time. A positive view of this characteristic is a potential similarity to the regular time structure of formal education.

From a scientific perspective, four major characteristics identify a SNGs [47, p. 35f]:

1. *Asynchronous play* was identified as one important characteristic for a SNG. It allows players to (socially) interact via the game, e.g., by exchanging items or favors, but they do not need to be within the game at the same time. Additionally, each player plays on her own speed, intensity and duration without direct drawbacks or benefits based on intensity (e.g., no other player destroys achievements while oneself is offline). *Asynchronous play* also leads to a game play design of *infinite play* in most cases, where no victory conditions exist and the game never ends. Instead, quests and missions exist and the game world evolves continuously in coverage and features [71].

2. *Casual Multiplayer* is a summarizing term for the possibility to play the SNGs individually (single-player) without strict dependency on others. Still, there is the awareness of the activities of others and interplay with them, e.g., based on item exchange, messaging, manipulation of the game world or shared game space. Together with *asynchronous play*, *casual multiplayer* leads mostly to a *turn-based design* of SNGs [65].

3. *Beneficial Social Media Interaction* characterizes SNGs as integrating the structure of the underlying OSN into the gameplay to allow players interactions via the game. Such interactions are based on the four base interactions in social media: networking, publishing, sharing, and discussing (or commenting). [43, cf. Design Framework for SNGs in]. This implies the beneficial use of the underlying social graph and the evolved community of the OSN [71].

4. *Coopetition* is the competition of the players for best results while at the same time collaborating (or at least cooperating) to achieve such results faster, easier, with less effort [6]. More references and details about the differences of collaboration and cooperation is given in Sect. 2.4.2. The competition is indirectly by leaderboards or levels of achievements, but no direct drawbacks for individual players appear (like loss of status or end of game). Players cannot directly harm each other. This appears to be a key difference compared to traditional multiplayer games.

2.3   Problematic Issues of Commercial Social Network Games

The requirement of easy accessibility—Fields analyzes in detail, how the process of accessing a game is streamlined [27, p. 40ff]—has led to phenomena of commercial SNG, which are discussed critically. Avoiding the barrier of initial payment supports easy access. Besides advertisements, as being one possibility of funding, an alternative model, Free-To-Play F2P, has been established and is transforming the gaming industry [68]. F2P allows the player to play a game in its core game mechanics without any payment. In order to enable revenues for the game developer, so called *in-game items* are offered. A common example for such an in-game item is to switch off advertisements [86]. In-game items are a kind of virtual goods, which provide an additional value for the player. This can also be an aesthetically value with no impact on the game results of the player. A more discussed type of in-game item influences the game play, when it enables faster progress in the game. An example is the *Arborist*, a *consumable*[4] from *FarmVille*. It harvests all trees at once—an action which was supposed to be done originally click-by-click tree-wise. So if the player buys such a *consumable*, demanded efforts on time and game play are substituted by money. This contradicts the common conception of game success as depending only on skills and cleverness of a player, but not on his financial resources.

Furthermore, it opens the door for severe misuses of SNGs. Video games are considered to cause addiction in a small group of players [89]. The F2P model extends such an unrestricted consumption of a game to a financial dimension. Like in gambling, players are endangered to receive existentially negative consequences of their uncontrolled play.

In general, the F2P payment model evokes the phenomenon that payment are made by only a small faction of players [27, p. 65ff] [86]. Kelly quantifies this group to less than 1 % of the players, who will spend comparatively large amounts of money [45]. In this context an US-$ 100 offer in *FarmVille* (see Fig. 1) can be considered as an exemplification for at least two issues. First, it demonstrates a questionable pricing approach, which follows the F2P model and which becomes even more questionable as the player gets in return for the money only a small fraction of available achievements in *FarmVille*. Furthermore, the offered discount ("A $600 value for $100 only") indicates the extraordinary huge amounts of money, which can be spent in SNGs. Compared to conventional pricing approaches of video games (e.g., licenses or subscriptions), some commercial SNGs offer almost unlimited possibilities to spend money.

Another characteristic of SNGs are simple game mechanics. Often, SNGs issue rewards for clicking, i.e., rewards are directly linked to basic player actions, not requiring any cognitive effort. This leads game critics to associate SNGs with *Skinner boxes* [77], i.e., instruments to train animals, and to the derecognition of the perception of a game. Ian Bogost sharpened this criticism in a satire of basic SNGs game mechanisms, where he used timers, the F2P concept for buying game progress, and interactions via OSNs user feed posts: his Facebook game *Cow Clicker*[5] [4] contributed to the discussion about SNGs (e.g., [3,51]). Lewis et al. analyze motivational patterns in order to explain why *Cow Clicker* not only got the attention of game experts, but was considered as a real, motivating game by certain people [53]. Interestingly, the phenomenon of Skinner box-like

---

[4] A *consumable* is defined as an item which depletes itself when it is used.
[5] https://apps.facebook.com/cowclicker/.

Fig. 1. FarmVille: $ 100 in-game offer

game mechanics is not limited to SNGs, as Yee observes in *EverQuest* [96]. So it seems to be again a matter of game design—and not of the game genre—if there are simple game mechanics. In the case of SNGs these criticized simple game mechanics increase the appeal to a large target group and therefor facilitate the developers' profit seeking.

Further it is stated that in SNGs fellow players are merely seen as resources, which facilitate one's own success. An example is given by *FarmVille*: So-called voting-buildings are intended to gather fellow players opinions about one's personality traits (see Fig. 2). However—as there were different rewards for different kinds of personality traits—we observed players instructing anonymously co-players to *vote* for a certain kind of trait [78]. In consequence, a game mechanic, which was designed to give a player insights into her reputation, and therefore foster social presence, has been (mis)used just to collect further items. However,

Fig. 2. FarmVille: voting building *Tea Time Personality*

considering fellow players as resources is not an issue limited to SNGs: Yee has observed a similar phenomenon for MMOGs: they "turn 'friends' into fungible, disposable resources" [95, p. 193ff]. As there exist SNGs, which foster relationships between players (cf. case study about *Fliplife* in Sect. 3.1), we argue that this phenomenon depends on the game design.

2.4   Foundations for Researching Social Network Games

In the context of serious game research the foundations focus on two major areas valuable to become familiar with before starting research with SNGs. First, the aspects of learning theories related to social interactions and peer education, then, second, the specifics of multiplayer games, especially game design for collaboration or cooperation.

2.4.1   Learning Theories: Connectivism and Peer Education

For general introduction to learning theories, more specifically socio-cognitive learning in constructivism theory refer to chapter *Games for Learning*, Sect. 2. For the design of SNGs we briefly introduce further models and concepts of learning.

Connectivism is a model for learning based on the fact that the human is a networked individuum. The learning is primarily informal and appears to be unstructured as content, structures and connections evolve collaboratively within the social network in general [76]. Connectivism connects to socio-cognitive constructivism and adds a perspective that results from the technologies used for learning nowadays. With social media and the OSNs behind, user-generated content can be seen as learning content when it is published, shared, commented and connected within a learning scenario (context). In such *connected learning* scenarios learning happens among peers which create tasks (questions) and solutions (user-generated content) in an informal learning context that has personal relevance to them [42].

The concepts of *peer education* existed before. The circumstances under which they lead to desired learning outcomes is discussed in brief by Damon in [16]. He differentiates *peer tutoring* and *peer collaboration*. An additional third concept *cooperative learning* is somewhere between the other two [17, cf.]. Prerequisites for these concepts are summarized by Damon as the levels of equality and mutuality as described in the following paragraphs.

If peers are very similar in the level of knowledge they have (high equality) [20, p. 7] and can benefit equally from each other by amending each other's knowledge in specific areas (high mutuality) [2], then *peer collaboration* is possible to succeed. It leads to increase in problem-solving competency of all participants. Consequently, it can be applied best for problem-solving where not only one correct result exists and the peers in the group collaboratively put together their individual strength and insights to come to a solution.

On the contrary, *peer tutoring* is suitable if a peer has a higher level of knowledge than the other(s) and can teach them (low equality). It is rather

Table 1. Peer education concepts and their characteristics.

	Aspect	Peer tutoring	Cooperative learning	Peer collaboration
Prereq.	Equality	Low	High	High
	Mutuality	Low	Varies	High
Outcome	Methodical skills	High	Varies	Low
	Problem-solving competency	Low	Varies	High

suitable for methodical knowledge transfer from a more experienced tutor to an unskilled tutee. Complex problem solving is seldom experienced in peer tutoring as for the taught topics secured correct ways of reaching solutions (or making progress) are known. It is recommended that peers change their roles after a while (or circle in the group) such that all participants profit from being taught in (different) topics.

Table 1 summarizes the three concepts of peer education, the prerequisites as well as the primary intended learning outcomes (based on [16,17]).

Both, connectivism and peer education, clearly state the importance of knowledge transfer among learners. For SNG design they imply that new connections among learners should be facilitated (probably based on social media interactions). For peer collaboration a proper matchmaking is needed to ensure high equality and mutuality for gameplay. Likewise, with low equality and low mutuality SNGs can provide peer tutoring tasks (and revenues) to players.

2.4.2 Multiplayer, Cooperation, and Collaboration

A main feature of SNGs is the social aspect. This means that those games are never singleplayer games, but multiplayer games with a strong focus on the social aspect. This social aspect can manifest in various ways. Some of those can be a focus on cooperation or collaboration, two elements which are fundamental to multiplayer games.

Historically, multiplayer games are as old as mankind (cf. illustration in Fig. 3). Children playing catch are technically playing a multiplayer game. Also, one of the oldest known board games, named *Senet*, dated to 3100 B.C. in Egypt [66], is a multiplayer game and thus a social game (cf. Sect. 2.1). For digital games, *Tennis for Two*[6] (1958) is considered to be the first multiplayer game. One of the most *well known* multiplayer games is *Pong* which can be considered a simple competitive game for two players. Multiplayer games evolved during the last 50 years which strongly impacted the way they were played. While in the 70es, multiplayer games were mainly played on arcade machines, later, in the early era of personal computers (C64, Atari, Amiga), multiplayer games were usually played on one machine. Hence, players played either simultaneously (using a shared screen or a split screen) or they had to take turns.

---

[6] Developed by William Higinbotham in 1958, using an analogue computer and an oscilloscope as monitor.

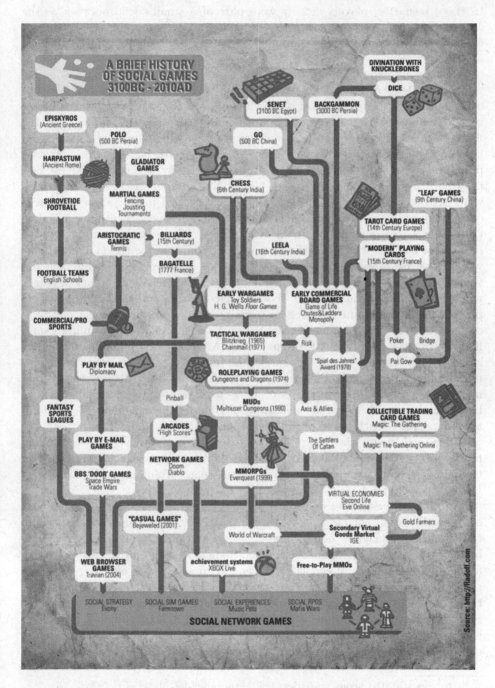

Fig. 3. History of Social Games with examples from each time period. © Jon Radoff, http://radoff.com

In those scenarios, players usually were part of a small social network as the common scenario was to play with a friend. Today, game consoles (although most of them having online functionality) have inherited this concept of local multiplayer games.

With the upcoming of network technology and later the Internet, a new multiplayer paradigm emerged where players each played on one machine connected to other machines. Early examples of this include Multi-User Dungeon (MUDs)—text-based multi-player adventure games—or first strategy games like *OCEAN*. A major milestone is the first person shooter *Doom* which despite being indexed in many countries started a new genre of competitive online games. At this point, players of multiplayer games often were closely socially linked because they had to know each other to start an online session. An exception to this were MUDs, where a player usually joined a server of many (often unknown) other players. This transfers to the concept of Massively Multiplayer Online (Role-Play Game)s (MMOs). In MMOs, players join a game of thousands to millions of players, which initially they are not connected with via a social network. However, those games are usually played in an instanced version, meaning that players play on a 'copy' of the game world with a smaller number of games whereas hundreds to thousands of those copies exist in parallel. Here, the players playing regularly on one instance are usually more closely connected and tend to play together on a regular basis [8,11]. Modern competitive online games like Multiplayer Online Battle Arena game (MOBAs) or First Person Shooter game (FPSs), usually contain a complex matchmaking system which is able to pair players with equally-skilled players. This means that players usually are matched with foreign players. However, even in those games, social networks between players exist—usually in form of a friends list and many players tend to play regularly with players from their social network.

In general, many players are attracted by the competitive nature of many multiplayer games (e.g., MOBAs, strategy games, FPSs) which is reflected in the numbers of active players of those games (e.g., 67 million active League of Legends players in 2014)[7].

Another core aspect of multiplayer games is certainly the social aspect that comes with playing with friends, either competitively or cooperatively. Especially those who enjoy playing cooperative games are a growing group of players. During the last years, many games developed dedicated cooperative modes (co-op) for multiplayer games. Whereas early versions usually were a singleplayer version able to be played by more than one players (usually against AI opponents), recently game developers focus on designing games with a focus on collaboration. Those games require players to work together in a coordinated way which is beyond simply playing through a level together, but instead requires close coordination and communication (e.g., *Portal 2*[8], *Left 4 Dead*[9], *Spelunky*[10]).

---

[7] http://www.statista.com/statistics/329015/number-lol-players/.
[8] http://www.valvesoftware.com/games/portal2.html.
[9] http://www.valvesoftware.com/games/l4d.html.
[10] http://www.spelunkyworld.com/.

In literature, often the terms *collaborative* and *cooperative* are used inter-changeably. However, many authors do make a distinction between those [20]. Here, a distinction will be made to clarify how a collaborative game is more complex in terms of interaction or teamwork than a cooperative game.

Dillenbourg defines *cooperation* in the following way: "In cooperation, part-ners split the work, solve sub-tasks individually and then assemble the partial results into the final output" [20, p. 8]. A common definition of *collaboration* is "a coordinated, synchronous activity that is the result of a continued attempt to construct and maintain a shared conception of a problem" [73, p. 70]. Usu-ally, this manifests in form of a synergy effect where the result of collaboration is more than the sum of the individual actions. Dillenbourg defines *collaboration* as follows: "In collaboration, partners do the work 'together'." [20, p. 8], whereas the 'together' refers to the synergy effect mentioned. In conclusion, the term *collaboration* contains a much stronger relatedness between the participants in terms of teamwork or understanding of the common work and how the single contributions work together and create synergy effects, which goes beyond the simple distribution of work in *cooperation*.

So, the above mentioned collaborative games require a much more inten-sive coordination (e.g., team composition, strategy, or communication between players) than the more simple co-op games.

A lot of research deals with collaboration in games. Collaborative games are well suited to utilize the motivation of social aspects of gaming like teamwork or a common goal [97], but also many components of collaborative learning scenarios [92].

Manninen and Korva [59, p. 3] define a core feature of collaborative games as "[...] players to cooperate to achieve a common goal against an obstructing force or natural situation [...]". Zagal et al. [97] analyzed one of the most popular collaborative board games, the *Lord Of The Rings* board game. The main feature of a collaborative board game is, that players do not play against each other but against the game. Therefore, either everybody wins or everybody loses together. The core design features identified by Zagal et al. are grouped in the following lessons and pitfalls:

Lesson 1: To highlight problems of competitiveness, a collaborative game should introduce a tension between perceived individual utility and team utility.

Lesson 2: To further highlight problems of competitiveness (which makes for a more interesting game as collaboration is no longer trivial when there is a personal gain in the game, e.g., a score), individual players should be allowed to make decisions and take actions without the consent of the team.

Lesson 3: Players must be able to trace payoffs back to their decisions.

Lesson 4: To encourage team members to make selfless decisions, a collaborative game should bestow different abilities or responsibilities upon the players.

Pitfall 1: To avoid the game degenerating into one player making the decisions for the team, collaborative games have to provide a sufficient rationale for collaboration.

Pitfall 2: For a game to be engaging, players need to care about the outcome and that outcome should have a satisfying result.

Pitfall 3: For a collaborative game to be enjoyable multiple times, the experience needs to be different each time and the presented challenge needs to evolve. (cf. [97])

Those lessons and pitfalls, as well as Manninen and Korvas statements about collaboration, can be affiliated to positive interdependence which is considered a key design element for collaboration in games [5,12]. Although it can be assumed that players who decide to play a collaborative game, want to play in a collaborative manner, the same is not necessarily true for Serious Games which are played in an educational setting. Positive interdependence is implemented in some examples of collaborative serious games [5,37]. Core features are making players depend on each other in a crucial way, creating a need to share knowledge, require coordination in order to solve (time- or space-related) puzzles. Rocha et al. present a set of design patterns for cooperative games based on an analysis of successful commercial games [72]. Those are amongst others complementary roles, synergies between abilities, and shared goals.

Examples of collaborative serious games are *Escape From Wilson Island* [91] or *TeamUp*[11]. Moreover, the complexity of teamwork in raids[12] in MMOs can be considered collaborative as it requires an extensive amount of coordination and communication between participants. The same is valid for most Multiplayer Online Battle Arena games (MOBAs). In brief, collaboration as a game concept is being used in many commercial games today.

Social Network Games (SNGs) by definition contain the perfect prerequisites for collaboration. As the players in an SNG are strongly connected via their social network, one can assume that the ability and readiness to collaborate is higher when playing with players from one's social graph than when playing with foreign players. Hence, SNGs are perfectly suited as collaborative games, given that the games follow the relevant design guidelines for collaborative games.

3   Case Studies

3.1   Fliplife—A Simple, Browser-Based Game with Social Network Features

Fliplife [28] is an example for an SNG beyond mainstream Facebook games. It employs a few game elements of typical SNGs, like an experience point-measured level and simple click-and-reward timer-based game mechanics. But, in addition, there are a lot of characteristics which are not commonly attributed to SNGs. So it uses its own web-platform and is technically based on HTML5. Its GUI is simplified, an example is shown in Fig. 4. *Fliplife* has been launched in 2010 as a means of storytelling platform for companies, therefore it can be considered as a so-called *advergame*. In consequence it is extensible: the metaphor of a *Career*

---

[11] http://www.thebarngames.nl/teamup/teamup.

[12] A game element where up to 30 players try to defeat a strong opponent in an encounter of up to four hours.

Fig. 4. *Fliplife*: Example of a Project (texts in German)

allows any company to provide its own story to the platform. This results in a modified business model also: besides selling a SNG-typical 'hard currency' [45], further revenues are generated from premium accounts and additionally from companies maintaining a digital dependence in *Fliplife* (namely, e.g., *Daimler*, *Bayer*, and *Ernst & Young*).

Uncommonly is also its definition of the term friendship, which depends on the number of common interactions. Game metaphors like *Projects* and spare-time activities require common interactions between players. The more activities two players have accomplished together, the better will be the reward for further interactions ('social experience points'). Friendship is categorized in different levels. Like in real life, the level of friendship decreases again, if there are no common activities any longer. Social interactions have been strengthened by offering the game feature of a *Department*—a formal means to foster closer groups of players. A *Department* comprises a group of up to 25 players, which are organized using formal roles like leader, member and apprentice. A *Department* is equipped with its own, customizable 'corporate identity' and is subject to competitions, spurred further by game-wide ranking lists.

The applied game mechanics can be considered as an example of a rudimentary game-provided framework, which has to be filled by players interactions and leads to emergent game play. An example is the metaphor of a *Project*. Players work together on a project, which means that they have to enroll themselves on this project, and thereafter to collect their reward within a certain time frame. If only one of the project members does not collect its reward in time, all the other team members will lose their reward, too. This rule has two major implications. In the short run, it leads to communication between players, who are regulating each other [80]. In the longer run, it lets players strive to do *Projects* only with reliable co-workers. Furthermore, it increases the meaning of *Departments*: being accepted here is a meaningful and precious achievement, which may be beneficial for both the motivation to participate in the *Department* and to maintain social relationships with fellow department members.

The sociability of this game is fostered further by specific durations of projects. Long-running *Projects* (1, 2, or 3 days) require almost daily logins. If players are synchronously online in the game, they are prone to start 'farming sessions'. This is a specific game play of repetitive common participation in short, 5-minute *Projects* for the purpose of gaining *Material*. Because *Material* can be applied as reward boosters to *Projects*, generating *Material* is essential for efficient game play ('*Bonus Projects*', cf. following paragraph). Those farming sessions lead to communication and sociability. In consequence, *Fliplife* can be considered as a virtual third place. [84]

As a kind of emergent game play, we have observed so-called *Bonus Projects*. These are projects, which are equipped by players with a huge number of *Material* in order to receive enormous amounts of rewards. In order to carry out such a project, players have to save their rewards for a long period of time, typically one or two months. We consider this as an example that SNGs can support delayed gratification—it is a matter of game mechanics. [81]

Despite of its simple game mechanics, due to our estimation most types of learning goals can be served with *Fliplife*: Besides cognitive learning outcomes also affective goals can be reached, as its purpose of an advergame suggests. Even simple psychomotor learning objectives are supported, when it comes to managing multiplayer online-events (*Parties*). Furthermore, the described metaphor of a *Project* apparently fosters meta-skills as teamwork and collaboration. [85]

Summarizing, *Fliplife* was—it has been shut down in 2014—an excellent example that SNGs provide a broad range of opportunities in serious contexts (here: storytelling, learning and community building). Furthermore, it used a dynamic, interaction-dependent model of friendship and demonstrated that SNGs players are able to defer gratification. All these phenomena are not commonly described in the context of SNGs. They are a matter of purposeful game design.

3.2 QuizUp—Illustrating Rhythm of Play, Matchmaking, and Derived Online Social Networks

The mobile app *QuizUp*[13] started as one competitor in the buisness field of mobile trivia quiz apps in 2013. At that time *Quizkampen*[14] had already come to public attention. It has made the field of mobile trivia quiz apps popular[15].

---

[13] http://www.quizup.com.

[14] http://www.quizkampen.se/ (Engl.: *QuizClash* (http://www.quizclash-game.com/).

[15] As of February 2016 the app indicated the number of German accounts as more than 27 millions. In order to give an impression of the enormous dissemination of this app: this number is equal to around a quarter of all native German speakers.

In the following, the two are compared to describe specific aspects of *QuizUp* with regard to OSNs.

3.2.1   *Match* as Core Game Mechanic

One common game mechanic of both apps are matches: a player competes with another player in choosing the correct answers to a set of Multiple Choice Questions (MCQs). However, the mode of the matches differ. While *Quizkampen* employs an asynchronous match mode, the prevalent mode in *QuizUp* is synchronous. Using *Quizkampen*, a player has to answer first three questions, than it is the opponent's turn to answer the same three questions and additionally another package of three questions. The player with the most correct answers from six rounds wins the match. In general a player has to answer a package within 48 h, so a match can last multiple days. Matches in *QuizUp* consist of seven questions, which are answered question by question synchronously—each question within ten seconds at most. So the different match modes lead to a different rhythm of play. In *Quizkampen* there can be multiple matches which probably span multiple days, whereas in *QuizUp* there is only one single match at a certain point of time, lasting for just over 90 s. In both cases a match potentially triggers social interactions. Thus it is a means of fostering social presence.

3.2.2   Strategies of Matchmaking

Both apps require matchmaking. Various strategies can be observed here: *Quizkampen* lets the user choose an opponent either from his *Facebook* friends or from her in-app list of friends. A third possibility is a random, system-provided opponent. In this case, the player gets assigned an opponent, who is currently online. The initiated match is basically still asynchronous. However, as both opponents can respond immediately to their turns, the match gets also a synchronous, turn-based characteristic.

Apparently, players are not matched according to their play level. At the same time, there is no a priori system-provided indication of the experience of a player, except for top ranking lists. Only the reward of a match reveals a posteriori the play level difference of both competitors. In contrast, *QuizUp* provides an open, recognizable topic-specific level, which aggregates the match results without any regard to the play level of opponents.

3.2.3   Content as a Determining Factor of Matchmaking and OSNs

Another, substantial difference between both apps is the categorization of the content. In both apps each question is assigned to a topic. *Quizkampen* lets the player choose a topic for each turn from a random choice of three topics. Therefore, all players have to deal with all topics. In contrast, in *QuizUp* a match is limited to the questions of a player-selected topic.

In early 2015, *QuizUp* has introduced further social network service features (e.g., post feeds and likes) [57]. So *QuizUp* now is able to accommodate a complete OSN. A relevant feature, which contributes to both matchmaking and OSN, is the requirement and the possibility to follow a topic. As mentioned above, a match focuses on the questions of a certain, player-chosen topic. Therefore, on account creation, a player is required to choose initially a set of preferred topics. Based on common topics, *QuizUp* suggests other players to follow. So common topics can be considered as an additional defining characteristic of the OSN (cf. [94]). This mechanism is intended, as the slogan "Connecting people through shared interests" confirms[16].

3.2.4   Links Between Players

The applications differ in the way they implement links between players. Social networks are according to the definition (cf. Sect. 2.1) given by interactions (or inter-dependencies) between individuals. Often there is a formal and persistent representation of such a network, e.g., in the OSN *Facebook* these links are called *Friendship* or the two involved individuals are called *Friends*. Those formal links between individuals occur in various manifestations in the context of SNGs. Table 2 summarizes attributes, which categorize these links.

Table 2. Characteristics of formal links between individuals in OSNs

Attribute	Description	Example
name	How is the link named?	*Facebook*: *Friendship*, *Twitter*: *Follower*
directed	Is the link directed or undirected (mutual)?	*Twitter*: directed (*'Follower'*), *Facebook*: mutual (*'Friendship'*)
confirmable	Is a confirmation of the targeted individual required?	*Twitter*: No confirmation required; *Facebook*: Friend-request has to be confirmed.
visible	Is the link visible to the targeted individual or others?	*Quizkampen*: Players see only their followed *Friends*, but not their followers. *Friendship* on *Facebook* is visible for other members.
dynamic	Is the link static or is it strength changed by further interactions?	The level of *Friendship* in *Fliplife* depends on current common interactions. *Friendship* on *Facebook* is static, it just requires a request and a confirmation

In *Quizkampen* the link is called *Friend*, it is defined directed, it needs not to be confirmed, and it is only visible to the originator. The link itself is static, however, for each *Friend* there is a statistic about wins, losses and draws. In contrast, *QuizUp* calls the directed link *Following* respectively *Follower*, it needs to be confirmed and therefore it is visible to the other individual. These

---

[16] http://www.quizup.com.

links determine the group of potential opponents of a player, besides randomly assigned ones.

3.2.5   Summary

As a consequence in contrast to first, genre-defining SNGs as *FarmVille*, *QuizUp* is an SNG, which does not depend on an OSN like *Facebook*, but tries to establish its own OSN. A *match* is the core game mechanic which leads to social interactions. Topics are used to structure and foster OSNs. Formal links between players are defined unusually: They are directed and need to be acknowledged. Further consequences of such an approach still have to be observed, but in general it takes into account that one major motivation of quiz app players is to compete with their friends [40,79,90].

3.3   Foldit—User-Generated Content is Rewarded and Unleashes New Gameplay Possibilites

Foldit[17] is a SNG with a serious purpose and thus a serious game. It was created by the Center for Game Science in collaboration with the Department of Biochemistry at University of Washington. The game's purpose is to find new protein foldings to solve real-life biomolecular problems. A protein is foremost a linear sequence of amino acids. However, in a cell, it is quickly bent into a 3D structure, which minimizes the forces between the different amino acids and with the environment. There is no known algorithm to compute this 3D structure in reasonable time, but it turned out that humans are quite good at guessing it. For example, if a protein is needed which detects and deactivates those proteins produced by an Human Immunodeficiency Virus (HIV), which enable its replication, the 3D structures of candidates are of great importance. The game *Foldit* poses the search for specific proteins and foldings as problems to players (see Fig. 5). The better are the characteristics of found solutions (precisely: proteins energy level) the more points they gain.

But the game offers more and aims for more: Players can save, share, reuse, and merge strategies (called *recipe scripts*) they use to reach promising states for their proteins. Even though the user-generated content is in this case primarily game-specific content, these interactions can be considered as *beneficial use of social media interactions*. While competing for the best solution and score, players also join groups to work together, continue to improve proteins submitted by other players and build up on successful strategies by others. As no player can destroy others' solutions, profit from each others' intermediate solutions, but compete for the best score, it is a typical *coopetition* design. All players can work on their new (creative) solutions in their own speed and intensity (asynchronous play), but still are aware of the community activity and solutions submitted in the mean time (*casual multiplayer*). Thus, we can consider it a *social serious game*. The OSN behind is *Foldit*'s own community network consisting of more

---

[17] http://fold.it.

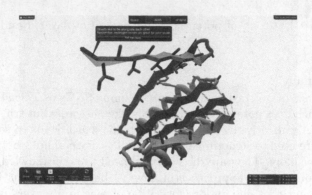

Fig. 5. Foldit: A tutorial problem with guidance to the solution

than 57,000 players in 2010 [14, p. 760]. Several publications report that players found solutions for tough problems, e.g., a problem scientists worked on since more than 15 years [23,46].

From the perspective of research on SNGs we can conclude that serious problems can be tackled by a SNG approach that unleashes the power of the crowd (crowdsourcing). "Compared with games, reality is disconnected. Games build stronger social bonds and lead to more active social networks" [61, p. 82]. It can be argued that the possibility to create own content as new proposed solutions and recipe scripts for strategies allowed players to explore completely new paths of the game unforeseen by the designers. The user-generated content was used as problem solutions and in the same time as new problems to others (as a intermediate solution that can possibly be improved to find an even better solution). Unfortunately, until now no studies about the earning effects to players' strategic skills and knowledge about proteins are published.

Other (not so serious) examples with a similar approach are the games Spore[18] by ElectronicArts or LittleBigPlanet[19] from Sony Computer Entertainment. The former allows sharing of new created species (creatures) to populate other players' worlds, the latter allows sharing of created levels. Finally, we want to point out an additional example using the game mechanics of SNGs to activate the community to solve a serious problem. In 2009 the English newspaper Guardian has launched a game to classify about 700,000 scanned receipts which have been handed in by parliament members to get refunds. The Guardian wanted to find the high expenses and thus claim irregularities[20]. Within three days the game attracted over 20,000 players, which assisted in the data analysis challenge and had finished classifying about 24 % of the documents already [61, p. 219f].

It can be concluded that these examples of SNGs fulfill all criteria to be *Social Serious Game*. The focus of the case study was on Foldit, a game whose

---

[18] http://www.spore.com/.

[19] http://littlebigplanet.playstation.com/.

[20] http://www.theguardian.com/news/datablog/2009/jun/18/mps-expenses-houseof commons.

serious purpose aims not for improvement (learning) of the players primarily, but rather for understanding protein folding and then use of these folding skills to find new protein candidates for curing diseases. In this context it remains a challenge to create games that balance between optimal learning outcome for the individual and valuable (reusable) produced results. At it's best solutions can be found that combine both, learning outcomes and high quality results for reuse. Additionally, in more open game scenarios without a complex physical world model behind, it can be challenging to decide how good a solution of a player is. Imagine creative tasks or assessment of ideas. In these serious game scenarios, the challenge of multiplayer-matchmaking gains importance to bring the right players together for collaboration and peer education efforts (cf. Sect. 4).

4 Challenges in Social Network Game Design and Development

The three challenges described here arise primarily in case concepts of SNGs are used for creating serious games. It is undoubted that direct, individual feedback is valuable to support learning progress [38], but the basis is a thoroughly made diagnosis of learners' abilities and, especially, existing misconceptions. Open-format tasks can be a valuable source for diagnosis. For problem-based learning and discussions about alternative solutions, the social aspects and interconnection of peers comes into account. All these aspects are discussed in Subsect. 4.1. As for SNGs players are connected to each other and play together, exchange content or discuss game-related topics, the challenge of matching the players for the best possible learning outcome arises and is discussed in Subsect. 4.2. Finally, if players are interacting within games or outside of games, toxic behavior may arise and threaten the beneficial outcomes for all players. Thus, the challenge of toxicity in multiplayer online games is discussed in Subsect. 4.3.

4.1 Enable Deep Learning by Provision of Open-Format Problems

To support players of educational games to become connected and collaborative problem solvers (see Sect. 1) game designers reach a certain barrier quickly. Traditionally quests and problems posed to the players are predefined and part of the storytelling, gameplay and flow. The problems are selected (and adapted) based on progress and skills. Correct and incorrect solutions to these are as well predefined. Algorithms check the conditions and if true, players proceed or otherwise get a (constructive) feedback. Maybe easier problems are selected in the end to allow progress. This approach limits by design the learning possibilities of players. Several researchers recognized this problem and proposed first solutions. [35, p. 89] highlights the importance of problem-space exploration for players, [32, p. 70f] demands *peer education* concepts to be integrated into serious games to support collaborative development of creative solutions and reflection on ones own state of knowledge.

An open-format problem is thus a challenge provided to the player where no closed, pre-specified list of correct solutions exist. It is open which solutions evolve and might prove themselves to be good. For example, the quest to 'explain the term SNG by a self-painted picture' is an open-format problem. Who can say which set of solutions is valid or wrong? The discussion about proposed solutions (user-generated content) to such problems and the final agreement among peers may lead to *deep learning* (cf. Sect. 1). Such problems exist in manifold areas, e.g., math (Which proof is written most elegant?) or computer science (What system architecture should be preferred?). It can clearly be seen that the main problem is not the creation of such quests for players, but the validation of the proposed solutions. To be more precise, most interesting are under-specified open-format problems. These leave open several parts of the problem specification which must be amended by players' interpretation. For example, the game could leave out some of the side restrictions in an computational optimization problem and ask the player to define additional (meaningful) restrictions and argue why they are needed.

Instead of algorithmic assessment of the solutions, *peer education* might be a valuable approach. Based on *connectivism* and the technological solutions to connect participants in OSN easily, first proposals and approaches have been made to integrate social media for peer education into educational games [47]. Still, it remains open how such quality assessment and feedback to solutions of open-format problems can be supported algorithmically. Encouragement and hints how these challenges can be tackled may be taken from other disciplines, e.g., approaches for automated quality assurance for Wikipedia articles [26] or machine learning in player role classification [22].

The research topic becomes even more relevant when user-generated content is not only an answer to a problem, but is also (re)used as a posed problem for other players [50]. Evaluation and assessment of peer-provided tasks and solutions (i.e., user-generated content) is an implicit part of situated learning [52]. A technical requirement are platforms, where learners can collaborate, i.e., produce and consume user-generated content. Such platforms form—or are at least similar to—OSNs. In the following paragraph we name examples.

The Q&A-Platform *StackOverflow*[21] can be considered as a working example of gamified, collaborative knowledge engineering. Participants refine knowledge step by step till a question has been answered sufficiently and exemplarily [63]. Another example of common knowledge engineering are game-related wikis, which are built up and maintained by players. Such wiki articles foster skills to assess and verify content and to suggest improvements. Thus participation in these processes can be considered as supporting skill acquisition [82]. There are commercial games, which provide *level editors* in order to encourage users to generate their own content. Examples are *LittleBigPlanet*[22] or *Portal*[23]. Another gaming-related, educational platform, which builds on a community is *Scratch*[24].

---

[21] http://www.stackoverflow.com.

[22] http://littlebigplanet.playstation.com.

[23] http://www.thinkwithportals.com - Educational level editor: http://www.teachwithportals.com.

[24] http://scratch.mit.edu.

All these platforms rely on the principle to provide a framework which can be filled by user-generated content. Quality assurance is accomplished by fellow players, who thereby increase their competency in parallel. Thus such platforms are scaling, i.e., additional participants do not lead to further supervision demand, but increase the number of peers. They can be considered as fruitful in common knowledge generation and for solving domain-specific problems [83]. However, they are still rare in the context of SNGs, although there are promising approaches. The *Reading Game* [70] is an epistemic game, which relies on MCQs as user-generated content. Players have to generate questions and have to evaluate questions of their fellow players. Although answering MCQs is not an open-format problem, the purposeful design and rating of MCQs can be considered as tasks with a high complexity. In general, such platforms provide manifold learning opportunities: when learning content is created, when tasks are solved and when artifacts are rated.

Still, all of these thoughts do not contain the influence to game mechanics. When players can create new assets for the game that contain specification of influences to game parameters (e.g., strength, durability) semantic enrichment is needed to allow an algorithmic use later on. Such approaches would allow players to create even more new (specific) problems (quests) for others. This could help in answering one main question serious games generally have to face: Where will all the content come from?

Research Questions

RQ1 How can the quality of answers to open-format problems be assessed in serious games? This includes the challenge to find game mechanics that can cope with delays until the assessment is done. For which game genre are which type of questions more suitable? Is there a mapping from game mechanics to intended learning outcome?

RQ2 If user-generated content becomes part of the gameplay, how can the accuracy, quality and level of difficulty be assessed beyond analysis of usage statistics?

RQ3 How can a model look like to generate new quests and story from contributed user-generated content?

RQ4 What are requirements of purpose-specific OSNs? How can their implementation be fostered? Can and how can these OSNs integrated into larger OSNs?

4.2   Bringing the Right Learners Together: Social Matchmaking

Traditionally, matchmaking focuses on the the player score to find opponents (or team partners) that may be suitable to play together. Emerging from the board game chess, the Elo system became famous and is still used in computer games, too. It basically calculates the winning probability of pairwise players and in case of a win increases the score of the predicted loser more than the score of the predicted winner [24]. Improvements like Glicko rating or TrueSkill from Microsoft were proposed recently [33, 39].

Quickly it was evident that score (or level of skill) is not the only relevant dimension for matchmaking. In team play, other factors like characteristics of an avatar or level of fun play a role [18]. As multiplayer games are nowadays not played in local area networks any more, but worldwide and even in mobile wireless networks, latency became a relevant factor for matchmaking [1,60].

If now additionally the serious aspect of gaming comes into play, optimization of the learning outcome for all players becomes a relevant aspect of matchmaking. Unfortunately, prediction of learning outcome or how much players will benefit from each other for learning is not directly measurable as a one-dimensional factor. Depending on the intended learning outcome, the similarity or difference in level of knowledge, area of knowledge, personality traits, learning style preferences, team orientation, motivation, etc. can be relevant and a weighted factor to find the best peers for playing a serious game. A more detailed discussion of criteria and algorithms can be found in [47, p. 16f].

Optimized *learning group formation* for serious games is an NP-complete problem [15, p. 325]. Consequently, computer science came up with agent based approaches that can satisfy the manifold restrictions and criteria [15]. Other approaches use semantic structures to build optimized learning groups. Ontologies of the learning domain and learner behaviors are considered by solver algorithms to find the best matches [41,67]. A third field of approaches uses analytic optimization algorithms based on the participants' criteria values represented as multidimensional vectors. Group-specific criteria, like group size, are respected as side conditions. If only those criteria are of importance, where homogeneity is beneficial (players are expected to be similar), clustering algorithms can be used [69]. Otherwise heuristics or genetic algorithms are used [7].

All of the cited approaches ignore the fact that for serious games scenarios like classroom learning or use of SNG in massive open online courses, not only the manifold criteria need to be matched (some homogeneous, some heterogeneous), but also there is a need that all created groups may be of similar quality and that all participants benefit equally from the other group members. Likewise, the weighting of the different matching criteria is seldom supported. Recently, the *GroupAL* algorithm has been proposed which satisfies these needs and outperforms most of the related algorithms mentioned before [48].

Still, all mentioned approaches above form learning groups at a certain time point. New approaches are needed for continuous group formation, re-grouping and update of existing groups as learners' characteristics change over time, group members drop out or learning goals change (e.g., in the game). It seems promising to combine valuable aspects of the approaches named here with Social Network Analysis (SNA) and hybrid recommender systems as discussed by Terveen and McDonald for non-learning scenarios [87].

Research Questions

RQ1 By which metrics (personality, goals, intensity, interaction, etc.) can players be matched to create a win-win situation that works for learning *and* playing?

RQ2 How can matchmaking be supported via recommender algorithms? What is
the relation between asynchronous matchmaking compared to optimal group
quality? Can both be achieved?

4.3 Toxicity in Multiplayer Online Games

Toxicity or toxic behavior is a form of cybermobbing with the goal of influencing fellow players negatively. It contains insulting or harassing fellow players or
disrupting game play in a way such that it negatively impacts other players'
perceived fun. Different kinds of toxic behavior can be observed:

The first is related to *communication* between players and contains insults and
harassment (i.e., racism, sexism, death threats, etc.).

The second is called *griefing* and contains negative behavior which is related
to how players intentionally disrupt a game through their behavior. This
involves steps to intentionally lose a game or help an opposing team to get
an advancement over the own team. A special form of griefing is called power
imposition. This form of toxic behavior can be observed in MMOs, where a
stronger player repeatedly 'kills' a weaker player's avatar on purpose and
just for the sake of fun, hence keeping that player effectively from playing
the game. Another form of griefing is called *scamming*, which means that
one player defrauds another player by obscuring important information or
abusing the fact that the other player is simply not experienced enough
to foresee the consequences of a trade between two players. This is a core
difference to strongly competitive games (with a small amount of players)
where in order to win the game one needs to defeat the opponent. In MMOs,
players play next to each other not against each other. Hence, in order to
'win' the game (i.e., leveling up, gathering valuable equipment, defeating boss
enemies) one does not depend on other players to lose. Subsequently, harming
a player usually has a serious negative impact on that player's perceived fun
which is the reason why in many modern MMOs most areas of a game world
do not allow players to fight and kill each other. Usually, this is only allowed
in so-called Player-Vs-Player (PVP) areas.

The topic of toxic behavior has become more and more important in recent years
due to the rise of MMOs and MOBAs. "In competitive multiplayer games, social
interaction determines if a player continues to play or quit. Players are up to
320 % more likely to quit a game, the more toxicity they experience." [55].

Many reasons for the occurrence of toxic behavior exist: The most important
is probably anonymity on the Internet [55]. As players can remain incognito,
the barrier towards negative behavior diminishes. This is a common problem in
social media. According to Jeffrey Lin, another aspect is that players are getting
used to toxic behavior and consider it as normal [55].

Because toxicity is such a big problem in current multiplayer games, various
countermeasures have been developed up until today with mixed success. First
methods were user-centered. Those usually included a vote system for other

players to decide over a possibly toxic player. This either took place in the game to exclude ('kick') that player from the ongoing game, or it was based on a report system to complain about malicious behavior after a game session. Initially, special operators reviewed those reports and decided about a penalty. Later, there were different systems designed to have the player community decide about this. A prominent example is the former *League of Legends Tribunal*, a system in which registered players could vote on if a reported player should be punished, making this decision essentially crowd-sourced [54]. Although the system was a big improvement, it had various flaws, the biggest probably being the time between the moment of toxic behavior and the actual punishment which often was months later due to the amount of reports.

A different approach contains positive reinforcement, i.e., rewarding players for positive behavior. Moreover, a study by Riot games showed that players could effectively be primed towards a positive or toxic attitude by showing messages at the start of a game session in either comforting (green), aggressive (red) or neutral (white) color and with provocative, positive, or neutral content [54].

Recently, machine learning is being used to automatically recognize toxic behavior in terms of gaming patterns or even language recognition. Lin [55] explained how a neural network which is learning human language is able to correctly identify toxic players with a false positive rate of less than 1 %. An important finding here is that toxic behavior propagates through game sessions meaning that if a player encounters toxic behavior in a game, hence being negatively affected, that player is more likely to be toxic herself in subsequent games.

This is related to the findings of Cheng et al. which shows that content creators in online communities more likely negatively comment on fellow contributors once they received negative comments themselves and become more likely to produce lower quality in future [9]. Another successful method used in social networks or forums for this problem is to use 'shadow bans' for toxic content creators - banning them without letting them know that they are banned, making their negative content invisible to other users without them realizing it [55]. Following those insights, in League of Legends it was decided to disable chat with the enemy team per default, so players can not be taunted or insulted by players of the opposing team. Moreover, one of the most effective punishments for toxic players was a chat ban (i.e., forbidding a player to chat for a set amount of games) which significantly improved toxic player behavior.

Also, findings from the same source state that one of the most important aspects in countering toxic behavior is immediate and clear feedback. In the context of SNGs, the finding is that players are less toxic when they play with friends from their social graph. As a result, game designers try to motivate players to play with friends by, e.g., giving them some kind of reward (like bonus experience points). Proposals for a combined game and community achievement system that rewards socially conform behavior are made [49].

However, the problem of toxicity in MMOs still contains many open research questions. A better understanding of player behavior and why players tend to be toxic is necessary, as well as efficient, algorithmic counter-measures to prevent toxic behavior in the first place.

Research Questions

RQ1 Which behavior of players in MMOs can support detection of toxic behavior?

RQ2 How can toxic behavior be recognized automatically, potentially using machine learning methods?

RQ3 Which game mechanics can prevent toxic behavior?

RQ3 Which social mechanics in and around games can prevent toxic behavior?

5 Conclusion and the Future

This chapter introduced *Social Network Games (SNGs)* as a modern and important field of serious games research. The introduction outlined the benefits of a *connected* and *collaborative* game play for deep and meaningful learning experiences. SNGs gain even more importance by the ongoing trend to mobile gaming and learning. Section 2.1 defined *Social Games*, *SNGs*, and *Social Serious Games* among other terms.

Section 2.2 introduced the distinguishing *characteristics of SNGs*. Primarily, the easy access with nearly no monetary or device-specific hurdles allows SNGs to be played by casual and hard-core gamers alike. SNGs typically have simple game mechanics and foster a *casual multiplayer* atmosphere. The section introduces *asynchronous play* and the connection to an OSN as additional characteristics that support scaling and *endless game play*. The often used *Free-To-Play (F2P)* model raises issues of monetary dependency if not carefully implemented (cf. Sect. 2.3).

The connecting and collaborative aspects of SNGs are discussed from different discipline perspectives in Sect. 2.4 on *foundations*. From a pedagogical point of view learning theories can be amended by the interconnecting functionality of the Internet and the resulting networked learning, as proposed by the *Connectivism* model. Likewise, the potential of *peer education* can be used to improve knowledge exchange in SNGs if game mechanics consider *cooperation* and *collaboration* wisely. These two terms, their importance for serious games and supporting game mechanics are deduced in Sect. 2.4.2 based on a brief look at the *history of social games* dating back to ancient times. The section closes with derived *lessons and pitfalls* to consider for game design on collaboration.

Three case studies examine the characteristics and success of the SNGs Fliplife, Quizup and Foldit in Sect. 3. Even though the games originated in different eras and focus different serious gaming aspects, the studies conclude for all games the beneficial use of social interactions to improve problem-solving competency as well as deep, connected learning. At the same time *three important challenges*, to be tackled by future research, can be conducted from the findings as outlined in the final Sect. 4.

First, learning is strongly related to assessment and diagnosis. For deep learning to happen (in the sense of learning researchers like Fullan and Langworthy Fullan and Langworthy [29, p. 6]), open-format tasks are valuable, but algorithmic assessment is not yet possible in a satisfying quality (and generality).

Second, in multiplayer scenarios for learning, all learners within a group should progress and benefit from the knowledge exchange, but how can matchmaking for games be extended to consider multi-dimensional (learning) aspects beside expertise of play? *Third*, SNGs include social interactions per definition and thus have to face the challenge of toxic behavior of players. This problem is not genuine to SNGs but endangers all multiplayer games and even all interactions in social media. Approaches have to be found to prevent—or at least detect and stop—toxic behavior inside and outside of games. For each of the challenges related research questions are formulated as a starting point.

Complementary reading suggestions can be found in the following books and articles sections. The literature is thoroughly selected as a good starting point to investigate the research field of Social Network Games further.

Further Reading

Books

Fields, T. (2014). *Mobile & Social Game Design: Monetization Methods and Mechanics* (2nd ed.). A K Peters/CRC Press.
This book consists of a valuable overview to the different market strategies and concepts needed to create successfull games for the social media (and network) market.

Bartle, R.A. (2003). *Designing Virtual Worlds.* New Riders.
This book is a classic one about the differences in playing style preference. Bartle's model has been extended in the meanwile, but this work with multiuser dungeons in mind is a good foundation.

Lehdonvirta, V., and Castronova, E. (2014). *Virtual economies: Design and analysis.* The MIT Press.
In this book two of the leading experts give an overview about developing virtual currencies, an essential aspect of commercial SNGs.

Crumlish, C., and Malone, E. (2009). *Designing Social Interfaces: Principles, Patterns, and Practices for Improving the User Experience* (Animal Guide). Sebastopol, USA: OReilly Media.
This book summarizes manifold design patterns for social media sites which are also applicable to the design of SNGs.

Articles

Lehdonvirta, V., and Ernkvist, M. (2011). *Converting the Virtual Economy into Development Potential: Knowledge Map of the Virtual Economy.* infoDev / World Bank. Washington: The World Bank.

McPherson, M., Smith-Lovin, L., and Cook, J. M. (2001). *Birds of a Feather: Homophily in Social Networks.* Annual Review of Sociology, 27, 415444. doi:10.1146/annurev.soc.27.1.415

Granovetter, M.S. (1973). *The Strength-of-Weak-Ties Perspective on Creativity: a Comprehensive Examination and Extension.* The American Journal of Sociology, 78(6), 13601380. doi:10.1037/a0018761

Damon, W. (1984). *Peer Education: The Untapped Potential.* Journal of Applied Developmental Psychology, 5(4), 331343. doi:10.1016/0193-3973(84)90006-6

van Dijck, J. (2009). *Users like you? Theorizing Agency in User-Generated Content.* Media, Culture & Society, 31(1), 4158. doi:10.1177/0163443708098245

Dillenbourg, P. (1999). *What do you mean by Collaborative Learning?* In P. Dillenbourg (Ed.), Collaborative-learning: Cognitive and Computational Approaches (pp. 115). Oxford: Elsevier.

Rossi, L. (2009) *Playing Your Network: Gaming in Social Network Sites* in Breaking New Ground: Innovation in Games, Play, Practice and Theory. Proceedings of DiGRA 2009.

Softic, S. (2012). *Towards Identifying Collaborative Learning Groups Using Social Media.* International Journal of Emerging Technologies in Learning (iJET), 7(Special Issue FNMA). Retrieved from http://online-journals.org/i-jet/article/viewArticle/2325.

References

1. Agarwal, S., Lorch, J.R.: Matchmaking for online games and other latency-sensitive P2P systems. ACM SIGCOMM Comput. Commun. Rev. **39**, 315 (2009)
2. Albert, D., Lukas, J.: Knowledge Spaces: Theories, Empirical Research, and Applications. Psychology Press, Hove (1999)
3. Alexander, L.: Ian Bogost's Troubling Experiences With Cow Clicker (2010). http://www.gamasutra.com/view/news/30835/GDC_Online_Ian_Bogosts_Troubling_Experiences_With_Cow_Clicker.php
4. Bogost, I.: Cow Clicker - The Making of Obsession (2010). http://www.bogost.com/blog/cow_clicker_1.shtml
5. Bonsignore, E., Kraus, K., June, A., Amanda, V., Fraistat, A., Druin, A.: Alternate reality games: platforms for collaborative learning. In: Proceedings of the Tenth International Conference of the Learning Sciences. International Society of the Learning Sciences, Sydney (2012)
6. Brandenburger, A.M., Nalebuff, B.J.: Co-Opetition. Currency Doubleday, New York (1997)
7. Cavanaugh, R., Ellis, M.: Automating the process of assigning students to cooperative-learning teams. In: Proceedings of the 2004 American Society for Engineering Education Annual Conference & Exposition (2004)
8. Chen, V.H.-H., Duh, H.B.-L., Phuah, P.S.K., Lam, D.Z.Y.: Enjoyment or engagement? role of social interaction in playing massively mulitplayer online role-playing games (MMORPGS). In: Harper, R., Rauterberg, M., Combetto, M. (eds.) ICEC 2006. LNCS, vol. 4161, pp. 262–267. Springer, Heidelberg (2006). doi:10.1007/11872320_31
9. Cheng, J., Danescu-Niculescu-Mizil, C., Leskovec, J.: How community feedback shapes user behavior. arXiv preprint. (2014). arXiv:1405.1429
10. Chiapello, L.: Formalizing casual games: a study based on game designers professional knowledge. In: DiGRA 2013 - Proceedings of the 2013 DiGRA International Conference, DeFragging Game Studies, pp. 1–16 (2014)

11. Cole, H., Griffiths, M.D.: Social interactions in massively multiplayer online role-playing gamers. CyberPsychology Behav. **10**(4), 575–583 (2007)
12. Collazos, C.A., Guerrero, L.A., Pino, J.A., Ochoa, S.F.: Collaborative scenarios to promote positive interdependence among group members. In: Favela, J., Decouchant, D. (eds.) CRIWG 2003. LNCS, vol. 2806, pp. 356–370. Springer, Heidelberg (2003). doi:10.1007/978-3-540-39850-9_30
13. Consalvo, M.: Hardcore casual: game culture Return(s) to Ravenhearst. Proceedings of the 4th International Conference on Foundations of Digital Games. FDG 2009, pp. 50–54. ACM, New York (2009)
14. Cooper, S., Khatib, F., Treuille, A., Barbero, J., Lee, J., Beenen, M., Leaver-Fay, A., Baker, D., Popović, Z., Players, F.: Predicting protein structures with a multiplayer online game. Nature **466**(7307), 756–760 (2010)
15. Cunha, L.M., Fuks, H., de Lucena, C.J.P.: Setting groups of learners using matchmaking agents. In: Uskov, V. (ed.) International Conference on Computers and Advanced Technology in Education, Rio de Janeiro, pp. 321–326 (2003)
16. Damon, W.: Peer education: the untapped potential. J. Appl. Dev. Psychol. **5**(4), 331–343 (1984)
17. Damon, W., Phelps, E.: Critical distinctions among three approaches to peer education. Int. J. Educ. Res. **13**(1), 9–19 (1989)
18. Delalleau, O., Contal, E., Thibodeau-Laufer, E., Ferrari, R.C., Bengio, Y., Zhang, F.: Beyond skill rating: advanced matchmaking in ghost recon online. IEEE Trans. Comput. Intell. AI Games **4**(3), 167–177 (2012)
19. Diestel, R.: Graph Theory (Graduate Texts in Mathematics), 3rd edn. Springer, New York (2006)
20. Dillenbourg, P.: What do you mean by collaborative learning? In: Dillenbourg, P. (ed.) Collaborative-Learning: Cognitive and Computational Approaches, pp. 1–15. Elsevier, Oxford (1999)
21. Dolwick, J.S.: 'The Social' and beyond: introducing actor-network theory. J. Marit. Archaeol. **4**(1), 21–49 (2009)
22. Eggert, C., Herrlich, M., Smeddinck, J., Malaka, R.: Classification of player roles in the team-based multi-player game dota 2. In: Chorianopoulos, K., Divitini, M., Hauge, J.B., Jaccheri, L., Malaka, R. (eds.) ICEC 2015. LNCS, vol. 9353, pp. 112–125. Springer, Heidelberg (2015). doi:10.1007/978-3-319-24589-8_9
23. Eiben, C.B., Siegel, J.B., Bale, J.B., Cooper, S., Khatib, F., Shen, B.W., Players, F., Stoddard, B.L., Popovic, Z., Baker, D.: Increased diels-alderase activity through backbone remodeling guided by foldit players. Nat. Biotechnol. **30**(2), 190–192 (2012)
24. Elo, A.E., Sloan, S.: The Rating of Chess Players. Past and Present. Ishi Press, New York (2008)
25. Entertainment Software Association (ESA): Essential Facts about the Computer And Video Game Industry, Technical report, Software, Entertainment Association (ESA) (2015). http://www.theesa.com/article/150-million-americans-play-video-games/
26. Ferretti, E., Errecalde, M.L., Anderka, M., Stein, B.: On the use of reliable-negatives selection strategies in the PU learning approach for quality flaws prediction in wikipedia. In: DEXA Workshops, pp. 211–215 (2014)
27. Fields, T.: Mobile & Social Game Design: Monetization Methods and Mechanics, 2nd edn. A K Peters/CRC Press, Natick (2014)
28. Fliplife: Fliplife (2011). http://fliplife.com/

29. Fullan, M., Langworthy, M.: Towards a New End: New Pedagogies for Deep Learning, Technical report, June, Collaborative Impact, Seattle, USA (2013). www.newpedagogies.org/Pages/assets/new-pedagogies-for-deep-learning--an-invitation-to-partner-2013-19-06.pdf

30. Goodman, A.: A Bayesian Approach to A / B Testing (2012). http://blog.custora.com/2012/05/a-bayesian-approach-to-ab-testing/

31. Garton, L., Haythornthwaite, C., Wellman, B.: Studying online social networks. J. Comput. Mediated Commun. 3(1), 1–9 (2007)

32. Gee, J.P.: Deep learning properties of good digital games. In: Ritterfeld, U., Cody, M.J., Vorderer, P. (eds.) Serious Games: Mechanisms and Effects, Chap. 5, 1 edn., pp. 67–82. Routledge, New York (2009)

33. Glickman, M., Ittenbach, R., Nick, T.G., O'Brien, R., Ratcliffe, S.J., Shults, J.: Statistical consulting with limited resources: applications to practice. CHANCE 23(Special Issue: What Is Jeopardy!?), 35–42 (2010)

34. Goad, L.: Facebook Users: 55% Play Social Games, 19% say They're addicted. Technical report, Games.com News citing a Lightspeed Research Survey (2010). http://blog.games.com/2010/09/13/facebook-users-55-play-social-games-19-say-theyre-addicted/

35. Graesser, A., Chipman, P., Leeming, F., Biedenbach, S.: Deep learning and emotion in serious games. In: Ritterfeld, U., Cody, M.J., Vorderer, P. (eds.) Serious Games: Mechanisms and Effects, Chap. 6, 1 edn., pp. 83–102. Routledge, New York (2009)

36. Granovetter, M.S.: The strength-of-weak-ties perspective on creativity: a comprehensive examination and extension. Am. J. Sociol. 78(6), 1360–1380 (1973)

37. Hämäläinen, R., Manninen, T., Järvelä, S., Häkkinen, P.: Learning to collaborate: designing collaboration in a 3-D game environment. Int. High. Educ. 9(1), 47–61 (2006)

38. Hattie, J., Timperley, H.: The power of feedback. Rev. Educ. Res. 77(1), 81–112 (2007)

39. Herbrich, R., Minka, T., Graepel, T.: True skill(TM): a bayesian skill rating system. Adv. Neural Inf. Process. Syst. 20(20), 569–576 (2007)

40. Hou, J.: Uses and gratifications of social games: blending social networking and game play. First Monday 16(7) (2011). ISSN 1396-0466, http://firstmonday.org/article/view/3517/3020

41. Inaba, A., Supnithi, T., Ikeda, M., Mizoguchi, R., Toyoda, J.: How can we form effective collaborative learning groups? In: Gauthier, G., Frasson, C., VanLehn, K. (eds.) ITS 2000. LNCS, vol. 1839, pp. 282–291. Springer, Heidelberg (2000). doi:10.1007/3-540-45108-0_32

42. Ito, M., Gutiérrez, K., Livingstone, S., Penuel, B., Rhodes, J., Schalen, K., Schor, J., Sefton-Green, J., Watkins, S.C.: Connected Learning. Digital Media and Learning Research Hub LSE (2014)

43. Järvinen, A.: Social Game Design for Social Networks (2010). http://playgen.com/game-design-for-social-networks/

44. Kaplan, A.M., Haenlein, M.: Users of the world, unite! the challenges and opportunities of social media. Bus. Horiz. 53(1), 59–68 (2010)

45. Kelly, T.: CityVille explained, part 1 (2010). http://gamasutra.com/view/feature/134615/cityville_explained_part_1.php?print=1

46. Khatib, F., Cooper, S., Tyka, M.D., Xu, K., Makedon, I., Popovic, Z., Baker, D., Players, F.: Algorithm discovery by protein folding game players. Proc. Nat. Acad. Sci. USA 108(47), 18949–18953 (2011)

47. Konert, J.: Interactive Multimedia Learning: Using Social Media for Peer Education in Single-Player Educational Games. Springer, Heidelberg (2014)

48. Konert, J., Burlak, D., Steinmetz, R.: The group formation problem: an algorithmic approach to learning group formation. In: Rensing, C., Freitas, S., Ley, T., Muñoz-Merino, P.J. (eds.) EC-TEL 2014. LNCS, vol. 8719, pp. 221–234. Springer, Heidelberg (2014). doi:10.1007/978-3-319-11200-8_17

49. Konert, J., Gerwien, N., Göbel, S., Steinmetz, R.: Bringing game achievements and community achievements together. In: Proceedings of the 7th European Conference on Game Based Learning (ECGBL) 2013, pp. 319–328. Academic Publishing International, Porto, Portugal (2013)

50. Konert, J., Richter, K., Mehm, F., Göbel, S., Bruder, R., Steinmetz, R.: PEDALE - a peer education diagnostic and learning environment. J. Educ. Technol. Soc. 15(4), 27–38 (2012)

51. Lantz, F.: [Insert Cow Pun Here] (2011). http://gamedesignadvance.com/?p=2383

52. Lave, J., Wenger, E.: Situated Learning: Legitimate Peripheral Participation. Cambridge University Press, Cambridge (1991)

53. Lewis, C., Wardrip-Fruin, N., Whitehead, J.: Motivational game design patterns of 'ville games. Proceedings of the International Conference on the Foundations of Digital Games - FDG 2012, pp. 172–179 (2012)

54. Lin, J.: The Science Behind Shaping Behavior in Online Games. Electronic (2013). http://gdcvault.com/play/1017940/The-Science-Behind-Shaping-Player

55. Lin, J.: More science behind shaping player behavior in online games. Electronic (2015). http://www.gdcvault.com/play/1022160/More-Science-Behind-Shaping-Player

56. Loreto, I.D., Gouaïch, A.: Social Casual Games Success is not so Casual. Technical report, LIRMM. University of Montpellier - CNRS, Montpellier, France (2010). http://hal-lirmm.ccsd.cnrs.fr/lirmm-00486934/fr/

57. Lowensohn, J.: QuizUp is trying to reinvent itself by turning into a social network (2015). http://www.theverge.com/2015/5/21/8633007/quizup-jumps-from-trivia-to-social-networking

58. Mahajan, A.: Rapidly Developing FarmVille (2010). http://de.slideshare.net/amittmahajan/rapidly-building-farmville-how-we-built-and-scaled-a-1-facebook-game-in-5-weeks

59. Manninen, T., Korva, T.: Designing puzzles for collaborative gaming experience-case: escape. In: Castell, S., Jennifer, J. (eds.) Selected papers of the Digital Interactive Games Research Association's Second International Conference (DiGRA 205), pp. 233–247. Digital Interactive Games Research Association, Vancouver (2005)

60. Manweiler, J., Agarwal, S., Zhang, M., Roy Choudhury, R., Bahl, P.: Switchboard: a matchmaking system for multiplayer mobile games. In: Proceedings of the 9th International Conference on Mobile Systems, Applications, and Services - MobiSys 2011, p. 71 (2011)

61. McGonigal, J.: Reality Is Broken: Why Games Make Us Better and How They Can Change the World. Penguin Press HC, New York (2011)

62. Miller, P.: SimCity launch debacle comes down to mismanaged expectations (2013). http://www.gamasutra.com/view/news/188575/Opinion_SimCity_launch_debacle_comes_down_to_mismanaged_expectations.php

63. Nasehi, S.M., Sillito, J., Maurer, F., Burns, C.: What makes a good code example? a study of programming Q&A in stack overflow (2012)

64. Nutt, C.: A Philosophy That Extends Eastward: Social Games Zynga-Style (2011). http://www.gamasutra.com/view/feature/6280/a_philosophy_that_extends_.php

65. O'Neill, N.: What exactly are social games? (2008). http://www.socialtimes.com/2008/07/social-games/

66. Orsini, L.: History of Social Games (2010). http://kotaku.com/5548105/history-of-social-games

67. Ounnas, A., Davis, H., Millard, D.: A framework for semantic group formation. In: Eighth IEEE International Conference on Advanced Learning Technologies, pp. 34–38 (2008)

68. Paavilainen, J., Koskinen, E., Hamari, J., Kinnunen, J., Alha, K., Keronen, L., Mäyrä, F., Pirinen, T., Järvinen, A.: Free2Play Research Project Final Report, Technical report. University of Tampere, School of Information Sciences (2016). http://free2playproject.wordpress.com

69. Paredes, P., Ortigosa, A., Rodriguez, P.: A method for supporting heterogeneous-group formation through heuristics and visualization. J. Univ. Comput. Sci. **16**(19), 2882–2901 (2010)

70. Parker, R., Manuguerra, M., Schaefer, B.: The reading game encouraging learners to become question- makers rather than question-takers by getting feedback, making friends and having fun. In: Carter, H., Gosper, M., Hedberg, J. (eds.) 30th ascilite Conference 2013 Proceedings, pp. 681–684. Macquarie University (2013)

71. Radoff, J.: Game On: Energize Your Business with Social Media Games. Wiley, Hoboken (2011)

72. Rocha, J.B., Mascarenhas, S., Prada, R.: Game mechanics for cooperative games. In: ZON Digital Games 2008, pp. 72–80 (2008)

73. Roschelle, J., Teasley, S.: The construction of shared knowledge in collaborative problem solving. In: O'Malley, C. (ed.) Computer-Supported Collaborative Learning, vol. 128, pp. 69–97. Springer, Heidelberg (1995)

74. Saatchi & Saatchi: Engagement Unleashed: Gamification for Business, Brands and Loyalty, Technical report, Saatchi & Saatchi (2011). http://saatchi.com/en-us/news/engagement_unleashed_gamification_for_business_brands_and_loyalty

75. Scott, J.: Social network analysis. Sociology **22**(1), 109–127 (1988)

76. Siemens, G.: Connectivism: a learning theory for the digital age. Instr. Technol. Distance Learn. **2**(1), 3–10 (2005)

77. Skinner, B.: Science And Human Behavior. Free Press, New York (1965)

78. Söbke, H.: Gaming a Non-Game? A Long Term (Self-)Experiment about FarmVille. Well Played **4**(1 (DiGRA & GLS)), 215–262 (2015)

79. Söbke, H.: Space for seriousness? In: Chorianopoulos, K., Divitini, M., Hauge, J.B., Jaccheri, L., Malaka, R. (eds.) ICEC 2015. LNCS, vol. 9353, pp. 482–489. Springer, Heidelberg (2015). doi:10.1007/978-3-319-24589-8_44

80. Söbke, H., Bröker, T.: A browser-based advergame as communication catalyst: types of communication in video games. J. Commun. Soc. **27**, 75–94 (2015)

81. Söbke, H., Bröker, T., Kornadt, O.: Social gaming just click and reward?. In: Felicia, P. (ed.) Proceedings of the 6th European Conference on Games Based Learning, No. Snow, pp. 478–486. Academic Publishing Limited (2012)

82. Söbke, H., Corredor, J.A., Kornadt, O.: Learning, reasoning and modeling in social gaming. In: Pan, Z., Cheok, A.D., Müller, W., Iurgel, I., Petta, P., Urban, B. (eds.) Transactions on Edutainment X. LNCS, vol. 7775, pp. 243–258. Springer, Heidelberg (2013). doi:10.1007/978-3-642-37919-2_15

83. Söbke, H., Hadlich, C., Bröker, T., Kornadt, O.: Concept of a gaming platform for domain-specific user-created content. In: Gouscos, D., Meimaris, M. (eds.) 5th European Conference on Games Based Learning, pp. 759–766. Academic Publishing Limited, Athens (2011)

84. Söbke, H., Londong, J.: A Social network game as virtual third place: community enabler in virtual learning environments?. In: Proceedings of World Conference on Educational Multimedia, Hypermedia and Telecommunications 2015, pp. 518–531. Association for the Advancement of Computing in Education (AACE) (2015)

85. Söbke, H., Londong, J.: Educational opportunities of a social network game. In: Göbel, S., Ma, M., Baalsrud Hauge, J., Oliveira, M.F., Wiemeyer, J., Wendel, V. (eds.) JCSG 2015. LNCS, vol. 9090, pp. 63–76. Springer, Heidelberg (2015). doi:10. 1007/978-3-319-19126-3_6

86. SOOMLA: mobile gaming insights report - a complete analysis of in-app. Purchases in F2P games, Technical report, SOOMLA (2016). https://soom.la/resources/2016-q1-insights-report

87. Terveen, L., McDonald, D.W.: Social matching. ACM Trans. Comput. Hum. Interact. **12**(3), 401–434 (2005)

88. Transparency Market Research (TMR): Social Gaming Market - Global Industry Analysis, Size, Share, Growth, Trends and Forecast, 2013–2019, Technical report, Transparency Market Research (TMR) (2015). http://www.transparencymarketresearch.com/pressrelease/social-gaming-market.htm

89. Van Rooij, A.J., Schoenmakers, T.M., Vermulst, A.A., Van Den Eijnden, R., Van De Mheen, D.: Online video game addiction: identification of addicted adolescent gamers. Addiction **106**(1), 205–212 (2011)

90. Wei, P.S., Lu, H.P.: Why do people play mobile social games? an examination of network externalities and of uses and gratifications. Internet Res. **24**(3), 3 (2014)

91. Wendel, V., Gutjahr, M., Göbel, S., Steinmetz, R.: Designing collaborative multiplayer serious games. Educ. Inf. Technol. **18**(2), 287–308 (2013)

92. Wendel, V., Hertin, F., Göbel, S., Steinmetz, R.: Collaborative learning by means of multiplayer serious games. In: Luo, X., Spaniol, M., Wang, L., Li, Q., Nejdl, W., Zhang, W. (eds.) ICWL 2010. LNCS, vol. 6483, pp. 289–298. Springer, Heidelberg (2010). doi:10.1007/978-3-642-17407-0_30

93. Wohn, D.Y., Lampe, C., Wash, R., Ellison, N., Vitak, J.: The "S" in social network games: initiating, maintaining, and enhancing relationships. In: 2011 44th Hawaii International Conference on System Sciences, pp. 1–10 (2011)

94. Yang, S.H., Long, B., Smola, A., Sadagopan, N., Zheng, Z., Zha, H.: Like like alike: joint friendship and interest propagation in social networks. Proceedings of the 20th International Conference on World Wide Web. WWW 2011, NY, USA pp, pp. 537–546. ACM, New York (2011)

95. Yee, N.: The Proteus Paradox: How Online Games and Virtual Worlds Change Us And How They Don't. Yale University Press, New Haven (2014)

96. Yee, N.: The virtual skinner box (na). http://www.nickyee.com/eqt/skinner.html

97. Zagal, J.P., Rick, J., Hsi, I.: Collaborative games: Lessons learned from board games. Simul. Gaming **37**(1), 24–40 (2006)

Pervasive Games

Leif Oppermann[1]([✉]) and Michaela Slussareff[2]

[1] Fraunhofer Institute for Applied Information Technology FIT,
Schloss Birlinghoven, 53757 Sankt Augustin, Germany
leif.oppermann@fit.fraunhofer.de
[2] Institute of Information Studies and Librarianship, Charles University,
U Kříže 8, 158 00 Prague 5, Czech Republic
michaela.slussareff@ff.cuni.cz

Abstract. Pervasive games are bridging the physical and digital worlds through the use of mobile devices, positioning technology, and mobile networks. They received an uptake since the Global Positioning System (GPS) became available for public use in May 2000. Since then, pervasive games have been studied in a number of research projects and have reached the mass market by now. Furthermore, their concepts have been applied to mobile augmented learning experiences which makes them very relevant also for the design of serious games. This chapter provides a historical introduction and highlights aspects of pervasive games illustrated by examples. It continues with a discussion of what pervasive games are made of, how they are built, and which recurring issues have to be considered when building and deploying them. The chapter concludes with considerations about how pervasive games went from research to application and how that relates to budget and marketing efforts. Finally, it provides recommendations for further reading and some research questions towards using pervasive games in mobile educational research.

Keywords: Pervasive games · Location-based experiences · GPS · Mobile technology · Augmented learning · Technology enhanced learning · History · Authoring concepts · Design considerations

1 Introduction

Pervasive games are technology mediated experiences that take place in our everyday environment. Pervasive games are mostly played using mobile devices, such as smartphones, smart glasses, or other wearables. In contrast to traditional computer and console games, they generally do not require their players to move to and stay in a specific situation, like at an office-desktop or in front of a TV. Such settings might be a part of a pervasive game, but in that case there would normally be other mobile interfaces, as otherwise one would generally not speak of a pervasive game. Pervasive games are often designed for several players sharing the same game-space and are then inherently multi-player

© Springer International Publishing AG 2016
R. Dörner et al. (Eds.): Entertainment Computing and Serious Games, LNCS 9970, pp. 475–520, 2016.
DOI: 10.1007/978-3-319-46152-6_18

and networked. In contrast to traditional mobile games that are just played on a handheld and which otherwise offer no relation to the surrounding environment, pervasive games are mostly also location-based and thus provide for game interaction with regards to the current context of the user. From a technical perspective, pervasive games can thus be seen as bridging the physical and the digital in mobile entertainment [15], often by reimagining classic game designs with wireless positioning and communication technology on wearable devices and usually employing a range of different interfaces. From a social perspective, pervasive games are defined as extending Huizinga's magic circle of play [58] in spatial, social, and temporal dimensions [78, 79]. So instead of having to meet with other players for a limited period of time at a certain place, a pervasive game could potentially be played anytime, anywhere, and with anybody; even with people who are not knowingly part of the game.

Pervasive games are highly relevant to the topic of entertainment computing and serious games, as they provide a glimpse of the future today. While wireless mobile communication and orientation is already a reality for most of us with our smartphones, many serious games are still designed with a classic desktop-metaphor in mind. It is thus the purpose of this chapter to go beyond that current state of the art and provide a guided overview of pervasive games, summarize how they are made, and discuss their wider implications and limitations.

1.1 Background

Curiosity, playfulness, and a bit of faith in science fiction have fueled technological development in the past, and will likely continue to do so in the future. "What can we do with this technology?", or "how can we play with it?" are basic questions that circumvent the evolution of entertainment computing. With regards to pervasive gaming and our everyday use of technology, one must also add the question: "what is real and what is a game, what is fiction?". The more technology pervades our everyday lives, the more the line between reality and fiction gets blurred. This is not said to be a bad thing, but has rather been at the core of fiction and entertainment since ages. Telling a story and giving people a good time is what a theatre play is all about. If the audience forgets about their reality and all its problems for a while, they get immersed in the play. Later, with the movies, the same principle applied. People are getting immersed, or sucked into the story and forget about their surroundings for a moment. It has to be noted that a theatre play and a movie are usually staged in designated rooms. But what if one would not have to go to a specific place in order to get immersed? What if the content of the story would be applied as an additional layer to the world that

A seminal, albeit non-computing-related example of how this blending of reality and fiction might look like if taken to an extreme can be found in the 1997 movie *The Game* by David Fincher. If you have not seen it, yet, and are interested in this topic, it can be highly recommended! Of course, *The Game* was not a game, but a fictional movie, but it pioneered many of the ideas that can be found in later pervasive games, and have inspired some as well.

On a conceptual and social notion, this is the blurring of the line between in-game and out-of-game - as in real world - experiences (compare to Huizinga's magic circle), which is at the core of alternate reality games (ARGs). A seminal example of an ARG is the commercial video game *Majestic* by Electronic Arts from 2001, which was themed around a conspiracy theory (which generally works well). This game was played over a range of communication interfaces like websites, email, instant messages, phone, or fax. Players of *Majestic* had to solve different riddles that were given out in a pre-timed script in order to follow the complex story line. The game was paused in the wake of 9/11 and officially discontinued in 2002. Nevertheless, the reason for the discontinuation of the game is unlikely to be found in those historic events alone, but rather in problems with the game design, such as the pre-timed script which reportedly hindered participation, as the game was not "always on".

Relating back to the movie *The Game*, but on a more technical notion, it is similar to the blurring of the line between the virtual and the real environment which is at the core of pervasive games [15]. Pervasive games decouple their computer-mediated interaction from "going to a computer or console" and instead using the real world as a stage. Much like in a Flashmob, where musicians are entering a public space, e.g. a shopping mall, and slowly taking over the public attention with their professional performance, pervasive games blend into the world and people's daily routines by means of mobile and wireless technology, esp. positioning technology. They received a huge boost since precise GPS became publicly available on May 2nd, 2000 and subsequently became available in consumer electronics and smartphones.

The prototypical pervasive game with GPS is called *Geocaching*. It is a treasure hunt game that uses a simple set of rules centered around finding hidden caches via their GPS coordinates. It was proposed on the same day as GPS became publicly available and has been played by millions since then. The mechanism of *Geocaching* is to find those hidden locations, share small presents through the caches, and log one's personal contact with them via a paper notebook and the web. As caches are hidden, they must not be accidentally revealed to non-players who are referred to as muggles. This term is obviously inspired by the famous *Harry Potter* books by J.K. Rowling, where it denotes normal people who are not part of the magic circle.

1.2   Relation to Computing History and Serious Games

Serious games and entertainment computing, just like pervasive games, will eventually follow the general trend in computing history towards ubiquituous computing, a.k.a. ubicomp. Mark Weiser famously stated that "The most profound technologies are those that disappear. They weave themselves into the fabric of everyday life until they are indistinguishable from it" [114].

The evolution of computing technology and integrated circuits makes computers ever so faster, smaller, lighter, and thus more portable. This can be illustrated when relating the early computers from the 1940s, such as the Zuse Z3, the Colossus, or the ENIAC, to the computers as we know them today. Those early computers filled whole rooms and have been operated by many people to perform a single task. The more sophisticated main-frame (a.k.a. time-sharing) machines of the 1950s and 1960s still filled large parts of a room, but allowed for many users to use the computing power of that machine from remote via interactive terminals. Then came the home-computer revolution of the 1970s and 1980s which provided one computer per user; the personal computer as we still know it today, which stands on a desktop, and often actually takes the form of a notebook. People usually have many more computers and gadgets than one desktop. These post-desktop devices are untethered from the desk, as they are small and portable. Many of them today are smartphones or other wearables. They contain a remarkable number of sensors that can be used for communication and positioning purposes beyond telephony, like GPS, Wi-Fi, Bluetooth, etc. The smartphones of today are ubicomp device according to the notion of Mark Weiser, as they have become such an integral part of our everyday life that they are indistinguishable from it. With parts of the computing power, sensors and interfaces now moving over to smaller, even more portable and easier to reach devices, such as glasses, watches, fitness-belts, or clothing, it can be stated that the end of the line has not been reached, yet. Perhaps, at some point in the future, our current work on the Internet of Things will ultimately lead to smart dust, or controllable matter? An early mention of such a vision was noted in Ivan Sutherland's original article on *The Ultimate Display* [107] from 1965.

But regardless whether or not mankind will ever manage to build such an ultimate display, it is safe to state that serious games and entertainment computing will see a shift from the traditional desktop to more mobile interfaces in the foreseeable future and thus provide for a more untethered and situational support. As pervasive games have already paved this way over the past 15 years, they are thus highly relevant to the development of future games, in particular games with a purpose beyond pure entertainment, namely serious games.

1.3   Historical Backdrop

In order to better situate pervasive games within the context of traditional computer games and serious games, this section provides a short historical backdrop.

From Computer Games to Adgames. Some early forms of serious games can be found in the adgames of the 1990s. Commercial point and click adventure games, such as the ones by LucasArts or Sierra, were very popular on home computers at that time. It thus seemed like a natural evolution that companies and organizations started to pay for the development of games that were themed around their brand or cause, and then given away for free to their customers in order to get their attention and raise brand awareness. Seminal examples of the early game development and advertising agency The Art Department include games made for a German telecommunication company, food suppliers, several banks, several ministries, and even political parties. This evolution was peaked in popularity by the *Moorhuhn* game for a beverage company, which became a

German national phenomenon at the turn of the century and is an established brand in its own even until today. While these adgames are akin to pure product placement in games (like for example in many racing games or shooters), they are not just merely presenting a brand, but inviting for a more playful and thus more personable communication that is still effective in terms of transporting their message and not being filtered out on their way to the intended audience [105]. It is notable that they had been developed for the mass-market computers of their time and were all geared towards a young and tech-savvy audience.

From Adgames to Computer Based Training (CBT). Some serious games follow a similar pattern as these adgames, as they try to convey their message in a more playful and personable way. Similar designs can be found in the edutainment sector, where learning games for kids try to present educational content in an entertaining fashion. In a more "serious" context for grown-ups, this same approach is often called computer-based training (CBT), or simulation and training. CBT is one of the main strands of serious games and, for example, used in further education and on the job training [77].

From CBT to Mobile, Pervasive Gaming. In light of this perspective on the development of serious games based on traditional computer games in a desktop environment, it is then especially interesting to look at the move of computer games and entertainment into the mobile domain and see that as an analogy for the development of serious games on mobile devices. It is a common place that mobile phones and smart phones have become a mass phenomenon – they are even considered to be the 7th mass medium [4]. We carry them around and care for them. Mobile phones are thus intertwined with our everyday life and have become an integral part of it. They pervade it in this sense!

Researchers have long come up with the notion of pervasive computing, which is nowadays mostly used as a synonym for the already mentioned ubiquitous computing (the two prestigous and aptly named conferences on Pervasive Computing and Ubiquitous Computing even merged under the name Ubicomp in 2013). With relation to gaming, there have been a number of large research projects, such as the British EPSRC-funded Equator, and the EU-funded Integrated Project on Pervasive Gaming (IPerG). IPerG used an artist-led approach to designing new gaming experiences with a multitude of different human-computer interaction approaches beyond the traditional desktop metaphor. The consortium was led by the Swedish Institute of Computer Science SICS and included key partners from industry, such as Nokia Research and Sony NetServices, as well as academia, such as Nottingham University's Mixed Reality Lab, as well as artists from Blast Theory, their long-time cooperation partners. Building on their tradition of evolving simple and well-known gaming-mechanisms into new mobile experiences – their seminal *Can You See Me Know?* [11] was essentially a game of catch spread between online and on the street players – the team developed pervasive games that seemed remarkably simple. For example, *Single Story Building*, a personalized audio-story that made use of automated call-center software, or *Day of the Figurines*, a slow, narrative-driven game for mobile phones using text messaging [48].

2   Aspects and Examples of Pervasive Games

Broadly spoken, pervasive games use the world as a game board, both from a social, as well as from a technical perspective. To further illustrate what they are, this section provides a guided overview of examples that is categorized after certain pre-dominant aspects which are found in many pervasive games, usually as a mixture.

2.1   Adapt Concept to Space

The most straight forward and simplest approach to creating a pervasive game is to take an existing game-concept and adapt it to real-word space in combination with digital media. For example, the aforementioned *Geocaching* [27] is an adaptation of a treasure hunt (Fig. 1, left). The classic arcade game *Pacman* has seen several spatial adaptations over the years, such as *Human Pacman* [33], *Pacmanhattan* [68], or *Pac-Lan* [93], amongst others. Each of these works posed slightly different research questions and used different positioning technologies, but the basic mechanism was exactly the same as in the original game, i.e. eat pills and do not get caught by the ghosts, unless you temporarily switched mode by eating a certain power-up (Fig. 1, right).

 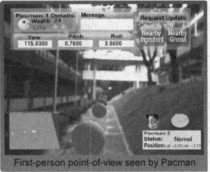

Fig. 1. *Geocaching* (left) with open cache (inset), Screenshot of *Human Pacman* (right);   (Credits: own, Mixed Reality Lab, National University of Singapore)

Similarly, *AR Quake* [108] is an adaptation of the 3D ego-shooter hit *Quake*. The game uses the same game-engine which was made possible as the original creators id Software made it available as open-source several years after the game's release. Based on that, the developers of *AR Quake* integrated bespoke positioning and orientation sensors, computer vision algorithms, and remodeled parts of their campus to match the digital game and the real environment.

As a third example for the concept-adaptation strategy, there was a series of so-called "geo-games" which was largely based on taking existing game-concepts, like *Poker*, or *Tic-Tac-Toe*, and applying them to a digital, mobile, and spatial context [100].

2.2 Location-Based Content Layer

Adding an additional, location-based content layer on top of the natural environment is a common approach for building pervasive games. It can already be found in the above mentioned *Geocaching*, but also in many more elaborate examples. Location-guides using additional informational layer over selected locations is one of the obvious and classic ideas that reaches back to even before precise GPS became publicly available. It is also a recurring topic ever since in various incarnations, ranging from tour-guides to museum-guides and everything in between. The early *Cyberguide* project from Georgia Tech researched into applications for location-aware computing. Using off-the-shelf technology, where possible, they built a number of prototypes. An infrared-based indoor-system was designed to guide visitors at the university's open day. Their early GPS-based outdoor system provided guidance on campus and also to local bars. Both systems employed the Apple Newton, which was an early PDA and as such a precursor to the smartphones and mobile phones of today [2]. Other notable early systems include the *Touring Machine* from the MARS project [44], the *Lancaster GUIDE* [34], which provided for campus tours and city tours respectively. The electronic guide *Hippie* is an early application for an adaptive information system in a museum setting [91]. More recent studies covered softer aspects, such as gamifying whole science centre visits [17] and group interactions in museum visits [110].

As well audio-clips can provide a rich and relatively easy to produce content layer. The seminal *Riot! 1831* was a mobile audio experience that was staged at Queen Square in Bristol for three weeks in 2004. During its history, the square had seen a number of riots and the audio-experience was designed to eavesdrop on a "sea of voices" [95], short location-based audio-clips that told small parts of the story of one particular riot in 1831 and which were solely triggered and volume-controlled based on GPS-coordinate proximity. Similar designs have also been reported in the *Mobile Urban Drama* [53].

In gamified or game-based projects riddles are a common interaction mechanic that works well in a range of secretive, conspiracy- or crime-driven narratives. Much like in the classic Lucasarts and Sierra point & click computer adventure games of the 1980s and 1990s [51], players would have to go to certain locations and perform actions of various kinds in order to advance the story-line of the game. For example, players of *Inspector Tripton* (see Fig. 2) were roaming pre-defined areas of Berlin to interrogate virtual characters in a murder-mystery plot, while at the same time learning more about the city. The game used stylised 2D images for the characters which were super-imposed on a live-camera view as a simple form of Augmented Reality. Similarly, players of *Murder at Harvard* were roaming the area of Harvard to unfold the location-based story-line which was presented with video-clips.

Fig. 2. Scene from *Inspector Tripton*; (Credits: Sprylab)

Claiming territory is another typical interaction mechanic that works particularly well with pervasive games, esp. when they are multi-player games. Here, the story-line is usually less location-specific than with the audio and riddle examples, and uses the world as playground. The seminal *Noderunner*, an artistically-inspired race game, asked participants to find free Wi-Fi hot-spots, take a picture of the area and submit it digitally via the hot-spot to a central server for scoring and claiming that spot on a spectator interface. *Mogi* was an early and relatively widely deployed collection game in Japan. Much like in *Geocaching*, player could find resources at real world locations, but here they were digital resources that players could also trade with other players. They could also make friends with other players and ask them to collect something for them [61]. Although *Mogi* ultimately failed due to expensive mobile-data tariffs in the early days of the mobile Internet, similar designs later followed with much more success. Depending on their personal preference for either fantasy, futuristic, or comic scenarios, players later preferred games like *Parallel Kingdom*, *Ingress*, or *Pokémon Go*, which had millions of players.

2.3 Multi-Player

Botfighters was one of the first commercial location-based games. It was a massively multi-player online role-playing game that utilized the location-based aspect offered by mobile phones and was played via SMS [39]. Player could configure their *BattleTech*-like robots on a website and then take them to battle with other players' robots on the streets. Other than *The Majestic*, this game was always on, so players might get attacked and receive messages in the middle of the night. Although *Botfighters* is also a good example of how an engaging pervasive game design might work with as little as a text-display, it is the marketing strategy that is most striking about the game. Long before GPS-enabled smart phones became available, the game launched via the mobile phone operators, who would look up their players' positions using operator-based positioning.

The game was launched in 2001 and had 40.000 registered. It was played in Sweden, Finland, Ireland, Russia, and China.

2.4   Mix Online and on the Streets (with Performers)

This approach is going one step further than simply adapting an existing concept for the location-based space on mobile devices. The idea here is to provide at least two interfaces that link the traditional with the new setting. A good example of this is *Can You See Me Now?* (*CYSMN*) which is a digital adaptation of a game of catch. The game is spread between online players, operating from remote via a Shockwave 3D game-world in their browser, and runners on the street that are equipped with GPS-enabled mobile devices and are hunting the online players (see Fig. 3, left). Using their additional walkie-talkie communication channel, the runners broadcast a live audio-stream and verbally performing in the sense that they greet each online personally once they decided to catch him, which greatly enhanced the overall experience [11].

CYSMN was designed in co-operation with a group of digital performance artists that have a background in theater. It therefore emphasized on the performative qualities in the sense that it can be seen as a stage-performace that has been spilled out onto the city streets and its online counterpart. The experience is critically acclaimed as an archetypal example of this genre. Later works, such as *Uncle Roy All Around You* (Fig. 3, right) extended on this by also providing mobile, on-the-street interfaces for the players themselves, and requiring cooperation between the online and on the street players [36].

Fig. 3. Performer on the street in *Can You See Me Now?* (left), Player in the office in *Uncle Roy All Around You* (right); (Credits: Blast Theory)

2.5   Acting It Out

Acting is an inevitable consequence of the aforementioned approaches. While traditional online multi-player games generally separate their players' online beings and social context from their physical bodies and actual social context (which can lead to its own set of problems, as some parents will know), pervasive game designers actually have to consider the physical context of their players as part of their design responsibility, as those games are staged in the world around us, which has people in it.

Maybe the players should keep the magic circle closed and not introduce the secret game to bystanders? This approach can be seen in *Geocaching*, where the location of the cache must under no circumstances be revealed to the "muggles". As a side-effect, players of geocaching, or at least those that are bad actors, can sometimes be spotted intensively searching for something by walking around using their smart phones as a guide; and then suddenly, when they found what they were looking for and now became mindfully aware of the muggles around them, starting to look remarkably unconspicious. Variations of this espionage-like theme can be found in other pervasive experiences, e.g. in *Uncle Roy All Around You*, where players were sometimes asked to shadow passer-bys without them noticing, or searching for clues in offices (see Fig. 3, right).

Instead of hiding the magic circle of the game, one might also purposefully amplify the effect of staging the game in a public setting [94]. Notions of this can be found in the design of *Rider Spoke*, a touring pervasive experience for cyclists that is played in a city at dusk [89]. Here, riders would stop their bike for recording answers to guided questions. There is an element of acting in the answers they give, as they will become part of the piece and available for other riders to listen. And there is another element of the riders phyically standing with their bike in a city at dusk that can be witnessed by bystanders, so that the player become performers themselves.

A specific form of this category are the so-called technology enhanced live action role-playing games (LARP). They are a variation of traditional LARPs where players impersonate their game-characters dressed up in historic costumes and which are often staged at fitting locations, like a medieval castle, or in the woods. More futuristic or para-normal scenarios lend themselves to using technological artifacts. A game called *Momentum* was staged in and around an abandoned nuclear reactor in Stockholm, Sweden. In there, players could contact dead people through technical interfaces such as the Electronic Voice Phenomenon which was attached to an old steel-bed on which players had to strap themselves [87, pp. 59–63]. Another technology enhanced LARP is the *Monitor Celestra*, which was situated in the Battlestar Galactica universe and physically staged on an abandoned Battle Ship [16]. LARPs are pre-dominantly conceived and played in Scandinavian countries, but can also be found in other countries. Although *Momentum* made a decent effort of expanding the magic circle in all three dimensions in order to be a pervasive game, LARPs are usually not very pervasive in this sense: they are often staged for a fixed time-frame at a given location, and are only accessible for registered players.

2.6   Alternate Reality Games

While the commercial game *The Majestic* had some problems to survive as a paid-for experience, its novel cross-media-design lived on in a number of similar experiences that were paid for from a big marketing budget. These campaign experiences were based on blurring the line between reality and game content for the players, making it hard to tell what was real and what was fictional. These so-called alternate reality games are made to create a high player involvement and experience. Their goal is to give its players something exclusive and something that they can identify themselves with, mostly by tapping into the story-lines of the advertised product, such as a movie. And because of that exclusivity and identification aspects, alternate reality games are leading players to continue and amplify the initial media campaign on their own channels, thus ultimately turning it into a viral campaign, and ideally into a hype.

The Beast by Microsoft was an early such cross-media campaign-game that prepared the media ground for the release of the 2001 Steven Spielberg movie A.I. - Artificial Intelligence. The campaign was doing marketing across a number of channels, including web-sites, email, phone, fax, and live events. According to the authors' own website, the campaign reached 3 million active participants and generated 300 millon page impressions for the movie. The same team later formed a company called 42 entertainment and created a similar campaign called *I Love Bees* that supported the launch of the Microsoft X-Box game *Halo 2*. The campaign was triggered by a short mention' of the project website (www.ilovebees. com) at the end of the *Halo 2* trailer. While the website appeared to be a bee farmers site at first sight, which did not make sense in the context of a multi-million dollar tech-marketing campaign, it looked hacked at closer inspection. Participants soon found out that the website revealed a list of coded coordinates and time-stamps that would lead players to public phone booths (see Fig. 4, left). Apparently the phones were ringing at the given time, which was also quickly discovered by the community. The community organized themselves to capture every call, as they advanced the story-line bit by bit. The company continued to design similar viral marketing campaigns on big budgets, amongst others for movies like Disney's *TRON: Legacy* (see Fig. 4, right) or Warner Brothers' *The Dark Knight*, but also for car-makers and other organizations.

2.7   Additional Interfaces

Pervasive Games are not fixed to any particular interface technology. Usually any combination of sensing, communication, and digital human-computer interface provides for a valid technological basis. Alternate reality games were built on this to a certain extent and provided a range of interfaces, usually utilizing well established mass-communication channels. Other, more research-oriented demonstrators, were built on more bespoke technology.

The Epidemic Menace was an event-based pervasive game that was designed to research into cross-media interaction by incorporating a range of different interfaces into the same game-space. The story was themed around a campus

Fig. 4. Players taking a call at a public phone booth in *I love Bees* (left), secret venue "Flynn's Arcade" in the *Flynn Lives* campaign for *TRON: Legacy* (right); (Credits: Andrew Sorcini, Loren Javier)

which was virtually infected with deadly viruses by a villain scientist. The players were divided into two groups and acted as SWAT teams of medical experts that had to liberate the campus. The available game interfaces included two GPS-enabled mobile interfaces (one of them a *Ghostbusters-like* mobile Augmented Reality kit with smart glasses that could destroy the virus), a large interactive touch-board with a map overview, instant-messaging, security cameras with overlaid AR graphics, and a Sony Aibo robot-dog (see Fig. 5). The game also included live-actors and video clues, and was staged at an actual science campus around Castle Birlinghoven in Germany. [70,115].

Fig. 5. Some of the player interfaces in *Epidemic Menace*: mobile AR with GPS and smart glasses (left), audio with GPS (middle), instant-messaging with text and audio at the headquarter (right); (Credits: Fraunhofer FIT)

2.8   Adaptive Interfaces

Adding additional interfaces provides for more flexibility and variety, but does not automatically reduce the physical, cognitive, and social affordances required to interact with a system. The related adaptive interfaces try to mitigate these affordances and adapt to the context and routine of the user.

Fig. 6. *Day of the Figurines* game-board (left), *Professor Tanda* calling (right); (Credits: Blast Theory & Fraunhofer FIT, Blast Theory)

Adapting to the daily routine is a typical approach. The aforementioned *Day of the Figurines* was an SMS-based game for mobile phones that was staged before smart-phone use became ubiquitous. It was very different from prior pervasive gaming designs, because participants could play it anytime from their private phones for a prolonged time of 24 days by just sending and receiving text messages. The game was staged multiple times and usually installed in a cultural venue. The fictional game-world of a decaying town with many different locations and events became tangible at the venue where players were required to be present at least once at the beginning, select their figurine and place it on the game-board (Fig. 6, left). Subsequent interaction was then via SMS. Operators updated the players virtual positions on the physical game-board at every hour, performing like croupiers.

In a similar vein, *Prof Tanda's Guess-A-Ware*, an early context-aware smartphone game, tried to lure its participants into conducting ecologically themed activities and quizzes. The game would call its participants several times a day (Fig. 6, right), but they could decide if they wanted to interact at that time or deny the call [29]. Amongst others, this allowed the game to effectively learn opportune moments for interaction on private smartphones. This field was later further studied, trying to understand receptivity to interruptions in mobile human-computer interaction [45].

More mundanely, some game interfaces were designed to adapt to the environment of the player, i.e. weather and time-of-day. Early notions of this can be found in the 1999 Sega Dreamcast game *Shenmue*, where time and weather had an influence on the game world and its characters. In pervasive gaming, this principle was later applied in *Epidemic Menace*, where wind-direction and temperature affected the spread of the virtual viruses by means of live weather-data being incorporated into the game. An extreme counter-example, where the link between actual weather and game tasks has not been made (which admittedly is the rule rather than the exception), can be found with *I Love Bees*. The urge to advance in the game must have been quite strong, as one person reportedly even braved a Florida hurricane in order to take a call from the game [40]!

More recently, there have been strands of work trying to adopt to the user themselves. Such projects are usually trying to figure certain bits of information about the user in an attempt to offer them "a more personalized" experience. We put this phrase in quotes, as it also has a very commercial side, which is often overseen in public discourse. Not speaking about intelligence services, who are obviously active in this field by their very nature, this is of course what companies have been doing for a long time: trying to find out more about their customers. And this is what big Internet companies are doing all the time: profiling their users on a massive scale to create valuable meta-data (a.k.a. Big Data). On a smaller scale, and coming back to the topic, similar techniques have been used to do personality profiling in the video- and questionnaire-driven, artistically-inspired smartphone-app *Karen is my life coach* [1].

2.9 Augmented Learning

Learning more about the user's context can also help to acustom a user-interface to their current needs and provide them with a personalized learning environment [121]. Coupled with findings from pervasive gaming research and mobile computing technology, this provides the means for augmented learning. While this term has been increasingly used in recent years since the 2000s [63, 103], presumably facilitated by the fact that the required mobile technology for augmenting learning was readily available, the concept behind it actually is a recurrent theme that guided innovations in computing through the 20th century! It can be found in Vannevar Bush's initial idea of the *Memex* from 1945 [23], a (theoretical) device which stores an individual's documents and communication, as well as in Douglas Engelbart's guiding framework on augmenting the human intellect from 1962 [41] which paved the way to his foundational 1968 "mother of all demos" where he presented the essential elements of personal computing as we know it today [69]. In 1972 Alan Kay wrote a comprehensive description of *Dynabook* a portable suite of hardware, software, programming tools and services offering an ultimate creative environment for kids of all ages. *Dynabook* became an inspiration for Nicholas Negroponte's *One Laptop per Child* project, but was never constructed. Kay has repeatedly stated that despite the technological progress (portable laptops, tablets and smartphones), our tools lack software supporting creative learning through "symmetric authoring and consuming" which was the primary intent of *Dynabook*. The idea of augmenting the human intellect via technology is also core to the work of Fred Brooks, who compared the computer scientist to a toolsmith that makes tools for intelligence amplification. He also stated the thesis that "IA > AI", i.e. that intelligence amplification systems will always outperform artificial intelligence [20].

With this background in mind, there are a number of augmented mobile learning experiences with different causes. From a technical perspective, they can be broadly divided into learning experiences that primarily rely on Augmented Reality, and those that rely on location-based triggers and physical movement.

Augmented Reality. A seminal example from the first category is Mark Billinghurst's *Magic Book*, which provided a digitally augmented view of a physical book through a hand held device [18], e.g. for teaching science facts to children. Another typical and early example is the *AR-PDA*, which used a Personal Digital Assistant (PDA) as a magic lens to provide additional information about consumer products. This included examples to learn about how a digital camera worked, and configuration options for an integrated oven [50]. In the industrial application domain, projects like ARVIKA [49] and AVILUS [101] researched and created prototypes for job-related learning support, e.g. visualisation of machine data to workers and engineers alike. Augmented Reality technology was also used to facilitate learning for school children in museums [102] as well as in class [22], by visualising complex physical relations, providing a tangible interface to modifying them, and seeing the effect of the manipulation right away. The examples depicted in the figure below show a model wing in a science centre as well as a miniature version thereof (created through 3D printing) for use in school classes called *Science Centre To Go*. In both versions, the user can modify the angle of the wing in relation to the airstream and see the resulting forces that allow a plane to fly, thus providing a playful direct manipulation interface to the formulas of the Bernoulli effect (Fig. 7).

Fig. 7. AR on a Science Centre exhibit of a wing (left), *Science Centre To Go* (right); (Credits: Fraunhofer FIT)

Mobile, Location-Based Experiences. In the second category, there are a number of examples that studied pervasive learning experiences. *Savannah* was an educational pervasive game played by groups of school children on their sports ground (Fig. 8). The ground was virtually divided into seperate areas that were meant to represent different areas in a virtual savannah. The children were equipped with GPS-enabled and networked mobile computers; one per child. They were acting as little lions and had to survive in their virtual environment, which included finding water and hunting for prey. Small prey could be caught by a single child, but the more interesting prey required a coordinated attack from several children in the same location [15]. *EcoPhone* by Danish milk company Arla was a QR-code based rally that users could play on their own smartphones during their visit to an organic farm. When scanning those tags at five designated locations, the app provided comic-strips to explain how the farm worked from the perspective of the cow, and quizzes and polls as further interaction metaphors. The location-based experience was built as part of a larger campaign, advertised on the milk cartons in advance, and the content later presented to a wider audience without requiring to be on location [53]. Also in the food domain, the *MILE* project strives to educate teenagers about nutrition via a range of missions. Each mission is themed, e.g. about bread-making, and integrated into a guided extra-curricular activity that is endorsed by a public good-food campaign. Volunteers are preparing the missions using an authoring tool that they have been trained to use and participating teenagers are welcome for an afternoon of playful mobile learning and eating [99].

Fig. 8. *Savannah* trial, showcasing positioning technology problems; (Credits: Mixed Reality Lab, University of Nottingham)

Also from this category are a number noise and pollution monitoring projects that involve their players in experiments, data-collection, and reflection. Participating schools involved children from primary and secondary schools in environmental data-collection, such as pollution and temperature, and presentation of the geo-coded results [31]. Similarly, but with an artistic background, *Bio-Mapping.net* produced digital maps annotated with biosensed-data of its users, paired with their comments.

Learning Theories in Pervasive Gaming. Pervasive games (in the educational field sometimes just called location-based games) might play an important role in formal and non-formal education in the future. Mobile devices allow educators to bring additional information and new immersive activities to the field. Thanks to mobile and augmented reality technologies, the user experience becomes more complex and fluid at the same time. The learning process grows from continuous interaction between the environment, technology and learners' prior knowledge. Their mutual diffusions and consequences are sometimes hard to control, but as many studies indicated [35, 42, 64, 96], in a well modeled and contextualized augmented environment highly stimulating and knowledge-rich experiences can occur. In such situation "[...] all learning takes place within a specific context and the quality of the learning is a result of interactions among the people, places, objects, processes, and culture within and relative to that given context" [103]. Most studies focusing on pervasive or augmented learning build on the theory of constructivism and situated learning. Learning activities following the principles of situated learning draw upon previous experience and prior knowledge of the learner, and often are problem-based. These problems should be inherently meaningful and motivating to the people involved [64]. Situated learning firmly embedded in real-world context and/or the community around the activity. Many succesfull games are connected with the places that are very well known to their players. The scenario of the game *Environmental Detectives* [64]was set into the players' university campus and positioned them into the role of environmental scientists who need in the time limit of 90 min indicate a possible cause of new toxin just found in the campus groundwater. In *Mad City Mystery* (sometimes called augmented mystery game by its authors; [104]) a dead body is found in the city lake. Players need to interview virtual characters to get more clues about this mysterious case. In this game each student gets a different role receiving different information, so it is impossible to finish the game without collaboration.

The central claims of situated learning are as follows:

1. action is grounded in the concrete situation in which it occurs
2. knowledge does not transfer between tasks
3. training by abstraction is of little use
4. instruction must be done in complex, social environments [7].

In such experience-based learning mostly little information is fed in the players by their devices, they rather must create that knowledge and understanding through exploration [63]. Anderson et al. [7] point out that not all those characteristics support better knowledge acquisition and transfer as it is overstressed [5, 103]. Research repeatedly indicates that minimally guided learning is less effective than instructional approaches placing a strong emphasis on guidance of the student learning process. Furthermore some studies show that in less guided approaches students generate more elaborate explanations, but less coherent and with more errors. It as well seems that knowledge is more linked with the specific learning content and the knowledge transfer is not very effective [62]. Accordingly, designers or implementers of educational pervasive games should strongly focus on efficient instructional design and learning assessment.

Nevertheless, many evaluation studies show promising data on location-based games used in different areas of learning, for example context-aware language learning [56], knowledge acquisition [35, 43, 57], academic competencies [104], and specific learning motivation [26, 35, 57].

2.10   Health and Fitness Games

The health and fitness domain is another interesting category of serious pervasive games. Continuing the tradition of computer supported collaborative work
(CSCW), computer supported collaborative play (CSCP) [60] and computer
supported collaborative sports (CSCS) [122] try to link players in playful and
physical activities, rather than work. Just like CSCW is providing collaboration
support over a distance (as well as co-located), many examples are striving to
facilitate sports over a distance [81].

Using the same technology and mechanics, and additionally incorporating
heart-rate sensors, pervasive games like '*Ere be Dragons* (a.k.a. *Heartlands* later
on) were an early venture into the domain of heartfelt gaming, i.e. incorporating
sensor-data from the participants as input into the game [37]. '*Ere be dragons*
sought to research into the use of pervasive gaming to get people "their daily
20 min" of exercise and to listen to their heart-beat. Their physical movements,
tracked via GPS, basically acted as the game controller, and their hearts were
the fire button. In order to build territory in the game, the heart-rate had to
be in the optimum range. And in order to conquer territory from other players,
one's heart had to go faster than the other's. The game also specifically included
stages that required the player to calm down and reduce their heart-rate. The
game had an artistic, as well as a medical side. Players of different age and fitness
levels could compete against each other, as the game employed a notion of an age-
related optimum heart-rate-range like a golf handicap. The game also included
a spectator interface, so that people could witness the game going on outside
from inside the venue. Likewise, but much more reduced, the artistic running
experience *I seek the nerves under your skin* presents a poem to the player, but
only when they physically move around to keep it alive. It is noteworthy that
it is impossible to experience the whole poem, as the requirements are steadily
increasing, and so basically everyone fails at the end [74].

3   Discussion

The above list of pervasive games and best practice examples is by no means
complete. Nevertheless it should provide a general idea and give a fair overview
of the possibilities. It can thus serve as the basis for the following discussion.

So it is now time to look behind the curtain and see what these pervasive
applications are made of, how they are built, and which recurring issues have to
be considered when building and deploying them.

3.1   Enabling Technologies

Although GPS-enabled smartphones with data connectivity are the obvious platform choice for building pervasive games, they are not the only one.

Mobile Devices. When it comes to untethered, mobile devices with computational power, smartphones and tablets are the obvious choice. And this is unlikely to change anytime soon. However, other smart wearables are currently on the uptake, such as glasses, or wrist watches; and others will follow. Researchers have already begun turning other accessories into pervasive computing devices, such as shoes, belts, gloves, rings, or umbrellas. Smart textiles look like a promising new avenue as well, maybe even chip implants at some point.

Positioning Technology. GPS - the Global Positioning System - is certainly the most well-known positioning technology of today. This is due to the fact that it was the first publicly available global navigation satellite system (GNSS). Developed by the U.S. Department of Defense, it was developed since the 1970s as a successor to the Transit system. GPS reached full operational capability in 1995 and was initially reserved for military use. This changed when U.S. president Bill Clinton announced on May 1st 2000 that the selective availability of GPS would be turned off and the system became publicly available the day after. Other notable global navigation satellite systems that are currently being build are the Russian GLONASS, the Chinese BeiDou, or the European GALILEO. Their importance will raise once they reach their full operational capacity.

But even with this variety of GNSS in the world, it is important to understand that other positioning technologies exist and can be readily used today. Basically anything that emits a signal that can be received and interpreted can act as positioning technology. This especially includes other radio-based system, such as wireless local area networks (WLAN), GSM Cell-ID, or Bluetooth which can all be processed on modern smartphones and used to determine proximity. The latest Bluetooth Low Energy standard also supports the use of so-called Beacons, which are small battery powered transmitters that can be placed at designated locations and whose signals can be received and processed by current smart phones. Other notable, radio-based technologies include wireless personal area network (WPAN), radio-frequency identification (RFID), near-field communication (NFC), and ZigBee.

Apart from radio-signals, computer vision based approaches, like QR-Codes, marker-based augmented reality and natural feature-tracking can be easily used for working out a position coordinate that is relative to a point of reference. This is not necessarily an absolute coordinate that is unique to the whole planet, like with GPS. But that might not be required, and GPS is not as universal as it might sound. GPS is not very precise when it comes to determining altitude, so it could not be used to distinguish between different floors on a building, not even in theory. Because in practice, GPS requires a direct line of sight to the satellites and thus does not work indoors!

In their 2005 study [67], the Place Lab project reported on an experiment that tested the availability of three positioning technologists throughout the daily routines of their participants. They concluded that GPS would only produce a usable coordinate reading in 4.5 % of their participants' daily time, opposed to 99.6 % for GSM, and 94.5 % for WLAN. In essence: GPS does not provide a positioning solution for most of our daily time. Technologies like GSM, WLAN, and Bluetooth usually provide a more coarse grained position reading. But in practice this is generally not a problem. The seminal Cyberguide and GUIDE projects [2,34] already found that

1. positioning technology does not have to be overly precise in order to effectively support a location-based experience
2. the context of the current location is often more important than absolute position coordinates

It is often more interesting to know what somebody is looking at than to get a "high" precision coordinate reading.

Communication Technology. Sending data from A to B became much easier with the ubiquitous availability of wireless networking such as WLAN, or Bluetooth. But it is often overlooked that these network connections are not always available. This is similar to the argument stated above about the daily availability of positioning technology. The state of disconnection in wireless communication technology must not be seen as an insignificant flaw or a temporary error. Much rather, it is an inherent characteristic feature of wireless networking and must be embraced in the design of systems [28]. This means that systems with mobile clients should not break when a network disconnection occurs. The devices will eventually reconnect later, so state synchronisation could possibly be post-poned until then by using a local buffer.

Moreoever, there is a cost-factor involved, as wireless network bandwidth is a limited resource and usually paid-for, at least on the mobile web. Users are unlikely to appreciate an app that carelessly eats up their bandwidth allowance and forces them to surf slower or pay more for the rest of the month.

3.2   Building

Like with any game development process, building a pervasive game requires a number of different skills, such as game design, programming, asset creation, and content authoring. The mobile target platform is also usually not the only platform that has to be developed for, as a typical system usually includes a server component, and maybe even a desktop component. There is no single way to build this magnitude of examples, but some recurring tasks can be identified, some of which are even supported by specialised tools.

Programming. With the rapid pace of development in mobile computing, and personal preference, it is impossible to give the definite advice with regards to programming languages. One would be generally well advised to use a programming language that is officially recommended for the platform in question, regardless of wether it is a compiled or interpreted language, or if it runs directly on an actual CPU or in a virtual machine, such as CLR, JVM, or ART.

Programming for all aspects of a distributed system, like a pervasive game, then still requires a lot of different components and their associated tricks to be mastered. This usually includes a selection of different programming languages (Java, Objective-C, C#, PHP, Perl, Python, Ruby, JavaScript, etc.), data-exchange formats (XML, JSON, plain text), databases, multi-media asset formats, user-interface toolkits, web application frameworks, and device administration. Mastering this mountain of technology can be difficult to handle for small teams which could even be groups of students. Different strategies have been proposed to tackle this complexity problem in an ever-changing landscape: "Prioritise strong server support", "Support very flexible communication", "Use a loosely coupled software approach", "Migrate functionality from the server to more capable handsets" [52], and "Strive for using a single programming language for all parts of the distributed system" [85].

Programming is required, because the programming task cannot be underestimated when building pervasive games (the same probably true for any software-related project). There might be tools that help you out, but they are the equivalent of good kitchen tools and recipes vs. the state of being a kitchen chef, i.e. a person that learned the tricks of the trade and thus can put it to creative use, also under new conditions. Just using the frying pan of a famous chef do not make you a good cook. The same is true for complex software that somebody else wrote. If you don not know what that piece of code does, be it a library, a framework, or just a code-snippet, you are unlikely to get anything out from simply using it. You have to learn it, or have somebody else on the team who has the required know-how. Building a pervasive game often involves developing for new platforms. This naturally limits the tool-support in those early phases to a working development environment and compiler tool-chain.

Game Design. Despite all technicalities, designing pervasive games should not be done only with a technology in mind. Technology serves as a tool to mediate content or an experience to the player. Wetzel et al. [119] point out that the choice of technology should as well respect ambience, time period and theme of the game.

High augmentation in such games is not a need, contrary interaction with real environment is a valuable part of the experience; location and physical objects should serve as an integral part of the pervasive game playground. The game design should be driven by the aim to support a fluid interaction across the physical and the digital domains [83]. Players may also enjoy interacting with virtual characters as well with other players, non-players and actors [115].

Within educational pervasive games, the designers need to consider that the nature environment provides many unexpected stimulus thus the learning experience cannot be completely controlled, the players are in the position of independent learners so not the application provides learning outcomes but the individual outdoor experience itself. For this reason the tasks should be designed as open-ended challenges or stories [63,64] that give the players a freedom to enfold the activity with their preliminary knowledge and individual outdoor experience.

Content Creation. Once the game design has been made and cross-checked with the technical feasibility, the time has come for content creation. This includes all visible and audible digital assets, such as text, pictures, videos, 3D objects and animations. All of this data needs to be created in available programs that are fit for the purpose. Since the range of programs on the mass-market is so vast and everyone has their favourite tools, we are not even trying to highlight any particular programs or approaches. Much rather, it is more interesting to consider the process of creation in a team, and how teams of game developers are organising themselves when putting it all together [65].

3.3   Authoring Concepts

That being said, there are a number of authoring concepts that can help building pervasive games and putting their content into structure. As these are often conceived as location-based experiences, the underlying principle of these approaches are mostly similar. It generally consists of a map of the area of interest on which the author marks smaller areas of interest that trigger further audio-visual content. The triggering is often done if the user approaches those trigger zones, interacts within them, or leaves again. GPS is still the most used technology for defining such trigger zones (usually a point and a radius) in a location-based context, but other sensors are gaining more importance, as outlined above. Nevertheless, the basic concept also applies to the authoring of Augmented Reality experiences. The following section provides a general overview of the main concepts.

Trigger-Zones on Maps. With the advent of web-based mapping tools came the option to place points of interest (POI) on them, export the structured data somehow, and use that as a simple authoring solution. While chronologically, digital online maps only became available after some of the later presented approaches, they provide for the simplest logical form of spatial authoring in the sense of defining areas on maps. Such authored data can be easily exported to the XML-based KML format. KML stands for Keyhole Markup Language as Keyhole was the name of a company that Google acquired in 2004 and which developed a desktop program that is now known as Google Earth. Since then, the programm did not only become widely used, but also received a web-based compagnion: Google Maps. Moreover, KML became an official standard of the Open Geospatial Consortium (OGC).

Figure 9 shows a typical view with POIs defined for the cycle-based experience *The Sillitoe Trail* in Google Earth and Google Maps. An account of how a location-based audio-tour has been devised using these tools is provided by Rowland et al. [97].

Trigger-Zones on Maps with Full Tool Support. Figure 10 shows a screenshot of the seminal Mobile Bristol authoring tool, a.k.a. *Mediascapes* [59]. It consists of several trigger-zones defined on top of a map of. This desktop authoring

Fig. 9. POIs from *The Sillitoe Trail* on Google Earth (left), and Google Maps (right)

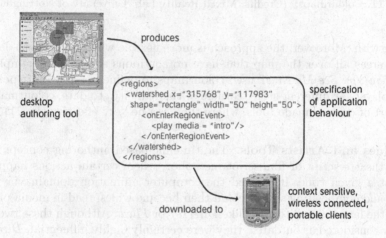

Fig. 10. *Mediascapes* workflow; (Credits: HP Labs and University of Bristol)

tool produces an XML-file that contains all trigger- and event-logic and thus specifies the application behaviour. This file and the associated media can then be downloaded into a player-app on mobile devices and played back on location.

Mediascapes is an early example of fully integrated authoring and deployment solution that spans desktop, server, and mobile components. Other, very similar examples are *CAERUS* [82], *Tidy City* [118], and *ARIS* [55].

Colourmaps. Colourmaps allow for content configuration by painting with different colours on geo-referenced bitmaps with indexed palettes [46]. The idea is inspired by artist tools like Photoshop that allow working with different layers of graphical information. The colourmap is usually aligned on top of a map-layer. The limited number of colours in the indexed palette (usually 256) is not a problem as the number of different regions that need to be defined is typically a lot lower. The big advantage of using colourmaps over vector-based tools like Mediascapes is that it allows artists to work with the tools that they are already

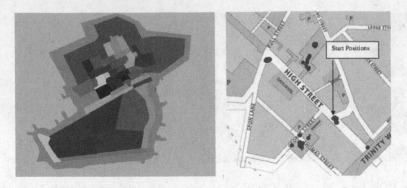

Fig. 11. Colourmaps; (Credits: Mixed Reality Lab, University of Nottingham)

familiar with. Moreover, the approach is more flexible when it comes to defining similar areas all over the map that have no continous shape. For example, the game *Can You See Me Now?* used colourmaps to define possible start-points of online players at different street corners of the real city. To date, colourmaps are only part of custom made tools, where they can be very effective (Fig. 11).

Timelines and Artists Tools. The timeline-based authoring concept stems from a theatre-script or film-script metaphor, where certain actions happen on stage at a given time. It entered the computer animation domain via video-editing and compositing software and then became widespread in media production in the late 1990s with tools like *Director* or *Flash*. Although these two tools are now considered as outdated, they were certainly highly influential. *Director's* flexible architecture allowed researchers to integrate AR tracking via an extension, thus providing for a rich authoring tool for marker-based AR-experiences called the *Designer's Augmented Reality Toolkit* [71]. With *Flash* being far more popular than *Director*, it naturally found its way to pervasive game creation as well. Although there were also *Flash*-based *AR Toolkit* bindings like *FLAR-ToolKit*, *Flash* has arguably been mostly used to create good-looking user-interfaces on mobile devices in pervasive games on pre-iPhone mobile devices, e.g. on a Nokia N800 tablet in *Rider Spoke* [30,89]. The main advantage, again, was that the tool was already familiar to the artists and so they could put it to good use.

Nowadays, the artist tool that is probably most oftenly for the same reasons is *Unity 3D*. Being a very graphical tool, it does not support all features of mobile devices, but is especially useful for authoring 3D content for desktop and mobile devices. *Unity 3D* is often used to create VR and AR content, also for current generation head mounted displays like the Oculus Rift or the GearVR.

Web-Based Authoring. With the advent of browser-based maps through Open Street Map since 2004 and Google Maps since 2005, the authoring of location-based content on maps naturally also moved into the browser. While a

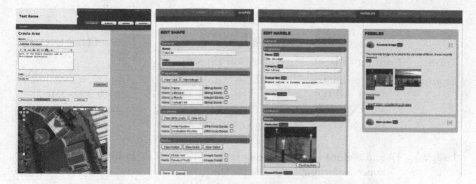

Fig. 12. *Game Creator* (left), *TOTEM.Designer* (right); (Credits: Swedish Institute of Computer Science, Fraunhofer FIT)

browser-based interface cannot provide the full flexibility of a custom-made desktop program, its ease of use outweights that disadvantage. Potential users just need a browser and register on the website, without further software installation. The required map-data is loaded on demand, and the resulting configuration is stored in the web, usually in a standard format like XML, CSV or JSON. Google Maps itself can and has been used to configure points of interest for location-based content, but it lacks support for any more sophisticated actions. Specialised tools like *Game Creator* [111] or *TOTEM.Designer* [116] allow for importing digital media assets like images, sounds, videos, or 3D objects, and wiring them together by associating these assets to certain locations and other trigger conditions (Fig. 12).

The Cycle of Creation. Like all other tools, authoring tools for pervasive games are created with the intent to facilitate certain recurring tasks. Unfortunately, with ever improving technology those tasks are often shifting slightly so that they are not as tight a fit like a hammer and a nail. The cycle of creation in computer game programming usually starts with making it work in the first place and see if it is well received, then eventually facilitating certain tasks when doing it again. With home-computer games, archetypical tools are the *Shoot Em Up Construction Kit* (*SEUCK*), the *Scripting Utility for Maniac Mansion* (*SCUMM*), or the many popular *Doom* level editors. These tools make it a lot easier to create content for the game-engines that they are associated with. But they cannot be used to create different things on new platforms. This is where programming is required again and why there are by large no games where no programmer was involved. And this is especially true for pervasive games which are targeting ever changing hardware.

3.4   Considerations for the Design Process

This section, as well as the following sections, provides an overview of relevant findings that circumvent the design and the staging of pervasive games.

Table 1. Position, location, place

	Metric level	Abstract level	Interactional level
Term	Position (Space)	Location (Space)	Place
Example	GPS coordinates, GSM cell ID, Wi-Fi fingerprint, Beacon ID	"House"; an empty shell; needs to be filled with meaning, i.e. content and regions in our case	"Home"; a location with associated semantics
Usage	Define regions in space according to a particular metric	Links the metric level with the interactional level	Point of interaction with end user

Position, Location, Space, Place. As many, but not all, pervasive games are also location-based experiences, it is important to have a terminology to speak about locations and their related terms. Based on the literature and on our own experiences, we propose using the terms *position* and *location* in combination with *space* and *place*.

Position specifies a point in a coordinate system and can be defined either in absolute or relative coordinates. (50.749° latitude, 7.2056° longitude) is an example for an absolute position that is defined in the World Geodetic Coordinate System (WGS84), which is the standard for GPS.

Location is an opportunity to associate meaning. Locations are more humane in the sense that they are easier to grasp and talk about, but they might be ambiguous. The previously defined absolute GPS position could refer to a location called "Castle Birlinghoven".

Thus, a location is a disembodied concept, whereas a position is a more tangible definition that is directly linked to its underlying metrics (e.g. GPS coordinates, Beacon IDs, etc.). A similar distinction of related terms has previously been introduced to the computer supported cooperative work (CSCW) community by Harrison and Dourish, who distinguished between space and place [54]. They argued that people "are located in *space*, but act in *place*" and that "*place* is generally a *space* with something added". We previously argued that this distinction should be used and appropriated for the design of location-based experiences [86]. Designers of such experiences ultimately strive to provide meaningful locations to their users, i.e. they are designing for places in the sense of Harrison of Dourish. Table 1 provides an example of how these terms can be associated within this context.

Mind the Environment. No matter which technological choice is made for a location-based experience, it will have to deal with a number of issues that arise from the coupling of digital content to the real environment. First and foremost: can the digital *content be reached* (triggered) on location? Because producing content that cannot be reached is a pointless exercise, if you think about it.

Often overlooked in this respect are natural boundaries, like rivers, big changes in altitude, like hills, or simply a triggering condition that is too sensitive for the chosen technology, e.g. GPS radius too small, received signal strength too high, etc.

Second, any such coupling is subject to *temporal variations*. How long will the coupling be valid? Will the signal still be there when you expect it to? Will your plan be interrupted by events that turn the same space into a totally different place? Or do you maybe want to design especially for the different case, e.g. for a festival (think about the Burning Man festival which for only eight days every year turns a salt-lake desert into *Black Rock City*)?

Third, think about *how closely coupled* your content is to the environment [115]? Is it really specific to that location, e.g. because it refers to an archeological site or something else that can only be found *there*? Or is it maybe universally valid and only needs to be triggered on location-categories *like this*, which could be meaningful for example for areas that are found everywhere, like parks, city-centres, suburbs, etc.? Or do you maybe intend to build something that just needs a spatial spread, like *Human Pacman*, where you collect pills and otherwise have no real relation to the environment?

Fourth, consider the *weather* and other external factors. Although common-sense, this is all too often overlooked. People arguably prefer good weather when playing pervasive games. But if it is too sunny, the screen of the mobile device might not be readable. Likewise, people might want to protect their device (and themselves) and not to take it out when it is raining or cold. Moreover, you might want to consider adapting the content to the wether to meet the expectations of your users.

Fifth, spaces are usually filled with people which provide it with a social and semantic context. This has a direct effect on how the technology can be used and how your users will operate in this space. With *Geocaching*, this is just the simple problem of the muggles, as mentioned above, which calls for a bit of care while playing and is actually part of the fun as you are making sure that no one else is witnessing how you open the cache. But the social conduct of people is highly different for other use-cases and has to be taken very seriously. Consider a location-based collection game like *Pokémon Go* that makes use of the smart-phone camera. It might be great in outdoor places, but it might be not so well received in saunas or at cemeteries. Also not everyone at the same space is there for the same reasons (consider a waiter and a customer). Moreover, some people might not be allowed to ignore your gaming behaviour for professional reasons, e.g. police men, security staff, medical staff, or cleaners [112]. Just because you are building something with new technology does not make you own the space!

Sixth, there is a tension for the user to give attention to either the screen space or the environment. If the design is very visual, this might lead to the user focussing on the screen space and forgetting about the environment. This has even been witnessed when the location-context provided a perfect fit for the game-content. In the game *Time Warp* there was a wedding scene which was staged in front of a real church. On one occassion the real space was even lined by a group of people while the digital ceremony went on. When the researchers,

Fig. 13. Players of *Time Warp* surrounded by bystanders (left), in-game wedding scene in front of Great St. Martin Church, Cologne (off-screen to the right)

being a little proud of that seemingly fitting combination, asked the users about their experience in that moment, they replied that they did not notice the people around them while they were focussing on the screen space [117] (see Fig. 13).

Seventh, due to effects like this, it is your responsibility as the designer to make the experience safe for its users. *Time Warp* was already purposefully build as a two-player experience where both players had different capabilites: an AR-view and a map-view navigator. The navigator role was designed to make the experience safer which worked quite well. It was also found that the users stood still while experiencing the AR content. It can be learned from this that bespoke content does not have to be available all the time. More generally, it is also the designers responsibility to consider safe routes for their participants through the experience.

Eightly, location-based experiences like pervasive games cannot be authored without going on location or in situ. This is not only for all of the above reasons, but also for neurological reasons. Studies confirmed that knowledge and stories about locations are best recalled at those locations, even when the person in question is a professional tour guide or a teacher. Thus, it can be generally advised to go on location for authoring purposes [113].

Ninth, you might have a cause for going into specific locations. That is: your design might not only want to tap into the existing space, but also create an attitude towards that location [90].

Tenth, protect your players lifes. Pervasive games are staged in the real environment rather than on a screen, and here your players only have one life! Even though the players will act on their own behalf, it is your professional duty to make the inherent risks of participation assessible to them [112].

Do Not Compete with Reality is a general recommendation regarding your graphics budget. One strand of computer graphics is concerned with creating life-like, photo-realistic animations with perfect lighting, and this is all interesting and great in its own right. You will know such graphics from the latest blockbuster movie or Playstation or X-Box AAA title. But these kind of graphics cost a lot of money that you probably do not have available if you are building

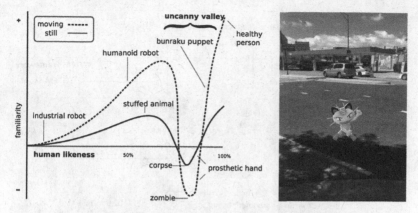

Fig. 14. Uncanny valley (left), virtual character from *Pokémon Go* on a street (right); (Credits: Masahiro Mori, Topher McCulloch)

a pervasive game. And if you strive to build them without the required budget, chances are that your graphics are going to look a tad boring at best and rather destroy the illusion that you were possible trying to create. The little money that you have available is better invested in other areas, like the story, the audio, etc. And regarding your graphics, it can be recommended to strive for a more abstract, maybe even comic-style look. The theory behind this is called the "uncanny valley" and was described by Japanese robotic researcher Mori (see Fig. 14, left) [80]. He found that the more life-like he was designing his robots, the more accepted they were by humans; but only to a certain extend. As soon as the robots became almost life-like, but not quite right, his test persons were alienated by the robots appearances. In essence, they looked like zombies, even more, when they were moving in a non-human way. This area is called the uncanny valley, and getting out of it can be a really costly matter. It can be learned from this that it is easier to stay on the save side, like Nintendo did, and choose a less photo-realistic and more comic-style look.

Another argument for the same recommendation can be learned from comic theory, where the characters are often depicted as abstract figures in front of a more real background to allow for a better identification with the figure [75]. With pervasive games in general and Augmented Reality views in particular, the background is already real, so it is a good idea to choose an abstract look for the foreground actors. Nintendo has recently proved this with the style of their *Pokémon Go* (see Fig. 14, right). You might even go as far as having only text, or even no graphics at all, depending on the type of experience and the device that you are building for, which might be a small additional wearable like in the case of Pokémon Go Plus.

Seperate Development Tasks into Roles. Building pervasive games is often done in small teams. If none of the existing tools completely support the intended scenario, custom programming will become necessary. If then no specific thought

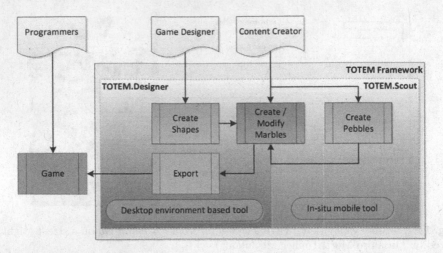

Fig. 15. TOTEM framework workflow; (Credits: Fraunhofer FIT)

is given to the share of tasks under this constellation, it is all too quickly decided that the programmer(s) will integrate everything under one hood and the other team members will *support* them. From our experience, this support is best given by outsourcing certain core, but not programming tasks to people other than the programmer(s). One particular approach to this was proposed by the TOTEM project. In their framework [116], there would be three main roles: *game designer*, *content creator*, and *programmer* (see Fig. 15). The game designer has the overall lead on the story, designs the game model from the available capabilities, and creates templates that can be filled to populate the game. The content creator takes these templates and fills them with content, but cannot modify the templates. Finally, the resulting dataset can be exported in standard web-formats and consumed by the game programmer.

This framework is based on the understanding that app development requires developers. It purposefully denies the approach of just having "an easy to use authoring tool" that fits all use-cases and rather tries to provide workflows that support the team collaboration. The framework goes as far as auto-generating source-code to access the game-data, but leaves the implementation of the actual user interface as a task on its own.

Test and Deploy. Testing often and early is good craftsmanship for any program, and thus also for location-based pervasive games. It is absolutely mandatory to test them in the actual use-situation, so probably outside or at least away from the deskop. Testing a prototype like this and then seeing it break down is the most effective way to improve its design. We often take background equipment for granted and only appreciate its existence in the case of a breakdown [120].

Of course, testing the overall integration under real life conditions is very time-consuming and costly. So the developers will need to consider ways of quickly testing their code under simulated conditions. This might take different forms. The Mobile Bristol project already used an emulator where the user could click on a map to move around a virtual character and test the game. Another practical form of integration testing is to write a test-suite in any of the available test frameworks like JUnit, or unittest, which covers the most typical uses of the code in a simulated usage-scenario (e.g. player starts, moves to position, content triggers). Due to its physically distributed nature it is hard to do integration testing of location-based content. But neglecting this important topic will result in a lot of extra work and lead to a lot of walking in order to debug the app.

Deploying to your final users has become a lot easier with the advent of app stores. But for testing, you might not want to go through the store, or maybe cannot even, for legal puposes. So it has to be considered how the newly made creation will reach the target audience. Will the devices be provided by your testers or by you? How will the software get installed and the users registered? And considering that your creation is mobile and thus your users will be out and about: how will you get technical feedback and maybe even provide support in case something breaks down? There are a number frameworks (e.g. Hockey) to support this task and you are well advised to consider using them, if you are not programming the required functionality on your own.

3.5 Further Considerations and Wider Implications

Once a pervasive game is deployed it will usually provide its creators with further insights into the matter that have not been considered before. This section presents an overview of some of the findings gained from earlier examples.

Bandwidth and Cost. It was already stated above that wireless network connectivity is not always available. Much rather, the state of disconnection is part of the wireless material. In addition to this, the speed of a mobile data-connection, once available, greatly varies between several megabytes and a few kilobytes per second. Moreover, it usually has a price-tag attached to it, as data-plans in most countries are not entirely flat, but actually limit the monthly data-use to certain number of mega- or gigabytes. This has huge implications on the design of mobile applications, as their users will not appreciate apps that will empty their data-plan and leave them surfing at slow speed, or increased costs, for the rest of the month.

Data-Collection. Much like traditional serious games, their mobile siblings can be used to not only transport a certain message in one direction, but also to collect valuable business data in the other direction. This can be illustrated by case of collecting data about wireless access points and other aspects of our environment (pictures, routes through areas, even pollution). In the research domain, a pervasive game called Feeding Yoshi was designed to identify and log wireless access points in a playful manner [9]. The Yoshi figures are little animals which can be virtually discovered when coming near to secured access points. They demand for particular food which can be harvested from plantations that are located at unsecured wireless networks. The process of mapping a wireless network was thus woven into a game activity. On a much larger commercial scale, this data collection is the main reason for the existence of the massively-multi-player online role-playing game Ingress by Google. Hidden in a compelling story about the discovery of alien artefacts and the struggle for power, Google employs millions of users to map out the environment for them for free, in return for a good gaming experience. It can be learned from this that there needs to be a perceived benefit for the user that makes him pay with data.

Boundaries. When designing trigger areas for location-based content, one usually designs the game-state to be changed upon the players entering, dwelling in, or leaving those areas. If you think about it, this puts more importance on the boundaries of those areas, and this effect has been found in the evaluation of Savannah. As the players were gathering in teams to hunt for big prey, not all of them were in the same area when they tried a coordinated attack. This happened due to a socio-technical effect. The players would have been searching the game areas for their prey as a team. Once the first player found it, she would have told everyone about it right away, making all players stop. To better coordinate their attack (pressing buttons on screen at the same time) they would form a circle that would eventually overlap with another area, because they stood at a boundary. As an effect of this, not all players would be in the same area and their attack failed [43]. This effect is similar to crowds gathering right near the door when leaving a venue.

Uncertainty. The issue of uncertainty is closely related to the effect of disconnection in wireless networks and the boundaries problem. As a designer of a location-based experience, you are often unsure about the characteristics of the utilised wireless infrastructures, especially their limited coverage and accuracy, which have a major impact on the performance of your experience. Seminal studies suggest that there is more to designing a location-based experience than assigning trigger-conditions to map areas. The analysis of the game *Can You See Me Now?* revealed the inherent patchiness and limited coverage of wireless systems such as Wi-Fi and GPS, how it affected the game experience, and how the supporting staff dealt with these issues [12,36,47]. Discussed problems included areas without either GPS or Wi-Fi, areas with reportedly bad GPS reception, as well as a temporal drift of these conditions, which was found to be caused by GPS shadows in build-up areas resulting from the satellites' movement through the orbit (see Fig. 16). In essence, it was described that the GPS reception in an area could change within a few minutes from good to bad. It can be learnt from this that even when the user is outside, one can not be certain that GPS will be available.

More details about the problem of uncertainty can be found in the cited papers. The main-author of this chapter also provides a more in-depth summary

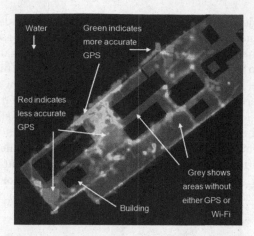

Fig. 16. GPS and Wi-Fi coverage and accuracy from *CYSMN* Rotterdam; (Credits: Mixed Reality Lab, University of Nottingham)

of the problem in his PhD thesis [87, pp. 111–116], and proposes to provide a layer of infrastructure information to the authors of location-based experiences [88] to mitigate the amount of uncertainty.

Modes of Transport. Our way through an environment is hugely influenced by the mode of transport that we choose. Seminal location-based experiences were often designed to be used on foot. Naturally, the finding would differ for other modes of transport like bicycles, cars, busses, trains, boats, planes, etc.

For this, the effect of different modes of transport on location-based experiences has not been studied too well, yet. But a few works exist. The aforementioned *Rider Spoke* was a game for cyclists. As another artist-led game, this game emphasizes the effect of riding a bike and exploits its unique characteristics as part of the design. The experience has been studied and compared to another cycle-based experience called *The Sillitoe Trail* to elicit these characteristics and condense them into design guidelines [97]. Interestingly from a technical point of view, *Rider Spoke* was also an early example of using wireless network signals rather than GPS for deploying and locating its content. Studies for pervasive games for other modes of transport are still in its infancy, but a small body of work exists on using the car as an arena for gaming, mostly from the backseat [106], and on persuasive gaming which aims on changing peoples behaviour in transport [66].

Recognizing modes of transport is a related problem. It has been proposed and studied to use GPS [8, 21, 92] and other sensors [6] available on mobile phones for this purpose and this approach has already reached the mass-market on Android and iOS phones. But practical experiments show that the recognition is far from perfect and thus also bears a lot of uncertainty and potential for future work.

Trajectories. Trajectories in human-computer interaction describe the user's journey through a number of related interfaces. The idea is based on the finding that complex software, and even more so complex pervasive games, usually have many different interfaces that form some kind of journey. Initial contact to a traditional software, for example, might be initiated through a recommendation, a review, or an advertisement, then it will be acquired, installed, and used. These are already at least four different contact points which might still be followed by data-migration and software de-installation. Pervasive games have at least the same complexity, put potentially differing interfaces on mobile devices. Core to the idea of trajectories is the understanding that a user's route (the *participant trajectory*) through a sequence of interactions and the author's intended route (the *canonical trajectory*) might differ from each other and that this needs to be managed [14].

Social Acceptance. People do not look to look like fools when appearing in public settings. As pervasive games embrace the public setting in their design, care has to be taken to mitigate this potential problem. One simple approach to this is to make them collaborate in teams. Not being alone while walking around stuffed up with lots of technology in *Time Warp* was frequently mentioned as a good idea that helped players to cope with the setting [19]. Other mentioned that they actually liked using fancy technology in public (and being followed by a camera team used for video observations) as it made them feel a bit like celebreties. While this might not be the same case for everyone, the players did feel socially accepted in both examples.

When designing a pervasive game for location with a strong cultural or natural heritage value or a cultural event, keep in mind that participants will rather consider the game as a social event. They may search for interesting information they can discuss about and funny social activities. Families, group of friends and colleagues often search for new kinds of playful activities to gather and share their free time. Therefore the experience should provide players with engaging collaboration options, and not just insist on a canonical trajectory. Studies of museums guides have confirmed that people actually like to deviate from any given route, be it to delve into a discovered detail, skip over certain aspects, plan ahead, or to reflect on what they have experienced while having a cup of coffee and share it with their acquintances [98].

Finally, for any interface produced to be staged in a public setting, it is interesting to consider if the interface *manipulations* should be rather hidden (secretive) or amplified, and if the resulting *effects* should be hidden or amplified. To illustrate the taxonomy resulting from usings these two terms as a lens for analysing public interfaces from a spectator perspective, consider a telescope and a guitar solo by Eddie Van Halen. The telescope will showcase very much amplified manipulations as the user of the telescope leans over, looks through the glass and rotates it on the tripod. The effects of this manipulation, however, are hidden from the spectator, as the resulting view is only visible to the user of the telescope. The famous guitar solo by Eddie Van Halen is the complete opposite and has hidden manipulations (at least initially) and max-imised effect. When first playing with his new technique, the famous guitarist reportedly turned his back at the audience to hide from them how he achieved his signature sound, as he was afraid that it would be copied by others all too easily. Thinking about these two terms, manipulation and effect, can help to plan for the relation between your users and their social environment when designing an interface for public settings [94].

Learning. Mobile devices have a great potential to extend learning opportuni-ties of today's learners. We can be constantly connected to shared knowledge, volumes of raw data and information. Almost ubiquitous connection to data allow people search information about the location they are, but as well based on location they are in a moment. These and many others technological oppor-tunities have brought new possibilities for education and engaging students in learning - it does not need to happen exclusively at school and through teachers. The term 'digital divide' originally understood as a gap between the technology rich and technology poor, both within and between societies; is today shifting into new digital divide, that can be seen as symptomatic of a much broader phenomenon a widening gulf between children's worlds outside school and the emphases of many education systems. Some educators react very well on this reality by integrating technologies to the classrooms, but pervasive games and other educational mobile applications let us to go beyond; by bringing the class-room outside, and even outside students' school time. *Environmental Detectives* [64] or *Mad City Mystery* [104] were nice examples of involving students into out-of-school playful project-based activities where put into challenging tasks they learned through interacting with their familiar environment and solving com-plex problems. Other projects such as *Mentira* [56] invited students of Spanish language courses to explore a Spanish-speaking neighborhood with a location-based game app on their mobile devices. As the out-of-school task the students followed the game revealing a mystery murder story throughout four weeks. The application was of course in Spanish, players needed to use Spanish to play it, but as well it provided players by real opportunities to use Spanish in an authentic environment.

Formal schooling systems often struggle with classic obstacles such as limited class time, unsufficient technical equipment, and specifics of national school cur-ricula. Educators thus often choose to embed a pervasive game into their school trip or out-of-school student activity. They need to cover a wide variety of roles to ensure an efficient learning process: technical assistant, motivator, leader of opening and closing game activity and last but not least evaluator within final debriefing. Most of today students dispose of their own smart mobile device which might turn into an advantage, whereby Chen et al. [32] revealed that students with higher mobile device attitudes (less anxiety and higher degree of mobile device fondness), showed higher learning achievements. For the same rea-son, students who are equipped by school mobile device should be provided by the basic training assuring sufficient technology literacy.

4 Conclusion

This chapter sought to provide a wide overview of pervasive games in the sense of location-based experiences and highlight their characteristics and typical surrounding issues. As the future of computing is mobile, it is believed that some of the findings from the presented seminal work in the field will be transferable to entertainment computing at large, and serious games in particular, once they tend to become more mobile.

4.1 From Research to Application

Over the last ten years or so, we have not only seen the world-wide adoption and thus triumphal procession of social media, but also a number of buy-outs and reincarnations of location-based social media. Google bought the once popular *Dodgeball*, then discontinued it, presented *Latitude* and later *Google+*. The founders of *Dodgeball* created *Foursquare*, basically a social networking app that had the location check-in as the core component. This was lately seperated into another app called *Swarm*. Facebook bought out *Gowalla*, shut it down, thereby eliminating a competitor to their *Facebook Places* feature, and lately presented *Nearby Friends* as a feature to their main social media app. With currently 1.59 billion users of Facebook alone at the end of 2015, the importance of the combination of location-features and social media cannot be underestimated.

Over about the same time-frame, we have also seen the uptake of seminal research project work in commercially successful software. Massively-Multiplayer Online Role Playing Games (MMORPG) on mobile phones had already been studied in the IPerG project between 2004 and 2008. In 2011, the commercial social gaming-app *Shadow Cities* had an acclaimed presentation at the Game Developers Conference. The game looked remarkably similar to the later Ingress, which is to date the most widely installed MMORPG with about 7 million players. *Shadow Cities* closed down in 2013 due to lack of popularity. *Ingress* developed Niantic Labs was part of Google for most of their time so far. Niantic recently became independent and secured a deal with Nintendo to jointly produce *Pokémon Go* app that has been released in July 2016 and which can be complemented by a low-cost wearable device called the Pokémon Go Plus. Given the importance of the Pokémon franchise to the traditional gaming business, this is surely an interesting development which will have an impact on gaming as well as on traditional commerce.

The health-domain looks like another interesting contestant for the commercial evolution of early research results. Apps like *Mobota* and games like *Heartlands* pioneered the use of location technology in the health sector. Commercial applications like the Nike+ Running App, or the more recent mobile location-based audio-game *Zombies, Run* took these ideas to the mass market. *Zombies, Run* overlays the real world running experience with a digital world story layer in which your area is infected by zombies that basically run behind you. Roaming the areas during their run, the players listen to the story like in a location- and activity-based audio-book and get different tasks, which are basically way points and running challenges that they have to solve. Given people's interest in new technology, fitness, self-presentation, and the "quantified self", it looks like the health-domain might provide interesting opportunites for studies.

4.2   Budget and Marketing

Other than traditional computer games, pervasive games are generally not directly paid for by their users. That is, their revenue is not generated through the classic and simple "units sold * margin" formula and usually does not cover the development costs. Much rather, pervasive games are paid for in other ways, usually one of the following:

1. funded research and education
2. data
3. in-app purchases
4. indirect revenue generated from brand awareness.

Most of the seminal work and work done in university courses belong to the first category. If the game is available at no charge, but you are running around and collecting stuff that is send back to a central server, chances are that it belongs to the second category. In-app purchases might still be available and save you some time when advancing in the game (note how this replaces skills that once had to be acquired through practice with skills that now can be acquired through purchases). The fourth category is related to marketing and can be better understood when reflecting about the earlier mentioned examples like *The Beast*, *I Love Bees*, or the *EcoPhone*. Here, the money was clearly coming from a big budget (for a movie, a game, and a milk-company respectively) in a marketing mix. These experiences based on new technologies were all used to promote their brand by associating it with an innovative image. Seeing that some companies have been doing it for over a decade, it can be learned that this seems to work quite well. It also appears that research in this area is a favourite topic of the media for much the same reasons. Seeing that serious games are generally also not paid for by their users, it will be interesting to see how findings from the area of pervasive games might be applied to serious games in the future.

One particular pattern that stems from the cross-media nature of pervasive games is evident over a number the presented examples, e.g. *EcoPhone*, *Love City*, and most of the 42 Entertainment experiences: a media campaign. It first creates interest in the experience via existing channels, be it packaging, videos, or classic advertisement. Then there is an exclusive on location part that only a chosen few, or those that sign up, can be part of. This is flanked by online activites, and then preserved for those who took part and especially presented to the mass audience via existing media-channels.

4.3   Outlook

Pervasive games take the world as a playground and wrap everyday, common meaning of objects, places, and people in a virtual layer with its own logic. Pervasiveness therefore leads to new kinds of immersion, play engagement, but also boundaries arising from the fuzzy mixture of game and real-life environment. Even though pervasive games have already a long history there is not a comprehensive body of research within this area. Mostly applied studies and evaluation of new pervasive projects are available, but it has yet to be proven how it can help mankind to cope with complex and urgent problems (to say it with the words of Doug Engelbart). This will be subject to further studies. However, it is also okay to take smaller steps and advance the subject one step at a time, then see how its findings might be applied to other application areas.

Pervasive games with augmented reality and wearable devices open the door to completely new user experiences over a wide area of application domains which makes it difficult to simply derive outcomes from other research areas. Thus, there will continue to be a need for building prototypes in a cooperative fashion, checking their fit for the intended purposes, and then applying the gained insight to the next iteration of prototypes [24,25]. For further reading about pervasive gaming, we recommend these books and publication series: PERVASIVE GAMES: THEORY AND PRACTICE [79], FUTURE LOCATION-BASED EXPERIENCES [10], PERFORMING MIXED REALITY [13], the proceedings of the PERGAMES workshop series that ran from 2004–2008 and the books that resulted from it: CONCEPTS AND TECHNOLOGIES FOR PERVASIVE GAMES and PERVASIVE GAMING APPLICATIONS [72,73]. An extensive project overview is provided by IASLONLINE [38,39]. A jargon buster and an in-depth literature review of seminal experiences, their technological underpinnings and development processes is provided in the doctoral thesis of Leif Oppermann: FACILITATING THE DEVELOPMENT OF LOCATION-BASED EXPERIENCES [87].

With regards to educational research utilising pervasive games there are still a lot of open questions. Answers to questions like "for which types of learning goals is a pervasive game more efficient than a computer game", "what kinds of tasks and instructional design support the best process of learning and knowledge transfer" and "how to design the best assessment mechanics built-in game" will be a valuable source for educators and pervasive game designers. For a start, we recommend reading AUGMENTED LEARNING: RESEARCH AND DESIGN OF MOBILE EDUCATIONAL GAMES [63].

Finally, speaking about the words *pervasive* and *games*, it has been argued to revisit the terms and evaluate what constitutes a pervasive game afterall [84]. In the late 1930s, Huizinga once famously argued about the play element of culture and how a society member learns through playing [58]. His *magic circle* and *homo ludens* are often cited primal principles in the pervasive game literature. However, he was no pervasive games researcher. There is an ongoing discourse of applying elements of gaming to the "real world" [76] (as opposed to the game world), i.e. *gamification*, or solving problems as a by-product of the gaming process, i.e. *games with a purpose* [3]. Seeing how this gets increasingly applied to future work scenarios, it appears interesting to revisit the terms *homo sapiens* (knowing man), *homo ludens* (playing man) and *homo faber* (crafting man) altogether, and see how they relate to our world of constant change [109].

Acknowledgements. This work would not been possible without the main-author's involvement in pervasive gaming related research projects such as: the British EPSRC Interdisciplinary Research Collaboration focused on experiences integrating physical and digital interactions (Equator), the European Integrated Project on Pervasive Games (IPerG), the European Integrated Project on Interactive Storytelling for Creative People (INSCAPE), the European Integrated Project on Interaction and Presence in Urban Environments (IPCity), and the French-German project on Theories and Tools for Distributed Authoring of Mobile Mixed Reality Games. We are indebted to all our collaborators and project leaders for the provided research opportunities. Many thanks also to the organizers of the Dagstuhl seminar on *Entertainment Computing and Serious Games* where this chapter originates from.

References

1. Karen | Blast Theory (2015). http://www.blasttheory.co.uk/matt-adams-on-psychological-profiling-in-karen/

2. Abowd, G.D., Atkeson, C.G., Hong, J., Long, S., Kooper, R., Pinkerton, M.: Cyberguide: a mobile context-aware tour guide. Wirel. Netw. **3**, 421–433 (1997)

3. von Ahn, L., Dabbish, L.: Designing games with a purpose. Commun. ACM **51**(8), 58–67 (2008)

4. Ahonen, T.: Mobile as 7th of the Mass Media: Cellphone, Cameraphone, Iphone, Smartphone. Futuretext, London (2008)

5. Alnuaim, A., Caleb-Solly, P., Perry, C.: A mobile location-based situated learning framework for supporting critical thinking: a requirements analysis study. In: Sampson, D.G., Ifenthaler, D., Spector, J.M., Isaias, P. (eds.) Digital Systems for Open Access to Formaland Informal Learning, pp. 139–158. Springer, Heidelberg (2014). doi:10.1007/978-3-319-02264-2_10

6. Anderson, I., Muller, H.: Context awareness via GSM signal strength fluctuation. In: Pervasive Computing, Dublin, Ireland (2006)

7. Anderson, J.R., Reder, L.M., Simon, H.A.: Situated learning and education. Educ. Res. **25**(4), 5–11 (1996)

8. Ashbrook, D., Starner, T.: Learning significant locations and predicting user movement with GPS. In: ISWC, Seattle, Washington (2002)

9. Bell, M., Chalmers, M., Barkhuus, L., Hall, M., Sherwood, S., Tennent, P., Brown, B., Rowland, D., Benford, S., Hampshire, A., Capra, M.: Interweaving mobile games with everyday life. In: CHI, pp. 417–426, Montréal, Québec, Canada (2006)

10. Benford, S.: Future location-based experiences, vol. 17, August 2009

11. Benford, S., Crabtree, A., Flintham, M., Drozd, A., Anastasi, R., Paxton, M., Tandavanitj, N., Adams, M., Row-Farr, J.: Can you see me now? ACM Trans. Comput. Hum. Inter. **13**(1), 100–133 (2006)

12. Benford, S., Crabtree, A., Reeves, S., Sheridan, J., Dix, A., Flintham, M., Drozd, A.: The frame of the game: blurring the boundary between fiction and reality in mobile experiences. In: Proceedings of the SIGCHI Conference on Human Factors in Computing Systems, CHI 2006, pp. 427–436. ACM, New York (2006)

13. Benford, S., Giannachi, G.: Performing Mixed Reality. The MIT Press, Cambridge (2011)

14. Benford, S., Giannachi, G., Koleva, B., Rodden, T.: From interaction to trajectories: designing coherent journeys through user experiences. In: Proceedings of the SIGCHI Conference on Human Factorsin Computing Systems, CHI 2009, pp. 709–718. ACM, New York (2009)

15. Benford, S., Magerkurth, C., Ljungstrand, P.: Bridging the physical and digital in pervasive gaming. Commun. ACM **48**(3), 54–57 (2005)
16. Bergström, K., Björk, S.: The case for computer-augmented games. Trans. Digital Games Res. Assoc. **1**(3) (2014). http://todigra.org/index.php/todigra/article/view/32
17. Bergström, K., Waern, A., Rosqvist, D., Månsson, L.: Gaming in the crucible of science: gamifying the science center visit. In: Proceedings of the 11th Conference on Advances in Computer Entertainment Technology, ACE 2014, pp. 2:1–2:10. ACM, NewYork (2014)
18. Billinghurst, M., Clark, A., Lee, G.: A Survey of Augmented Reality. Now publishers Inc., Breda (2015)
19. Blum, L., Wetzel, R., McCall, R., Oppermann, L., Broll, W.: The final TimeWarp: using form and content to support player experience and presence when designing location-aware mobile augmented reality games. In: Designing Interactive Systems, Newcastle, June 2012
20. Brooks Jr., F.P.: The computer scientist as toolsmith II. Commun. ACM **39**(3), 61–68 (1996)
21. Brunauer, R., Hufnagl, M., Rehrl, K., Wagner, A.: Motion pattern analysis enabling accurate travel mode detection from GPS data only. In: 2013 16th International IEEE Conference on Intelligent Transportation Systems (ITSC), pp. 404–411 (2013)
22. Buchholz, H., Brosda, C., Wetzel, R.: Go, science center to: a mixed reality learning environment of miniature exhibits. In: Epinoia, pp. 85–96, Rethymno, Greece (2010)
23. Bush, V.: As we may think, July 1945
24. Buxton, B.: Sketching User Experiences: Getting the Design Right and the Right Design. Morgan Kaufmann, San Francisco (2007)
25. Buxton, W., Sniderman, R.: Iteration in the design of the human-computer interface. In: 13th Annual Meeting, Human Factors Association of Canada, pp. 72–81 (1980)
26. Cabrera, J.S., Frutos, H.M., Stoica, A.G., Avouris, N., Dimitriadis, Y., Fiotakis, G., Liveri, K.D.: Mystery in the museum: collaborative learning activities using handheld devices. In: Proceedings of the 7th International Conference on Human Computer Interaction with Mobile Devices & Services, MobileHCI 2005, pp. 315–318. ACM, New York (2005)
27. Cameron, L., Ulmer, D.: The Geocaching Handbook. Globe Pequot Press, Falcon (2004)
28. Chalmers, M., Galani, A.: Seamful interweaving: heterogeneity in the theory and designof interactive systems. In: Designing Interactive Systems, Cambridge, Massachusetts (2004)
29. Chamberlain, A., Benford, S., Greenhalgh, C., Hampshire, A., Tandavanitj, N., Adams, M., Oldroyd, A., Sutton, J., Tanda, P.: Greener gaming & pervasive play. In: Proceedings of the 2007 Conference on Designing for User eXperiences, DUX 2007, pp. 26:1–26:16. ACM, New York (2007)
30. Chamberlain, A., Oppermann, L., Flintham, M., Benford, S., Tolmie, P., Adams, M., Row-Farr, J., Tandavanitj, N., Marshall, J., Rodden, T.: Locating experience: touring a pervasive performance. Pers. Ubiquit. Comput. **15**(7), 717–730 (2011)
31. Chamberlain, A., Paxton, M., Glover, K., Flintham, M., Price, D., Greenhalgh, C., Benford, S., Tolmie, P., Kanjo, E., Gower, A., Gower, A., Woodgate, D., Fraser, D.S.: Understanding mass participatory pervasive computing systems for environmental campaigns. Pers. Ubiquit. Comput. **18**(7), 1775–1792 (2013)

32. Chen, C.-P., Shih, J.-L., Ma, Y.-C.: Using instructional pervasive game for school children's cultural learning. J. Educ. Technol. Soc. **17**(2), 169–182 (2014)

33. Cheok, A.D., Goh, K.H., Liu, W., Farbiz, F., Fong, S.W., Teo, S.L., Li, Y., Yang, X.: Human pacman: a mobile, wide-area entertainment system based on physical, social, and ubiquitous computing. Pers. Ubiquit. Comput. **8**(2), 71–81 (2004)

34. Cheverest, K., Davies, N., Mitchell, K., Friday, A., Efstratiou, C.: Developing a context-aware electronic tourist guide: someissues and experiences. In: CHI, pp. 17–24, The Hague, The Netherlands (2000)

35. Chou, T.-L., Chanlin, L.-J.: Location-based learning through augmented reality. J. Educ. Comput. Res. **51**(3), 355–368 (2014)

36. Crabtree, A., Benford, S., Rodden, T., Greenhalgh, C., Flintham, M., Anastasi, R., Drozd, A., Adams, M., Row-Farr, J., Tandavanitj, N., Steed, A.: Orchestrating a mixed reality game 'on the ground'. In: CHI, pp. 391–398, Vienna, Austria (2004)

37. Davis, S.B., Moar, M., Jacobs, R., Watkins, M., Shackford, R., Capra, M., Oppermann, L.: Mapping inside out. In: Magerkurth, C., Röcker, C. (eds.) Pervasive Gaming Applications-A Reader for Pervasive Gaming Research, Shaker, vol. 2 (2007)

38. Dreher, T.: IASLonline NetArt: pervasive games (2008). http://iasl.uni-muen chen.de/links/NAPG.html

39. Dreher, T.: IASLonline NetArt: sammeltipp, August 2009. http://iasl.uni-muen chen.de/links/TippSammel1-3.html

40. Edery, D., Mollick, E.: Changing the Game: How Video Games Are Transforming the Future of Business. FT Press, Upper Saddle River (2008)

41. Engelbart, D.: Augmenting human intellect: a conceptual framework (1962)

42. Etxeberria, A.I., Asensio, M., Vicent, N., Cuenca, J.M.: Mobile devices: a tool for tourism and learning at archaeologicalsites. Int. J. Web Based Commun. **8**(1), 57–72 (2012)

43. Facer, K., Joiner, R., Stanton, D., Reid, J., Hull, R., Kirk, D.: Savannah: mobile gaming and learning? J. Comput. Assist. Learn. **20**(6), 399–409 (2004)

44. Feiner, S., MacIntyre, B., Höllerer, T., Webster, A., Machine, T.: Prototyping 3D mobile augmented reality systems for exploring the urban environment. In: International Symposium on Wearable Computing, pp. 74–81, Cambridge, Massachusetts (1997)

45. Fischer, J.E., Yee, N., Bellotti, V., Good, N., Benford, S., Greenhalgh, C.: Effects of content and time of delivery on receptivity to mobile interruptions. In: Proceedings of the 12th International Conference on Human Computer Interaction with Mobile Devices and Services, MobileHCI 2010, pp. 103–112. ACM, New York (2010)

46. Flintham, M.: Painting the town red: configuring location-based gamesby colouring maps. In: Advances in Computer Entertainment Technology (ACE), Valencia, Spain (2005)

47. Flintham, M., Anastasi, R., Benford, S., Hemmings, T., Crabtree, A., Greenhalgh, C., Rodden, T., Tandavanitj, N., Adams, M., Row-Farr, J.: Where on-line meets on-the-streets: experiences withmobile mixed reality games. In: CHI, pp. 569–576, Ft. Lauderdale, Florida (2003)

48. Flintham, M., Smith, K., Benford, S., Capra, M., Green, J., Greenhalgh, C., Wright, M., Adams, M., Tandavanitj, N., Row-Farr, J., Lindt, I.: Day of the figurines: a slow narrative-driven game for mobile phones using text messaging. In: PerGames, Salzburg, Austria (2007)

49. Friedrich, A.W.: Augmented Reality in Entwicklung, Produktion und Service. Publicis Corporate Publishing, Erlangen (2004)

50. Geiger, C., Kleinnjohann, B., Reimann, C., Stichling, D.: Mobile AR4all. In: IEEE and ACM International Symposium on Augmented Reality (ISAR), New York (2001)

51. Gilbert, R.: Why adventure games suck and what we can do about it. J. Comput. Game Des. 3(2), 4–7 (1989)

52. Greenhalgh, C., Benford, S., Drozd, A., Flintham, M., Hampshire, A., Oppermann, L., Smith, K., Tycowicz, C.: Addressing mobile phone diversity in ubicomp experience development. In: Krumm, J., Abowd, G.D., Seneviratne, A., Strang, T. (eds.) UbiComp 2007. LNCS, vol. 4717, pp. 447–464. Springer, Heidelberg (2007). doi:10.1007/978-3-540-74853-3_26

53. Hansen, F.A., Kortbek, K.J., Grønbæk, K., Drama, M.U.: Interactive storytelling in real world environments. New Rev. Hypermedia Multimed. 18(1–2), 63–89 (2012)

54. Harrison, S., Dourish, P.: Re-Place-ing space: the roles of place and space in collaborative systems. In: CSCW, Boston, Massachusetts (1996)

55. Holden, C.: ARIS: augmented reality for interactive storytelling. In: Mobile Media Learning, pp. 68–83. ETC Press, Pittsburgh, PA, USA (2015)

56. Holden, C.L., Sykes, J.M.: Leveraging mobile games for place-based language learning. Int. J. Game Based Learn. (IJGBL) 1(2), 1–18 (2011)

57. Huizenga, J., Admiraal, W., Akkerman, S., ten Dam, G.: Mobile game-based learning in secondary education: engagement, motivation and learning in a mobile city game. J. Comput. Assist. Learn. 25(4), 332–344 (2009)

58. Huizinga, J.H., Ludens, H.: A Study of the Play-Element in Culture. Beacon Press, Boston (1939)

59. Hull, R., Clayton, B., Melamed, T.: Rapid authoring of mediascapes. In: Davies, N., Mynatt, E.D., Siio, I. (eds.) UbiComp 2004. LNCS, vol. 3205, pp. 125–142. Springer, Heidelberg (2004). doi:10.1007/978-3-540-30119-6_8

60. Ishii, H., Wisneski, C., Orbanes, J., Chun, B., Paradiso, J.: PingPongPlus: design of an athletic-tangible interface for computer-supported cooperative play. In: Proceedings of the SIGCHI Conference on Human Factors in Computing Systems, CHI 1999, pp. 394–401. ACM, New York (1999)

61. Joffe, B.: Mogi: location based services - a community game in Japan. In: von Börries, F., Walz, S.P., Böttger, M. (eds.) Space Time Play, pp. 224–225, Birkhäuser (2007)

62. Kirschner, P.A., Sweller, J., Clark, R.E.: Why minimal guidance during instruction does not work: an analysis of the failure of constructivist, discovery, problem-based, experiential, and inquiry-based teaching. Educ. Psychol. 41(2), 75–86 (2006)

63. Klopfer, E.: Augmented Learning: Research and Design of Mobile Educational Games. The MIT Press, Cambridge (2011)

64. Klopfer, E., Squire, K.: Environmental detectives-the development of an augmented reality platform for environmental simulations. Educ. Technol. Res. Dev. 56(2), 203–228 (2007)

65. Koleva, B., Tolmie, P., Brundell, P., Benford, S., Rennick-Egglestone, S.: From front-end to back-end and everything in-between: work practice in game development. In: Proceedings of the 2015 Annual Symposium on Computer-Human Interaction in Play, CHI PLAY 2015, pp. 141–150. ACM, New York (2015)

66. Krachel, M., McCall, R., Koenig, V.: Playing with traffic: an emerging methodology for developing gamified mobility applications. In: Emerging Perspectives on the Design, Use, and Evaluation of Mobile and Handheld Devices, Advances in Wireless Technologies and Telecommunication (AWTT) (2015)

67. LaMarca, A., Chawathe, Y., Consolvo, S., Hightower, J., Smith, I., Scott, J., Sohn, T., Howard, J., Hughes, J., Potter, F., Tabert, J., Powledge, P., Borriello, G., Schilit, B.: Place lab: device positioning using radio beacons in the wild. In: Gellersen, H.-W., Want, R., Schmidt, A. (eds.) Pervasive 2005. LNCS, vol. 3468, pp. 116–133. Springer, Heidelberg (2005). doi:10.1007/11428572_8

68. Lantz, F.: PacManhattan. In: Pervasive Games: Theory and Design. Morgan Kaufmann Game Design Books, pp. 131–136. CRC Press (2009)

69. Levy, S.: Insanely Great: Life and Times of Macintosh, the Computer That Changed Everything. Penguin Books Ltd, London (1995)

70. Lindt, I., Ohlenburg, J., Pankoke-Babatz, U., Ghellal, S., Oppermann, L., Adams, M.: Designing cross media games. In: PerGames Workshop, Munich, Germany (2005)

71. MacIntyre, B., Gandy, M., Bolter, J., Dow, S., Hannigan, B.: Dart: the designer's augmented reality toolkit. In: IEEE and ACM International Symposium on Mixed and Augmented Reality, pp. 329–330, Tokyo, Japan (2003)

72. Magerkurth, C., Röcker, C.: Concepts and Technologies for Pervasive Games: A Reader for Pervasive Gaming Research, vol. 1. Shaker, Aachen (2007)

73. Magerkurth, C., Röcker, C.: Pervasive Gaming Applications: A Reader for Pervasive Gaming Research, vol. 2. Shaker, Aachen (2007)

74. Marshall, J., Benford, S.: Using fast interaction to create intense experiences. In: Proceedings of the SIGCHI Conference on Human Factors in Computing Systems, CHI 2011, pp. 1255–1264. ACM, New York (2011)

75. McCloud, S., Comics, U.: The Invisible Art. William Morrow Paperbacks, New York (1994)

76. McGonigal, J.: Reality Is Broken: Why Games Make Us Better and How They Can Change the World. Penguin Press HC, New York (2011)

77. Metz, M., Theis, F.: Digitale Lernwelt - SERIOUS GAMES: Einsatz in derberuflichen Weiterbildung. W. Bertelsmann, Bielefeld (2011)

78. Montola, M.: Exploring the edge of the magic circle: defining pervasive games. In: Design Automation Conference, Copenhagen, Denmark (2005)

79. Montola, M., Stenros, J., Waern, A.: Pervasive Games: Theory and Design. Morgan Kaufmann, Burlington (2009)

80. Mori, M.: Bukimi no tani [the uncanny valley]. Energy 7(4), 33–35 (1970)

81. Mueller, F.F., Stevens, G., Thorogood, A., O'Brien, S., Wulf, V.: Sports over a distance. Pers. Ubiquit. Comput. 11(8), 633–645 (2007)

82. Naismith, L., Sharples, M., Ting, J.: Evaluation of CAERUS: a context aware mobile guide. In: mLearn, Cape Town, South Africa (2005)

83. Nam, Y.: Designing interactive narratives for mobile augmented reality. Cluster Comput. 18(1), 309–320 (2014)

84. Nieuwdorp, E.: The pervasive discourse: an analysis. Comput. Entertain. 5(2), 13 (2007)

85. Oppermann, L.: On the choice of programming languages for developing location-based mobile games. In: Mobile Gaming Workshop, Informatik 2008, vol. 2, pp. 481–488, Munich, Germany (2008)

86. Oppermann, L.: An abstract location-model for mobile games. In: Mobile Gaming Workshop, Informatik 2009, Lübeck, Germany (2009)

87. Oppermann, L.: Facilitating the development of location-based experiences. Ph.D. thesis, University of Nottingham, Computer Science, Nottingham (2009)

88. Oppermann, L., Broll, G., Capra, M., Benford, S.: Extending authoring tools for location-aware applications with an infrastructure visualization layer. In: Dourish, P., Friday, A. (eds.) UbiComp 2006. LNCS, vol. 4206, pp. 52–68. Springer, Heidelberg (2006). doi:10.1007/11853565_4

89. Oppermann, L., Flintham, M., Reeves, S., Benford, S., Greenhalgh, C., Marshall, J., Adams, M., Farr, J.R., Tandavanitj, N.: Lessons from touring a location-based experience. In: Lyons, K., Hightower, J., Huang, E.M. (eds.) Pervasive 2011. LNCS, vol. 6696, pp. 232–249. Springer, Heidelberg (2011). doi:10.1007/978-3-642-21726-5_15

90. Oppermann, L., Jacobs, R., Watkins, M., Shackford, R., von Tycowicz, C., Wright, M., Capra, M., Greenhalgh, C., Benford, S.: Love city: a text-driven, location-based mobile phone game played between 3 cities. In: Magerkurth, C., Röcker, C. (eds.) Pervasive Gaming Applications - A Reader for Pervasive Gaming Research, vol. 2. Shaker (2007)

91. Oppermann, R., Specht, M.: A nomadic information system for adaptive exhibition guidance. Arch. Mus. Inf. 13(2), 127–138 (1999)

92. Patterson, D.J., Liao, L., Gajos, K., Collier, M., Livic, N., Olson, K., Wang, S., Fox, D., Kautz, H.: Opportunity knocks: a system to provide cognitive assistance with transportation services. In: Davies, N., Mynatt, E.D., Siio, I. (eds.) UbiComp 2004. LNCS, vol. 3205, pp. 433–450. Springer, Heidelberg (2004). doi:10.1007/978-3-540-30119-6_26

93. Rashid, O., Bamford, W., Coulton, P., Edwards, R., Scheible, J.: PAC-LAN: mixed-reality gaming with RFID-enabled mobile phones. ACM Comput. Entertain. 4(4), 4 (2006)

94. Reeves, S.: Designing Interfaces in Public Settings: Understanding the Role of the Spectator in Human-Computer Interaction. Human-Computer Interaction Series. Springer, London (2013)

95. Reid, J., Hull, R., Cater, K., Fleuriot, C.: Magic moments in situated mediascapes. In: Advances in Computer Entertainment Technology (ACE), Valencia, Spain (2005)

96. Rosenbaum, E., Klopfer, E., Perry, J.: On location learning: authentic applied science with networked augmented realities. J. Sci. Educ. Technol. 16(1), 31–45 (2006)

97. Rowland, D., Flintham, M., Oppermann, L., Koleva, B., Chamberlain, A., Marshall, J., Benford, S., Perez, C.: Ubikequitous computing: designing interactive experiences for cyclists. In: Mobile HCI, Bonn, Germany (2009)

98. Savidis, A., Zidianakis, M., Kazepis, N., Dubulakis, S., Gramenos, D., Stephanidis, C.: An integrated platform for the management of mobile location-aware information systems. In: Indulska, J., Patterson, D.J., Rodden, T., Ott, M. (eds.) Pervasive 2008. LNCS, vol. 5013, pp. 128–145. Springer, Heidelberg (2008). doi:10.1007/978-3-540-79576-6_8

99. Schaal, S., Bartsch, S., Brosda, C., Oppermann, L.: Location-based games with smartphones - developing a toolbox for educators. Madrid (2016)

100. Schlieder, C., Kiefer, P., Matyas, S.: Geogames: designing location-based games from classic board games. IEEE Intell. Syst. 21(5), 40–46 (2006)

101. Schreiber, W., Zimmermann, P.: Virtuelle Techniken im industriellen Umfeld: Das AVILUS-Projekt - Technologien und Anwendungen. Springer, Berlin (2011)

102. Sotiriou, S., Anastopoulou, S., Rosenfeld, S., Aharoni, O., Hofstein, A., Bogner, F., Sturm, H., Hoeksema, K.: Visualizing the invisible: the CONNECT approach for teaching science. In: Sixth International Conference on Advanced Learning Technologies, pp. 1084–1086 (2006)

103. Squire, K.D.: From information to experience: place-based augmented reality games as a model for learning in a globally networked society. Teach. Coll. Rec. **112**(10), 2565–2602 (2010)

104. Squire, K.D., Jan, M.: Mad city mystery: developing scientific argumentation skills with a place-based augmented reality game on handheld computers. J. Sci. Educ. Technol. **16**(1), 5–29 (2007)

105. Stuke, F.R.: Wirkung und Erfolgskontrolle von Werbespielen. Ruhr-Universität Bochum, Bochum (2001)

106. Sundström, P., Wilfinger, D., Meschtscherjakov, A., Tscheligi, M., Schmidt, A., Juhlin, O.: The car as an arena for gaming. In: Proceedings of the 14th International Conference on Human-Computer Interaction with Mobile Devices and Services Companion, MobileHCI 2012, pp. 233–236. ACM, New York (2012)

107. Sutherland, I.: The ultimate display. In: Proceedings of IFIP Congress, pp. 506–508 (1965)

108. Thomas, B., Close, B., Donoghue, J., Squires, J., De Bondi, P., Piekarski, W.: First person indoor/outdoor augmented reality application: ARQuake. Pers. Ubiquit. Comput. **6**(1), 75–86 (2002)

109. Thomas, D., Brown, J.S.: Learning for a world of constant change: homo sapiens, homo faber & homo ludens revisited. In: University Research for Innovation. Economica (2010)

110. Tolmie, P., Benford, S., Greenhalgh, C., Rodden, T., Reeves, S.: Supporting group interactions in museum visiting. In: Proceedings of the 17th ACM Conference on Computer Supported Cooperative Work & Social Computing, CSCW 2014, pp. 1049–1059. ACM, New York (2014)

111. Waern, A.: IPerG Deliverable D14.5 Appendix: Gamecreator Tutorial (Showcase - Boxed Pervasive Games), August 2009

112. Waern, A.: The ethics of unaware participation in public interventions. In: Proceedings of the 2016 CHI Conference on Human Factors in Computing Systems, CHI 2016, pp. 803–814. ACM, New York (2016)

113. Weal, M.J., Hornecker, E., Cruickshank, D.G., Michaelides, D.T., Millard, D.E., Halloran, J., De Roure, D.C., Fitzpatrick, G.: Requirements for in-situ authoring of location based experiences. In: MobileHCI, Helsinki, Finland (2006)

114. Weiser, M.: The computer for the 21st century. Sci. Am. **265**(3), 66–75 (1991)

115. Wetzel, R., Blum, L., Broll, W., Oppermann, L.: Designing mobile augmented reality games. In: Furht, B. (ed.) Handbook of Augmented Reality, pp. 513–539. Springer, New York (2011). doi:10.1007/978-1-4614-0064-6_25

116. Wetzel, R., Blum, L., Jurgelionis, A., Oppermann, L.: Shapes, marbles and pebbles: template-based content creation for location-based games. In: IADIS International Conference Game andEntertainment Technologies, Lisbon, Totem, July 2012

117. Wetzel, R., Blum, L., McCall, R., Opperman, L., ten Broeke, S., Szalavari, Z.: IPCity Deliverable D8.4: Final Prototype of TimeWarp application. Deliverable D8.4, April 2010

118. Wetzel, R., Blum, L., Oppermann, L.: Tidy City: a location-basedgame supported by in-situ and web-based authoring tools to enable user-created content. In: International Conference on the Foundations of Digital Games, pp. 238–241. ACM, Raleigh, June 2012

119. Wetzel, R., McCall, R., Braun, A.K., Broll, W.: Guidelines for designing augmented reality games. In: Proceedings of the 2008 Conference on Future Play: Research, Play, Share, Future Play 2008, pp. 173–180. ACM, New York (2008)
120. Winograd, T., Flores, F.: Understanding Computers and Cognition: A New Foundation for Design. Addison-Wesley, Reading (1986)
121. Wolpers, M., Najjar, J., Verbert, K., Duval, E.: Tracking actual usage: the attention metadata approach. Educ. Technol. Soc. **10**(3), 106–121 (2007)
122. Wulf, V., Moritz, E.F., Henneke, C., Al-Zubaidi, K., Stevens, G.: Computer supported collaborative sports: creating social spaces filled with sports activities. In: Rauterberg, M. (ed.) ICEC 2004. LNCS, vol. 3166, pp. 80–89. Springer, Heidelberg (2004). doi:10.1007/978-3-540-28643-1_11

Storytelling in Serious Games

Antonia Kampa[1]([✉]), Susanne Haake[2], and Paolo Burelli[3]

[1] RheinMain University of Applied Sciences, Wiesbaden, Germany
antonia.kampa@hs-rm.de
[2] University of Education Weingarten, Weingarten, Germany
haake@md-phw.de
[3] Aalborg University Copenhagen and Tactile Entertainment APS,
Copenhagen, Germany
pabu@create.aau.dk

Abstract. This chapter about storytelling and interactivity in storytelling first explains on various serious games examples foundations of storytelling. Then storytelling in Interactive Media with regard to serious games is described. Further the current state of the art on Interactive Digital Storytelling is presented including example experiences, authoring tools and challenges in the field combined with examples of serious games. This chapter closes concluding with open storytelling challenges and opportunities in serious games development and recommending further literature on the subject.

Keywords: Narrating techniques · Serious games · Interactive media · Interactive digital storytelling

1 Introduction

Nearly all nations formulate their identity by narrating stories [44]. Stories, firstly being oral narrated, represent an important aspect of culture since the beginning of human being. Stories help to connect cultural values and learning or moral items in a meaningful correlation and they make them recountable and understandable. Therefore, using storytelling means recording and distributing histories, myths, and values of nations. Many types and different genres of narrations exist today, from oral histories, literature, films to games. This opens an interdisciplinary research field, from cultural and literature studies to media science and game studies.

According to Henry Jenkins not all games tell stories, but many games have narrative aspirations [34]. Particularly in a serious games context stories play an important role. They help to connect serious context with playing games. By using narrations the game designer is able to transport the 'serious sense' behind the play, mostly an educational sense or training items. But this must not be a big linear story like an epos or a drama in literature. The original serious text information has to be transformed to game action. For this narration helps besides other didactic aspects to add serious context into games [34].

© Springer International Publishing AG 2016
R. Dörner et al. (Eds.): Entertainment Computing and Serious Games, LNCS 9970, pp. 521–539, 2016.
DOI: 10.1007/978-3-319-46152-6_19

"A discussion of the narrative potentials of games need not imply a privileging of storytelling over all the other possible things games can do, even if we might suggest that if game designers are going to tell stories, they should tell them well. In order to do that, game designers, who are most often schooled in computer science or graphic design, need to be retooled in the basic vocabulary of narrative theory" [34]. To analyze narrating parts of serious games, it is necessary to understand narrating techniques, the "basic vocabulary", as Jenkins emphasizes. Essential storytelling basics are significant in all kind of narrating types, also in games. In Sect. 2, important storytelling basics, mostly linear told, are presented: the narrative structure, the narrators perspective, time and place of narration and characters. Furthermore, their meaning for serious games context and significant characteristics are added.

While the basic principles of storytelling are fundamental to understand and design narratives for serious games, the interactive natures of games rises further challenges. Even if the story is not meant to change through the interaction, the actions performed by the player have to be take into account for the story presentation. Section 3 gives an overview of the challenges and the research work performed on the presentation of a story in an interactive medium though the lenses of discourse and user interaction.

Section 4 furthers the analysis of implications of storytelling in serious games by analyzing the technical and design challenges of designing stories that dynamically adapt to the player's actions. A series of games examples and research works are presented to report the state of the art of both interactive storytelling experiences and of authoring tools, which allow designers to produce content for the engines.

Lastly, Sect. 5 concludes the chapter with a short overview and an analysis of the future of the field, with open research questions and potential research directions.

2   Storytelling Basics

Narrative structure means a literary element and describes the structural framework that shows the order and manner of a narrative. Two items are necessary to distinguish: plot versus story. Plot contains the sequence of events inside a story, connected by the principle of cause and effect. The story represents the meaning, which the reader constructs behind the plot, a second-level-construct [7]. Literature about narrative structure has to be read carefully. There exist different meanings and terminologies. In the structuralist terminology the what of the narrative is called story, the how it is told is called discourse [14].

In game design not all story elements have to be written before a game starts. This second item story is important to analyze in serious game context, particularly to analyze the meaning behind constructed by the authors of games. This could be demonstrated at the alternate reality game World without oil, designed i.a. by Jane McGonnigal and settled for a few weeks in 2007 via a website [25]. A serious game for a public good, could be read the official website.

Fig. 1. The official website world without oil

The big story behind this game with a strong serious context concludes a fictional global oil crisis. The gamer have to find solutions to live without oil and save the nature within their personal living conditions. The stories and ideas were incorporated into an official narrative, posted daily. Gamer could post their solutions as videos, images or blog entries. While playing the big story were added by hundreds of personal narratives. These narratives were compressed to a central paper with solutions how we can manage our lives without wasting oil [48] (Fig. 1).

But how story and plot points could be structured? The most famous narrative structure until today represents the drama structure originally developed by the Greek philosopher Aristotle in 335 B.C [32]. The author emphasizes the important role of plot or mythos for drama, particularly the type of tragedy. He subdivided the tragedy in three different narrating parts: Exposition, middle part including the climax and finally the resolution. The connection between the three acts is called plot points or turning points.

The German writer Gutav Freytag expand the plot structure into five stages in his developed Freytags pyramid in 1863. His theoretical work subdivides the tragedy into: exposition, rising action, climax, falling action, retarded moment and denouement [27]. Both structures are compared in Fig. 2, referring to Aristotle and Freytag [27,32].

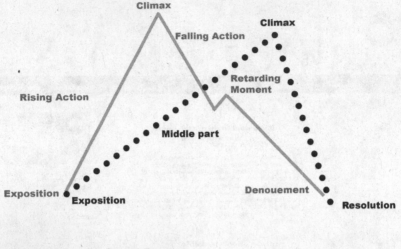

Dramastructure by Gustav Freytag

Dramastructure by Aristotle

Fig. 2. The drama structure by Aristotle and Freytag

Until today narrators, also in media field, refer to Aristotle three-act-structure or Freytags pyramid, particularly the most famous American screenwriter Syd Field. This is the structure of the Syd Field "Paradigm" in three acts: Passing the first plot point in the first act the main character protagonist is faced with a goal to achieve. The main conflict is settled. The second act is named the "confrontation" and contains a midpoint. At this turning point the character fortune changes dramatically. The last act includes a climatic struggle to achieve the settled goal, or not [26].

Game Designer have been inspired by this drama structure by developing the level structure until today. This does not mean simply copying this structure, originally coming from literature. They have to find a way to install a suspense line considering the nature of game playing. The interaction while playing influences the length of the different acts, for example. In many games a big challenge can be found at the end, according to the climax of a traditional narrative structure. A good structured suspense line can increase users involvement, but have to respect players freedom of choice. So game designer have to find the right balance between reception of the story and playing.

2.1   The Time of Narration

The time of narration has to do with the relation between the narration and the story. The time regulates the narrator's temporal position relative to the events being told. The French specialist of narratology Gerard Genette gave some methodological choices referring the time to writers: they can vary (1) the order of the narrative, (2) the speed of the narrative and (3) the frequency of events [28]. Changing the order of a chronically narration often means to create suspense. The most popular techniques of changing the order of time in narration are: previews or flashbacks. The narrative speed means how detailed or abbreviated a passage of a story is told and the frequency, how often a single or periodic detail is told. Gerard Genette's theoretical work based on studies about Marcel Prousts "In Remembrance of Things Past" [52]. It fits into the German and Anglo-Saxon academic tradition and contains a culmination and a renewal of this school of narratological criticism [52]. Flash backs and forecasts is also a famous film technique. Looking back or forth in a stories increases the dramatic suspense line and because of this the involvement of the audience. But changing the order of time in narration assumes a linear reception of a story. If it is possible to arrange a change of order of time in games, has increased a discussion in game design: Using Quake as an example, Jesper Juuls argues that flashbacks are impossible within games, because the game play always occurs in real time [34]. Yet, this is to confuse story and plot. Games are no more locked into an eternal present than films are always linear. Many games contain moments of revelation or artifacts that shed light on past actions. Carson suggests that part of the art of game design comes in finding artful ways of embedding narrative information into the environment without destroying its immersiveness and without giving the player a sensation of being drug around by the neck [34]. Looking at the time in games, it seams to be difficult to find similarities. Player could influence the time of narration via interaction. But narrating clips or textual based fadings inside a game contain this technique for increasing the motivation to play a game to the end. So you could see the kidnapped princess at the beginning of Super Mario Land to demonstrate the mission of the game at the intro [49]. At the field of serious games this narrating parts are used to show the sense behind the game, often at the beginning or end of a level.

2.2   The Place of Narration Environmental Storytelling

Beyond the time the setting is essential to formulate a story. Environmental storytelling uses techniques of architectural or exhibition design to tell stories. Stories are told or established in particular spaces. The most famous author is Jury Lotman, a Russian structuralist [42]. He subdivided a story environment mostly in good and worse. In his opinion places have a profound meaning for the storyline. Particularly in game design the environment is useful to settle narration parts into a game. In open world games this technique is often found today. There are virtual environments in which computer games are played, which are designed by computer game authors. The story isnt linear, it is being constructed by players interaction through the game environment. "Game designers don't simply tell stories; they design worlds and sculpt spaces. It is no accident, for example, that game design documents have historically been more interested in issues of level design than plotting or character motivation. A prehistory of video and computer games might take us through the evolution of paper mazes or board games, both preoccupied with the design of spaces, even where they also provided some narrative context" [34]. The serious game Global conflict

Palestine represents an example for this [56]. The user plays the character of a freelance journalist. The goal is to write an article for a newspaper by collecting quotes from the dialog during the game. The player has to act carefully respecting both sides of the conflict. So important serious aspects are to take different perspectives and learn more about the people within the conflict. The game is used in educational context, including a teachers manual and further resources. The storyline seems to be a didactic play by the German writer Berthold Brecht. While playing it the people understand the didactic aspects.

So famous patterns of environmental storytelling can be discovered by analyzing games. They "fit within a much older tradition of spatial stories, which have often taken the form of hero's odysseys, quest myths, or travel narratives" [34]. The American mythological researcher Joseph Campbell analyzed the structure of mythological texts all over the world [12]. His results he formulated in the heros journey, which includes basic stages every hero quests goes through. His theoretical work influenced successful Hollywood filmmakers like George Lucas writing the story for Star Wars, but also game designer. "The Star Wars game may not simply retell the story of Star Wars, but it doesn't have to in order to enrich or expand our experience of the Star Wars saga. We already know the story before we even buy the game and would be frustrated if all it offered us was a regurgitation of the original film experience. Rather, the Star Wars game exists in dialogue with the films, conveying new narrative experiences through its creative manipulation of environmental details. One can imagine games taking their place within a larger narrative system with story information communicated through books, film, television, comics, and other media, each doing what it does best, each relatively autonomous experience, but the richest understanding of the story world coming to those who follow the narrative across the various channels" [34].

2.3   Changing the Perspective

Mostly narrators present their story from one of the following three perspectives: first-person, third-person limited or omniscient. They are also called narrative modes. The Austrian expert of storytelling Franz Stanzel developed a circle of narrators perspectives as a central point of writing a story [60].

In Stanzel's typological circle contains "three typical narrative situations", including various possibilities of structuring narratives: "mode", "person" and "perspective". These can be subdivided into three oppositions "narrator/ reflector", "first person/third person" and "internal perspective/external perspective". The first narrative situation is "authorial narrative situation", which can be described by the dominance of the external perspective. In the second narrative situation "First-person narrative situation" the story is presented by a "narrating I", who is part of the action. The last narrative situation is "The figural narrative situation" and it can be described by the dominance of the reflector mode.

Learning social skills means to be able to change perspectives and this could be done by serious games very easily. There are different characters, which can

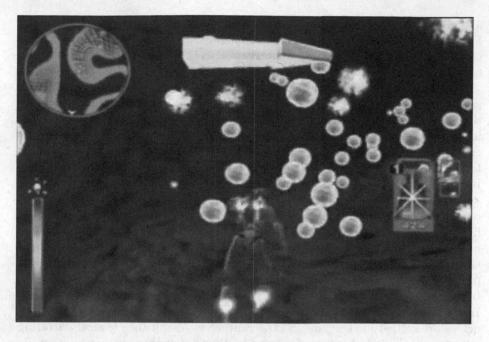

Fig. 3. Screen shot of the game "Re-Mission"

be chosen. Project Peacemaker is a government simulation game about the Israeli-Palestinian conflict [33]. The player can choose the perspective of the leader of Israel and the Palestinian Authority. The serious meaning of the game is a better understanding of the long time conflict and promoting peace. The most popular perspective in game design is the "narrating I" perspective, that contains a high involvement by the player, well known in the Ego-Shooter-Games. Also serious games use this perspective, for example the game Re-Mission. In the health game player, often young ill children, fight against cancer and win. They flight in ego-shooter-perspective through a human being body and kill cancer cells [54] (Fig. 3).

2.4   Characters and Archetypes The Role of Empathy

The importance of characters for a narration is very simple. Characters bring action into the story. Their relationship is important for the development of a story. Conflicts between characters, for example, cause an increasing suspense line. Joseph Campbell did researches about famous archetypes often found in myths, influenced by the Swiss Psychiatrist Carl Jung [12]. The central figure of a myth are heros. Their antagonist represents so called shadows or enemies. In some cases the enemy is within the protagonist, his dark site. Mentors guides the hero through the challenges. Herald brings the call to adventure. This could be also an event. Threshold guardians stand in the way at important turning points. They inhibit like jealous enemies, professional gatekeepers the heros journey. Sometimes they are inside the main character, representing the heros own fears and doubts. Shapeshifters, creatures like vampires or werewolves, change shape. Further tricksters are clowns and troublemakers. Allies help the hero throughout the quest. And finally woman a temptress: This is a female character, a femme fatale, which offers often danger to the hero.

These archetypes also can be found in serious games. Interesting characters keep the gamer playing and a high involvement can be reached by identification with the characters. Characters differ according to game genre. For example in serious games for health context medical experts are needed as an intelligent agent. Dealing with emotional items like cancer in a competent way causes big challenges in character design. One famous character in health context is Roxxi [54]. In the game Re-Mission gamer fight from a ego-shooter-perspective against cancer by this nano-robot and learns besides more about this illness. The narrators perspective is important in this kind of game, because ill children could fight actively against their cancer. Studies proved an increasing self-powerness of the gamer [44]. Roxxi has an friend as a learned guide inside, a Holographic Guidance. This simulated holographic companion provides audio suggestions and occasional guidance through a holographic navigational arrow. The interaction between Roxxi and her holographic friend are also generating funny sequences. Besides Roxxi and the Holographic Guidance there friendly and enemy characters are settled in the game. So the characters install the classical narrating structure of the fight between good and bad guys. For this, characters are a big opportunity and also challenges for serious game designer.

3   Storytelling in Interactive Media

The idea of interactive narrative is not strictly bound to digital and interactive media; however, with the advent of these technologies and the development of fields such as artificial intelligence, computer graphics or sound synthesis a number of new forms of interactive narratives became possible (e.g. computer games or training simulations). For instance, real-time computer graphics [2] allows the generation and modification of the visual representation of the story in response to story changes and user actions; techniques such as planning or machine learning can be used to automatise some narrative theories and and enable real-time story generation [69].

One of the fundamental challenges in developing and in designing and developing interactive narratives using digital media is the contrast between the freedom of interaction of the user and the designer's control of the principles of drama. As pointed out by Szilas [62], these two aspects of interactive narrative are often in conflict as the user has potentially the freedom to disrupt the principles of drama by, for instance, not looking at a specific character in the virtual world or by not triggering a specific event in a specific moment. The vast majority of the research work in the area attempt to directly or indirectly addressing this contrast by improving the freedom of interaction and, at the same time, introduce more intelligent algorithms able to adapt the narrative so that it is consistent with the both user actions an the principles of drama.

This adaptation is implemented at different levels either handling the changes in the story or the ones in the discourse [15, 70]: in the first case the narrative experience adapts to the user actions by changing the events composing the story, while, in the second case, the adaptation is focused on the way the events are presented to the user. This section focuses in the latter case, while the adaptation of the story events is covered in Sect. 4.

3.1 Computational Discourse

Game discourse plays a fundamental role in enabling serious games to correctly engage the players and effectively achieve their purpose [54, 68]. To achieve this result all of its components have to be correctly designed an implemented.

El-Nasr [23, 24] identifies three different aspects affecting the discourse in games: camera shots, light effects and character movements. She further analyses the challenges of designing an interactive narrative architecture in which story generation is separated from story presentation, which is handled by a "Director Agent" controlling the virtual camera, the lights and the characters.

Following similar architectures, many researchers have focused on different aspects of discourse generation and their combination. One of the most developed areas in this field are probably virtual cinematography and camera control [18], in which researchers have been studying for many years the process of translating the cinematographic language to interactive media. Drucker et al. [21, 22] initially addressed this problem by defining a language to translate cinematographic shots into instructions processable by a machine; this involved defining a domain specific language for the shot description and a series of algorithms to interpret these descriptions and translate them to camera movements. Since this initial work, research in virtual camera control has evolved mainly in two directions. On one side, researchers focused on finding methods and algorithms to allow computers to design the overall visual discourse, such as shot plans, transitions and cuts [17, 36, 41]. On the other side, researchers have focused on finding efficient algorithms to animate and accurately place the camera in real-time in response to the given shot plans [6, 10, 53].

Tightly connected to virtual cinematography research are the studies on automatic lighting of three-dimensional virtual scenes. One of the first works in the area is CameraCreature by Tomlinson et al. [63]: in their work, they envision visual discourse as a multi-agent process, in which a team of ethologically-inspired agents control cameras and lights according to their motivations and their emotional state. El-Nasr [23], instead, proposes a more top-down architecture in which a unified system controls the overall lighting of the scenes following formalised principles of lighting such as the ones described in [64]. The process of formalising such principles and automatising the light placement has itself been focus of research works such as [57] or [31].

The third element of visual discourse identified by El-Nasr [23] is character animation: good character animations are clearly a major contributor to the visual quality of an interactive narrative and automatising the process of animation has been a major research topic in computer graphics for a long time [43].

Within the field of computer graphics, researchers have studied different problems problems connected to automatic character animation, such as the realistic generation of facial expressions [13], body movements [5] or the synchronisation of realistic lips movements with the characters speech [8]. Many of these technologies are now commonly employed in commercial animation products or game engines (e.g. Autodesk Maya or Unity3D).

Beyond the aspects of discourse enlisted by El-Nasr [23], we can identify many other aspects that contribute to the presentation of a story in a digital audio-visual media: for instance, Jowel [35] proposed a system that generates automatically a sound track given an annotated version of a cinematographic animation. Another example of area related to story presentation is procedural generation of virtual environments in games: a number of works in this area have attempted a story-driven approach, in which the environment is generated to support the completion of a number of quests composing the games story [3,20].

3.2   Discourse and Interaction

In a combination, the aforementioned technologies and methods can be used to generate automatically full story visualisations and implementations such as [36, 41] are two examples of such visualisation based on slightly different approaches. However, the idea that discourse and interaction are connected only by changes of the storyline and that, therefore, the discourse can be directly generated from a formal representation of the story is insufficient to capture the full extent of an interactive narrative experience.

As shown by the studies conducted by Martinez et al. [45] and Burelli [9], visual discourse in interactive experiences as a profound impact on the user experience; therefore, potentially affecting the ability of the user to interact with the digital narrative and to perceive the story narrated [36]. Furthermore, examples of adaptive visual discourse based player interaction and playing style [11] show that interaction can be used to drive camera movements improving the quality of the interactive experience.

The extents of the interplays between story, interaction and discourse revealed by the aforementioned studies highlights even further the importance of studying the relationship between the designer's control of the narrative experience and the user's freedom of interaction, not only at story level, but also at discourse and interaction level. This would allow to envision interactive narratives in which, not only the story itself, but the way in which the user interacts with the story and the way the story is presented can evolve during the experience. For instance, due to a twist in the narrative a first-person perspective game could switch to a third-person view while changing the color palette a lowering the pace of interaction to support a more contemplative phase of the experience.

4   Interactive Digital Storytelling

Interactive Digital Storytelling (IDS) or Interactive Digital Narrative (IDN) is a diverse interdisciplinary research field. Various definitions for concepts of IDS

Fig. 4. Left, Faade [46]: Trip and Grace arguing. Right, Prom Week [47]: decision result forecast

exist so far. Spierling [58] assumes for her working definition of interactive storytelling that "during the interactive experience of a story, members of the audience become participants in a storyworld that enables the resulting story. They take a more or less active role right within that storyworld that grants them some degree of influence on the plot as one possible outcome." [38] states that in Interactive Digital Narrative (IDN) "digital means enable interactive forms of narrative." [38] An IDS experience only exists by the time the user in experiencing. On the other hand there is Emergent Narrative which was called an improvisation by [4] that is interpreted as a plot based on the users life experience, also see Heider and Simmel Film from 1944[1]. Two notable IDS experiences are Faade [46] and PromWeek [47] providing non-linear storytelling through conversation. Faade Fig. 4 was the first non-linear IDS experience giving users free input choice by providing free text input. Prom Week Fig. 4 is a game providing complex non-linear IDS experience by letting the user choose conversation components and for the first time providing end result forecasts for the user to base decision-making on. Chris Crawford [19] states that in games the user interacts mainly with object while in IDS experiences users interact with other characters.

We can conclude there are various approaches on interactivity in narratives shaped by the audiences experience where (A) in IDS the audience actively enables the experienced story and (B) in Emergent Narrative the audience where the narrative emerges from abstract storytelling based on users life experience. Its necessary to mention that in IDS a story does not exist as one finished product to be consumed by the user like movie or a book but a reactive media form like games or serious games and the users choices produce a story with in the system, meaning every user can experience a different story. Some serious games implemented IDS [29,55]. Different stories in IDS consist of different actions, characters and events shaping each individual story. The sequence of actions is called a plot. Changing the plot will not change the story. Opposite to serious games IDS experiences have no additional goal adding to entertaining

---

[1] Film available online, e.g. https://www.youtube.com/watch?v=VTNmLt7QX8E.

the end-user. IDS is a feature that can be implemented in serious games. As in games an engine enables the experience. In IDS the engine mostly is called story or storytelling engine.

Koenitz [38] writes: "Interactive Digital Narrative (IDN) connects artistic vision with technology." In IDS information and methods are coming from different domains following different ontology of highly creative fields such as of film writers, film directors or pedagogues. Thats also the case in serious game development where all content apart from program code comes from experts of other domains such as pedagogy (E-Learning), health experts (Exergames) or hydraulic engineers as in project SECOM[2] This interdisciplinary constellation produces a collaboration problem tackled by authoring models and their implementation called authoring tools or authoring systems [59].

4.1   Authoring

Spierling [58] states: "the situation for story creators approaching highly-interactive storytelling is complex. There is a gap between the available technology, which requires programming and prior knowledge in Artificial Intelligence, and established models of storytelling, which are too linear to have the potential to be highly interactive." Producing IDS experiences needs process structures of interdisciplinary development. So far several approaches deal with creative input of content and non-linear stories structures by non-programmers [58, 61] called authors weather they are technical and content producing [1] or narrative [58] or other authors who are non-expert in software engineering [1]. Some authoring tools enable children to input stories like the Heider and Simmel Interactive Theater [30] and the Wayang Authoring Tool [67] both evaluated with undergraduates. The question of who is an author and what skills an author should possess and if this must be taken into account when designing authoring tools [1] is still undefined for IDS [58,59]. Opposite to that authors can learn how to program and implement their own idea of an IDS experience but this approach excludes authoring by non-programmers and is therefore not discussed here.

The process of authors entering data or narrative structures into the IDS system tailored for a storytelling engine to run on is called authoring. Producing a game with storytelling and especially with interactive storytelling characteristics involves various steps of designing, authoring, capturing, media production and programming [50]. Researching and writing stories for the game comes before dramatically rendering and translating content into visual content, which then is produced renders the production to an interdisciplinary task. With regard to expensive production costs many prior steps must be prototyped, which makes the interdisciplinary task an iterative process argues [59]. As authors expertise and skills vary, input models called authoring models vary as well as authoring methods implemented in authoring tools. In many systems XML and dialects of it describe non-linear story structures [16,39,40,65,66].Entering XML structures is a task included in the authoring model and can be implemented by using a text

---

[2] https://www.secom20.eu/.

editor or a graphical user interface [66]. In all cases a XML experienced author can fall back on a text editor entering XML structures. But graphical user interfaces open a window for non-expert authors widening the target group of authors for an IDS system. That is the wide-spread goal of authoring tools [1,40,66].

The concept of authoring is determining "the relationships between generative technologies underlying Interactive Storytelling engines, and the actual description of narrative content"[51]. Entering other creative content and information for a storytelling engine creates a bottleneck [51,59] in production process. So far approaches like generating input [58] and output by input combination using Artificial Intelligence based on discourse analysis in conversational systems as well as game-and simulation design [58], as well as component-based approaches [1] did not solve this bottleneck. While using different approaches and models for authoring IDS experiences all works on authoring tools agree on the necessity for all authors including programmers and non-programmers of instant testing of entered content [1,66].

4.2 Authoring Tools as Technical Challenges in IDS Production

Authoring for IDS systems follows various models depending on the executing system delivering the interactive experience depending on the storytelling engine [51] used. An authoring tool should not only support the presentation of the used technology states [1], but also allow for authors with different backgrounds to create IDS experiences. The author himself should not need to create the underlying structure from scratch, but can fall back on a story template provided by the authoring tool. An authoring tool can also be an authoring toolkit MR Toolkit, [66] The relevant tasks that the author has to fulfill are then reduced to his core domain and competencies, which include selecting and combining components, adapting multimedia content, and calibrating visual representations of components with the appropriate real world objects. says [1].

But there are problems with visualizations of programming structures for non-programmers as [65] states: "The limitations of a single graph to model a complex non-linear scenario are obvious, because an author is forced to define all possible paths through the story in detail." Describing a fallback to programming structures opposite to creative methods creating narratives. The goal of an authoring tool is to provide communication interfaces between technology experts, storytelling experts and application domain-experts [1]. Szilas and Spierling [59] describe a vicious circle in the process of creating authoring tools between listening to authors and adjusting the authoring tool suggesting that the creation of an authoring tool is rather an iterative building process than a nonrecurring process. Easy to use interfaces are needed for defining complex structures. "The Heider-Simmel Interactive Theater[3] [30] allows novice users to easily author movies intended to convey rich narratives that involve various physical, social, and psychological concerns." Gordon2014 states. This authoring tool can be used by undergraduates as well as the Wayang Authoring Tool [67]

---

[3] Heider Simmel Interactive Theater: http://hsit.ict.usc.edu/.

but both authoring tools produce no IDS system operated by storytelling engines but a complete product to watch by the audience though non-expert input by graphical user interfaces are provided by these authoring tools.

StoryTec environment [29] is an example of an authoring tool in the serious game domain where non-programmers like "medical doctors, fitness coaches or members of other user groups can either define fitness programs and game-based applications for sports and health from scratch or retrieve preconfigured programs and templates from the database (repository) and customize those to the needs and characteristics of individuals and groups." Ergo Active, Y-Move and SunSports Go are serious games developed with StoryTec [29].

Apart from enabling input for non-programmers authoring tools are mainly developed for specialized storytelling engines. StoryNet [55] using hypertext for IDS and HTML browsers as storytelling engines. This is the only project using standardized software and markup language for IDS. Most IDS projects use XML or a self-made XML dialect for describing story structures and content [66], MR Toolkit. [40] and use specialized storytelling engines implementing several planning algorithms [61]. We conclude authoring tool development is a diversified research field of different authoring models and methods providing access to non-expert authors of various domains and an interdisciplinary task with the goal of tackling the authoring bottleneck [59].

5   Conclusions and Outlook

In Summary, this article draws a line from linear told stories to highly non-linear stories in Interactive Media and Interactive Storytelling by showing their importance for serious games. Beginning with the storytelling basics, fundamental narrative techniques are presented, corresponding to traditional and mostly linear told stories. Narrative techniques like narrator perspective, dramatic structures and Character Design are also important for Game Design. Further the chapter "Storytellung in Interactive Media" includes interactive theories related to narrative aspects. The interferences between story, interaction and discourse has to be researched, considering the relationship between the designer's control of the narrative experience and the user's freedom of interaction. This has to be done in three levels, the story level, but also at discourse and interaction level. In addition to this, Interactive Digital Storytelling is presented. Various definitions exist today. Working definitions of Interactive Digital Storytelling had been published [38,58], some incorporating specialized authoring methods [58,61] and some implemented Authoring Tools like Scenejo, Heider Simmel Interactive Theatre and MR Authoring Tool [1,30,66] according to authoring models and specific authoring processes. A general definition is missed until now. According to Interactive Digital Storytelling also authoring tools and their particular items are illustrated.

Using storytelling in serious games context opens challenges and opportunities. According to Jenkins not all games tell stories, but many games have narrative aspirations. [Jenkins] First of all, narrative techniques particularly in serious games design have to be defined. The presented storytelling basics have to be examined in game context. In the serious game context narratives are essential to transport the serious sense behind the game. There exist different ways to work with narrating parts in serious games. Not all parts have to be told by the author. The serious game World without oil, in which the user tell their own stories how to deal with the oil crisis, is a good example for that. But how correspond this with the immersion, game designer want to reach? This opens a new research field: How influence dramatic storylines or character design the immersion level of the player? And how could we measure this?

Further, interference between interaction and reception in serious games have to be analyzed in detail, considering the players freedom of choice. This also means the mixture between linear and nonlinear elements. Balancing the reception of the story with the interaction with game elements is an important challenge in designing games, but an opportunity as well. New forms of storytelling according to Interactive Digital Storytelling opens prospects for learning. Self-determined learning needs a freedom of choice, given by Interactive Storytelling. So, gamer learn serious content as a coauthor by active doing and trying it out. This is represented for example by roleplaying in the highly interactive game Faade or discovering the Saalburgs spirit on players own ways with the mobile location-based serious game Spirit. This opens an important research field: How narrative parts and the freedom of choice influence the learning aspects in serious games? It has to be analyzed, how much a guidance is useful for transporting serious sense.

Further, authoring tools are often specialized on certain IDS systems and authoring methods producing different IDS experiences from other authoring tools. Today there is no comprehensive media format for IDS experiences but many IDS approaches mostly implemented as prototypes. Unlike HTML as format for Hyperfiction a IDS format of the 80 s and 90 s [39] today formats diverge seemingly according to different technologies like mobile gaming, theater performances, location based technology, HMDs, Google glass and desktop PCs used for IDS experiences. The question here is weather these diversions are only technical diversions or is there a mutual core of IDS in those models, authoring methods and authoring tools and if yes what is this core? Also, authoring in a game design process opens new challenges: How to visualize realize the concept of interactive storytelling in a game to the author to enable the authoring process in the interdisciplinary team?

Many years of research and discussion have passed, but the coupling of narration and interaction can still spark provocative debates requiring our attention. Therefore further work on the practical and ontological analogies and differences between interactivity and narration is necessary. [38] In Interactive Digital Storytelling the authoring bottleneck up to this point is still left unsolved [59].

Last but not least, Learning, Gaming and Storytelling have to be examined as an unity. A big challenge is how to evaluate learning aspects transported by narration in prospect. Single evaluations already exist, particularly in heal care. The 2008 study by Kato, Cole, Bradlyn and Pollock [37] about the serious game Re-Mission represents a good example for this. But there is no focus on narration parts. It is a common sense that serious games using storytelling can help to understand in a learning context, but their is no general method to evaluate this connection.

Further Readings

We recommend Lee Sheldon's 2013 book "Character Development and Storytelling for Games" for game designing and writing because the highlights the fundamental importance of characters and storytelling for all types of games. "The hero with a thousand faces" (Vol. 17) by 2008 by Joseph Campbell, New World Library combines the insights of modern psychology with Joseph Campbells unique understanding of comparative mythology and is a good book with many insights into storytelling as well as Henry Jenkins's book "Game Design as Narrative" in Computer, 44 from 2004. On Interactive Digital Storytelling we recommend two books: "Chris Crawford on Interactive Storytelling" [19] by Chris Crawford is a second edition from 2012 in New Riders updating his fundamental thesis and understanding of Interactive Storytelling. Koenitz's 2015 book "Interactive Digital Narrative: History, Theory and Practice" [38] in Routledge provides a broad overview of current issues and future directions in the multi-disciplinary field of Interactive Digital Storytelling, it covers history, theoretical perspectives and varieties of practice including narrative game design and it assembles the voices of leading researchers and practitioners in the research field.

References

1. Abawi, D.F., Reinhold, S., Dörner, R.: A toolkit for authoring non-linear storytelling environments using mixed reality. In: Göbel, S., Spierling, U., Hoffmann, A., Iurgel, I., Schneider, O., Dechau, J., Feix, A. (eds.) TIDSE 2004. LNCS, vol. 3105, pp. 113–118. Springer, Heidelberg (2004). doi:10.1007/978-3-540-27797-2_15
2. Akenine-Möller, T., Haines, E., Hoffman, N.: Real-Time Rendering, 3rd edn. A. K. Peters Ltd., Natick (2008)
3. Ashmore, C., Nitsche, M.: The quest in a generated world. In: Digra International Conference, pp. 503–509 (2007)
4. Aylett, R.: Narrative in virtual environments - towards emergent narrative. In: AAAI Fall Symposium on Narrative Intelligence, pp. 83–86 (1999)
5. Baran, I., Popović, J.: Automatic rigging and animation of 3D characters. ACM Trans. Graph. 26(3), Article no. 72 (2007)
6. Bares, W.H., Gregoire, J.P., Lester, J.C.: Realtime constraint-based cinematography for complex interactive 3D worlds. In: Conference on Innovative Applications of Artificial Intelligence (1998)
7. Bordwell, D.: Narration in the Fiction Film (1986)
8. Brand, M.: Voice puppetry. In: ACM SIGGRAPH International Conference on Computer Graphics and Interactive Techniques, pp. 21–28. ACM Press, New York (1999)

9. Burelli, P.: Virtual Cinematography in Games : Investigating the impact on player experience. In: International Conference on the Foundations of Digital Games, Chania, Greece, pp. 134–141. Society for the Advancement of the Science of Digital Games (2013)

10. Burelli, P.: Implementing game cinematography: technical challenges and solutions for automatic camera control in games. In: William, H., Bares, M.C., Ronfard, R. (eds.) Eurographics Workshop on Intelligent Cinematography and Editing, Zurich, pp. 59–63. Eurographics Association (2015)

11. Burelli, P., Yannakakis, G.N.: Adaptive virtual camera control trough player modelling. User Model. User Adapt. Interact. **25**, 155–183 (2015)

12. Campbell, J.: The Hero with a Thousand Faces. MJF Books, New York (1949)

13. Cassell, J., Vilhjálmsson, H.H., Bickmore, T.: BEAT: the behavior expression animation toolkit. In: Life-Like Characters, vol. 137, pp. 163–185. ACM Press, New York (2004)

14. Chatman, S.B.: Story and Discourse: Narrative Structure in Fiction and Film, 1st edn. Cornell University Press, Ithaca (1978)

15. Chatman, S.B.: Story and Discourse: Narrative Structure in Fiction and Film. Cornell University Press, Ithaca (1980)

16. Cheong, Y.-G., Jhala, A., Bae, B.-C., Young, R.M.: Automatically generating summary visualizations from game logs. In: AAAI Conference on Artificial Intelligence in Interactive Digitale Entertainment, pp. 167–172 (2008)

17. Christianson, D., Anderson, S., He, L.-W., Salesin, D.H., Weld, D., Cohen, M.F.: Declarative camera control for automatic cinematography. In: AAAI, pp. 148–155. AAAI Press, Portland (1996)

18. Christie, M., Olivier, P., Normand, J.M.: Camera control in computer graphics. Comput. Graph. Forum **27**(8), 2197–2218 (2008)

19. Crawford, C.: Chris Crawford on Interactive Storytelling, vol. 5334. New Riders, Berkeley (2012)

20. Dormans, J.: Adventures in level design. In: Workshop on Procedural Content Generation in Games, pp. 1–8. ACM Press, New York (2010)

21. Drucker, S.M., Galyean, T.A., Zeltzer, D.: CINEMA: a system for procedural camera movements. In: Symposium on Interactive 3D Graphics, pp. 67–70. ACM (1992)

22. Drucker, S.M., Zeltzer, D.: Intelligent camera control in a virtual environment. In: Graphics Interface, pp. 190–199. ACM, Alberta, Canada (1994)

23. El-Nasr, M.S.: Story visualization techniques for interactive drama. In: AAAI Spring Symposium, pp. 23–28. AAAI Press (2002)

24. El-Nasr, M.S.: An interactive narrative architecture based on filmmaking theory. Int. J. Intell. Games Simul. **3**(1), 49–62 (2004)

25. Electric Shadow: World without oil (2007)

26. Field, S.: Screenplay. Delacorte, New York (1982)

27. Freytag, G.: Die technik des dramas. Hirzel, Leipzig (1872)

28. Genette, G.: Narrative Discourse: An Essay in Method, vol. 9. Cornell University Press, Ithaca (1980)

29. Göbel, S., Hardy, S., Mehm, F., Wendel, V.: Serious games for health - personalized exergames. In: 18th ACM International Conference on Multimedia, pp. 1663–1666. ACM (2010)

30. Gordon, A.S., Roemmele, M.: An authoring tool for movies in the style of Heider and Simmel. In: Mitchell, A., Fernández-Vara, C., Thue, D. (eds.) ICIDS 2014. LNCS, vol. 8832, pp. 49–60. Springer, Heidelberg (2014). doi:10.1007/978-3-319-12337-0_5

31. Ha, H.N.: Automatic lighting design. Ph.D. thesis, University of Newcastle (2008)
32. Höffe, O.: Aristoteles: Poetik. Oldenbourg Verlag, Munich (2009)
33. Impact Games: PeaceMaker (2007)
34. Jenkins, H.: Game design as narrative. Computer **44**, 53 (2004)
35. Jewell, M.O.: Motivated music: automatic soundtrack generation for film by. Ph.D. thesis, University of Southampton (2007)
36. Jhala, A., Young, R.M.: Cinematic visual discourse: representation, generation, and evaluation. IEEE Trans. Comput. Intell. AI Games **2**(2), 69–81 (2010)
37. Kato, P.M., Cole, S.W., Bradlyn, A.S., Pollock, B.H.: A video game improves behavioral outcomes in adolescents and young adults with Cancer: a randomized trial. Pediatrics **122**(2), 305–317 (2008)
38. Koenitz, H.: Interactive Digital Narrative: History,Theory and Practice. Routledge, New York (2015)
39. Koenitz, H., Chen, K.-J.: Genres, structures and strategies in interactive digital narratives – analyzing a body of works created in ASAPS. In: Oyarzun, D., Peinado, F., Young, R.M., Elizalde, A., Méndez, G. (eds.) ICIDS 2012. LNCS, vol. 7648, pp. 84–95. Springer, Heidelberg (2012). doi:10.1007/978-3-642-34851-8_8
40. Kriegel, M., Aylett, R.: Crowd-sourced AI authoring with ENIGMA. In: Aylett, R., Lim, M.Y., Louchart, S., Petta, P., Riedl, M. (eds.) ICIDS 2010. LNCS, vol. 6432, pp. 275–278. Springer, Heidelberg (2010). doi:10.1007/978-3-642-16638-9_41
41. Lino, C., Christie, M., Lamarche, F., Schofield, G., Olivier, P.: A real-time cinematography system for interactive 3D environments. In: ACM SIGGRAPH/Eurographics Symposium on Computer Animation, pp. 139–148. The Eurographics Association (2010)
42. Lotman, J.M.: Notes on the structure of a literary text. Semiotica **15**(3), 199–206 (1975)
43. Magnenat-Thalmann, N., Primeau, E., Thalmann, D.: Abstract muscle action procedures for human face animation. Vis. Comput. **3**(5), 290–297 (1988)
44. Marr, A.C.: Serious Games für die Informations- und Wissensvermittlung - Bibliotheken auf neuen Wegen (B.I.T. online - Innovativ) Band 28 (2010)
45. Martinez, H.P., Jhala, A., Yannakakis, G.N.: Analyzing the impact of camera viewpoint on player psychophysiology. In: International Conference on Affective Computing and Intelligent Interaction and Workshops, pp. 1–6. IEEE (2009)
46. Mateas, M., Stern, A.: Interaction and narrative. In: The Game Design Reader: A Rules of Play Anthology, pp. 642–669. MIT Press, Boston (2005)
47. McCoy, J., Treanor, M., Samuel, B.: Prom week: social physics as gameplay. In: Proceedings of the 6th International Conference on Foundations of Digital Games, pp. 319–321. ACM (2011)
48. McGonigal, J.: Reality is broken: why games make us better and how they can change the world, vol. 22, p. 400. New York (2011)
49. Nintendo: Super Mario Land (1989)
50. Nisi, O.I., Valentina, M.H.: Places, location-aware multimedia stories: turning spaces into places. In: Artech, International Conference on Digital Arts, pp. 72–82. Universidade Cátolica Portuguesa (2008)
51. Pizzi, D., Cavazza, M.: From debugging to authoring: adapting productivity tools to narrative content description. In: Spierling, U., Szilas, N. (eds.) ICIDS 2008. LNCS, vol. 5334, pp. 285–296. Springer, Heidelberg (2008). doi:10.1007/978-3-540-89454-4_36
52. Proust, M.: In Search of Lost Time. Random House, New York (1932)
53. Ranon, R., Urli, T.: Improving the efficiency of viewpoint composition. IEEE Trans. Vis. Comput. Graph. **20**(5), 795–807 (2014)

54. Realtime Associates Inc.: Re-Mission (2006)
55. Schäfer, L., Stauber, A., Bokan, B.: StoryNet: an educational game for social skills. In: Göbel, S., Spierling, U., Hoffmann, A., Iurgel, I., Schneider, O., Dechau, J., Feix, A. (eds.) TIDSE 2004. LNCS, vol. 3105, pp. 148–157. Springer, Heidelberg (2004). doi:10.1007/978-3-540-27797-2_20
56. Serious Games Interactive: Global Conflicts Palestine (2007)
57. Shacked, R., Lischinski, D.: Automatic lighting design using a perceptual quality metric. Comput. Graph. Forum **20**(3), 215–227 (2001)
58. Spierling, U.: Implicit creation non-programmer conceptual models for authoring in interactive digital storytelling. Ph.D. thesis, University of Plymouth (2010)
59. Spierling, U., Szilas, N.: Authoring issues beyond tools. In: Iurgel, I.A., Zagalo, N., Petta, P. (eds.) ICIDS 2009. LNCS, pp. 50–61. Springer, Heidelberg (2009). doi:10.1007/978-3-642-10643-9_9
60. Stanzel, F.K.: Theorie des Erzahlens. Vandenhoeck & Ruprecht, Göttingen (1995)
61. Szilas, N.: IDtension: a narrative engine for interactive drama. In: Technologies for Interactive Digital Storytelling and Entertainment (TIDSE) Conference, pp. 183–203. Fraunhofer IRB Verlag (2003)
62. Szilas, N.: Interactive drama on computer: beyond linear narrative. In: AAAI Fall Symposium on Narrative Intelligence, vol. 144, pp. 150–156 (1999)
63. Tomlinson, B., Blumberg, B., Nain, D.: Expressive autonomous cinematography for interactive virtual environments. In: International Conference on Autonomous Agents, Barcelona, Spain, p. 317 (2000)
64. Viera, J.D., Viera, M.: Lighting for Film and Electronic Cinematography. Wadsworth Publishing Company, Belmont (1993)
65. Wages, R., Grützmacher, B., Conrad, S.: Learning from the movie industry: adapting production processes for storytelling in VR. In: Göbel, S., Spierling, U., Hoffmann, A., Iurgel, I., Schneider, O., Dechau, J., Feix, A. (eds.) TIDSE 2004. LNCS, pp. 119–125. Springer, Heidelberg (2004). doi:10.1007/978-3-540-27797-2_16
66. Weiss, S., Müller, W., Spierling, U., Steimle, F.: Scenejo – an interactive storytelling platform. In: Subsol, G. (ed.) ICVS 2005. LNCS, pp. 77–80. Springer, Heidelberg (2005). doi:10.1007/11590361_9
67. Widjajanto, W., Lund, M., Schelhowe, H.: A web-based authoring tool for visual storytelling for children. In: 6th International Conference on Advances in Mobile Computing and Multimedia (MoMM), pp. 464–467. ACM (2008)
68. Wouters, P., Van Oostendorp, H., Boonekamp, R., Van Der Spek, E.: The role of game discourse analysis and curiosity in creating engaging and effective serious games by implementing a back story and foreshadowing. Interact. Comput. **23**(4), 329–336 (2011)
69. Michael Young, R.: Creating interactive narrative structures: the potential for AI approaches. In: AAAI Spring Symposium. Narosa Publishing House (2000)
70. Young, R.M.: Story and discourse: a bipartite model of narrative generation in virtual worlds. Interact. Stud. **8**(2), 177–208 (2007)

Author Index